TEXT AND READINGS

# Marketing

# in Business Management

STEVEN J. SHAW

*and*

C. McFERRON GITTINGER

*Steven J. Shaw is Professor of Marketing and Editor,*
Business and Economic Review, *Bureau of Business
Research, School of Business Administration, University of South Carolina*

*C. McFerron Gittinger is Professor of Marketing and
Head, Marketing Department, School of Business
Administration, University of South Carolina*

THE MACMILLAN COMPANY, NEW YORK
COLLIER-MACMILLAN LIMITED, LONDON

*Second Printing, 1964*

Library of Congress catalog card number: 63-13130

THE MACMILLAN COMPANY, NEW YORK
COLLIER-MACMILLAN CANADA, LTD., TORONTO, CANADA
Divisions of The Crowell-Collier Publishing Company

*Printed in the United States of America*

Designed by Frank E. Comparato

# Preface

$\mathcal{B}$*USINESS MANAGEMENT* is in the process of radical reorganization as it seeks to adapt itself to a post-War II environment of intense domestic and world competition. In company after company, the marketing function is being upgraded as management strives to bring its thinking into closer focus with consumer needs and wants. Business leadership is increasingly aware that it must become completely marketing oriented to survive and prosper in today's severely competitive world economy.

To keep abreast of the many significant developments in marketing, it is necessary to read numerous professional journals and trade publications. The problem of staying current in the field is, however, a difficult task because of the large volume of literature that is being published and the varying quality and repetitious content of many of the writings. An enormous amount of professional study is needed just to maintain contact with what is being published and to bring to light those articles that contain new and important ideas or that synthesize known information more effectively.

In the field of business administration, it is believed desirable for both students and practitioners of business to read the significant current literature in marketing, but there is today a serious problem of having available an adequate number of copies of the leading periodicals to serve the needs of the rapidly growing number of scholars. The purpose of this book, therefore, is to make available in a single volume the articles which, in the opinion of the authors, represent many of the most significant developments in the practice of modern marketing. The selections that appear in this book of readings have been screened from an initial list of over 1,000 articles, all of which have been published within the last four years in professional journals and business periodicals.

This book can be used in a number of different ways in the academic and business worlds. It can be used for instance, as a basic textbook for marketing majors in schools of business administration. Again, it can be used very conveniently as a supplementary text in any of the general marketing and management courses. It also can serve very effectively as a book of readings in case or problem courses. Questions at the end of each article, and an extensive bibliography at the end of each chapter have been added to stimulate further thinking, discussion and research.

In the business world, this book can serve as a basic text or reference source on management training programs. It can also be very helpful to the busy executive who wants to keep abreast of new developments in marketing.

Many helpful suggestions were received in the compilation of this book of readings. James A. Morris, John MacDonald, A. C. Flora, Charles Edwards, Robert King, Clinton Baker, James Hilton and William Wesson, all of the School of Business Administration faculty deserve special mention for their assistance.

For their toil and patience in the preparation of this manuscript for publication, the authors wish to thank Ann Merline and Mildred Allen, Bureau of Business and Economic Research secretaries.

The authors are also deeply indebted to the professional staffs of the University Library and the University Printing Service for their generous assistance.

STEVEN J. SHAW
C. McFERRON GITTINGER

*Columbia, South Carolina*
*January, 1963*

# Contents

# I. Modern Marketing Concept

*To SURVIVE,* business has always had to be more or less consumer oriented. Adam Smith and the classical economists established the fact that the purpose of an enterprise is to satisfy human wants and that profit is merely a reward for faithful service. But at first there was a great scarcity of goods and a firm had to find a way of producing useful merchandise inexpensively. So it needed to be production oriented. The development of mass production finally converted our economy from one of scarcity to one of relative plenty.

At first a businessman could determine consumer wants quite accurately through personal contacts with his customers. However, as the small business grew into a large plant serving regional, national and international markets, the wants of the customers near the home plant did not always reflect accurately the wants of the majority of his customers.

The first marketing departments were sales promotion departments with personal selling and advertising serving as the communication link between a producer and his expanding universe of customers. But with many competing producers, consumers could now pick and choose and sales resistance developed.

Clearly, the businessman that could most accurately gauge the preferences of the majority of his customers before producing his goods would have an advantage over his competitors. So marketing research came upon the scene. But the first researchers were frequently buried in the sales promotion oriented department and their recommendations were not taken seriously. After World War II, however, with domestic and foreign competition intensifying, business sought to rid itself of its marketing myopia, and the modern marketing department began to emerge.

Under the new marketing concept, top management realizes that almost every decision in the operation of a business must be made in the light of consumer needs and preferences. Organizationally, the marketing department is placed on an equal footing with production and finance as marketing decisions have to be made at the beginning as well as at the end of the production cycle. The sales forecast and marketing planning precede physical production. Marketing determines for the engineer, the designer and the manufacturer what the customer wants in a given product, what price range is acceptable, etc. Thus, marketing gains in authority in product planning, production scheduling, and inventory control as well as in sales, physical distribution and servicing of the product.

The essence of the modern marketing concept is the substitution of research-based planning for intuition and guesswork, and the effective integration and coordination of all business activities with marketing. Thus, the modern marketing manager must be actively involved in long-range planning of new products and company expansion as well as in the programming of current marketing strategy.

To feed reliable information to management on a vast range of pre-production, physical distribution and servicing problems, the marketing department must rely heavily on research.

Fortunately for marketing management, there have been a number of significant advances in research technology. Today the marketing research director can call on the skills of accountants, statisticians, behavioral scientists and business mathematicians for a joint attack on complex company problems.

# 1. Marketing Myopia*

Theodore Levitt, Lecturer in Business Administration, Harvard Business School

*In practice many businessmen only pay lip service to the marketing concept. For one thing they are still under the illusion that population growth results almost automatically in market growth. To correct its myopia, management must completely accept and implement the view that industry is a customer-satisfying process, not a goods-producing process.*

Every major industry was once a growth industry. But some that are now riding a wave of growth enthusiasm are very much in the shadow of decline. Others which are thought of as seasoned growth industries have actually stopped growing. In every case the reason growth is threatened, slowed, or stopped is *not* because the market is saturated. It is because there has been a failure of management.

## FATEFUL PURPOSES

The failure is at the top. The executives responsible for it, in the last analysis, are those who deal with broad aims and policies. Thus:

The railroads did not stop growing because the need for passenger and freight transportation declined. That grew. The railroads are important today not because the need was filled by others (cars, trucks, airplanes, even telephones), but because it was *not* filled by the railroads themselves. They let others take customers away from

them because they assumed themselves to be in the railroad business rather than in the transportation business. The reason they defined their industry wrong was because they were railroad-oriented instead of transportation-oriented; they were product-oriented instead of customer-oriented.

Hollywood barely escaped being totally ravished by television. Actually, all the established film companies went through drastic reorganizations. Some simply disappeared. All of them got into trouble not because of TV's inroads but because of their own myopia. As with the railroads, Hollywood defined its business incorrectly. It thought it was in the movie business when it was actually in the entertainment business. "Movies" implied a specific, limited product. This produced a fatuous contentment which from the beginning led producers to view TV as a threat. Hollywood scorned and rejected TV when it should have welcomed it as an opportunity—an opportunity to expand the entertainment business.

Today TV is a bigger business than the old narrowly defined movie business ever was. Had Hollywood been

* Reprinted from the *Harvard Business Review*, July–August 1960, p. 45.

customer-oriented (providing entertainment), rather than product-oriented (making movies), would it have gone through the fiscal purgatory that it did? I doubt it. What ultimately saved Hollywood and accounted for its recent resurgence was the wave of new young writers, producers, and directors whose previous successes in television had decimated the old movie companies and toppled the big movie moguls.

There are other less obvious examples of industries that have been and are now endangering their futures by improperly defining their purposes. I shall discuss some in detail later and analyze the kind of policies that lead to trouble. Right now it may help to show what a thoroughly customer-oriented management *can* do to keep a growth industry growing, even after the obvious opportunities have been exhausted; and here there are two examples that have been around for a long time. They are nylon and glass—specifically, E. I. duPont de Nemours & Company and Corning Glass Works:

Both companies have great technical competence. Their product orientation is unquestioned. But this alone does not explain their success. After all, who was more pridefully product-oriented and product-conscious than the erstwhile New England textile companies that have been so thoroughly massacred? The DuPonts and the Cornings have succeeded not primarily because of their product or research orientation but because they have been thoroughly customer-oriented also. It is constant watchfulness for opportunities to apply their technical know-how to the creation of customer-satisfying uses which accounts for their prodigious output of successful new products. Without a very sophisticated eye on the customer, most of their new products might have been wrong, their sales methods useless.

Aluminum has also continued to be a growth industry, thanks to the efforts of two wartime-created companies which deliberately set about creating new customer-satisfying uses. Without Kaiser Aluminum & Chemical Corporation and Reynolds Metals Company, the total demand for aluminum today would be vastly less than it is.

### ERROR OF ANALYSIS

Some may argue that it is foolish to set the railroads off against aluminum or the movies off against glass. Are not aluminum and glass naturally so versatile that the industries are bound to have more growth opportunities than the railroads and movies? This view commits precisely the error I have been talking about. It defines an industry, or a product, or a cluster of know-how so narrowly as to guarantee its premature senescence. When we mention "railroads," we should make sure we mean "transportation." As transporters, the railroads still have a good chance for very considerable growth. They are not limited to the railroad business as such (though in my opinion rail transportation is potentially a much stronger transportation medium than is generally believed).

What the railroads lack is not opportunity, but some of the same managerial imaginativeness and audacity that made them great. Even an amateur like Jacques Barzun can see what is lacking when he says:

"I grieve to see the most advanced physical and social organization of the last century go down in shabby disgrace for lack of the same comprehensive imagination that built it up.

[What is lacking is] the will of the companies to survive and to satisfy the public by inventiveness and skill."[1]

## SHADOW OF OBSOLESCENCE

It is impossible to mention a single major industry that did not at one time qualify for the magic appellation of "growth industry." In each case its assumed strength lay in the apparently unchallenged superiority of its product. There appeared to be no effective substitute for it. It was itself a runaway substitute for the product it so triumphantly replaced. Yet one after another of these celebrated industries has come under a shadow. Let us look briefly at a few more of them, this time taking examples that have so far received a little less attention:

**Dry Cleaning.** . . . This was once a growth industry with lavish prospects. In an age of wool garments, imagine being finally able to get them safely and easily clean. The boom was on.

Yet here we are 30 years after the boom started and the industry is in trouble. Where has the competition come from? From a better way of cleaning? No. It has come from synthetic fibers and chemical additives that have cut the need for dry cleaning. But this is only the beginning. Lurking in the wings and ready to make chemical dry cleaning totally obsolescent is that powerful magician, ultrasonics.

**Electric Utilities.** . . . This is another one of those supposedly "no-substitute" products that has been enthroned on a pedestal of invincible growth. When the incandescent lamp came along, kerosene lights were finished. Later the water wheel and the steam engine were cut to ribbons by the flexi-

bility, reliability, simplicity, and just plain easy availability of electric motors. The prosperity of electric utilities continues to wax extravagant as the home is converted into a museum of electric gadgetry. How can anybody miss by investing in utilities, with no competition, nothing but growth ahead?

But a second look is not quite so comforting. A score of nonutility companies are well advanced toward developing a powerful chemical fuel cell which could sit in some hidden closet of every home silently ticking off electric power. The electric lines that vulgarize so many neighborhoods will be eliminated. So will the endless demolition of streets and service interruptions during storms. Also on the horizon is solar energy, again pioneered by nonutility companies.

Who says that the utilities have no competition? They may be natural monopolies now, but tomorrow they may be natural deaths. To avoid this prospect, they too will have to develop fuel cells, solar energy, and other power sources. To survive, they themselves will have to plot the obsolescence of what now produces their livelihood.

**Grocery Stores.** . . . Many people find it hard to realize that there ever was a thriving establishment known as the "corner grocery store." The supermarket has taken over with a powerful effectiveness. Yet the big food chains of the 1930's narrowly escaped being completely wiped out by the aggressive expansion of independent supermarkets. The first genuine supermarket was opened in 1930, in Jamaica, Long Island. By 1933 supermarkets were thriving in California, Ohio, Pennsylvania, and elsewhere. Yet the established chains pompously ignored them. When they chose to notice them, it was with such derisive descriptions as

[1] Jacques Barzun, "Trains and the Mind of Man," *Holiday*, February 1960, p. 21.

"cheaply," "horse-and-buggy," "cracker-barrel storekeeping," and "unethical opportunists."

The executive of one big chain announced at the time that he found it "hard to believe that people will drive for miles to shop for foods and sacrifice the personal service chains have perfected and to which Mrs. Consumer is accustomed."[2] As late as 1936, the National Wholesale Grocers convention and the New Jersey Retail Grocers Association said there was nothing to fear. They said that the supers' narrow appeal to the price buyer limited the size of their market. They had to draw from miles around. When imitators came, there would be wholesale liquidations as volume fell. The current high sales of the supers was said to be partly due to their novelty. Basically people wanted convenient neighborhood grocers. If the neighborhood stores "cooperate with their suppliers, pay attention to their costs, and improve their service," they would be able to weather the competition until it blew over.[3]

It never blew over. The chains discovered that survival required going into the supermarket business. This meant the wholesale destruction of their huge investments in corner store sites and in established distribution and merchandising methods. The companies with "the courage of their convictions" resolutely stuck to the corner store philosophy. They kept their pride but lost their shirts.

### SELF-DECEIVING CYCLE

But memories are short. For example, it is hard for people who today confidently hail the twin messiahs of electronics

and chemicals to see how things could possibly go wrong with these galloping industries. They probably also cannot see how a reasonably sensible businessman could have been as myopic as the famous Boston millionaire who 50 years ago unintentionally sentenced his heirs to poverty by stipulating that his entire estate be forever invested exclusively in electric streetcar securities. His posthumous declaration, "There will always be a big demand for efficient urban transportation," is no consolation to his heirs who sustain life by pumping gasoline at automobile filling stations.

Yet, in a casual survey I recently took among a group of intelligent business executives, nearly half agreed that it would be hard to hurt their heirs by tying their estates forever to the electronics industry. When I then confronted them with the Boston streetcar example, they chorused unanimously, "That's different!" But is it? Is not the basic situation identical?

In truth, *there is no such thing* as a growth industry, I believe. There are only companies organized and operated to create and capitalize on growth opportunities. Industries that assume themselves to be riding some automatic growth escalator invariably descend into stagnation. The history of every dead and dying "growth" industry shows a self-deceiving cycle of bountiful expansion and undetected decay. There are four conditions which usually guarantee this cycle:

1. The belief that growth is assured by an expanding and more affluent population.
2. The belief that there is no competitive substitute for the industry's major product.
3. Too much faith in mass production and in the advantages of rapidly declining unit costs as output rises.
4. Preoccupation with a product that lends itself to carefully controlled

[2] For more details see M. M. Zimmerman, *The Super Market: A Revolution in Distribution* (New York, McGraw-Hill Book Company, Inc., 1955), p. 48.
[3] *Ibid.*, pp. 45–47.

scientific experimentation, improvement, and manufacturing cost reduction.

I should like now to begin examining each of these conditions in some detail. To build my case as boldly as possible, I shall illustrate the points with reference to three industries—petroleum, automobiles, and electronics—particularly petroleum, because it spans more years and more vicissitudes. Not only do these three have excellent reputations with the general public and also enjoy the confidence of sophisticated investors, but their managements have become known for progressive thinking in areas like financial control, product research, and management training. If obsolescence can cripple even these industries, it can happen anywhere.

## POPULATION MYTH

The belief that profits are assured by an expanding and more affluent population is dear to the heart of every industry. It takes the edge off the apprehensions everybody understandably feels about the future. If consumers are multiplying and also buying more of your product or service, you can face the future with considerably more comfort than if the market is shrinking. An expanding market keeps the manufacturer from having to think very hard or imaginatively. If thinking is an intellectual response to a problem, then the absence of a problem leads to the absence of thinking. If your product has an automatically expanding market, then you will not give much thought to how to expand it.

One of the most interesting examples of this is provided by the petroleum industry. Probably our oldest growth industry, it has an enviable record. While there are some current apprehensions about its growth rate, the industry itself tends to be optimistic. But I believe it can be demonstrated that it is undergoing a fundamental yet typical change. It is not only ceasing to be a growth industry, but may actually be a declining one, relative to other business. Although there is widespread unawareness of it, I believe that within 25 years the oil industry may find itself in much the same position of retrospective glory that the railroads are now in. Despite its pioneering work in developing and applying the present-value method of investment evaluation, in employee relations, and in working with backward countries, the petroleum business is a distressing example of how complacency and wrongheadedness can stubbornly convert opportunity into near disaster.

One of the characteristics of this and other industries that have believed very strongly in the beneficial consequences of an expanding population, while at the same time being industries with a generic product for which there has appeared to be no competitive substitute, is that the individual companies have sought to outdo their competitors by improving on what they are already doing. This makes sense, of course, if one assumes that sales are tied to the country's population strings, because the customer can compare products only on a feature-by-feature basis. I believe it is significant, for example, that not since John D. Rockefeller sent free kerosene lamps to China has the oil industry done anything really outstanding to create a demand for its product. Not even in product improvement has it showered itself with eminence. The greatest single improvement, namely, the development of tetraethyl lead, came from outside the industry, specifically from General Motors and DuPont. The big contributions made by the industry itself are confined to the technology of oil exploration, production, and refining.

### ASKING FOR TROUBLE

In other words, the industry's efforts have focused on improving the *efficiency* of getting and making its product, not really on improving the generic product or its marketing. Moreover, its chief product has continuously been defined in the narrowest possible terms, namely, gasoline, not energy, fuel, or transportation. This attitude has helped assure that:

• Major improvements in gasoline quality tend not to originate in the oil industry. Also, the development of superior alternative fuels comes from outside the oil industry, as will be shown later.

• Major innovations in automobile fuel marketing are originated by small new oil companies that are not primarily preoccupied with production or refining. These are the companies that have been responsible for the rapidly expanding multipump gasoline stations, with their successful emphasis on large and clean layouts, rapid and efficient driveway service, and quality gasoline at low prices.

Thus, the oil industry is asking for trouble from outsiders. Sooner or later, in this land of hungry inventors and entrepreneurs, a threat is sure to come. The possibilities of this will become more apparent when we turn to the next dangerous belief of many managements. For the sake of continuity, because this second belief is tied closely to the first, I shall continue with the same example.

### IDEA OF INDISPENSABILITY

The petroleum industry is pretty much persuaded that there is no competitive substitute for its major product, gasoline —or if there is, that it will continue to be a derivative of crude oil, such as diesel fuel or kerosene jet fuel.

There is a lot of automatic wishful thinking in this assumption. The trouble is that most refining companies own huge amounts of crude oil reserves. These have value only if there is a market for products into which oil can be converted— hence the tenacious belief in the continuing competitive superiority of automobile fuels made from crude oil.

This idea persists despite all historic evidence against it. The evidence not only shows that oil has never been a superior product for any purpose for very long, but it also shows that the oil industry has never really been a growth industry. It has been a succession of different businesses that have gone through the usual historic cycles of growth, maturity, and decay. Its over-all survival is owed to a series of miraculous escapes from total obsolescence, of last-minute and unexpected reprieves from total disaster reminiscent of the Perils of Pauline.

### PERILS OF PETROLEUM

I shall sketch in only the main episodes:

First, crude oil was largely a patent medicine. But even before that fad ran out, demand was greatly expanded by the use of oil in kerosene lamps. The prospect of lighting the world's lamps gave rise to an extravagant promise of growth. The prospects were similar to those the industry now holds for gasoline in other parts of the world. It can hardly wait for the underdeveloped nations to get a car in every garage.

In the days of the kerosene lamp, the oil companies competed with each other and against gaslight by trying to improve the illuminating characteristics of kerosene. Then suddenly the impossible happened. Edison invented a light which was totally nondependent on crude oil. Had it not been for the growing use of kerosene in space heaters, the incandescent lamp would have completely finished oil as a growth industry at that time. Oil would have been good for little else than axle grease.

Then disaster and reprieve struck again. Two great innovations occurred, neither originating in the oil industry. The successful development of coal-burning domestic central-heating systems made the space heater obsolescent. While the industry reeled, along came its most magnificent boost yet—the internal combustion engine, also invented by outsiders. Then when the prodigious expansion for gasoline finally began to level off in the 1920's, along came the miraculous escape of a central oil heater. Once again, the escape was provided by an outsider's invention and development. And when that market weakened, wartime demand for aviation fuel came to the rescue. After the war the expansion of civilian aviation, the dieselization of railroads, and the explosive demand for cars and trucks kept the industry's growth in high gear.

Meanwhile centralized oil heating —whose boom potential had only recently been proclaimed—ran into severe competition from natural gas. While the oil companies themselves owned the gas that now competed with their oil, the industry did not originate the natural gas revolution, nor has it to this day greatly profited from its gas ownership. The gas revolution was made by newly formed transmission companies that marketed the product with an aggressive ardor. They started a magnificent new industry, first against the advice and then against the resistance of the oil companies.

By all the logic of the situation, the oil companies themselves should have made the gas revolution. They not only owned the gas; they also were the only people experienced in handling, scrubbing, and using it, the only people ex-perienced in pipeline technology and transmission, and they understood heating problems. But, partly because they knew that natural gas would compete with their own sale of heating oil, the oil companies pooh-poohed the potentials of gas.

The revolution was finally started by oil pipeline executives who, unable to persuade their own companies to go into gas, quit and organized the spectacularly successful gas transmission companies. Even after their success became painfully evident to the oil companies, the latter did not go into gas transmission. The multibillion dollar business which should have been theirs went to others. As in the past, the industry was blinded by its narrow preoccupation with a specific product and the value of its reserves. It paid little or no attention to its customers' basic needs and preferences.

The postwar years have not witnessed any change. Immediately after World War II the oil industry was greatly encouraged about its future by the rapid expansion of demand for its traditional line of products. In 1950 most companies projected annual rates of domestic expansion of around 6% through at least 1975. Though the ratio of crude oil reserves to demand in the Free World was about 20 to 1, with 10 to 1 being usually considered a reasonable working ratio in the United States, booming demand sent oil men searching for more without sufficient regard to what the future really promised. In 1952 they "hit" in the Middle East; the ratio skyrocketed to 42 to 1. If gross additions to reserves continue at the average rate of the past five years (37 billion barrels annually), then by 1970 the reserve ratio will be up to 45 to 1. This abundance of oil has weakened crude and product prices all over the world.

Management cannot find much consolation today in the rapidly expanding petrochemical industry, another oil-using idea that did not originate in the leading firms. The total United States production of petrochemicals is equivalent to about 2% (by volume) of the demand for all petroleum products. Although the petrochemical industry is now expected to grow by about 10% per year, this will not offset other drains on the growth of crude oil consumption. Furthermore, while petrochemical products are many and growing, it is well to remember that there are nonpetroleum sources of the basic raw material, such as coal. Besides, a lot of plastics can be produced with relatively little oil. A 50,000-barrel-per-day oil refinery is now considered the absolute minimum size for efficiency. But a 5,000-barrel-per-day chemical plant is a giant operation.

Oil has never been a continuously strong growth industry. It has grown by fits and starts, always miraculously saved by innovations and developments not of its own making. The reason it has not grown in a smooth progression is that each time it thought it had a superior product safe from the possibility of competitive substitutes, the product turned out to be inferior and notoriously subject to obsolescence. Until now, gasoline (for motor fuel, anyhow) has escaped this fate. But, as we shall see later, it too may be on its last legs.

The point of all this is that there is no guarantee against product obsolescence. If a company's own research does not make it obsolete, another's will. Unless an industry is especially lucky, as oil has been until now, it can easily go down in a sea of red figures—just as the railroads have, as the buggy whip manufacturers have, as the corner grocery chains have, as most of the big movie companies have, and indeed as many other industries have.

The best way for a firm to be lucky is to make its own luck. That requires knowing what makes a business successful. One of the greatest enemies of this knowledge is mass production.

## PRODUCTION PRESSURES

Mass-production industries are impelled by a great drive to produce all they can. The prospect of steeply declining unit costs as output rises is more than most companies can usually resist. The profit possibilities look spectacular. All effort focuses on production. The result is that marketing gets neglected.

John Kenneth Galbraith contends that just the opposite occurs.[4] Output is so prodigious that all effort concentrates on trying to get rid of it. He says this accounts for singing commercials, desecration of the countryside with advertising signs, and other wasteful and vulgar practices. Galbraith has a finger on something real, but he misses the strategic point. Mass production does indeed generate great pressure to "move" the product. But what usually gets emphasized is selling, not marketing. Marketing, being a more sophisticated and complex process, gets ignored.

The difference between marketing and selling is more than semantic. Selling focuses on the needs of the seller, marketing on the needs of the buyer. Selling is preoccupied with the seller's need to convert his product into cash; marketing with the idea of satisfying the needs of the customer by means of the product and the whole cluster of things associated with creating, delivering, and finally consuming it.

[4] *The Affluent Society* (Boston, Houghton Mifflin Company, 1958), pp. 152–160.

In some industries the enticements of full mass production have been so powerful that for many years top management in effect has told the sales departments, "You get rid of it; we'll worry about profits." By contrast, a truly marketing-minded firm tries to create value-satisfying goods and services that consumers will want to buy. What it offers for sale includes not only the generic product or service, but also how it is made available to the customer, in what form, when, under what conditions, and at what terms of trade. Most important, what it offers for sale is determined not by the seller but by the buyer. The seller takes his cues from the buyer in such a way that the product becomes a consequence of the marketing effort, not vice versa.

### LAG IN DETROIT

This may sound like an elementary rule of business, but that does not keep it from being violated wholesale. It is certainly more violated than honored. Take the automobile industry:

Here mass production is most famous, most honored, and has the greatest impact on the entire society. The industry has hitched its fortune to the relentless requirements of the annual model change, a policy that makes customer orientation an especially urgent necessity. Consequently the auto companies annually spend millions of dollars on consumer research. But the fact that the new compact cars are selling so well in their first year indicates that Detroit's vast researchers have for a long time failed to reveal what the customer really wanted. Detroit was not persuaded that he wanted anything different from what he had been getting until it lost millions of customers to other small car manufacturers.

How could this unbelievable lag behind consumer wants have been perpetuated so long? Why did not research reveal consumer preferences before consumers' buying decisions themselves revealed the facts? Is that not what consumer research is for—to find out before the fact what is going to happen? The answer is that Detroit never really researched the customer's wants. It only researched his preferences between the kinds of things which it had already decided to offer him. For Detroit is mainly product-oriented, not customer-oriented. To the extent that the customer is recognized as having needs that the manufacturer should try to satisfy, Detroit usually acts as if the job can be done entirely by product changes. Occasionally attention gets paid to financing, too, but that is done more in order to sell than to enable the customer to buy.

As for taking care of other customer needs, there is not enough being done to write about. The areas of the greatest unsatisfied needs are ignored, or at best get stepchild attention. These are at the point of sale and on the matter of automotive repair and maintenance. Detroit views these problem areas as being of secondary importance. That is underscored by the fact that the retailing and servicing ends of this industry are neither owned and operated nor controlled by the manufacturers. Once the car is produced, things are pretty much in the dealer's inadequate hands. Illustrative of Detroit's arm's-length attitude is the fact that, while servicing holds enormous sales-stimulating, profit-building opportunities, only 57 of Chevrolet's 7,000 dealers provide night maintenance service.

Motorists repeatedly express their dissatisfaction with servicing and their apprehensions about buying cars under the present selling setup. The anxieties and problems they encounter during the auto buying and maintenance processes are probably more intense and widespread today than 30 years ago. Yet the automobile companies do not *seem* to listen to or take their cues from the anguished consumer. If they do listen, it must be through the filter of their own preoccupation with production. The marketing effort is still viewed as a necessary consequence of the product, not vice versa, as it should be. That is the legacy of mass production, with its parochial view that profit resides essentially in low-cost full production.

### WHAT FORD PUT FIRST

The profit lure of mass production obviously has a place in the plans and strategy of business management, but it must always *follow* hard thinking about the customer. This is one of the most important lessons that we can learn from the contradictory behavior of Henry Ford. In a sense Ford was both the most brilliant and the most senseless marketer in American history. He was senseless because he refused to give the customer anything but a black car. He was brilliant because he fashioned a production system designed to fit market needs. We habitually celebrate him for the wrong reason, his production genius. His real genius was marketing. We think he was able to cut his selling price and therefore sell millions of $500 cars because his invention of the assembly line had reduced the costs. Actually he invented the assembly line because he had concluded that at $500 he could sell millions of cars. Mass production was the *result* not the cause of his low prices.

Ford repeatedly emphasized this point,

but a nation of production-oriented business managers refuses to hear the great lesson he taught. Here is his operating philosophy as he expressed it succinctly:

"Our policy is to reduce the price, extend the operations, and improve the article. You will notice that the reduction of price comes first. We have never considered any costs as fixed. Therefore we first reduce the price to the point where we believe more sales will result. Then we go ahead and try to make the prices. We do not bother about the costs. The new price forces the costs down. The more usual way is to take the costs and then determine the price, and although that method may be scientific in the narrow sense; it is not scientific in the broad sense, because what earthly use is it to know the cost if it tells you that you cannot manufacture at a price at which the article can be sold? But more to the point is the fact that, although one may calculate what a cost is, and of course all of our costs are carefully calculated, no one knows what a cost ought to be. One of the ways of discovering . . . is to name a price so low as to force everybody in the place to the highest point of efficiency. The low price makes everybody dig for profits. We make more discoveries concerning manufacturing and selling under this forced method than by any method of leisurely investigation."[5]

### PRODUCT PROVINCIALISM

The tantalizing profit possibilities of low unit production costs may be the most seriously self-deceiving attitude that can afflict a company, particularly a "growth" company where an apparently assured expansion of demand already

[5] Henry Ford, *My Life and Work* (New York, Doubleday, Page & Company, 1923), pp. 146–147.

tends to undermine a proper concern for the importance of marketing and the customer.

The usual result of this narrow preoccupation with so-called concrete matters is that instead of growing, the industry declines. It usually means that the product fails to adapt to the constantly changing patterns of consumer needs and tastes, to new and modified marketing institutions and practices, or to product developments in competing or complementary industries. The industry has its eyes so firmly on its own specific product that it does not see how it is being made obsolete.

The classical example of this is the buggy whip industry. No amount of product improvement could stave off its death sentence. But had the industry defined itself as being in the transportation business rather than the buggy whip business, it might have survived. It would have done what survival always entails, that is, changing. Even if it had only defined its business as providing a stimulant or catalyst to an energy source, it might have survived by becoming a manufacturer of, say, fanbelts or air cleaners.

What may some day be a still more classical example is, again, the oil industry. Having let others steal marvelous opportunities from it (e.g., natural gas, as already mentioned, missile fuels, and jet engine lubricants), one would expect it to have taken steps never to let that happen again. But this is not the case. We are now getting extraordinary new developments in fuel systems specifically designed to power automobiles. Not only are these developments concentrated in firms outside the petroleum industry, but petroleum is almost systematically ignoring them, securely content in its wedded bliss to oil. It is the story of the kerosene lamp versus the incandescent lamp all over again. Oil is trying to improve hydrocarbon fuels rather than to develop *any* fuels best suited to the needs of their users, whether or not made in different ways and with different raw materials from oil.

Here are some of the things which nonpetroleum companies are working on:

Over a dozen such firms now have advanced working models of energy systems which, when perfected, will replace the internal combustion engine and eliminate the demand for gasoline. The superior merit of each of these systems is their elimination of frequent, time-consuming, and irritating refueling stops. Most of these systems are fuel cells designed to create electrical energy directly from chemicals without combustion. Most of them use chemicals that are not derived from oil, generally hydrogen and oxygen.

Several other companies have advanced models of electric storage batteries designed to power automobiles. One of these is an aircraft producer that is working jointly with several electric utility companies. The latter hope to use off-peak generating capacity to supply overnight plug-in battery regeneration. Another company, also using the battery approach, is a medium-size electronics firm with extensive small-battery experience that it developed in connection with its work on hearing aids. It is collaborating with an automobile manufacturer. Recent improvements arising from the need for high-powered miniature power storage plants in rockets have put us within reach of a relatively small battery capable of withstanding great overloads or surges of power. Germanium diode applications and batteries using sintered-plate and nickel-cadmium techniques promise to make a revolution in our energy sources.

Solar energy conversion systems are also getting increasing attention. One usually cautious Detroit auto executive recently ventured that solar-powered cars might be common by 1980.

As for the oil companies, they are more or less "watching developments," as one research director put it to me. A few are doing a bit of research on fuel cells, but almost always confined to developing cells powered by hydrocarbon chemicals. None of them are enthusiastically researching fuel cells, batteries, or solar power plants. None of them are spending a fraction as much on research in these profoundly important areas as they are on the usual run-of-the-mill things like reducing combustion chamber deposit in gasoline engines. One major integrated petroleum company recently took a tentative look at the fuel cell and concluded that although "the companies actively working on it indicate a belief in ultimate success . . . the timing and magnitude of its impact are too remote to warrant recognition in our forecasts."

One might, of course, ask: Why should the oil companies do anything different? Would not chemical fuel cells, batteries, or solar energy kill the present product lines? The answer is that they would indeed, and that is precisely the reason for the oil firms having to develop these power units before their competitors, so they will not be companies without an industry.

Management might be more likely to do what is needed for its own preservation if it thought of itself as being in the energy business. But even that would not be enough if it persists in imprisoning itself in the narrow grip of its tight product orientation. It has to think of itself as taking care of customer needs, not finding, refining, or even selling oil. Once it genuinely thinks of its business as taking

care of people's transportation needs, nothing can stop it from creating its own extravagantly profitable growth.

## "CREATIVE DESTRUCTION"

Since words are cheap and deeds are dear, it may be appropriate to indicate what this kind of thinking involves and leads to. Let us start at the beginning—the customer. It can be shown that motorists strongly dislike the bother, delay, and experience of buying gasoline. People actually do not buy gasoline. They cannot see it, taste, it, feel it, appreciate it, or really test it. What they buy is the right to continue driving their cars. The gas station is like a tax collector to whom people are compelled to pay a periodic toll as the price of using their cars. This makes the gas station a basically unpopular institution. It can never be made popular or pleasant, only less unpopular, less unpleasant.

To reduce its unpopularity completely means eliminating it. Nobody likes a tax collector, not even a pleasantly cheerful one. Nobody likes to interrupt a trip to buy a phantom product, not even from a handsome Adonis or a seductive Venus. Hence, companies that are working on exotic fuel substitutes which will eliminate the need for frequent refueling are heading directly into the outstretched arms of the irritated motorist. They are riding a wave of inevitability, not because they are creating something which is technologically superior or more sophisticated, but because they are satisfying a powerful customer need. They are also eliminating noxious odors and air pollution.

Once the petroleum companies recognize the customer-satisfying logic of what another power system can do, they will see that they have no more choice about working on an efficient, long-lasting fuel (or some way of delivering present fuels without bothering the motorist) than the big food chains had a choice about going into the supermarket business, or the vacuum tube companies had a choice about making semiconductors. For their own good the oil firms will have to destroy their own highly profitable assets. No amount of wishful thinking can save them from the necessity of engaging in this form of "creative destruction."

I phrase the need as strongly as this because I think management must make quite an effort to break itself loose from conventional ways. It is all too easy in this day and age for a company or industry to let its sense of purpose become dominated by the economics of full production and to develop a dangerously lopsided product orientation. In short, if management lets itself drift, it invariably drifts in the direction of thinking of itself as producing goods and services, not customer satisfactions. While it probably will not descend to the depths of telling its salesmen, "You get rid of it; we'll worry about profits," it can, without knowing it, be practicing precisely that formula for withering decay. The historic fate of one growth industry after another has been its suicidal product provincialism.

## DANGERS OF R & D

Another big danger to a firm's continued growth arises when top management is wholly transfixed by the profit possibilities of technical research and development. To illustrate I shall turn first to a new industry—electronics—and then return once more to the oil companies. By comparing a fresh example with a familiar one, I hope to emphasize the prevalence and insidiousness of a hazardous way of thinking.

In the case of electronics, the greatest danger which faces the glamorous new companies in this field is not that they do not pay enough attention to research and development, but that they pay *too much* attention to it. And the fact that the fastest growing electronics firms owe their eminence to their heavy emphasis on technical research is completely beside the point. They have vaulted to affluence on a sudden crest of unusually strong general receptiveness to new technical ideas. Also, their success has been shaped in the virtually guaranteed market of military subsidies and by military orders that in many cases actually preceded the existence of facilities to make the products. Their expansion has, in other words, been almost totally devoid of marketing effort.

Thus, they are growing up under conditions that come dangerously close to creating the illusion that a superior product will sell itself. Having created a successful company by making a superior product, it is not surprising that management continues to be oriented toward the product rather than the people who consume it. It develops the philosophy that continued growth is a matter of continued product innovation and improvement.

A number of other factors tend to strengthen and sustain this belief:

(1) Because electronic products are highly complex and sophisticated, managements become top-heavy with engineers and scientists. This creates a selective bias in favor of research and production at the expense of marketing. The organization tends to view itself as making things rather than satisfying customer needs. Marketing gets treated as a residual activity, "something else" that must be done once the

vital job of product creation and production is completed.

(2) To this bias in favor of product research, development, and production is added the bias in favor of dealing with controllable variables. Engineers and scientists are at home in the world of concrete things like machines, test tubes, production lines, and even balance sheets. The abstractions to which they feel kindly are those which are testable or manipulatable in the laboratory, or, if not testable, then functional, such as Euclid's axioms. In short, the managements of the new glamour-growth companies tend to favor those business activities which lend themselves to careful study, experimentation, and control—the hard, practical, realities of the lab, the shop, the books.

What gets shortchanged are the realities of the *market*. Consumers are unpredictable, varied, fickle, stupid, shortsighted, stubborn, and generally bothersome. This is not what the engineer-managers say, but deep down in their consciousness it is what they believe. And this accounts for their concentrating on what they know and what they can control, namely, product research, engineering, and production. The emphasis on production becomes particularly attractive when the product can be made at declining unit costs. There is no more inviting way of making money than by running the plant full blast.

Today the top-heavy science-engineering-production orientation of so many electronics companies works reasonably well because they are pushing into new frontiers in which the armed services have pioneered virtually assured markets. The companies are in the felicitous position of having to fill, not find markets; of not having to discover what the customer needs and wants, but of having the customer voluntarily come forward with specific new product demands. If a team of consultants had been assigned specifically to design a business situation calculated to prevent the emergence and development of a customer-oriented marketing viewpoint, it could not have produced anything better than the conditions just described.

### STEPCHILD TREATMENT

The oil industry is a stunning example of how science, technology, and mass production can divert an entire group of companies from their main task. To the extent the consumer is studied at all (which is not much), the focus is forever on getting information which is designed to help the oil companies improve what they are now doing. They try to discover more convincing advertising themes, more effective sales promotional drives, what the market shares of the various companies are, what people like or dislike about service station dealers and oil companies, and so forth. Nobody seems as interested in probing deeply into the basic human needs that the industry might be trying to satisfy as in probing into the basic properties of the raw material that the companies work with in trying to deliver customer satisfactions.

Basic questions about customers and markets seldom get asked. The latter occupy a stepchild status. They are recognized as existing, as having to be taken care of, but not worth very much real thought or dedicated attention. Nobody gets as excited about the customers in his own backyard as about the oil in the Sahara Desert. Nothing illustrates better the neglect of marketing than its treatment in the industry press:

The centennial issue of the *American Petroleum Institute Quarterly,* published in 1959 to celebrate the discovery of oil in Titusville, Pennsylvania, contained 21 feature articles proclaiming the industry's greatness. Only one of these talked about its achievements in marketing, and that was only a pictorial record of how service station architecture has changed. The issue also contained a special section on "New Horizons," which was devoted to showing the magnificent role oil would play in American's future. Every reference was ebulliently optimistic, never implying once that oil might have some hard competition. Even the reference to atomic energy was a cheerful catalogue of how oil would help make atomic energy a success. There was not a single apprehension that the oil industry's affluence might be threatened or a suggestion that one "new horizon" might include new and better ways of serving oil's present customers.

But the most revealing example of the stepchild treatment that marketing gets was still another special series of short articles on "The Revolutionary Potential of Electronics." Under that heading this list of articles appeared in the table of contents:

- "In the Search for Oil"
- "In Production Operations"
- "In Refinery Processes"
- "In Pipeline Operations"

Significantly, every one of the industry's major functional areas is listed, *except* marketing. Why? Either it is believed that electronics holds no revolutionary potential for petroleum marketing (which is palpably wrong), or the editors forgot to discuss marketing (which is more likely, and illustrates its stepchild status).

The order in which the four functional areas are listed also betrays the alienation of the oil industry from the consumer. The industry is implicitly defined as beginning with the search for oil and ending with its distribution from the refinery. But the truth is, it seems to me, that the industry begins with the needs of the customer for its products. From that primal position its definition moves steadily backstream to areas of progressively lesser importance, until it finally comes to rest at the "search for oil."

### BEGINNING AND END

The view that an industry is a customer-satisfying process, not a goods-producing process, is vital to all businessmen to understand. An industry begins with the customer and his needs, not with a patent, a raw material, or a selling skill. Given the customer's needs, the industry develops backwards, first concerning itself with the physical *delivery* of customer satisfactions. Then it moves back further to *creating* the things by which these satisfactions are in part achieved. How these materials are created is a matter of indifference to the customer, hence the particular form of manufacturing, processing, or what-have-you cannot be considered as a vital aspect of the industry. Finally, the industry moves back still further to *finding* the raw materials necessary for making its products.

The irony of some industries oriented toward technical research and development is that the scientists who occupy the high executive positions are totally unscientific when it comes to defining their companies' over-all needs and purposes. They violate the first two rules of the scientific method—being aware of and defining their companies' problems, and then developing testable hypotheses about solving them. They are scientific only about the convenient things, such as laboratory and product experiments. The reason that the customer (and the satisfaction of his deepest needs) is not considered as being "the problem" is not because there is any certain belief that no such problem exists, but because an organizational lifetime has conditioned management to look in the opposite direction. Marketing is a stepchild.

I do not mean that selling is ignored. Far from it. But selling, again, is not marketing. As already pointed out, selling concerns itself with the tricks and techniques of getting people to exchange their cash for your product. It is not concerned with the values that the exchange is all about. And it does not, as marketing invariably does, view the entire business process as consisting of a tightly integrated effort to discover, create, arouse, and satisfy customer needs. The customer is somebody "out there" who, with proper cunning, can be separated from his loose change.

Actually, not even selling gets much attention in some technologically minded firms. Because there is a virtually guaranteed market for the abundant flow of their new products, they do not actually know what a real market is. It is as if they lived in a planned economy, moving their products routinely from factory to retail outlet. Their successful concentration on products tends to convince them of the soundness of what they have been doing, and they fail to see the gathering clouds over the market.

## CONCLUSION

Less than 75 years ago American railroads enjoyed a fierce loyalty among astute Wall Streeters. European monarchs invested in them heavily. Eternal wealth was thought to be the benediction for anybody who could scrape a few thousand dollars together to put into rail stocks. No other form of transportation could compete with the railroads in speed, flexibility, durability, economy, and growth potentials. As Jacques Barzun put it, "By the turn of the century it was an institution, an image of man, a tradition, a code of honor, a source of poetry, a nursery of boyhood desires, a sublimest of toys, and the most solemn machine— next to the funeral hearse—that marks the epochs in man's life."[6]

Even after the advent of automobiles, trucks, and airplanes, the railroad tycoons remained imperturbably self-confident. If you had told them 60 years ago that in 30 years they would be flat on their backs, broke, and pleading for government subsidies, they would have thought you totally demented. Such a future was simply not considered possible. It was not even a discussable subject, or an askable question, or a matter which any sane person would consider worth speculating about. The very thought was insane. Yet a lot of insane notions now have matter-of-fact acceptance—for example, the idea of 100-ton tubes of metal moving smoothly through the air 20,000 feet above the earth, loaded with 100 sane and solid citizens casually drinking martinis—and they have dealt cruel blows to the railroads.

What specifically must other companies do to avoid this fate? What does customer orientation involve? These questions have in part been answered by the preceding examples and analysis. It would take another article to show in detail what is required for specific industries. In any case, it should be obvious that building an effective customer-oriented company involves far more than good intentions or promotional tricks; it involves profound matters of human organization and leadership. For the present, let me merely suggest what appear to be some general requirements.

### VISCERAL FEEL OF GREATNESS

Obviously the company has to do what survival demands. It has to adapt to the

------

[6] *Op. cit.,* p. 20.

requirements of the market, and it has to do it sooner rather than later. But mere survival is a so-so aspiration. Anybody can survive in some way or other, even the skid-row bum. The trick is to survive gallantly, to feel the surging impulse of commercial mastery; not just to experience the sweet smell of success, but to have the visceral feel of entrepreneurial greatness.

No organization can achieve greatness without a vigorous leader who is driven onward by his own pulsating *will to succeed*. He has to have a vision of grandeur, a vision that can produce eager followers in vast numbers. In business, the followers are the customers. To produce these customers, the entire corporation must be viewed as a customer-creating and customer-satisfying organism. Management must think of itself not as producing products but as providing customer-creating value satisfactions. It must push this idea (and everything it means and requires) into every nook and cranny of the organization. It has to do this continuously and with the kind of flair that excites and stimulates the people in it. Otherwise, the company will be merely a series of pigeonholed parts, with no consolidating sense of purpose or direction.

In short, the organization must learn to think of itself not as producing goods or services but as *buying customers,* as doing the things that will make people *want* to do business with it. And the chief executive himself has the inescapable responsibility for creating this environment, this viewpoint, this attitude, this aspiration. He himself must set the company's style, its direction, and its goals. This means he has to know precisely where he himself wants to go, and to make sure the whole organization is enthusiastically aware of where that is. This is a first requisite of leadership, for *unless he knows where he is going, any road will take him there.*

If any road is okay, the chief executive might as well pack his attaché case and go fishing. If an organization does not know or care where it is going, it does not need to advertise that fact with a ceremonial figurehead. Everybody will notice it soon enough.

## QUESTIONS

1. What is the population myth?
2. Frequently what is the engineer-manger's viewpoint of consumers?
3. A narrow preoccupation with low unit production costs can lead to marketing blindness. Explain.
4. As the author views it, what caused the present dilemma faced by the railroad industry?
5. There is no such thing as a growth industry. Explain.

# $\mathcal{Z}$. A Changing World Requires New Marketing Concepts*

Charles S. Roberts, Manager, Marketing Services, Ebasco Services Incorporated

*Marketing considerations have a direct influence on the performance of other major functions of the company, such as manufacturing, engineering, research and development, and financial. Instead of the traditional functional fragmentation of corporate activities, the marketing management concept is a unifying concept with all the functions of the company oriented and guided by the market and its requirements.*

In 1959, just a year ago, a new inspirational phrase was heard throughout our land—The Soaring Sixties. The recession of 1958, and the protracted steel strike of 1959, was a disappointing finish for the decade of the '50's. But the decade of the '60's—ah, that will be another thing! Just view the controversy that goes on today. "As election fever mounts, everybody running for office stands four-square against Sin, Payola—and Economic Stagnation. Just as surely, from now to November the air will be rent with oratory extolling Virtue, Motherhood—Economic Growth. Nobody is anti-growth. The controversy is not whether we will have growth but about the question 'How much'?"[1]

Here are some forecasts made by *Fortune* magazine for the decade of the sixties.

Any long-range forecasts of market growth must take into consideration popu-

lation. The growth of population has always been interpreted as a bullish factor. *Fortune's* estimate, surrounded by a host of qualifying clauses, sets the 1970 United States population at 208,000,000 persons.

*Fortune's* estimate of American economic growth as measured by Gross National Product is a comfortable middle-of-the-road estimate of an annual average rate of growth of about 4% in the 1960's. Under a Republican administration during the past eight years, growth has been at an average annual rate of 3%. The Democrats insist it will have to be 5% if we are to keep up with Soviet growth.

A difference of only two percentage points can make an enormous gap in Gross National Product targets over the long pull. A 5% growth rate is calculated to yield a projected real Gross National Product in 1975 of about $1,100 billion, whereas a 3% growth rate would yield only about a $700 billion Gross National Product in 1975.

*Fortune* estimates "investment" and defense expenditures together should rise from $177 billion in 1957 to $195 billion in 1960 to $260 billion in 1965 and $315

---

* Reprinted from *The Commercial and Financial Chronicle*, 25 Park Place, New York, 7, New York, October 13, 1960, p. 9. (Originally, a talk by Mr. Roberts at the Twenty-fourth Annual Client Companies Marketing Conference, New York City.)
[1] "The Great Growth Debate." *Dun's Review*, Vol. 76, No. 1, July, 1960, p. 34.

billion in 1970 (inflation would raise all the figures).

It also estimates an immense increase in consumption outlays. Total consumption should increase from $275 billion in 1957 to about $355 billion in 1965 and $436 billion in 1970.

## WILL MARKETING KEEP PACE?

I certainly have no quarrel with these forecasts. They are based on hypotheses acceptable to the magazine, and represent its best thinking as to what lies ahead. We must recognize, however, that in addition to numerical forecasts and trend analyses of such matters as capital formation, population and output per man-hour which have gone into these statistical growth calculations, there is an underlying and basic assumption to which no numerical value is assigned.

*This assumption is that our marketing ability will keep pace with our growth opportunities.*

The first nine months of 1960 do not offer assurance that this assumption is valid. The current concern regarding the possibility of a recession in 1961 is even less reassuring. If industry fails to recognize the need for improving our marketing competence to keep pace with our growth opportunities "The Soaring Sixties" may go down in history as "The Sagging Sixties."

There is no need to review our economic history in painstaking detail in order to recognize that our problem is no longer one of production but one of consumption. It became obvious in World War II that we could meet the war material needs of ourselves and that of our allies—and still increase the standard of living of our people. We were able to afford both guns and butter. We have continued to expand production and raise our standard of living through one crisis

after another—Korea, Quemoy, Suez, and into the age of missile rattling.

Thus, as we stand here today and peer into the future, the major problem confronting industry is the expansion of consumption to keep pace with the growth in productive capacity. It is not enough to satisfy present wants; industry must stimulate and "create" new wants. Only by continuing and expanding consumption can we realize the growth projected for the decade of the '60's. The sole end and purpose of production is consumption, and marketing is the handmaiden of consumption.

The general problem confronting American Industry is deceptively simple. The effectiveness of marketing has not kept pace with our increase in productive capacity. To repeat, the extent to which we improve our marketing effectiveness will determine whether the decade of the '60's will go down in history as "Soaring" or "Sagging."

## MARKETING MANAGEMENT CONCEPT

Before you begin to conclude that I am a prophet of doom, I will hasten to add that I believe that American Industry will rise to meet the marketing challenge which faces it. In my judgment, American Industry will meet the challenge by increasing acceptance and implementation of the Marketing Management Concept as a fundamental philosophy of business operation.

The thinking embodied in the Marketing Management Concept is not particularly new nor revolutionary. What is new is that more and more companies are examining their traditional sales thinking with jaundiced eyes and finding their ideas outmoded and obsolete.

The Marketing Management Concept implies that top management thinking is market oriented. Marketing considerations have a direct influence on the performance of other major functions of the company, such as manufacturing, engineering, research and development, and financial. Instead of the traditional functional fragmentation of corporate activities, the Marketing Management Concept is a unifying concept with all the functions of the company oriented and guided by the market and its requirements.

There is no universal agreement, as yet, as to what the Marketing Concept includes. One good definition is that of the General Electric Company, a leader in the implementation of this concept. G.E. defined the Marketing Concept as the introduction of ". . . the marketing man at the beginning rather than at the end of the productive cycle and (the integration of) marketing into each phase of the business. Thus marketing, through its studies and research, will establish for the engineer, the designer, and the manufacturing man what the customer wants in a given product; what price he is willing to pay; and where and when it will be wanted. Marketing would have authority in product planning, production, scheduling, and inventory control, as well as in the sales, distribution and servicing of the product."[2]

## A FAR CRY FROM TRADITIONAL VIEW OF SELLING

Although controversy may continue for some time about what, exactly, is a good definition of the Marketing Management Concept, there is little doubt that the importance of marketing considerations as they affect other functions of the company is becoming more and more appreciated in the business philosophy of a growing number of companies.

As we can see in the G.E. definition,

[2] The General Electric Company. Annual Report 1952.

the customer is King in determining what, how, where, when, and for how much, a company will sell its products and services. This is a far cry from the traditional view of selling that the function of the sales department is to persuade individual customers to buy whatever product the company produces, or wants to produce.

The customer-oriented philosophy of the Marketing Management Concept importantly influences the actions of all corporate functions. Engineering has to employ all its ingenuity to design products, not only to meet engineering requirements, but also to be acceptable to the customer in regard to appearance, size, complexity, service, and final cost. Manufacturing must schedule, produce, and maintain inventory consistent with forecasts of customer demand. Research and Development must orient its activities toward products with a predetermined favorable market opportunity rather than toward products that are "interesting" but whose market acceptance is undetermined. Financial Management must consider the financial requirements of the company in the light of sales forecasts, investments in plant, work in process, and inventory levels, as they are determined by market requirements. And Sales Management, of course, must gear its activities, selling, merchandising, advertising, servicing, etc., to the demands of the market.

## MARKET KNOWLEDGE

A prime requisite of the Marketing Management Concept is knowledge of markets. We must know the answers to broad questions—How big is the market? What are the growth potentials? What are the characteristics of the market? What are the characteristics of the competition? We must know the answers to questions of detail—What are the functional and physical specifications required of the product? What are the price considerations? How should the product be marketed? What are the service requirements? What other products will our product compete with? Without such knowledge the Marketing Management Concept is just a string of words. It can't work and may do more harm than good.

Thus, the success of the Marketing Management Concept is significantly dependent on the findings of soundly conceived and well performed marketing studies and marketing research findings. You may recall in G.E.'s definition of the Marketing Concept, it was stated that ". . . Thus marketing, through its studies and research, will establish for the engineer, the designer, and the manufacturing man what the customer wants in a given product; what price he is willing to pay; and where and when it will be wanted, etc."

The emphasis, therefore, of the Marketing Management Concept is on the customer. Here is an example of how one of our clients used market research to guide its product development, establish prices, and establish its sales forecast.

## AN ILLUSTRATION

This company planned to add to its line a portable instrument used extensively in metal working plants. The engineers had designed an extremely compact instrument weighing only two pounds as compared to the conventional 11 pounds. For purposes of evaluating the new design, we performed a study in which users were offered a choice of three instruments, all identical in function, quality, and price but differing in size. Contrary to the expectation of our client's engineers, a larger instrument weighing four pounds was preferred substantially over the two-pound instrument. The findings

were of this order: 55% of the users selected the four-pound instrument as their first choice compared to 25% who selected the two-pound instrument. Equally significant, perhaps, was the finding that 16% of the users stated that the two-pound instrument would be unacceptable compared with less than 2% of the users expressing this attitude regarding the four-pound instrument.

The reasons for the marked differences in preference and lack of acceptance might be considered as irrelevant by an engineer yet readily understood by a marketing man. Two important reasons militated against the two-pound instrument:

(1) Its very small size would make it easy to steal.

(2) It did not look as though it was worth as much as the four-pound instrument.

An analysis of the market potential by various price levels revealed that the increase in sales potential as the price level declined was not enough to affect the profitability favorably. From the research findings, the client was able to establish its selling price at a level which would yield 26% more net profit with 19% fewer unit sales.

Thus, in a single study, this company was able to establish that there was an attractive market for the product it was contemplating, it was able to establish design criteria to ensure maximum customer acceptance, it was able to establish price on a realistic basis, and it was able to set up forecasts of sales and profitability of the new product line.

Let us turn our attention to the market forecasts for the electric utility industry. As you recall, The Edison Electric Institute's study earlier this year revealed that the electric companies expect their output to be 1.2 *trillion* kilowatt-hours by 1970, more than double that of last year. By

1980 the annual output forecast was estimated to reach an estimated 2.3 *trillion* kilowatt-hours. *Can* these forecasts be realized? I believe they can! *Will* these forecasts be realized? Well, that is another matter.

### WILL ELECTRIC SALES INCREASE?

In referring to electric space heating as the big market opportunity of the Sixties, one of the industry's representatives[3] said "I believe to promote successfully in this kind of competitive market, utilities really have to wake up and get up!" It is obvious that he does not think that the forecasted increase in kilowatt-hour consumption will just happen. He thinks the industry will have to go to work if it is to achieve its goals.

We must not permit ourselves to be lulled into thinking that our product is indispensable, that all we have to do is to stand by and let others do our marketing for us. We cannot afford to ease up just because we may agree with the financial community that the electric utility industry is an industry with a truly impressive growth record and an equally impressive growth prospect.

There is quite another, and bearish, evaluation of the electric utility industry: "This is another one of those supposedly 'no-substitute' products that has been enthroned on a pedestal of invincible growth. When the incandescent lamp came along, kerosene lights were finished. Later the water wheel and the steam engine were cut to ribbons by the flexibility, reliability, simplicity, and just plain easy availability of electric motors. The prosperity of electric utilities continues to wax extravagant as the home is converted into a museum of electric gadgetry. How can

anybody miss by investing in utilities, with no competition, nothing but growth ahead?

### SUBSTITUTE FOR ELECTRICITY

"But a second look is not quite so comforting. A score of nonutility companies are well advanced toward developing a powerful chemical fuel cell which could sit in some hidden closet of every home silently ticking off electric power. The electric lines that vulgarize so many neighborhoods will be eliminated. So will the endless demolition of streets and service interruptions during storms. Also on the horizon is solar energy, again pioneered by nonutility companies.

"Who says that the utilities have no competition? They may be natural monopolies now, but tomorrow they may be natural deaths. To avoid this prospect, they too will have to develop fuel cells, solar energy, and other power sources. To survive, they themselves will have to plot the obsolescence of what now produces their livelihood."

We may not agree fully with this viewpoint, expressed by an economist[4] in a recent issue of the *Harvard Business Review,* but it should make us realize that no industry is inviolate, that managerial imaginativeness and audacity are essential ingredients in the success of a company and an industry.

Even though we may agree that utility companies as we know them today are far from obsolete, it becomes pretty clear when we look at the figures that the utility industries must embark on a diversified program of marketing activity if they are to achieve their goals. Now that rural electrification is practically complete there is no big segment of the population to be opened up as new electric customers. The

---

[3] Thomas G. Ayers, Vice-President, Commonwealth Edison Company.

[4] Levitt, Theodore, "Marketing Myopia," pp. 46–47. *Harvard Business Review,* Vol. 38, No. 4. Also included in this text, pp. 1-19.

future increase in nonindustrial electric customers is dependent, practically entirely, on the increase in population and household formation.

Thus, increases in the consumption of energy, at least the form of energy you prefer to sell, can come about in several different ways.

## WHAT MUST BE DONE

(1) You must capture an increasing share of load builders from your competitors selling different forms of energy—electric, gas, and the fossil fuels. Thus, space heating by electric has hardly scratched the surface, and both electric and gas compete with oil and coal to fill this need.

(2) You must promote and encourage the purchase and use of load builders still in fairly limited use, from a saturation level at least—room and central air conditioning, dishwashers, clothes dryers, dehumidifiers, etc.

(3) You must encourage increased use of existing load builders—better lighting for example.

But over and above all of these activities it is clear that the utility industries must embark on a program of creating new wants for energy. As the accepted uses of energy approach saturation, it becomes imperative that utilities take a direct hand in creating new consumer wants, which will be satisfied by new appliances, which will create additional energy demands. Although, traditionally, nonutility companies have performed this function of creating new wants, the utility industries must ask themselves whether the time has come to break with this tradition. If nothing else, the tremendous investments in plant and facilities make it mandatory that utilities play a more positive role in creating their own future.

In summary, then, we believe that the marketing ability of American Industry will keep pace with our growth opportunities by a revolution in marketing procedures. Whether we call it Marketing Management Concept, Total Marketing, or Customer-Oriented Marketing, the end result will be the same. More and more companies will direct their activities to giving the customer what he wants. More and more companies will adopt the scientific approach and use studies and marketing research to provide the bases for sound management decisions.

## QUESTIONS

1. On what other major management functions of the company do marketing considerations have a direct influence?

2. Since product planning in most established firms is still production oriented and organizationally under the engineering department, what practical steps might be taken to make it more market oriented?

3. What specific studies can be conducted by the marketing research staff to keep top management informed on changes in customer requirements?

4. Why must the naturally monopolistic electric utility industry embark on a diversified program of marketing activity?

5. Does the fact that the United States will have 30 million more people by 1970 mean that new and better markets will automatically follow?

# 3. The Marketing Revolution*

Robert J. Keith, Executive Vice President, The Pillsbury Company

*Business today is in the throes of a marketing revolution. This revolution is based on a change of philosophy and one of its effects will be the emergence of marketing as the dominant function in American business.*

The consumer, not the company, is in the middle.

In today's economy the consumer, the man or woman who buys the product, is at the absolute dead center of the business universe. Companies revolve around the customer, not the other way around.

Growing acceptance of this consumer concept has had, and will have, far-reaching implications for business, achieving a virtual revolution in economic thinking. As the concept gains ever greater acceptance, marketing is emerging as the most important single function in business.

## A REVOLUTION IN SCIENCE

A very apt analogy can be drawn with another revolution, one that goes back to the sixteenth century. At that time astronomers had great difficulty predicting the movements of the heavenly bodies. Their charts and computations and celestial calendars enabled them to estimate the approximate positions of the planets on any given date. But their calculations were never exact—there was always a variance.

Then a Polish scientist named Nicolaus Copernicus proposed a very simple answer to the problem. If, he proposed, we

* Reprinted from the *Journal of Marketing*, national quarterly publication of the American Marketing Association, Vol. 24, No. 3, January 1960, pp. 35–38.

assume that the sun, and not the earth, is at the center of our system, and that the earth moves around the sun instead of the sun moving around the earth, all our calculations will prove correct.

The Pole's idea raised a storm of controversy. The earth, everyone knew, was at the center of the universe. But another scientist named Galileo put the theory to test—and it worked. The result was a complete upheaval in scientific and philosophic thought. The effects of Copernicus' revolutionary idea are still being felt today.

## A REVOLUTION IN MARKETING

In much the same way American business in general—and Pillsbury in particular—is undergoing a revolution of its own today: a marketing revolution.

This revolution stems from the same idea stated in the opening sentence of this article. No longer is the company at the center of the business universe. Today the customer is at the center.

Our attention has shifted from problems of production to problems of marketing, from the product we *can* make to the product the consumer *wants* us to make, from the company itself to the market place.

The marketing revolution has only begun. It is reasonable to expect that its implications will grow in the years to come, and that lingering effects will be felt a century, or more than one century, from today.

So far the theory has only been advanced, tested, and generally proved correct. As more and more businessmen grasp the concept, and put it to work, our economy will become more truly marketing oriented.

## PILLSBURY'S PATTERN: FOUR ERAS

Here is the way the marketing revolution came about at Pillsbury. The experience of this company has followed a typical pattern. There has been nothing unique, and each step in the evolution of the marketing concept has been taken in a way that is more meaningful because the steps are, in fact, typical.

Today in our company the marketing concept finds expression in the simple statement, "Nothing happens at Pillsbury until a sale is made." This statement represents basic reorientation on the part of our management. For, not too many years ago, the ordering of functions in our business placed finance first, production second, and sales last.

How did we arrive at our present point of view? Pillsbury's progress in the marketing revolution divides neatly into four separate eras—eras which parallel rather closely the classic pattern of development in the marketing revolution.

## 1st ERA—PRODUCTION ORIENTED

First came the era of manufacturing. It began with the formation of the company in 1869 and continued into the 1930s. It is significant that the *idea for* the formation of our company came from the *availability* of high-quality wheat and the *proximity* of water power—and not from the availability and proximity of growing major market areas, or the demand for better, less expensive, more convenient flour products.

Of course, these elements were potentially present. But the two major elements which fused in the mind of Charles A. Pillsbury and prompted him to invest his modest capital in a flour mill were, on the one hand, wheat, and, on the other hand, water power. His principal concern was with production, not marketing.

His thought and judgment were typical of the business thinking of his day. And such thinking was adequate and proper for the times.

Our company philosophy in this era might have been stated this way: "We are professional flour millers. Blessed with a supply of the finest North American wheat, plenty of water power, and excellent milling machinery, we produce flour of the highest quality. Our basic function is to mill high-quality flour, and of course (and almost incidentally) we must hire salesmen to sell it, just as we hire accountants to keep our books."

The young company's first new product reveals an interesting example of the thinking of this era. The product was middlings, the bran left over after milling. Millfeed, as the product came to be known, proved a valuable product because it was an excellent nutrient for cattle. But the impetus to launch the new product came not from a consideration of the nutritional needs of cattle or a marketing analysis. It came primarily from the desire to dispose of a by-product! The new product decision was production oriented, not marketing oriented.

## 2nd ERA—SALES ORIENTED

In the 1930s Pillsbury moved into its second era of development as a marketing company. This was the era of sales. For the first time we began to be highly conscious of the consumer, her wants, and her prejudices, as a key factor in the business equation. We established a commercial research department to provide us with facts about the market.

We also became more aware of the importance of our dealers, the wholesale and retail grocers who provided a vital link in our chain of distribution from the mill to the home. Knowing that consumers and dealers as well were vital to the company's success, we could no longer simply mark them down as unknowns in our figuring. With this realization, we took the first step along the road to becoming a marketing company.

Pillsbury's thinking in this second era could be summed up like this: "We are a flour-milling company, manufacturing a number of products for the consumer market. We must have a first-rate sales organization which can dispose of all the products we can make at a favorable price. We must back up this sales force with consumer advertising and market intelligence. We want our salesmen and our dealers to have all the tools they need for moving the output of our plants to the consumer."

Still not a marketing philosophy, but we were getting closer.

## 3rd ERA—MARKETING ORIENTED

It was at the start of the present decade that Pillsbury entered the marketing era. The amazing growth of our consumer business as the result of introducing baking mixes provided the immediate impetus. But the groundwork had been laid by key men who developed our sales concepts in the middle forties.

With the new cake mixes, products of our research program, ringing up sales on the cash register, and with the realization that research and production could produce literally hundreds of new and different products, we faced for the first time the necessity for selecting the best new products. We needed a set of criteria for selecting the kind of products we would manufacture. We needed an organization to establish and maintain these criteria, and for attaining maximum sale of the products we did select.

We needed, in fact, to build into our company a new management function which would direct and control all the other corporate functions from procurement to production to advertising to sales. This function was marketing. Our solution was to establish the present marketing department.

This department developed the criteria which we would use in determining which products to market. *And these criteria were, and are, nothing more nor less than those of the consumer herself.* We moved the mountain out to find out what Mahomet, and Mrs. Mahomet, wanted. The company's purpose was no longer to mill flour, nor to manufacture a wide variety of products, but to satisfy the needs and desires, both actual and potential, of our customers.

If we were to restate our philosophy during the past decade as simply as possible, it would read: "We make and sell products for consumers."

The business universe, we realized, did not have room at the center for Pillsbury or any other company or groups of companies. It was already occupied by the customers.

This is the concept at the core of the marketing revolution. How did we put it to work for Pillsbury?

THE BRAND-MANAGER CONCEPT

The first move was to transform our small advertising department into a marketing department. The move involved far more than changing the name on organizational charts. It required the introduction of a new, and vitally important, organizational concept—the brand-manager concept.

The brand-manager idea is the very backbone of marketing at Pillsbury. The man who bears the title, brand manager, has total accountability for results. He directs the marketing of his product as if it were his own business. Production does its job, and finance keeps the profit figures. Otherwise, the brand manager has total responsibility for marketing his product. This responsibility encompasses pricing, commercial research, competitive activity, home service and publicity coordination, legal details, budgets, advertising plans, sales promotion, and execution of plans. The brand manager must think first, last, and always of his sales target, the consumer.

Marketing permeates the entire organization. Marketing plans and executes the sale—all the way from the inception of the product idea, through its development and distribution, to the customer purchase. Marketing begins and ends with the consumer. New product ideas are conceived after careful study of her wants and needs, her likes and dislikes. Then marketing takes the idea and marshals all the forces of the corporation to translate the idea into product and the product into sales.

In the early days of the company, consumer orientation did not seem so important. The company made flour, and flour was a staple—no one would question the availability of a market. Today we must determine whether the American housewife will buy lemon pudding cake in preference to orange angel food. The variables in the equation have multiplied, just as the number of products on the grocers' shelves have multiplied from a hundred or so into many thousands.

When we first began operating under this new marketing concept, we encountered the problems which always accompany any major reorientation. Our people were young and frankly immature in some areas of business; but they were men possessed of an idea and they fought for it. The idea was almost too powerful. The marketing concept proved its worth in sales, but it upset many of the internal balances of the corporation. Marketing-oriented decisions resulted in peaks and valleys in production, schedules, labor, and inventories. But the system worked. It worked better and better as maverick marketing men became motivated toward tonnage and profit.

## 4th ERA—MARKETING CONTROL

Today marketing is coming into its own. Pillsbury stands on the brink of its fourth major era in the marketing revolution.

Basically, the philosophy of this fourth era can be summarized this way: "We are moving from a company which has the marketing concept to a marketing company."

Marketing today sets company operating policy short-term. It will come to influence long-range policy more and more. Where today consumer research, technical research, procurement, production, advertising, and sales swing into action under the broad canopy established by marketing, tomorrow capital and financial planning, ten-year volume and profit goals will also come under the aegis of marketing. More than any other function, marketing must be tied to top management.

Today our marketing people know more about inventories than anyone in top management. Tomorrow's marketing man must know capital financing and the implications of marketing planning on long-range profit forecasting.

Today technical research receives almost all of its guidance and direction from marketing. Tomorrow marketing will assume a more creative function in the advertising area, both in terms of ideas and media selection.

### CHANGES IN THE FUTURE

The marketing revolution has only begun. There are still those who resist its basic idea, just as there are always those who will resist change in business, government, or any other form of human institution.

As the marketing revolution gains momentum, there will be more changes. The concept of the customer at the center will remain valid; but business must adjust to the shifting tastes and likes and desires and needs which have always characterized the American consumer.

For many years the geographical center of the United States lay in a small Kansas town. Then a new state, Alaska, came along, and the center shifted to the north and west. Hawaii was admitted to the Union and the geographical mid-point took another jump to the west. In very much the same way, modern business must anticipate the restless shifting of buying attitudes, as customer preferences move north, south, east, or west from a

liquid center. There is nothing static about the marketing revolution, and that is part of its fascination. The old order has changed, yielding place to the new—but the new order will have its quota of changes, too.

At Pillsbury, as our fourth era progresses, marketing will become the basic motivating force for the entire corporation. Soon it will be true that every activity of the corporation—from finance to sales to production—is aimed at satisfying the needs and desires of the consumer. When that stage of development is reached, the marketing revolution will be complete.

## QUESTIONS

1. Describe the four evolutionary stages in the marketing revolution at Pillsbury.
2. Were most firms of the nineteenth century production or marketing oriented? Why?
3. The brand-manager idea is the very backbone of marketing at Pillsbury. Explain.
4. What additional management responsibilities must marketing men be prepared to take on in the future at Pillsbury and other consumer oriented companies?

# 4. Marketing Decision Making: A Management Revolution Under Way*

Charles C. Slater, Director of Consumer Marketing Services, Arthur D. Little, Inc.

*The development in marketing decision-making appears to be a coordination of presently available skills far more than it is replacement of present skills by new methods. Behavioral scientists and operations researchers are beginning to pool their skills in joint attack on marketing problems.*

When one thinks of a revolution in marketing decision-making, the parallel of the Industrial Revolution comes to mind. Economic historians now, in retrospect, seem to agree that one of the inventions that triggered the Industrial Revolution was the development of co-ordinated specialization of production. With this coordinated specialization of production it was possible to make interchangeable parts, thus gaining the increase in output that this system permits. Evidence indicates that a similar revolution has begun to emerge in the marketing field—the coordination of specialists in marketing working together to solve large-scale, fundamental marketing problems.

This development in marketing decision-making appears to me to be a coordination of presently available skills far more than it is replacement of present skills by new methods. In order to place these developments in the appropriate perspective, the very significant contributions of research studies based on individual discipline approaches must be fully recognized. Behavioral scientists making studies in depth of sub-optimal problems have yielded important contributions to marketing science. Studies of consumer attitudes and behavior and the more recent developments in the study of consumer motivation could be cited at length —each a contribution to the solution of specific marketing problems. Many are contributions to the general understanding of human behavior. The importance of the individual study based on the approaches found in one of the social sciences is in no way depreciated by this emerging coordination. Sub-optimal studies based on each of the behavioral sciences will continue to be of value but a new level of marketing problem is emerging, one that requires application of several science approaches. The ability to tackle problems as broad and basic as, for example, "What is the optimum long-run distribution system for a particular large firm?" or "What is the optimum distribution of sales effort among several market outlets over the next decade?" require that the research be the product of specialists working as a team.

Merely recognizing the need for information that is beyond the technical

* Reprinted from *Dynamic Marketing for a Changing World*, Proceedings of the Forty-third National Conference of the American Marketing Association, June 15–17, 1960, p. 173. Edited by Robert S. Hancock.

capacity of any one of the several research disciplines involved does nothing more than provide the incentive for coordination. In my opinion there are two factors that have been crucial in the development of coordinated research. First, students of each of the behavioral disciplines seem to be growing in their awareness of the fact that all of the other disciplines share the same basic scientific method of testing hypotheses. Behavioral scientists with specific training in sociology, psychology, cultural anthropology, economics, and marketing as well as the newly emerging discipline of operations research can all communicate effectively and relatively economically with the language of statistics. Thus, there is the possibility of exchanging information about their work and sharing as specialists in the tasks of hypothesis generation, research design, and the testing of these hypotheses. Furthermore, certain of the specialists trained in marketing and economics are capable of working on the assignments closely enough so that they get some grasp of all the research procedures employed and at the same time can undertake to guide the implementation of research findings.

The whole family of new data processing techniques is the second innovation which has made possible the revolution in marketing decision making. These techniques make it possible to test many propositions that had been treated as only academic and marginal possibilities before the development of the data processing capacity of modern electronic machines.

I have had an opportunity to observe some of the modest beginnings in our own organization of these more general and broader joint attacks on marketing problems. The following two cases illustrate the interdependence of the separate specialties in the behavioral sciences working on what appear to be fundamental

rather than sub-optimal marketing problems. Most of these techniques are not new to the major utility and energy industries. Petroleum companies have for some time been utilizing these techniques in dealing with problems of minimizing supply costs and at the same time trying to gain share in their markets.

The first case deals with a consumer goods manufacturer selling in an oligopolistic market with independent distributors and retailers handling their product. The industry is characterized by rapid product modification to achieve minor and seemingly temporary differentiation. The study was prompted by the Long-range Planning Committee composed of young executives of a large corporation who were asked to recommend the optimum product policy, distribution policy, and merchandising plan for the corporation over the next ten years. In effect, they were charged with the responsibility of developing a long-range marketing plan for the corporation. We were asked to aid them in organizing broad theses which could be tested and thereby develop an over-all long range marketing plan.

First, a man trained in marketing indicated that in his opinion, the changes in distribution channels that had been observed reflected a growing consumer appreciation of the differences in the costs of physical handling of large outlets versus small outlets. Many important consumer attitude problems could be studied to probe further into this proposition, but for purposes of these studies these questions were temporarily held in abeyance and the proposition was accepted that consumers are willing to go further to shop in order to get to the necessarily larger and lower priced outlets. Reasoning from this, it was decided that lowering costs of physical handling all along the channels of distribution would improve their brand's chances of being the best comparative value.

An operations research specialist was the next contributor in the sequence of this study. A transportation model with nearly a dozen production points and an additional near dozen distribution centers was planned to identify nearly one hundred wholesale distribution points. Then an economist, using multiple regression methods, developed a forecast of demand for each major product for the next ten to fifteen years for each of the nearly one hundred local markets. One of the inputs to this regression was a periodically conducted survey of purchase intentions and replacement schedules for the products. Thus, measurement of demand changes over time required the interdependent actions of economists and marketing survey specialists.

One other aspect of the problem brought into play marketing specialists concerned with the costs of selling and why it varied from area to area. Their study considered variations in the cost of selling by area and established an estimate of the rate of change of sales cost with changes in volume. The increase in sales cost for a given increase in volume was, in fact, greater in some areas than in others. This information together with the information from the economic forecasts of aggregate demand were employed in the transportation model to determine the optimum locations for sources, routes and destinations for all products—and the optimum distribution of promotional expenditures among the many market areas. These studies are providing a general frame of reference for the firm to continuously refine their physical distribution plan and to assess the relative effectiveness of their sales expenditures in each market.

The product line policy remained to be considered. This work is now being pursued in two separate but interdependent attacks. Production cost changes due to changes in product line modifications are being examined by the use of a linear program of the plant system. While simulation permits examination of changes in inventory and production cycles, the impact of changes in product line upon market penetration and marketing cost must be assessed by test markets. In this phase of the work it is planned to deliberately thin down the varieties of products offered in selected markets and see whether the loss in sales offsets savings in production.

This illustration of interdependent work by behavioral researchers trained in various disciplines tied the work of half a dozen separate fields together to answer fundamental questions of marketing policy asked by management. To be sure, this treatment falls short of considering strategic gains due to sharp shifts in policy that could mislead competition and it falls short of providing answers to the quest for creative advertising themes.

In the second case a large firm asked us to examine by this interdisciplinary approach the problem of establishing the optimum market share objectives for several marketing outlets. This is a firm with operations in many areas. On the one hand, the problem consisted of establishing the hypothetical operating costs that would be associated with changes in relative importance of the several operations considered. The other side of the problem consisted of determining the changes in sales performance that were associated with variations in sales effort. In this way we were able to establish the likely levels of sales expenditures that would be required to compensate for loss of volume that might be expected to result from market organization changes.

First, the estimate of cost reductions due to consolidation of operations was put in the hands of engineers trained in economic procedures. The determination of the changes in sales costs associated with variations in sales effort was made the responsibility of economists interested in marketing problems. Several questions remained that had to be answered by survey research approaches. For instance, would there be added costs due to dealer defection if marketing policies were changed? Were the observed variations in the apparent efficiency of marketing effort of competing sellers due to measurable differences in consumer attitude, or must the variation be treated as the random influence of unexplained variation? A group of survey research people worked on these aspects of the problem. Finally, a very simple simulation model was devised that permitted us to examine the profitability likely to follow from various alternative courses of action. The important point to be drawn from these two very limited examples of coordinated research is that they are attacks upon fundamental marketing decision problems and not isolated studies of sub-optimal problems.

I do not hold either of these examples up to be unique, nor do I consider them to be outstanding examples of research procedure, but they do represent a new kind of marketing study, a study which depends on the interdependent activity of marketing research specialists trained in several different behavioral sciences. Other similar instances could be cited of

very broad and penetrating questions being asked of marketing research people. Management is beginning to ask broader questions and the researcher is given a chance to solve problems that optimize long run profitability of the firm rather than researching to find the answer to small and often transitory problems by independent and uncoordinated use of specialists.

## QUESTIONS

1. Behavioral scientists and operations researchers can communicate their findings to one another through what common tool of measurement?
2. Describe in some detail one example of interdependent research by behavioral scientists and operations researchers.
3. Distinguish between the professional training of behavioral scientists and operations researchers.
4. An interdisciplinary research attack on distribution problems will trigger a marketing revolution similar to the industrial revolution which was stimulated by the development of coordinated specialization of production. Comment on this statement.

# 5. An Interpretation of the Marketing Concept*

Robert L. King, Associate Professor of Marketing, University of South Carolina

*The marketing concept is defined as a managerial philosophy concerned with the mobilization, utilization, and control of total corporate effort for the purpose of helping consumers solve selected problems in ways compatible with planned enhancement of the profit position of the firm.*

## INTRODUCTION

During the 1950's, especially since 1955, trade and business publications and conferences attended by businessmen and business academicians have devoted a quantity of space and time to consideration of the meaning, implications, and implementation of something called "the marketing concept." As is true of many such discussions, it is probable that the heat generated has substantially exceeded the light.

Some writers and speakers have criticized "the jargon" which has accompanied these discussions; yet, few have offered precise, comprehensive definitions. Others have been more concerned with whether or not "the marketing concept" embodied or proposed something really new, most often, however, failing to take time to find out exactly what is included or what is being proposed. Still others have concentrated attention on the historical origins of the concept and on the forces which have emphasized its relevance to business management. The purpose of this paper is not to explore the concept's origin or its age. Rather, this inquiry is concerned with construction of a definition of "the marketing concept" which not only stresses its relevance to business management, but which, further, may serve as a foundation for implementation of the concept by firms' managements.

## INTERPRETATIONS IN THE LITERATURE

Business publications and conferences of businessmen and business academicians have been very effective in generating interest in, and concern with, "the marketing concept." It appears, however, that they have been less effective in disseminating the meaning of the concept. Definitions of the marketing concept are few, and generally they are vague. Most articles platitudinize the basic role of consumer and profit orientations, or enumerate a series of physical manifestations by which some persons apparently judge the degree to which a firm has implemented the concept. Manifestations most frequently named are: (1) creation of formal marketing departments, headed by vice-presidents in charge of marketing or marketing directors, who coordinate strong central marketing staffs; (2) formal written marketing planning, with emphasis on

* A paper presented at the Thirty-first Annual Conference, Southern Economic Association, Memphis, Tennessee, November 10, 1961. This paper is based upon an unpublished doctoral dissertation deposited in the Michigan State University Library, 1960.

35

product planning and development and profit planning and control; and (3) increased use of the marketing research function. A number of writers appear to base implementation of the concept solely on the organizational structuring of the marketing operation. Marketing concept literature content may be summarized as concerned primarily with partial analyses of the implications of the concept to marketing management, and with over-emphasis of certain physical manifestations which allegedly indicate implementation of the concept. While frequent and occasionally heated discussion of the preceding aspects has shed some light on the concept's meaning, its failure to provide widespread understanding is based upon the literature's lack of comprehensiveness of scope, and the lack of integration of reported data into a meaningful total system.

## DEFINITION OF "THE MARKETING CONCEPT"

Based upon a review of marketing concept literature, a series of interviews with members of corporate management, and this writer's interpretations, "the marketing concept" is defined as a managerial philosophy concerned with the mobilization, utilization, and control of total corporate effort for the purpose of helping consumers solve selected problems in ways compatible with planned enhancement of the profit position of the firm. More specifically, the marketing concept involves:

1. Company-wide managerial awareness and appreciation of the consumer's role as it is related to the firm's existence, growth, and stability. As Drucker has noted, business enterprise is an organ of society; thus its basic purpose lies outside the business itself. And the valid definition of business purpose is the creation of customers.

2. Active company-wide managerial awareness of, and concern with interdepartmental implications of decisions and actions of an individual department. That is, the firm is viewed as a network of forces focussed on meeting defined consumer needs, and comprising a system within which actions taken in one department or area frequently result in significant repercussions in other areas of the firm. Also, it is recognized that such actions may affect the company's equilibrium with its external environment, e.g., its consumers, its competitors, etc.

3. Active company-wide managerial concern with innovation of products and services designed to solve selected consumer problems.

4. General managerial concern with the effect of new-product and service introduction on the firm's profit position, both present and future, and recognition of the potential rewards which may accrue from new product planning, including profits and profit stability.

5. General managerial appreciation of the role of marketing intelligence and other fact-finding and reporting units within, and adjacent to the firm, in translating the general statements presented above into detailed statements of profitable market potentials, targets, and action. Implicit in this statement is not only an expansion of the traditional function and scope of formal marketing research, but also assimilation of other sources of marketing data, such as the firm's distribution system and its advertising agency counsel, into a potent marketing intelligence service.

6. Company-wide managerial effort, based upon participation and interaction of company officers, in establishing corporate and departmental objectives, which are understood by, and acceptable to

these officers, and which are consistent with enhancement of the firm's profit position.

7. Formal short- and long-range planning of corporate goals, strategies, and tactics, resulting in defined and coordinated effort of the firm's functional areas.

8. Creation, expansion, termination, or restructuring of any corporate functions as deemed necessary in mobilizing, utilizing, and controlling total corporate effort toward the solution of selected consumer problems in ways compatible with enhancement of the firm's profit position.

## "THE MARKETING CONCEPT" AND MANAGERIAL ACTION

The relationship and significance of the marketing concept, as previously defined, to business management can be demonstrated schematicaly as a closed-system model. The model illustrates (1) the firm's product-service offering in the market place, (2) the conscious sensitivity of corporate management to imbalance in market offering and market demand, and (3) the mechanism through which balance is regained by management.

Essential features of the model are the "sensitivity monitor" and the "bases of managerial action." The "sensitivity monitor" represents the firm's total, integrated marketing intelligence force, including company units and external agencies. Included, for example, are marketing and logistics research which are engaged in the collection of market information and the interpretation of this data into market intelligence. A broader area than traditional marketing research is implied, with its focus directed toward the market offering-market demand balance. "Managerial action" refers to corporate management's selection from a number of alternative decisions a course of action consistent

with the firm's dual objectives implicit in the definition of "the marketing concept."

Functioning of the concept model may be summarized as follows. In accordance with the bases of the marketing concept, management determines the firm's initial market offering. When this offering is presented in the market place, the sensitivity monitor functions continuously to evaluate the balance existing between the firm's market offering and the market demand. The monitor is sensitive not only to existing and predicted imbalance, i.e., "problems," but further it is sensitive to existing and potential opportunities. While balance exists between market offering and market demand, the firm continues normal operations. In effect, the monitor confirms the validity of management's plans, and remains as a sentinel, watchful for the appearances of any element in the market place which may affect the position of balance.

Whenever the monitor detects imbalance or new opportunity, this information is passed on to management, thereby causing a break in the system's offering-demand flow. Ultimately, the result is a modified or revised market offering. Whether the information requires corrective action within the bounds of existing company policy, i.e., "routine action," or whether basic policy changes are indicated, i.e., "policy action," resultant decisions and actions are based upon the precepts of the marketing concept.

## SUMMARY

The widespread interest in "the marketing concept" which has developed among businessmen and business academicians during the past decade is evidenced by the appearance of numerous articles and papers on the subject, organizational restructuring of firms' mar-

# MODEL OF THE MARKETING CONCEPT

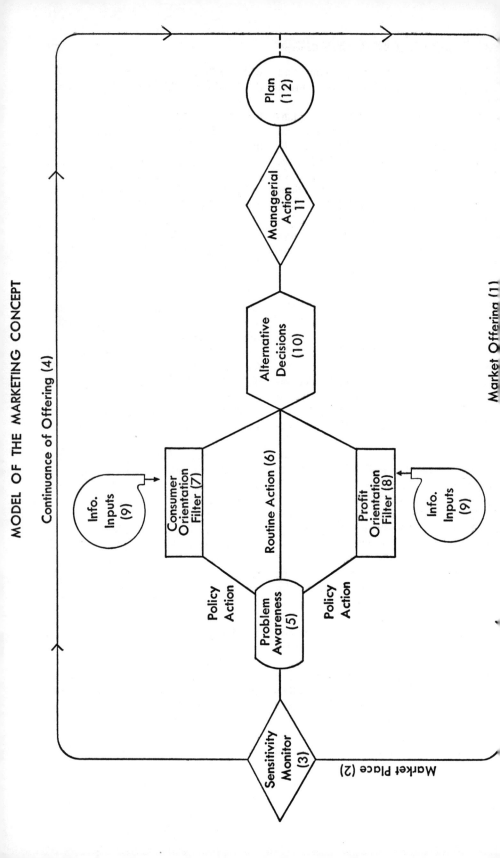

Continuance of Offering (4)

Plan (12)

Managerial Action 11

Alternative Decisions (10)

Consumer Orientation Filter (7)

Profit Orientation Filter (8)

Routine Action (6)

Info. Inputs (9)

Policy Action

Policy Action

Problem Awareness (5)

Sensitivity Monitor (3)

Market Place (2)

Market Offering (1)

keting departments, and title changes involving marketing officers.

While the literature has established almost universal acquaintance with the term, "marketing concept," general understanding of the term has not developed. Most treatments of the concept have dealt with its impact only in selected areas of marketing management. Typically, articles may be categorized as concerned with the philosophical bases of the concept, i.e., consumer and profit orientations, or with certain physical manifestations described as basic to implementation of the concept. The latter is exemplified by the appearance of numerous articles concerned with marketing department organization. Apparently, to many executives, the concept suggests little more than establishment of coordinated central marketing staffs headed by persons titled "marketing vice president."

Three features of the literature are primarily responsible for its failure to present a clear meaning of the concept. First, unwarranted emphasis has been given to certain physical manifestations, such as organizational changes, which are allegedly indicative of implementation of the concept. Second, only negligible attention has been given to the company-wide aspects of the concept. The role of the chief executive in winning acceptance of the philosophy, and the implications regarding participation and perceptions of management in functional areas other than marketing, have been largely ignored. Third, there has been little coordination and integration of the numerous articles

concerned with limited aspects of the concept's meaning and implementation.

Nevertheless, the literature has made a significant contribution to understanding of the concept. Varying degrees of emphasis have been placed upon the dual nature of the firm's objectives, management by objectives, the role of marketing planning and research, significance of the profit contribution of new products, and the lack of coordination and control of marketing effort.

A speaker at the December 1958, conference of the American Marketing Association concluded that the marketing management concept is "an old suggestion that has become popular." It is hoped that this definition of the concept will lead to better understanding of the philosophy, and to meaningful implementation of it in the business world. It is only upon the concept's performance under these conditions that its popularity can be justified.

## QUESTIONS

1. Explain each of the eight subpoints listed under a definition of the marketing concept.
2. What are the company-wide aspects of the marketing concept?
3. Under the marketing concept what roles are played by research and planning?
4. How can the market-oriented firm keep up its communications with customers?

# *6.* Marketing and Management Decision*

Wroe Alderson, Director of Research and Planning, Alderson Associates, Inc.

*Marketing considerations are fundamental to any decision on business plans and policies. The business firm must be visualized as an operating system with inputs and outputs. Staff specialists, including market analysts, operations researchers, and cost accountants can perform their service to management with greater insight by adopting this system perspective.*

Marketing is extremely simple in essence. The goals of scientific marketing are market expansion and marketing efficiency. The whole business of the marketing consultant is to assist management in expanding sales or in controlling or reducing marketing costs in order to have something left for profits. But the breadth of perspective and the refinements of techniques in seeking these ends have developed with breath-taking speed in the postwar period. Major developments include the application of operations research to inventory control and production scheduling, to the evaluation of advertising results, and in measuring the efficiency of other forms of marketing effort. Systematic problem-solving and formal planning have arisen to implement what is known as the marketing concept. Electronic data processing has opened up new avenues of attack on all of the problems mentioned. Analysis of every aspect of market opportunity and marketing effort is carried on with increased speed, precision, and promise of payoff.

All of these improvements in techniques rest on a fundamental conceptual advance. Marketing men come to see the

business firm as an operating system, to analyze it in terms of its inputs and outputs, to understand its destiny as an organic and growing entity in its marketing environment. The application of systems analysis to business activities is the common element of contemporary developments in marketing counsel, operations research, and cost accounting. One aspect of an effective operating system is the flow of information and analysis to facilitate decisions. The market analyst, the operations researcher, and the cost accountant can perform their services to management with greater insight by adopting this systems perspective. A system has some analogy to a machine or a living organism. It differs drastically in the way that it achieves coordination through the collection and transformation of information. The analyst, meditating on his role within the system, might think of the information either in terms of where he gets it or how it is going to be used.

## INTERNAL AND EXTERNAL DATA

The first view leads to dividing the informational problems of a firm into ex-

* Reprinted from *Cost and Profit Outlook,* January 1960.

ternal and external studies. This division is related to the way that information is obtained rather than to the way it is to be used. Internal studies pertain to the resources and activities within the firm. This phase of the informational service to management would include the normal accounting records and analytical studies based on these records. External studies pertain to the relations of the firm to its environment and particularly to its markets. Typical would be the forecasts and studies of demand for the company's products ordinarily carried on by a marketing research department. Accounting came first for a number of reasons, including the fact that data on what was going on inside were more readily available. It was only some fifty years ago that management began to grasp the possibilities of gaining reliable information about the external relationships of the firm through such methods as consumer surveys.

This division into internal and external studies is convenient because it corresponds roughly to the distinction between accounting and marketing research, two disciplines which have required quite different training and technical skills. Perhaps the distinction is all too pat and has served to keep people apart who should have made more progress in working together. Some on either side have recognized that internal and external studies are necessary complements to each other. Both are essential elements in the informational groundwork for decision-making. In fact, the art of management might be said to consist precisely of taking account simultaneously of the inner workings of the firm and its interaction with external forces. The most vocal and effective advocates of this view have been the operations researchers who entered the field of business analysis with a healthy disregard for the traditional boundaries between analytical disciplines.

## FUNCTIONAL CLASSIFICATION OF DATA

An alternative approach is to classify information along functional lines, or in other words, according to the types of decision-making in which it will be used. It will be helpful to go back to the analogy of a machine to point up the differences in a three-way functional classification of information useful to management. First to be considered is the information used in the current and short-run control of a machine, whether it be an automobile or a turning lathe. Take for example the drift of an automobile toward the side of the road in rounding a curve. The feedback of information to the driver normally leads to slight corrective pressures on the steering wheel.

Next is the situation of uncertainty resulting in a slowdown or stoppage of the operation. The driver has now paused at a cross roads not knowing which fork to take. He looks at his maps, asks questions of passersby and considers alternatives if the predetermined route turns out to be impassable. Another example of a problem situation is the driver who has stopped at a repair station because he is doubtful about the performance of his car.

The third type of functional need for information is that in which the car or the lathe is being observed or operated experimentally by an engineer or designer to determine its faults and limitations. His goal is to create a new design which will achieve improved performance. In terms of general systems analysis, the three types of decision-making might be called control, problem-solving, and planning and development.

Control works on the principle of feedback from current operations for minor adjustments designed to keep activities on target. Problem-solving combines internal and external data, often collected for the specific occasion, to resolve uncertainties as to the general direction which activities should be taking. Planning undertakes to design a new system which diverges in greater or lesser degree from the present system. In its more limited phases, planning would only attempt to modify the amounts of various inputs going into the system. In the more comprehensive and long-range versions of market planning, both the character and the amounts of inputs and outputs are wide open for review and recommended changes. The planner might be said to be designing a new model of the operating system each time he submits a general operating plan.

The dual, inside-outside character of informational needs pervades all aspects of informational needs although it may be least obvious in the case of control data. A full realization of this principle should promote fuller cooperation among staff analysts in the several fields of accounting, marketing research and operations research.

## INFORMATION AND CONTROL

Consider, for example, some of the most basic aspects of control information in business, such as quality control, inventory control, and budgetary control. The *procedures* of quality control are carried out in a laboratory, whereas the *policies* are imbued with marketing considerations. Products have been priced out of the market due to control of quality at a higher level than consumers demanded. Other products have been misdirected due to control on qualities which were of relatively little moment to the consumer.

Operations researchers have sometimes worked out perfectly good formulas for inventory control, lacking only one small piece of information which they assumed could be supplied by someone else. This was an estimate of the cost to the company of losing sales which enables the analyst to decide on the level of service to plan for. Obviously the cost of lost sales requires marketing information and a high level of marketing judgment. The sales department may think that it wants nothing less than perfect availability of goods to customers at least until it has heard how much it would cost to provide this level of services.

Budgetary control has an honorable tradition as an aid to management and has been carried out successfully, relying largely on data generated internally. This may still be feasible if budgets are regarded solely as a set of financial limitations imposed by management. A more advanced view of a sales or advertising budget is that it reflects a two-way commitment between top management and the department head. Management pledges resources, and the responsible executive pledges organized effort, both being related to agreed-upon objectives. More and more the sales or advertising executive is being required to submit a written plan in support of his budget request. Marketing plans which will stand up under critical review must make use of information derived from external studies of the company's markets. Once more, inside and outside sources appear to be inseparable in providing an adequate foundation for control decisions.

## INFORMATION AND PROBLEM-SOLVING

In the problem-solving area, marketing is generally reaching for some sense of direction either as to the markets to be cultivated or as to the marketing methods to be used. With companies not accustomed to the use of market surveys to estimate demand, the chief reliance is likely to be on trends in company sales and industry-wide forecasts prepared by outside organizations. Making the best use of either type of data is obviously a problem in market analysis. Studies of marketing costs can sometimes produce useful results, relying on existing internal records or data which can be generated without external research. This is particularly true for the operations of retailers and wholesalers whose expenditures for influencing consumer demand are relatively modest. It also holds for some aspects of marketing by manufacturers such as the physical distribution of goods. But suppose the analyst is asked to determine the optimum amount to be spent for advertising or some other form of marketing effort. To answer this he must estimate the consumer response function, and draw the curve relating expenditures to results. Here he cannot do a wholly adequate job without external marketing research and marketing experiments.

## INFORMATION AND PLANNING

It is the third area of decision-making —that concerned with planning and development—which has the greatest need for synthesis of data drawn from many sources. To develop the disciplines of marketing and business planning which management requires, it will be necessary to utilize the techniques of all types of staff specialists, including accountants and marketing researchers. The need for marketing to employ concepts and techniques originating in accounting is represented by the currency of certain phrases in marketing circles. A prime example is the adaptation of methods of cost analysis first applied in production to marketing cost analysis. More recently market analysts have developed the concept of the marketing audit, with several refinements

and variations such as the pre-plan audit. The latter term implies a careful evaluation of the firm's present position before the planner begins to consider strategies for improving its position.

Another way in which the planner in marketing draws on accounting concepts is the growing use of pro forma operating statements as a major tool of planning. The goals of business planning may be stated as the effort to reach certain operating levels during some specified future time, which might, for example, be the calendar year 1965. Surely it is not enough to forecast company sales volume for that year. Management also needs a forecast of the price level relating dollar volume and physical volume of output. Profits for the firm in 1965 will consist of the margin of sales volume over the total of all the constituent elements of the cost or expenditure side of the operating statement. The pro forma statement, so conceived, is a summary presentation of a set of forecasts for dollar volume, prices, costs and profits. These forecasts cannot be made without various types of information derived from marketing research and planning. Some accountants are not too happy in seeing these tools applied in areas which involve a substantial margin for error. A more constructive view is that the methods borrowed from accounting may bring a little more precision into the hazardous but unavoidable task of guessing about the future.

A pro forma statement for 1965 must be supported by a similar statement for 1964 and so on backward to the present. To set up such a series of statements merely as a projection of last year's figures would be an almost trivial exercise. Costs are incurred in one year with the purpose of augmenting sales and profits in following years. A target as to dollar volume requires a level of marketing expenditures estimated to stimulate that level of demand. The costs of providing the product demanded must be covered by what is left before there is anything for profits. The forward look at what it is going to cost for materials, labor, and productive equipment will carry both the accountant and the marketing researcher into fields which have been explored by very few in either camp.

## MARKET AND BUSINESS PLANNING

It is safe to say that marketing considerations are fundamental to any decisions on business plans and policies. Investment and capital budgeting come back to the kind of facilities which will be needed to supply the markets of the future. Personnel recruitment and training is preparation to perform the tasks which the consumer needs of tomorrow will impose. Budgets for technical research and development will increasingly be devoted to product ideas where there is some evidence of promising markets. Marketing forecasts and programs on the other hand will necessarily take on more of the quantitative and precise detail which is familiar in accounting. Loose concepts, such as market potential, must be translated into market response functions showing sales expectations at various prices and various levels of marketing expenditure.

Accounting was undoubtedly the first staff function generating aids for management judgment. It anticipated by some years the doctrine now accepted by various types of analysts that the business firm should be viewed as an input-output system. As a matter of fact, a business is a dual system relating respectively to flows of money and flows of goods. From the financial viewpoint there are inputs of investment and current expenditure and outputs of profits. From the operating point of view there are inputs of

goods or materials purchased from suppliers and outputs of goods sold to customers. Accountants, by virtue of their traditional role, have tended to emphasize one aspect, and market researchers the other. Market planners need to be reminded that no plan is valid which does not point to a specific profit objective. Accountants may need to be reminded that the only ultimate source of profits is market demand for the company's products and services. Both need greater skill either in direct collaboration or in translating their results into a form that is useful to the other.

Let us return to the analogy previously suggested between business planning and the design of a new and improved version of a machine. Every staff analyst would be well advised to consider the outlook for his own firm and try to picture what it will look like in 1965. If its present products are sold largely to some limited age group, such as the home-makers of from 20 to 40 years, then over a quarter of its customers for 1965 are not yet in the market today. If the firm is technologically progressive and determined to grow through new product introduction, more than half of its sales in 1965 may come from products which are not now in its product line. If the turnover in the sales force is as great as many large companies experience, its sales in 1965 will largely be made by salesmen the firm has yet to employ. The importance of planning decisions for management is underscored by the fact that the success of most any business in 1965 will rest in a very major way on the efforts of new salesmen (men it has not yet hired) selling new products (products it has not yet introduced or perhaps has not yet even designed) to serve the needs of new customers (customers who have not yet matured to the point of being prospective users of the company's products).

Planning can be described in many

ways, but one part of its responsibility is to match resources against prospective opportunities as they will exist in the business environment at some future date. Attempting to balance effort and opportunity five years from now may seem like a hazardous extension of the known into the unknown. But planning is coming forward rapidly because the hazards of planning are not as great as the hazards encountered without planning. Progress in any area usually comes through an act of the imagination. Perhaps the establishment of a central planning unit can be described as a systematic attempt to equip the firm with an active imagination of its own. One of its functions is to generate visions of future possibilities which can then be screened through experienced judgment.

Another major development in handling information for decision-making is electronic data processing. Many firms have installed large scale computers but continue to use them primarily for relatively routine accounting tasks. Their possibilities in the areas of planning and problem solving are being realized more gradually. Problem solving applications in marketing include the evaluation of advertising expenditures, the optimum deployment of salesmen, more effective and continuous marketing-cost analysis, time series analysis for market forecasting and the simulation of marketing programs to assess the consequences of alternative policies and strategies.

To the possibly fanciful notion that formal planning endows a business with imagination, might be added the suggestion that electronic data processing vastly expands the company's memory capacity and equips it with a form of reason. One of the most impressive facts about the big computers is the amount of information which can be stored in them or on rolls of magnetic tapes for their use. In this sense it is theoretically feasible for a computer to remember everything about the history of a company and the markets in which it operates, or at least everything which is assumed to be pertinent to questions asked by management. With these data at hand, the machine can be programmed to transform the data into answers to questions. Management may, in effect, ask the machine a question such as the following: "Given a complete history of the business and what we have just told you about the marketing plans we now have under consideration, what do you infer as to the results we can expect?" Experimental use of computers for this purpose is under way by several leading business firms and research groups in the universities. At MIT during July a two weeks seminar in market planning will be held. The program will include a major demonstration of the use of electronic computers in planning.

Management decision-making will draw increasingly on the advancing techniques for gathering and sorting information, for drawing logical and quantitative inferences from data, for constructing new operational patterns from available components, and for testing these new strategies and programs before they are adopted.

In summary, it can be said that the newer concepts of information for decision-making start with an investigation of the business firm as an input-output system. Staff analysts can in turn understand their own function in terms of inputs and outputs of information. The outputs can be classified functionally as designed for control, problem-solving, and planning. The new discipline of systematic business planning, in conjunction with the mechanical aids of electronic data processing tend to endow a business with imagination, memory and reason. Or, stated more literally and accurately, they serve to expand tremendously the outreach of these functions of the human mind.

1. Distinguish between operations research, marketing research and cost accounting as techniques for gathering information for management decision-making.

2. What are some of the basic functions of marketing in management decision?

3. What is meant by the systems concept of business?

4. Enumerate some of the internal and external studies which supply the information for management decision.

# 7. Marketing Has a New Look*

Arthur L. Boschen, Vice President—Finance, Richardson-Merrell Inc., and President of Controllers Institute

*Recognizing that many of the traditional approaches to planning and control are ineffective when applied to marketing, the Controllers Institute Research Foundation conducted a study of leading companies to determine how controllers might serve marketing management more effectively. This article presents some of the findings.*

In recent years there has been a significant change in the attitude of top management regarding the position and responsibility of the marketing department. There has been a departure from the traditional concept of marketing as the sales arm of a business disposing of goods developed and manufactured with only a secondary reference to market needs. The "new marketing concept," places marketing at the beginning of the process—assigned the task of determining what goods are needed on the market, their selling prices, and when, and under what conditions, the goods are to be delivered.

* Reprinted from the *Controller,* February 1962, p. 60. Published monthly by the Financial Executives Institute.

This extensive shift in authority is accompanied by a significant increase of responsibility for the corporate well-being. Where it has taken place, marketing has gone beyond a mere sales-getting operation and is more concerned with costs, profits and an adequate return on investment. Considering the role of marketing management in this concept, and its strategic impact on the over-all budget, the quantitative analyses directed to marketing management encompass more than the limited area traditionally envisioned as marketing. Thus, financial and manufacturing cost implications must be conveyed to marketing management through analyses that provide an effective basis for planning and budgeting.

Recognizing that many of the traditional approaches to planning and control are ineffective when applied to marketing, Controllers Institute Research Foundation conducted a study in depth of 28 companies to review the marketing functions and problem areas and the applications of controllership in each case. The findings are reported in the book, *Financial Management of the Marketing Function,* to be published by the Foundation in the near future. The report was written by Dr. Michael Schiff of the New York University School of Business Administration, who directed the research team, and was reviewed periodically by CIRF's research director, W. J. Littlefield.

## THE CONTROLLER'S APPROACH

The report makes clear that the controller cannot merely transfer the tools developed in the production sphere to marketing as a total system, but must begin anew with fundamentals. Before attempting to develop an information flow system, he must review the functions assigned to marketing in his particular company. He must study the organization of the marketing department and the delegation of specific tasks to members of the marketing team. Above all, he must recognize the need for a flexible system because the marketing department is subject to frequent organization change in its attempts to meet the changing needs of marketing in a dynamic economy. The relative lack of organization stability in marketing, as contrasted with production, has been noted by controllers and seems to be inherent in the nature of the operation rather than in the qualities of the personnel involved.

## THE CONTROLLER'S GUIDANCE

Over the ten-year period from 1947 to 1958, distribution costs, as a percentage of sales, rose from 12 per cent to 16 per cent, an increase of 33⅓ per cent. As a percentage of gross margin, they rose from 55 per cent to 79 per cent, or approximately 44 per cent. These comparisons underscore the importance of marketing costs to manufacturers. They also indicate that marketing management, generally speaking, needs additional guidance from the controller in the form of analyses and reports like those now being rendered in regard to production, investment and other phases of the business.

In developing reports and deciding on form and frequency, their usefulness to the persons to whom they are directed must be studied. An understanding of the kinds of decisions made by marketing people, and the nature of the activities to be controlled, will lead to more effective reporting. Once this logical approach is followed, the Foundation study points out, education in effective reporting for delegated profit responsibility will follow.

## ASSIGNING RESPONSIBILITIES

Definition of the responsibilities assigned to marketing management and association of these responsibilities with organizational units are the primary steps in deciding how the controller can best serve marketing management. This must be followed by a delineation of the problems associated with such delegation. Only then can one determine the quantitative information necessary and its usefulness to the existing situation.

The field study reveals that assignment of profit responsibility to the marketing operation is not a frequent occurrence. It was observed in practically every case, however, that there is an awareness of profit implications in decisions such as those concerning sales mix, customer mix, packaging, quotas, etc. This suggests a sort of transition from the view of sales volume as the only goal to an acceptance of profit responsibility. Other beginnings of profit responsibility are the field sales quota, expressed by products and by customer class, and the development of incentive compensation plans geared to profit contribution. The study showed, however, in the majority of cases that evaluation of field sales performance is still based on total dollar volume.

## FORECASTS AND QUOTAS

The details in which sales goals and the marketing effort are budgeted are significant for production and financial budgeting. The controller's familiarity with the latter areas positions him for educating and motivating marketing management regarding detailed sales goals and marketing plans; which in turn will permit better use of the controller's reports and set the stage for evaluation of results.

Marketing is responsible for the sales forecast and sales goal, and also for the budget of the associated marketing effort. Obviously, as Professor Schiff observes, the sales-budgeting process does not proceed without consideration of the nature, mix and cost of the marketing effort required to achieve the sales goal. Selection of marketing methods and the right mix is part of the over-all task of budgeting.

Some executives interviewed in the study held that the establishment of sales goals and quotas is not the concern of the controller—his task being to accept and report. Yet the very fact that the controller's department is the center for quantitative reports and analyses does provide him with adequate reason for understanding the quota-setting process, even though he has no active participation in the process. For example, in discharging his responsibility to marketing management, he prepares reports measuring salesmen's performance and revealing the percentage

of sales quota they achieved. The quota must be an effective yardstick.

The controller's efforts that improved factory standards and standard costs, must also be directed towards the use of effective sales quotas. Forecasts are preferable to history. Detailed quotas which recognize the need for selling a balanced product mix, as well as the profit implications (gross margin differential) are preferable to aggregate dollar totals.

## FIELD FORCE ASSIGNMENTS

The problems of setting work load assignments for the field force are different and more complex than those encountered in the factory. Yet the controller's skills can be harnessed with the know-how of field sales management and marketing research to produce the most effective assignment of tasks and to develop the control reports essential to effective management. Participation in developing assignments will enhance the controller's ability to produce meaningful reports.

Assigning work loads involves consideration of (1) the need for thorough coverage of the market; (2) giving each salesman a reasonable task; and (3) routing which will minimize the cost of solicitation in each territory.

Effective work-load assignments facilitate the budgeting of related costs and supply the criteria for evaluating performance. When possible, accomplishment of the assigned work load within the budgeted expense allowance must be associated with sales profit objectives.

## SALESMEN'S COMPENSATION

Quotas and profit objectives are assigned to salesmen for purposes of motivation, evaluating performance and, at times, to provide a basis for compensation. Important factors to be included are: (1) Responsibility for quotas and the basis for establishing them, (2) the manner in which the quota is stated, (3) assignment of profit objectives to salesmen, and (4) control of salesmen's expenses. The controller generally supplements the control and analysis measures used by the field organization with reports of sales and salesmen's expenses, or gross margin and salesmen's expenses.

The controller should be concerned with salesmen's compensation and the related measures of performance, because the development of quantitative measures and the preparation of sales performance reports to sales management fall within his area of responsibility. Decision areas regarding compensation involve establishing its level and the differential among salesmen and areas, as well as the plan of compensation—straight salary, salary plus incentive, or straight commission.

## EXPENSES, TURNOVER, AND REPORTS

The controller is usually well informed about salesmen's expenses, through the flow of expense vouchers and disbursements and the resulting accounting actions. In addition, his role as coordinator of the budgeting process keeps him informed of the appropriation side. The typical expense reports which he furnishes to sales management indicating actual and budgeted expenses round out this role.

The cost and profit implications of the recruitment, selection and training of salesmen should be brought to the attention of marketing management by the controller. Analyses that reveal the full cost of turnover or expansion and contraction of the field force should be made available to marketing management.

Having established goals, work loads and expense budgets for salesmen, the measures of performance adopted must reveal clearly whether the goals are being achieved. The incentive plan should prompt performance in accordance with goals, and reward should be related to contributions to the profit of the enterprise.

## COMMUNICATION IS A MUST

A noteworthy fact brought out in the study is the lack of integration between measures used by the field organization and the controller's reports relating to salesmen's activity. If such measures included "cost per call," "cost per customer," "cost per order," "order size needed to break even," "sales per call," etc., they shed light on profitability, work load assignments, quotas and compensation problems.

Communication between the field sales force and the supervisory field offices and home office is essential, if the field force is to carry out the policies and plans of the home office, and if control is to be maintained over salesmen's activities. Information gathered in field contacts enables the home office to evaluate plans in the light of a changing environment. To prevent the loss of valuable selling time spent on report preparation, the value of the reports called for should be carefully determined.

## NEGLECTED AREAS

The Foundation study casts light on what is termed "neglected areas" of reports on field sales administration—studies of customer, channel or market profitability. In their absence, the study continues, decisions affecting the selection and management of channels of distribution and the adding or dropping of customers, or of extending or contracting the field force effort, are reached without full awareness of cost and profit results. The report also adds that the needs of special marketing managers are passed over, although their responsibilities tend to increase.

## JUSTIFYING FIELD INVESTMENT

Justification of field investment is another marketing area in which the controller can be helpful. The decision to enter a new market or to expand sales in an existing one involves a number of considerations which are not unlike those encountered in acquiring capital equipment. Both include the investment of a significant amount of money and they extend over long periods of time. The tools of capital budgetary control can be applied to expenditures for securing markets.

The planned costs of developing markets are known and, if capitalized, can be related to profitability along with those of the plant turning out goods for the market. Specifically, decisions on where to invest market-wise, what to expect in the way of profits, and the relation of actual performance to plan can be applied to investments to secure and expand markets, in the manner they are extended to investments in plant and equipment.

Managing and evaluating marketing performance are continuous tasks. Once the initial decision has been made to penetrate a market, measurement of performance, in terms of return on investment, provides a tool for evaluation. This requires decisions relative to the assets (type and valuation) to be assigned to markets.

In developing return-on-investment reports for sales districts or territories the investment or assets employed generally include physical equipment, average in-ventories, average receivables, but not the value of the territory or district. As the report points out, however, assigning an investment value to the sales territory will aid in more effective control of territorial penetration or expansion. Then the salesman responsible for a territory is viewed as a manager responsible for marshaling its resources to realize the highest net return on the investment in the territory.

Assigning an investment value to the sales territory is superior to the frequently used method of "share-of-market potential" in an area. It gives recognition not only to potential but also to competitive conditions and the costs associated with market penetration.

## DISTRIBUTION PROBLEMS

Problem areas in the administration of the physical distribution function are related to the activities generally included as part of it, such as, finished goods inventory control, warehouse location and operation, finished goods handling and packaging, and the movement of finished goods to customers. In general terms, the nature of the problem may be stated as one of providing the best customer service in the shipment of goods, and optimum support to the selling function at a cost consistent with profit goals, and within the framework of the firm's over-all financial plan.

In essence, the problems of physical distribution are not unlike other areas of the marketing operation, because the selection of methods of operation from various alternatives, and the planning, controlling and evaluating of performance are essential to management. However, the intangible nature of selling methods and their impact on measurement and evaluation do not plague the physical functions. To this extent, the report makes plain, it would be reasonable to expect a wide application of the use of quantitative analysis in this area.

## MARKETING RESEARCH

While the technical problems of marketing research lie beyond the controller's scope, adequate budgetary controls within the marketing research department are within his responsibility. Planning of manpower and projects by marketing research, as well as their timing, provides a basis for estimating the cost of operations and integrating it into the over-all marketing budget. Control reports issued to marketing management during the period may relate costs to the budget on a period as well as a project basis.

The study confirms that the evaluation of marketing research is difficult indeed. The controller can contribute through reports that indicate the cost of the various tasks assigned to marketing research and the units of organization or segments of business activity for which they are performed. It is then possible to compare the costs with those of alternative methods of obtaining the same information.

## QUESTIONS

1. Why are many of the traditional approaches to planning and control ineffective when applied to marketing?
2. How can the controller contribute to the establishment of a more equitable system of salesmen's compensation?
3. In what specific ways can the Controller's Department be of assistance to marketing research?
4. In what other areas of distribution can the controller give valuable assistance?

## BIBLIOGRAPHY FOR CHAPTER I

ARTICLES:

Bund, Henry, and Carroll, James W., "The Changing Role of the Marketing Function," *Journal of Marketing,* Vol. XXI, No. 3 (January 1957), pp. 270–325.

Houser, T. V., "True Role of the Marketing Executive," *Journal of Marketing,* Vol. 23, No. 4 (April 1959), pp. 363–9.

Keeler, F. T., "What Does Management Expect of Marketing?" *Industrial Marketing,* Vol. 43, No. 12 (December 1958), pp. 56–59.

Kniffin, Fred W., "The Modern Concept of Marketing Management: Its Implications and Problems," *Indiana Business Information Bulletin 31,* Indiana University Bureau of Business Research, 1958, pp. 9–10.

Lazo, Hector, "The Marketing Manager: Who the New Executive Is and What He Will Do," *Printers' Ink,* Vol. 262, No. 1 (January 3, 1958), pp. 29–31.

BOOKS:

Bursk, Edward C., *Text and Cases in Marketing: A Scientific Approach.* Englewood Cliffs, N.J.: Prentice-Hall, 1962.

Davis, Kenneth R., *Marketing Management.* New York: Ronald Press, 1961.

Faville, David E., *Selected Cases in Marketing Management.* Englewood Cliffs, N.J.: Prentice-Hall, 1961.

Holmes, Parker M., *Marketing Research: Principles and Readings.* Cincinnati, Ohio: South-Western Publishing Co., 1960.

Lazer, William, and Kelley, Eugene J., *Managerial Marketing: Perspectives and Viewpoints.* Homewood, Ill.: Irwin, 1962.

Lazo, Hector, and Corbin, Arnold, *Management in Marketing.* New York: McGraw-Hill, 1961.

Levitt, Theodore, *Innovation in Marketing: New Perspectives for Profit and Growth.* New York: McGraw-Hill, 1962.

Mauser, Ferdinand F., *Modern Marketing Management: An Integrated Approach.* New York: McGraw-Hill, 1961.

McCarthy, E. Jerome, *Basic Marketing: A Managerial Approach.* Homewood, Ill.: Irwin, 1960.

Otteson, Schuyler F. (ed.), *First International Seminar on Marketing Management.* Special Supplement of *Business Horizons,* School of Business, Indiana University, 1961.

Tousley, Rayburn, Clark, Eugene, and Clark, Fred, *Principles of Marketing.* New York: Macmillan, 1962.

Westfall, Ralph, and Boyd, Harper W., *Cases in Marketing Management.* Homewood, Ill.: Irwin, 1961.

# II. The Organizational Structure

*NOT EVEN* for companies in the same industry is there a single ideal organizational structure for effective implementation of the marketing concept. The organization for the individual firm must be custom built, paying attention to such factors as bigness of the company, size of its market and number of products planned for sale.

In planning the organizational structure, sufficient attention must be given to the external as well as the internal needs of the business. That is, the planners must not only consider the company's own objectives or marketing tasks but must give adequate attention to such external facts as competition, social forces and political climate. They must think in terms of an organization that is effectively oriented toward planning for the future: an organization that can effectively administer operational strategy in the present and, finally, one that can efficiently evaluate past performance through statistical analysis. In developing the organizational structure, it is helpful to visualize all the interrelationships through a compact organization chart. First, the functions of the marketing department such as sales, advertising, sales promotion, market research, forecasting and planning, warehousing and distribution are determined, then the relationships between these functions can be shown clearly through the drawing of the formal chart. The chart must not only show the relationships of the marketing functions among themselves but how these marketing functions integrate with the other key functions of the enterprise. In many large companies, marketing can become an effective part of the total business organization only when given top management authority and responsibilities equal to those of production and finance.

When the functions are grouped together in a logical manner, the resulting organizational structure may give the appearance of efficiency on the organizational chart, but we must never lose sight of the fact that the main purpose of management is to operate the business efficiently through people. The traditional view of organizations puts too much emphasis on a logical arrangement for the work, the people and the workshop. However, a more modern behavioral concept of organization is emerging. The behavioral view stresses the system of cooperative relationships among individuals and groups which can only be established by close attention to individual and group feelings, perceptions, inducements, motivations and interactions.

People cannot function effectively if organized into permanently fixed relationships like cogs in a wheel. Relationships between people are subject to slow perceptible changes. Some need the opportunity to move ahead through acceptance of greater responsibility, others are content to stay put and still others retrogress. Also, many people perform better when working alone, as individuals; others work better when part of a team, and the best organization is the one that allows for such differences in behavior. Thus, the structure must be reviewed periodically and kept flexible to allow for changes. In staffing a new marketing organization, it is well to maintain flexibility and not finalize position descriptions until an evaluation of the potential incumbents' abilities can be made.

While it is common practice to refer to four principal types of departmental organization: financial, production, marketing and geographic, a company can organize in an almost unlimited number of ways to operate under the marketing concept. In the post World War II era among the large diversified companies, there has been a definite trend toward decentralization into self-contained divisions. However, in the future, more thought will probably be given to developing a better balance between centralization and decentralization, for at this writing, there is a noticeable trend towards a "recentralized decentralization" in an effort to establish a more effective central office control over marketing and product planning, analysis and strategy.

# $8.$ Factors That Shape the Organization*

Wendell R. Smith, President, Marketing Science Institute

*An effective marketing organization is oriented toward planning for the future, controlling operations in the present, and evaluating what has transpired in the immediate past.*

Since no two enterprises have the same, or even very similar, marketing tasks to perform, it would be sheer coincidence if any one marketing organizational structure proved the most suitable for more than one business. This paper will discuss some of the marketing factors and circumstances that determine what is needed organizationally to establish total effective marketing and achieve volume and profit goals.

Marketing considerations are fundamental to virtually all decisions regarding business plans and policies. Investment and capital budgeting decisions revert to the kinds of facilities needed to supply the markets of the future. Personnel recruitment and training are preparation for the tasks that the customer needs of tomorrow will impose. Budgets for technical research and development will be devoted increasingly to product ideas that afford evidence of promising markets. This central role means that marketing plans and programs must include more of the quantitative and precise detail common in areas such as accounting.

The facts and insights provided by quantitative marketing research and sales analysis do not offer automated or even

mechanized marketing management. They do serve, however, to limit the uncertainty with which executives must grapple. Decision-making time can then be concentrated upon resolving key issues; it is not dissipated over broad areas because of lack of information as to what the key issues and action alternatives really are.

One might well ask, "Why is it that scientific marketing came to the fore much later than scientific management in the area of production?" Many reasons could be given, but the most important is to be found in our shift from an economy of scarcity, during which production considerations were stressed, to an economy of relative abundance, which tends to bring market and sales considerations to the foreground and into proper perspective. It seems clear, then, that the rational approach to marketing management is one in which effective use is made of the following: (1) forecasts, and plans and programs designed to chart the future course of business; (2) checkpoints by means of which marketing operations can be controlled; (3) established criteria or yardsticks by means of which marketing results and man power can be evaluated at the appropriate times.

Marketing research and planning techniques and procedures can be applied to

* Reprinted from the First International Seminar on Marketing Management, p. 9. Published as a Special Supplement to *Business Horizons*, School of Business, Indiana University, February 1961.

**55**

almost every phase of the business operation. They have been used successfully in connection with problems ranging from capital budgeting and financial planning on the one hand, to provision of a rational basis for the deployment and use of sales man power and determination of advertising requirements on the other. Much time could be devoted to detailed discussion of the diverse applications of the art; however, emphasis should be put on the three primary functions of planning, operational control, and evaluation of marketing and sales results. I should also like to suggest what an organization designed to provide a rational approach to these functions holds for the future of marketing and sales management.

An effective marketing organization is oriented toward planning for the future, controlling operations in the present, and evaluating what has transpired in the immediate past.

## THE ORGANIZATION

### PLANNING

Marketing planning, in its initial phases, draws heavily on industry and company records and other sources of internal data. If past procedures are continued, the latter sources of data can be analyzed to indicate marketing performance in the year ahead. These preliminary projections are then adjusted for expected changes in economic activity, in product line, product design, or other company actions that will affect marketing and sales.

Such adjusted forecasts are then ready for discussion and review. We may simply accept the marketing results indicated as our goals and request budgets for the time, money, and effort necessary for their achievement. More frequently, however, the reaction will be, "Surely we can do better than that," and a series of dis-

cussions will get underway on what can be done to sharpen the marketing effort in order to make a forecast of improved performance feasible. Fully developed marketing plans, then, which include realistic estimates of sales performance, furnish important guides for the planning of the production and financial aspects of the business.

Estimating the results of marketing new products creates special problems in planning. Frequently these problems can be partly solved through analysis of marketing information contained in government reports and trade association publications. In other instances, specially designed field projects must be initiated.

The end product of marketing planning, of course, is a detailed blueprint of the marketing actions to be taken during the period covered by the plan. Such a blueprint will include specifications of product line, plans and schedules for advertising and sales promotion, as well as strategies, plans, and programs for the use of the company's sales force. It is truly a flight plan designed to meet in advance the thunderstorms and cross-winds that may be encountered along the way. Its objective is to minimize the crises and waste that are common where marketing is not planned and to save the panic button for real emergencies over which we have no control.

### OPERATIONAL CONTROL

The marketing plan will be incomplete if it fails to specify bench marks of expected performance against which actual performance can be checked at specified times. Just as the aircraft pilot periodically checks back with flight control, marketing personnel must check their progress against the plan or the "par" that has been established. Deviations from planned performance (quotas) may indicate that someone is falling down on the job or that predetermined plans are now unrealistic in terms of changed conditions. If the latter turns out to be the case, plans must be revised. One may very well ask, "What is the good of having plans if they are constantly being revised?" It is a fact that "meeting developments" by revising plans results in a more successful and rational adjustment to changed conditions than is true of the business that is not planned ahead and thus is constantly "flying by the seat of its pants."

### EVALUATION

At the close of each month and in greater detail at the close of each quarter of the business year, it is desirable to compare the marketing results with the goals that were set in the marketing plan. This procedure allows consideration of basic points of emphasis in connection with future operations. Evaluation of this sort, of course, is done by almost all business organizations; but in those that do not have marketing plans and continuing analysis of marketing activity, the standards or criteria against which performance is evaluated are vague and based largely on judgment. Only if objectives have been clearly defined can it be determined whether or not those objectives have been achieved. This is true of the marketing program as a whole and also for its important elements such as advertising and personal selling.

## INTERACTION

There is little argument among sales and marketing managers as to the general desirability of engaging in planning, control, and evaluation of sales and marketing activities. However, it is not generally recognized that it is just as dangerous to plan, control, and evaluate by intuition as it is to dispense altogether with these functions. These three closely interrelated concepts imply the need for a rational approach if they are to be successful. A plan based upon hope alone is often worse than no plan at all, because others often take plans seriously as bases for budgeting and production planning.

The almost complete interdependence of successful planning, operational control, and evaluation is not generally understood. Plans are of little value unless they become the basis for controlling operations and evaluating results. Effective control of operations is impossible without the bench marks that can be provided by the plan, and control is weakened unless it is understood that it will be followed by evaluation of results in terms of both programs and the performance of people. Similarly, evaluation is futile, in fact impossible, unless control records over a period of time are available for evaluation against the performance objectives defined in the plan.

Once the sales or marketing manager becomes convinced that planning, control, and evaluation are tools that make it possible for him to utilize his creativity and imagination more fully, he benefits from the rational approach. First, and perhaps most important, rationality (in an area of the business often thought to carry an aura of mystery and hucksterism) goes a long way toward securing for marketing management a place at the conference table where over-all, company-level policies are being made. For many years, we complained vociferously that top managements were production oriented in their thinking, and as a result the leadership that could be provided by the people in marketing was going unused. Today, however, most successful top managements are market oriented. The doors of executive committee and board rooms are open to marketing and sales executives who can back up their judgments with facts and analysis, rather than resting their case upon an intuitive "feel of the market" or the opinion of the last distributor they happened to talk to.

## SETTING OBJECTIVES

Much has been said about the sequence of steps involved in the development of sound marketing plans. The first step is usually identified as the determination of goals or objectives to be accomplished by means of the marketing action that is being planned. This step presupposes, of course, that the firm or division has in its possession the results of a careful audit or review of its present position as a foundation upon which to determine realistic goals. If the firm is not fully aware of the "characteristics" of the launching pad from which it is planning to get into orbit, such planning analysis must precede the process of goal definition.

Those experienced in the planning of marketing activities tend to approach the finalizing of goals cautiously and often come to regard alternative sets of goals somewhat in the light of hypotheses to be tested, with the selection of the appropriate alternative as an important product of the planning operation. This is true because the feasibility of a goal can be evaluated best by careful consideration of the plan of action necessary for its achievement. It is at this exploratory, perhaps experimental, stage in the planning process that considerations of marketing strategy begin to play their part in the development of the final plan of action with timetables, budgets, campaigns, and schedules for the distribution of personnel. These products of the planners' art become the specifications within which advertising, sales promotion, and sales management use the marketing tools that they administer with skill and precision to produce the planned objective. The marketing plan embraces specifications for all selling activities as elements in the planned marketing mix.

## MARKETING STRATEGY

Marketing strategy, however one defines it, is primarily concerned with the creative elements of a goal-directed marketing plan. It describes the way the firm or division plans to get from where it is to where it wants to be. Marketing strategy, then, becomes the factor that integrates and coordinates the many and diverse tactics to be stipulated in the marketing plan itself. While marketing strategies are inherently creative, a genius is not needed to conceive and develop them. In fact, an orderly method of developing strategic concepts is one of the most basic aspects of total marketing. In general, marketing strategies evolve from studying the firm itself, the competition, and the market.

The generation of marketing strategies begins essentially with a careful review of present position in relation to competition and to the markets. Such analysis rather quickly reveals whether the strategy should be essentially defensive—that is, designed to compensate for and to correct weaknesses in the present operation—or offensive in the sense of leading to plans designed to capitalize upon the relative strengths or advantages of the firm. A defensive strategy might well be one designed to eliminate a weakness, thereby increasing the profitability of an existing volume of sales. An offensive strategy is often oriented toward increasing profits by pumping additional products into the market with disproportionately small increases in total marketing costs.

Many marketing strategies are developed with principal reference to the present and future behavior of competition. Again strategy may be essentially defensive insofar as it may be influenced by present or expected competitive threats, or it may be offensively directed at points at which competition is or is expected to become vulnerable. Such elements are probably present in most strategic concepts whether stated or not. The most important and fundamental of marketing strategies, however, are those that are related directly to the accomplishment of goals that are defined in terms of the market itself. Solid knowledge of the market is the basis of such strategies.

Much time could be spent in elaboration of the almost unlimited list of market-based strategies that could be developed and adopted as guides to the planning of marketing activities. Obviously, strategies generated from market study must be feasible in view of the characteristics of the firm and the competition. Let us look at two examples of the ways in which market data may suggest an orderly method or approach to strategy generation.

First, analysis of trends in demand for present products or services is fundamental. An unfavorable trend in demand suggests a choice between a strategy designed to reverse the trend or one to accept and adjust to this development. A favorable trend suggests a choice of strategies concerned with how the firm can profit most from this happy state of affairs without overextending or producing imbalance.

Second, analysis of market structure will reveal whether the market is characterized by *homogeneity,* a situation where the requirements of consumers or users are very much the same, or *heterogeneity,* where the varied individual requirements cause dissatisfaction with a limited or proprietary offering. In the first case, one would logically follow a strategy designed to make individual market demands converge on a single product or limited product line. This is usually accomplished by differentiating the product from competition through heavy advertising and promotion, and presenting it as "all things to all people." On the other hand, if the structure of the market is characterized by heterogeneity, the decision may be to accept this divergent demand as a market characteristic and to adjust product lines and marketing strategy accordingly. This may result in a long line or a production-to-order situation. Whatever the choice, knowledge of market structure is essential to strategy determination.

To summarize, it has been my purpose here to suggest, first, that the hard core of the total marketing concept that is attracting so much attention today is effective and scientific use of market planning; second, that the first, and perhaps crucial, phase of the planning process is the generation of marketing strategies or strategic concepts that guide the specifics of the planning operation and offer the essential links between the present market position and the predetermined goal. Last, this creative component of planning, marketing strategy, is developed by study of the firm, competition, and market.

Total marketing has five organizational implications:

1. The position of the marketing organization within the firm or the division must provide for effective coordination of the marketing planning with that being done in connection with all other functions, specifically, product, finance, facilities planning, and production scheduling.

2. Each division or firm must carefully evaluate the appropriateness of its organization to the achievement of effective planning, control, and evaluation of marketing operations. Further, we must be willing to accept the fact that it is more important for marketing organizations to

be in tune with the tasks they have to perform and the markets they serve than to conform with some traditional, or popular pattern. To be sure, there are many general principles of marketing organization that must be respected, but tailor-made organizations, like tailor-made suits, fit best.

3. The all-important functions of planning, control of operations, and evaluation of results must be specifically assigned. From experience, we know that planning activities in particular will get shoved aside unless we can create a sense of urgency about planning for the future that is comparable to the urgency we feel for current operations.

4. The organizational structure must make specific provision for effective co-ordination and integration of both plans and operations concerning the product line, channels of distribution to be used, personal selling effort required, and the advertising and promotional support to be applied.

5. The organizational structure should be designed so as to accommodate, without revolutionary change, the addition or deletion of products, product lines, or whole businesses.

A company must have, particularly from a marketing point of view, maximum flexibility, adaptability, and sensitivity to new opportunities for growth and profit.

These are the specifications that marketing organizations must meet if they are to survive and operate profitably in the 1960's. Two crucial points may well mean the difference between success and failure: the firm must be able to adjust continuously to the dynamics of the markets that it serves, and it must also be able to gain lead time on crises in such a way that a rational plan for future action is a matter of urgency.

## QUESTIONS

1. What five organizational implications does total marketing have?
2. What specific current company activities are determined by marketing planning?
3. Distinguish between marketing planning and marketing strategy.
4. What tools can help the marketing manager utilize his creativity and imagination more fully?
5. Effective control of operations is impossible without the bench marks that can be provided by the marketing plan. Explain.

# 9. Making the Marketing Concept Work*

Arthur P. Felton, Director of Marketing, American Brake Shoe Company

*The author describes some of the organizational pitfalls which have befallen companies that have rushed into the marketing concept. The president need not be a marketing man but top management must have sufficient comprehension of marketing to be able to think, plan and administer efficiently all aspects of the marketing program.*

Since the time of World War II, American business has passed through the popular fads of *linear programing, statistical quality control, operations research,* and *long-range planning,* into the throes of *diversification* and *motivation research,* and now the currently popular *marketing concept.*

Sometimes it seems as though American business as a whole is as subject to stylish fads as is the women's dress industry. Not that this is necessarily bad, but (as in the case of the unfortunate husbands of wives who buy dresses) it is liable to be very expensive.

Many American businesses have rushed into reorganization, mergers, diversification, "total marketing," and the like, without being fully aware of certain underlying company conditions which may lead to organizational failures or prevent the establishment of a completely successful integrated program.

## INTEGRATED MARKETING

I propose to discuss some of the mistakes which companies have made when attempting to employ integrated marketing, and to outline the necessary steps to

* Reprinted from the *Harvard Business Review*, July–August 1959, p. 55.

avoid those mistakes. Unless companies realize the implications of the marketing concept, the outcome will inevitably be drastically reduced profits and dividends, or continued losses.

### IMPORTANT INGREDIENTS

A description of the marketing concept can be provided in the following definition:

A corporate state of mind that insists on the integration and coordination of all of the marketing functions which, in turn, are melded with all other corporate functions, for the basic objective of producing maximum long-range corporate profits.

Let us consider the component parts of this definition in greater detail:

(1) *The most important ingredient in a formula for marketing success is the proper state of mind.* A business organized along the lines of a proven successful formula will fail, or at least operate far below proper efficiency, if the corporation does not develop the proper marketing state of mind. The board of directors, the chief executive, and the top-echelon executives must appreciate the need to develop this

marketing state of mind. It is a lack of understanding of this need that is currently causing many corporations untold anguish in the execution of their marketing plan. Without this conditioning, all that is accomplished organizationally in the textbook manner is of no avail.

(2) *Another important condition that must be met is an* actual *integration and coordination of all the marketing functions.* These functions, in turn, must be fully coordinated with production, personnel, finance, and all other functions in today's modern, complex corporation.

(3) *Finally, professional and executive skills of a high order must be utilized.* It is necessary to take all of this complex functioning and make it work, so as to produce the optimum long-range profit as set forth in a well-developed long-range plan.

### CAUSES OF FAILURE

There is a tendency for most executives to oversimplify the basic implications of operating under a total marketing concept. For an executive to say that a company embraces the marketing concept and, accordingly, relates all its thinking to the consumer's needs, or for a company to suddenly consider itself "customer-oriented," is just as apt to create marketing overemphasis now as was the danger in the past to create production or financial overemphasis. In American business today, in short, there is too great a tendency to get on the marketing concept bandwagon per se, and too little concern for making it work at a profit.

Just where do these danger spots show up and what can a company do about them? Or, expressed another way, what are the pitfalls that face a firm embracing the marketing concept?

### INEXPERIENCED EXECUTIVES

Many boards of directors, executive committees, and presidents lack experience in marketing because they have come up through the ranks of production, finance, or the like. This situation is apt to exist in the company that was originally established in the governmental or industrial market, as well as in certain companies in the consumer field where the chief executive has risen through other than marketing channels. Now this must not be interpreted as meaning that only marketing men should become presidents. The point is merely that situations do exist in which top executives and boards of directors do not fully understand the tremendous complexity of modern marketing, and hence are unable to give proper guidance and direction to the operation. For instance:

Executives of many industrial goods manufacturing companies often fail to understand the psychology of the distributor and the retailer, or the company's obligation to the consumer regarding product servicing, or the different sales personality involved, as well as the dissimilar manner of remuneration. Many a company has been prevented from gaining an equitable share-of-market because of the executives' reluctance to spend the necessary amounts on advertising, sales promotion, trade deals, salesmen compensation plans, and so forth, for what they feel to be a relatively low volume of unit sales.

The industrial goods producers do not have a monopoly on marketing myopia. Time and again, we see old-time consumer packaged goods companies which suffer in modern marketing competition because they fail to appreciate fully the dynamic and ever changing character of, let us say, certain channels of distribution; or they fail to realize the need for a highly professional integration of package design, trade and consumer promotions, and advertising with the direct selling effort.

Because of scattered elongations of the seller's market, there are some older top executives who have not been exposed to the steady increase in customer services and the growing subservience to the customer that most companies have experienced. They find it difficult, therefore, to adjust when hit with a buyer's market.

### ERRORS IN PROMOTION

Many companies slavishly follow the policy of "promotion from within," which may result in unqualified men filling newly created positions. This is particularly dangerous if a corporation is attempting to stay in or enter the more fiercely competitive fields. For example:

A large industrial chemical company formed a new consumer division charged with the responsibilities of packaging basic chemicals, developing a consumer line, and launching new products as consumer goods. Quite obviously this posed a complex marketing problem.

Organizationally, the company made the right start. It established five product managers, an advertising department, a sales promotion department, and a marketing research department. The company also set up seven divisional sales offices. A national sales manager was appointed over the seven field sales managers. The organization chart was workable.

However, only three men out of the entire head office staff had the necessary experience to fulfill their particular jobs. The five product managers

came out of the field sales force, basically with a background of selling bulk chemicals to other manufacturers; and the sales promotion managers came from either the laboratory or the industrial sales force.

The sales manager himself came from one of the industrial divisions where for 15 years he had been the sales manager directing six men selling to 56 large users who bought on an annual contract basis. He was an excellent personal salesman, a loyal company man, but (a) had never directed a sales force of any size, and (b) had no experience with wholesalers or retailers in any field. His principal qualification was years of successfully writing multimillion-dollar carload orders personally.

As one company executive put it: "This is like sending a Little League championship team against the Yankees."

### DEMANDS OF THE JOB

In many cases, sales management is a very obvious source of manpower for the new coordinating position. However, a successful sales manager does not always make a good marketing director. A basic qualification for good sales management is the ability to plan, to organize, and to select and lead other salesmen.

The duties of a modern and advanced director of marketing require that he be much broader than the successful sales manager. The following are areas in which he must be qualitatively different:

He must think in corporate terms rather than dollar or unit sales.

Not only must he have a higher degree of analytical ability than that normally required (or even advisable) in sales management; but, most importantly, he must have the ability to define problems for research and then capably analyze results and develop the indicated plans and policies.

He must have a high degree of capability and experience in planning and organization, to be able to integrate and coordinate the many other marketing functions that must be performed in today's competitive situation.

He must be able to get the best out of his director of marketing research as well as his advertising, sales promotion, and product managers.

He must, in addition to all this, be a man who can sit down with the production director, the personnel director, the treasurer, the lawyer, the president, and, in many cases, the board of directors, and put the interests of the corporation first, while representing the broad marketing aspects of the business.

In many cases, because of the particular personality, breadth of technical know-how, and ability to effect integrated operations required of the director of marketing, the aggressive, dynamic "leader of the troops" type of sales manager completely falls apart when promoted to that position.

Frequently, an advertising manager, a marketing research manager, a product manager, or a sales promotion manager is similarly promoted over his head. In these situations, the personal failings often stem from insufficient aggressiveness in dealing with other executives or even with their own department heads rather than from the lack of planning ability. They may be outmaneuvered at the conference table or unable to resolve interdepartmental conflicts.

## INCOMPLETE INTEGRATION

This train of thought leads to another type of pitfall which we might call the lack of complete integration of teamwork. There are some companies organized in the approved marketing concept manner, properly departmentalized, staffed by individually competent people, and perhaps even with soundly conceived integrated marketing plans—which still fail to attain maximum profits. This type of company can be likened to a potentially national championship college football team which never quite lived up to its preseason ratings. Why? Because every man did his job most of the time but all eleven did not do their best job at the same time.

Failure in these circumstances stems from a lack of complete integration and coordination between executives, as well as an absence of clear-cut channels of communication. Such a situation may reflect the fact that certain department heads are not sufficiently competent to carry their weight on the team; the solution is obvious. There is more room for constructive action when the men are capable but are held back by personality clashes and/or battles for personal power, or by the fact that they are not yet accustomed to working together.

### PERSONALITY CLASHES

There are two danger signs to look for in this situation. One is the case of the introvert or the nonconformist who is so right on so many things (in some cases including things which are not within his jurisdiction) that he stirs up antagonism among the other department heads. The other danger area centers around the executive who dedicates himself exclusively to what he thinks is his own personal advancement; often his tactics are subtle in that he gives lip service to team effort at various meetings, but then proceeds to undercut his teammates.

Today in integrated marketing programs, the need is so great for precise timing and sequential operations that three or four departments often have to do business with each other and depend on each other for supplementary help. When one or more of the men belong to what Mr. Khrushchev referred to as the "cult of the individual," coordination falls by the wayside.

Many such unintegrated situations fall largely within the province of the director of marketing. His solution of the problem must provide for the development of a mutually cooperative attitude and for the coaching of all of his men on their teamwork. Often this is 80% of the value of the director of marketing to his company. Consider the following case in point:

There is an East Coast consumer goods manufacturer selling a line of products distributed exclusively through grocery stores. The product line of the company falls into one of the most competitive categories within one of the most competitive industries, so the need for close coordination is paramount. Management was so completely uncoordinated two years ago that in the months of March and April $200,000 was devoted to one of the company's major products in TV and magazine advertising; the sales promotion manager was running a dynamic $100,000 promotion involving coupons for a second major product totally unrelated to the first; while the sales manager was running a salesman contest awarding prizes for the sale of a third product line.

Such an uncoordinated operation inevitably dilutes profits.

### ONE-MAN DOMINATION

There are also those companies which are dominated by autocratic, "one man" operators. Although these men, by and large, have been outmoded by fully and professionally developed techniques of integrated marketing, they still exist. For example:

A large and well-known cosmetic company called in one of the leading management consulting firms at the insistence of its bank. It received a thorough analysis and a new, well-designed marketing organization, complete with advertising manager, brand managers, marketing research department, merchandising department, marketing administration section, and a reorganized sales force. Professionally competent marketing men with specialized qualifications were added, some of the least competent incumbents were let go, and other old-time employees were reassigned duties and responsibilities under the new organization chart—in short, a virtually perfect textbook solution.

Only one thing was missing—a proper state of mind on the part of the president. He still made all the decisions; he still second-guessed the professionals; he still was out of touch with the current marketing problems. As a result, at the end of two years the company was still functioning in the same manner that it had for the previous twenty years. The entire marketing group, which by and large represented at least average if not above average individual competence, was never allowed to function in a professional manner.

This is not an isolated case history. The situation is duplicated among hundreds of overly self-sufficient executives, including marketing directors. Companies which fail to develop a smoothly coordinated marketing team can find themselves in the almost incongruous position whereby the more complete, detailed, and sophisticated the marketing plan, the greater the chance for failure.

MIS-DIVERSIFICATION

Certainly no study of the problems and failures of the marketing concept would be complete without mention of that business monstrosity, the mis-diversified company. Such a company, as a result of helter-skelter, illogical diversification, finds itself beset with a multitude of virtually insoluble marketing problems.

The most common types of diversification which lead to marketing problems are these:

- Companies that have no common manufacturing or marketing economies, or have purchased, or merged with, equally weak companies.
- Companies which have purchased virtually any salable company, to take advantage of their tax loss carry-forward, or that have purchased other manufacturers to add the assets to their balance sheet in order to work financial manipulations.
- Companies which have purchased other companies showing good past earnings but that were going "over the hill" at the time they sold out.
- Companies which have purchased, with management retention agreements, other companies that had already outgrown the capacity of their managements.

There is also the situation in which brokers or security houses have sold the idea of mergers under the guise of diversification when the real goal was the commission on the sale of securities or a finder's fee.

Whatever the reasons for mergers or purchases (and they may have seemed valid and logical at the time), those companies that subsequently develop serious marketing problems generally find their troubles stem from one or both of two fundamental sources:

1. *The product lines acquired prove to be incompatible from the marketing standpoint.* This situation is typified by the corporation with divisions which have little or no similarity in the type of product, channels of distribution, type of sales force, and so forth. In such a case, the merger has not strengthened the marketing position of any division, and each of the individual units still finds itself beset with the problems it had hoped would be cured by the merger.

2. *Personality characteristics of individual division managers may impede the development of an integrated marketing operation.* In many cases, a man who might now be vice president in charge of a division was the owner, operator, or manager of a smaller independent company. He probably became the owner or manager of this smaller company because of his individual productivity, forceful driving personality, and fiercely independent spirit—an entrepreneur. He does not find it easy to become a corporate man. So we find a multidivisional diversified company which is composed of many fiercely independent managers who refuse to take any guidance or direction from corporate headquarters.

For example, a company in the building materials field has purchased, since World War II, 14 independent manufacturers, all of whom make similar products stemming from common raw materials which can logically be sold through the same set of outlets by the same sales force. However, at the end of eight years, less than half of these companies have been brought under a common letterhead, to say nothing of an integrated marketing operation. As recently as 1957, one of the divisions went to considerable expense and trouble to reprint a two-year supply of letterheads which virtually eliminate mention of the parent company.

When dissimilar companies with individualistic managers merge or are purchased, the two problems are often increased by the square of the two. Top management of the headquarters company has so little knowledge of all its subsidiaries' fields that it is unable to help when individual divisions get into trouble. This situation frequently occurs when the small businessman has sold out to the corporation at about the time he has got in over his head in trying to run his own business. By his various efforts to maintain autonomy, he does continue to keep the parent company staff at arm's length while he runs his own business. But when a sales recession hits, he is not capable of coping with the situation; even more unfortunately, the parent company is also incapable because it has not had an opportunity to really learn the business of its subsidiary.

### REMEDIAL MEASURES

Any company can embrace integrated marketing; it has been done successfully by many companies—large and small— and is becoming an absolute must for survival in some industries. There is no particular magic formula. The unresolved question with most companies which do not adhere to it is not whether they can, but whether they are *willing,* to take the necessary steps to break through the roadblocks. Those who have been successful and those who wish to integrate their marketing effort profitably must effect the following:

1. The proper state of mind.
2. The proper organization.
3. The proper balance of professional talent.
4. Adequate direct and indirect controls.

A more detailed discussion of these conditions is called for.

## STATE OF MIND

If this requirement is not met, the other three are valueless. Since the proper corporate state of mind is a fundamental need in understanding and making integrated marketing work, it follows that the chief executive officer and the board of directors come up for review first.

### BOARD OF DIRECTORS

It should be quite obvious that in many companies the board needs to be "beefed up" by adding mature, topflight, marketing-oriented directors. These men may be directors or top-level officers of other successful noncompetitive corporations, retired executives with broad marketing experience, professors in business schools, or consultants. A recent trend has been to pay substantial fees for active participation by men who act as director-consultants.

The use of this technique for strengthening a board of directors need not be confined merely to the marketing area. Any company can derive great benefit from strengthening its board with equivalent types of men for its other areas such as finance, production, and the like. According to E. Everett Smith, a director of the management consulting firm of McKinsey & Company, Inc.:

> "It is easy to turn to insiders because of their ready availability and knowledge of the business. . . . We justify the action by pointing to exceptional circumstances where men have worn two hats successfully. . . . All this is merely a way to postpone facing up to the real issue of making the board a functioning and effective organ. The first step in this process is to begin to

inject people who can bring a fresh viewpoint, who are not subordinate to the chief executive, and who will act as independent judges."[1]

In this connection, Smith-Corona Marchant, Inc. has an interesting board of directors:

At Smith-Corona Marchant, a unique and close-working relationship opens up direct channels of communication between the president, the board, and the staff executives. It puts the president's and directors' knowledge and experience at the disposal of the operating executive. Moreover, the vice president in charge of marketing can call on a director without going through the president or the board chairman. This organizational structure paves the way for support of marketing objectives and the marketing concept at the top level.

By way of further background, two and a half years ago only one of the present seven vice presidents was with the company, and of its 19 directors, 13 were not associated with it at that time. President Elwyn L. Smith started looking around for new men and new lines in 1956, and Dr. Edward H. Litchfield was named board chairman in September.

Dr. Litchfield recruited several outside men for the board, including Clarence Francis, formerly chairman of the General Foods Corporation. The board was then organized into eight working committees to parallel the major fields of operation. Each committee works directly with the vice president in its designated field.

The chairman of the board marketing committee is Clarence Francis. The vice president in charge of marketing is not a director but is the sixth member and secretary of the committee. The marketing committee convenes periodically, and it makes objective appraisals of marketing, sales, advertising, and promotional plans. The final approval for the marketing program must come from the operating committee, headed by the president. Any major step is thus reviewed and coordinated with the corporate long-range plan at one of the weekly meetings.

The marketing function is, therefore, well integrated at the top level. The marketing and operating committee provide control, as well as consultation on all marketing decisions.

### THE PRESIDENT

The chief officer and the key executives of a company, on the other hand, have to initiate their own self-improvement program. We must recognize the fact that all presidents (including some excellent ones) are not born with an innate appreciation and understanding of an integrated marketing operation. How can they compensate? Consider the following:

One effective tool is the long-range corporate plan. Perhaps the greatest benefit to a company developing such a plan is the *education* the executives get from the fact-finding and analysis requisite for the development of the plan.

This research includes studying future growth characteristics of the country in general and technical and economic growth trends in the specific industry, as well as in related firms.

An evaluation of competitive trends to determine what niche the company should carve out for itself over the next five to ten years is also a part of the background work.

This study is normally followed by

---

[1] "Put the Board of Directors to Work!" HBR May–June 1958, pp. 42–43.

detailed yearly sales forecasts for current products.

Then specific plans for new product additions, diversification, and mergers are incorporated.

And finally this future planning is tied in with similar planning by the production, personnel, research, and financial departments to form a carefully integrated and coordinated, but flexible, long-range plan.

Executive exposure to this type of analysis and planning aids in developing a state of mind that insists on planned, coordinated efforts in the marketing areas. Such a plan, however, is only the *foundation* for the proper corporate attitude.

While a long-range plan will give direction in broad terms, executive officers must be imbued with an understanding of the specific problems faced by the integrated marketing operation, and the reasons the marketing functions are performed as they are. The president need not be a "marketing man," but top management must have *sufficient* comprehension of the marketing aspects of business to effectively carry out these functions:

- Establishing objectives.
- Directing the attainment of these objectives.
- Measuring the results.

Implied is a knowledge of product planning, advertising, merchandising, selling, distribution channels, servicing, and a myriad of other carefully integrated functions.

In this connection, I should like to make a positive recommendation:

I would suggest an educational course for top-echelon corporate managers, specifically designed to offer instruction in the broad aspects of integrated marketing closely tied to long-range corporate planning. (Courses for junior executives should also be developed as they are indicated.)

This type of program should be administered by a good business school with personnel experienced in business and consulting, who are also skilled in teaching case histories, leading discussion groups on business policy, and conducting problem-solving sessions. The cases used might be drawn up from the personal experience of the attending executives.

It would also be advisable to call in outside speakers who would themselves be top-level executives, consultants, and other men skilled in specific fields. The sessions could vary in length from long weekends to five- to ten-day periods.

Certainly the experience of the advanced management programs now held by many business schools has shown that mature executives can absorb a tremendous amount of material in short concentrated courses. The attending executives feel that they benefit as much from their association with other executives during this period as from the course itself.

## ORGANIZATIONAL PLAN

First and foremost, the organizational plan for the marketing department or division requires a basic concept. A violation of good organizational principles is often the main cause for failure, rather than a lack of ability or product. As the management consulting firm of Barrington Associates, Inc., points out in one of its brochures:

"The current shift from a Sales Management to a Marketing Management concept increases substantially the number and complexity of the problems and decisions facing the Divisions Chief Executive. He is more than ever before, a key member of the Top Management Group, and he must be capable of thinking, planning and administration of the highest order. For that reason, it is imperative that the Vice President–Marketing's job be analyzed meticulously, and that his basic function, his major responsibilities and key duties be stated in the most precise terms. When this is done, he is in position to delegate the component responsibilities and authorities specifically, and to follow through regularly and efficiently to insure their effective performance by his subordinates.

"Such a position analysis must be carried out in greater depth than is usually the case for a conventional 'Job Description.' . . ."[2]

### ASSIGNING RESPONSIBILITIES

In most cases, final responsibilities must be assigned in the light of the character of the total operation, and modified by the experience and personality of the executives available. The personalities and experience of the team members must complement and balance each other.

Top management must first clearly resolve whether the director of marketing is to have complete responsibility for all the necessary marketing functions, including sales, or whether he should be, in fact, a director of marketing services or of marketing planning. In many companies, the integration of the marketing effort is brought about by the president or owner of the company. In other cases, it is carried out by the executive vice president or vice president in charge of sales. In such companies, the director of marketing may be in a staff position, and, as such, be responsible for all the marketing functions *except* sales, which becomes the responsibility of another ex-

ecutive who is charged with directing the sales force, sales training, sales analysis, and product servicing.

In a multidivisional company, the director of marketing may be even further removed from the intimate direction of departmental operations of such functions as marketing research, advertising, sales promotion, and so on. He often functions primarily as an over-all marketing coordinator and as a consultant to the president.

### CLEAR DEFINITION

Let me stress the importance of clearly defining the basic responsibilities of the marketing director, because this has such a strong bearing on the background and personality of the man selected for the position. For instance:

One very large multidivisional corporation was looking for its third director of marketing in five years. One reason the first two marketing directors were unable to handle the job was the lack of definition of duties and responsibilities. The last man selected had come from a background of divisional sales, national sales, and eventually director of marketing of a large national manufacturer. The requirements for this corporation, however, were those of being an adviser and coordinator to the president, being the adviser to thirteen divisions, and participating, in a loosely defined manner, in the marketing aspects of an acquisition program.

In many cases, he was called on a "panic button" basis to attempt to solve detailed sales promotion problems for strongly autonomous divisions in an unbelievably wide range of different types of industries. Consequently, he was never able to function effectively in any one area.

---

[2] Barrington Associates, Inc., *The Kind of Executive Needed for the Position of Vice President–Marketing* (New York, 1957), p. 1.

In trying to determine more exact man specifications in preparation for the search for the new director of marketing, two of the top officials in the corporation still had widely divergent ideas of what the functions of this man should be. One official was looking for a man with stature in the industry, sales experience, and skill in public speaking. The other official put more stress on analytical ability, marketing research know-how, and a wide range of experience in consumer and industrial goods industries.

The most difficult problem which this company had not resolved was recognition of the fact that no one man could probably fill the two divergent specifications.

### SIZE AND COMPLEXITY

Additional factors that bear on definition of responsibilities arise from the nature of the corporation itself. Here are two important ones:

1. *Large vs. medium-size company.* The top marketing man in a large company is more likely to be a coordinator, planner, and "corporate thinker." Thus, the marketing director for a broad multiproduct line needs great skills in administration and over-all planning. He need be only sufficiently experienced in the various marketing functions to be able to give adequate direction to and, more particularly, evaluation of the performance of his various department heads. On the other hand, one finds that the marketing executive of a smaller company must actually *perform* a wider variety of marketing functions himself. He should have a more intimate connection with the daily work; therefore he should have greater experience in specific technical marketing skills.

2. *Multidivisional corporation.* The basic requirements for the marketing director of a multidivisional corporation put the greatest emphasis on long-range planning skill, coordinating competence, and human relations. In a personal letter to an executive recruiting agency, the board chairman of a large multidivisional company searching for a broad-gauged director of marketing explained these requirements when he stated:

". . . Our chief requirement is for a man with sufficient knowledge of the principles of marketing research, merchandising, advertising, sales, etc., to be able to help set objectives and evaluate the work of his own department heads as well as those in each of our divisions. Even more important is the ability to exercise across-the-board coordination and quality control while at the same time aggressively represent marketing interests at our top management level, and, to put it bluntly, sell the marketing concept to our divisional presidents."

### MAN SPECIFICATIONS

To avoid trouble, every company should take a careful look at its particular job requirement; develop a complete job description with clearly delineated duties and responsibilities; and then draw up a man specification before rushing out to hire a man or to promote one from within.

Here are excerpts, drawn from several professional sources, of the job descriptions for three basic types of marketing directors:

*A True Director of Marketing.* ". . . The basic function of this position is to: plan and manage *all aspects of the marketing program*; maintain and equip a well-trained organization to carry out the program; and direct all marketing operations so as to attain stated objectives within company policy and budgets.

"Major Responsibilities:

1. Sales Planning and Policy
2. Sales Organization, Training and Compensation
3. Sales Forecasts, Quotas, Budgets and Controls
4. Selling Operations
5. Industry and Customer Relations
6. Pricing
7. Advertising, Sales Promotion, Publicity and Public Relations
8. Product and Market Research and Development
9. Sales Operations Research
10. Employee Relations."[3]

*Director of Marketing Services— Marketing Planning.*

"Basic Function . . . responsible for administering, coordinating, and controlling all aspects of planning the total marketing program for his assigned product lines and *for assisting the sales organization* in successful implementation of the program. . . .

"Specific Responsibilities:

1. To develop and recommend for approval of the Vice President a complete marketing program pertaining to his assigned product lines, including a factual analysis of the markets, an enumeration of problems and opportunities, specific marketing objectives, advertising and promotion plans, packaging and brands, selling methods, forecasts of sales, cost of sales, and profits for at least the ensuing year.
2. To direct the Product Managers in conducting similar marketing planning activities for the assigned products.

3. To organize and chairman planning meetings of representatives from Research and Development and from Production, together with the Product Managers, for purpose of expediting the development and production of present products as well as the coordinated development of new and improved products. . . .
4. To represent his assigned product lines in the product-planning sessions of the Executive Product Committee. . . .
5. To work with Research and Development and with Production in the development of improved products by interpreting the needs and preferences of the market.
6. To work with Finance and accounting in providing recommended budget estimates and accounting controls necessary to determine the profitability of present products and methods of marketing, as well as to measure current marketing performance in relation to objectives.
7. *To work with the General Sales Manager* and the Regional Sales Managers in the development of all aspects of marketing planning. . . ."[4]

*Vice President of Marketing— Multidivisional.* "As vice-president of marketing, the successful candidate will report directly to the president. Primary responsibility is the co-ordination, in a staff capacity, of all sales and related activities among twelve autonomous manufacturing and sales divisions. The vice-president of marketing may have acquired a broad knowledge of sales methods and market research as a top staff man in a company producing both consumer and industrial goods, or as a management consultant. He must be

---

[3] Barrington Associates, Inc., *op. cit.,* p. 2.

[4] From a report prepared by Bruce Payne & Associates, Inc. (Westport, Connecticut, 1958).

able to recognize and cure duplication of sales or allied efforts between divisions without creating friction. He must act as the profit center conscience of the entire company's distribution system. He must be highly creative and have the ability to use all the knowledge gleaned from divisional sales personnel to benefit the company's over-all planning and scheduling."[5]

## BALANCE OF TALENT

The next job is that of filling in the blocks on the preliminary organization chart with men possessing the proper combination of executive ability, technical marketing competence, and personality. The final definitions of duties and responsibilities should wait upon the selection of the men, so that the written descriptions will be a realistic blending of personalities and capabilities with the required duties and responsibilities.

One major error which should be avoided if possible is staffing from the bottom up. This is the type of situation in which a new organization chart is developed and the company fills all or most of the positions *before* it hires a director of marketing, or it fills jobs in a department before hiring the department head. Trouble develops when the new top man finds his subordinates are incompatible, or his prehired department does not have the proper balance of ability and personality.

### PERSONALITY REQUIREMENTS

There still is a great deal of merit in carefully considering the personality requirements of your director of marketing, despite the recent derision of the "corporate man." A new director of marketing, particularly if he fills a newly created

[5] Ward Howell, "Marketing Managers Wanted: Big Rewards, Key Responsibilities for Right Men," *Printers' Ink*, March 21, 1958, p. 61.

position, will be faced with many human relations problems. He will have to contend with any one or all of the following situations in almost any company:

He will be resented by any unsuccessful internal candidates for the position, and may experience great difficulty in securing their cooperation.

He will be viewed with suspicion and apprehension by division and department heads who automatically will fear any dilution of their highly cherished prerogatives.

He may be considered an intruder, if selected from the outside, particularly if his peers have arrived at their positions via a long-time company policy of promotion from within and form a tightly knit group.

The ability of the new executive to handle these situations may well be the key to his success, rather than his professional competence and experience.

The marketing director must be sufficiently aggressive to hold up his end of the corporate give-and-take, in addition to seeing that the jobs within his division get done on time. And at the same time he must be sufficiently flexible to relate successfully to these same people. In the smaller company, a man with ability to make quick decisions based on undocumented pros and cons is needed. In the larger company where more staff assistance and more facts are generally available, the requirement is for a more analytical, more moderate personality—a man who will weigh the pros and cons carefully and then effectively *communicate* his decisions throughout the organization.

In a company with several plants and many offices, the integration of all the efforts once a decision is made becomes a high-level exercise in executive ability —particularly if maximum profits are to be made. In this situation, bull in the china shop tactics can be ruinous. It is extremely important that the man "fit" with the rest of the top executive team. Unprofessional as it may seem, the human factors will often govern the effectiveness of the teamwork.

## HIGH-LEVEL CONTROLS

Every corporation has a difficult problem in achieving over-all marketing efficiency. There are, however, a number of steps that a corporation (particularly a multidivisional one) can take, which serve as operating controls of a high-level nature.

### LONG-RANGE PLANS

Each division should develop its own long-range plan as a part of the corporate long-term project previously discussed. There is this additional benefit to a diversified corporation in having the divisions develop individual long-range plans: top management will be more completely informed about present and future industry trends and each division's intrinsic corporate problems, as details of the long-range plan are reviewed.

For closer control in greater detail, an annual marketing plan, by product lines, is often used. This type of plan is based on extensive research and analysis, complete with monthly forecasts; it defines the marketing strategy and its implementation on a month-by-month basis. The simple act of sending a copy to headquarters, plus monthly or quarterly progress reports (which the division should have anyway) gives headquarters current information.

### GROUPING AND REALIGNING

Often, a corporation comprising a wide range of companies can improve its marketing efficiency by organizing those companies into logical industry groups and by dropping and adding companies within each group. Here is an example of such grouping and realigning:

One large, nationally prominent corporation purchased 12 companies between 1938 and 1955. The individual companies were in such widely diversified operations as: the manufacture of automatic processing machinery; atomic energy research; industrial OEM components in electronic instruments; parts for automobiles; and consumer goods sold through hardware, sporting goods, and grocery stores.

A careful analysis of the groups of the companies showed that they could logically be combined in such a way as to benefit from common research, manufacturing, and/or marketing efforts. They consequently formed a research and development group, a recreational industry group, a machinery automation group, and an industrial electronics group.

The company is now proceeding to divest itself of divisions which do not contribute to or benefit from a common research, manufacturing, or marketing setup. They are also purchasing companies which will complement and round out the operation in each industry group.

In the recreational and machinery automation groups in particular, the greatest emphasis is being placed on developing new products (either through acquisition or through research and development) that will have common channels of distribution and also will lend themselves to benefiting from a common advertising campaign in order to achieve maximum marketing efficiency.

Such moves made during the first year of this general shakedown operation showed very promising indications of improved operating efficiency and are being reflected already in better net profit and earnings per share.

## UNIFORM SYSTEM

The concept of a uniform control system should afford means of determining goals and limitations, as well as proper yardsticks with which to measure progress made in achieving these goals. This represents more than standardized balance sheets and profit and loss statements usually prepared by the financial department. The control system should result in clear, concise charts or report forms which not only provide facts and figures but show them in relation to past records and in comparison with forecasts, so that top management can see problems developing before they get to the danger point, rather than after.

A reporting *system* must be developed which gives corporate headquarters current information on exactly what is happening from an operating standpoint in all operations of each subsidiary division in time to take action. This type of financial reporting can be so set up as to be automatically and painlessly extracted from each division's own operating figures (which they should have for their own use anyway) and management can be adequately informed as to the exact efficiency of a division without appearing to breathe down the neck of a division manager or encroach on his prerogatives.

An excellent publication providing both the philosophy and several examples of such a control system is: *How The DuPont Organization Appraises Its Performance.*[6]

## CORPORATE CHARACTER

One of the most effective ways of securing stronger corporate control over independent divisions, as well as improving marketing efficiency, is through a carefully designed corporate advertising and public relations program.

Under certain circumstances, a diver-

[6] American Management Association, Inc., Financial Management Series, Number 94 (New York, 1950).

sified corporation finds it economically advisable to establish a strong "corporate character" among various specific publics in such a way that the name or insignia of the parent company becomes a definite marketing tool for the individual companies. Often, when properly promoted, the corporation's name or insignia becomes so much of a competitive advantage that even the hard-bitten, fiercely independent former owner or manager rushes to tie in.

## CONCLUSION

Professional marketing techniques are being developed so rapidly in so many industries, both consumer and industrial, that those companies which do not devote their full efforts to making the integrated marketing concept work will soon find themselves dropping behind in the procession.

However, even among those companies which have embraced the concept, there are those that do not recognize certain organizational weaknesses which impede profitable functioning in this area. Most of these basic failings can be grouped under four headings:

1. Lack of comprehension of the highly professional marketing job necessitated by today's competitive market.
2. Unsound organizational structure.
3. Lack of top executive ability.
4. Overconcern with personal aggrandizement.

These problem situations can be countered by means of the following suggestions:

- Better determine the true nature of the marketing operation.
- Develop, with the help of consultants, the proper organizational structure.
- Strengthen the board of directors by

bringing in outside members with specific skills.

- Staff with the proper balance of ability, experience, and personality.
- Sponsor executive educational courses to develop the practice of coordinating modern integrated marketing techniques with long-range planning.
- Require written long-range plans and annual product-line plans.
- Set up operating controls that will tell you what you are actually doing and whether or not you are meeting your planned objectives.

But, first and foremost, a company must possess the proper corporate state of mind in regard to integrated marketing thought, or all attempts to solve such problems become academic.

## QUESTIONS

1. What criteria might be set up to determine whether to promote from within or hire from the outside to fill a management opening?
2. What personality clashes might impede the development of a smoothly coordinated marketing team?
3. Do most firms that adopt the modern marketing concept assign the same responsibilities to the top marketing manager? Comment in detail.
4. What specific suggestions does the author give for avoiding the organizational weaknesses described in his article?
5. What organizational problems frequently arise due to mergers or purchases?

# 10. New Organization Patterns for Marketing*

Edward G. Koch, Professor of Business Administration, University of California

*Reorganizations that implement the marketing concept are particularly significant in corporations with decentralized operations. Recently there has been a strong trend toward a "recentralized decentralization" with a marked tendency for strong central-office control over marketing and product planning, analysis and strategy.*

What's so new about the "marketing concept"? The term has been discussed and written about so much that the uninitiated might be forgiven for assuming that the marketing concept is a dramatic and revolutionary theory that has recently burst upon the management scene; actually, of course, most of the ideas it embodies have been around for some time. What *is* new—at least for many companies—is the emphasis on making marketing a central part of the business philosophy of the company and elevating

* Reprinted from *Management Review*, February 1962, p. 4. Published by the American Management Association.

the marketing function to a pre-eminent position in the organization.

There was a time when most companies were production-oriented: First they produced the product, then they made a market for it. Selling was thus the important concept—and the difference between selling and marketing is more than a semantic exercise. Selling focuses on the needs of the seller, marketing on the needs of the purchaser. Selling means moving products; marketing means obtaining customers. In production-oriented companies, management tells the sales department, in effect, "You get rid of the products; we'll worry about the profits." In contrast, the marketing-minded company makes every effort to create goods that customers will want to buy at a reasonable profit to the company.

We have had marketing-minded companies with us for some time; such pioneer companies as Sears, Roebuck, John Wanamaker, J. C. Penney, and General Foods have understood and practiced the so-called marketing concept for many years. Today, however, more and more companies are adopting this point of view; management thinking is becoming more customer-oriented, and profitable selling is replacing sales volume as the primary objective of the marketing program.

## A MATURE MARKET

The reasons for this changing emphasis are not difficult to determine. During the past decade and a half, the United States market, although by no means saturated, has become mature. A great many U.S. consumers have satisfied their basic needs for products and goods. They have become more discerning buyers, and they can afford to pass up products that do not completely meet their desires

and standards. Moreover, they are spending a larger proportion of their income on services than ever before. Thus, producers of consumer goods must compete not only with each other, but with the growing appeal of vacation trips, higher education, better medical care, and the wide array of services that are becoming part of the "good life" to the American consumer.

## FOCUS ON THE CONSUMER

Faced with this situation, many companies are finding that they cannot afford a hit-or-miss approach to marketing problems. The consumer has become the pivot point about which the entire business must move. This shift in emphasis requires more research expenditures, greater product-development activities, and increased attention to the short- and long-term planning of marketing activities. Marketing plans have become the basis for the design and erection of total corporate planning. Future market plans and sales potentials, for example, serve as premises for the planning of advertising expenditures, sales and promotion efforts, plant expansion and location, financial requirements, and other short- and long-term business commitments.

At the same time, sheer sales volume is no longer considered the key to corporate profitability. As competition increases and profit margins shrink, many companies have found that their marketing plans, policies, and strategies must be designed chiefly for their contribution to profits, rather than predicated on sales-volume objectives alone. And marketing goals must be consistent with over-all company objectives in order to contribute most to the long-range benefit of the firm. This means that the marketing function must be more closely coordinated and integrated with the other activities of the company, and the marketing responsibility has been expanded and reorganized to interlock all functions of the company into greater effectiveness.

## ORGANIZATIONAL CHANGES

In short, the modern marketing concept demands that the activities of the entire business be directed toward the satisfaction of consumer needs at a profit, and to accomplish this goal it has often become necessary for a company to rearrange its organizational structure. Although the changes that have been made have varied widely from company to company, depending on the peculiar circumstances in which they may operate, enough experience has been logged to identify several basic types of organizational set-up that have been established by companies who have adopted this management philosophy.

## SIMPLE PRODUCT LINE

In companies with a narrow product line, relatively simple problems of distribution, and a single channel of distribution, marketing and selling activities are often diffused among the various functions making up the business. Usually, the product-planning function reports to the production or engineering departments, the pricing function reports to the finance or accounting department, and sales and advertising are separate departments. Sales forecasting and budgeting are often under a separate department or report to the finance or accounting departments.

When such a company adopts the marketing-management concepts, all these activities, which obviously bear on the consumer, are properly moved to the direction and control of a marketing director or manager. This executive is under the general supervision of top management and at the same level of delegated authority as production, engineering, and finance.

The specific arrangement of the marketing-management function will be determined by the particular needs and scope of the company's operations. In some companies, for example, some of the technical activities related to the product or product group—such as product development or product research—are not under the direct control of the marketing director but are a responsibility of the production or engineering organization. Other companies place technical product activities in his care, even, in some cases, locating the repair service work with him rather than with production or manufacturing. In all instances, however, the tendency has been toward a task-force approach to departmentalization, giving the marketing director full charge of such activities as market research, advertising, sales promotion, product planning and budgeting, and sales management.

## THE MARKETING DIRECTOR

This increased centralization of marketing functions requires a marketing executive who is more than the traditional sales manager. The marketing director must think in corporate terms, rather than confining himself to building up sales volume; he must define problems for research, analyze results, and develop the indicated policies, plans, and strategies. In doing this, he must integrate the activities of other functions into the overall plans, working harmoniously with all members of top management and with the board of directors.

Such men are not always easy to find; in fact, the chief difficulty many companies experience in adopting the marketing-director form of management is obtaining the right executive for the job. Executive recruiters indicate that the specifications most frequently sought in a marketing manager are these:

1. Ability to plan and coordinate the entire marketing activity on a profit-minded, businesslike basis.
2. Working familiarity with both manufacturing and research.
3. Sufficient knowledge of finance and accounting to be able to judge merger and acquisition possibilities intelligently.
4. Ability to set up and carry out long-range plans for new markets.

## COMMITTEE SYSTEMS

It is quite possible that a company lacking such executive talent but desiring to go ahead with a reorganization under the marketing concept might start with a committee system. Indeed, even companies with highly capable managers often prefer the committee approach, believing that it facilitates communication and coordination among the various functions of the business. In Dennison Manufacturing Company, for example, the president serves as chairman of a marketing committee composed of the marketing manager, the general merchandise manager and his assistant, the research and development director, and the controller. Meetings are held at least every other week to discuss profits, make concrete plans, and decide on courses of action. In other companies, marketing committees are composed of the top executives from sales, advertising, market research, finance, and production.

The advantage of the committee system is that it eliminates many obstacles to interdepartmental coordination. The problems of communication between activities are greatly lessened because each, through active participation, is constantly abreast of the problems, needs, and findings of the other activities represented on the committee. But many companies find committees unwieldy, and they prefer to pinpoint the marketing management responsibility under the line authority of a single corporate marketing director.

## DIVERSIFIED COMPANIES

Although the reorganizations that implement the marketing concept are significant in functional-type companies, they are even more dramatic in corporations with decentralized operations, many of which have shown a decided movement away from the General Motors type of decentralization. This is not to say that all companies with this marketing approach have changed their organizational patterns; some, like General Electric, adhere to the decentralized structure of self-contained divisions. But more often than not there is a strong trend toward a "recentralized decentralization" under the modern marketing concept.

To see how this trend changes organizational patterns, we can examine the effect of adoption of the marketing-management concept in four types of decentralized companies: (1) those with a package of complementary products or services using the same channel of distribution; (2) those with similar products using separate channels of distribution; (3) those with dissimilar products using the same channels of distribution; and (4) those with dissimilar products using different channels of distribution.

## COMPLEMENTARY PRODUCTS— SAME CHANNELS

Companies with a package of complementary products using the same channels of distribution often centralize the marketing-management activity and geographically decentralize selling operations.

In these cases, the pure selling functions are decentralized under regional or territorial line managers for reasons of economy, selective selling, and expanded penetration. Top marketing management reports to the chief executive officer and operates on a staff basis, with "functional authority" over *all* marketing and selling activities. This pattern of organization is well suited to a company selling complementary products through common distribution channels because the company is often more concerned with marketing a "whole idea" rather than individual products.

It is not difficult to find examples of large corporations that have reorganized in this fashion. Among the companies that are now emphasizing centralized marketing are the following:

• Burroughs Corporation, after a three-year tryout of product-line decentralization in which each division was responsible for its own marketing, manufacturing, engineering, and the like, abandoned this structure and set up a single marketing activity at headquarters to oversee the marketing of almost everything the company produces.

• Illinois Tool Works also centralized its marketing management and decentralized its product groups, which are responsible for their own selling.

• Monsanto Chemical revamped its organization to centralize marketing at the top corporate level. This reorganization was designed to bring marketing and production closer together and to get better-coordinated product planning.

• Humble Oil consolidated six operating affiliates into one, with centralized marketing management at the headquarters office and decentralized field selling operations in four regions across the country. Company management anticipates that over-all sales volume can be increased appreciably in the years ahead

through the use of a single marketing organization and a company-wide trademark or symbol. The new organization will be able to make use of national advertising and promotion, to enter new marketing areas where none of the separate affiliates operated before, and to expand the network of marketing facilities in some areas where present representation is comparatively light.

## SIMILAR PRODUCTS— SEPARATE CHANNELS

A second type of marketing organization in decentralized companies can be found in companies with similar products and separate channels of distribution. Under this kind of organization, production and marketing are centralized activities and selling is a responsibility of the divisions. Examples of this pattern are evident in the automobile industry, where Ford Motor Company and Chrysler Corporation—and, to some extent, General Motors Corporation—are moving toward this kind of "recentralized decentralization."

In 1955, Ford Motor Company planned to set up separate, self-contained car divisions to compete line by line with General Motors. Within four years, the company created four new divisions—Continental, Lincoln, Mercury, and Edsel—and dismantled them because sales volume was not robust enough to absorb the divisional overhead. In 1957 and 1958, Mercury, Edsel, and Lincoln were combined into one division. In 1959, Ford dropped the Edsel line and transferred the Lincoln-Mercury division's assembly, purchasing, and production to the Ford division, leaving Lincoln-Mercury merely a sales organization. In 1960, the company took all assembly, purchasing, and production-engineering operations out of the Ford division and placed them in a new centralized automotive activity. This was the final step in centralizing all production, keeping market planning and strategy centralized at headquarters, disbanding self-contained profit centers, and assigning only selling responsibilities to the divisions.

Chrysler Corporation experienced a similar evolution in its organization structure. In 1950, Chrysler was structured on the simple lines of any manufacturing plant of an earlier generation, with a chief executive officer and vice-presidents for finance, engineering, and sales—all operating executives. Reorganizing was a gradual process that started with a program of divisionalization to get control of costs. In 1956, sales responsibilities were taken from the divisions and given to the central staff, evidently to obtain marketing information for headquarters. The system got another upheaval in 1958, when manufacturing operations were taken from the car divisions and put into centralized functional groupings, and the divisions were once more given responsibility for sales. As a result, Chrysler now has a strong policy, market-analysis, and planning staff at the top corporate level, and a centralized manufacturing activity to handle all production. The divisions have no other task than to sell automobiles.

General Motors is the least consolidated of the "Big Three." Each GM car division has its own engine, suspension, and assembly facilities, and Chevrolet and Buick have their own transmission operations. However, a dispersal of activities has started: Now Buick and Oldsmobile share an engine, Chevrolet makes trans-axle and rear suspension parts for Pontiac, and Pontiac produces differential parts for Oldsmobile. It is conceivable that the future will see a changing pattern of "recentralized decentralization" in General Motors as it seeks to gain more of the advantages of the modern marketing

concept and, along with them, the paring of burdensome divisional overhead costs.

At all three major automotive companies, responsibility for breaching new markets, capitalizing on new-product diversification, and utilizing the modern marketing concept is lodged in a separate office—next door to the chief executive.

## DIFFERENT PRODUCTS-SAME CHANNELS

A third type of recentralization occurs in companies with dissimilar products but common channels of distribution. In this structure, selling operations are centralized under a sales division, because selling methods are the same for all products, but marketing and production functions are delegated to various separate product divisions. Although these divisions are responsible for enterprising efforts and expanded profits on their respective lines, their activities are subject to stringent central-office control by the vice-president of marketing, who oversees marketing management throughout the organization. He approves all short- and long-term planning of the product divisions, including advertising appropriations, sales-promotional deals, pricing policy and strategy, and expense budgets. In addition, he is usually responsible for marketing research, advertising research, and broad consumer-research functions.

Companies with this type of organization—among them, General Foods Corporation, Pillsbury Company, H. J. Heinz Company, and Procter & Gamble Company—depend heavily on consumer and product research to guide them in producing products that meet consumer needs and desires, thus attuning the entire corporate effort to the consumer. Such companies are truly "marketing managed." They utilize research to define needs or desires that a product might be designed to fulfill. New-product ideas come from interpretation of consumer surveys or from astute anticipation of consumer needs. Product divisions, working with the central office of research and development, are responsible for initiating product ideas and improvements; pure research is left to the central R&D activity.

During a product's lifetime, the product division uses research to analyze the quality and value it represents to the consumer, so the company can predict or ward off competitive inroads. Should a product develop trouble, it is the job of the product division and central R&D to determine how much of the problem lies in the product and how much is created by outside pressures. Even when products are successful and trouble-free, product divisions continue to study them for opportunities to redesign or repackage them, or otherwise to improve their salability and expand their market penetration. The "marketing managed" companies are most sophisticated in the use of research and the marketing concept to satisfy today's mature consumer needs at an adequate return to the company.

## DIFFERENT PRODUCTS— DIFFERENT CHANNELS

A fourth type of recentralization is found in companies with dissimilar products using different channels of distribution. Even though product responsibilities may be delegated separately—e.g., for consumer and industrial products—they are often controlled by a top management executive operating under the modern marketing concept, as is the case with Du Pont, Borden, and General Mills.

Companies with a wide variety of products, both consumer and industrial, must always be alert to the possibility that their profit position may be impaired even while their total sales are growing. Top-heavy selling and marketing activities can be a serious drain on company resources, sometimes to the point where it is actually more profitable to eliminate some lines than to have too many irons in the fire. It is interesting to note that Monsanto Chemical Co. developed an excellent consumer product in "All," a home-laundry detergent, but sold it outright because the product did not fit their line, used a different channel of distribution, and required a separate selling effort.

## RECENTRALIZED DECENTRALIZATION

All these organizational realignments, different as they are, have a common element: a marked tendency for strong central-office control over marketing and product planning, analysis, and strategy. This strict marketing direction from the top, which is akin to the rigid central-staff financial control found in the General Motors type of organization, is a feature of the organization of an increasing number of companies.

The revolution in marketing management, along with the revolution in information technology, may very well portend a reversal of the trend to decentralization and a strong recentralization of major business functions in the corporations serving the markets of the sixties.

## QUESTIONS

1. What is meant by "recentralized decentralization" under the modern marketing concept?
2. What are the specifications most frequently sought in a marketing manager according to executive recruiters?

3. A third type of recentralization occurs in companies with dissimilar products but common channels of distribution. Explain.

4. The consumer has become the pivot point about which the entire business must move. Comment.

5. The difference between selling and marketing is more than a semantic exercise. Comment.

# 11. Changes in the Marketing Organization in Selected Industries—1950 to 1959*

Robert E. Weigand, Chairman of the Department of Marketing, DePaul University

*The author reveals some of the findings of a study into the nature and causes of change in the organizational structure of firms in the electric and non-electric machinery, fabricated metals, chemicals, and instruments industries. Particular emphasis was directed toward the problem of coordination of activities within the marketing department.*

During the nineteen fifties considerable literary attention was directed toward changes in organization which performed the marketing task. Various terms were used to describe these changes but probably the most popular were "the marketing concept" and "integrated marketing." Part of the basic meaning of these terms centered on giving more attention and effort to measuring and adapting to market tastes and preferences; this idea was often referred to as "market orientation."

Those concerned with implementing the concept, however, often stated that changes in the organization structure were an essential step toward market orientation. The most identifiable change was the extent to which firms were attempting to coordinate closely related activities under a single marketing executive. Many suggested that market orientation could be achieved to the fullest extent when all of the marketing activities in a firm became a part of a unified marketing plan.

## PURPOSE OF THE STUDY

There was evidence in the literature that changes in the marketing organization structure were occurring. Notices of job title changes (usually from a "Sales" to a "Marketing" position), examples of "old" and "new" organization charts, and

* Reprinted from *The Social Responsibilities of Marketing,* Proceedings of the Winter Conference of The American Marketing Association, December 27–29, 1961, p. 475. Edited by William D. Stevens.

statements by those in a position to observe the business scene were common. But none of these sources presented a comprehensive and specific view of what was occurring. The purpose of this study was to investigate the nature, extent, and causes of organizational changes in five selected industries.

## SCOPE OF THE STUDY

This study empirically investigated certain changes in the marketing organization structure and the responsibilities of the chief marketing executive in the electric and non-electric machinery, fabricated metals, chemicals, and instruments industries. In addition, it was limited to the internal formal organization of firms with a net worth of at least one million dollars.

The period investigated was limited to the years 1950 through 1959. The same type of field evidence was gathered for both 1950 and 1959 in order that the nature of organizational changes could be identified and the extent of change measured. The results were fruitful, although there were obvious methodological problems involved in gathering information for the earlier period.

## METHODOLOGY

Empirical evidence was gathered by mailed questionnaires, further correspondence with the respondents, and a series of field interviews. Analysis of the questionnaires returned by mail revealed a variety of changes, but attention in this paper will be restricted to reviewing the extent to which closely related activities are coordinated by a single marketing executive, indicating the relationship of organizational changes to various size categories, and citing the major causes of change.

## THE FINDINGS

There appeared to be almost as many different types of organization structures as there were firms which answered the mailed questionnaire or cooperated on a personal interview. At the risk of oversimplification, however, three organizational structures were identifiable:

First, in a decreasing per cent of firms the top marketing executive supervised only a sales force. Any other marketing activities were performed personally by the top marketing executive without the aid of a specialized staff, by those in another department, or by those outside the firm such as an advertising agency or consulting firm. This method was most popular among firms with a yearly sales volume under $10,000,000. Most of the smaller firms and more certainly the larger firms, however, had graduated to the second method of organizing the marketing department.

Second, in a method used by a large and slightly increasing per cent of firms, the chief marketing executive supervised the line sales force but also had at least one specialized staff assistant. Advertising and research were the most frequent activities to warrant a staff appointment.

Third, in a very small but rapidly growing per cent of firms the individual designated as the top marketing executive was *not* responsible for supervising the line sales force. Rather, he limited his attention to managing a headquarters marketing staff. This staff included such activities as advertising, sales promotion, marketing research, product development, market planning, and long- and short-range forecasting. About half of the largest firms, defined as those with yearly net sales over $100,000,000, organized in this manner.

The tendency toward dividing line sales and staff marketing activities is based upon a sound principle of organization.

The literature of management has long recognized that there is a limit to the number and variety of activities which a manager can supervise effectively. Such factors as the increasingly recognized complexity of marketing problems, the decentralized nature of many marketing duties, greater specialization of job duties, and product diversification, as well as the executive's personality, training, and interests influence his effectiveness in supervising the marketing task as being so formidable that it cannot be managed by a single executive.

In dividing the supervision of line sales and staff marketing activities there is danger that coordination will be impaired. But the same problem can also arise when the marketing executive's span of management becomes so broad that it is unwieldy. Further investigation indicated that coordination between line sales and the marketing staff was achieved by group conferences and daily contact of individuals. However, a significant and increasingly used method of achieving unity of direction, one which was more prevalent among larger firms, was marketing planning. Where marketing executives have been relieved of time-consuming duties, particularly supervision of the personal sales force, they are expected to allocate considerable time to integrating the activities of the sales force with other elements of the marketing system.

There was a major exception to the tendency toward functionalizing the various marketing activities under a single executive. No evidence was found to indicate that either traffic or warehousing decisions were the responsibility of the marketing executive. Indeed, in only a relatively few firms was he expected to express his views concerning problems in these areas. For the most part he did not even share in decision-making responsibility. Most marketing textbooks list transportation and storage as two func-

tions in the marketing process. Whether businessmen agree with this view is not very important. But it is exceedingly important that they be aware of the interrelatedness between the two physical supply functions and other marketing activities. The assignment of supervisory responsibility for these two activities clearly did not reflect any such awareness.

The marketing organization became much more complex between 1950 and 1959 because many activities, perhaps long performed, became formalized or identifiable parts of the organization. Analysis of the activities indicated that managements were increasingly aware of a need for more information before making decisions. Advertising historically has been the activity which first and most frequently has warranted specialized staff attention. But marketing research and long-range forecasting and planning were clearly the fastest growing activities.

From this brief review of what occurred in marketing organizations during the period 1950 to 1959 two factors are dominant. First, management was seeking a more unified marketing system. Both the literature of the period and the empirical evidence indicated this was an advantage sought by management in making certain changes. The literature of marketing has repeatedly emphasized the importance of bringing all the elements of the marketing mix together both in terms of balance of effort and timing. Coordination was clearly a managerial objective in making some of the organizational changes during this period. Second, managements were also seeking greater accuracy of business decisions. Response to direct questions about some of the organization changes indicated that management was concerned with risk reduction by gathering and analyzing information about the market and other elements of the marketing process. This conclusion was further evidenced by noting job titles on the organization charts for 1950 and 1959. There were substantially more job titles involving such terms as *market research, marketing research, market analysis,* and *product research and development.*

But if these were the objectives which management sought in making organizational changes, what were the factors which stimulated management to an awareness that there was need for change?

One of the most easily identified causes of change in the marketing operating system was growth in the net sales size of the firm. Growth of the total marketing task inevitably accompanies an increase in sales. As the firm becomes larger, the character of the marketing organization tends to undergo fundamental changes. It is not always a matter of adding personnel to the system who perform the same activities and report to the same individual as others have been doing. Rather, intrinsic changes occur because management recognizes that an organization which is adequate for a smaller firm may not be appropriate for performing the marketing task in a larger firm. Size of firm and the operational difficulties associated with an organization which has been out-grown was the most readily identified cause of organizational change.

In a substantial number of instances changes in personnel caused changes in the marketing organization. Various writers have suggested that top managements too frequently select an individual for a position with less than adequate regard for the organization structure. The empirical evidence corroborated this view and amplified it considerably. Changes in either the president or the top marketing executive sometimes resulted in changes in the marketing system. In several firms changes in the marketing organization were attributed not to changes in the marketing executive but to a new presi-dent. The new president often interpreted the needs of the system much differently than his predecessor. To an extent the system tends to adjust or to be adjusted to the abilities or interests of the newly appointed executive.

In a few firms renewed attention was centered on the marketing organization because the firm was more diversified than in earlier years. Product or industry diversification implies that growth should follow. While it is improbable that diversification will occur without at least a degree of growth, it is suggested that it can take place without excessive and, more important, without immediate growth. Hence the complexity of operations, resulting from diversification rather than sales growth, may sometimes be a cause of change in the marketing organization.

One of the healthiest signs was admission by a few management groups that changes were made in the marketing organization because of a recently acquired appreciation of the complexity of marketing decisions. Apparently these managements are only now beginning to identify the array of strategic factors which significantly influence the success or failure of a business decision. Certain organizational changes, particularly those designed to result in more accurate marketing decisions, were influenced by managements' increased capacity for identifying and coping with factors which are a part of the decision-making environment.

A final factor seems to have made managements more aware of the need for centering attention devoted to the organizing activity by the business press tended to encourage change. This factor did not necessarily bring about changes which would not otherwise have occurred, but it seems reasonable to believe that this increased literary attention accelerated changes in the marketing organization.

Such attention to organization must

also be considered a healthy sign. Many writers have indicated that managements often attribute operating difficulties to factors other than organizational faults. Too little time and attention, so it is said, is spent determining and working toward the most effective organization structure and definitions of job responsibilities. Yet the individual, either businessman or academician, who is familiar with organization concepts views the organizing process and growth of the firm as reciprocally related. The relationship between manufacturing or financial capacity and growth of the firm is easily recognized. No firm could hope that its net sales would increase substantially without assessing the appropriateness of its ability to manufacture for or to finance this growth. But the need for compatibility of the marketing organ-

ization and the volume of sales the organization is expected to move has not been so apparent to management. Publicity concerning organization changes, however, has had the healthy effect of bringing renewed attention to the organizational needs of the firm.

### QUESTIONS

1. Describe the three organizational structures identified by this study.
2. What are some of the principal causes of changes in the marketing organization?
3. What future developments in marketing organization might be predicted from the study findings?

# 12. Experimental Marketing: Corporate Pivot*

Seymour Kroll, Weyerhaeuser Company

*Whereas research and development is production oriented, the problems of the firm are frequently market oriented. To shift to a market orientation an experimental marketing department could be created. This new department would be responsible for carrying out long and short range market planning, including the development of marketing strategy, the evaluation of new marketing ideas, and the coordination of marketing with production and research.*

A new mechanism must be installed in the corporate organization if companies are to make the transition from production-orientation to the marketing-orienta-

* Reprinted from *Printers' Ink,* October 13, 1961, p. 32. Copyright 1961 by Printers' Ink Publishing Corp., 635 Madison Ave., New York 22, N. Y.

tion demanded today. This mechanism I call "experimental marketing."

Experimental marketing will have five important functions:

1. It will act as the central intelligence unit of the company, to determine if

policies and products are in tune with the needs of the market.

2. It will objectively evaluate creative marketing ideas submitted by personnel throughout the company, to determine if they will improve the company's marketing methods.

3. It will develop new marketing strategies that will keep the company ahead of its competition.

4. It will train the company's marketing management to use new marketing techniques and tools.

5. It will assist the president in coordinating the activities of marketing, production and research and development, so that all three are operating at optimum efficiency.

How will experimental marketing carry out these functions? Primarily by the application of research methods and procedures already being used effectively in the technical fields. The research must be both basic and applied.

In basic research, the highly theoretical approach, the scientific researcher has been given no specific commercial specifications or objectives. Basic research requires creative thinking and recognizes the need for experimentation. This same freedom to think, to theorize, to experiment, to test—essential to basic technical research—is equally important in the field of marketing. A corporation, in the future, must rely more and more on creative thinking to keep it one step ahead of its competitors. Experimental marketing will act as a clearing house for creative ideas and will evaluate them objectively. Currently, companies do not have such a mechanism, and as a result, creative thinking has been stymied by ultra-conservatism on the part of corporate management. Major changes in marketing policies only occur after there has been a major reorganization.

Applied research, the second approach, involves scientific investigations directed to the discovery of new concepts and theories that have specific commercial objectives.

With its dual approach, experimental marketing will fill a vacuum that has existed for many years. It will give a company a mechanism to develop effectively and carry out long-range market planning. It will act as a catalytic agent to stimulate creative thinking. And it will also bridge the gap between the theoretical and the practical, through necessary field tests, and trained management personnel who will use the techniques as they are developed and proven.

Where does the experimental marketing group fit into the corporate organization? To operate effectively, this group must have direct communication with the chief executive. It must have stature within the company. The man to head the group must be a highly qualified professional marketing man. He must know how to use effectively management tools such as marketing research and economics. And he must also be able to transform theoretical concepts into practical programs. In fact, he should be qualified himself to fill the top executive post of the firm.

The major sections of the experimental marketing group must be marketing research, economics, operations research, product planning and operations marketing.

Marketing research would play a very important role in carrying out the group's functions. It would aid in screening all new ideas and concepts. It would conduct market surveys. It would spend considerable time evaluating the effectiveness of the marketing programs that are being market-tested or that have been fully commercialized. Market research would be used both as a creative tool during the development of new marketing programs as well as a constructive critic of existing strategies. Including market research in the experimental marketing group assures that the data obtained from market studies will be more effectively integrated into marketing programs. This would be a refreshing contrast to marketing research's present ineffectiveness as a management tool.

The economist would be included in the experimental marketing group for much the same reason. Today the economist is isolated within the organization, and his talents cannot be tied in effectively with long-range market planning. All too often, top management doesn't know how to use the information that is developed by the economist.

Few companies have an operations research department, which I indicated would also be part of the group. I believe, however, that in the decade ahead this department will be recognized as a valuable marketing tool and many more companies will establish such departments.

Operations research will be able to make significant contributions in many areas. Here are three:

The design and analysis of marketing strategies, especially for the movement of consumer goods, but possibly for movement of industrial goods also. This could involve forecasting of consumer demands and the allocation of

the advertising budget among different types of media.

The training of executives, by use of training games.

Determination of optimal inventory policies for both raw materials and finished goods.

Product planning, another member of the proposed group, would effectively integrate the activities of research and development into the company's long-range marketing plans. But not only would the new products be developed by experimental marketing, but the marketing strategies necessary to successfully launch them would also be developed and tested by the new group. This function would be the responsibility of the last department shown on the chart.

The final section of the experimental marketing group would be operations marketing. This is a brand-new function, and one that I believe is an essential ingredient if the experimental marketing concept is to be effective. It would be the link between the theoretical and the practical. The operations marketing manager would have responsibilities similar to the R&D project director. He would be assigned marketing problems. To solve these problems, he would utilize the professional skills of market research, opera-

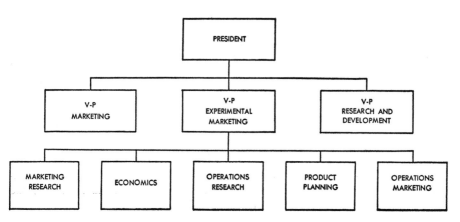

tions research and economics. In addition, he would work with product planning in the development of marketing strategies required for the introduction of new or improved products. The operations marketing manager would not operate in a vacuum. In order to effectively carry out his broad responsibilities, it would be essential that he work closely with other departments within the corporate organization, such as the line organization, advertising, R&D and manufacturing. It is imperative that he prove to these other departments that the function of experimental marketing is to help them do a more effective job. The operations marketing manager must not only have a creative imagination, but he must be able to translate marketing theories into practical and profitable marketing programs.

For example, if a company that had been selling consumer goods decided to market an industrial line of products, its operations marketing manager would not only develop the marketing strategy but he also would be responsible for setting up the sales organization and doing whatever else was necessary to set the program into motion. Once it was successfully launched, the operations marketing manager would step out of the picture, leaving in charge the line executive, who would be responsible for the continued success of the program.

Another function of the marketing manager would be to teach marketing management new marketing techniques as they are developed.

From this description, it might appear that experimental marketing is designed for the large corporation only. This is not true. A smaller corporation also can afford such a group. In this case, the group might consist of only two people; but it is the concept of experimental marketing that counts, not the size of the department.

The group's very first assignment would be to study and evaluate the objectives of the company. In many companies, objectives have not been revised in 20 years. In other cases, they are so general that the objectives cannot be used effectively to guide the corporation in its long-range market planning. Until a corporation has its basic objectives clearly defined, experimental marketing cannot work effectively.

Here are some other projects that would be assigned to experimental marketing:

1. Develop a method to increase the effectiveness of the sales force.

2. Examine the company's distribution policy to determine if it is in tune with the needs of the market.

3. Determine if the company should establish a warehouse system.

4. Determine if the company should diversify.

5. Evaluate product X to determine if it should be added to the line.

6. Develop a more effective marketing strategy to sell product Y.

7. Determine if the sales force should be increased in size within the next five years.

8. Determine if new plants should be built in the next five years.

9. Forecast major changes in the market. Then develop a marketing plan to take advantage of these changes.

10. Determine if the company's advertising budget is adequate to accomplish its objectives.

11. Develop a plan that would increase the effectiveness of the company's advertising.

12. Develop a marketing strategy for the company's new line of industrial products.

This is far from being a complete list of experimental marketing's broad responsibilities, but it does indicate that the group is primarily concerned with to-morrow's corporate marketing problems. Of course, the responsibilities, as well as the methods and procedures of experimental marketing, would vary from company to company. To be effective, it must be custom-designed.

Experimental marketing is not being presented here as a theoretical concept. It can be a profit-making function for the corporation if top management is agreeable to three things:

Top management must be completely sold on the experimental marketing concept before setting up the department.

Highly qualified personnel must be hired for the various positions. This will not be an easy task.

The board of directors and the president must give the experimental marketing group their complete support after the group has been established. It must have time to prove to the skeptics that its activities are both practical and profitable, and top management must give it that time.

If a corporation follows these procedures, then I believe that experimental marketing will become a new and valuable tool of the chief executive.

## QUESTIONS

1. Why is research and development still production oriented in many firms even though top management is trying to focus executive thinking on the consumer?
2. What useful purposes might an experimental marketing department serve?
3. In your opinion do you need to separate marketing research from operations research as seen on the organization chart?
4. Experimental marketing could act as a clearing house for creative ideas and evaluate them more objectively than the research and development department. Do you agree?
5. Might the experimental marketing department be an effective mechanism for carrying out long-range market planning?

## BIBLIOGRAPHY FOR CHAPTER II

ARTICLES:

Bund, Henry, and Carroll, James W., "The Changing Role of the Marketing Function," *Journal of Marketing*, Vol. XXI, No. 3 (January 1957), pp. 270–325.

Mapel, E. B., "What is the Marketing Concept?" *Sales Management Magazine*, Vol. 79, No. 1 (July 5, 1957), pp. 34–38.

"The Myth of the Organization Chart," *Dun's Review and Modern Industry*, Vol. 75, No. 2 (February 1960), pp. 38–41.

BOOKS:

Argyris, Chris., *Understanding Organizational Behavior*. Homewood, Ill.: Dorsey Press, 1960.

Bursk, Edward C., *Text and Cases in Marketing: A Scientific Approach*. Englewood Cliffs, N.J.: Prentice-Hall, 1962. Section Six.

Buskirk, Richard H., *Principles of Marketing*. New York: Holt, Rinehart and Winston, 1961. Chapter 26.

Howard, John A., *Marketing Management*. Homewood, Ill.: Irwin, 1957. Chapter 1.

Lazo, Hector, and Corbin, Arnold, *Management in Marketing*. New York: McGraw-Hill, 1961. Chapter 3.

Levitt, Theodore, *Innovation in Marketing: New Perspectives for Profit and Growth*. New York: McGraw-Hill, 1962. Chapter 6.

Mauser, Ferdinand F., *Modern Marketing Management: An Integrated Approach*. New York: McGraw-Hill, 1961. Chapters 11 and 12.

McCarthy, E. Jerome, *Basic Marketing: A Managerial Approach*. Homewood, Ill.: Irwin, 1960. Section G. 1.

Otteson, Schuyler F. (ed.), *First International Seminar on Marketing Management*. Special Supplement of *Business Horizons*, School of Business, Indiana University. pp. 9–29.

Pfiffner, John McDonald, and Sherwood, Frank P., *Administrative Organization*. Englewood Cliffs, N.J.: Prentice-Hall, 1960.

Rubenstein, Albert Harold, and Haberstroh, Chadwick J., *Some Theories of Organization*. Homewood, Ill.: Dorsey Press, 1960.

# III. Planning in Marketing

*HE HARD* core of the modern marketing concept is planning. While not new, marketing planning historically has been neglected by business management. In the early nineteenth century, J. B. Say, a noted economist and leading entrepreneur on the continent popularized the idea that a product created its own demand. While this idea was discredited by later economists, it seems to have persisted in business thinking.

Motion pictures and railroads are examples of industries which are now in difficulty due to marketing shortsightedness. In today's complex competitive environment, looking ahead and trying to anticipate marketing developments which might have an impact on company operations is absolutely essential for the survival and growth of most industries.

Through foresight and planning, modern marketing management tries to improve its decision making. A carefully planned sales forecast is an essential step in both short- and long-range planning. It provides the foundation for most other planning. In most companies, a very short-range forecast is required for planning production. Every company needs a forecast for budgeting and planning purposes, looking ahead at least a year. This forecast is the basis for cash budgets and many other planning activities such as workforce changes, purchasing requirements, inventory needs, and working capital.

Long-range predictions of business and economic changes are the basis for planning of new and the deletion of old products, plant expansion or contraction, capital investment and personnel expansion.

Short-range planning is formalized by the establishment of a system of work programs embracing a multitude of activities, many of which are simply an elaboration and extension of the long-range planning of a few years before. Short-range plans are, of necessity, more detailed and specific in nature. In a sense they become the operating instructions for carrying on any changes in operation. The establishment of special studies, training programs, or new methods and procedures are all matters which require greater or lesser amounts of planning by marketing.

Long-range planning is becoming more necessary and more critical to the successful conduct of business in today's rapidly changing, highly competitive market. Five-year programs are most common and probably make up the bulk of what is called long-range planning. But 10, 15 and 20 year plans are becoming increasingly frequent.

The marketing plan can be the cornerstone in the long-range planning of a company. Long-range estimates of customer demand, geographical trends, price stability, and industry requirements are the basic ingredients of over-all company plans for the future.

Total company planning, including the planning for capital requirements, product planning, share-of-market planning, personnel needs and operations, requires more than a mere projection of today's needs or activities. Long-range planning, for the foreseeable practical future often results in a complete change of company philosophy, products, techniques and facilities far beyond the existing situation.

Plans confined to the operation of the marketing division must be tailored to the demands of the company as a whole. There is a tendency for departments to get involved in detailed planning for their own units without first having a clear understanding of over-all company plans and objectives. For this reason, it is essential that company planning be organized on a committee or other basis where marketing, production, and finance are all represented.

# 13. Awesome Array of Forces Bearing on Future Marketing*

Benjamin F. Stacey, Vice-President, The First National Bank of Boston, Boston, Mass.†

*A dispassionate appraisal of the varied powerful economic and social forces shaping our future growth and challenging as never before American marketing management's know-how in the decade and a half ahead. Certain basic assumptions are postulated and predictions about 1975's dimensions are offered against which four broadly grouped forces of marketing structure, government's role, world environment and technology are scrutinized.*

Although our forward look ccmes at a critical and disturbing time—when we can be less sure of any estimate or trend—we must, nevertheless, look and plan ahead. First, we should establish several basic assumptions even though the uncertainties of the moment make some of them extremely tenuous—

(1) There will be no thermonuclear war, although the "cold" war will continue unabated, even taking on many new forms.

(2) There will be at least a stand-off with communism—a live and let-live accommodation.

(3) There will be no great depression, although minor ups and downs similar to those of the past decade should be anticipated, despite expanded Government counter-cyclical actions.

(4) Technological advance and eco-nomic growth, with reasonably full resource employment, will continue within a free market system.

That we can look forward to a 1975 economy enormously larger and infinitely more complex than today's is evident from some of its broad dimensions that show through the growth and momentum of today's America.

## THE "NUMBERS" GAME

There is a great temptation—to which I shall yield only very briefly—to discuss the long-range outlook for the economy as a "numbers" game, for numbers can appear very impressive and memories are so short that one's "guestimates" will be forgotten.

Some of the dimensions of the future are fairly certain of realization, for they are based to an extent upon people already here and trends with a high degree of validity—

* Reprinted from the *Commercial and Financial Chronicle*, 25 Park Place, New York 7, N. Y., October 5, 1961, p. 5.

† An address by Mr. Stacey before the Annual Marketing Conference of the National Industrial Conference Board, New York City, September 21, 1961.

By 1975 we shall almost surely have:

45 million more consumers;

14 million more families—including un-attached individuals;

21 million more in the labor force, with roughly 50% more entrants each year than during the Fifties;

6 million more persons 65 years of age and over;

17 million more persons under 30 years of age.

(Together these make up the de-pendent age groups—and account for roughly one-half of the 15-year total population increase).

Other measures depend upon econom-ic factors about whose myriad combina-tions we can only speculate. Some diverse projections with significant marketing im-plications, based upon reasonable exten-sions of recent trends, suggest that by 1975 we may expect—

$1 trillion GNP—in 1960 dollars;

20 million additional homes;

30 million more motor vehicles on the highways;

15–16 million families with incomes of $10,000 or over;

10 million additional college graduates with a minimum of a bachelor's de-gree;

1.150 million more scientists and engi-neers.

It serves no useful purpose to extend these numbers here. Such projections de-pend upon many variables, and The Na-tional Industrial Conference Board and other capable groups provide periodic up-dating of such information. Then, too, in view of the wrenching world changes we are now witnessing daily, we may be sure that new modifying forces will come into play. And, generally speaking, each forecaster and planning strategist likes to apply his own particular formulas and de-rive his own projections.

While we can easily agree that the numbers will be vastly larger in 1975, big-ger numbers alone will not tell us what kind of a country we shall be living—and marketing—in; what social and moral environment, living standards, or world role we shall experience.

## QUALITATIVE FORCES

I should like to direct your attention to some of the qualitative forces—involving consumers, managers, workers, and gov-ernments—that will determine the climate in which marketing management operates over the years to the mid-Seventies.

Some of these economic forces—now assuming shape after a rather obscure birth and retarded development during the Fifties—seem likely to become so powerful that they will challenge as never before the skill and ingenuity which has long characterized American marketing know-how—calling forth new skills and insights, greater imagination and adapt-ability to change than we now imagine we possess.

These forces may be roughly grouped into four broad categories. Without at-tempting to assign any order of impor-tance, these are: Market Structure, Role of Government, World Environment, and Technology.

Let us look at each of these in turn, even though they are thoroughly inter-mingled in their influence on our eco-nomic and marketing environment.

**(1) Market Structure.** . . . Market struc-ture will be subject to rapid and far-reaching shifts during the Sixties and be-yond. The demographic changes reflected in the number, sex, age, location, labor force participation and occupational dis-tribution of a population expected to be one-fourth larger by 1975, represent a minor part of the challenge. The techno-logical and cultural revolution—in being and accelerating—and the rising educational level of the labor force will combine to change many personal values and tastes, and radically alter spending priorities.

In the near future the suburban population will exceed the urban, and more money will be spent on the wide array of personal services than on nondurable goods. Leisure time will expand markedly if the work week continues to shrink by roughly two hours per decade, absorbing a part of our increasing productivity. Consumer adjustments to such sociological forces will increasingly plague marketers in their planning and operations.

Income will expand along with the greater skills and higher productivity accompanying a more complex and mechanized economy. Greater stability should also result with relatively less of aggregate income arising from agriculture and manufacturing and relatively more from services and professions. By 1975, after-tax family income may exceed $9,000—in 1960 terms—40% greater than today. The shift up the income scale should continue, so that 14 years hence less than one-third of spending units will be receiving under $5,000, compared with nearly one-half in 1960. Such income changes should be reflected in even more dramatic gains in discretionary spending power—helping to support the new products and services sure to be conceived in abundance.

**(2) Role of Government. . . .** Today we have a "mixed economy"—one in which government is increasingly involved in stimulating and regulating business enterprise. Big government seems destined to become bigger, not only because of its involvement with expanded defense spending, but also because of the trend toward providing more welfare services, both in quantity and breadth. In the process, governments will become more important customers for many nondefense goods and services, thus vitally affecting market planning. The Federal Government, through its regulatory and investigative commissions, is also likely to become more deeply involved with private business policy decisions, in the process affecting distribution strategy.

The present expansion of spending on defense and associated space age activities furnishes a most dramatic example of fluctuating demand for many goods and services, as we move unevenly toward a higher degree of preparedness for any eventuality. Although we do avoid a shooting war, the defense market over the years to 1975 will present many changes to marketing. The shifting balance among research and development contracts and production runs, new weapons systems, radical changes in geographical areas of expansion to allow for the huge spending on such activities as Project Apollo—the moon shot, upon which we seem committed to lavish billions as if they were millions—all these and more will have a bearing on sales organization and personnel needs directly, and on market growth indirectly.

### NEARING $100 BILLION FEDERAL BUDGET

The Federal administrative budget is rapidly moving toward $100 billion, and that for state and local units is approaching $65 billion. By 1975, assuming the same relationship to GNP, these totals could nearly double. But the disturbing current philosophy that in our affluent society more of our resources should be allocated to social or public goods and services, as dictated by some central planning authority, suggests this ratio may increase. Marketing men have a vital stake in this struggle, for their professional talents would wither under a totalitarian welfaristic state.

Although government is becoming bigger, the same tendency of private institutions is called increasingly into official question. Anti-merger attitudes, a crusading role on pricing policies and profit margins, an "investigative" complex which leads to the harassment of particular industries—these serve to divert valuable management time and frequently reduce the flexibility of marketing in matters of products, design, price, and customer selection.

(3) **World Environment.** . . . While political and economic decisions must increasingly be made in an international setting, paradoxically, the Sixties and Seventies will witness a less dominant role for the United States in the Free World. Free-handed foreign policies of military and economic aid have helped to rebuild the productivity of many of our allies, and our domestic tolerance for labor monopolies and wage increases in excess of productivity gains have been major factors in raising our unit costs of production. Now, marketing—at the very time it needs to focus increasingly on world markets to provide dynamic growth and contribute to redressing our unfavorable balance of payments—will experience a period of the most intense competition in our history, with the most efficient industrial nations of all time.

## OPPORTUNITIES IN FOREIGN TRADE

Exports and imports, which in the Fifties averaged 5% and 4.7%, respectively, of our gross national product, will each achieve new importance. Wide sales opportunities exist in foreign markets. In the more advanced nations, as incomes rise, demand will broaden to include many products formerly beyond the reach of the masses. In the underdeveloped countries, if investment funds are available as expected, capital goods requirements will provide the stimulus for sales-minded firms. Increasing attention may be expected to establishing manufacturing facilities abroad, or entering into licensing or royalty arrangements, especially if long-standing tax considerations are not altered to meet temporary conditions, unduly reducing the incentive.

A widening range of goods from abroad, many with strong price advantage, may be anticipated in the Sixties. Imports will be stimulated by periods of rising business activity, by the need to replenish dwindling domestic material resources, by the need to absorb some of the expanding output of the world's developing nations, and perhaps most of all by the hunger of competitive marketers abroad for a share of the rich and varied American market. The latter force has already affected enough products to call forth a rising swell of protectionist sentiment, sure to provide a major legislative battle in the next session of Congress, which faces the renewal of the Reciprocal Trade program or adoption of a substitute.

The trend toward a closer economic, and even political, union of peoples in various parts of the world through blocs and associations is bound to exert a strong influence on trade development and will require extremely close scrutiny. Successful association of the United Kingdom with the European Common Market—possible only after delicate negotiations that conceivably could fail—would create a powerful economic bloc of upwards of 300 million persons. Over the years ahead, such a bloc could become less and less closely linked with the United States, and more and more competitive in world markets. The current tendency toward a high degree of centralized planning of the industrial economy—successfully practiced by France in recent years and about to be embraced by Britain, could further complicate price, product, and market planning on a world basis for our free competitive economy.

## PRESSURES ON TRADE PATTERNS

Overriding in importance all these forces is the ideological conflict with communism—so determined on world domination that it will not desist until exhausted or defeated. An increasing part of this conflict is likely to be fought out on economic grounds—causing the most intense pressures on trade patterns. A totalitarian system—able to sell at any price, or give goods away, and spread its losses on the backs of a rigidly controlled and uninformed people—can easily upset carefully planned private marketing programs where attention to quality, service, and the necessity for an energizing and motivating profit are essential. And marketing must also be equally concerned over the battle of ideas. It should dedicate more of its great promotional talents to the successful export of free enterprise— our most important product—for a recent report to the Western European Union said "if means of combatting Communist propaganda techniques are not found, the West will no longer have to seek a *raison d'etre,* it will no longer exist." Clearly the political and economic ferment faces us with hard, tough, and awesome questions in an era when we must increasingly seek to penetrate world markets.

(4) **Technology.** . . . An eminent authority has said that roughly scientific knowledge is doubling about every nine years; technological effort is doubling about every ten years; and more advances have been made in science in the past 50 years than in all preceding history.

Total spending upon research and development of some $13 billion per year is six times the amount spent 15 years ago. Industry alone is performing more than double the research done five years ago. The outlook is for annual outlays to approach $30 billion by 1975.

The population explosion, here and worldwide, will place greater pressure on resources and facilities. These trends point to urgent research needs—and eventual market impact—in such fields as synthetic foods, geriatrics, nonfossil energy sources, air and water pollution control, traffic control, resource conservation, desalting of water, and even planned parenthood.

## ROLE OF AUTOMATION

Automation—simply defined as "increased efficiency resulting from technological improvement"—will be an important factor in conserving labor and increasing productivity, and will require substantial new capital investment. Computer systems and electronic processing equipment for operating factories and providing more meaningful data for management decisions will loom large in this respect. The 4,500 computer systems operating or installed in the United States on Jan. 1, 1961, may by the end of 1965 number 19,000 valued at $8 to $10 billion.

New scientific knowledge, sure to be accelerated because of our contest with the Soviet and the approach to the space age, can be readily translated into new industrial technology, much of it with civilian applications, sooner or later. It is altogether likely that products not yet on the market may account for as much as one-third to one-half of total manufacturers' sales by 1975.

The depth and variety of our research and technological achievements, one of the greatest assets of the West as well as the best hope for increasing economic growth, properly coordinated, will also provide one of the basic ingredients for successfully increasing sales.

This rather awesome array of varied economic forces which will bear so heavily upon our future growth—all too briefly set forth—presents a mixture of the good, the bad, and the uncertain. The population explosion and the many related sociological forces, changed tastes of a nation with a markedly higher educational level, a desire for security and an enlarging role for government, a drastically altered world environment, and a flood of now unimagined new products and services insure an era of rugged competition. The spread of such devices as automatic merchandising and leasing of consumer products, the probable extension of nonprice competition, a continued squeeze on profit margins will force many innovations in distribution.

Marketing as "the creation and delivery of a standard of living," can succeed in the growing economy of the Sixties only by being highly imaginative and skillfully creative. Only through expert, determined, flexible management of our economic affairs will we succeed in preserving the benefits and vigors of our free market system and in achieving sustained, sound economic growth in a rapidly changing world. Only with confidence that, despite threatening pressures, we and the West will continue to exist and to advance through adhering to the principles free men live by can we muster the strength we shall need.

## QUESTIONS

1. What are the four awesome forces which bear on future marketing?
2. Evaluate the quantitative predictions made for 1975 by the author. Do you disagree with any of them?
3. Is there any evidence that computer systems and electronic processing equipment will play a strategic role in future marketing management?
4. What might be done to increase our opportunities in foreign trade?
5. What changes in our market structure are expected by 1975?

# 14. The Role of Planning in Marketing*

Wendell R. Smith, President, Marketing Science Institute

*The hard core of the so-called marketing concept is effective use of market planning. Perhaps, the crucial phase of the planning process is the generation of marketing strategies. This creative component of planning is developed by study of the firm, competition, and the market.*

Perhaps the most important innovation being discussed in management meetings and conferences these days is the marketing management concept, sometimes referred to simply as the marketing concept. Marketing people, both teachers and businessmen, are simultaneously pleased and puzzled by this development. They are pleased that at long last the necessity for a more professional approach to marketing management and general management is gaining recognition. They are puzzled by the relatively sudden, almost explosive, rate of acceptance of a philosophy neither new nor revolutionary to thoughtful students of marketing theory and practice.

Some of the more meticulous professionals in marketing are also disturbed by an apparent lack of precision in many of the statements being made about this marketing concept—disturbed by the fact that its many proponents are not in agreement as to just what the concept means and implies.

At present, the so-called marketing concept appears to be an umbrella term used to describe one, several, or even all of the following developments in the basic components of effective marketing operations:

* Reprinted from the Fall 1959 issue of *Business Horizons,* p. 53. Published by the School of Business, Indiana University.

1. A marked increase in the degree of market orientation of top management thinking. Specifically, marketing considerations are increasingly coming to provide the framework within which other factors such as engineering, finance, and manufacturing are positioned and analyzed.

2. An increased recognition of the importance of planning marketing activities in a systematic way and using marketing plans as the springboard for over-all plans and budgets.

3. The emergence of the notion that innovations in marketing (new outlets, channels, and so on) are just as revitalizing as new products.

4. A trend toward positioning marketing executives in the organization structure in ways compatible with effective market orientation and planning.

Probably the last trend provides the most readily observable evidence that something new has been added. The appointment of directors of marketing or vice-presidents for marketing who, in addition to the usual "downstream" responsibility for determination of the marketing mix and directing marketing action, are also responsible "upstream" as members of the general management team shows that the marketing concept is more than just a currently popular expression. However, important as organizational recognition of the marketing concept may be, the success of the concept in increasing marketing productivity will depend largely on the second component—scientific marketing planning.

## MARKETING PLANNING

Planning in marketing, in its broadest terms, may be thought of as the exercise of analysis and foresight to increase the effectiveness of marketing activities. Planning, therefore, is necessarily concerned with (1) the goals or objectives that the firm seeks to attain; (2) the operating system through which the firm is attempting to achieve these goals; (3) the quantity and quality of effort needed for their achievement; and (4) the firm's capacity for generating this effort.

This is not to say that, prior to the emergence and recognition of the marketing concept, marketing operations were necessarily fortuitous and unplanned. Perhaps the crucial point is that developments in the economy, and in society generally, have operated so as to stimulate the emergence of planning as a conscious or explicit function. Among these developments are (1) the increasing complexity of products, services, and marketing operations and the environment in which they exist; (2) acceptance of the expectation of change—substantial change —as part of the "normal" operating environment; and (3) our ability, through research, to identify and control certain factors (images) in the marketing situation.

The recent period of business recession revealed the need for planning in some companies where that need had previously been concealed by the rapid growth caused by great technological advances or other external factors. In other instances, the recession caused planning to be elimi-

nated or put on the shelf. Because management identified the concept narrowly, planning was regarded as a tool of growth rather than as a rational means of achieving the most profitable adjustment to current and future market conditions, regardless of the stage of the business cycle.

## MARKETING STRATEGY

Much has been said and written about the sequence of steps involved in the development of sound marketing plans. The first step is usually identified as the determination of the goals or objectives that are to be accomplished by the marketing action being planned. This is true only to the extent that the firm has the results of a careful review of its present position as a foundation upon which to determine realistic goals and feasible objectives. If the firm is not fully aware of the characteristics of its current position in the market, such preplanning analysis must precede the process of goal definition. Hence, determination of goals and objectives may turn out to be the second step in planning instead of the first. While it is often true that the mere identification and statement of goals and objectives puts the firm well on its way toward their achievement, it is likewise true that those experienced in the planning of marketing activities tend to approach this step cautiously. Alternative sets of goals and objectives are regarded somewhat in the light of hypotheses to be tested, and the selection of the appropriate alternative becomes an important product of the planning operation itself. The feasibility of a goal can be evaluated only by review of the action plan necessary for its achievement. Therefore, in practice, the initial stages of the planning process may merge with the final steps in research and development until the criteria of feasibility have been satisfied. At this exploratory, perhaps experimental, stage in the planning process, strategy considerations become paramount as a true prelude to the development of the action plan that will finally emerge, complete with timetables, budgets, campaigns, and schedules for personnel deployment.

There are many ways in which the nature of marketing strategy can be described. Regardless of definition, however, marketing strategy is primarily concerned with the creative elements of a goal-directed marketing plan. It describes, in general terms, the basic elements of the way in which the firm plans to get from where it is to where it wants to be. Marketing strategy then becomes the central theme that integrates and co-ordinates the many and diverse components of effort to be stipulated in a marketing plan.

## PLANNING OBJECTIVES

It is worthy of note that the product line of today's marketing planners is exceedingly broad. At any given time, a firm can have one big plan or many little plans. Plans may emerge routinely, almost unnoticed, as the first stage of budgeting activities, or their development may represent a special, sometimes herculean, effort that has been triggered by anticipation of change in the firm's marketing situation. However, the great majority of firms find that their planning activities result largely from the desire to develop rational programs to achieve one or more of several objectives. These objectives may be grouped into two basic categories; the distinction between the categories depends on time considerations.

The first group is comprised of objectives giving rise to recurrent and continuous planning associated with appropriate procedures for control and evaluation. These objectives are:

1. Enabling the firm to maximize profits for a stated operating period by increasing sales or margins and/or by reducing marketing costs. This is the classical economic motivation that accounts for recurrent and regular attention to the planning function.

2. Gaining or maintaining a desired share of the market. This is an objective that has emerged concurrently with the rise of imperfect and monopolistic competition.

The second category is made up of objectives giving rise to special (*ad hoc*) planning. Such objectives include:

1. Bringing about a change that will influence the performance of marketing functions by means such as:

    a. Improving the layout of a store or warehouse

    b. Accomplishing a more appropriate geographic allocation of sales effort

    c. Installing a more smoothly operating marketing organization structure.

2. Preparing for the future by developing a program that will be activated when and if a specific contingency arises, such as:

    a. The lapse of a patent or franchise

    b. Movement of competition in a particular direction

    c. Release of a new product for marketing

    d. A substantial change in the economic environment.

3. Preparing for a major change in the direction or in the scope of the firm's activities, such as would result from major construction, acquisition, merger, or entering a new channel of distribution.

Implicit in all of these planning objectives is acceptance of the idea that "flying by the seat of the pants" is definitely impractical and that there are still enough unanticipated hazards to make the future exciting even though full advantage is taken of all of the aids to planning that contemporary marketing research techniques can provide.

## DEVELOPING STRATEGIES

While, in my opinion, marketing strategies are inherently creative, this does not mean that the process of their generation depends on the availability of an inspired genius. As a matter of fact, an orderly method for developing strategic concepts is one of the most basic aspects of the modern approach to marketing. In general, marketing strategies evolve from study of the firm itself, from study and analysis of competition, and from study of the market.

As was pointed out earlier, the generation of marketing strategies essentially begins with a careful review of the present position of the firm in relation to competition and in relation to the markets that it serves. Such analysis reveals rather quickly whether or not the strategy should be essentially defensive—that is, designed to compensate for and to correct weaknesses in the present operation—or offensive, in the sense of leading to plans designed to capitalize fully on the relative strengths or advantages that the firm enjoys. A defensive strategy might be one designed to eliminate a relative weakness, hence to increase profits, thereby increasing the profitability of an existing volume of sales. On the other hand, an offensive strategy would be oriented toward increasing profits by pumping additional products through an existing marketing mechanism, hence producing disproportionately small increases in total marketing costs. While strategies may vary in terms of the degree of rationality that they represent, they necessarily provide the creative sense of direction essential to planning.

As contemporary economists have so eloquently pointed out, many marketing strategies are developed with primary reference to the present and prospective future behavior of competition. Again, strategy may be essentially defensive insofar as it may be influenced by present or expected future competitive threats; or it may be offensively directed at points at which competition is or is expected to become vulnerable. Whether stated or not, such elements are probably implicit in most strategic concepts.

From my point of view, the most important and fundamental marketing strategies are those directly related to the accomplishment of goals or objectives defined in terms of the market. Solid marketing research is the stuff out of which such strategies can be built.

Much time could be spent in elaboration of the almost unlimited list of market-based strategies that could be developed and adopted as guides to the planning of marketing activities. Obviously, strategies generated from market study must be feasible from the point of view of the characteristics of the firm and competition. Let us look at two examples of the ways in which market data may suggest an orderly method or approach to strategy generation.

In the first place, analysis of trends in demand for present products or services is fundamental. An unfavorable trend in demand suggests a choice between strategies designed to reverse the trend or to accept and adjust to the development. Similarly, a favorable trend suggests a choice of strategies concerned with how the firm can profit most from this happy state of affairs without overextending itself or producing imbalance in its situation.

Second, analysis of market structure will reveal whether or not the market is homogeneous, a situation in which the requirements of consumers or users are very much the same; or heterogeneous, a situation in which individual requirements vary and hence would be imperfectly satisfied by a limited offering to the market. In the first case, the situation of homogeneity, one would logically follow a strategy designed to bring about the convergence of individual market demands on a single or limited offering to the market. This is usually accomplished by product differentiation, achieved through advertising and promotion. On the other hand, if the market is heterogeneous, it may be better to accept divergent demand as a market characteristic and to adjust product lines and marketing strategy accordingly. Such a strategy has been referred to as a strategy of market segmentation, which consists essentially of approaching a heterogeneous market as if it were a group of smaller homogeneous markets (market segments) with different product needs and preferences.

This strategy also often involves substantial use of advertising and promotion, but the objective becomes that of informing the market segments of the availability of goods or services produced or presented as meeting their needs with greater precision. Whereas a strategy of product differentiation may be classified as essentially a promotional strategy or approach to marketing designed to produce the convergence of demand compatible with mass production, market segmentation is essentially a merchandising strategy. It subordinates the desirability of production economies to the desirability of simplifying the demand manipulation component of the marketing process.

## CONCLUSION

To sum up, I have tried to suggest, first, that the hard core of the so-called marketing concept that is attracting so much attention today is effective and scientific use of market planning. Second, the first, and perhaps crucial, phase of the planning process—the prelude—is the generation of marketing strategies or strategic concepts to provide the essential linkage between where you are and where you want to be by guiding the specifics of the planning operation in the appropriate direction. Finally, this creative component of planning—marketing strategy—is developed by study of the firm, competition, and the market. Strategy provides the vehicle for plans to enable the firm to move toward realization of its market opportunity in ways that are feasible, because they have been designed only after full consideration of the firm's strengths and weaknesses and the competition it must face.

This, then, is the new marketing that is emerging—emerging as the logical outgrowth of the acceptance of marketing research and development as the partner of the technical research and development that is the pride and not (we hope) the despair of our times.

## QUESTIONS

1. What is the role of marketing strategy in marketing planning?
2. How is marketing strategy developed?
3. According to the author, the marketing concept is an umbrella term used to describe what four developments in distribution?
4. Distinguish between the two types of planning objectives described by the writer.

# 15. Application of Planning to Marketing*

Carrol Ehlers, Chairman of the Department of Marketing, School of Business Administration, Georgia State College

*Among other things the master marketing plan will establish objectives for volume, share of market, margins, and profits; it will determine the product line, select the best channels of distribution, and formulate effective policies in regard to sales, pricing, and advertising and promotion.*

Many economists and business observers believe the decade of the 1960's is destined to become the "decade of marketing" in the same sense that the decade of 1900-1910 was "the decade of finance" and the decades 1910 to 1950 were "decades of production." The decade 1950-1960 may well be termed the "decade of evolution." During this period, industrial productivity in America increased at the rate of approximately three per cent per annum.

**The Lag in Distribution. . . .** However, productivity in distribution has lagged, relatively, since it has been estimated as having shown an increase of only one per cent per annum.[1] For the national economy to continue to expand and to meet the challenges of a rapidly increasing population, accompanied by an unprecedented increase in consumer purchasing power, marketing productivity must be brought in line with industrial productivity.

**Application of Management Techniques to Marketing. . . .** The author believes that the application of the same scientific management techniques to marketing that have proved so effective in industrial production may indeed offer business executives the necessary tools to bring about this increased marketing productivity. Three of the major functions of management are (1) planning, (2) organizing, and (3) controlling. Thus, three articles in the Marketing Center will deal with the application of these three functions, respectively, to the field of marketing management. This article examines the managerial activity of planning in marketing and the measures which can be taken by marketing executives to improve marketing performance through the application of the basic tenets of effective management.

## SELECTED AREAS OF PLANNING IN MARKETING

Most companies could benefit from a review of their marketing setups to see whether they have provided for the kinds and quality of marketing planning that will ensure their future in an increasingly competitive economy.

Most companies could improve their profits by an organized approach to planning in the following areas:

* Reprinted from the *Atlanta Economic Review*, February, 1962, p. 6. Published by the Bureau of Business and Economic Research, School of Business Administration, Georgia State College.

[1] Hector Lazo and Arnold Corbin, *Management in Marketing* (New York: McGraw-Hill Book Company, Inc., 1961), p. 8.

### (1) THE PRODUCT

Product planning determines the characteristics of products best meeting the consumers' numerous desires, characteristics that add saleability to products. Sales resistance can be lowered at the start by planning the product's features—appearance, form, shape, color, name, price, package—to meet consumer demand.

### (2) THE MARKET

One of the most important phases of marketing management is market planning. Sales programs cannot be executed economically and effectively without planning the market. Such planning provides a manufacturer with facts about how, when, and where to apply effective sales effort.

### (3) CHANNELS OF DISTRIBUTION

Plans for establishing effective channels must be predicated upon a thorough factual analysis of the product, the market, the functions of distributors and dealers, the comparative costs of different methods of distribution, and the application of sound marketing principles. The problem varies with the different marketing situations of each manufacturer, but the use of the factual approach and principles is helpful in solving the distributive problems of all companies.

The most practical way to plan effective methods of distributing products is to *study the market and work back to the factory*. This approach is the opposite of that generally followed in planning distribution: channels usually develop more or less fortuitously from the factory to the market. Salesmen are sent to find or accept orders from any and all types of distributors and dealers willing to buy from the company and pay their bills. Selecting channels of distribution by such a method leads, to say the least, to inefficient distribution.

### (4) THE SALES MANAGEMENT FUNCTIONS

Prior to efficient and effective performance of sales management functions, a great deal of detailed planning is required in such areas as recruiting, selecting, training, assigning, compensating, establishing territories, determining sales quotas and market potentials, supervising, equipping, and motivating.

### (5) THE ADVERTISING PROGRAM

This planning activity is concerned primarily with short-range plans (usually no more than a year ahead) for such things as promotion, contests, advertising media and schedules, new markets to be entered, and sales and advertising budgets.

Many companies perform this type of planning effectively. This is because it has to be done in some form to prepare marketing budgets for management; it is also an area with which marketing executives are intimately acquainted; and it requires less coordination with other departments of the business than do many other types of planning.

### (6) SALES PROMOTION FUNCTIONS

Modern sales planning and administration reaches its climactic point with the development of a properly executed sales promotion program. Such a program provides the drive and the follow-through necessary to turn advertising and personal selling efforts into sales. A soundly planned and executed sales promotion program unifies all of a company's selling activities, integrates all phases of the firm's sales plan. Specifically, the primary purpose of sales promotion is to coordinate and to implement the work of the manufacturer's salesmen, advertising staff, and distributors and dealers in the field to the end of attaining the maximum potential sales volume.

### (7) MARKET RESEARCH

The need to plan for market research in an organized manner is often overlooked. Too often marketing research is viewed as a service department for putting out problem fires and to be called on as the need arises. The result is emphasis upon immediate operational problems with insufficient attention being paid to the longer range concerns.

It is management's obligation to assist in planning research for the long range and then to give its efforts definite support. Part of such planning is the establishment of priorities for research. Once priorities are established, management should review them periodically in the light of changes in markets and in the company.

Planning should call for both internal and external research. The internal is often overlooked. Every company has an accumulation of data on which marketing research can be based. Such things as sales analyses, sales forecasts, cost studies, and marketing-mix expenditure patterns are based entirely or in large measure on internal analyses. They often shed light on areas which will respond to attention.

### (8) SALES FORECASTING

Sales forecasting provides the foundation for most other planning. Short-range sales forecasts provide the basis for manufacturing schedules and manpower needs, sales controls, purchasing requirements, inventory needs, and working capital and profit forecasts. Long-range sales forecasts provide the basis for facilities planning, capital investment, research needs, and organization and personnel planning.

Sales forecasts should be carried on continuously. Since many of the factors entering into forecasts are subject to change, the forecasts themselves must be adjusted regularly if they are to be of value. When forecasts are not adjusted with changes in conditions, the manufacturing and other departments tend to take matters into their own hands and make their own estimates of the situation. The damage to profits can be almost as serious as when no forecasting is done at all.

### (9) CREDIT

The increasing use of consumer credit has brought about a need for planning in an area formerly of interest to only a handful of industries. In the oil industry, for example, consumer credit was only a minor factor until recently. Now the number of credit accounts for the larger companies runs into the millions. Questions of whether to use credit, how far to extend it, and whether to finance through company funds or through lending institutions—all are problems offering important areas for study. Closely allied are the questions arising in the areas of distributor and dealer financing. The frozen food industry, in order to build a distributor system for its products, found it necessary, in effect, to finance distributors through liberal inventory credit terms. Some tire companies assist new dealers to finance their inventories in order to broaden their dealer selection base. Electrical supply distributors' inventories are placed on consignment by some electrical manufacturers. Such practices can tie up sizable amounts of a company's capital and as a result pose the need for striking a delicate balance between cost to the company and the sales advantage to be gained.

## (10) INVENTORY

Finished inventories are properly the responsibility of the marketing side of the business. Marketing must be sure that inventories are available in the right place at the right time to provide satisfactory customer service. At the same time, inventories in excess of requirements are costly. They tie up capital—capital for which the company is paying interest or capital that could be invested elsewhere at a profit.

Important as the cost of capital invested in inventories is, however, a common fault of the company management is to look only at the size of the investment in inventories and, if it seems high, to order an arbitrary percentage reduction in finished inventories. But this practice overlooks the fact that investment in inventories may be less costly than investment in facilities required to meet peak production periods.

## (11) PLANT LOCATION

Markets are people geographically dispersed. Since merchandising includes getting products to the right place, it involves the movement of physical products through space. Getting goods to the right place is an adjunct of profit maximization; it is sometimes the most important key to profit realization. By proper use of the space dimension, cost reductions and spatial advantages can be achieved. The space dimension is a competitive one, although frequently not viewed in that manner by market planners.

In addition, business actions related to the expansion and contraction of plant locations have major reverberations for virtually every function of the community. Government tax bases are affected; city services must be shifted; transportation facilities may be overtaxed or may atrophy for lack of use; land use changes affect the character of neighborhoods—indeed, there are few decisions made by business leaders that have more widespread effects on a community. Therefore, it is imperative that the location programs of businesses be tied in with long-range regional planning.

## ONE EXAMPLE— PLANNING THE PRODUCT

Each of the above eleven marketing areas, for which planning should take place, can be divided into many subareas. To illustrate, aspects of "product" planning are shown below:

### DESIGN

Perhaps product planning's most important problem is product design. An attractively planned package, a satisfactory price, an appealing brand name, and other acceptable product characteristics do not overcome the sales resistance to a poorly designed product. Product planning should begin, therefore, with product design.

All firms should design their products with consumer buying motives and habits, and with improvements in the designs of competing products, in mind. New designs of products when (and usually) protected by patent effectively increase sales insofar as they cannot be copied by competitors. There is little value in changing designs for the sake of change alone; but if a changed design enables nonusers to make use of a product and increases the satisfaction of the users, thus widening the market, the change is economically and socially sound.

### NAME

Manufacturers spend millions of dollars annually advertising brand names; the problem of planning this name cannot be overlooked. Sales may be restricted by the poor name under which the product is sold.

### PRICE

Pricing is an area of merchandising greatly influenced by factors outside of the market place. Thus, price policy and pricing are keenly affected by production, development engineering, transportation, accounting, finance, competition, and public relations. In spite of these limits placed on price, it still offers considerable merchandising range.

Pricing is one of the most obvious of the merchandising tools and is often the first to be used. Prices are adjusted when a change seems to be called for. In spite of the heavy reliance of merchandisers on pricing and the great amount of literature about it, pricing is not really well understood. The great complexity and power of it and the ease with which prices can be changed make pricing a much abused and misused merchandising tool.[2] The great error comes mainly from the use of pricing as a tactical tool rather than as a strategy force. Its strategy significance implies that only when the particular market target is defined clearly and brought sharply into focus can the planner decide how price is to be best used.

Price cannot be considered separately from all the other factors making up the value a customer is expected to consider when purchasing. Consumers do not react to price; they react to value. Hence, there is no consumer price decision; it is a consumer *value decision*. It is this latter decision which becomes the merchandiser's true objective.

Pricing involves decisions beyond the mere establishment of what the ultimate

customers will pay. Tied to pricing are such questions as: (1) How many price lines should be featured? (2) What is to be the gap between prices for different lines? (3) Should cash and volume discounts be given? (4) What margins should be allowed in order to get required distributor cooperation? (5) Should services and guarantees be coupled with price? (6) Should merchandise be price fixed and prepriced? (7) Should products be priced as a line or separately? All questions should be answered in relation to long-range price-strategy plans leading to maximum over-all long-range profits. A tactical price maneuver to gain a quick profit or temporary market advantage can often do irreparable long-run damage.

Before determining ranges within which prices are to be set, it is necessary to calculate profit results at different price levels. Profits should be tied to capital investment rather than to sales volume.

### NEW USES

An important but neglected aspect of product planning is that of analyzing and determining new uses of the product. New uses lead to new markets, improved merchandising methods, improved old products, and even new products. Promotion of new uses increases the consumption of present users and also attracts new users.

Consumers often find ingenious uses of a product which are unknown to the manufacturer. Effective sales planning, however, requires that manufacturers be aware of and exploit all possible uses of their products.

### COLOR

Color sells products. The selection of colors for a product or package is a task for the expert stylist or designer. Manufacturers should have definite reasons for

[2] Ferdinand F. Mauser, *Modern Marketing Management* (New York: McGraw-Hill Book Company, Inc., 1961), p. 66.

using color in their products. They must determine the objectives to be attained in using color.

Numerous factors have contributed to color consciousness of consumers. Higher income levels, higher standards of living, and increased leisure time have enhanced aesthetic appreciation and provided the means of satisfying this interest. Magazine articles and advertising educate consumers to a greater appreciation, a clearer understanding, and a more intelligent use of color. Home economics courses and fine arts courses in schools and colleges develop in youth an appreciation of art. Chemical research has made available a limitless range of colors and has improved the application of chemicals, dyes, paints, and finishes.

### DISTINCTIVE FEATURES

An often neglected phase of product planning is that of exploiting the promotional value of distinctive product features. In some cases a manufacturer's product already has distinctive features that are not being adequately promoted. Product analysis aids in the discovery of distinguishable characteristics, the promotion of which frequently stimulates sales by arousing the interest of the salesmen, distributors, and dealers in the product; encouraging more intensive selling; inducing dealers to give the product better display; and aiding the manufacturer in breaking through competition.

### BRANDS

Billions of dollars are spent annually to popularize and protect the use and ownership of brands or trademarks. There are many reasons for using brands. Trademarks enable consumers to identify the product itself; and, if satisfied, they can buy the same product. Conversely, if they are not satisfied, they can avoid repur-

chasing the product. Brands help consumers to protect themselves against purchasing poor quality merchandise, a risk in unidentified products.

Formulating a brand policy becomes complicated when a manufacturer who produces a line of products plans to advertise the line under brand names. The question arises whether all of the products in the line should be advertised and sold under the same brand or whether each product in the line should be advertised and sold under distinctive brand names.

There are, in general, four brand policies manufacturers should consider when formulating brand strategy:

(1) Application of different brands to products of different quality

(2) Application of the same brand to products of the same quality (blanket or family brand policy)

(3) Application of different brands to products of the same quality (individual brand policy)

(4) Application of the same brand to products of different quality.

### PACKAGE

One of the important problems involved in product planning is that concerned with the type of package in which a product is sold.

Packaging is continually changing. A product becomes "dated" if its package is not in line with the latest design trends. Planning a package's design is a highly technical problem. There are too many ramifications to entrust the work to inexperienced and untrained people. It is important for advertising and sales executives to have some familiarity with the factors involved in package design and to work cooperatively with the designers.

Planning the design of a package includes consideration of a number of special packaging problems. If packaging is to be fully exploited as a sales device, every opportunity must be explored to make the greatest possible use of the package to stimulate sales. Factors to be considered in designing a package are numerous and varied: (1) the product's physical characteristics, (2) materials of which the package is to be constructed, (3) the shape, (4) size, (5) color, (6) cost, (7) copy and illustrations on the package, and (8) closure of the package.

In planning sales campaigns, special uses might be made of packaging, such as specialty, dual-use, combination, gift, novelty, juvenile, sample, cross-packaging, and kaleidoscopic packaging.

## SUMMARY

### THE STRUCTURE OF CUSTOMER-ORIENTED PLANNING

Customer-oriented planning calls for a functional organization structure wherein all management decisions are made in the light of customer needs. The process starts and ends with the customer.[3] Of necessity this implies that the marketing program and the marketing process are based on a sound knowledge of customer requirements, determination of who the customer is, what the customer wants, where and how he will buy, and how much he will pay for the product. Market research, market analysis, and forecasting for the future precede the formu-

---

[3] Edward S. McKay, "Blueprint for an Effective Marketing Program," Marketing Series 91, American Management Association, 1954.

lation of the marketing program. The total marketing organization is based on such research which accumulates all available facts for management decision. Such is the meaning of "customer orientation."

Planning, under such circumstances, establishes objectives, selects policies and techniques to attain these objectives, and sets up standards for the measurement and control of the effort necessary to attain the objectives. The master marketing plan, therefore, will establish objectives for volume, share of market, margins, and profits; it will determine the product line; it will select the best channels of distribution; it will formulate the best policies in regard to sales, pricing, advertising and promotion, personnel training and development; it will set up standards for evaluation of the total effort; and it will make provision for continued study and research to maintain all operations up to date, practical, and economical. Without planning, it is impossible to attain coordinated, integrated performance at optimum profit levels for the company as a whole.

## QUESTIONS

1. Why is the sales forecast so important in short-range planning?
2. What concrete steps might be taken to eliminate or lessen the lag in distribution?
3. Into what subareas can product planning be divided?
4. Into what subareas might the planning of sales promotion be divided?

# *16.* Sales Forecasting: Key to Integrated Management*

**William Lazer, Professor of Marketing, College of Business and Public Service, Michigan State University**

*The marketing planning process starts with sales forecasting. The sales forecast assists management to integrate its objectives, its operating programs, and its targets with potential market opportunity.*

Business organizations are increasingly adopting the marketing management concept. This philosophy of business operation places greater emphasis on marketing planning and forces business executives to design marketing strategies and program marketing effort to achieve realistic and predetermined objectives.

Sales forecasting can aid management greatly in implementing the marketing management approach. It is a basis for developing co-ordinated and goal-directed systems of marketing action. The sales forecast is one of the vital tools of marketing planning since adequate planning and the effective deployment of marketing resources are based on sales forecasting data.

Sales forecasting promotes and facilitates the proper functioning of the many segments of a firm's total spectrum of business and marketing activities. It influences almost every other prediction of business operations. It is used in establishing budgets and marketing controls. Sales forecasts help determine various limiting conditions for management decisions and programs and are useful tools

for co-ordinating the integral aspects of business operations. They provide bases for evaluating the functioning and productivity of various segments of business activity. They can guide marketing and other business action toward the achievement of implicit and explicit objectives.

This article investigates three aspects of sales forecasting as a key to integrated management action: (1) sales forecasting as a component of the marketing planning process, (2) sales forecasting as a focus for integrative planning, and (3) the basic components and procedures of a comprehensive sales forecasting program.

## IN MARKETING PLANNING

Figure 1 illustrates the strategic role of sales forecasting in gathering information for marketing planning. Effective planning of marketing activities can be achieved only if adequate marketing-related information is available. Marketing planning is concerned with the application of analysis and judgment to available information and the prediction of likely occurrences and trends during some future period.

Marketing-related information can re-

* Reprinted from the Fall 1959 issue of *Business Horizons*, p. 61. Published by the School of Business, Indiana University.

113

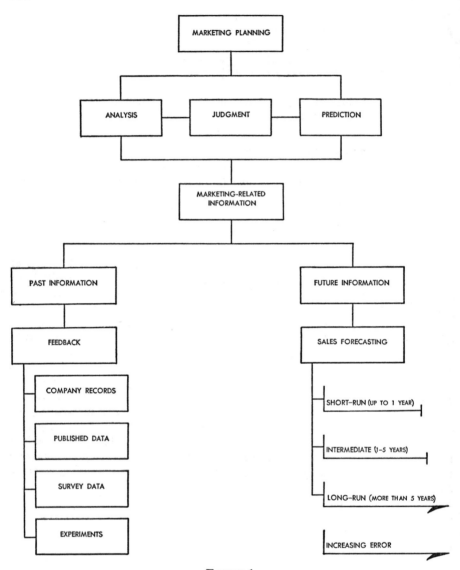

FIGURE 1

fer to either the past or the future. Information about past activities is often referred to as factual information. Information about the future is anything but factual, and might be characterized as assumptive. Past information is available to every business if it has an adequate record-keeping process. It is also available from other secondary data sources, such as information reported by governmental bureaus, university research bureaus, and trade associations. Past information may also be assembled through the use of various primary data-gathering research tools, such as surveys and experiments.

Future information requires the utilization of forecasting techniques and processes. Nevertheless, it is based on past data and is usually the result of the application of predictive tools to available past information.

Whenever a business gathers future data, varying degrees of error are bound to exist. Regardless of the forecasting techniques used and the degree of sophistication achieved, future conditions will always deviate to some degree from the predictions of the forecasters. Thus, management must expect future information to contain some error.

For effective marketing planning, both types of information must be available for executive use. From a planning and decision-making point of view, future, or nonfactual, information may be more significant than information about the past. This becomes clear if one considers that plans and decisions made today are actually based on executive expectations of what will happen during some future period.

If we consider sales forecasting from the point of view of furnishing marketing-related information, we can state that management gathers information as a result of two complementary processes: feedback and sales forecasting. Feedback consists of relating information about past events and relationships back to management. Through the use of such factual data, management can adjust existing operations and plans and thereby improve the effectiveness of all business action.

Sales forecasting furnishes management with information about what market conditions will probably be like during a future period. Management can then use this information as a basis for planning broad company goals and the strategies to achieve them. Sales forecasting data are used in establishing various types of potential volume and profit targets that become the bases for guiding and controlling operations.

Past and future information, however, are constantly blending. A sales forecast, although it furnishes future information, eventually takes the form of feedback information. Once this happens, a comparison may be made between actual and forecast sales for a specific period. Through such an audit, deviations may be noted and explanations sought for them. This information can, in turn, help refine the assumptions about future sales forecasts and increase the total effectiveness of the forecasting procedure.

The various predictions made may take the form of short-run sales forecasts of less than a year, intermediate forecasts of from one to five years, and long-run forecasts for periods of more than five years. Generally, the longer range the predictions, the greater the forecasting error.

## IN INTEGRATIVE PLANNING

Another facet of sales forecasting and its role in marketing planning is its position in the integrative planning process. A sales forecast is a useful tool for integrating the external business environment with the internal forces of the company. It reduces to workable management dimensions the external business environment over which management has relatively little control. It delimits those constraints that establish the boundaries within which a company must make decisions and operate and translates them into company programs.

Figure 2 portrays sales forecasting as an aid to integrative planning. It indicates the controllable, partially controllable, and noncontrollable factors that management should integrate and take into account in making effective sales forecasts.

The noncontrollable forces determine

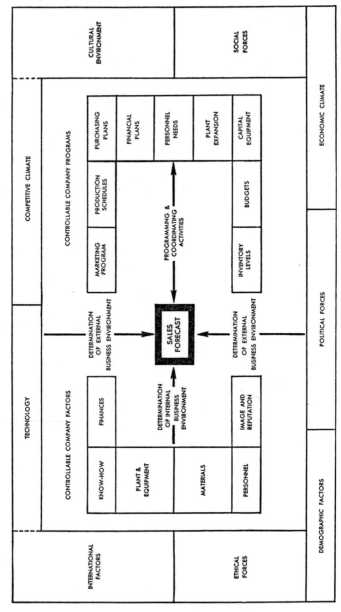

FIGURE 2. Sales Forecasting: a focus for integrative planning.

the broad environmental limits within which the company will operate. These factors include cultural forces, the economic environment, demographic forces, political factors, ethical and social forces, and various international conditions. They cannot be influenced to any degree by company action; at best, they may be recognized and appraised in an intelligent manner.

On Figure 2, broken lines separate the competitive environment and technological factors from other noncontrollable factors. This is to indicate that management action may have some influence over at least these two external forces, which are considered partially controllable factors. However, even though company action can affect competition and technology, the forces *beyond* company control generally have a more significant impact.

As forecasts become longer run in nature, the necessity of recording the existing external climate becomes more imperative since, in the future, it will be these noncontrollable factors that set the over-all constraints and boundaries within which companies survive and grow or fail. Through an evaluation and projection of external forces, management attempts to make realistic assumptions about the future environment. These assumptions about noncontrollable and partially controllable factors are the foundations of sales forecasts, and intelligent sales predictions can be made only by implicitly or explicitly assuming relationships about these factors.

Management should not consider this initial step of determining the external company environment as merely a theoretical exercise that is of little use in practical sales forecasting. The external variables are factors that must be dealt with practically and realistically. Their influence cannot be ignored.

As an example of the importance of external forces, consider the development of a controlled shopping center. Several years may elapse from the initiation of the original idea and the first inquiry concerning site location until the actual opening of the center. Choices must be made from among alternative sites, and considerable negotiations may follow to obtain the property and construct and finance the center. Then there are a host of operating details to attend to, including the actual leasing of stores.

The profitability of the total investment and the sales realized by retail stores in the shopping center will be affected by external forces. Existing and potential competition, for example, can have great influence on future sales. Demographic and economic forces in the form of population shifts and income trends will shape the retail sales potential of the center. Existing and potential industrial development of the surrounding territory will influence employment and income and will be reflected in marketing opportunity.

Municipal, state, and federal regulations will have an impact on future pricing tactics, on the use of various promotional devices including trading stamps, on store hours, and even on the types of merchandise that may be sold in particular kinds of stores.

Other examples could be presented concerning such industries as wood products, chemicals, mining, petroleum, transportation, the power industry, and communications.

After determining the external business climate for a future period, the sales forecaster must estimate the impact that internal business factors will make on potential markets. This involves an evaluation of those factors over which the company has direct control. They can be adjusted over the longer run by the company itself.

For an effective forecast, the company's know-how, its financial position, the plant capacity, the material resources and personnel available, and the company's reputation, image, and position in the market place must all be evaluated. The market position that a company eventually earns and the sales that it achieves will depend on the impact made by the internal business factors as they are combined into planned management programs carried out within the external business system. A consideration of both climates, external and internal, will give management some guides by which to judge the potential sales opportunity for a company. Through the use of various analyses and by the application of sound judgment, management may map out a company's future sales position.

Thus, sales forecasting helps integrate the management-controllable and management-noncontrollable factors, or the given elements of a total business system within which the company operates and the internal factors of the business itself.

The sales forecast is also a device by means of which management may integrate its objectives, its operating programs, and its targets with potential market opportunity. This can be done by translating the sales forecast into specific profit and sales-volume goals to be realized in a given future period of time. The sales forecast thus becomes a basis for marketing programs, purchasing plans, financial budgets, personnel needs, production schedules, plant and equipment requirements, expansion programs, and perhaps most other aspects of management programming.

The right half of Figure 2 presents sales forecasting as a vehicle for translating the noncontrollable, partially controllable, and internal business environments into specific controllable management programs. The figure also emphasizes the interrelationships between sales forecasts and company programs.

## FORECASTING PROGRAM

The table opposite outlines the elements of a total sales forecasting program. Four major stages of forecasting, the specific procedures to be followed, and their sequence are presented. These stages are: assembling the forecasting information; evaluating and projecting the data; applying the sales forecast operationally; and auditing the forecast. These four steps are broken down further, and some of the techniques that may be utilized at each stage and the results achieved are described. The table starts with the noncontrollable business environment and internal business climate and works down through the various predictions about controllable business plans, programs, and objectives.

The first step in a comprehensive sales forecasting program is assembling forecasting information. This involves the recognition of noncontrollable and partially controllable environments through observation and listing of significant external factors. The result is the identification of pertinent social, cultural, ethical, economic, political, demographic, international, technological, and competitive forces that will influence the projections.

Next, information can be assembled about these noncontrollable factors and an investigation made of such outside sources of information as governments, industries, and universities.

The third step in assembling forecasting information is that of gathering information about the controllable company environment, which involves research into company records. This should result in the selection of relevant company forecasting information.

After forecasting information has been assembled, the data must be evaluated and projected. This activity has two components: analyzing the data and making the actual forecast. To analyze the data,

# A TOTAL SALES FORECASTING PROGRAM

| Stages of Process | Techniques | Results |
|---|---|---|
| **Assembling Information** | | |
| Recognize noncontrollable and partially controllable business environment | Observe and list significant external factors | Identification of pertinent cultural, social, economic, political, demographic, competitive, ethical, international, technological forces |
| Gather information about noncontrollable and partially controllable forces | Investigate outside sources of information | Selection and gathering of data from government, industry, university research, Federal Reserve Board, company records |
| Gather information about controllable forces | Investigate company records | Selection of relevant company forecasting information |
| **Evaluating and Projecting Data** | | |
| Analyze data | Apply analytical tools: time series analysis, least squares, simple correlation, multiple correlation, input-output tables, breakeven charts | Determination of patterns and relationships: lead and lag indicators, cycles, seasonal indexes, trend lines, co-variation |
| Forecast future sales | Employ extrapolation, constant percentage of increase, end-use analysis, executive opinion, historical analogy, panel of experts, grassroots techniques, surveys, models, experiments, samples, hunches, judgment, and crystal ball | Prediction and definition of future dollar sales, unit sales, maximum and minimum ranges |
| **Operationally Applying Forecast** | | |
| Refine sales forecast | Break sales down by volume and profit control units: product lines, territories, customers, salesmen | Establishment of specific sales targets |
| Translate specific targets into operational programs | Establish and co-ordinate plans: marketing program, production schedules, purchasing plans, financial requirements, personnel needs, plant expansion, capital equipment budgets, inventory levels | Identification of controllable business environment |
| **Auditing the Forecast** | | |
| Review forecast | Compare actual and forecast sales regularly and analyze discrepancies | Determination of reasons for deviations |
| Modify forecast and forecasting procedures | Re-evaluate projections and adjust forecasting techniques | More accurate sales forecasting |

such analytical tools as time series analysis, least squares methods of fitting a straight line, fitting curves, simple and multiple correlation, the use of input-output tables, and breakeven charts may be used. This leads to the determination of patterns and relationships through lead and lag indicators, cycles, seasonal indexes, trend lines, and measures of covariation.

The actual sales projections may be made through extrapolation, a straight percentage increase in sales, executive opinion polls, end-use analysis, historical analogy, a panel of experts, the grass-roots approach, samples and surveys, models, experiments, hunches, judgments, and the oft-used crystal ball. After these projections have been made, the prediction and definition of future dollar and unit sales, and maximum and minimum sales ranges is possible.

Then the forecast must be applied operationally, which involves refining the sales forecast. This is done by breaking it down on the basis of volume and profit control units by product lines, salesmen, customers, territories, and other managerial units. Specific sales targets can thus be established, and sales forecasting data become the basis for programming, marketing, production, purchasing, finance, plant expansion, capital equipment acquisition, personnel, and inventory needs. Controllable business programs have now been really determined.

The last step in a comprehensive sales forecasting program is that of auditing the forecast. This involves reviewing the forecast by comparing actual and forecast sales and analyzing any deviations or discrepancies. The purpose here is to determine the reasons for the deviations. Then future forecasts and even the forecasting techniques can be modified. The end result is more accurate sales forecasts.

The total sales forecasting process is one of refinement. It starts with the more general factors—the external noncontrollable environment and the internal business environment—quantifies them, and finally · establishes specific operational goals and targets.

Marketing planning often suffers because management does not develop an effective sales forecasting program. One of the great inducements to ignore or neglect sales forecasting is the difficulty of making predictions. It is a trying task for anyone to try to determine future relationships and their implications for potential sales. It is much more comfortable to turn to the consideration of current operating problems, which are more concrete, are somewhat easier to grasp, and for which some corrective action may be initiated almost immediately.

However, professional marketing management cannot afford to neglect the sales forecasting process. It must become concerned with the development of well coordinated, planned, and forceful systems of business action. It must plan the use of company resources so that a firm can establish itself in the market place and grow.

The future marketing climate is likely to be one of keener competition, an exhilarating pace of market change, heavier fixed costs, and an increasing emphasis on innovation. Adequate marketing planning will become the foundation for integrated marketing action. Since one of the basic components of effective marketing planning is sales forecasting, it seems obvious that in the future an increasing amount of time and resources will be spent by companies in developing more adequate sales forecasts.

## QUESTIONS

1. A sales forecast is a useful tool for integrating the external business en-

vironment with the internal forces of the company. Explain.

2. Distinguish between noncontrollable and partially controllable external factors or environment.

3. List and describe the four major stages

in a comprehensive sales forecasting program.

4. Explain how feedback and sales forecasting can serve as two complementary processes.

# 17. Short-, Medium-, and Long-Range Forecasting: Requirements and Objectives*

James B. Meredith, European Representative, General Economics Department, Standard Oil Company

*The business man who hopes to make his business prosper has no choice but to make guesses about the future. The function of forecasting—to the extent that it is a formalized activity—is simply to make this guessing process as informed as possible. It is conventional to categorize forecasting as being short-, medium-, or long-range in nature.*

Forecasting, as all who have tried it know, is a very difficult business. And, unfortunately, its difficulties cannot be entirely removed by hard work and intelligence. Whether we are considering the sales of a particular firm or the movement of an entire economy, we deal with phenomena which have, or appear to have, much of a random nature about them. The basic premise in forecasting is that, by and large, the forces which operated in the past to produce certain results will continue to be associated with these results in the future. We must make this assumption, or we have no basis for looking ahead.

The real difficulty lies in timing. Knowing that the total output of goods and

* Reprinted from *The Marketing Job.* Published by the American Management Association, Inc., New York, 1961, p. 139.

services in the economy increases at a rate of approximately 3 per cent each year does not allow us to infer that we will be above, below, or on the trend line in, let us say, 1970. Our knowledge of the relevant odds in economic forecasting is rudimentary. But there is the advantage that events in the economic sphere are related over time in a more or less logical way, instead of being independent of one another.

## THE FUNCTION OF FORECASTING

Fundamentally, the calculation of odds in forecasting serves the purpose of maximizing strategy. In war, games, or business, the successful operators are those who are most skillful in anticipating future developments. The business man who hopes to make his business prosper has no choice but to make guesses about the future. He may not do it explicitly, but he does it nevertheless. The function of forecasting—to the extent that it is a formalized activity—is simply to make this guessing process as informed as possible.

These rather general remarks apply to almost all kinds of forecasting. Certainly they apply to general economic and sales forecasting.

The specific uses to which the latter may be put will vary from firm to firm. The range and complexity of the problems confronting the company will be the predominant factors in determining how ambitious a program of sales forecasting it undertakes. Giant international organizations such as Standard Oil Company (New Jersey) are faced with an array of problems, and many of their policy decisions hinge on estimates of future markets.

Standard Oil and its affiliated companies produce, refine, transport, and market a great variety of crude petroleums and petroleum products. They operate in many countries of the world and transact their business in many currencies. They must worry about matters of political stability, the availability and strength of different currencies, and the impact of tariffs at home and abroad. All these matters have a bearing on future business. Purely domestic firms manufacturing one standard commodity, on the other hand, have a narrower range of problems—which is not to say that they are any less important to the firm in question.

Large or small, however, the firm that prospers is the one that anticipates the future, foresees the problems and opportunities lying ahead, and takes measures to be prepared. Ideally, more is involved in this strategy of preparation than mere-

ly making the best possible forecast. This, of course, is necessary; but, were we to base future plans for our business on it alone, we would often make strategic errors. Every forecaster knows how easy it is for his forecast to go wrong. This is an occupational hazard. What is required, therefore, is that we consider several directions of development which the future might take, and attempt to assign relative degrees of likelihood to each. That is the first step.

We must then calculate what is implied for the operations of our firm under each forecast: whether we expand, curtail, or remain at status quo. Next, we assume that each forecast, in turn, is inaccurate, and we appraise the cost to our firm of gearing its operations to an erroneous estimate of the future. We may overbuild in anticipation of markets which do not materialize, and find ourselves with excess capacity on our hands; or we may underestimate the market, and be unprepared to grasp opportunity when it presents itself. On some suitable basis, we attempt to assess the cost of making such errors.

When all this is done, we bring together the various data we have calculated: the rewards of being right, the penalties of being wrong, and the likelihood of different occurrences. Then we try to determine what, on balance, our optimum strategy is. Admittedly, this is an ideal course of action. In most cases, we only approximate it. Nevertheless, it is what we should have in mind as a target in business planning. Sales forecasting cannot achieve all this alone. It is just a part—although a very vital part—of the over-all operation.

## PATTERNS OF CHANGE

It is conventional to categorize forecasting as being short-, medium-, or long-range in nature. This is not a very precise breakdown, however; since the terms mean different things to different companies, it is difficult to generalize about them. Owing to the possibility of confusion which the use of these terms affords, it is wise to go beyond the words and consider the nature of the underlying economic phenomena to which they relate.

Are there, in the real world, sets of economic movements which have different time dimensions attached to them and which call for different varieties of consideration from the business organization? It is clear, I think, that there are such movements. There are, to begin with, seasonal fluctuations which in one way or another affect most businesses: the automobile companies produce less during the change-over months; the oil companies have different patterns of demand in summer and winter; and there are many other examples. This type of fluctuation tends to be highly regular, so that one can usually prepare for it.

A second major type of business fluctuation is the business cycle. There are all sorts of business cycles, of course. The one most commonly thought of is the so-called "inventory cycle," which in the postwar period has averaged 2½ to 2¾ years in length. This cyclical variety of fluctuation is more difficult to forecast. Both the timing and the magnitude tend to be more irregular. Moreover, the impact on business varies noticeably from industry to industry.

Finally, there is a truly long-run pattern of change in the economy. This is the rate of change which derives from basic growth factors—population change, productivity increase, and the like. It is convenient to think of this long-run rate of change as being represented by some growth curve, and it is about this curve that cyclical variations occur.

During normal periods, these are the major regular varieties of change in the level of economic activity and, therefore, the major determinants of demand for the goods we sell. There often are, naturally, random developments which no one can foresee. Wars, earthquakes, and fads occur and have major effects on the business climate of many firms.

If we so choose, we may identify the need for short-, medium-, and long-range forecasting with seasonal, cyclical, and trend movements, respectively. This, however, would be a great simplification. The long and the short run for most firms depend primarily on the nature of their business. For firms using raw materials whose prices vary drastically in the space of days or weeks, a couple of months may be a long run. For firms whose capital installations take several years to complete, anything under two years may be a short run.

Whatever the situation of the individual firm, the distinction between long and short run is usually meaningful, and—within the context of the problems which the firm faces—little confusion between the two is likely to arise. Frequently, problems have aspects of both the short and the long run about them. We typically assign these to the somewhat vague medium-term future.

## HOW MUCH OF WHAT KIND?

In formulating business plans, sales forecasting offers help in a variety of directions. It helps top management frame its general policy. It facilitates the establishment of budgets and the determination of sales goals. Basically, however, it is concerned with the question of *how much of what kind of goods to produce*. This is the core of the problem. And it is in these terms that the distinction between long and short run can most fruitfully be examined.

Over any given short-run period, a firm

has available for productive purposes a relatively fixed amount of plant and equipment. With this, it is possible to turn out varying amounts of product—depending on the amount of labor employed, the number of shifts worked, the flow of materials to the factory, and the like. To schedule the proper level of production over, say, the next six months, management must know how many of the variable factors to employ. It must therefore have a short-range sales forecast.

What the short run is for the firm in question depends largely on how long it takes for new plant and equipment to be brought into operation. Within limits, it is possible—over the short run—to vary the product mix which the firm sells and to vary the total amount produced. Major changes in productive potential, however, can take place only in the long run—that is, over a period sufficiently long to permit important alterations in the capital structure of the firm. Since major capital expansion programs are costly undertakings, they must, of course, be carefully weighed—hence the necessity for long-range sales forecasts.

The first task for the forecaster who wishes to clarify these matters is to discover, in as much detail as possible, to what factors the sales of his company's product are related. The hope is that, sooner or later, he will hit on something which is not only related to sales of the product in question but somewhat easier to forecast.

The relationships on which the forecaster settles will vary with the nature of the product. If it is completely new and different, there is little to go on. Products, however, are rarely this new; ordinarily the forecaster will find a relationship of some sort. Occasionally there will be only one major determinant of sales, but usually more than one determinant will be involved. And, in some cases, there may be so many that forecasting them all is equivalent to forecasting the movement of the entire economy.

## GENERAL ECONOMIC FORECASTS

It is for the reasons cited that many large business organizations have come to rely increasingly on general economic forecasting as a basis for their sales estimates. Consider for a moment the range of factors on which the sale of Jersey Standard's products depends. In the overall pattern, petroleum sales are closely related to the total demand for all forms of energy. We must therefore be concerned about trends in the demand for and supply of coal, hydroelectricity, and other competing fuels. The total demand for energy is a function of the level of over-all economic activity, particularly of industrial activity. Hence the latter must be estimated. But oil products are also sold to the consumer for pleasure driving and home heating, and to the government for military purposes. Consequently, automobile sales, home construction, and the progress of the cold war must be appraised!

Moreover, because Jersey Standard does business in many parts of the world, it is confronted with problems of an international character. Should it build a refinery in this foreign country or in that one? There may be many reasons for choosing whether or not to develop a particular market, and high among them may be the question of what currency must be accepted in payment. Some currencies are weak and cannot be exchanged for dollars. Others may be on the verge of devaluation. In such cases, should liquid assets in the countries concerned be removed or left where they are? And so it goes, through an array of considerations which ramify throughout the entire economy. Obviously, a general economic forecast is basic to answering many of these questions.

## METHODS OF APPROACH

Assuming that by now we know both why we want a forecast and what the sales of our product are related to, where do we go from here? How do we actually make a forecast? The answer depends on the resources at the disposal of the forecasting department, and on the skills and inclinations of the forecasters. There is a good deal of technique, both statistical and economic, which can be brought to bear on the problem. Here are several broad approaches which are most commonly used:

1. *The leading-indicator approach.* This technique involves finding an economic series which is related to the one being forecast, and which moves up or down in advance of it. Having found such a series, we depend on it for signals to action. This method is frequently useful in picking directional moves; it has the disadvantage of telling little about the magnitudes of change to be expected.
2. *The survey approach.* This is a matter of sampling buyer opinion. It has been employed extensively by the Survey Research Center at the University of Michigan in the area of consumer purchases, and by the Securities and Exchange Commission and the McGraw-Hill Company in the area of capital spending. Although still unproved as a scientific forecasting device, the method has promise. Its principal weakness derives from the fact that people are always heavily influenced in their plans for the future by the prevailing

state of business. With a shift in the wind, their plans may change substantially.
3. *The GNP (gross national product)-model approach.* This is used only in those cases where it is thought that the direction of the total economy is an important determinant of the series being forecast. It may be some sort of mathematical model or a relatively loose model which depends on a series of successive approximations for its results.
4. *The trend or rate-of-growth approach.* The idea is to use a growth curve which will be taken as indicative of the average growth to be expected in the future. Typically, such growth curves are fitted to historical data, then extrapolated.
5. *The "glandular" approach.* The technique here is straightforward. You simply ask yourself, "Where would I go if I were next year's sales?" and see what comes to mind. This is an important ingredient of all forecasting, because—try as we may to be "scientific"—personal judgment continues to be a vital element. Usually, the quantitative evidence will carry us only a certain distance in our attempts to penetrate the future, and we have no choice but to make a judgment. When the latter derives from experience and knowledge, it may be invaluable. When it is a mere cover for an inbuilt pessimistic or optimistic bias, however, it can be dangerous.

The first three forecasting approaches mentioned—the leading-indicator, the survey, and the GNP-model techniques—are primarily useful for forecasting no more than 12 to 18 months ahead. The principal use of trends, on the other hand, is in long-range forecasting. The last technique, the so-called "glandular" approach, is employed in any and all kinds of fore-casting. These methods are not mutually exclusive, of course; in general, it is ad-visable to use all those which afford any hope of improving the quality of the fore-cast.

## FACTORS DETERMINING THE APPROACH

I do not think it necessary to dwell at length on why we use different approaches to short- and long-range forecasting. The reasons are inherent in the nature of the data we use. The long run being further away, we see it less clearly and can spec-ulate about it only more generally. In the short run, we are interested in economic forces subject to relatively quick change. In the longer run, we expect these to average out; so we look to the more slowly evolving forces as determinants of growth.

In the short run, for instance, we may be concerned about an excessively high level of outstanding consumer credit or about a too rapid increase in inventories. We are unlikely to worry so much about the stock of physical capital or the rate of population growth. The latter are im-portant, but they are unlikely to change sufficiently over a short period to have much effect on short-run economic fluctu-ations. In the longer run, however, the emphasis is reversed. Few forecasters worry about the amount of consumer credit likely to be outstanding in 1970. On the other hand, capital stock and population level are important in our thinking for a decade ahead.

A major difficulty in both short- and long-range forecasting is the problem of discerning when something new is about to take place. As a matter of fact, it is sometimes difficult to tell when something new has *already* taken place. It is a max-im among professional forecasters that the safest forecast is always one in which the next time period behaves about the same as the previous period. If things were going up last month or year, it is safe to predict that they will be doing the same next month or year. If a forecaster follows this rule consistently, he will be right more often than he is wrong (at least if the time period for which he is forecasting is relatively short). Only at the turning points does he run into diffi-culty. Unfortunately for this school of forecasting, it is a change in the direction of economic activity—the "something new" that is about to take place—which creates the big problem for business.

This is obviously true in the case of cyclical swings in business. It matters a great deal to most business firms whether they operate under conditions of pros-perity or recession. Perhaps less obvious but no less important are the conse-quences of shifts in long-run growth curves. If, for instance, a firm is con-templating the installation of facilities to serve such increases in demand as may develop over the next five to ten years, a minor variation in the annual rate of growth assumed for this period can make a major difference by the time the end of the period is reached: the difference, let us say, between an excess of capacity and a shortage of capacity, each of which is costly in its way.

Therefore, predicting such changes in the direction of the general economy is the most valuable service a forecast can provide.

# 18. A New Approach to Sales Forecasting and Production Scheduling*

John Parkany, Marketing Research Manager, Formica Corporation

*The potential contributions of short-term sales forecasts to production economies are often overlooked. The short-term behavior of the manufacturer's shipments can be anticipated with accuracy once the constant interaction of the sales of stock-carrying intermediaries, the changes of inventories of such intermediaries, and the order pattern of such intermediaries are known and understood.*

The monthly shipments curve of a manufacturer usually is an imperfect reflection of his order curve. If a certain volume of orders is assumed, then the volume of shipments is governed on the one extreme by the peak capacity and on the other extreme by the unwillingness of production management to operate with less than a pre-set minimum of order backlog. This will result in sharply fluctuating production schedules, factory shipments, and accounts receivable—factors detrimental to the profitable operation of a manufacturing company.

This wasteful practice can be traced to the inability of the sales department to make reliable short-term forecasts. The production department of the typical manufacturing company—often after a number of disappointments with sales forecasts produced by the sales department—usually has reached the point where it refuses to accept any estimate for its production scheduling other than that which could be derived from the order backlog of the company. The net result is the waste caused by hectic pro-

duction rates, unsatisfactory finished-goods inventories, poor deliveries from suppliers of basic materials, and unsatisfactory relationships with customers.

## NEED FOR RELIABLE SHORT-TERM FORECASTING

What is needed to overcome such difficulties is not merely improved short-term sales forecasts, but short-term sales forecasts which are reliable. If it is known that the short-term forecast will agree with the actual sales experience, such sales forecasts will prove a great deal more useful to both sales and production.

Most manufacturing companies reach their customers by selling through intermediaries. Selling through intermediaries (such as stock-carrying distributors) has profound effects on production schedules. The sales of the intermediaries are much smoother than those of the manufacturers which supply them, for reasons which will be discussed.

The attack on the problems resulting from uneven production schedules must be two-fold. First, the incoming orders must be so utilized as to provide much

* Reprinted from the *Journal of Marketing*, national quarterly publication of the American Marketing Association, Vol. 25, No. 3, January 1961, pp. 14–21.

smoother production and shipment schedules. Second, the sales and production departments of the manufacturing company must be provided with a reliable forecast of shipments on a continuous ("rolling") 3-months basis, and preferably on a monthly basis as well, in order to anticipate accurately changes in the rate of production and shipments.

While the production and marketing characteristics of manufacturing products vary greatly from each other, the following characteristics may be typical of an important number of manufactured products:

1. Short production cycle
2. Production of stock-items rather than job-order items
3. Marketing primarily through stock-carrying distributors

The factory shipment curve of the manufacturer of such products will depend on two factors: *the current trend of sales at the distributor's level;* and *the constant fluctuations in the aggregate volume of distributor inventories.*

## FACTORS AFFECTING SHORT-TERM SALES FORECASTING

The chief hazard of sales forecasting is that, during the period for which the forecast is prepared, many events will happen which are not foreseeable at the time of the forecast. This statement is inapplicable to sales forecasts for periods not exceeding three months. A sales forecast prepared for the forthcoming three months will reflect *primarily* past events rather than events which will occur during any part of the three month period.

The difficulty in the preparation of a short-term sales forecast is not the occurrence of unforeseeable and unpredictable events during the short-term period, but *rather the lack of knowledge at the outset of the forecast period of the exact past facts* which collectively will determine the course of sales during the forecast period.

### IMPORTANCE OF DISTRIBUTOR INVENTORY FLUCTUATIONS

The aggregate volume of inventory held by a company's distributors varies continually. The fluctuations are due to numerous causes. In fact, so many factors influence the level of distributor inventories that it is surprising that the inventories do not fluctuate more than they actually do. Distributor orders are extremely poor indicators of the current rate of sales by distributors.

In a nutshell, once the company sells through stock-carrying distributors, its monthly shipments will reflect the rhythm of the purchases by its distributors, rather than the rhythm of the purchases of the customers of the distributors. Fortunately, the rhythm of the purchases of distributors is predictable, thus making accurate short-term sales forecasting possible *once the current trends of distributor sales and of the cumulative inventory changes of the distributors are properly identified at the time of their occurrence.*

## EXISTENCE OF FOUR CONCURRENT CYCLES

Four cycles are running concurrently in the marketing of a manufacturer who sells primarily through stock-carrying distributors:

Cycle   I: *Sales of distributors to their customers*

Cycle  II: *Inventory changes of distributors*

Cycle III: *Orders by distributors from manufacturer*

Cycle IV: *Shipments by manufacturers to the distributors*

There is a constant interaction among these four cycles. All of them have their own characteristic behavior.

Usually the manufacturer attempts to project his orders and shipments in the forecast period on the basis of the known behavior of orders and shipments in the immediate past. However, the behavior of the orders and shipments cannot be understood even in retrospect without reference to the volume of sales and inventory changes at distributor levels. The orders of distributors taken by themselves cannot reflect the volume of *their* sales. Hence, the manufacturer must know the past behavior of all four cycles up to the beginning of the forecast period.

### CYCLE I: SALES OF DISTRIBUTORS TO THEIR CUSTOMERS

The first cycle is influenced by the myriad factors affecting the manufacturer's sales volume. In virtually all instances there are seasonal factors influencing sales. There exists the constantly changing influence of competitive pricing. The increase or decline in public acceptance of the products sold might be an important factor, and the effectiveness of the manufacturer's advertising and marketing program will have its constant ebbs and flows. Economic events directly related to the consumption of the manufacturer's products might be of particular importance.

Although sales of distributors to their customers fluctuate within rather wide limits, on a month-by-month basis or on on a quarter-to-quarter basis, this cycle, on the whole, is more stable and shows less fluctuations than the typical wider variations in the manufacturer's monthly shipments.

### CYCLE II: INVENTORY CHANGES OF DISTRIBUTORS

Every manufacturer attempts to persuade his distributors to carry an ample inventory. Nevertheless, the distributors' inventories fluctuate constantly within wide limits.

Some products have strong and weak selling "seasons" at the distributor level. This causes distributors to stock up in anticipation of the strong season and leaves inventories either in a strong or weak position following the end of the season, depending upon the ability of the distributors to predict accurately their "strong season" sales. Anticipations of good or poor business conditions by the distributors will cause them continually to increase or deplete their inventories. Production holdups at the factory level, or conversely speed-up of factory deliveries, will cause substantial variations of distributor inventories. An important cause of changes in distributor inventories is often the inefficient methods applied in purchasing.

To a large extent, the current volume of distributor inventories is the accidental by-product of the sales by distributors and of the factory shipments to the distributors. While the distributors frequently "plan" higher or lower levels of inventories, the changes of the sales of distributors and the changes in the delivery dates of manufacturer suppliers will result in "unplanned" inventory changes.

### CYCLE III: ORDERS BY DISTRIBUTORS FROM MANUFACTURER

The replacement of products sold by the distributors is brought about through orders placed by the distributors with the manufacturer. Distributors do not mechanically reorder the volume which they have been selling. The causes for inventory fluctuations outlined in the preceding section affect orders, together with such additional factors as impending changes in the product line and hold-ups in factory deliveries.

### CYCLE IV: SHIPMENT BY MANUFACTURERS TO DISTRIBUTORS

At the outset, it was suggested that the shipments by the manufacturer to the distributors are an imperfect reflection of the orders received by the manufacturer. The levels of finished-goods inventory, the peak capacity, and unwillingness to reduce the order backlog beyond a minimum point are the principal factors influencing the manufacturer's shipments in any given month.

The constant changes in the delivery dates by the manufacturer can themselves influence the orders received by the manufacturer. If the sales of distributors are at a lower rate and factory deliveries are known to be prompt, the distributors are willing to carry smaller inventories because they can assume prompt factory shipments. Once the factory is extending delivery dates over a longer period of time, the distributors will both increase their inventories and place orders covering their needs for a longer period of time because they know that the factory cannot be relied upon for prompt shipments. In fact, one of the more characteristic events after a period of strong factory sales is the abrupt falling off of orders received by the factory. This usually happens when the factory is in a position to shorten delivery dates on the orders received. This will cause a huge increase in the inventories of the distributors and will prompt the distributors to decrease their inventories to much lower levels—a process helped by the known promptness of factory deliveries of the new orders.

## DETERMINATION OF SHORT-TERM SALES FORECASTS

The four cycles discussed will determine the actual factory shipment volume in any short-term period. For the manufacturer, it is necessary to know the exact behavior of the first three cycles in order to predict the factory-shipment cycle (Cycle IV) with accuracy.

Some manufacturers receive periodic, often monthly, reports from their wholesalers on their sales. These reports are valuable, but often are not much help in forecasting the behavior of the four cycles. Monthly reports are usually received during the month which follows the month for which they are prepared, and they are as much as sixty days "dated" when these monthly reports are complete.

### ESTABLISHMENT OF WEEKLY TELEGRAM REPORTING

It is necessary to know the current behavior of all four cycles. Hence, it is essential to obtain reports by telegram each Monday regarding the sales volume at the distributor level during the preceding week. The comparison of the factory shipments of the previous week with the sales of the distributors will result in the computation of the changes in the aggregate volume in distributor inventories.

Once the manufacturer obtains weekly telegram reports from the distributors regarding the sales of the distributors, the manufacturer will know the exact behavior of the sales and of the net inventory changes of its distributors in any past period. In order to make short-term sales forecasts for a period of one to three months, it will be necessary to make some assumptions regarding the sales and the future net inventory changes of the distributors during the forecast period.

PROJECTION OF SALES OF DISTRIBUTORS
IN FORECAST PERIOD

The necessity to make forecasts of the future sales of distributors might suggest that the advantages of the forecasting system proposed are purely manipulative ones. Such a suggestion disregards the fact that the sales of distributors are more stable and predictable than the volume of factory shipments. Furthermore, any forecasts of factory shipments prepared in the absence of an exact knowledge of the sales of distributors is guesswork.

If it is our assumption that the sales of distributors are a relatively stable series

with predictable variations, then we might anticipate that the skilled forecaster will be able to prepare "better than rough" (in fact, consistently close) estimates of the sales of distributors in the forecast period. The knowledge of the exact level of current sales and of general business and industry conditions, together with the known influence of the seasonal factors, will permit the forecaster reasonably accurate projections of the sales of the distributors in the forecast period. Such projections must be extended to include reasonable estimates of inventory changes, also.

While these projections still include elements of subjective calculations, they

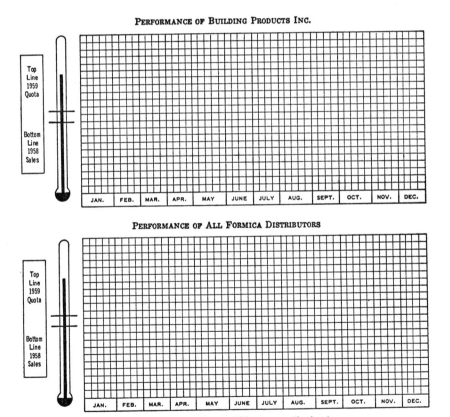

PERFORMANCE OF BUILDING PRODUCTS INC.

PERFORMANCE OF ALL FORMICA DISTRIBUTORS

Average 1958 sales (Base Period) and 1959 quota expressed in sales out
of warehouse (Factory Shipment Value)

FIGURE 1

are on sufficiently solid grounds to permit effective manipulation of the *existing order backlog, the current rate of production,* and *the current rate of shipments.*

## MANIPULATION OF MANUFACTURER'S ORDER BACKLOG

While the rate of incoming orders is not subject to the manufacturer's direction, all of the foregoing three factors are subject to such direction. If adequate information on the current rate of sales by distributors is available, the manufacturer might consciously use his existing order backlog to provide for a predictable and stable rate of production. Both the orders received as well as the orders anticipated by the manufacturer can be used much more intelligently, once the true sales of the distributors and the inventory changes of the distributors are known.

Practically all manufacturers experience uneasiness about delays in receiving heavy orders from the distributors just prior to the beginning of the usual heavy seasonal buying of distributors. Such delays often cause unnecessary additional production expenses and shortages in distributor inventories. If the current sales volume of the distributors as well as their inventory position is known, the manufacturer can utilize better his order backlog and produce in anticipation of incoming orders, irrespective of the slowness of the orders of the distributors at times when such orders should be coming in but are late.

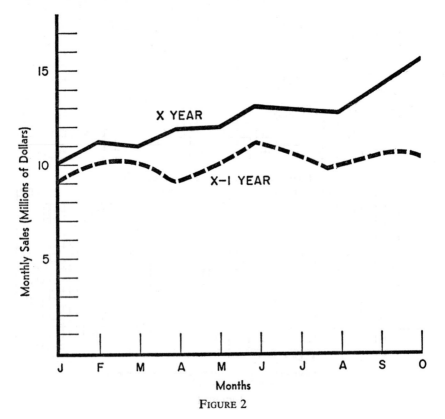

FIGURE 2

INFORMATION ON COLLECTIVE SALES
OF OTHER DISTRIBUTORS

Wholesalers in certain lines of business (usually those concerned with the wholesaling of "big-ticket" items or of large volume package goods) are used to periodic reporting of their sales to their manufacturer supplier. It is possible to establish weekly telegram reporting plans in other lines of business by having well conceived plans of appealing to the self-interest of the distributors.

Distributors in any line of business are eager to obtain information on questions such as: What is the current sales performance of other similar business concerns? How does his own performance compare with the performance of other similar concerns?

The writer is associated with a company selling a product which is a well-known building material. All distributors of his company's products have been asked to report their sales for the previous week by telegram each Monday. In the course of the same week, the distributors will receive by mail a 2-part chart with the following information: The top chart shows in bars the relative performance of the distributor in the past week. The bottom chart shows the relative performance of all distributors in the past week. (See Figure 1.)

Both charts are cumulative and show the average performance through the past week. On the left side, lines show last year's average performance objective (sales quota). At a glance, the distributor is able to determine how his performance each week up to the last week compares with last year's sales performance and this year's sales objective. Each distributor has this information available for the aggregate performance of all other distributors of the same product as well.

In a recession, such a chart will show all distributors how this product was affected by the recession. Likewise, in a period of business expansion it shows how the expansion directly affected the distributors of the product, and how the individual distributor's performance stands up compared with the others.

THE OPERATION OF A TELEGRAM
REPORTING PROGRAM

Thus, a telegram-reporting program in an industry which is not experienced with it has several advantages: information to field sales management on distributor sales performance; supply of information on national sales trends to distributors to secure their participation; and continuous use of data for forecasting short-term sales.

The distributors' participation is assured, because they are convinced that they obtain practical benefits through feeding back information to the manufacturer.

Top management of the manufacturer obtains the following information every Monday afternoon regarding the previous week's performance:

1. Total sales of the distributors
2. Total factory shipments to the distributors
3. Net distributor inventory change (that is, the difference between the two foregoing items)
4. Net inventory change for an accumulated period
5. Net distributor orders

## VAGARIES OF DISTRIBUTOR INVENTORY CHANGES

There are many apparent advantages in establishing such a weekly telegram reporting system. An example illustrates this. In a recent year shipments of a manufacturing company showed the pat-

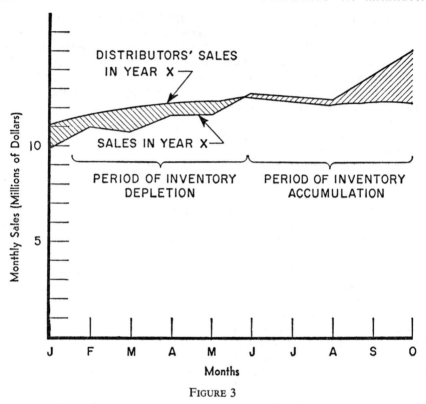

FIGURE 3

tern illustrated in Figure 2. The increase in sales throughout the year led management to believe that the demand for the product increased substantially. There was a small percentage increase in sales at the distributor level. Initially, the distributors did not step up their purchases in response to the slightly increased demand. Consequently, inventories started to deplete and after some months had passed, the distributors stepped up their orders.

At this time the factory was forced to put a 6-day and soon a 7-day work week into effect, and to continue to lengthen the delivery period of new orders. Distributors, realizing this delay, put in orders for a longer period of time in advance. The factory further stepped up production and, once additional capacity was available, was able to make a real "dent" in the backlog of distributors.

It took distributors some time to realize that the factory was catching up with the order backlog and was shortening the delivery period on new orders. At this time inventories were not only replenished, but showed a considerable increase over the volume prevailing before the depletion of inventories started.

The manufacturer knew that orders and shipments had been increasing tremendously, but was unaware of the fact that all the time there was a nominal increase in distributor sales and a substantial depletion and accumulation of inventories. (See Figure 3.) Sales forecasts for the next year based upon peak shipments at the end of this period were misleading and false.

## IN CONCLUSION

The existence of selling intermediaries, namely, distributors, might bring about less smooth factory shipment schedules than otherwise might be the case. This is true because distributor inventories vary constantly.

The object of the approach outlined in this article is to change the weakness of fluctuating distributor inventories into a possible asset to the manufacturing company. More specifically, it is to use the distributor inventories to act as "shock absorbers," and to have such inventories permit smoother factory production schedules rather than to cause them to accentuate fluctuations.

Once factory shipments to the distributors are identified as to current distributor sales and distributor inventory changes, this information can be readily translated into reasonably accurate projections of sales to distributors in any forthcoming three months period.

The existence of the 2-way system of communication, consisting of the dispatch of weekly telegrams and the return of sales charts, can be used to many advantages. In the introduction of a new product, for example, separate reports of the sales of such new products can be added to the weekly telegrams. Thus, the orders of the distributors for the new product can be broken down between orders for stocking and orders for replacement of sold stock. Such information is quite valuable in determining the early acceptance of a new product.

## QUESTIONS

1. Distributor orders are extremely poor indicators of the current rate of sales by distributors. Why?
2. For the manufacturer it is necessary to know the exact behavior of what three cycles in order to predict its factory-shipment cycle? Discuss.
3. Explain how a telegram reporting program can improve the accuracy of short-term sales forecasts.
4. What are some of the drawbacks of the system proposed by the author.

# 19. The Marketing Plan as the Cornerstone of the Corporate Plan*

Edmund Greene, Assistant Director of Marketing Services, Monsanto Chemical Co.

*The marketing plan should be the cornerstone of the corporate long range plan but can serve that purpose only if it starts with a clear statement of objectives, states the assumptions on which all forecasts are based, and spells out what changes must be made in the marketing mix to reach forecast levels of sales.*

What I propose to do this afternoon is to describe what characteristics a marketing plan must have and what information it must contain to make it a cornerstone of the corporate long range plan.

In our company, corporate planning is the major responsibility of a separate committee headed by a vice president and reporting directly to the president and the executive committee. None of its members come from marketing. This means that the marketing plan is the principal medium of communicating marketing's intentions to the committee.

To put it mildly, our planning committee does not isolate itself. It keeps in frequent contact with all aspects of our company and receives written and verbal communications containing supplementary information. But the committee can always come back to the formal marketing plan—if it's a good one—as the cornerstone of their planning.

In companies organized differently to handle long range corporate planning, the formal marketing plan may or may

not hold quite so pivotal a position; but the corporate planners—whoever they may be—are going to need the kinds of information, in the detail I describe, if they are to build a good plan for the company. I might add parenthetically that I know of no better way to make sure they have those facts than to include them in the written marketing plan—but I don't want to belabor the point.

First off, a marketing plan solid enough to serve as the foundation for a corporate plan must be truly a plan.

It cannot be just a forecast. It must include a forecast, of course, but it must also spell out specifically how the marketer proposes to reach the forecast level —what new expenses will be incurred, what changes will be necessary in the organization, what other people and functions must accomplish by what dates for sales to reach the forecast. The plan can't just assume that "everybody's on the marketing team" or that "everybody knows that to double sales we've got to double the number of salesmen." The plan must spell out all the specifics.

Also, the marketing plan can't be just a collection of quotas for salesmen. If you want to indulge in sales manage-

* Reprinted from *Marketing Precision and Executive Action*, Proceedings of the Forty-fifth National Conference of the American Marketing Association, June 20–22, 1962, p. 92. Edited by Charles H. Hindersman.

ment's traditional device of always setting quotas a little beyond the reach of salesmen, use that device with any group you think will be fooled by it. But don't try to fool your corporate planning group. Your plan should be challenging, yes, but it must also be realistic. Assume that, on the basis of your plan, your company is going to commit cash, to build plants, to hire men. Let's not kid each other when these kinds of resources are involved.

I am not going to dwell—and I probably don't have to dwell in this group— on this need for realism in the marketing plan. But it is the criticism I hear most frequently of marketing plans. In writing realistic marketing plans we have an excellent opportunity to break the old stereotype of the ever-optimistic peddler and to prove our capabilities as responsible men of management.

The second most frequent criticism leveled at marketing plans is they lack specificity. They call for more salesmen but don't say how many more. They call for more warehouses but don't say where these warehouses should be. You can't build a corporate plan on the shifting sands of such generalities.

I also think that we as marketers, in fairness to a corporate planning group, should set some sort of *values* on the successful execution of each element of the plan. If research makes us a detergent that dissolves more quickly, *we* must estimate how much we could increase our sales. While we will have difficulty putting even approximate values on some of these parts of the plan, it will be easier and better for us to do so than to have a corporate planning group actually or indirectly set their own values.

In addition to setting values, the plan should establish clear-cut *priorities*. No company has enough cash nor enough other resources to do everything called for in everyone's plans. If we are most

knowledgeable about our company's marketing, we are best qualified to set these priorities honestly and realistically to guide corporate planning in the allocation of these resources.

A good marketing plan should have two other characteristics: It should set deadlines, preferably by year and month, for each important phase of the plan and establish an expected sequence of interrelated events. Second, it should set the measures by which the success of each element of the plan will be judged. Shall we judge sales by dollar volume or by share of market? Shall we judge advertising by number of inquiries or by the changes it effects in readers' attitudes? These deadlines and measures are extremely valuable, if not downright essential, to good marketing management. The corporate planning group may not need them so badly but I know of nothing that would so inspire confidence in the marketing plan as a series of checkpoints and standards which, as time passed, would show that the plan was being followed and that it was on schedule.

Brevity may be the soul of wit but it is the curse of plans. Better to burden your planning committee with a page of extra reading than to frustrate them— and to generate misgivings about the adequacy of the whole plan—by omitting important elements. If these omissions are by intent, not by default, say so. The fact that you are *not* planning a change in your channels of distribution for one line of products, for example, can be as significant as the fact that you *are* planning a change for another line.

So much for what a plan should be— now for some specifics as to what it should contain.

First, of course, it should contain a statement of your objectives, set down in tough, specific, quantified terms. Sometimes the objectives are quite apparent from the plan itself, but often they are not. For example, the plan may call for dropping unprofitable products from your line, but in the longer term, you may want to build a longer line of products. You may wish to try selling your products through only a few distributors for a year or two as a test to see whether in the longer term, you might sell entirely through distributors. Your corporate planning group has a right to know your objectives. How else can they ascertain whether they are consistent with the objectives of the whole company?

Next, of course, the plan should contain the forecast, in both units and dollars, for the period of the plan. Implied in forecasting *both* these bases is a price forecast.

This price forecast is the *acid* test of the realism you build into your plan. In rereading the plans we made several years ago I find we thought we were being pretty hard-headed in forecasting prices below which no competitors in their right minds would think of cutting the price—but cut the prices they did. The far-reaching changes we had to make in our operations have dramatized for us the pivotal importance of the price forecast.

The plan should also contain a forecast of profitability. The cost data will, of course, have to come from manufacturing and other sources, but including it in the marketing plan is a stern reminder to the planner of the facts of life he will be facing. Its inclusion is also evidence to management that we don't think just of sales volume, that we are just as oriented to profits as our colleagues in other functions and that we are keeping our eye on the lifeblood of our business.

Somewhere in the plan—or in a document clearly associated with it—must be two kinds of information for the corporate planner:

1. Some guides to the reliability of the forecasts, and

2. a statement of the principal, significant premises on which the forecasts are based.

Planning groups are understandably wary of the sales curve which takes off to the stratosphere not next year, perhaps, but the year after. And they tend to apply their own deflation factors to the forecasts of a sales group which consistently overestimates its sales by wide margins. If yours is *the* product in a hundred which really is going to take off, or if your sales fluctuate widely with weather or other variables, your planning committee should be told this, not left to guess it or, more likely, to discount the forecast entirely.

So give them enough history on your sales and industry sales that they will have confidence in your forecasts. If your previous forecasts have been wide of the mark, explain why and what steps you have taken to improve their accuracy.

The planning committee should also be told the assumptions on which you based your forecast. Social and economic trends; the import threat, if any; the probabilities of your principal customer's making their own raw materials or being bought out by a competitor.

Some marketers feel that they will be accused of "hedging," of not having the courage of their convictions, if they qualify their forecasts in any way. But if your plans assume that eight million cars will be produced in 1967 and the planning committee thinks the figure will be six million, it's better to find that out in '62 than in '67.

Also, if you're realistically assuming prices are going to drop another 10%, that tariffs are going to be cut, that three new producers are going to enter your market—say so. It will show that you are facing the facts—and might prevent your brass from panicking every time they read an adverse item about your products in the *Wall Street Journal*.

Next, I would urge you to devote some space to the competitive climate in which you expect to be operating. To use a term in current vogue, you know what kind of an s.o.b. your competitor is, but does your planning committee?

I'd give more than the bare bones of your estimates of their capacity and past sales. I'd try to present their strengths and weaknesses—in production, research and marketing—as realistically as possible.

This is an area where qualitative judgments are every bit as important as hard numbers. To forecast what your competitor might do, put yourself in his position and try to determine his objectives. Tell your planning group:

Is your competitor trying to enter the market, gain position or hold leadership?

Is he trying to find outlets for raw materials, dump by-products, dispose of temporarily excess capacity or upgrade intermediates?

How important is this product to his business?

Equally important, how important to his ego?

How do his accountants calculate costs for raw materials, depreciation, incremental sales?

Against this background, then, of your long term objectives and the social, economic and competitive climates in which you expect to be selling, what do you in marketing propose to do to reach your forecast sales and profitability levels?

How many salesmen will you need?

What kind of men will you recruit—technical; college seniors or experienced?

How trained? How long more to train? Where will you put them?

Sales forces aren't found, ready-made under cabbage leaves. They take time to recruit, to train, to get to know their territories, to learn to work well with their district managers. As Dick Alt has mentioned, the operations researchers have some ingenious critical path scheduling programs for complex timing problems, but it just takes common sense to know that we all have to anticipate our manpower needs.

Show your corporate planning group that you *have* anticipated these needs and budgeted the necessary money for recruiting and training far enough in advance of your needs.

Similarly for other aspects of marketing:

Technical Service
Application Research
Distribution Facilities
Customer Service
Advertising
Sales Promotion
Marketing Research

For all those elements of your marketing mix—get specific. Define the problems and estimate the costs of each. If your mix is going to change—Why? How? How will the charges affect costs —and results?

These, of course, are the vitals of the marketing plan and perhaps I should devote more time to discussing them. But Dick Alt has covered many of them and it has been my experience that this is the part of the plan that gets most attention and is usually the best written. Except to repeat the need for realism and for specificity, I'd like to move on to three more areas which need more attention.

First is dropping unprofitable products. There is almost always money to be saved—and, more important, sales effort more profitably re-directed—by judicious pruning of dead wood.

Beware the argument "we need this product to fill out the line"—it almost never holds water.

Corporate planning is concerned because functions other than marketing are involved—in this case, production—and any savings can be maximized if the product is dropped according to a plan and not precipitously.

Second, the possibilities of integrating forward should be mentioned in the plan. If you see this as a possible solution to your marketing problems—and I must add that it isn't always so easy a solution as it appears on the surface—by all means say so in the plan. If integrating forward involves acquisition, cash and organization changes are involved. If you plan to extend your own operations, a plan integrating facilities, people, capital and research must be built upon your plan.

Finally, but most important, your plan must contain a clear, detailed, specific statement of what you expect of research and development: first, in the area of model changes and keeping your present products competitive, and, second, in the really vital area of really new products.

We know our financial futures depend on these new products. We deplore the mistakes R&D sometimes make in developing new products for which there are no markets. But how often do we give R&D the constructive guidance they want and need?

Corporate planning is vitally concerned because new products may—in fact are intended to—lead us into new markets,

require new facilities, lead to still more and different R&D.

In meetings such as this—or more informally at the bar—we marketing men plead for "marketing orientation" of our companies. But are we prepared to provide the direction and leadership that term implies?

To write the kind of plan I have described will take time and honest sweat—but it's the best opportunity I know to orient our companies to our markets and to provide a solid cornerstone for building a sound corporate long range plan.

## QUESTIONS

1. Can you think of any reasons why a top marketing man is not on the corporate planning committee at Monsanto?

2. What are some of the criticisms leveled at marketing plans by corporate long range planning committees?

3. The price forecast is the acid test of the realism you build into your plan. Why?

4. Why is a corporate long range planning committee concerned in dropping a product according to plan?

5. In summarizing this paper, is it fair to say that long-range marketing plans prepared by marketing departments are considered weak for long-range planning?

# $\mathcal{20}.$ Long Range Planning*

Robert E. Brooker, President, Whirlpool Corporation

*Long range planning must go beyond forecasts of five or ten years. It must establish future goals for all parts of the company, in terms of results to be accomplished, at the same time that it allocates physical, human, and financial resources throughout the company to attain these goals.*

Long range, or long term, planning is a concept which requires analysis to insure that its meaning and value for business concerns is clearly defined. The phrase is frequently used quite loosely by economists, market researchers, analysts, and professional consultants just as the terms "automation" and "professional management" have been used without true analysis. I propose to define the kinds of planning that may be considered long term with illustrations drawn from companies whose background and history are well known, and then to describe the organization and background of the Whirlpool Corporation, and its long range planning activity.

Long range planning must go beyond forecasts of five or ten years, although such forecasts, along with short and medium term forecasts, have a considerable value and are necessary in the operation of a company. Forecasting has a secondary function in that it provides a criterion for a company to compare its market growth on a competitive basis, and also to appraise the growth of its industry market to determine whether or not the industry's growth is faster or slower than that of the national income or the per capita income. Where a company lags in growth in either of these two instances, there is a warning sign. If it should lag in the first respect, it clearly indicates that the company is losing out to its competition, and this suggests a change in sales policy or one of distribution. In the second instance, if its industry is growing at a slower rate than the economy and the industry is obtaining a decreasing portion of the country's spending power, then here is a situation where planning would suggest a change in the direction of the company. This example may suggest that short range planning will deal primarily with the existing activities of the company to capture a larger share of the market on a more profitable basis than its direct competitors, and that longer range planning will relate to the progress of the firm compared with the general economy. The function of management planning in an organization is to establish goals for all parts of the company, in terms of results to be accomplished, at the same time that it allocates physical, human, and financial resources throughout the company to attain these goals. In the case history of our own long range planning activities, it will be seen that in our consideration we directed our activity toward maximizing the return

* Reprinted from *Business Topics*, Summer 1961, p. 28. Published quarterly by the Graduate School of Business Administration, Michigan State University.

141

on investment on the capital employed in our business and utilizing the specializations we have in manpower, facilities, and systems of distribution.

## ILLUSTRATIONS OF PLANNING

### DOUGLAS AIRCRAFT CORPORATION

The first time that the term "long range planning" penetrated my consciousness was during the latter period of the Second World War. At that time, the Douglas Aircraft Corporation set up a long range planning function to study potential diversification for using facilities, management, and work force that had been greatly expanded for production of military aircraft. This long range planning task force explored many consumer durables, which they felt might be adapted to the facilities and skills of the Douglas organization. As it turned out, these plans came to naught with the tremendous post-war growth of commercial and private aviation. Douglas, whose commercial business had been concentrated largely in the DC–3, entered the market with a series of new products to meet this newly-created demand. This started with the DC–4, quickly changed to the DC–6 with several modifications of this ship, followed with the DC–7 with several modifications, and their latest work, the DC–8 Jet Liner, which, with other similar ships, has revolutionized long distance travel. I am sure the long range planning task force of Douglas, during the war period, was not in a position to anticipate the change in growth that would occur in the next ten, fifteen, or twenty years, and yet the management of the company had the ability to adjust itself to the change as technological advancement occurred and as the markets developed. It is interesting to note that aircraft manufacturers, as the result of missile programs, are again concentrating on long range planning.

### GENERAL MOTORS CORPORATION

The largest industrial corporation in the United States has had an interesting growth pattern, and much of its planning resulted from the vision of individuals. Mr. Durant and Mr. Sloan, jointly, acquired the companies that now produce the General Motors line of automobiles —Chevrolet, Pontiac, Oldsmobile, Buick, and Cadillac. They acquired by acquisition the companies that have integrated into the manufacture of automobiles, beginning with Fisher Body and extending through Warner Electric, Delco, A. C. Sparkplug, Packard Electric, Rochester Products, a tubing company, transmission and other components. Now that General Motors has 50 percent of the total passenger car market and bigness may become a liability, the company has expanded its growth in other fields of land transportation, which has included its Electromotive Division, manufacturer of Diesel railroad engines, its Euclid Division, manufacturer of earth moving equipment and construction machinery, and its consumer durables, where the Frigidaire Division and Delco Division are factors in appliances and heating. The growth of the General Motors International Division, with its decision to establish manufacturing plants abroad rather than relying on exports, indicates the vision of the planners many years ago in this phase of their growth pattern. Trade releases indicate that the long range planners in this industry today are mindful of the potential of gasoline turbine driven cars and wheelless automobiles which would render engine, transmission, and frame facilities obsolete.

SEARS, ROEBUCK AND COMPANY

The present long term planning of this firm is an outgrowth of many years' experience in the general merchandising business. In the 1920's, General Wood had the vision to recognize that the movement of people from farm to urban areas required that the mail order business be supplemented by a retail business and that the specialized talents of the buyer developed in mail order could apply equally effectively to the retail store system. The original stores followed the familiar location pattern in central areas with heavy foot traffic. Again, General Wood had the vision and courage to move retail stores out of the congested areas into locations that would serve automotive travel and provide large parking facilities. Once this pattern proved successful, it was then possible for Sears to set up a longer range planning program which was to determine its growth for many years to come. Its Market Research Department was able to determine population growth and movement trends and anticipate national income. Experience had taught Sears the percentage of each market that could be developed with decentralized locations handling a full line of general merchandise and related services, and with these being available on satisfactory credit terms. An analysis of the projected growth and income of the major markets in the country readily determined the retailing space requirements to fully cover the market.

The long range planning of distribution required provision for selling area, offices, warehouses, and parking. The cost of this expansion can be determined on a square foot basis. An additional requirement was retail fixturing and merchandising. This too can be related to the square footage required. Experience had shown that just as retail sales depend on a square foot basis, the capital required to finance the time payment accounts can also be anticipated based on the square footage requirement. Together with all factors related to the square footage of the selling area, the planners had to provide for facilities, merchandise, and money, and then a growth of organization to man these facilities. In addition, it was necessary to provide a back-up of sources to provide consistent merchandise values in volume to support the growing rate of sales.

This plan is well established in Sears, and the mechanics of providing the location, designing and erecting the buildings, while flexible, are usually planned four or five years in advance. Each annual report of this company indicates the growth in the number of retail units.

OTHER COMPANIES

In this field, Penney's has had a similar program of long range planning and as a result their progress and growth are apparent. A contrast to this is Montgomery Ward where there was a long period of no growth and no planning, and it is only recently that this company has moved forward in a long range concept and, because the program is late, at considerable expense. These examples of planning long term growth in a few well known companies lead into the concept of planning that we have used in Whirlpool.

## A PLANNING PROGRAM

The Whirlpool Corporation of today is the result of a merger made five years ago. Prior to 1955, Whirlpool Corporation manufactured laundry products only and distributed them through Sears, Roebuck and Co. under the Kenmore label and through its own distributors under the Whirlpool brand. The Seeger Corporation made refrigerators and freezers for Sears under the Coldspot brand, and the Estate Range Company made ranges which they sold through RCA distributors along with RCA air conditioners. Combining these companies into the present Whirlpool Corporation made us a manufacturer of a full line of major domestic appliances. In addition, we acquired the use of the RCA trademark and changed our name brand to RCA Whirlpool for major appliances. This line is distributed through distributors, the majority of whom handled the RCA line of electronic products—that is radio, television, etc. The sales volume of the companies being merged approached $400 million per year, and currently the company has sales of $450 million.

### THE TASK FORCE

The first four years of this combined operation did not provide much time for planning. The problems of integrating the organization and bringing out an entirely new line of major appliances, under the full line concept, occupied every minute of the time of a very energetic and effective management team. A little more than a year ago, during a period when we were enjoying the most successful year since the merger, we paused to reflect on the longer range outlook for the company and decided that a planning program was timely and necessary. Both Mr. Gray, the Chairman, and I had been exposed to longer range planning functions of other companies where these functions had been separated from the top executive offices. We felt that planning functions tended to lose the dynamic qualities needed for change and leadership when it was assigned to a regular staff category. It was

Mr. Gray's thought, and it proved to be a very good one, that we select from our organization a group of promising young men in various functions of the business, whose qualifications might indicate they would become the managers in the next ten years, and that they be given the assignment, with their regular duties, of working out a ten year plan for the growth and development of our company.

Six men were selected and they became known as our Long Range Planning Task Force. They were given a year to make their study. There was no restriction on the amount of assignments given people within the company, providing time was available, nor the monies to be spent on outside consultants where such consultation was deemed necessary in specialized areas. The men were in an age bracket between 35 and 42 years, and their experience included manufacturing, engineering, sales, and finance. At the initial meeting, it was established that the plan would not go beyond specialization in major appliances and products functionally associated with major appliances, or such products as might come from our Research and Development, as were compatible with our general skills. This did not mean that our long range planning would not eventually go beyond this stage, but we felt there was ample opportunity within this specification to provide a growth pattern which was proper for our present operation.

### NATURE OF THE STUDY

The Long Range Planning Task Force organized itself with a Chairman and Secretary, who scheduled the meetings and kept a record of the discussions. Meetings were held bi-weekly, generally for a full day and on occasion for several days. The group divided their study into six phases:

They determined their objectives.

They arrived at a method of analyzing the problems.

They went about securing the background information.

They assigned specific projects to members of the group and, where necessary, enlisted support from inside talent or obtained outside consultation.

They reviewed and discussed the findings on the individual projects and came to an agreement on the recommendations they would make.

They summarized their work and made a report to the Chairman and the President.

Within the company, the Market Research Department was able to make what we hope will be accurate forecasts of the markets for major appliances for the next ten years. The family formation growth rate is available from a number of sources, the expected income per family rate is available. We in the appliance industry have a complete record of the saturation of each of our products, and we have fairly accurate records of the replacement rate, except as innovation and changes may accelerate replacement. This means that the Task Force, without providing for any innovation or change, could anticipate the overall market for appliances during the next ten years, and then determine whether the systems of distribution could increase our share of these markets, whether the share would merely be held even or whether there was some possibility of losing position in the market.

INVENTION AND RATE OF CHANGE

The technical changes that might accelerate the rate of replacement have several effects on long range planning. If a manufacturer had a technical change that made all other products obsolete and he had this exclusively, he might increase his market share disproportionately. Experience has shown that this is an unlikely set of circumstances in the appliance industry.

The rate of change through innovation has been very slow. In the washing machine, there have been two major innovations in the last fifty years. One was the agitator principle of washing, which is fifty years old or older and the second was the automatic washing machine, which is now approximately twenty-five years old. The acceptance of these changes was only accomplished as several manufacturers entered the field with a like principle. Many of the other improvements that have come along in laundry appliances are developed by one manufacturer, and where the innovation provides a real benefit to the consumer other manufacturers quickly follow, either through licensing or by copying the idea. The same is true of refrigerators. The major basic change in the refrigerator was the introduction of the hermetic sealed system, which came in the middle twenties. The dual temperature boxes, that is a refrigerator with a freezer compartment, were introduced in the thirties, but it is only within the last five years that the temperature in the freezer compartment of a dual temperature box has been held below 10°, which is the requirement for proper storage of frozen foods.

ASPECTS OF TECHNICAL DEVELOPMENT

There may be technical changes that would not only affect the consumer buying of a product but might also change the facilities required to produce the appliances. Ultrasonic washing is a subject that has been thoroughly explored, and it is now pretty well accepted that ultrasonic washing of clothing is not likely to revolutionize this industry, because a sound wave hitting a fabric suspended in a liquid is not meeting a solid object, and, therefore, is not as effective as a sound wave against metal parts where the principle is well established in commercial practice. Ultrasonic washing may be practical in the dishwashing field where china, glassware, and silverware provide a solid object to bounce the sound wave against.

Another area where technical development could bring about change is in the development of thermoelectric heating and cooling. It is quite probable that the day will arrive when we can economically cool thermoelectrically by the simple transfer of electricity into cooling without going through the process of using a compressor, evaporator, and condenser as now used in refrigerator systems. When this day arrives, the facilities required for refrigerators, freezers, air conditioners, and like products may be greatly changed. Our own work in thermoelectrics is well advanced and we estimate that such a contingency might be outside of the ten year scope of this plan.

Obviously, developments of this type must be reviewed currently and plans be flexible enough to anticipate such change. Today's mass production of durable goods requires substantial lead time for product change. The development, tooling, and testing of a new product require long periods. Time is required to provide the capital equipment, most of which is tailored for automatic or semi-automatic production. This means that companies must today take action which commits manpower and resources for longer periods of time. Long range planning must provide this, avoiding the prospect of having to maintain a partially idle labor force free of write-off obsolescent plans and equipment.

## THE DISTRIBUTIONAL STUDY

Once the Task Force got into the assignment of projects, they found that the critical area for growth within this ten year period would be the problem of appliance distribution. The growth of distribution through our brands manufactured for the mass distributional arm of our system was related to its growth of facility, the expansion of its service, our ability to supply value in the product and a serviceability that would encourage the replacement of each of the Coldspot and Kenmore products in the field by a new Coldspot and Kenmore, and through this reputation of service and dependability bring new customers to these products. The Sears system of distribution is well refined to eliminate elements of handling costs, and passes these savings along to the consumer. This does not mean that further refinements are not available in the distribution of the products through Sears, but the opportunity for taking costs out of their distribution method is far less than opportunities available to the distributor-dealer system.

The Task Force found that the whole system of independent distribution should be carefully reviewed and for this purpose employed an outside consultant to work with our own Market Research Department. This work resulted in an economic forecast of the geographical distribution of sales that could be achieved by 1970. They then set up a mathematical model of distributional facilities to serve independent dealers most economically with this geographical distribution of sales. Currently, we distribute through 78 distributors located to serve roughly 10,000 dealers. The distributional pattern is a familiar one. The goods are manufactured and warehoused in the manufacturing location and drawn out in carload lots by the distributor where they are again warehoused. They are ultimately shipped to the dealer and he makes the sale and installation to the consumer.

### THE GATEWAY SYSTEM

The distribution study was directed to eliminate some of this handling and the related expenses. A further objective was to bring complete stocks closer to the consumer. The study developed a regional system of warehouses, which we chose to call gateway warehouses. These warehouses might ultimately replace the stock at the manufacturer's plant and the stock at the distributor's establishment so that goods would be shipped off the ends of the manufacturing lines into a gateway warehouse, and then as sold delivered to the consumer; or they would follow the present pattern to a dealer and then be delivered to the consumer.

The gateways have the advantage of bringing the factory inventory closer to the consumer, and this provides for mixing shipments of all appliances when shipment is made to the dealer. Carload freight rates are available to ultimate destinations even though the shipment is interrupted at the gateway for storage. This proposal would eliminate inventories at distributorships but would increase factory-owned inventories since these would be held in gateway warehouses. Our study showed that fewer gateway warehouses would meet our distribution needs and provide delivery no later than the second day. The gateway system also provides a means of leveling factory manpower and securing maximum production economies.

### OTHER RECOMMENDATIONS

Our Task Force, recognizing the potential in the international field, author-ized an extensive study of product market practices and competition in several countries. This developed a recommendation to participate in these markets and suggested priority for certain areas.

The Task Force also considered some of the other products that have already been developed from research such as the coin-op dry cleaning machine, which is being introduced this year and ice-makers, which are being introduced both in refrigerators and as separate appliances.

## REORGANIZATION

Once these parts were set into an overall recommendation, the need for study of the organization became apparent. When a company has grown big, it tends to become inflexible and is slow to change because of its structure and routine. Long range planning should have the objectivity to cut across established functions and procedures, to stimulate a change in direction and where necessary suggest changes of policy, procedure, and methods. The task force recommended a reorganization of manufacturing, a reorganization of distribution that developed from their study, a reorganization of the customer service and quality assurance development to complement distribution, and a reorganization of the International Division.

The recommendations all appeared valid; it was then necessary to determine whether earnings would provide the financial growth necessary to support this expansion. The net result of the financial study indicated that it was possible to substantially increase our business within 10 years, provide for additional facilities to support this added volume, and provide for the international expansion, if we are able to realize an 8 to 10 percent profit on sales during the period and retain 50 percent of the total earnings, or, if we confine our dividends to 50 percent of earnings. Experience has proven that we are able to earn 8 to 10 percent on sales over long periods, and we have followed a policy of limiting our dividends to 50 percent of earnings. The increase of our potential sales is in line with our present market penetration and somewhat below our rate of growth in the market.

### IMPLEMENTING CHANGE

The Task Force at the conclusion of their study made their presentation to Mr. Gray and me. We have accepted many of their recommendations and are in the process of putting them into effect. The reorganization of manufacturing into product groups has been accomplished. The distribution recommendation for regional warehouses is under way through a pilot operation. The international recommendations are being explored and may be followed presently much along the lines of the long range recommendations. The customer service and quality assurance function has been reorganized to achieve the objectives recommended by the Task Force.

Top management planning has the responsibility for initiating change of the total company system, moving forward as a coordinated whole, in an evolutionary sense in response to changes in environment in which the company must survive and grow. The Long Range Task Force recommended that we establish long range planning as a permanent function. We have not accepted this recommendation yet as we would like to hold the long range planning responsibility as one belonging to the two top officers. We have arranged to meet with the original Task Force after the first year of operation under their recommendations and let them discuss the accomplishments and any new recommendations that may have come to them in their day-to-day work.

### DEVELOPMENT OF LEADERSHIP

It is interesting that of the six men who made up the Task Force, four have been promoted to officers, a fifth has been made a Division Manager, and a sixth is Assistant to the President. We feel that our selection of men to do this work was well justified by their performance, and we look to these men to play an important part in the future of our company. This does not exclude other men who are demonstrating ability as they have equal opportunity, but, obviously, these six have had a great broadening of their outlook on all phases of activity, and they have been given opportunity to demonstrate their qualities of leadership. In many ways our long range planning activities fall into a category of intermediate planning with the only breakthroughs being in the area of distribution and international.

The execution of this program will require the doubling of our management force. Currently, we have slightly more than 2,000 men in a management category to carry out these objectives which will require more than 4,000. At the conclusion of this review, we took our long range planning to the entire management group to point out not only the opportunity for growth in the company and the opportunity for the individual, but also the requirement that the individual management develop people to carry this additional load.

At the time of the merger five years ago, we made a five year plan of what we expected to accomplish. A review of this plan shows that we have substantially accomplished all objectives; although, quite frankly, they were not all achieved on the scheduled dates. We think our ten year program is one that is an attainable objective, but, here again, we recognize that progress will not follow a straight line. There will be some periods when we make more progress than in others; the essential thing is to have an objective, to be moving forward, and to have everyone in the organization recognize the goal.

## QUESTIONS

1. The rate of change through innovation has been very slow in the appliance industry. Why?

2. What techniques did the Long-Range Planning Task Force at Whirlpool use to determine the desirability of the gateway system of warehousing?

3. Describe the long-range planning system at Sears, Roebuck and Company.

4. In contrast, why did Montgomery Ward fail to expand and grow?

5. From your study of the case histories described in the article, what do you believe are some of the basic requirements for success in long-range planning?

## BIBLIOGRAPHY FOR CHAPTER III

ARTICLES:

Alderson, L. W., "Theory and Practice of Market Planning," *Cost and Profit Outlook,* Vol. XI, No. 4 (July–August 1958), pp. 1–6.

Anderson, Henry, "Scientific Sales Forecasting and Its Problems," *Western Business Review,* Vol. 5, No. 2 (May 1961), pp. 19–24.

Buell, Victor P., "Organizing for Marketing Planning," *The Journal of Marketing,* Vol. XXI, No. 1 (July 1956), pp. 68–71.

Crisp, R. D., "Product Planning for Future Profits," *Dun's Review and Modern Industry,* Vol. 71, No. 3 (March 1958), pp. 34–36.

Levitt, Theodore, "Blue-Skies Approach to Tomorrow's Marketing," *Business Horizons,* Vol. 1, No. 2 (Spring 1958), pp. 120–128.

Smith, W. R., "Marketing Strategy; What Preparations Should Precede the Marketing Concept?" *Printers' Ink,* Vol. 264, No. 13 (September 26, 1958), pp. 37–38.

Wickstrum, R. H., "Sales Management's New Horizons," *Commercial and Financial Chronicle,* Vol. 188 (August 7, 1958), p. 505.


BOOKS:

Alderson, Wroe, *Marketing Behavior and Executive Action.* Homewood, Ill.: Irwin, 1957. Chapter 14.

Alderson, Wroe, and Green, Paul, *Planning and Problem Solving in Marketing.* Homewood, Ill.: Irwin, 1962. Chapter 14.

Bursk, Edward C., *Text and Cases in Marketing.* Englewood Cliffs, N.J.: Prentice-Hall, 1962. Section Six.

Crisp, Richard D., *Sales Planning and Control.* New York: McGraw-Hill, 1961.

Davis, Kenneth R., *Marketing Management.* New York: Ronald, 1961. Chapter 15.

Ewing, David W. (ed.), *Long-Range Planning for Management.* New York: Harper, 1958.

Ferber, Robert, and Verdoorn, P. J., *Research Methods in Economics and Business.* New York: Macmillan, 1962. Chapter 10.

Holmes, Parker M., *Marketing Research: Principles and Readings.* Cincinnati, Ohio: South-Western Publishing Co., 1960. Chapters 10 and 18.

Howard, John A., *Marketing Management.* Homewood, Ill.: Irwin, 1957. Chapters 2 and 6.

Lazo, Hector, and Corbin, Arnold, *Management in Marketing.* New York: McGraw-Hill, 1961. Chapter 2.

LeBreton, Preston P., and Henning, Dale A., *Planning Theory.* Englewood Cliffs, N.J.: Prentice-Hall, 1961.

**150**

Levitt, Theodore, *Innovation in Marketing.* New York: McGraw-Hill, 1962. Chapters 6 and 7.

McCarthy, E. Jerome, *Basic Marketing: A Managerial Approach.* Homewood, Ill.: Irwin, 1960. Section G. 2.

Phelps, D. M., and Westing, J. H., *Marketing Management.* Homewood, Ill.: Irwin, 1960. Chapters 10 and 15.

Spencer, Milton H., Clark, Colin, and Hoguet, Peter, W., *Business and Economic Forecasting.* Homewood, Ill.: Irwin, 1961.

Theil, Hans, *Economic Forecasts and Policy.* Netherlands: North-Holland Publishing Company, 1958. Parts 2, 4, 5, and 7.

# IV. Research in Marketing

*HE MODERN* marketing manager needs information for planning and policy formulation. Marketing research is one of the principal tools through which management is supplied with the data necessary for intelligent decision making. Marketing research informs business management where the company stands in its industry, and predicts and analyzes industry trends. It is not only an essential marketing management tool in appraising and improving current marketing strategy effectiveness but it can also be a most useful instrument in long-range planning activities such as the development of new products.

The role of marketing research as an information communication system for top management calls for its placement organizationally under the top marketing executive. In the past where the department has been placed under the direction of operating departments such as advertising, critical reports were frequently suppressed, preventing its profitable use by the company.

Although at the present time there is a dispute between the "sample" researchers of the traditional school and the "motivation" researchers of the behavioral school, there are signs that the two schools will merge for a joint attack on management problems. The behavioral scientists with specific training in sociology, psychology, and cultural anthropology are contributing new insights into consumer behavior, and they can communicate effectively and relatively economically with the "sample" researchers through the common language of statistics.

To serve top management better, marketing research must develop a broader orientation. Instead of being preoccupied exclusively with narrow investigations, it should be called on more to map out long-range plans which ultimately provide some of the data to guide the design of individual studies for today's decisions. Research departments which work only on requests brought to them tend to be occupied with routine, short-range operating problems. They are less likely to contribute to policy formulation, planning and innovation.

Marketing managers are becoming increasingly aware of the

whole new array of quantitative techniques which research departments can use to sharpen their analysis of problems. These techniques commonly identified under the broad name of operations research include a wide variety of mathematical and statistical procedures such as linear programming, queueing theory, search theory, information theory, system simulation, and statistical decision theory.

The utilizations of these quantitive research procedures by the marketing research department can strengthen marketing planning and bring more precise solution to such marketing problems as pricing, location of warehouses, inventory control, allocation of advertising budgets and forecasting.

The refinement of these new procedures is taking place with breathtaking speed due to the development of computers and electronic data processing which call for the quantification of data. Electronic data processing vastly expands the company's memory capacity. One of the impressive facts about the big computers is the amount of information that can be stored on magnetic tapes and later called up for analysis. With the computer's enormous capacity to handle information, it becomes increasingly possible to include consideration of many aspects of business activity which had to be excluded from consideration previously to keep the problems within bounds.

The development and implementation of a higher-quality intelligence system built around quantitative research and computers is the top challenge of marketing management for the immediate future.

# 21. Put Research into Marketing Decisions*

Joseph W. Newman, Professor of Business Administration, Graduate School of Business Administration, Stanford University

*The new concepts and skills from such varied disciplines as psychology, anthropology, sociology, semantics and economics must be integrated into the marketing research effort. Research generalists should be used as counselors, liaison men and communicators for a more effective integration of the new research power with decision making.*

For years, marketing men have called for better tools to help them in understanding and solving their problems. Now they are confronted with a burgeoning array of resources. However, at present, not enough is known about how to put them to work effectively in the decision-making processes of business organizations. As a result, there exists a serious administrative bottleneck which demands the attention of top management.

## KEEPING UP WITH PROGRESS

This challenging situation arose because of the substantial progress made in the past 15 years in the behavioral sciences, statistics, mathematics and electronics:

In psychology, sociology, and cultural and social anthropology, there have been significant contributions to knowledge of human behavior and ad-

vances in concepts and techniques for identifying and measuring factors related to behavior. Work of special interest to marketing has been done on perception, memory, attitudes, learning, personality, motivation, communication flow, opinion leadership, and social strata and mobility.

The field of statistics, which earlier developed probability sampling and experimental design, now offers a major new development called statistical decision theory. Departing from tradition, this approach shows how both judgment and statistical evidence should be combined in the making of decisions. It also offers an approch for deciding how much statistical evidence should be obtained before a decision can be made.

Power has been added to the analytical tools of mathematics which are being applied in the social as well as in the physical and biological sciences. Developmental work is under way on mathematical models designed to describe the functioning of economic units or systems and to predict the

* Reprinted from *Harvard Business Review*, March–April 1962, p. 105.

outcome of given inputs into the system. This approach promises to open the door to new understanding in such difficult areas as customer behavior and determination of how much to spend on advertising and sales promotion. Operational models are being successfully applied to somewhat less perplexing problems in sales forecasting, advertising, and sales and inventory management.

Speeding up progress has been the interdisciplinary movement that has led marketing to draw increasingly on other fields for new ways of thinking and new methods and skills for obtaining and interpreting data. As a result, marketing's stock of resources for generating a flow of useful information for decision making now is at a significant all-time high. Research has not, of course, suddenly become able to solve all of marketing's problems. Far from it. On the other hand, marketing research has acquired a considerable potential for helping management. And faster growth lies immediately ahead as the interdisciplinary movement gains momentum in the amazing new age of "intellectronics" which features the combined use of the intellect of man and the "intellect" of the computer.

### GETTING INTO THE ACT

All of this would foretell a new age of development in information for business management except for one highly disturbing fact; progress in developing tools has far outdistanced progress in learning how to get them used appropriately in the regular course of decision making. The administrative problem which now concerns us is really an old one which has been greatly accentuated and complicated by the burst of new developments. It is that of how to get the results of marketing research more into the decision-making act.

While the use of marketing research has grown, it still is applied on a very limited scale compared to the importance of marketing decisions which are made and to the capacity of research to be of help. As recently as 1958 the American Marketing Association found that 40% of the firms represented in its membership and the membership of other selected national associations had no marketing research departments at all. And among the companies which have such departments, there is a tremendous range in both the amount and nature of research activity. A few companies are well out in front, and there are a number of encouraging examples of recent growth. It is my observation, however, that this growth is coming much too slowly. Only in a relatively small number of companies has marketing research become a regular part of the making of important policy and operating decisions.

In companies with marketing research units, a wide gap typically separates research personnel and management personnel. As a result, many researchers complain that they are not understood. At the same time, many managers protest that the researchers do not understand practical marketing problems. These complaints should be regarded as symptoms of a complex problem.

It appears that we have not yet taken a comprehensive enough view of either research or decision making to understand what is involved in relating the two. In order to point up this problem and learn more about its nature, I have been engaged in an exploratory study during the past year. In my comments in this article, I shall be drawing on observations made both in this study and in my contacts with marketing research during past years.

## DIMENSIONS OF THE JOB

The usual starting point in discussions of how to use marketing research effectively has been the subject of research itself, so let us follow that route and see where it takes us.

Have you ever tried asking these questions of the key executives and the researchers in your company: What is research? And what role should it play? If not, do it sometime when you feel courageous. If your company is typical, you will find widely divergent conceptions—or, maybe, misconceptions. If they are not recognized and dealt with—and usually they are not—there is bound to be trouble in attempting to relate research and decision making.

Even in professional groups of marketing researchers it would be easy to prove that research means quite different things to different people. It is common, for example, for some researchers to see research as being the application of certain techniques—those techniques which they know how to apply. Great emphasis has been given to the technicalities, and this has affected the thinking of business executives as well as researchers. As a result, management tends to equate surveys and research and to ask about such things as sample size and cost before clarifying what it really wants to learn.

The main point is that many people in both research and management have been thinking too narrowly. Our emphasis has been on details or parts of research—and not on research itself. There is a widespread failure to visualize a continuing process of inquiry in which executives are helped to think more effectively. Research should stand for systematically approaching two essential tasks: (1) the getting of ideas and (2) the testing of these ideas. Research should bring to these tasks whatever concepts and methods promise to be of help.

In order to emphasize that research is much more than a question of techniques, I am using the term "research resources," which refers to ways of thinking, theories, knowledge, and skills, as well as methodology. Research resources will change over time as progress is made. What remains constant is the concept of careful search to generate a flow of ideas and information which will help executives make better decisions.

### IMPORTANCE OF PROCESS

It now appears that the logical starting point for our discussion of the use of research is not research itself but decision making. Otherwise we put the cart before the horse—or, perhaps, I should say the tool kit before the problem. This is a very common mistake—so common, in fact, that it constitutes a major barrier to relating research and decision making. It should be obvious that our success in relating these two functions depends on knowing what the decision-making process is. We need to know what decisions are made, by whom, when, and how. Then we can design a research function to bring appropriate research resources to bear on the important questions at the right time.

Thinking in terms of processes instead of techniques immediately broadens the horizon. It should help us see that research is not simply a matter of evaluating given alternatives, but that it can feed the creative process more directly. As this becomes apparent, research will be used more not only for short-run operating decisions but for longer run planning *and* for innovation. A systematic approach to innovation, for example, requires a methodical searching for opportunities and use of various means of gathering and interpreting data to stimulate a flow of ideas.

So far, I have pointed to a growing store of research resources and to our inability to make anything like full use of them. If we are going to correct this condition, we first must do two basic things:

1. Think more specifically in terms of an on-going process of decision making which requires a flow of inputs.

2. See research as the systematic application of a variety of concepts and methods which can be useful in generating these inputs.

Perhaps the reader has wondered, as I have, why the very nature of our business concerns has not automatically led us to marketing research. After all, our companies contrive to perform certain functions and to make profits, and they must do this in a competitive economy. Why are we not constantly studying the process by which our organizations function and seeking better inputs to improve performance? Marketing research departments are born more of the shock of necessity than of continuous positive thinking. What happens is that share of market shrinks, or profits drop, or competition steals a march. A consultant is called in. He notes the absence of systematic planning and recommends it along with research to generate needed information. This is the kind of sequence of events that gives rise to research organization.

## IMPEDIMENTS TO PROGRESS

Whatever its origin, marketing research inevitably faces a struggle to gain acceptance within the company. Why is this so? What are the factors that now impede relating research and decision?

Let me discuss some of the main barriers as I have seen them in my field observations.

### LIMITED BACKGROUNDS

The concepts of decision-making processes and research resources that I have described are unfamiliar to most business executives and to many marketing researchers as well. They were not taught when these people went to school, and they still are not taught to any appreciable extent. So a serious educational problem exists. Ways are needed to acquaint business people with the resources of related fields which are becoming part of the business scene and to help them to see marketing research as embracing a variety of data-gathering activities which can serve such management functions as are indicated by the following questions:

*What is going on?* This is the function of keeping management informed so that control may be exercised. Estimates of sales, share of market, and sales potential are examples. The figures reflect what is happening, but do not in themselves explain it.

*How do you account for it?* This is the idea-getting or hypothesis-formulating function. It may be served by research undertaken specifically to aid in the creative process by which ideas are brought into consciousness. It can involve any number of steps designed to reveal more about the nature of people, things, and relationships.

*Is the explanation valid?* The function here is that of checking on the soundness and importance of ideas and tentative explanations. Testing may be done in any of a variety of ways, depending on the subject.

*What, then, should be done?* This step involves reasoning from the evidence obtained as to the nature of the situation being studied and prescribing the alternative courses of action which appear to be appropriate.

*What results can be expected?* Various tests may be employed to serve the function of predicting the outcomes of the suggested alternative courses of action.

*How successful was the action, once taken?* The function here is that of evaluating how well the chosen course of action achieved its purpose. It may include an examination of sales figures or the use of tests to measure such things as advertising readership or changes in knowledge, impressions, and attitudes.

The main point is that research is not simply a matter of having a survey done from time to time as has been so typical in the past. Instead, it should be a continuous program designed to help management set its objectives, plan for their accomplishment, implement the plans successfully, and evaluate the outcome so that still better programs may be undertaken in the future.

#### RESISTANCE TO THREAT

A key barrier to the use of research is that business executives tend to see it as a threat to their personal status, and, therefore, they resist it. Unfamiliarity with research is part of the problem. More central are fears that research implies personal evaluation and that it will invalidate the assumptions the executive has regarded as his "knowledge" and which he believes justify his position.

There are good grounds for fear. The very nature of research is inquiry. It represents an attempt to put into specialized hands activities deliberately designed to produce new ideas and to test old ones. Unfortunately, it also is true that research has been used by ambitious people for personal advantage and by company presidents to build fires under key personnel. Line executives naturally shy at any suggestion that they will be undermined or that someone else will start telling them how to run their jobs.

We should not forget that the concept of professional institutional management with its division of labor and use of specialists is relatively new. Because of this, many executives have had little experience with using such staff services as research and planning. In fact, the alleged need for these services seems to contradict the honored assumption that a good business executive primarily is a born intuitive artist. True, he has to learn the business by working his way up; but once he has done this, he either has it or he doesn't. So why worry about things like decision-making processes and research?

The attitude just described is still widely held, often with devotion. I grant that intuitive artistry is highly important. Because of the limited state of business knowledge, executives have had no alternative but to operate largely as intuitive artists. The practice of business artistry, however, naturally leads to a strong vested interest in it. It then tends to be accompanied by a disinclination to distinguish between what is known and what is not known and to use systematic means of getting better information when they become available.

Executives rise to power either by making correct assumptions about uncertainty or by persuading others that they have done so. Typically, there are few specific checks on their judgments. If an executive thinks that others regard him as a good business artist, he can hardly be expected to welcome research which, in effect, challenges both the adequacy and the quality of his skills.

In the language of organization theory, the business executive has engaged in "uncertainty absorption" by making inferences about an uncertain situation and then communicating to others the inferences, not the evidence from which they were drawn, as certainty. This can be a highly effective technique for gaining power because of the great demand for assurance within business organizations which continually must act in the face of uncertainty. Inasmuch as one of the main purposes of research is that of removing some of the uncertainty, the introduction of a research function into an organization means some shift in location of the function of "uncertainty absorption," and thus it may also mean a loss of power for certain executives.

### ORGANIZATIONAL DEFECTS

I have been impressed repeatedly with the fact that few companies have specified what kinds of needs they are in business to satisfy and what kinds of organizations they want to be. If this were done, there would be more consistent efforts by executives to get better answers to questions important to the company's welfare.

In the absence of clear common goals, executives develop their own. Their opinions as to what the company should be tend to become the bases of political alignments in the internal struggles for power. Defense of their views, then, becomes very important. This means that the question of whether to use research can become a major political issue. Naturally, those who think that market research would enhance their positions will favor it while others will oppose it. Part of the challenge faced by the researcher is that of navigating the political waters so as to avoid torpedoes, and, preferably, win respect and support.

A related barrier is the widespread lack of adequate provisions for systematic marketing planning. It has been common practice to expect operating executives to be both planners and operators even though they frequently lack training and aptitude for planning. In addition, they are occupied by the immediate pressures of day-to-day routine, so little planning gets done. Since planning and research go hand in hand, if little planning goes on, no one is likely to be very interested in research. Under these circumstances, the marketing research department finds itself in the unenviable position of being the sole advocate of better planning. Not only is this a lonely place to be, but it is also risky because it implies that certain executives are not doing their jobs.

The absence of planning may reflect the failure of key executives to think in terms of continuous change and of keeping up with it. Progress consists of continually evolving new and better methods of viewing goals and achieving them. If executives do not accept this concept, they are likely to fear new ideas as implying some personal deficiency. Marketing research does not have much of a chance in this kind of situation.

Fortunately, there now is an encouraging trend toward putting planning in qualified hands as companies accept the "marketing concept." The change inevitably stimulates the demand for research.

### INABILITY TO USE SPECIALISTS

Only a few years ago, we tended to see the problem of relating research to decision making in terms of getting a statistician and a business executive to understand one another well enough to pull in the same direction. And that was no easy matter, either, but it now appears simple when contrasted with the latest methods of research which draw on a growing number of specialists from such varied disciplines as psychology, anthropology, sociology, semantics, economics, mathematics, and statistics. The need for greater understanding of how to productively employ specialists both individually and in combination is urgent. So is the need for learning how to handle the flood of data they can generate.

Here are the kinds of questions that are becoming increasingly important to answer:

• How can marketing learn about the resources of other disciplines that can be of help?

• What means can be used for determining when to get what specialists into the act?

• What constitutes a beneficial working relationship between marketing executives and outside specialists?

• How can the work of specialists, whose concepts and methods are unfamiliar to business people, be made part of the thinking of executives?

The trend to interdisciplinary approaches is compounding the highly difficult problem researchers always have had of communicating with top management. Some companies have instituted special communications units within their marketing research departments to help bridge the gap. While progress has been made, communication today clearly is inadequate and the future seems to demand substantially revised communication channels and methods.

The need for specialists will grow. Some companies will use them as outside consultants while others will bring them into the organization. In order to attract good professional people, it will be necessary to offer them more attractive working situations than have existed in the past. Among other things, this will entail changes in customary salary ranges and patterns of advancement for staff personnel. Typically, it has been necessary for a specialist to leave his specialty

and become a line executive in order to continue to advance in status and pay. There has been some movement to correct this condition. One large corporation, for example, has instituted parallel ladders of advancement for line and staff people to encourage specialists to develop professionally within their specialties.

## ISOLATION FROM MANAGEMENT

If research is to be an integral part of marketing decision making, research people must have close and continuous contact with the key executives. Progress is being made in this direction, but there is a long way to go. For one thing, marketing research departments typically have been handicapped by low organizational status. Also, they have been headed by people who have lacked the breadth of background and the skill in human relationships needed to work effectively with management.

Reflecting executives' lack of understanding of research and its potential contribution to decision making is the fact that research departments have tended to be technical job shops to which operating people could bring requests if they chose to do so. The weakness of this system is that it depends on the initiative of executives who are unfamiliar with research and who typically are unable to identify their problems well enough to ask for the help they need.

Research departments which work only on requests brought to them tend to be occupied with routine, short-range operating problems. They are unlikely to be contributing to policy formulation, planning, and innovation. They cannot become an integral part of the decision-making process because line executives do not look to research for that sort of participation. Without a close relationship with the decision makers, research cannot play much of an educational role.

Line executives usually cannot and will not come to it saying: "Here are my main operating assumptions. Check on them and help me develop better ones, will you?" Yet this is the very kind of activity needed if progress is to be made.

Even when research departments are not handicapped by isolation, they still have difficulty working well with management. A good many marketing research directors who, in my opinion, have been reasonably successful, spend at least half of their time consulting individually with executives and attending management meetings. In spite of this beneficial contact, however, they report that their main problems are: (1) finding out what management's problems really are, and (2) communicating effectively with management. Their experience highlights the necessity of developing better approaches. Clearly, past patterns are inadequate.

## METHODS OF ATTACK

The obstacles just described are large and basic. Together they pose a tremendous challenge to management. Meeting this challenge will require much effort over a period of time. Granted this, what can be done now toward solving the problems involved? Helpful action is possible on several fronts.

### PROGRAM OF RESEARCH

In the present period of significant technical progress, it is painfully apparent that the introduction of new tools does not automatically lead to their use. In fact, technical advances create administrative problems which remind us that we have a great deal to learn. The administrative aspects of employing research effectively must become a major area for study along with that of technical development.

Fortunately, the functioning of business organizations now is receiving greater research attention by social scientists. A promising start has been made on learning more about how the various marketing decisions actually are made. But much work is needed to provide specific descriptions which can serve as the basis for thinking about what information should be introduced and by what system this can best be done. The opportunity for related studies is large because the administrative front has been neglected. For example, communications problems await study as do the problems of working with specialists. Also needed is a detailed description of the role of the modern director of marketing research and the qualifications necessary for the successful discharge of his functions. My observations indicate that a good many conventional notions on this subject are obsolete.

The problem of supplementing limited backgrounds will require several measures:

Major program revisions are needed in the business schools that seek to train the marketing managers of tomorrow. Only a start has been made. (The effect, moreover, will not be felt for some years and business cannot afford to wait.)

Specially designed management development programs are needed for acquainting today's marketing managers with the newer concepts and techniques for research, planning, and decision making.

Management can bring into the organization researchers who have up-to-date technical backgrounds and who also are qualified by training and skill to be effective educators as they work with key executives from day to day.

Understanding of research, of course, is highly desirable. But must executives be able to understand research before their companies can use it effectively? The answer is no. In fact, understanding has followed acceptance more often than the other way around. Many of today's more advanced marketing research departments owe their initial acceptance to the interpersonal relations skills of their directors and to having scored important success stories which impressed top management.

### ORGANIZATION CHANGES

We can look forward to a multiplication of the current amount and variety of marketing research. In other words, the intelligence function will become a major one, offering a sharp contrast to the past practice of having a small research job shop located pretty much on the sidelines of the decision-making game.

The expansion will require changes in organizational provision for both research and planning. While the pattern remains to be developed, certain things can be said at this time. A much greater division of labor within marketing research is essential. Professional specialists from other disciplines will become a major part of the business research picture. They will be concerned largely with bringing the resources of their respective fields to bear in the design and execution of research and the interpretation of data. Efforts by teams of specialists will become much more the rule.

### RESEARCH GENERALISTS

Another major part of the picture has to do with effective administration to see that the new research power is hooked up to decision making. This is a vital matter which demands full-time attention. One way of providing for it is through expanded use of people who may be referred to as "research general-

ists." This is a relatively new occupational role which is rapidly gaining favor. It is an exacting one, and those who can fill it will find themselves in great demand at increasingly attractive salaries.

The responsibility of the research generalist should include such things as the following:

1. *Establishing a mutually satisfactory working relationship with the marketing manager, one characterized by friendliness, trust, and easy two-way communication*—If the researcher is regarded as an enemy, he will have no chance to be effective. The first order of business, then, is that of gaining personal acceptance. This is much more a matter of understanding the other person's feelings and of skill in interpersonal dealings than it is of technical research ability.

2. *Acquiring a thorough understanding of marketing problems and how the marketing executive thinks about them*—The executive makes decisions based on assumptions which stem from the view or "model" of the market place he carries in his mind. This model is a market simplification of reality, as it must be so that limited human faculties can deal with something which is highly complex. Yet the model needs to be reasonably accurate.

The executive does not consciously think in terms of an over-all model, nor is he aware of many of his operating assumptions. Over a period of time, the research generalist can piece together the model, the main features of which will be implicit in the executive's words and actions. The researcher then will be in a position to lead the executive to think more systematically and to distinguish between "knowns" and "unknowns."

3. *Suggesting and planning a research program which will help the*

*executive check his operating assumptions, make his model more complete, and keep it up to date with the constantly changing environment.*

4. *Making sure that the most appropriate technical specialists are called into action at the right time*—In order to do this, the research generalist must have a good background in a growing number of fields—particularly in the behavioral and the quantitative areas. While he need not be a specialist in any of these areas himself, he must know their main concepts and methods so that he can exercise his responsibility for their timely use and explain them and their contribution. Although the emphasis here is on administrative skill, the technical requirements also are high since the research generalist is responsible for research programs. And here we must be prepared for the fact that the technical requirements will increase as business people become more sophisticated in the use of research.

5. *Serving as middleman between the research technicians and the marketing manager during the conduct of the research*—He should make sure there is a common understanding of the problem and of what can be expected from the research. He should keep the marketing executive informed as work proceeds to avoid both misunderstandings and the often fatal mistake of suddenly coming up with a final report which is completely strange and bewildering to the executive.

6. *Helping the marketing manager understand the research, its strengths, and its limitations*—He should participate in discussions of the findings and their implications. Going from a research report which should represent an improved understanding of a situation to an improved program of action is a challenging creative process.

The research generalist can help the executive to provide for the steps that the process entails. He should make whatever recommendations he feels are warranted on the basis of the research, but he must remember that his function is that of helping the executive—not that of usurping the decision-making role. It is the marketing executive who must make the decision and who will get most of the glory or blame for the final outcome.

This means that the research generalist is not likely ever to receive full credit for his contribution. Therefore, he must be able to realize sufficient satisfaction out of facilitating a process designed to help someone else develop.

In summary, the research generalist acts as a friend and serves as a problem definer, an educator, a liaison man, a communicator, and a counselor. This is a large order, but it is an order demanding to be filled.

ADMINISTRATIVE DIRECTION

Most of what has been said about the research generalist can be applied to the marketing researcher or intelligence director of the future. This man must establish effective working relationships with top management and with the research generalists and technicians who work as members of his staff. He must direct, coordinate, and control the marketing intelligence effort and, at the same time, keep up with the growing number of new developments in related fields. In short, he must be a skillful administrator at a high level.

Improvements in the formal organizational placement of research can be expected in order to facilitate the integration of research with the functions of innovation, planning, and operations. While we tend to think in terms of one central research department, this setup may not turn out to be well suited to the informational systems of the future. Whatever the arrangement, a greater use of closely knit teams is probable—a team including a line manager, a planner, and a researcher.

## CONCLUSION

The development and implementation of a high-quality intelligence system is a top-management responsibility of prime importance. The signs are clear that we are entering a new era in research and information which will mean improved performance and competitive advantage for the firms that gear up for it. Now is the time, then, for top management to initiate a thorough review of the decision-making machinery of the marketing organization—including the process involved, the inputs needed, the provisions for generating the inputs, and the capacities of personnel to meet future requirements. Such information is basic to determining specifically what a company should do now to prepare itself for a future in which much heavier emphasis will be placed on research and planning.

Important advances in several fields have provided resources of high potential value to marketing management. Unfortunately, however, they have caught business unprepared for their use. As a result, there exists an urgent need for greater understanding of how to incorporate a variety of new concepts, skills, and methods in the marketing research effort, and of how, in turn, to integrate research into the decision-making process.

Solving the problems that are involved in meeting this need will require major efforts on several fronts. However, these efforts are fully warranted. At stake is our ability to realize the benefits of the interdisciplinary movement in a technological age.

## QUESTIONS

1. Whatever its origin, marketing research inevitably faces a struggle to gain acceptance within the company. Why is this so?
2. Specialists from what other disciplines can help to do marketing research?
3. Research means quite different things to different people. Explain.
4. Should the marketing research department take the initiative and look for management problems that need study, or should they wait for problems to come in?
5. Do you think that marketing research will be outmoded by the new skills and techniques developed by behavioral sciences, statistics, and mathematics?

# 22. How Can the Research Department Adapt to New Demands for Information?*

Wendell R. Smith, President, Marketing Science Institute

*Marketing departments will continue to adapt to the new demands for information by upgrading and diversifying their talent, becoming more closely identified with future planning, and integrating their operations with the decision-making process.*

I certainly support what appears to be the major hypothesis to be explored by this session, namely, that the demand for the kinds of information that can be developed by marketing research is changing both from a qualitative and from a quantitative point of view. The reason for the quantitative expansion of demand is quite obvious: it flows logically from the rather widespread trend toward acceptance and installation of the marketing management concept which places a premium upon effective marketing planning. More fundamental than the quantitative change, however, is the expansion and the change in the nature of informational requirements. This has important implications with reference to the organization of the marketing research function and its positioning within the company or the operating division.

If we accept the rather simple concept that the function of marketing research within the firm is that of providing the informational and analytical inputs necessary for: (1) effective planning of future marketing activity, (2) effective control of marketing operations in the present, and (3) effective evaluation of marketing results; the change can be identified quite simply as terms of an across-the-board quantity increase in demand associated with a requirement for both increased quantity and vastly improved quality in the inputs required for successful conduct of the planning operation. As a matter of fact, in some companies the conventional marketing research associated with control of current operations is being assigned to separate groups (Sales Analysis, Market Statistics, etc.), some of which are administered by the Director of Marketing Research, and some of which are becoming identified with the Controller's office.

More and more, it seems to me, the image of marketing research is becoming the image of a function that can introduce rationality and reduce the risks associated with the forward planning that has become so essential as the price of success in today's complex and ever-changing market situation. This is in sharp contrast to the image of the green eye shade and the compiling of voluminous data presented as a "service to management."

What, then, are the changes that must occur, or are occurring, in connection

* Reprinted from *Marketing: A Maturing Discipline,* Proceedings of the Winter Conference of the American Marketing Association, December 28–30, 1960, p. 345. Edited by Martin L. Bell.

with the orientation of marketing research towards its changing responsibility?

1. Recognizing the age-old truism that you "start from where you are," marketing research must tool up to furnish on a continuing basis a more detailed and more meaningful profile of the company's market position at the beginning of the period for which plans are being developed—position with reference to market saturation, market share, within the market segments and with reference to many other factors. These inputs are the foundation upon which effective marketing plans can be built.

2. By clarifying the picture of the expected future behavior of the economy, the industry, key competitors, and consumers or users; marketing research must be responsible for the availability of the forecasts and the projections on the basis of which realistic goals and feasible objectives to be achieved by the marketing program can be determined. In connection with this responsibility we must enlist the aid of the behavioral scientists, the financial analysts, and all others who can contribute to the precision and to the durability of such forecasts.

3. Once goals and objectives have been defined, marketing research must supply and analyze the information necessary for the construction of the bridge that links present position with the future goal—the bridge that we call marketing strategy—the strategy that describes in broad brush and in quite general terms the means by which we expect to get from where we are to where we want to be.

4. Marketing research must also furnish the inputs of data and analysis required for the development of the nuts and bolts of the marketing plan by spelling out the portion of the marketing task that can be achieved by advertising and promotion, by personal selling, and by the other marketing tools at our disposal.

Obviously, successful accomplishment of these activities will necessitate some changes in the organization and the capabilities of the marketing research department. Some of the more obvious of these changes are:

1. Bringing those who are responsible for the planning and administration of marketing research activities into intimate contact with the decision-making process. Increasingly, I think, the administrative head of marketing research for the operating unit will become an active participant in decision making by becoming the vehicle through which the increasingly complex and technical work done in marketing research can be communicated and applied to the development of marketing plans and programs. Marion Harper of McCann-Erickson called attention to this need in very dramatic fashion in this year's Parlin lecture delivered to the Philadelphia Chapter. Not only does the decision-making conference table require the presence of the marketing research administrator as a communicator of research findings to management, he must have sufficient involvement in decision making to become able to carry back to his department the specifications of that research program which will be most productive. Communication? Yes—two-way communication.

2. The increasing requirement that marketing research have a level of involvement in planning and decision making has important implications with reference to the organization of the function. It means that marketing research, generally speaking, must be centralized or decentralized to the degree that market-

ing management and general management are centralized or decentralized. To the extent, of course, that this proximity to decision making may impair effectiveness by imposing unrealistic limitations upon the size of a particular research operation, compromises will have to be made.

3. I think it also follows that marketing research departments within the firm, both at the divisional and corporate levels, will tend to become somewhat more dependent upon outside services for performing discrete portions of the total marketing research task. The volume of marketing research currently being carried on within our economy has given rise to the development of a wide range of outside services that have economies of scale and are causing the research director's "make or buy" decision to be made somewhat differently than has been true in the past.

4. Finally, to the extent that marketing research within the firm can respond to the invitation to shift its major impact from current operations to the planning of future operations, its activities should become somewhat less hectic and more capable of being planned or programmed. I am not naive enough to believe that any research department will completely escape the "fire department" end of operations that take so much of the time and energy of all of us. Any change in this direction, however, will I am sure be welcomed.

In summary, it is my belief that departments of marketing research will continue to adapt to new demands for information by:

1. upgrading and diversifying the capabilities represented within the department,

2. becoming more closely identified with future planning,
3. integrating their operations with the decision-making process,
4. accepting the invitation to join the executive family by evidencing a willingness to carry their end product beyond fact finding and bringing it to bear as an integral part of planning and decision making.

Business history provides many analogies to the situation under discussion. The engineer, for example, became an executive when he became associated with *research and development* instead of, or in addition to, factory operations. The accountant became an executive by changing his name and recognizing the need for the Controller's function. Marketing research can do likewise by making sure that the information developed is applied and presented within a framework of pertinence.

## QUESTIONS

1. If one of the functions of marketing research is that of providing the informational and analytical inputs necessary for effective control of marketing operations, will it replace the accounting department?
2. What role can marketing research play in the planning of future operations?
3. To what extent can the marketing research department adapt to new demands for information by farming out research tasks to outside services?
4. How can the marketing research department integrate its operations with the decision-making process?

# 23. The Probative Value of Motivation Research*

Morris J. Gottlieb, Arthur D. Little, Inc.

*Important advances in marketing will come from learning how to apply consumer motivational research results usefully to management decisions. This research should provide a basis for justifying the actions suggested. Such actions tested via control panels have probative value.*

Certainly much progress has been made during the past decade in understanding consumer motivations, and one can look forward to even more progress in this direction in the sixties. However, I feel that the important advances in marketing will be not so much in learning more about consumer motivations as in learning how to apply this kind of knowledge usefully to marketing management decisions.

To accomplish this we shall have to do more thinking about how management decisions are made and even more about how they should be made. The essential steps in the decision process are: (1) Bringing up for consideration all the relevant alternatives, (2) selecting the best alternative, and (3) evaluating the decision.

Motivation research has made important contributions towards the first of these questions. Certainly marketers have become more sophisticated about consumers and their behavior and this knowledge has increased the range of products and marketing strategies. However, often the recommendations stemming from motivation research are plausible rather than probative. Motivation research is

* Reprinted from *Effective Marketing Coordination*, Proceedings of the Forty-fourth National Conference of the American Marketing Association, June 19–21, 1961, p. 571. Edited by George L. Baker.

likely to suggest actions management would not have thought of otherwise; it is less likely to give management information that provides a basis for justifying such action to a reasonably skeptical Board of Directors.

I think I can communicate most successfully by using a fictitious example. The National Sassafras Council is disturbed by continuing low consumption of sassafras tea. It is considering such alternatives as investing in a program of product research and development to find new uses for sassafras, allocating a budget to lobby in Washington for high import duties on leaf tea and coffee in order to improve the competitive situation, or investing in a program of advertising and promotion to stimulate consumer demand. For the moment let's assume that the decision is to advertise.

In order to develop the most effective advertising theme the Sassafras Council engages an outstanding motivation research organization to study consumers' feelings and attitudes towards beverages and specifically towards sassafras tea. The research company conducts a study using group and depth interviewing, projective techniques, mathematical analyses including factor analysis and multiple regression. The relevant conclusions of the study are: On the negative side: Sassafras

169

tea has the image of being old-fashioned and feminine rather than masculine. People think of it as being rather medicinal. It is not considered as stimulating as coffee or as invigorating as leaf tea. Incidentally, the cultural anthropologist on the research team has suggested that the upper-lower, lower-middle, and middle-middle social classes, which offer the greatest potential market for sassafras tea —because there are more of them—are alienated from the product because they associate it with the upper-upper classes. On the positive side: Sassafras tea is thought of as wholesome and mild. It doesn't have any of the negative health aspects of coffee and tea nor is it as filling as milk or other food drinks. There's a suggestion that it may have snob appeal to the upward mobile. Finally, it is associated with American tradition and the home. In the ambivalent area: Sassafras tea is associated with childhood. On the one hand it carries connotations of guilt, parental chastisement and restrictions. On the other hand, memories of uninhibited fun and freedom from responsibility.

On the basis of these findings, the creative department of the advertising agency develops a campaign of full page life ads based on the theme—Enjoy the Innocent Pleasure of Sassafras Tea. The picture shows a wholesome American family featuring a very rugged masculine father complete with tattoo. The group is engaged in or relaxing from a very vigorous but status-y activity. In the background is a 1960 Thunderbird. The original version had a Rolls-Royce, but the cultural anthropologist suggested that this was too upward mobile for the upper-lower group.

What's wrong with this picture? Well, to start with, nothing was said about how well people like sassafras tea. We only discussed their image of the product. True, the problem was stated in such a way as to rule this out of discussion. Let me suggest that ignoring consumer reactions to the specific product is an easy trap to fall into. To illustrate the seriousness of this trap I'll quote a real case— that of the Edsel. That's fair game for everyone; and since I had nothing to do with the research planning of the Edsel, I am free to discuss it without revealing the confidence of a present or past client.

Considerable research was done by Edsel's marketing research department on the images of American cars and on studying what kind of an image should be projected for the Edsel. Incidentally, it turns out that his research played little or no role in any of the basic decisions about the Edsel, but that's another story and one you can read about in a series of two excellent articles on the Edsel that appeared in the NEW YORKER about a year ago. Now, until a few months ago I had understood that prior to the actual introduction of the Edsel no research at all had been conducted on consumer reactions to its design. Well, it turns out that this is almost true, but not quite. In June, 1957, three months before the Edsel introduction, a survey was conducted by Columbia's Bureau of Applied Social Research. In this survey people were shown sketches of the front and rear end of the Edsel. According to Dr. Lazarsfeld, the findings were definitely negative. One can certainly question the probative value of any research that recommends developing a certain image for a product that just won't support this image. It's hard to develop much enthusiasm for a doctor who's doing cosmetic surgery on a patient with a dangerously inflamed appendix, no matter how pretty the patient looks with a new nose.

Now, back to the motivational study of sassafras tea. People who have quarreled with this kind of approach have questioned matters that are really irrelevant to the kinds of decisions marketers have to make. For example, they may question whether the conclusions are based on a probability sample, whether one can state within given limits of error how many Americans view sassafras tea as being old-fashioned. While often valid, this kind of criticism is not too pertinent. The soundness of the premise—that people view sassafras tea as old-fashioned—is relatively unimportant in view of the large inferential gap between the premise and the conclusion that one should invest $2,375,845.59 in a campaign to promote the idea that it is a modern, masculine, invigorating beverage. The kind of consideration one needs here is whether 2 million odd dollars spent in such a campaign will yield a better return than if spent in some other way.

In a sense it doesn't matter whether the campaign theme was developed by motivational research, by an electronic digital computer, or by a ouija board. The question is—how good, that is how productive is it? That's not strictly true, of course. A plan of action supported by knowledge of how people behave certainly deserves a greater claim than an arbitrary action. But, while the kind of research we've been talking about can do much to establish the credentials of a general plan of action and support its plausibility, one still needs the intermediate step of proving out the specific recommendations.

True, the proper design of such tests calls for considerable ingenuity and resourcefulness. True, the results are sometimes inconclusive. Nevertheless, it is my feeling that they can often be carried out more simply than one would have thought, and that, at worst, the mental discipline of devising a test is a good way of forcing oneself to think through the meaning and consequences of a proposed course of action. Let's see how we could measure the effectiveness of the proposed sassafras tea Life magazine promotion

without regard to restrictions of time and budget.

To start with I'd select two panels of households—a test panel and a control panel. According to the established rules of statistical witchcraft I should start out by selecting a set of families paired in some way—let's say each pair consists of two names, six names apart in the files of Life subscribers. For each pair I flip a coin—heads, the first name is assigned to the test group, the second to the control group; tails, the other way around.

I use the word panel to designate a group of subjects that I will subject to various stimuli and whose reaction I will observe either continuously or at several different points of time. The essential point of a panel is that I should be able to observe the change in behavior or attitudes produced by a stimulus. In its simplest form the test would consist of including the proposed advertising in the copies of Life going to the test panel and withholding it from the control panel. The return on the advertising campaign is computed by comparing the per cent sales increases for the test control panel. Here, it is essential to be suitably precise, to consider carefully questions on sample size and design. In this connection, there is a growingly important school of modern statisticians, the Bayesian school, who believe that the customary tests of statistical significance are nonsense. They feel that sample size should be determined by what action you would have taken without a sample—by your prior estimate of the probable return on the various alternatives. On the basis of these prior estimates they would determine how much they should be willing to pay for a sample size, or for eliminating the risk of bias from the study design. In other words, they try to answer the question how much should you be willing to pay for a true probability sample. It is my conviction that Bayesian statistics is

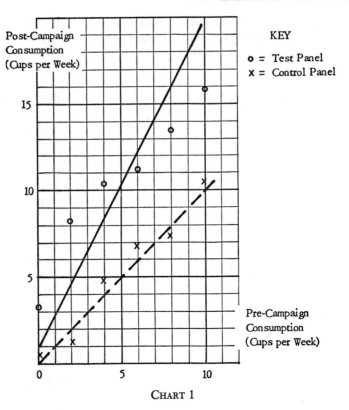

Post-Campaign
Consumption
(Cups per Week)

KEY

o = Test Panel
x = Control Panel

15

10

5

Pre-Campaign
Consumption
(Cups per Week)

0                 5                 10

CHART 1

more appropriate to business decision-making than the hypothesis testing approach currently favored by most statisticians.

If I may be permitted a digression in the form of a public confession, I'd like to say that the most dramatic failure of my professional life as a marketing researcher has been the inability to convince anyone except statisticians of the advantages of using the panel method involving repeated measures on the same subject in order to measure changes in behavior and attitudes. Come to think of it, the people who won't concede the desirability of using a panel approach always seem to be the ones who think you can't really measure advertising effectiveness. I wonder if there is any connection.

In Chart 1 each "x" represents a group

of control subjects. Each small circle a group of test subjects. The third "x" from the left stands for a group of control subjects whose average sassafras tea consumption before the campaign was 4 cups a week; after the campaign average consumption changed to about 4.2 cups a week. The third small circle represents a test group whose average consumption increased from 4 cups a week before the campaign to about 9.2 cups a week after the campaign. Notice that to make up this chart I need pre- and post-campaign data for the same individuals. True, it is less expensive to interview a different group before and after. I could do this and come up with a table like Table 1. But I'd be saving research money at the cost of information. First, in the obvious sense that the estimate of per cent in-

## TABLE 1
### Average Consumption
### (Cups per Week)

| | Test Panel | Control Panel |
|---|---|---|
| Post-Campaign | 10.5 | 7 |
| Pre-Campaign | 7 | 7 |
| Percent Increase | 50% | 0% |

crease in Table 1 has a higher standard error than that derived from Chart 1; the estimates are less reliable for the same sample size. Second, from Chart 1 you get more specific information. For example, you see that the campaign has produced a greater per cent increase among light drinkers than among heavy drinkers. Finally, by classifying subjects according to the amount of change it is possible to analyze out the effects of specific components of the promotion—you can get qualitative as well as quantitative information.

To make this kind of qualitative analysis I need to know more about the panel members. In addition to the level of sassafras tea usage for each subject, I want to know his specific beliefs about and attitude towards the product—his image of the product. Further, it might be useful to know the social class of each subject, his beverage consumption habits, his attitude towards life, whether he had a happy childhood, and so on. Just what I need to know depends on how much and what I want to learn from the analysis. How can the analysis answer such questions as: What aspects of the message were responsible for increasing sales—

the modernity, the masculinity, the class appeal?

Let me describe in rather schematic form how this is done. Please forgive the crudity of the presentation. All these things could be done in a more elegant, refined way. In the pre-campaign measurement, we had panel members express the extent of their agreement or disagreement with certain statements on a 7 point scale ranging from $-3$ for a disagree strongly through 0 for no opinion, to $+3$ for agree strongly. This was repeated in the post-campaign measure.

The statements are:

1. Sassafras tea is modern rather than old-fashioned
2. Sassafras tea is a masculine rather than a feminine drink
3. Sassafras tea is an appropriate drink for people in my social class

The results are summarized in Table 2. Additional information could be obtained by drawing up charts similar to Chart 1. However, the tables are sufficient to point out that the campaign did not successfully refute the belief that sassafras tea is old-fashioned. On the other hand, it did convince some people that

## TABLE 2

| Percent Agreeing with Statement | TEST GROUP | | | CONTROL GROUP | | |
|---|---|---|---|---|---|---|
| | After Campaign | Before Campaign | Diff. | After Campaign | Before Campaign | Diff. |
| 1 | 35% | 34% | 1% | 36% | 35% | 1% |
| 2 | 18% | 10% | 8% | 11% | 11% | 0% |
| 3 | 28% | 17% | 11% | 18% | 17% | 1% |

the product is masculine and that it is socially appropriate for them.

The next question is: Did the improved attitude of the masculinity of sassafras tea and its correct social position cause people to drink more tea? If we want to use the available evidence to answer this question Table 2 does not give us enough information. We need to know which people changed their beliefs about masculinity and social appropriateness in order to relate these changes to changes in usage. To this end we have examined charts 2 and 3. In this analysis we can ignore the control group. In Chart 2 the horizontal line is used to measure the change in the level of agreement with the statement sassafras tea is masculine. The first circle to the left represents a group whose opinion was unchanged by the campaign. The circle on the extreme right represents the groups that swung over from disagreeing very strongly to agreeing with it very strongly. Let me stress that we are concerned here with changes in agreement level rather than with any absolute measures. The vertical axis measures changes in consumption levels. The group whose agreement level did not change at all—represented by the first circle on the left—increased their consumption by .2 cups a week on the average. The group whose opinion changed radically, represented by the circle on the extreme right, increased their consumption by 1 cup per week.

Chart 2 tells us unequivocally that the masculinity of tea had no effect on the increased consumption. There was no more increased consumption among people who were convinced. On the other hand, Chart 3 leaves open the possibility that the correct social positioning of tea had an effect on increasing sales. On the basis of this data one might equally well infer that greater acceptance of the product produces the belief that it is socially correct. To settle the question of the direction of causality definitely it is necessary to expand the experiment by including a panel receiving advertising without a social class angle. The difference in increased consumption between this panel and the social class panel measures the effect of the social class message.

This kind of research has probative value. It provides a basis for calculating the sales and profit return associated with a specific course of action. Furthermore, it enables you to learn something from experience by analyzing out the effect of the various components of the action. It has been my experience that you always learn more from an analysis of this kind than you started to learn. As soon as you start looking analytically at some aspect of the communication process—no matter how limited—serendipity starts working for you.

I don't want to minimize the difficulties involved in this approach. Many of the obvious difficulties can be overcome by minor modifications. I'd like to quote a philosophical friend of mine: "People generally worry about the wrong things."

The important difficulties in measuring advertising are not the ones people generally bring up. Overcoming them is one of the exciting opportunities in the modern analytical approach to business problems. The key methods here involve not going more deeply into consumers' motivations but making the right kind of simplifying assumptions about their aggregate behavior.

The moral of this is that successful marketing demands all the imagination and insight that can be brought to bear on understanding consumer motivations. However, without probative research, management is at the mercy of the most plausible suggestion. Furthermore, what's even sadder, there's no way out because without probative research you can't learn from experience or what's worse, you may learn the wrong things.

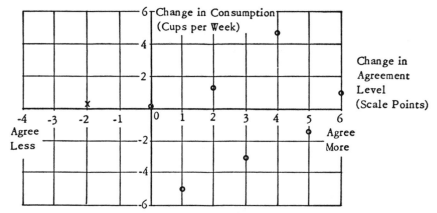

CHART 2. Change in Consumption Related to Change in Belief
About Masculinity of Product

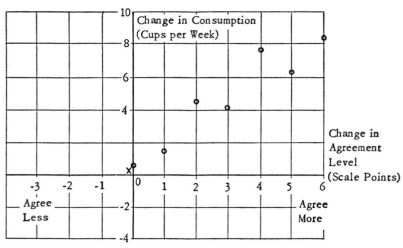

CHART 3. Change in Consumption Related to Change in Belief
About Social Appropriateness of Product

## QUESTIONS

1. Aside from the commonly assumed unconscious level, within every person there is also a *conscious* level which is a closely guarded private world. It is our private world of secrets, hopes, fears, and dreams. Comment.

2. What techniques can motivation research use to bring out some of these *conscious* but private thoughts?

3. How can we scientifically determine whether the feelings and attitudes uncovered by motivation research really motivate consumer behavior in the market place?

4. We need not go more deeply into consumers' motivation but should instead make the right kind of simplifying assumptions about their aggregate behavior. Comment.

# 24. Statistical Decision Theory in the Realm of Marketing Management*

Frank J. Charvat, School of Business Administration, Emory University

*Of all the mathematical models available to the marketer, statistical decision theory appears to have the widest applicability. This general purpose tool is used in the important case of decision making under uncertainty; and few functional areas of business operate in a more uncertain climate than marketing.*

## QUANTITATIVE METHODS

Accounting and classical statistics are analytical tools that marketing managers have used for years. These quantitative techniques have been taught in the normal business school program. Recently, a third tool variously labeled quantitative methods has been introduced. This new mathematical methodology, not more quantitative than accounting or statistics, is revamping business courses and curriculum. While this entire area is nebulous, quantitative methods basically are techniques that attempt to stimulate a business problem with a normative type of model and try to use actual or simulated data to see if the model does what it is supposed to do.

By definition a model is a representation of reality that attempts to explain the behavior of some aspect of it. There are many classifications and types of models—qualitative, quantitative, stochastic, problem solving, and optimal value models to name but a few. Some models are based on simple relationships. For example, assume that a firm has a linear relationship between price ($y$) and unit sales ($x$). This relationship can be expressed by the equation for a straight line:

$$y \text{ (price)} = mx \text{ (unit sales)} + b$$

The term $m$ (slope) and $b$ (vertical intercept) are the parameters. Once the parameters are known, the sales at each price can be established. Assume that sales of the product being sold will have a quantity zero at a price of $10. Then the term $b$ (vertical intercept) can be calculated by substitution in the equation and is found to be 10. Next the slope $m$ can be calculated by assuming values of $X$ and $Y$ and by substituting in the equation it is found to be $-1$. Under the given assumptions, this simple mathematical expression enables the firm to establish its demand curve. On the other end of the scale, the equation developed by Alfred A. Kuehn for consumer behavior in the purchase of frozen orange juice is:[1]

---

* A paper presented at the Thirty-first Annual Conference, Southern Economic Association, Memphis, Tennessee, November 10, 1961.

[1] Bass, Buzzell, Greene, Iazer, Pessemier, Shawver, Shuchman, Theodore, Wilson, *Mathematical Models and Methods in Marketing* (Homewood, Ill.: Irwin 1961), p. 334.

$$C_{i,T} = C_{c,T} \left[ \frac{\sqrt{m_i I_o b_{pda} (k - \bar{r}L + T^e) (p^k)^L k^{T-1}}}{C_{c,T}(1 - pr_i e) E_R (PD)_R} - \frac{1}{E_R (PD)_R} \right]$$

The development of the Kuehn model required (1) the solution of many complex difference equations, (2) the use of a computer, and (3) the past history data on consumer purchases of orange juice from the Market Research Corporation of America. This special purpose model is an example of one of the advanced techniques in quantitative methods open to marketing management.

## ELEMENTS OF THE STATISTICAL DECISION THEORY MODEL

Of all the models available to the marketer in this broad spectrum of quantitative methods, statistical decision theory appears to have the widest applicability. This general purpose tool is used in the important case of decision making under uncertainty; and few functional areas of business operate in a more uncertain climate than marketing.

Basic elements of this model are uncertainty, prior probabilities, payoffs, acts or strategies, events or states of nature, sampling decisions, and posterior probabilities. The decision maker is confronted with the use of alternative acts or strategies. He organizes his thinking about these courses of action in relation to uncertain states of nature or events that confront him. The prior probabilities, about these events occurring must be assessed; this can be based on a wide assortment of data ranging from extensive statistical evidence to pure judgment or guessing. The expected results of the acts and the events with their probability of occurrence are arranged in a payoff table or matrix for comparison purposes.

The decision maker selects the course of action deemed best according to the objectives established. If needed, additional data can be gathered through sampling, and the prior probabilities adjusted by the current data to form posterior probabilities. These new posterior probabilities are used to evaluate the former descision in the light of the new data. The original decision may be substantiated or revoked.

Consider a supermarket chain that has set as its objective an increase in volume and profits. One strategy available is the use of trading stamps. Management may have a diffuse prior probability as to the success of this device in attaining the desired increase in sales. The firm may rely upon data from various secondary sources including the stamp seller as to the chances of success. The states of nature or events are the possible increases in sales that may result which are dependent primarily upon consumers' and competitors' actions; both of these are out of the control of the decision maker. Management will have to assess the probability of different sales increases based on this diffuse information and calculate the expected profits as a result of its action. Assume the tentative decision is to adopt trading stamps pending the findings from an experimentally designed test market in which twenty randomly selected stores of the chain try the stamps. The additional findings from the sample can be used to calculate new probabilities called posterior probabilities as to the expected gain in sales. The revised expected profit from the use of stamps then can be calculated and the former decision modified as need be.

## ADAPTABILITY OF DECISION THEORY TO MARKETING MANAGEMENT

This new quantitative tool offers to the marketer a vast number of areas of application for its use. Basically, the marketing manager has a retinue of acts or strategies available that can be used to sell the product line. These variable factors generally referred to as the components of the "marketing mix" can be classified within the broad areas of merchandising, pricing, distribution, personal selling, advertising, and sales promotion. These are the variables—acts or strategies—that the marketing executive has at his command with which to perform the selling function.

However, marketing management generally is uncertain as to the success of attaining its objectives through the use of these variable factors, either individually or collectively. It faces a multitude of uncertain states of nature, both external to the company and internal in the firm, over which it has little or no control. The external factors that make for uncertainty can be classified within the broad areas of (1) competition, (2) business conditions, (3) consumer attitudes, (4) government, and (5) circumstances of nature. For example, if management acts to cut price in order to increase sales, what action will competitors take? Should management increase the size of its advertising budget when it is uncertain as to the amount of personal disposable income available? If trading stamps are adopted as a promotional tool, what will be the reaction of current customers of the store to this device? If a questionable advertising allowance is granted to meet competition, what action if any will be taken by the Federal Trade Commission? If a Christmas promotion is planned, will extraordinary weather conditions prevail to keep customers away?

Internally in the firm, marketing management must cope with the broad functional divisions in the business over which it has little or no control in the short run, such as production, research, financing, personnel, and administrative structure. Examples of conflict in these areas with resulting uncertainty are apparent. A sale may hinge on a certain delivery date; and yet the delivery rests in the hands of the production department. The marketing executive may desire large inventories to be carried for a special promotion; yet, the financial executive who is overdrawn at the bank may deem this an undue financial burden. The marketing executive may quote a special price to a particular customer; and yet, he has no control over the cost of production.

The statistical decision theory model offers the marketing executive a framework in which to organize his thinking. The tool can be used in selecting the best course of action for both simple as well as complex problems. It can be used in the example as to whether or not to use trading stamps; and it can also be used to select the best course of action in regard to the selection of overall promotional strategy, namely whether to use price, trading stamps, advertising, or the use of private brands to obtain the largest overall volume gain. The more accurately the states of nature or events can be forecast or predicted, the greater will be the degree of success that the acts of strategy employed by the decision-maker will operate to attain the objectives of the firm.

## EXAMPLE OF STATISTICAL DECISION THEORY

The following example is presented for the student who is interested in a more detailed approach to this type of analysis.

The problem was selected for simplicity in understanding the methodology and not for content.[2] Only basic concepts of Baysian statistics are given; the student is referred to detailed texts in this field.[3]

### THE PROBLEM

Assume a firm that operates a Coca-Cola vending business faces a problem in conjunction with machine servicing. Coca-Cola sells for ten cents a unit, and approximately 1,000 units are sold per week from each machine. An attendant services each machine every week. Assume each machine as a result of abuse makes conditionally independent errors in favor of the customer. The machines are not identifiable. If the machine is operating in its best condition for the week, only one coke for every 100 dispensed is given away free. But, if the machine is not in its best condition, it could give away five cokes per 100 dispensed; or in its worst service, it could give away ten cokes per 100 dispensed. These three settings or machine conditions are the possible states of nature or events; and they have probabilities of .01, .05, and .10 respectively, of making mistakes in favor of the customer. In addition, assume that for the service man to place weekly each machine in its best condition at the .01 setting will cost $1. The payoff as to the cost of either action in this problem is shown in Table 1.

If the service man checks every machine it will cost the company $2 regardless of the condition of the machine. One dollar will be for the ten free cokes out of every 1,000 units dispensed, and the other dollar is for the service cost. How-

**TABLE 1**

**Payoff Matrix for a Coca-Cola Machine**

| Act | Event .01 | .05 | .10 |
|---|---|---|---|
| Check the Machine | $2 | $2 | $2 |
| Do not Check the Machine | $1 | $5 | $10 |

ever, if the service man does not check the machine and it is set at its best possible condition, the cost incurred will be only $1 or ten free cokes out of the 1,000 sold. If the machine has been kicked or shaken by an irate customer, the possibility of five free cokes per 100 could appear at a total weekly cost of $5. Or, if the worst possible condition is in force, the cost to the company would be $10.

Should management have the attendant put the machine into its best condition on every service call? To remove pure guessing from the decision, management can gather statistical evidence on the machines to determine the frequency at which each condition is found. These historical data are shown in Table 2. The .01 setting is found 75% of the time, the .05 condition is found 15% of the time, and the worst condition of .10 is found only 10% of the time.

**TABLE 2**

**History of Fraction Defectives for the Coca-Cola Machine**

| Events | Frequency |
|---|---|
| .01 | .75 |
| .05 | .15 |
| .10 | .10 |
| | 1.00 |

[2] This type of problem was suggested by Harry V. Roberts, Graduate School of Business, University of Chicago, in his unpublished syllabus. *Statistics for Management.*

[3] The most complete treatment of statistical decision theory is found in Robert Schlaifer, *Probability and Statistics for Business Decisions* (New York: McGraw-Hill, 1960).

Armed with this information, management can calculate the expected costs of either action.

Expected cost of checking
$$= .75 \times \$2 + .15 \times \$2 + .10 \times \$2$$
$$= \$2.00$$

Expected cost of not checking
$$= .75 \times \$1 + .15 \times \$5 + .10 \times \$10$$
$$= \$2.50$$

From these equations it is obvious that in the long run it will be advisable to service each machine mechanically at every call inasmuch as the expected cost to the firm will be $2 on the average whereas the cost of not servicing will be $2.50.

THE COST OF UNCERTAINTY

On the evidence to date the decision to check every machine upon its weekly service is apparently the best action. If management knew the setting of every machine at the time of the weekly service, the cost of action in the light of perfect information could be ascertained. For example, if the service man knew the machine was set in the .01 condition, it would be better not to check the machine. However, if the machine were on the .05 or the .10 setting, then it would be better to service it mechanically.

Expected cost of perfect information
$$= .75 \times \$1 + .15 \times \$2 + .10 \times \$2$$
$$= \$1.25$$

Simply the cost of servicing would be $1.25 if the attendant knew the setting of the machine beforehand. The difference between the cost of checking each machine and the cost of perfect information is known as the cost of uncertainty. In this case, it would be the difference between $2 and $1.25 or $.75.

ADDITIONAL DATA THROUGH SAMPLING

In the light of our prior knowledge, the best course of action is to check every machine. However, supposing management had additional information about the machine at the time it is to be serviced that might change the prior knowledge about the condition. These new data could be obtained as the result of sampling. Suppose the service man places ten coins in the machine in succession and finds that the device worked perfectly in all cases. If the probability is .01 that this is the setting of the machine, then the probability of a single perfect operation is $1 - .01 = .99$. The probability of two perfect operations in a row is $.99 \times .99 = .9801$. By extending this reasoning to the ten perfect operations, the likelihood of ten perfect operations if $p = .01$ is $99^{10} = .904$. By similar reasoning if the machine is set at .05, then the probability of one perfect operation of the changer is $1 - .05 = .95$. The probability of ten perfects in a row in a sample is $.95^{10} = .599$. Similarly, if the machine is set for $p = .10$ then the probability of one perfect operation is $1 - .10 = .90$. The probability of ten perfect operations is $.90^{10} = .387$. These data are recorded in Table 3 in the likelihood column.[4]

The prior probability knowledge was determined from past history of the machines as shown in Table 2. The probabilities calculated from the additional sample or likelihoods can be considered as two separate actions with a resulting joint probability shown in Table 3. The joint probability is obtained by multiplying each prior probability by the likelihood. The joint probabilities are then totaled and found to be .807. Since probabilities total to 1, the joint probabilities are adjusted by dividing each separate joint probability by the total and recorded in the table as the posterior probability. These posterior probabilities are now the result of our prior knowledge about the machine coupled with the results of the sample.

The expected costs of checking vs. not

[4] Likelihood or conditional probabilities for the various kinds of sample results can be calculated from the binomial tables. The technique involved is not shown here.

### TABLE 3
#### Calculation of Posterior Probabilities for the Coca-Cola Machine

| p | Prior Probability | Likelihood | Joint Probability | Posterior Probability |
|---|---|---|---|---|
| .01 | .75 | .904 | .678 | .840 |
| .05 | .15 | .599 | .090 | .112 |
| .10 | .10 | .387 | .039 | .048 |
| | 1.00 | | .807 | 1.000 |

checking with the revised probabilities are calculated in the following equations:

Expected cost of checking based on posterior probabilities = .840 × $2 + .112 × $2 + .048 × $2 = $2.00

Expected cost of not checking based on posterior probabilities = .84 × $1 + .112 × $5 + .048 × $10 = $1.88

The additional information gathered from the statistics of the sample has improved the probability that the machine is in the .01 condition from .75 to .84 as shown by the data in Table 3. As a result, the expected cost of not fixing the machine based on posterior probabilities is now $1.88 or below the expected cost of servicing the machine mechanically weekly. As a result of this additional information, the management now would not have the machine checked every time it is serviced if the attendant can get ten perfect operations. Management could set up a system of sampling in such a way that the service man could establish whether the machine should be serviced or not from a certain number of sample results.

## PREREQUISITES FOR QUANTITATIVE METHODS

The basic concepts of statistical decision theory were illustrated by the Coca-Cola example. This tool can have wide use in the solution of both simple and complex marketing problems. However, for the marketing student to master this type of model, a thorough knowledge of Baysian statistics must be attained as a minimum prerequisite. In fact, for the student to be able to use models generally and work with them pragmatically, the mathematics requirements in business schools will have to include a basic knowledge of matrix algebra and a working knowledge of differential calculus as well as a thorough understanding of Baysian statistics. And, for a complex specific purpose model to be designed, the builder should have (1) an excellent knowledge of mathematics through numerical analysis and difference equations, (2) a substantial amount of business data available, and (3) a computer or computer time to solve the equations.

Courses in the function areas of business will have to be revamped to include the use of these mathematical tools in the analysis of cases and problems. A revision of texts, cases, and curriculums is in order.

## QUESTIONS

1. What are the basic elements of the statistical decision theory model?
2. The statistical decision theory model offers the marketing executive a framework in which to organize his thinking. Explain.
3. What is meant by the term, the cost of uncertainty?
4. To be able to work with models knowledgeably, with what types of mathematics must the student of business be familiar?

# $\mathcal{25}$. Mathematical Concepts for Marketing: Linear Programming*

Robert W. Rosen, Professor in School of Business Administration, University of South Carolina

*Linear Programming is a mathematical technique designed to identify the best way from among many possible alternatives of optimizing some objective. But marketing problems seem to be oversupplied with uncertainties, irregularities, nonlinearity, and plural objectives. Consequently, linear programming, and other similar mathematical devices, can offer only limited assistance to the solution of marketing problems.*

## WHAT IS LINEAR PROGRAMMING?

At the most fundamental level, it is a device for selecting the optimum program or line of action from out of many alternatives. Viewed still differently, it is a technique for allocating scarce resources among interdependent or competitive ends according to some criterion to be maximized.

What kinds of allocations, or rationing problems, are found in industry and hence offer opportunities for applying linear programming (LP) techniques? The entire realm of budgeting involves such problems as, for example, the marketing manager's need to decide how much of his available money to allocate among direct selling, advertising, direct mail, and other selling devices. Within the distribution sector one might face such problems as determining the most profitable sales mix which can be obtained from existing production facilities; or determining which factories should supply each warehouse in order to minimize the over-all cost of transporation between factories and warehouses. In the area of sales management, there is always the problem of determining the best allocation of each salesman's time among various customers, including the frequency of calls and the sequence for calling on different prospects.

## WHAT KINDS OF PROBLEMS DOES IT SOLVE?

In short, LP problems usually contain an objective to be maximized, such as profits or sales; scarce resources, such as money or time; alternative ways of dividing these resources among competitive ends; and interaction among the various activities. One may conclude, therefore, that LP can be applied to a wide range of business problems.

The mounting interest in LP techniques stems from its ability to surmount the limitations of more traditional methods, such as common sense, simultaneous equations, and differential calculus. Hence, comparisons with these three de-

* Reprinted from the *Atlanta Economic Review*, July 1961. Published by the Bureau of Business and Economic Research, School of Business Administration, Georgia State College.

vices may help to explain the increasing interest and contribution of newer techniques like linear programming.

From a practical standpoint, common sense methods are limited to small and fairly easy business problems. Even in these cases, however, there is no systematic way of determining whether the solution derived is optimum, and in many cases it is not. Conceptually, common-sense methods often fail because variables which are interrelated are treated in isolation from each other. Such procedures are often impossible and typically inexact. Economists have long recognized the interactions among economic variables and, consequently, the necessity for simultaneous methods, such as those embodied in the Law of Comparative Advantage and Walras' studies of general equilibrium. Thus, LP differs from common sense in at least four major respects. First, LP problems can be programmed on data computers so that solutions can be obtained for larger and more complex problems. Second, LP employs calculating techniques which automatically identify the optimum solution. Third, LP takes explicit account of the interrelationships among relevant variables by using simultaneous equations to arrive at the final solution. Fourth, LP techniques are oriented toward optimizing the system as a whole without regard for the welfare of any one or more parts of the problem. Indeed, LP proceeds on the uncommon assumption that optimum solutions can be achieved only if one or more parts of the problem are deliberately disadvantaged. When it is possible to optimize each activity in a system, then no LP problem exists. Such conditions are extremely rare, however, as would be the case where the most efficient machine has enough capacity to satisfy all sales requirements.

Traditional simultaneous equation methods also have limited applicability to business problems because negative numbers may appear in the solution. Such solutions might specify negative sales for a particular market region, or that the sales mix include a negative amount of a particular product. Obviously, solutions of this kind are neither practical or optimum. Traditional simultaneous equation methods are also incapable of coping with restrictions. For example, instructions from the marketing department placing a minimum or maximum range of shipments to a particular warehouse could not be incorporated into traditional simultaneous equation methods. Another characteristic of this method which is limited in applicability to business problems is that all committed resources must be employed and none may be left idle. Yet, the optimum solution to many business problems quite often leaves some resources idle. Another serious drawback is that business problems usually contain more unknowns than equations. As a result of these and other considerations, business problems frequently cannot be solved by traditional simultaneous equation methods.

Like simultaneous equations, differential calculus is not designed to cope with inequations and constraints. Moreover, where the data are linear and discontinuous, differential calculus is of limited usefulness. Thus, the three techniques discussed exhibit marked limitations when applied to business problems.

## WHAT UNIQUE ADVANTAGES DOES IT OFFER?

Linear programming employs four devices to overcome the limitations inherent in the three techniques just discussed. Specifically, those four devices or concepts are: inequalities; constraints; slack variables; and iterations.

"Inequalities" are statements that one

quantity need not equal some other quantity. For example, in a machine-loading problem, the statement "hours of work assigned to machine A may be equal to or less than the 200 hours available" is an inequality. Here, the hours of work assigned may be less than 200, thus permitting a degree of idleness, or slack, if that should be required for determining the optimum solution. Constraints are the right-hand side of inequations. In the example given, 200 hours is the constraint or restriction. Hence, the first function of inequalities is to permit some resources to remain idle if this condition is necessary to obtain an optimum, and to prevent solutions which require more resources than those available. The second function of constraints, or restrictions, is to allow management, rather than mathematics, to dictate certain requirements which must be met before a solution can be considered optimum. Thus, in designing a product to meet customers' preferences, management may specify certain requirements such as minimum or maximum boundaries of weight, length, cost, fragility, etc. In this way, the range of possible solutions is "restricted" or "constrained" to conform with the manager's specifications.

If the Simplex algorithm is to be used in calculating the optimum solution, then the inequalities referred to earlier must be converted into equations. This is done by introducing a fictitious activity, such as an imaginary product, called a "slack" variable. All resources not utilized in performing "real" activities are assigned to the "imaginary" or slack variable. Essentially, slack variables are only a mathematical device to facilitate computations requirements of the Simplex Method by converting inequalities into equations.

The last concept, "iteration," is the actual mechanics of calculating the optimum program. LP solutions are derived

by systematic trial and error, each successive trial coming closer to the final solution. Each such trial is called an "iteration." The iteration process is designed to obey all the restrictions and to prevent the appearance of negative numbers in the optimum solution. There are many iterative procedures ranging from the simplest, the index number method, to the most comprehensive, the Simplex Method. Normally, the iterative process itself indicates when the optimum solution has been derived.

Summarizing briefly, LP is a mathematical technique designed to identify the best way from among many possible alternatives of optimizing some objective. Thus, LP is a device for rationing or allocating scarce resources in the most efficient or profitable manner. Perhaps the most distinguishing feature and advantage of LP is its ability to cope with restrictions.

The discussion up to this point has illustrated some of the many contributions which LP has made to improve the decision making process. Like other techniques, however, LP is also subject to certain limitations.

## WHAT ARE ITS LIMITATIONS?

The first and most prominent limitation of LP is the requirement of linearity among the variables entering into the problem. Unless this linear relationship exists, then LP is either inapplicable or inexact. Two questions then are in order. First, what is a linear relationship? Second, to what extent are business variables related in a linear manner? Essentially, linear relationships are proportional relationships. If it takes $1 of advertising to create $10 worth of sales, then it would take $5 to create $50 worth of sales. Stated differently, marginal productivity remains constant at all levels of activity. To take one more illustration, if 100 units can be sold at a profit of $8 per unit, then 1000 units can also be sold at a profit of $8 per unit.

Both theoretical and empirical considerations suggest that business variables are not typically related in a linear manner. One would not expect marginal variable costs to remain constant at all levels of production, that profit margins would remain the same regardless of the volume sold, or that each added dosage of advertising would yield an equivalent return of sales or profits. Such considerations would seem to place a sharp limit on the applicability of linear programming to the solution of business problems. Before leaving the grave-site, however, prudence dictates that we examine LP's defense against these mortal charges.

A dedicated linear programmer is aware of and admits this defect—but not without a stout defense. His counterargument consists of two worthwhile points. First, a valid application of LP requires only that linearity occur in the range of normal solution, not along the entire range of relationships; and there is evidence to substantiate the existence of this point. For example, many researchers seem to find near constant marginal costs over a wide range of experienced output levels. Similarly, it is not inconceivable at all that some input-output relationships may remain fairly uniform at different levels of activity. In short, the LP'er may grant the rarity of perfect linearity but hold to the position that many situations approximate linearity closely enough to justify the assumption of strict linearity. This impasse is resolved, typically, by agreeing to the usefulness of LP—provided approximate answers are acceptable. And a reasonably approximate answer is acceptable, if not welcomed with joy, in many cases. Fur-

ther rapport is established by adding the caution that the linear programmer must not assume "reasonable" linearity without prior investigation.

Unfortunately, the rose of rapport comes equipped with thorns. Specifically, there seems to be no way to measure the schedule of errors introduced into the final solution by varying degrees of departure from linearity. Thus, the amount of confidence which can be placed in the final solution cannot be expressed quantitatively. Similarly, restricting the requirement of linearity to the "neighborhood" of the solution raises added difficulties. How does one identify the reaches of this "neighborhood" before solving the problem? As a partial assuagement of these doubts, the linear programmer closes his argument by suggesting that, however approximate the solutions might be, they are still more valid than any other practicable device available. Moreover, the LP'er notes that some progress has already been made towards adapting LP to problems containing nonlinear relationships.

Summarizing, because perfect linearity hardly ever exists, LP solutions are necessarily approximate. Unfortunately, there seems to be no way of estimating the amount of error introduced by varying degrees of departure from linearity. However, sight should not be lost of the real possibility that many of these approximate solutions may still represent considerable improvement over present practices.

A second factor limiting the applicability and usefulness of LP is its inability to cope simultaneously with plural managerial objectives. For example, LP could indicate the program which maximizes production, or profits, or utilization of facilities, or any other objective. But, LP cannot yield a solution where two or more of these objectives must be considered simultaneously. Viewed somewhat differently, the program which maximizes one objective is not the same program to maximize some other objective. This point is readily demonstrated. Using the same data and LP techniques, the optimum production schedules for two products, A and B, are as follows. The maximum profit program consists of all B units and no A units. Maximum production has the opposite program, no B's and all A's. Finally, maximum utilization falls about half way between the two previous solutions: about as many A's as B's. The ideal program might necessitate consideration of all three objectives. Linear programming, however, cannot generate such a program. Thus, two facts have been established. First, business problems typically involve consideration of several objectives; and, second, LP can optimize only one objective at a time. These considerations constitute another severe restriction on the use of LP. Two additional conclusions may be drawn from these findings. One, LP is only a suboptimizing device because of its inability to cope with all objectives pertinent to the problem. Secondly, and as a result, LP does not replace management. Only management can decide how much weight should be given to each objective in arriving at the final solution.

A dedicated LP'er might accept all or part of these charges—but, again, not without strenuous qualifications. As a starting point, he might agree that LP can optimize only one objective at a time and that business decisions typically involve several objectives. However, LP can show management the costs and returns associated with varying degrees of departure from some optimum program. For example, management might feel that the production program which minimizes cost would result in excessive labor turnover. LP could help management to resolve this impasse between conflicting objectives by indicating the cost increases associated with lesser degrees of labor turnover. Thus, although LP did not design the final solution, it did provide pertinent information about the costs and returns associated with alternative combinations of objectives. Here, better decisions would result because more of the vital facts were made known to management. Where more than two objectives are in conflict, which is the typical case, estimating the costs and returns from alternative combinations of objectives may be time-consuming and expensive, thus modifying LP's contribution in this area.

Conceivably, obstructions raised by conflicting objectives could be swept aside by weighing each of the different objectives. However, the difficulties here are not inconsiderable. How would one equate such diverse objectives as cost, labor turnover, speed of delivery, etc., when all might be relevant to a particular problem?

The last major limitation to be examined concerns the type of data which can be processed by LP methods. Since LP is a mathematical device, all factors pertinent to the problem must be expressible in quantitative and certain terms. Objectives, for example, must be stated unambiguously. "Profits must be increased" is not a properly stated objective for LP purposes. Rather, one must say, "Find the program which maximizes profits." Similarly, it is inadequate to state as a restriction that stockout must be kept to satisfactory levels. Rather, one must say, "stockout shall not exceed $10,000," or "one per cent," or some similar quantitative criterion. Although it may seem easy to quantify objectives or restrictions, such is really not the case. It is exceedingly difficult, for example, to estimate the true cost of stockout associated with various production or inventory schedules. Yet, if stockout, goodwill, morale, or any other factor is relevant to the problem, it must be expressed quantitatively. One can well imagine the misgivings any manager would have in trying to estimate these intangibles. Without such decisions, however, LP cannot deliver its full potential. Many managers seem to feel that quantitative estimates of the kinds just referred to are so fallible as to destroy the merits of any program based on such estimates. These considerations, in turn, have led some managers to reject LP. To this objection the LP'er has an effective counterargument. If it is necessary to include intangibles in the final analysis, wouldn't it be better to make such guesses explicit and thereby reap the benefits which LP offers? After all, if these elements are important, then the issues, however tenuous, cannot be side-stepped forever.

A more tangible limit on the type of data amenable to LP processing is the requirement of certainty. Certainty is the opposite of probability or stochastic systems. To illustrate: LP methods have not been applied very successfully to inventory problems because the stream of incoming demands tends to be irregular and uncertain. Efforts to solve this and similar problems have employed other decision making techniques like the Queue or Waiting Line Theory. Unfortunately, marketing problems seem to be oversupplied with uncertainties, irregularities, nonlinearity, and plural objectives. Consequently, the final conclusion seems to be that linear programming, and other similar mathematical devices, can offer only limited assistance to the solution of marketing problems.

## QUESTIONS

1. What is linear programming, and what unique advantages does it offer?
2. What are some of the principal limitations of linear programming in the solution of marketing problems?
3. To what types of marketing problems can linear programming give limited assistance?
4. Is linear programming and operations research the same thing?

# $26.$ Operations Research in Solving a Marketing Problem*

James S. Cross, Manager Statistical Research Department, Sun Oil Company

*An Operations Research task group was assembled at the Sun Oil Company to consider future product policies. Possible courses of action were: (1) To retain the policy of marketing only a single grade of gasoline. (2) To market a regular and a premium grade, similar to competition. (3) To market three grades of gasoline: regular, premium, and superpremium. (4) To continue the "Blue Sunoco" grade, but with an "octane concentrate" which could be custom blended at the pump to produce a wide range of fuels.*

*This article explains how the group provided management with the data necessary to make the decision.*

The Sun Oil Company is an integrated company, performing the functions of producing, refining, transporting, and marketing petroleum and its products. The marketing department serves consumer and industrial markets, both in this country and abroad, with a well-established sales organization.

When occasion demands, management forms task forces to undertake specific projects. These teams consist of company personnel who are able by virtue of their training and experience to contribute to the solution of the problem to be studied.

Several of the marketing problems handled by Operations Research teams fall into the classical Operations Research pattern. One of these problems was the question of where to locate a pipe-line terminal to supply ninety-one retail outlets in Michigan. A mathematical model was constructed to represent the distribution costs that would be incurred in supplying these service stations from any possible terminal location. The method used for determining distribution costs was that of measuring mileage, weighted by potential gallonage, from each retail outlet to each possible terminal location. A system of grid squares was superimposed over a map of the area studied.

The question then became: "Which terminal point would minimize distribution costs?" Using an electronic computer and employing a search technique, or area scanning, this point was established; and management was given the location of the theoretically optimum place to build the terminal.

A recent project arose out of the problem of customer delay at service stations. This research sought to determine the optimum number of service channels that should be provided in any given station. A service channel requires a car position,

* Reprinted from the *Journal of Marketing*, national quarterly publication of the American Marketing Association, Vol. 25, No. 3, January 1961, pp. 30–34.

a pump, and a serviceman. Thus, the number of channels limits the number of cars that can be simultaneously serviced.

The penalty for providing too many service positions is the loss involved in unused investment, or unearned wages. The penalty for providing too few service positions is the loss of sales due to the fact that customers are unwilling to be delayed. Since these costs are inverse to each other, the optimum solution should balance these factors to achieve the most profitable operation.

Empirical studies of service-station operations have clearly demonstrated that both automobile arrivals and the amount of time that it takes to service an automobile can be described by probability distributions. This justifies the application of queueing or waiting-line theory to a model of service-station operations. A model which is adaptable to Sun's service stations is now being constructed.

## THE CUSTOM BLENDING EXPERIMENT

The most ambitious Operations Research effort undertaken by Sun Oil Company was that which culminated in the adoption of a new gasoline marketing method—the Custom Blending System. As early as 1953, the executive committee had been concerned with the long-range question of whether Sun's traditional marketing policy for motor fuel could be maintained in the light of then current and possible future market developments. The traditional policy had been to supply one grade of motor fuel of a quality intermediate between regular and premium and selling at regular gasoline price. This single fuel, branded "Blue Sunoco," was designed to satisfy the antiknock requirements of 90 per cent of the cars on the road. The 10

per cent not satisfied was composed for the most part of the newer, higher-compression models.

Forecasts of future automobile engines indicated that the trend toward higher compression ratios would continue. In general, the higher the compression ratio of an automobile engine, the higher is its octane appetite. This trend, coupled with the fact that there would still be older cars on the road, pointed to a growing spread in octane requirements within the passenger car fleet. In 1953 there was a spread of about seventeen research octane numbers between the lowest and highest requirement cars. Today this range has increased to as high as twenty-five. It became obvious that to follow the single-grade policy would commit Sun to marketing a higher and higher octane fuel in order to continue to satisfy 90 per cent of the drivers on the road.

This policy appeared untenable for several reasons. First, the entire octane pool would have to be elevated. This would waste costly octane numbers on the bulk of the automotive fleet not requiring extraordinarily high quality. Second, the cost of raising octanes would become progressively more expensive as the octane number was increased. In addition, a considerable capital investment would be necessary to provide the refining facilities to manufacture the quality fuel required. From a manufacturing standpoint, it would be difficult to absorb the cost of added pool octanes within the competitive regular price structure. From a marketing point of view, the specter of raising the price above competition was even less attractive. Finally, motivational research suggested that Sun would have difficulty in selling to owners of new, luxury-model cars, even though the bulk of these cars could be satisfied with the single grade fuel.

An Operations Research task force,

composed of social and physical scientists, together with operating and administrative personnel, was appointed to consider the problem of what Sun's future marketing policy should be.

### POSSIBLE COURSES OF ACTION

Four possibilities were considered by the group: (1) To retain the present policy of marketing only a single grade of gasoline. (2) To market a regular and a premium grade, similar to competition. (3) To market three grades of gasoline: a regular, a premium, and a super premium. (4) To continue marketing the present "Blue Sunoco," but with an "octane concentrate" which could be custom blended at the pump to produce a wide range of fuels; this would permit the individual motorist to select the fuel best fitted to his car.

The concept of blending motor fuels at the pump, first proposed by the Chairman of the Board, was entirely new. Before this possibility could be considered as a realistic possibility, it was first necessary to determine whether a workable system could be devised. Accordingly, the attention of the Operations Research group was focused on the engineering aspects of the problem.

### TECHNICAL CONSIDERATIONS

The practicability of custom blending hinged on two technical questions: (1) Could an octane concentrate be produced in sufficient quantity and within a realistic cost framework? (2) Could a pump be developed that would effectively blend the two basic components?

The concentrate problem was handled by a subgroup composed of representatives of the Marketing and Research and Engineering Departments. Any proposed concentrate had to meet several stringent requirements. From a marketing point of view, the various qualities of fuel resulting from the blending process would have to satisfy the operating requirements of a wide range of present and future automobiles. The concentrate would have to possess properties, other than antiknock, which would be compatible with the base fuel so that any blend would be consistent in terms of such qualities as quick starting, fast warm-up, and good mileage. An additional requirement was to produce a concentrate commercially without incurring prohibitive costs.

The marketing requirements were met and proved out in many tests made on special test engines, and on cars under field operating conditions. At the same time refining techniques for producing these concentrates were developed. The economic evaluation of any proposed concentrate was an interesting Operations Research problem in its own right.

The operation of a refinery consists essentially of a flow process in which the output of one unit becomes input for other units and so on, until finished products are withdrawn from the system. Altering the operating conditions of any of the units thus affects the flows to the other units and eventually the product mix.

It is common to employ a technique called refinery simulation. This consists of programming the complex operations of a refinery on electronic computers. By supplying the computer with instructions as to the types of feed stock to be run and the operating conditions of each unit, it is possible to obtain the product output of the system. Experiments are conducted by altering the "through-put" or operating conditions or the sequence of unit processing.

By considering the market value of the products together with the operating costs, it is possible to choose an optimum range within which the desired product can be manufactured. After a considerable amount of laboratory, plant, and field research, an octane concentrate which satisfied the marketing and manufacturing requirements was developed. At the same time another subgroup attacked the problem of producing the blending pump. As in the octane concentrate problem, the group had to "balance" several requirements. The pump not only had to perform the usual operations of dispensing, measuring, and computing, but also had to be equipped with a mechanism which would accurately apportion two product streams so as to produce the exact blend required. In addition, it had to lend itself to mass-production methods, so that its production cost could be kept within reasonable limits. Two years of intensive research resulted in a pump that accomplished these objectives.

MEASURING CONSUMER AND
COMPETITIVE REACTIONS

After solving these technical problems, the task force turned to the question of how the motoring public would react to an entirely new concept in gasoline retailing. Since the Custom Blending system was so radically different, it was decided that the only possible way to evaluate consumer and competitive reaction was to perform actual tests at service stations.

Two and one-half years had passed since the inception of the project, and the work had been carried out with utmost secrecy. Only top management and the task-force employees had knowledge of the proposed changes in marketing policy. Although this had the advantage of keeping information from competition, there were two disadvantages: the loss of help that could have been gained from employees not on the task force, and the absence of market information.

An example of the first type of cost resulted when the Custom Blending pump was demonstrated to the marketing people. It soon became evident that the pricing mechanism was not flexible enough to handle all possible pricing situations. The price computer was subsequently redesigned to correct this deficiency. However, it was the lack of knowledge as to how the system would work in the market that resulted in the decision to conduct a pilot test; and so the cloak of secrecy was removed.

Sun's Southeastern Region, encompassing the states of Florida and part of southern Georgia, was selected as the site of the test for two reasons. First, it was an isolated area for the company, with little advertising "spill-over" from other Sun marketing regions. Second, the resort character of the area would expose the Custom Blending system to a diverse group of individuals and thus secure the reactions of consumers driving a wide variety of cars.

The first phase of the experiment began in February, 1956, in Orlando, Florida, and was extended throughout the region in June of the same year. Competitive reactions to the announced Custom Blending system were soon apparent. Within a short time several competitors were offering three grades of gasoline. Others stepped up their second grades to "super premium" quality and price.

Reactions of consumers to Custom Blending were highly favorable. Paired stations were set up, allowing comparisons to be made between competitive stations and Sun stations *with* Custom Blending, and between competitive stations and Sun stations *without* Custom Blending. By observing traffic through these paired stations, it was found that Custom Blending increased both the volume of sales and the proportion of sales made to high-priced, high-octane requirement cars at those Sun stations which had the new system.

This case study illustrates an important difference between a purely mathematical Operations Research approach and one more concerned with a dynamic marketing situation. When a mathematical model is set up, it is possible to perform experiments without altering it or the environment which it represents. However, once an experiment is performed on a system which operates in a social environment, no matter how hard one tries to keep the experiment "pure," the system and the environment in which it operates are usually subject to outside influences.

In the case of Custom Blending, two things happened. First, competitors altered their basic marketing strategy, for example, by selling three grades, which changed the "rules of the game." Second, they increased marketing pressure in advertising, promotion, and station building. Nonetheless, by careful examination of very small markets, it was possible to minimize considerably the effect of the changed environment.

### EVALUATION

The final task of the Operations Research group was to evaluate each of the possible policies. To accomplish this, a model was constructed to evaluate the rate of return on investment for a given sales volume for each system.

The problem was stated as follows: Consider three different alternatives to Sun's traditional single-grade motor fuel system:

1. Custom Blending.
2. The two-fuel system.
3. The three-fuel system.

For each system, at what point in sales volume will additional revenue:

a. Equal additional costs?
b. Yield 10, 15, or 20 per cent return on investment before taxes?

Measurements were made on an incremental basis. That is, the costs, investment, and revenue for each system were compared with the dollar sales that would have been generated by the traditional single-grade system as it would have been operated in the reference year. Only the incremental amounts were reported.

Detailed estimates of the capital requirements and operating costs for each system were obtained and substituted in the model. The marketing and manufacturing assumptions were varied in order to determine the effect of different sets of operating conditions. For example, separate computations were made for a two-fuel system, one assuming a 3-cent retail differential and another assuming a 4-cent differential. The expected results of a three-fuel system were calculated, using varying proportions of each grade. For the Custom Blending System, profitability estimates were made for a range of octane-concentrate ratios.

The final report did not specify an optimum solution, but rather presented management with the return on investment for each possible course of action, with a variety of sales volumes and sets of operating conditions. Management decided in favor of Custom Blending.

## FINAL CONSIDERATIONS

Here are some final considerations, developed during the course of the work on this project.

1. It is not always possible to construct a mathematical model to represent the system under study.
2. At almost every point there are conflicts of interest among functional units of a system. These should not be suppressed, but rather balanced so that an optimum solution for the entire system is achieved.

3. It may not be possible to supply an optimum solution because one or more of the essential variables of the system cannot be evaluated objectively. Under such conditions a plausible range of values may be stated. Within this framework possible values can be specified. The decision maker may then exercise his subjective judgment as to which is the most probable value, and the solution follows from this selection.

4. Provision should be made to cope with possible changes in conditions that may arise from conducting experiments in the market.

5. If it is desired to maintain a high degree of security over the research operation, the advantages and disadvantages of doing so should be carefully weighed.

6. Final decisions should not be made by the Operations Research team, but rather by management.

### QUESTIONS

1. Final decisions should not be made by the operations research team, but rather by management. Why?

2. Describe specific types of problems that an operations research team can solve.

3. What different types of research were used in the custom blending study?

4. Will operations research replace traditional marketing research in the near future?

# 27. The Use of Operations Research in a Small Company*

H. L. Baum, President, Noreen Incorporated

*The managements of small businesses can use operations research effectively. Specifically, the budgeting of advertising funds, sales forecasting, and inventory control are areas of management decision where operations research formulas can be used productively.*

Operations research is a huge and complex subject, and I should like to admit at the outset that I really do not know enough about it technically to feel entirely comfortable in discussing it. Nevertheless, I do have some convictions on the subject, and the little experience I have had with it has given me certain insights which I believe may be of some value to others.

My observations are strictly from the point of view of the small business firm, in which context only I have acquired

* Reprinted from the AMA Management Report No. 10, *Operations Research Reconsidered.* Copyright 1958 by the American Management Association.

whatever familiarity with OR I may have. In this context, then, I believe that the complexity of business organization and operations makes necessary the resolution of data into pieces that can be handled comfortably. I don't know how it is in a large company, but, in a small company, the problem of handling data is a major one. This, of course, is primarily because of the limited number of personnel. These people cannot possibly devote all their energies to understanding and using a vast amount of information; they have too many other hour-by-hour responsibilities. Thus, I have learned that the quality of our decisions is in direct ratio to the quantity and quality of assimilable data—with the emphasis on the word *assimilable* because, if the volume of data is so great that it cannot be assimilated, then the data are useless.

In our business, OR techniques put data into usable form. OR does not make decisions for us, but it places at our disposal relevant data, organized in logical sequence. In management, you have two choices: to base your decisions on organized data or to fly by the seat of your pants.

In the November 1957 issue of *Dun's Review* I came across an article on the subject of business failures. As to the cause of such failures, the author observed, "While the ways in which inexperience and incompetence were manifested cannot be narrowed into a single category, it is a matter of record that small enterprises are plagued most by inadequate sales and competitive weakness, whereas receivables and inventory problems play a large role in the failure of big concerns." I have a feeling that inadequacies in management decisions stemming from "seat of the pants" navigation are the fundamental causes of the problems referred to. Personally, I don't want to get involved in inadequate sales, competitive weakness, bad receivables, or messed-up inventories, and the only way I know how to protect myself is with objective, current data. In retrospect, it seems to me that my one chronic problem in management has been the constant struggle to get data—and get them while they are fresh.

## OPERATIONS RESEARCH AT NOREEN

Affecting this whole problem of data handling, of course, is the question of emphasis. At Noreen, for example, our primary problem was to sell; thus, all of our energies were devoted toward establishing a new product. Having successfully established the product, management emphasis then shifted to the company. In my view, during the establishment phase the company (or division) doesn't really exist. The collection of individuals becomes a company only once the product is successfully established. From then on, it is a fight to preserve the enterprise, which must maintain the position of its product, launch new products, go into other lines of business, or protect itself against the incursion of competitive products.

It is this shift in emphasis—from throwing everything to the wind to get the product established, to preserving and maintaining the planned progress of the company—that leads to complications. Although we started in the cosmetics business, we are now engaged in a number of completely dissimilar activities; for all I know, 50 years from now we might be refining selenium on the moon. When we began to move into other fields, the interplay of forces from these various new activities and the resulting pressures on our staff became insupportable, and I began to feel that we were losing touch with reality. In a word, the corporation was becoming neurotic, and we had to make a choice between suffering a nervous breakdown or getting some sort of practical, usable apparatus to enable us to keep functioning logically and according to some order.

The exigencies of wartime resulted in the application of mathematics to the solution of military problems; and the techniques involved have since been found to be adaptable to business. Since the conduct of a business essentially amounts to the control of interrelated forces, supposedly sequential and logical, it lends itself to mathematical analysis; but the properties of a dynamic system cannot be defined in terms of a static system. The Gestalt of dynamic mathematics, however—as opposed to the static mathematics which we all use in our bookkeeping departments—makes possible the representation of the factors in a business situation by mathematical symbols and the manipulation of this symbology by completely objective dynamic mathematical techniques to arrive at objective conclusions which can form the basis for decision and consequent planned action. That is how we define OR in our business: simply *the application of the discipline of dynamic mathematics to the solution of business problems.*

The head of our OR department reports to me—for the reason that there is no one else in our small organization to see that OR functions for the benefit of the total complex, rather than for the benefit of only a small part and to the possible disadvantage of the rest. The OR boss is involved in all aspects of the business, and it is up to him to take the initiative to apply his skills where needed (in consultation with me, so that I can help determine where emphasis should be placed). This function requires a professional mathematician, and we sometimes use consultants to reinforce the skills of our own people. For example, Booz, Allen & Hamilton helped us con-

siderably on an advertising project. If an amateur were to attempt such a job alone, he would inevitably end up groping for a mathematical straw.

We actually got into OR almost by accident. By sheer coincidence, we acquired a theoretical mathematician as an assistant bookkeeper. After a few months this man began to use his capabilities in other parts of the business, and we began to make our approach toward comprehension and control of our problem more rational. We didn't even realize that we were using OR! Subsequently, we formed an OR department, and we are now very formal.

To value this activity in terms of dollars and cents is difficult, but we have a few clues. We spend about 20 times as much money on advertising as our OR activity costs; thus, if OR is making our advertising only 5 per cent more effective, then it is paying for itself. Similarly, the application of OR to the production facility enabled us (as I shall describe later) to restructure our labor force to provide the manpower to launch a new product. As the sales volume of this new product grows, of course, we shall have to add more production people; but the value of the manpower we freed is approximately equal in dollars to the cost of our small OR function. (Perhaps our production vice president would have come up with this same approach on his own, but I am not so sure it would have happened as early as it did.) In still another instance, we were faced with the need for raising our prices—the second time we have done so in the history of the company. The first increase lost us some goodwill because we could not forecast its consequences far enough in advance to give our customers enough lead time to keep their inventories balanced; also, we had to make package exchanges of old pre-priced packages for new, which was very costly to us. This time, we had seven months' lead time as a result of OR forecasting. This actually increased customer goodwill, and also very greatly reduced the package exchange problem. On the whole, then, I feel that OR earns money for us.

Actually, I believe that any business unconsciously uses what is now called operations research. In most cases, however, it is simply not recognized or organized as such; it is floating around in the minds of the various company managers as they intuitively absorb data, collate them, compare them, and reach decisions. Through the application of OR techniques, such nebulous activity is anchored firmly in place—and this more disciplined OR approach produces more sales, plus actual dollar savings.

For the remainder of this discussion, I should like to describe three OR applications which seem to illustrate best the impact of this management skill on a small business. Specifically, the areas of management we shall consider are the budgeting of advertising funds, sales forecasting, and inventory control.

## BUDGETING
## ADVERTISING FUNDS

Advertising is important, of course, in any size or kind of enterprise. It is especially important to us at Noreen, because we are fighting for drugstore display space with many very large firms—and not necessarily those in the field of cosmetics alone. It is therefore extremely important that we spend our modest budget in an intelligent fashion. For years, we have made budget decisions with the aid of that instrument provided by nature and ordinarily modestly masked by a competent tailor—the seat of our pants. (Is it coincidence that a man commonly carries his wallet in this general anatomical area?)

This informal method of budgeting advertising funds was acutely disturbing to us, because we knew we were spending a much higher percentage of our sales dollar than was conventional (although the actual amount of money was comparatively modest). In addition, we had no way of evaluating the effectiveness of what we were doing. So we decided to apply OR techniques.

The first step was to define the problem. The second step was to create a mathematical model of our advertising complex which was so organized that we could control the manner in which it functioned, and which had the capacity of providing data in logical sequence and in a manipulable form.

We defined our problem as an attempt to balance the four different kinds of advertising or promotion activities we engage in—local advertising, national advertising, point-of-sale merchandising, and public relations—recognizing that they are all interrelated. The question was: Should we devote equal funds to all four? Or should the local-advertising allocation be very large and the other three small? Or what? On this subject, we had lots of opinions but no facts. The problem was further complicated by the influence of important forces which operate dynamically and fluidly on an integrated advertising campaign: competitors' activities, the frequency and continuity of the advertising program, the type of management response to a changing situation, and so forth. Although certain of these forces can be controlled, there are many that cannot be; however, we believe that these forces offset one another, and that the effects of those that cannot be controlled are insignificant.

Having defined the problem, we constructed a mathematical model, the components of which we could vary or hold constant at will. We decided to hold constant the point-of-sale merchandising and public relations budgets and to vary the local and national advertising expenditures. In the interest of simplicity, we divided the various force factors into constants and variables, on the basis of logic. We held as constants the quality of our advertising and sales effort. As for our competitors, we decided that they could not be any more active than they had been in the past, so that their activities were effectively constant as well. The variables we had to contend with were matters of time, area, balance, amount, continuity, and frequency.

Thus, we determined our constants and variables, working together or in opposition in a constantly changing, never-static relationship, all over the United States, which we divided into three zones for the purpose of this research. In each zone, we selected a major city in which we will do local advertising in varying amounts and types; at the same time, we will do national advertising with controlled variations. While all this is going on, we will be measuring the flow of merchandise at the retail level in the major and minor markets. This is all very complicated, but, in substance, what we will come up with can be thought of as a "black box" which has 27 interrelated complexes of data (including seasonal data): three geographic zones and nine different combinations of local and national advertising programs.

By means of a lot of complicated mathematics which I don't pretend to understand, our OR technicians will solve 27 different equations simultaneously. Or, in the terms of our black box, we will turn a crank and optimize the four most productive combinations (in terms of dollar sales) which discount all the constants and variables mentioned previously and which isolate the fixed effects of year, season, or area. Then we will take these four optimum solutions and go through a refinement of the previously described

process for 20 months, and we will end up with number values which are essentially a range of optimums ranked with respect to each other and which indicate the volume of sales to be expected for each dollar spent.

Although we have completed the design for this program, we are barely launched on the data-collecting stage. We have, however, already reaped some benefits. Our advertising agency has created a carefully planned 36-month integrated media program, whereas previously we worked on a year-to-year basis. All major copy themes and related graphics have been planned on a long-term basis, which makes possible a more consistent evolution and development of the concepts we wish to communicate to our buying public. And, finally, we know what our monthly financial commitments are for three years, rather than only for 12 months ahead.

## SALES FORECASTING

The management of any business is constantly faced with the need for making decisions. Since (unfortunate as it may be) our decisions affect only the future and never the past, they must be based on our evaluation of what we expect the future to hold. In our company, we have indulged in several different kinds of forecasting, as I shall relate below.

Our first attempt at forecasting was simply what business I thought we would do. This "guesstimate" was based on my 20-odd years of experience in the business, studies of salesmen's reports and general economic data—and a large proportion of hunch. Most of the time, I was pretty accurate, but once in a while I would be off by as much as 20 or 30 per cent. Even this wasn't too bad—or so I used to tell myself. But every once in awhile I would guess high on volume and low on expenses—a shattering experience! As a result of one of our young executives' attending an AMA course in forecasting, I fired myself as a forecaster —and we started our second kind of forecasting.

This was similar to the first, except that we tried to find various kinds of trends to use as correlations for prediction purposes, and we refined a lot of the guesswork out of what we had been doing. But our errors were still running as high as 10 to 12 per cent.

As a result of the impact of our captive mathematician, we entered our third kind of forecasting. Although nobody understands how it is done, this type of forecasting has an error range of from 2 to 5 per cent. We make a five-quarter forecast in terms of probability, showing upper and lower limits and the most probable dollar volume. Its usefulness is so obvious as to preclude discussion.

The reason the first type of forecasting was a failure was human fallibility. The reason the second kind of forecasting was relatively undependable was that we could find no reliable correlation trends except the amount of consumer disposable income, which offers no lead time; and without lead time, you merely know where you are now, not where you are going. In developing our present forecasting system, the first thing we had to do was dig into the availability of good data—which gives me the opportunity to warn others that the value of their research will be strongly influenced by the reliability of their basic data. We found, for example, that we cannot use our own sales-to-wholesalers figures because inventory fluctuations occur (either by plan or by accident) in the wholesale house. These artificial fluctuations create a false picture for us: Sales-to-wholesalers figures show a terrific drop at Christmas, whereas over-the-counter sales are substantially the same at Christmas as they

are at any other time. Obviously, a great deal of care must be taken to insure that the basic data are really correct and are not subject to outside influences which create a false picture.

What did we do with all these data when they were collected and verified? We made a projection. When I asked our mathematician how these data were projected, he made the following statement, upon which I shall not attempt to elaborate: "In selecting a medium for projection, we fitted our data to every type of curve known to us for short-term forecasting purposes and tested them by a least-squares fit, punctuated by common sense." When I attempt to understand what this really means, I throw a least-squares fit myself—punctuated by perplexity!

Having gone through the above procedure, our technicians discovered that a second-degree parabolic function won the contest hands down. Miss Second-Degree Parabolic Function, it seems, is not only well curved, but is also highly volatile— and dangerous if extrapolated too far. In English, I think this means that, while the second-degree parabola technique is useful for a five-quarter forecast, it is very dangerous if you try to use it to go years into the future. As a matter of practice, I know that our technicians review this entire procedure from time to time and make a continuous inspection of any particular area that appears to show unique deviations. Such deviations have so far been completely explainable upon analysis.

We drop a quarter and add a quarter every quarter, which means that what happens in the current quarter will influence our forecast for the next five quarters; thus, we have a truly dynamic and fluid system, because it is constantly changing as current data are fed into it.

We could do this on a monthly basis if we desired, but so far a quarterly basis has been frequent enough for our purposes. At quarterly forecasting meetings, the statistical analysis is carefully discussed in detail with the top marketing people in order to take into consideration any sales promotions or external factors which might influence our volume. We have been using this kind of forecasting technique for more than a year, and we feel that it has withstood the test of time.

The results? First, we have been able to organize all of our sales data into homogeneous form.

Second, since we now have a realistic basis for anticipating sales, we can more rapidly control cash flow. This releases cash for other business opportunities which would otherwise have to be held in reserve.

Third, we finally have a meaningful forecast of expenses—in other words, a usable budget. Without accurate forecasting, you can only guess what your sales volume will be, what your costs should be, and what the relation of your costs to your volume is. This situation leads to the imposition of an inflexible budget system, which may prevent you from spending money to increase sales—because you can't be sure you will have adequate future volume to provide money to pay for a present commitment—or may cause you to spend money needlessly because you cannot record or predict the impact of a proposed expenditure on future volume.

Fourth, we now have good control of inventory and production, which permits us to cut our investment to reasonable levels instead of having to hedge against the unknown.

## INVENTORY CONTROL

The problem of inventory control for our small manufacturing facility was completely frustrating. Our company is adequately capitalized, but about once or twice a year we would develop serious shortages of operating capital, at the same time suffering a tremendous inventory buildup—and we didn't dare lay off our workforce. In 17 years we had never solved this problem.

The first step in our OR approach was to determine all the factors of production and demand. (The production factors considered were our ability to produce and our capacity for holding goods in process, for warehousing raw materials and finished goods, and so forth. The demand factors had to do with seasonal fluctuations, unforeseeable peculiarities of the market, costs of distribution, and so forth.) The second step was to determine the costs of all these factors. The third step was to determine the flow of raw chemicals, semi-finished and finished chemicals, and packaging materials through the production process. The fourth and last step was to determine the flow of cash. (This was a function of demand, because demand fluctuations create sales fluctuations which in turn create cash-flow fluctuations.) The four types of data covered in these steps were all we needed.

Having acquired the data, we set up a linear program which determined the optimal relationship between amounts of inventory and cash, simultaneously taking into consideration all factors of supply and demand. This is an extremely difficult computation and could not have been done without making use of the mathematics of movement. Our linear program might be compared to two pots, both boiling furiously. The first pot gave us the optimum cost for the two largest-volume product lines, which means that the lowest-cost combination was a product mix consisting of $X$ of these and $Y$ of those. The second pot broke the above two major product lines into their 28 parts and solved each part for optimum cost in relation to the other 27; this was done 28 times.

Having developed the optimum costs for all items in all relationships, our technicians next plugged in the raw-material availability data and came up with a final solution for the whole operation. As the factory commences the manufacture of other items, data from them will be inserted into the above matrix, and over-all factory production and financing will be adjusted accordingly.

Our methodology in this program was as follows:

1. We established a minimum-cost standard work system for the manufacture of all products.
2. We established the cost of carrying inventory on the basis of returns from alternative uses of our marginal-investment dollar. To illustrate by oversimplification: If we have $100,000, the first $1,000 is not very costly to spend; but to commit the last $1,000 of that $100,000 might be extremely costly, because the same last $1,000 might be the $1,000 we need for research work to create a new product, or for some other purpose.
3. We established standard capacities of daily output for our productive resources. (In English, this means we determined how much of a particular item we can produce in one day.)
4. We forecast our demand for one year by quarters and translated the same into so many standard days' output for each product, including a 20 per cent safety factor. We also translated into standard production days our quarterly productive-re-

sources capacities, which are inventory lag time, normal production, and overproduction. Having a statement of demand in terms of standard days' output and a statement of production capacity in standard days' output, it is a relatively simple thing to match the two so as to reduce non-productive costs and operate the company at minimum over-all costs.

What have been the results of our OR approach to inventory control? Our finished-goods inventory now varies at reasonable levels in consonance with fluctuations in anticipated demand and in our cash flow. We get planning information as to the size of the inventory needed and the size of the labor force needed. We have restructured our production workers into teams, and we picked up enough man-hours to go into production on a new item without adding any more people. Of special significance to us, because of the limited size of our building, is that we have freed storage and production space for other products, so that we can continue our operation within the same building.

## QUESTIONS

1. Why does operations research seem to work at Noreen, Inc., but not at Rheem Manufacturing?
2. On what types of marketing problems has operations research seemed to work at Noreen?
3. What are the necessary components of an effective operations research department?
4. What was Noreen's operations research approach to inventory control?

# BIBLIOGRAPHY FOR CHAPTER IV

ARTICLES:

Adler, Lee, "Phasing Research into the Marketing Plan," *Harvard Business Review,* Vol. 38, No. 3 (May–June 1960), pp. 113–122.

Bogart, Leo, "The Researcher's Dilemma," *The Journal of Marketing,* Vol. 26, No. 1 (January 1962), pp. 6–11.

"How Important Has Marketing Research Become?" *Industrial Marketing,* Vol. 45, No. 9 (September 1960), pp. 164–166.

"I Predict; Research," *Printers' Ink,* Vol. 278, No. 1 (January 5, 1962), pp. 49–51.

Magee, John F., "Operations Research in Making Marketing Decisions," *The Journal of Marketing,* Vol. 25, No. 2 (October 1960), pp. 18–23.

"Mathematical Models and Marketing Strategy," *Television,* Vol. 17, No. 11 (November 1960), pp. 58–59.

BOOKS:

Alderson, Wroe, and Green, Paul, *Planning and Problem Solving in Marketing.* Homewood, Ill.: Irwin, 1962.

Alevizos, John P., *Marketing Research: Applications, Procedures, and Cases.* Englewood Cliffs, N.J.: Prentice-Hall, 1959. Chapter 12.

Baumol, W. J., *Economic Theory and Operations Analysis.* Englewood Cliffs, N.J.: Prentice-Hall, 1961.

Bursk, Edward C., *Text and Cases in Marketing: A Scientific Approach.* Englewood Cliffs, N.J.: Prentice-Hall, 1962. Section One.

Crisp, Richard D., *Sales Planning and Control.* New York: McGraw-Hill, 1961.

Ferber, Robert, and Verdoorn, P. J., *Research Methods in Economics and Business.* New York: Macmillan, 1962.

Ferguson, Robert, and Sargent Lauren, *Linear Programming.* New York: McGraw-Hill, 1958.

Frank, Ronald, Kuehn, Alfred, and Massy, William, *Quantitative Techniques in Marketing Analysis.* Homewood, Ill.: Irwin, 1962.

Holmes, Parker M., *Marketing Research: Principles and Readings.* Cincinnati, Ohio: South-Western Publishing Company, 1960.

Lazo, Hector, and Corbin, Arnold, *Management in Marketing.* New York: McGraw-Hill, 1961. Chapter 4.

*Operations Research Reconsidered.* AMA Management Report No. 10. New York: American Management Association, 1958.

Schlaifer, Robert, *Probability and Statistics for Business Decisions*. New York: McGraw-Hill, 1959.

Smith, George H., *Motivation Research in Advertising and Marketing*. New York: McGraw-Hill, 1954.

Tousley, Rayburn, Clark, Eugene, and Clark, Fred, *Principles of Marketing*. New York: Macmillan, 1962. Chapter 24.

# V. New Product Planning

*T*HERE is no one best organizational structure for product development as an organization is in part a function of company size, type of products, recency of establishment, and a host of other factors. Historically, product planning was usually production or engineering oriented, but under the impetus of today's marketing concept reorganization, there is considerable pressure toward placing product planning under the marketing department.

Some firms are setting up separate product planning departments. Product planning in these firms is being disassociated from production, engineering, marketing, or any other functional group since it is an important function and needs the continuous attention of able people who are not tied down with other major duties. Perhaps, an even more important argument for the separation is that those dealing with product planning should be entirely unbiased toward the position of anyone of the functional groups which might be in conflict regarding any product under consideration. For instance, marketing personnel might be favorable toward a new proposal while engineering or production might be against it, and neither could be expected to act in an unbiased manner if the product planning function was entrusted to their department.

The independent product planning department is given responsibility for initiation and reception of the product idea, preliminary screening, assignment of specific responsibilities to other functional groups, coordination of inter-departmental work, and recommendations for action to top management. This department is an arm of top management and reports directly to top executives. Authority from these top executives is needed to secure full support from all the functional departments.

Product innovations can be divided roughly into three categories based on the extent of planned differentiation.

*(1) Minor changes in styling of the old product.* The simplest of innovations is well illustrated in the automobile and

women's apparel industries where distinctiveness in appearance is important to consumers. Minor changes are made to date last year's style. The old style while still completely useful becomes psychologically obsolete.

*(2) Major product changes.*   This type of innovation generally calls for a radical change in design which offers the consumer a substantially improved product. In the automobile industry, for instance, this generally involves major improvements in the mechanical operation of the car as, for instance, the self-starter and the automatic shift. The research and development work for these radical improvements is very costly but must be undergone periodically to really make the older model obsolete.

*(3) Revolutionary product changes.*   Here the design and mechanical changes are so radical that you really have a complete new product for the same general use. Such new products at times make the old product obsolete. For instance, the development of the automobile brought about the retirement of the horse and buggy, but television did not displace either the movies or radio as was first thought by many.

Successful innovations of the major and revolutionary type are the ones that give individual companies their greatest competitive edge. As it stands today, product development is an extremely costly operation, and the failure rate of newly developed products is much too high. The challenge to both business management and marketing management is to find ways and means to bring these costs down.

# *28.* The Rise of Marketing in Product Planning*

E. Raymond Corey, Professor of Business Administration, Harvard University

*Product planning as a marketing activity has gained greatly in importance in the last decade due to the high rate of technological development, the postwar wave of mergers and acquisitions, increasing competition in world markets, and the mounting costs of new plants.*

The General Electric Annual Report for 1952 contained the following statement:

"In 1952, your company's operating managers were presented an advanced concept of marketing, formulated by the Marketing Services Division. This, in simple terms, would introduce the marketing man at the beginning rather than at the end of the production cycle and would integrate marketing into each phase of the business. Thus, marketing would establish for the engineer, the designer, and the manufacturing man what the customer wants in a given product, what price he will be willing to pay, where and when he will want it. Marketing would have authority in product planning, production scheduling and inventory control as well as the sales and distribution and servicing of the product. This concept, it is believed, will fix responsibility, while making possible greater flexibility and closer teamwork in the marketing of the company's products."

Is this in fact an "advanced concept"? If so, what underlies what appears to be

* Reprinted from the *First International Seminar on Marketing Management,* p. 79. Published as a Special Supplement to *Business Horizons,* School of Business, Indiana University, February 1961.

a fundamental change in approach to product planning?

Throughout its long and successful history, General Electric has been an engineering-oriented company, a technical pioneer in a wide range of activities. Whether by formal arrangement or simply by practice, the design of its product lines had become the responsibility primarily of the company's engineering personnel. Product planning was a laboratory-initiated activity. The products GE sales representatives took to the market were an expression, in good part, of the company's technical research achievements.

For General Electric and for many other technically strong U.S. corporations to conceive of product planning as a marketing function is to reverse a decision-making flow of long standing. Product planning becomes a market-initiated activity, and product lines, an expression of what marketing personnel have determined to be the needs of GE's customer groups.

## REASONS FOR THE CHANGE

What conditions, we may ask, have dictated this change for GE and for many other technically competent American

**205**

corporations? Four factors, at least, may be cited. *First,* the high rate of technical development has forced companies to pay more attention to their markets. Technical research has been a competitive weapon, surpassing in its power such traditional weapons as price cutting and increased advertising. New products, unseating existing ones in the markets they traditionally claimed, became the new face of competition. These new products brought hosts of new competitors—unorthodox in approach, unpredictable and undisciplined in the time-worn protocol of industry practice. For some, research was the cornucopia of new opportunity; for others research was an uncontrollable force disrupting stable markets. The essential point, however, is that for both the challenger and the challenged the question, more urgently asked than ever before, became: "What exactly should we make and sell?"

*Second,* the postwar wave of mergers and acquisitions has had the same disrupting effect in the market place. In many instances, mergers became the answer to the challenge of new products. Thus, for example, when aluminum began after World War II to move vigorously into applications traditionally held by copper, copper companies acquired aluminum-producing subsidiaries so they could continue to serve their existing customers. Can manufacturers, such as American Can and Continental Can, acquired affiliates supplying plastic containers and other forms of packaging. The question leading to many of these mergers was, what kind of a "package of products" makes sense in the market place?

A *third* factor that served to elevate the importance of product planning as a function, and to give this function a market orientation, was the huge dollar stakes for which the game was being played. In this day of mass production

for mass markets, large investments in plant and equipment could be committed by a single decision to add a new product to the line. In many cases, the manufacturing and marketing economies of scale were such that a company could ill afford to move half-heartedly into a new market. To be competitive, one needed low unit cost product; and the only low cost plants were large, highly automated facilities. Careful product planning and marketing research helped to provide cheap insurance against costly errors.

*Fourth,* even apart from the increasing rate of technical development and the wave of postwar mergers, the sheer intensity of postwar competition *per se* has provided a steady pressure in the direction of market-oriented product planning. In the sellers' market that we experienced in this country from the end of World War II to the early 1950's, we could tolerate considerable laxity in every dimension of marketing. When companies can sell all they make, managements sense no urgency when it comes to product planning.

Starting, however, in 1951–52, demand-supply conditions changed suddenly. Not only did domestic competition become intense, but European and Far Eastern competitors began besting us in world-markets. The quality of their products was good, and their prices were often low. It is not an overstatement to say that many domestic manufacturers were forced into sharp reappraisals of what they had conceived to be their competitive strengths. If we can give such reappraising a name and call it "product planning," there was a lot more of it after 1952 than before!

It may be useful to digress briefly at this point to ask what the term "product planning" means. In actual practice, it seems to involve dealing with a broad range of problems related to what a company makes and sells. At one end of the spectrum, product planning is concerned with the company's objectives and its over-all marketing strategy. At this end, we deal with such problems as: What are the basic functions that our product line is designed to perform? What are the groups and classes of customers for which this line is intended? Do we seek to serve our markets as full-line suppliers or limited-line specialists? Will we function primarily as a supplier of materials and components or as a manufacturer of end products? Will we attempt to take a position of technical leadership in our industry, or will we achieve greater success as a follower?

At the other end of the scale, product planning becomes concerned with the detail of carrying out the basic product policy. We deal at this end with such problems as: How many grades, models, and sizes do we supply in each product line? What exactly are the specifications of each item in the line? If Customer X requests certain modifications in the specifications to meet his particular needs, will we accede to this request?

By way of definition then, product planning is the determination of the company's basic product objectives, of what products the company will make and/or sell, and of what the specifications of these products will be.

## DECISION-MAKING CRITERIA

Product planning decisions often involve investigation and judgment in three areas: What does the market want? Can our company be competitively effective in this market? What will our making and selling the new product contribute to our total operations? Let us consider each of these areas in turn.

*What does the market want?* The late Charles Kettering, a pioneer in the automotive industry, was once asked in an interview whether he believed that "if a man made a better mousetrap, the world would make a beaten path to his door." Kettering replied, "The people who have mice will." This observation is striking for its clear and simple wisdom. Kettering stresses the necessity for orienting product development effort to market needs. He also suggests in his rejoinder that, in analyzing markets, we need to be conscious of the fact that every market is made up of segments. Each segment consists of a group of customers having homogeneous needs and buying motivations.

Our first task, then, is to identify the specific market segments with which we are concerned and to determine market needs as precisely as possible. We are then able to ascertain, first, whether the product under consideration actually has a market and, if so, what its specifications should be.

Simple enough to say, but we often encounter obstacles in making these judgments. In the first place, the market we have in mind may not be able to articulate its needs if the idea of the product is relatively new. How far would we get, for example, in determining the potential market for private space vehicles by interviewing our potential customer—the man in the street? He has no way of knowing how such a product would fit into his pattern of living, if in fact it ever will. The same fundamental difficulty is present even in investigating the needs for new products that might fit immediately into the customer's day-to-day activities.

Another difficulty often exists in identifying accurately those groups that will make the buying decisions and whose ideas may then determine product planning decisions. Take, for example, the dilemma of a manufacturer of heating and air-conditioning equipment who was interested in adding heat pumps to his line. The heat pump, based on the same principles of operation as the refrigerator, heats the home in the winter and cools it in the summer with the same unit doing both tasks. This equipment could be made in one large unit and installed in the house. Alternatively, it could be made in two parts with one in the house and the other outside. The choice involved such considerations as ease of installation, quality of performance, and noise levels. In attempting to resolve this question, the manufacturer recognized that homeowners, architects, builders, heating and plumbing contractors, and distributors would all be influential in buying decisions regarding the heat pump. It was unlikely, however, that each would appraise the relative advantages of the split and the integral designs in the same way. How, then, could he appraise the relative importance of these conflicting signals, and make a product design decision?

A third difficulty in analyzing markets for new products is presented by the changing and evolving nature of these markets. The market segments of which we speak may emerge only after a product is in commercial use for a period of time. Then different groups begin to exhibit distinguishing characteristics with regard to the purchase and use of the product. At the outset, however, market segmentation may be only a latent thing.

In the face of these problems, it may be difficult, but not impossible, to make some initial judgments regarding market needs. For lack of adequate market information, marketers and engineers may have to define, as objectively as possible, what market needs are likely to be. Interviews with a few potential customers, with the company's field sales engineers, and with representatives of technical trade associations may provide them with some broad guidelines. These ideas may be enough for a first approximation

of the market to be served and the product to be supplied.

The further refinement of these ideas then may come through the experience gained in the initial marketing of the product. It may be useful to recognize that the beginning phases of market development, when the new product is actually being made and sold to commercial customers, are at the same time a part of the market research effort. Introducing the product commercially, in other words, is part of the very process of finding out what we need to know about where the market exists and exactly what it wants.

*Can our company be competitively effective in this market?* It is axiomatic that, in defining its basic purpose and objectives, a company should "lead from strength." It should attempt to do those things that it can do well. In dealing, then, with product planning questions that fall at the "policy" end of the spectrum, we need to relate the company's strengths to the requirements of the specific job a management undertakes if it elects to make and market the new product.

It then becomes pertinent to ask questions such as these: Are there few or many potential customers? Can they be reached through the company's existing channels of distribution? Will extensive technical and engineering service be required by customers? Will the company need to establish new manufacturing and warehouse facilities? Are the supplier's trade reputation and brand name important considerations in the eyes of potential customers? Will market share depend significantly on maintaining a position of technical leadership? Will market position depend on low price or on level of quality? Are existing customers also potential customers for the new product?

Answers to these questions may go a long way toward determining whether the particular assets, skills, and relationships the company possesses can be effectively employed in marketing the new product.

There is one other dimension, however, with which to deal in appraising a company's capacity for marketing a new product. This is the matter of management interests and orientation. The degree of enthusiasm—or alternatively, the degree of resistance—that is generated internally by the idea of adding a new product can be a critical consideration. The new product may, for example, compete against the existing line for certain applications. In such instances, it may be true that the sense of psychological commitments to the current line literally disqualifies the management from doing an effective marketing job with the new product.

*What will our making and selling the new product contribute to our total operations?* Instinctively, the first question asked regarding the addition of a new product to the line is: How profitable will it be? While this may be an appropriate first question, it is often not the key question. And very often a product planning decision is made not simply to increase profit but to accomplish some other objectives related to the business as a whole.

It may be desirable, for example, to add certain products to have a full line of products going to certain customer groups. Or the product may be added because the company's distributors want it and will turn to other sources of supply if the company does not add it to the line. Again, improvements in product specifications may be made simply to meet the threat of a competitor's improved product and thereby to retain market position.

On the other hand, new product ideas may be considered and rejected because of their potentially adverse impact on some part of the company's business. Making and selling the new product may put the company in competition with some present customers. Or selling the new product might seem to existing customers to be in conflict with the company's image. A manufacturer of electric fork-lift trucks, for example, who had claimed for years in his advertising that electric trucks were superior to gas trucks would face some difficulty in adding gas trucks to his line.

Judgments regarding the impact of a new product on the company's total operations are not easily made. For one thing, it is often not possible to apply quantitative measures in this area. Nevertheless, tough-minded and objective judgment is called for to avoid making decisions based on emotion and short-run considerations.

Product planning may be defined as the determination of the company's basic objectives, of what products it will make and sell, and of what the specifications of these products will be. Product planning as a marketing activity has gained greatly in importance in the last decade. Reasons for the increase are the high rate of technological development, the postwar wave of mergers and acquisitions, increasing competition in world markets, and the mounting costs of new plants. These factors have tended to increase both the number and the significance of decisions corporate managements must make regarding what products the company should make and sell. They have forced management to give increasing effort to the task of designing competitively effective product lines.

In making product planning decisions, the relevant factors seem often to fall in three areas of consideration: What does the market want? Can the company be competitively effective in this market? What will making and selling the new product contribute to the company's total operations?

## QUESTIONS

1. Historically at General Electric, product planning has been a laboratory-initiated activity. Explain.

2. Describe some of the difficulties encountered in analyzing potential markets for new products.

3. What three criteria are used in deciding whether to launch a new product?

4. Why has product planning gained in importance in the last decade?

## 29. Why Are New Products So Costly?*

*The matter of profitability grows constantly and increasingly in importance, and marketing requirements have become the guiding consideration in successful product planning for that profitability. Few products fail because of technical deficiencies. In today's economy it is getting increasingly easier to make a product than sell it.*

Modest improvement in new-product performance could mean a major improvement in the profit position of many companies. But the failure rate of new products in industry generally remains high. The odds against the commercial success of a new product *idea* before it goes into development is about 50-to-one. After extensive and expensive development and testing, it still is even money that the product will fail in general distribution.

Why? The question that has plagued every company with a success rate lower than it would like was examined this week in a report by Booz, Allen & Hamilton, management consultants, New York. After reviewing the experience of

scores of companies, the firm has come up with a conclusion that puts the weight of responsibility for the basic decisions that influence the success or failure of a company's new products, squarely on the shoulders of top management.

The importance of top management in this respect is suggested by three familiar points made in the report:

"Business strategy is fundamentally product planning."

"Company plans are keyed to and made up of product plans."

And, "Throughout history, the underlying secret of business success has been to be in the right business at the right time."

This ability to be in the right business at the right time has taken on greater meaning during the postwar years. New products in increasing numbers have

* Reprinted from *Printers' Ink,* December 9, 1960, p. 48. Copyright 1960 by *Printers' Ink* Publishing Corp., 635 Madison Ave., New York 22, N. Y.

taken a growing share of total sales volume—consumer and industrial. And much more of the same is in store. The report estimated that 75 per cent of industry's increase in sales volume during the next three years will come from new products.

And perhaps, said the report, too much emphasis is placed on increasing sales volume through new products. For the fact is, it emphasized, sales tend to outrun profits. As a general rule, profits tend to start declining before the sales curve of a new product reaches its peak, because "sooner or later every product is preempted by another or else degenerates into profitless price competition." This, the report suggested, "means that as a business strategy, a company must plan to run ahead of price competition by differentiating its products and introducing new products that can command better margins."

The problem is the same for every company and likely to grow more so: to plan and organize in such a way as to "be in the right business at the right time."

But that is much easier to say than do. Even the more successful companies face serious, constant problems that reflect the need for fuller participation by top management, from the first step to the last.

The Booz, Allen report incorporated a survey of 70 large companies that have been "at least by popular repute, relatively successful with new products." The consultants found that the most urgent problem—listed by 84 per cent of the companies—was the general category of "problems with organization." It is interesting to note that very few companies complained of lack of new ideas, of creativity or of qualified personnel. After organizational problems, the top four problem areas noted were: poor control and follow-up, poorly defined new prod-

uct objectives, inadequate business analysis of proposed new products, and inadequate performance of one or more steps in the new-product program.

## WHAT THE PROBLEMS INVOLVE

Taking them one by one:

**Organization Problems.** . . . Most of these problems dealt with organizational structure, unclear definition of responsibilities and inadequate systems and procedures, communications and working relationships of people involved in new-product programs.

**Poor Control.** . . . Maintaining a program's schedule and costs, from screening of ideas through laboratory development, field testing and commercialization, would seem to be basic to new-product success. Nevertheless, more than one in four companies reported difficulties in holding to cost and time projections. "More breakdowns," noted the report, "seem to trace to poor planning than to poor supervision."

**Poorly Defined Objectives.** . . . This would seem to be too basic to the success of any product for discussion. But again, more than one in four of the 70 successful companies studied indicated failure to spell out objectives clearly enough to provide the needed guidance.

**Inadequate Business Analysis.** . . . Executives in almost one out of four (24 per cent) of these successful companies complained of insufficient facts regarding projection of sales, profit and return on investment prospects. Such faulty projections can be extremely costly. The consultant put heavy emphasis on the need for better and fuller market research and "more critical market evaluation."

**Inadequate Performance.** . . . The

Comparison of new product expenses for successful and unsuccessful products.
(Most new-product costs go to products that fail, and of those
costs, most is spent in the development stage)

failure of responsible people to do their job as scheduled generally occurs in the final stages of the product program: development, testing and commercialization. A prime problem here is "poorly written specifications."

In every case, problem-solving is aided and problems minimized, by an understanding and participating top management. There seems to be a clear relation between the degree of top management's participation and the degree of new product success, one following on the other. As the Booz, Allen report pointed out, there are at least five basic areas in which top management must exercise primary control. Top management must:

(1) set company objectives that provide criteria and direction to the product fields of primary interest for the company;

(2) make decisions on recommended product development projects to be undertaken;

(3) decide whether or not to test the new product and the extent to which testing will be done;

(4) make the decisions on commercialization; i.e., whether or not to undertake a full-scale marketing effort;

(5) decide on major changes in product or program once the product is on the market.

## MARKETING IS THE GUIDE

Prompt top-management action at any and each of these points can avoid costly losses and assure greatest profit potential. The matter of profitability grows constantly and increasingly in importance, and marketing requirements have become the guiding consideration in successful product planning for that profitability. For, as the report noted, "Few products fail because of technical deficiencies" and "In today's economy it is getting increasingly easier to make a product than sell it."

The top management that understands this basic truth is in a better position to shape the form and direction of a company's efforts to grow through successful new-product programs.

## QUESTIONS

1. Business strategy is fundamentally product planning. Explain.
2. Why are new products so costly?
3. For successful product development, top management must exercise primary control in what five basic areas?
4. The odds against the commercial success of a new product idea before it goes into development is about 50-to-one. Comment.

# 30. Integrating the Over-all Development Program*

D. W. Karger, Head Department of Management Engineering, Rensselaer Polytechnic Institute

*Standards of performance are met when marketing has an appropriate voice in the selection and development of new product ideas; when product innovations reflect the findings of marketing research and result in profitable sales; and when new items and lines are integrated into the company's portfolio without undue expense or effort.*

Products are developed to be sold, not to be kept on laboratory shelves as curiosities. The over-all development program must therefore include all the major functional elements of the enterprise; it cannot be restricted to the consideration of laboratory functions alone. In a word, it must be *integrated*. It is true, of course, that in most cases the actual process of integration involves organization; yet, if the place of need is known, the nature of the need defined, and the general objective established, a practical person with a general understanding of organizational principles can design the appropriate organization structure, assign the requisite duties and responsibilities, and staff the effort with whatever personnel are necessary.

## DETERMINING THE NEED FOR INTEGRATION

Marketing considerations are, of course, pre-eminently important in any development program. In this connection one hears such terms as "new features,"

* Reprinted from *The Marketing Job*, p. 211. Published by the American Management Association, Inc., 1961.

"product improvement," "modification," "innovation," "new product," "expanded market," and "new market" tossed about very casually these days, with little regard for precision or clarity. The chart on pages 214 and 215 is designed to help remedy this situation by identifying more specifically the relationship between the various degrees of product newness and market newness. With the help of this chart, it is hoped, management will be able to determine more precisely what in any given company should be considered a new product from the marketing point of view.

As the chart indicates, it is possible to achieve various degrees of product newness from a technological viewpoint without significantly affecting the market; conversely, it is also possible to develop new markets without developing new products. A relatively minor technical modification of an existing product can vastly expand its market; indeed, it can make such a product a great deal more important to the company than a new product involving radically advanced technology. Such minor technical modifications can also have a tremendous impact upon manufacturing costs, processing problems, and facilities requirements.

It seems quite logical, then, to evaluate each laboratory or engineering project from both a manufacturing and a marketing viewpoint to determine (1) whether the project deserves handling as a major development program and (2) which aspects of the project require special attention. Without such consideration, a project can have a disastrous impact or, at very least, fail to provide maximum benefits. My first recommendation, therefore, is to evaluate *every* research and engineering project—not merely major development programs—to determine whether they need over-all integration and, if they do, which aspects require special attention.

## INTEGRATION WITH MANUFACTURING FUNCTIONS

Most companies engaged in product development today, I am sure, have at one time or another had the sad experience of finding that the marketability of a new product in which considerable amounts of time, money, and manpower had been invested was severely limited because of excessive production costs. The creation of such monsters can often be prevented by bringing industrial engineering and/or production engineering into the development program at an early stage; at times, in fact, this is the only practical solution.

A rather simple but practical example in my own experience involved a Magnavox mercuric oxide battery. In its original prototype stage, this product consisted essentially of only six elements: two metal cans, a plastic separator, parchment paper, a cathode of compacted mercuric oxide, and an anode of gelatinized electrolyte containing zinc particles. The

engineering and development groups argued for a period of three years that the unit was so simple it could not help but be competitive. Despite the product's apparent simplicity, however, the engineering and development groups were unable to prove with legitimate cost estimates that the unit could be produced competitively. It was only after industrial engineering and production engineering had been integrated into the program, had identified the factors contributing to the high production costs, and had helped the engineering and development groups eliminate them that we were able to assure ourselves that we had a competitive product. True, the industrial and production engineers did not contribute to the basic design concept, but they were able to guide the original engineering thinking into more practical design channels.

The principal reasons, then, for integrating industrial and production engineering into the development program are (1) to cut costs and (2) to help get production started on schedule. The second reason can be just as important—and, in some cases, even more important—than the first.

All major companies today have some sort of established cost-estimating procedure; some even have a cost-estimating department. The function or functions involved are extremely important to successful new-product development, for excessive cost is a barrier to the success of any new product. The biggest problem in this area is generally not one of faulty procedures or incompetence but rather one of low morale stemming from a lack of understanding of the problems involved. Cost estimators are generally very precise and well-organized individuals, and they like to have their work come to them in the same fashion. Unfortunately, engineers have only partial

| | | | |
|---|---|---|---|
| Expansion of sales into new classes of customers. | No change in product, but new classes of customers reached. Probably involves finding some new uses for product. This type of market expansion may occur without expansion of sales to old classes of customers; it may even occur when sales to old classes of customers are decreasing. Finding new uses for product may involve technical or new-product assistance. | No change in product, but new classes of customers reached. Probably involves finding some new uses for product. This type of market expansion may occur without expansion of sales to old classes of customers; it may even occur when sales to old classes of customers are decreasing. Finding new uses for product may involve technical or new-product assistance. | Expanded sales to new classes of customers will not occur automatically. If they do occur, it will be principally for same reasons and in same manner that they could occur for an unchanged product. |
| Strengthened market in existing classes of customers. | Remerchandising and/or other efforts to expand sales result in selling to more customers of the same types previously served. | Remerchandising and/or other efforts to expand sales result in selling to more customers of the same types previously served. | Market coverage for present classes of customers is likely to increase because of improvements in product characteristics and merchandisability. The altered product characteristics could affect prices, but the general aim is always to reduce costs and increase profit margin, increasing prices only when absolutely necessary. |
| No market change. | No change in product characteristics and no change in market penetration. | No change in product characteristics and no change in market penetration. | Positive market change likely to result, but some adverse market parameters could hold sales constant or even let them slip. |
| | No product change. | Product characteristics unchanged in spite of changes in components, formulation, production techniques, etc. to keep costs in line and quality at same relative level. | Improvement in product characteristics to yield greater utility to customers and/or increase merchandisability through improved packaging, etc. |

INCREASING MARKET NEWNESS

INCREASING

| | | | |
|---|---|---|---|
| In effect, the marketing function is here concerned with what is essentially a new product and is faced with almost all the problems associated with a new product. | Opening of new markets does not automatically follow introduction of a replacement product. Unless changes in characteristics and/or price obviously open new markets, new applications must be actively sought and aggressively exploited in order to reach new classes of customers. | Addition of new items of products to a given product line can make it possible to attract new classes of customers, especially where a previously incomplete line made it necessary for certain classes of customers to buy from several manufacturers. When this barrier is removed, new customer classes can often be reached. This device also often operates to increase market penetration with existing classes of customers. | Sales of new products in a new product line obviously mean reaching new customers and, generally, new classes of customers. This is the extreme opposite of the "no product change, no market change" situation. |
| Not applicable; no previous market. | Replacement products usually lend themselves to a remerchandising campaign for the purpose of achieving greater penetration of existing markets. | Introduction of such new products strongly tends to strengthen sales to existing customers. | Not generally applicable; no previous market. (See comment above.) |
| Not applicable; no previous market. | Depth of market penetration could remain constant, but when product changes involved are drastic enough, they are likely to change market penetration. An example of a less drastic change which had comparatively little effect on market penetration was the substitution of synthetic resin for shellac in S. C. Johnson & Son's Glo-Coat in 1950. | Not applicable; no previous market. | Not applicable; no previous market. |
| Major modification of product characteristics to aim at new classes of customers for entirely new applications. Company might continue producing old product for existing class of customers. | Replacement of an existing product through new technology—for example, the replacement of a tube-type portable radio with a transistorized model. | Product line extension—for example, development by S. C. Johnson & Son of Emeral, a floor cleaner which extended the company's maintenance product line in 1953. The miniature electrolytic capacitor introduced by Magnavox late in 1957 is another example. | Diversification, or the addition of a new product line—for example, the introduction of Raid, a dual-purpose insecticide, by S. C. Johnson & Son, and of a high-speed sampling switch by Magnavox. |

**PRODUCT NEWNESS** ⟶

information when they evaluate a product still in the development stage; consequently, either they assume that the estimators will be able to deduce the necessary information from the unorganized and incomplete data provided them, or else they look upon the whole matter of cost estimation as an unnecessary chore. Couple this attitude with the necessity of going through this messy procedure many times for the same product, and you have the origin of a serious morale problem.

Knowing the problem and its origin is more than half the battle. Cost estimators must be brought in—not held off, as they so often are. If each party can be made to consider the other's problems and to understand their collective relationship in the effort, the problem will be whipped.

The way these functions are integrated into the development program depends not only upon the organization structure involved but also upon the individual personalities and capabilities involved. It is possible, for example, to assign industrial or production engineers to engineering and development teams working on projects for the future; they can also be assigned to a section chief in a staff capacity; and there are probably any number of other effective approaches. A certain amount of "hand holding" and careful explanation is also vital if these men are to work well together.

What is required for one particular development project is not necessarily required for another. If the product is such that only a low level of quality control will be required, for example, there is no need to bring in quality control people at an early point in the development program. If, on the other hand, the product is such that there are obviously going to be major problems in manufacturing which will be difficult to solve, the factory quality control function should be

integrated into the project at an early date. In short, although there are certain specific areas that should be considered, not all will pose integration problems for every development project.

Another important manufacturing function which needs to be considered is production supervision. When it appears that the techniques involved are going to be complex, it is often advisable to have production supervisors help the engineering department construct the pilot models. This procedure not only is a world beater for training purposes but also qualifies the participants as instructors. Moreover, each supervisor will be better able to understand the operator's problems.

## INTEGRATION WITH MARKETING FUNCTIONS

If our development program is to start off on a sound footing, marketing research must make a preliminary definition of the market. Although this step is obviously a necessity, many development programs have been started merely because one or two individuals thought it would be a good idea to work on a particular problem, or because an executive's request for an opinion was misconstrued as a suggestion to inaugurate a program.

The market is changing every minute in our dynamic world. Marketing researchers obviously cannot afford to sit back and consider any definition of the market as a final pronouncement. All too often, the market either contracts or expands suddenly because of the general economic situation, the appearance of competitive products on the scene, or a major change in related technology. In short, the marketing research function should be integrated into the development program in its initial stages and should continue to function from then on—throughout the life of the resulting product.

Advertising, another important marketing function, does not need to be integrated into the program early, but it should be pulled in prior to the program's completion. It takes time to plan advertising approaches, produce copy and artwork, make contracts with the various media to be used, develop new-product news releases, write technical bulletins, and prepare promotional campaigns. At just what point advertising should be integrated into the project depends to a large extent upon the amount of advertising work to be done. In other words, enough time should be allowed that the task can be completed in a satisfactory and well-organized manner.

Since a product is worthless if it cannot be sold, the sales function must, like marketing research, be brought into the picture at the inception of the development program. The marketing research and sales functions must work hand in hand with research, development, and engineering. The success of a product often depends upon its special features, and determination of the features the customer wants is generally the result of a joint effort on the part of the sales and marketing research functions. They must, however, be careful to determine the true economic worth, to the customer, of every special feature. It is possible to add so many features to a product that it is no longer an economical buy for the customer; engineering often tends to drift in this direction.

## ACHIEVING TOTAL INTEGRATION

Two other functions that are essential to the success of a product development program are accounting and finance.

These functions are involved not only in analyzing the investment required but also in establishing the project's budget, and the talents of financial and accounting personnel should be used to help keep that budget in line.

The integration of all these diverse functions cannot be achieved by waving a magic wand; each of the various organizational elements involved must be carefully combined with all the rest to form an effectively functioning team. Serious consideration should be given to assigning this task to a new-product development group, so placed organizationally that it can operate effectively throughout the company. This means, of course, that the function must report either to the chief executive or to the head of marketing or engineering, depending upon the product emphasis in the company concerned.

In addition to coordinating the efforts of the various organizational elements with regard to each development project, the new-product development function should also see that detailed schedules are established, and should measure performance against them. By "detailed schedules" I mean, not merely target dates for broad tasks, such as prototype construction or drawing, but precise timetables for each segment of a task, such as determination of the metal alloy needed or the degree of vacuum required.

It is true, of course, that many of the detailed tasks performed by any given function are likely to be interrelated, thus making completion-date forecasting difficult; it is also true, however, that detailed schedules provide a good basis for judging progress. My advice is: *Try them!*

## QUESTIONS

1. It is possible to achieve various degrees of product newness from a tech-

nological viewpoint without significantly affecting the market. Explain.

2. Why must industrial and production engineering be integrated into the product development program?

3. Enumerate and describe the various business functions that should be involved in product development.

4. What services can marketing research perform in the product development program?

# 31. Who Should Control New Product Development?*

*Should marketing control new product development in the industrial company? Or engineering? Or any other department of the company? A group of industrial company presidents give their answers.*

At American Air Filter, new and improved product responsibility rests with the marketing function. This assignment was prompted by two major considerations. First, our marketing people are closer than engineering to our customers and to the performance of our products. Changing customer needs are more quickly known and desirable improvements in product performance incorporated in the development program.

The second factor recognizes how important new and improved products are to the vitality and profitability of the company's operation. An effective program will be reflected in the volume of new orders received. Here, again, is a yardstick close to marketing whose performance is judged in part by their ability to increase their sales volume at optimum profit.

We see no lack of engineering contribution to new product ideas under our organizational setup. The skill of our

* Reprinted from *Industrial Marketing*, p. 129. Copyright 1959 by Advertising Publications Inc., 200 E. Illinois St., Chicago 11, Ill.

engineering group in these areas is recognized throughout the company. However, under marketing, better selection of products to be developed and a more noticeable sense of urgency are obtained.

Centralized control by management is retained through required approval of major new product research and development expenditures and through the establishment of priorities in an annual budgeting program. Research and development expenses represent major investment of company funds, and as such deserve the same management scrutiny that capital appropriations requests receive.

Exploration of new products outside existing product lines is handled as a function of central staff. They also serve as a control group through quarterly checks of progress against the forecasts for the research and development program.

The saleability of a product and its marketing limitations is, in our opinion, the most important consideration of a manufacturer; therefore it is our firm conviction that the director of sales should control new product development.

We follow that policy in our new product development program at Big Joe Manufacturing Co. Here's how the program works:

In delegating the individual responsibilities, we set up a new product program meeting to which we invite our sales manager, chief engineer, plant production manager, advertising manager, research and development team, legal counsel and top management.

The purpose of each original meeting is to set up a meeting series which has as its objective, the control of progress toward the marketing of new products so that all key aspects are accomplished at the proper time in relation to the release of the product to the market. This involves design, production, advertising, pricing and the functions relative to the release of a new product for which the men listed above are responsible.

The initial content of this group is intended to include those who have the most direct interest in the accomplishment of required work and whose participation will simplify communications.

The first meeting is intended to determine just what will be required in the long run.

After an initial review of our objectives in this meeting, we find it worth while to have the new product program meeting on a biweekly basis. Coordinating with each of the departments, the director of sales sets up the agenda for each meeting. In other words, the promotional letters, catalogs, operating and maintenance manuals, patents, registration of trademark, procurement, production and ability to ship on schedule, subsequent to the original development plans, are all definite responsibilities of the sales group who must have all of the answers ready for the customer. It is the sales group who contact the buyer of our product. It is the sales group who must be fully informed regarding the progress of a new product. It is, therefore, the director of sales who must control new product development.

In the field of steel strapping and allied items for use in package reinforcement, unitizing of articles for ease in handling, and securing shipments of goods, there are many factors to be taken into consideration. First, the variety of products which need securing into units that are easy to handle and ship is limited only by the imagination. Consequently, a great number of special applications and special tools for application of strapping, need to be provided.

Secondly, within many industries, practices have been developed for handling or shipping certain materials which require special tools or machinery or methods singular to that industry. Third, the development of new methods of producing many materials includes forming into shapes or conditions which now make strapping possible where previously the shape or form prevented a unitized or consolidated package for handling; for example, items handled and sold in bulk form.

The merchandising of strapping tools and machines for these myriad applications puts great demands on the ingenuity of the user as well as the seller. Over the years, the mechanical handling of products within a plant or in loading into a transport vehicle, or in handling at the destination point has shown a trend from small size containers and units to large size containers and units, and from the hand application of strapping to the semiautomatic or automatic machine-applied strap.

We believe that the development of new methods of band application, new tools for increasing operator efficiency and reducing cost of strapping application, and the increasing number of newer and more difficult items to be strapped calls for unceasing attention to these problems, and we look upon this attention as vital to our continued growth.

So vital is our development of tools, methods, materials and accessories, that we have organized this activity under a corporate vice-president whose sole and complete responsibility is in this development. The activity itself consists of three general categories of work; namely, Sales Engineering, Development Engineering and Application Engineering.

A development committee, consisting of the vice-president in charge of new products, vice-president in charge of marketing, chief engineer, superintendent of production and the products managers thoroughly discuss ideas for consideration by the development group prior to their actually being developed. All phases of manufacture, production, market determination and the like, are fully analyzed by this committee at the outset, and as a tool or machine is in the process of design and development. In this fashion, all of the techniques available to the marketing and sales group, the production group, and the engineering group are available to be applied to the problems of the development of new ideas.

In time, new product development may come into the sphere of marketing activity, which is normal in many companies. However, with the extreme importance of this activity in our particular business, it is currently and for sometime will continue to be the direct responsibility of a corporate officer reporting to the president of the company.

The strides that have been made in product development in the last several years have been assisted by the close attention of this committee to this activity, and have done much to stimulate growth in our company's sales.

In Dearborn Chemical Co., a new product usually stems from an "idea" that may come from anyone. While it is to be expected that most workable ideas will originate in our research, sales, or production engineering departments, we want the flow of ideas to be as free and uncontrolled as possible and we encourage everyone in the company to turn in "ideas" with as much preliminary substantiation of the worth of the idea as the individual can muster.

Our Product Planning Committee is the first control point. In order to keep new products from being dominated by either sales, laboratory, or engineering, the Product Planning Committee personnel is appointed annually from junior supervisory personnel to represent all facets of the company.

Where an idea can be adequately evaluated by the Planning Committee personnel they are empowered to act either by rejection or referral. If the project is one which envolves sizeable expenditures in research, engineering, or marketing it is submitted to our Product Policy Board, made up of senior personnel from all divisions of the company, including administration. At this stage, estimates must have been made on time and money to be spent and a survey made of marketing. We have a New Products Department to assist in this preparation.

An idea approved by the Policy Board and developed within the company to the stage of field testing and final customer approval is handled by the New Products Department before being released to Sales.

Our philosophy is to allow as much freedom as possible, while retaining an objective analysis of new product development to the end that time and money is not dissipated in a hit or miss fashion. We are also seeking to avoid domination by any one division of the company which could result in only "pet" projects moving ahead and what should be objective controls becoming unreasonable road blocks in the way of progress.

We believe that to put new products completely under the control of an existing division of the company or under a New Products Department without frequent review and administrative attention by the senior officers concerned with overall progress can impede what should be one of the company's most important activities.

## QUESTIONS

1. What departments are represented on the product planning committee at Dearborn Chemical Company?

2. In what essential ways does the development committee of the firm marketing steel strapping and allied items differ from the product planning committee at Dearborn Chemical Company?

3. What can go wrong if sales controls new product development?

# 32. New Products—Keys to Corporate Growth*

Taylor W. Meloan, Professor and Chairman, Department of Marketing and Transportation, Graduate School of Business, University of Southern California

*The management of new product development requires careful attention to new product idea sources and to methods of appraisal. Most concerns are still experimenting with organizational procedures and techniques for new product evolution.*

## IMPORTANCE OF NEW PRODUCTS

No phase of marketing management has received greater attention in industry during recent years than has new product planning, research, and development. The reasons for this stress are obvious. In most industries, competitive pressures require a constant flow of technologically

* Reprinted from *Marketing: A Maturing Discipline*, Proceedings of the Winter Conference of the American Marketing Association, December 28–30, 1960, p. 28. Edited by Martin L. Bell.

new goods or improvements in existing ones if corporate sales and profits are to be sustained or enhanced. In chemicals, metal working machinery, industrial installations, and transportation equipment, as examples, new products have accounted for 40 to 80 per cent of sales increases during the past five years. The same is true in many consumer goods markets. The drug, cosmetic, photographic, toy, and household goods fields have been especially prolific in new product introductions in the immediate past. Some relatively small firms have blossomed overnight on the basis of a single new development that has caught on.

The current softening of our economy is not likely to result in less emphasis on new products. Indeed, it will probably lead to an increase in over-all research and development and more new technology as firms continue to scramble for the consumer and/or the industrial dollar. There is every reason to believe that the Kennedy administration will implement its campaign pledge of increased government support for "basic" and military research from which commercially feasible developments may emerge. Thus, it seems logical to assume that over-all R & D budgets, which include allocations for new product research in most firms, will spurt ahead of the estimated current $10 billion annual total.[1]

## NEW PRODUCT
## BATTING AVERAGES

For years we have read that four out of five new products fail. This cliché stems from an early postwar study of 200 leading packaged goods manufacturers. Since respondents were asked about their success with products actually introduced, it is contended that the failure rate would have been even greater if those which never reached the commercialization stage, on which management spent considerable time and talent in laboratory, field, and office, had also been included in the calculations.[2] Also, since the sample was restricted to *large*

firms, it is often argued that the success ratio would have been much less had *smaller,* and presumably less sophisticated firms, been included in the survey. However, these are unproven hypotheses that are at least partially refuted by later data. In a survey completed in New England in 1954 of 82 firms making industrial goods, 357 of 515 new products introduced during the previous five year period were considered to be successful. Of this group, 45 per cent enjoyed sales equal to expectations, while 19.5 per cent exceeded projected volume.[3] Study of new product success ratios in the electronics field have produced similar conclusions.

**Success Criteria. . . .** In part, these differing ratios stem from lack of common norms for defining product success. While sales volume and profits are traditional ones, ancillary success criteria cited by marketing managers include the following: tapping new markets, making other orders possible, absorbing excess capacity, providing potential for expansion, reinforcing a firm's reputation as a leader, and reducing returns or complaints about performance. A high score on one or more of the foregoing criteria could result in a new product with a mediocre sales record being considered a satisfactory addition to a line.

**Failure Rates in Consumer Versus Industrial Fields. . . .** There is reason to believe that consumer goods producers often experience a higher new product failure rate than do those making industrial goods. Generally, there are more distribution variables to consider in successfully launching new consumer items than is the case with industrial products. Furthermore, the extensive promotional budgets required for many nationally distributed consumer

[1] See David Novick, "What Do We Mean by Research and Development," *California Management Review* (Spring, 1960), pp. 9–14 for a discussion of the components of R&D budgets and their non-comparability from firm to firm.

[2] Ross Federal Research Corporation, "A Survey of 200 Leading Package Goods Manufacturers on Experiences and Problems Prevalent in the Introduction of a New Product" (New York: Ross Federal Research Corporation, 1945), p. 4.

[3] Wm. B. Martz, "A Survey of Reasons Behind the Introduction of New Industrial Products" (Cambridge, Massachusetts: School of Industrial Management, Massachusetts Institute of Technology, unpublished manuscript, 1954), p. 37.

goods in highly competitive lines create difficult-to-achieve breakeven points which are not common in job-order industrial fields where limited markets and small volume do not necessarily spell failure. Admittedly, however, large research investments in technologically new industrial products can lengthen pay-out periods unduly, thereby creating situations comparable to those faced by new consumer goods in intensely competitive markets.

## NEW PRODUCT
## POLICY GUIDES

Although many firms now have written statements covering their new product emphasis or objectives, there is considerable evidence indicating that these policy guides are frequently so broad that they are of limited value in channeling effort. Product scope, desirable mix, and profitability criteria are too often inadequately covered. The marketing managers of other concerns indicate that written product policy statements are unnecessary because of the close rapport among members of the top management team; but, when they give differing replies to questions about new product plans, there is obvious reason to question their agreement.

**Clear Cut Goals Needed. . . .** The first and most elementary step in achieving new product planning, research, and development maturity is to formulate logical accomplishment goals. This implies a complete audit of company strengths and weaknesses. An objective analysis of production capacity, availability of materials, adequacy of labor, management talent, and distribution facilities provides the basis for future planning. What one firm may reasonably expect to accomplish may be a pie-in-the-sky dream for another.

**Production and Marketing Fit. . . .** In many successful companies, the key factor influencing the selection of new products for development and commercialization is the degree to which they fit or mesh with the present line. A high degree of production accord exists when present plant, labor, equipment, and manufacturing processes can be used in making new products. Acceptable adjustment requires minimum additions or alterations in one or more of these production categories. Such firms also consider it desirable when a contemplated addition to the line can be manufactured with materials and components identical or similar to those used in current production. This is the rationale of the Ekco Products Company, which is probably best known to most of us for its housewares and cutlery. Because of this firm's production know-how with metals, its primary areas of product interest are other houseware items and builders' hardware.

From a marketing standpoint, new product harmony exists when established distribution outlets and sales organizations can be used to move a new good or line through the pipelines. Helene Curtis Industries, Inc., for example, is interested chiefly in new products that may be sold through drug, grocery, department, and variety stores—its traditional channels. The possibility of using the same service or repair facilities and personnel enhances the fit between current products and new ones as does blanket brand identification. The recent introduction of the Hoover Company's new floor polisher was facilitated by the firm's half century image as a leader in home cleaning equipment.

**Decisions Depend Upon Objectives. . . .** Lack of a high degree of production or marketing adjacency between established products and contemplated new ones does not necessarily mean that new product ideas should be discarded. This decision depends upon a firm's objectives. As the Cheshire Cat commented to Alice (in Wonderland), where one goes depends a great deal on where he wants to get to. Smoothing out seasonal fluctuations in sales was reported to be a prime consideration behind the purchase of the assets of the Inserting and Mailing Machine Company by Bell and Howell. Textron-American, Inc. has sought to overcome low profits in the textile field by moving into industries where 20 per cent after taxes on net worth may be earned. Virtually all West Coast aircraft companies have established commercial products divisions largely because of short run insecurity over cold war temperature changes and also the longer run phasing out of military air-frame construction. In short, there are many pertinent and often inter-related reasons why firms move into new lines or industries.[4]

**Propagation and Acceptance of Criteria. . . .** In most companies, including those previously cited, product scope and mix are usually determined on the basis of multiple criteria. Regardless of what they are, such considerations should be *recorded, disseminated, understood, promoted,* and *accepted* by all appropriate personnel through the intermediate management levels of the enterprise. The establishment of product-line parameters should not stifle management imagination, but rather guide it in directions designed to maximize the achievement of company objectives. Consideration of ideas which clearly fall outside of the boundaries that have been set up should require exceptional justification.

Annual review of product policy statements is desirable to make sure that they continue to reflect corporate objectives.

[4] See Thomas A. Staudt, "Product Diversification," *Harvard Business Review* (November–December, 1954), pp. 122–123 for a list of 43 reasons for diversification.

If they have been carefully drafted initially, only minor changes should be needed from time to time in the absence of an abrupt shift in management thinking.

## NEW PRODUCT IDEA SOURCES

Study of a large number of new product case histories fails to show any single source of ideas as the most fruitful one. Generally, however, internal sources are cited more often than external ones as creative seedbeds. Some companies seem to have a dearth of suggestions while others are deluged with them. The key factor stimulating the internal flow of ideas appears to be an innovationist philosophy which pervades the entire organization. A highly motivated management team in a permissive organization that is known to be willing to accept the risks of new product evolution is almost sure to be more productive of ideas than equally competent men in an authoritarian, or "fat and tired" firm that is primarily interested in maintaining the status quo.

In part, however, the number of product ideas available for consideration is a function of a firm's definition of "newness." Concerns that limit product change to minor variations in operation, design, color, or packaging are likely to have more ideas to consider than those that seek true technological newness. Companies with well structured R&D facilities and engineering laboratories typically get more worthwhile ideas internally than do smaller companies that perforce often turn to external sources such as customers, raw material suppliers, competitors, firms in allied fields, government agencies, consulting organizations, research institutes, or free lance product analysts.

**Independent Idea Screeners. . . .** Organizations that specialize primarily in generating new product ideas and/or analyzing those submitted by outsiders for clients are a relatively new breed of business service. Because of the cost and complexity of finding worthwhile product ideas, 140 Los Angeles metal products manufacturers of everything from wheelbarrows to missile components belong to Associated Specialists, Inc.—a former trade association that actively solicits new products for its members.[5] In Boston, the Product Development Corporation screens for its 12 clients between 300 and 400 suggestions submitted weekly by outsiders. According to PDC, one idea of practical merit can be winnowed from every 1,000 submitted.[6] About two per cent of those received by Associated Specialists are worthy of development.

**Legal Hazards. . . .** Use of such outside agencies can mitigate to some degree the legal hazard of having a confidential relationship thrust upon a company for alleged or actual use of an unsolicited idea. Cautious firms that decline to consider unpatented suggestions from outsiders often return such letters with covering notes stating that mail clerks stopped reading when the nature of the correspondence became apparent. Other companies return suggestions with release forms for the signature of those submitting ideas. Generally these waivers disclaim liability if the company examines the proposal. They specify further that payment shall be at the firm's sole discretion and shall not exceed a stipulated amount. The obvious purpose of these steps is to preclude a confidential relationship developing unless and until

agreement is reached regarding compensation, if any, for the idea.

Rather than enter into royalty arrangements with outsiders, many companies prefer to buy outright ideas or information which interests them, or they may escrow the proposition with a third party who is technically qualified to evaluate its merits. In any event, most attorneys consider it highly unwise to submit unsolicited ideas to a panel or a committee of technical or management personnel for evaluation prior to limiting corporate obligations to the outsider.[7] On the other hand, some marketing managers argue that so few ideas from outsiders have any real merit that a critical review of all confidential disclosures can hardly put a firm in serious legal danger. This is more likely to be true in smaller firms, and especially those making industrial goods, than it is with large, well-known manufacturers of consumer products. Many prominent companies receive hundreds of suggestions weekly from outsiders. Without the use of legal safeguards in handling them, it is almost a foregone conclusion that certain of them would result in lawsuits.

**Advertising for Ideas. . . .** A few companies combine their search for new products with institutional advertising. A recent American Machine and Foundry Company display advertisement in the *Los Angeles Times* identified the firm as creators of leisure time products for the consumer, and manufacturers of chemical and electromechanical equipment for industry and defense. Readers were invited to telephone for an appointment to discuss ideas for new products that might fit within the marketing and manufactur-

[5] Interview with C. W. Farrar, Executive Secretary, Associated Specialists, Inc., Los Angeles, California on December 10, 1960.
[6] Interview with William Donohue, Vice President, Product Development Corporation, Boston, Massachusetts on December 18, 1960.

[7] See Bessie A. Lepper, "Ideas From Outsiders Can Be Dangerous," *Chemical Week* (August 17, 1957), pp. 107–112, and John W. Bohlen, "Legal Considerations in Product Development and Introduction," in *Establishing a New Product Program* (New York: American Management Association, 1958) pp. 30–36.

ing capabilities of an AM&F division, or that could form the basis for an entirely new product line. About 300 replies were received, of which 50 merited further consideration. AM&F contemplates repeating this experiment in other cities.[8]

**New Products by Merger.** . . . Companies that seek new products or lines via merger also sometimes make known their interests in acquisitions by print advertising, especially in business and trade publications. Generally, however, they rely on brokers, consultants, bankers, business friends, and aggressive "scouting" for leads. For example, The L. A. Young Spring and Wire Company, a diversified producer of seats and mattresses, power tail gates, dump truck bodies, and electronic equipment, has compiled a mailing list of 1,500 influential businessmen and community leaders around the country who are reminded occasionally of Young's interest in other enterprises.[9]

Securing acquisition leads is no less difficult than generating ideas for internal development. However, well financed, respected companies that are considered to be merger conscious apparently do not lack for candidates from whom to choose. The Glidden Company and Purex Corporation are reported to be contacted regularly by firms that wish to affiliate with them. While it may be presumed that there are many "cats and dogs" among the list, well managed, desirable firms are also available for consideration. Sometimes they favor merger with a larger and stronger company in order to secure new capital for continued growth. In many other instances, the management of a closely held corporation may want to sell out in order to realize a capital gain, or to make possible an exchange of stock that has inheritance tax advantages.

## ORGANIZATION FOR ACTION

Regardless of whether a firm expands its line by development of products within the firm, through purchase of existing business or products, or by pursuing an ambidextrous policy, organization for action is necessary. Without *motivation, direction,* and *coordination* of staff specifically charged with new product responsibility, it is unlikely that anything will happen. In many firms, initial discussions about the desirability of new products have not led to the creation of appropriate plans and procedures for internal development because executives were too absorbed in day-to-day operations.

**New Product Departments.** . . . In recognition of the importance of new product evolution as a full time activity, more and more firms are setting up new product planning departments. As yet, they rarely exceed four or five managerial members. In fact, many of them initially consist of only a director. The key purposes of these managers and departments are to mesh the gears of the new product creation process and to insure continuity of effort. Liaison between technical and marketing research and development must be maintained, as well as multidirectional communication between staff and line production, finance, and sales personnel. Frequently, too, the work of independent design, marketing, or management consultants must be coordinated with that of the company. Usually product planning managers report directly to top management; common alternatives provide for reporting to the president or executive vice president, to the vice president of

[8] Interview with Hamilton Herman, Vice President, Research and Development, American Machine & Foundry Company, New York, New York on December 22, 1960.
[9] Russell B. Robins, "New Products by Proxy," *Marketing's Role in Scientific Management* (Chicago: American Marketing Association, 1957), pp. 74–78.

research and development, or to the vice president of marketing or sales.[10]

**Use of Committees.** . . . Because of the inter-functional nature of successful new product evolution many companies use one or more kinds of committees to facilitate action in addition to or in lieu of product planning personnel. In some firms, product idea teams plus product screening or evaluation committees have been set up. Creative, divergent thinkers are sought for the former groups, while the latter committees are usually composed of those with analytical, convergent minds who review critically the output of the idea teams. In other firms, these functions are performed by one committee. It generates ideas of its own, passes judgment on those submitted by others within the firm, and reviews suggestions from outsiders that have been cleared by the legal department. If the company has a product planning department, one or more members are usually assigned to each committee. Often the product planning manager is either chairman or secretary of idea and/or screening committees. He seeks to establish a creative climate and a sense of momentum in their deliberations. This is important because committee members usually have day-to-day responsibilities that often seem more pressing. Another common responsibility of product planning department members who are assigned to committees is the maintenance of records about group decisions. Such committees may also be chaired by a member of general management, marketing management, or by an R&D officer. In any event, all of the foregoing areas plus marketing research, finance, production, and sales are likely to be represented.

While the use of committees and/or new product departments are the prevailing ways of expediting new product evolution, this responsibility is borne in some companies solely by the research and development department, by the sales department, or by a member of top management, even the president. The Stauffer Chemical Company is a successful case in point. The president directs all new product activities personally.

**Initial Appraisal.** . . . Preliminary screening is an obvious initial step in winnowing new product wheat from chaff. Regardless of whether it is done by a committee, a department, or an individual, experience and judgment are used at this stage far more than formal research. If a firm has established its overall objectives and scope of product interest, the delineation of preliminary screening criteria should not be too difficult. Ideas are considered in the light of these factors. Reference tools largely consist of the telephone, knowledgeable people in the firm, and the reference library.[11] In many companies, from one hour to two days is a common range per idea. Of course, obviously inappropriate ones are rejected immediately.

**Feasibility Analyses.** . . . Ideas that survive preliminary screening are generally subjected next to more detailed technical and marketing analyses. To facilitate research and inter-departmental communications, product proposals are usually prepared at this stage describing the idea and its purposes in concrete terms. Some companies have forms for this purpose that are quite detailed. That of Beckman Instruments is eight pages long. Like many others, it provides space to record the results of research and the estimates of functional specialists about project feasibility. A majority of companies use checklists of some sort for this

---

[10] See Jerome E. McCarthy, "Organization for New Product Development," *The Journal of Business* (April 1959), pp. 128–132 for a review of new product organization structures.

[11] "Survey Report: How to Plan New Products" *The Iron Age* (October 17, 1957), p. 88.

purpose. Those that conduct analyses-in-depth commonly include sections covering the project cost and time schedule, the target date for completion, estimated average return on investment, patent possibilities and restrictions, projected sales in dollars and units for X years, pricing, product life, the effect, if any, on the current line, the competitive situation, manufacturing fit, channels of distribution, promotional investment, and a project P & L statement or break-even chart.

**Evaluation Formulas. . . .** A few companies have experimented with numerical formulas or equations to secure a quantitative indication of an idea's worth. They include the Quaker Oats Company, Monsanto Chemical Company, Olin Industries, Inc., and American Alcolac. In most of these schemes, the rater assigns a point score from a specified range to each of a series of product criteria. In some of them, plus and minus values are used. Others require simple mathematical calculations, but they all provide a total point score or an index number. Their purpose is to establish priorities for developmental consideration. A few firms using new product rating systems have scored past projects, successful and unsuccessful, as bench marks for comparison. These schemes have been controversial. Opponents argue that they are arbitrary and lack flexibility. Supporters rebut with the contention that they force consideration on an organized basis of all of the key variables influencing product success. They point out also that the ratings can be supported or refuted by other data.

The foregoing implies that all companies conduct a detailed study of projects that have survived preliminary screening. This is not always the case. Some firms seek only a broad spectrum of executive opinion about ideas under consideration. They reserve more detailed analysis until the project has been authorized. In

other companies, the depth of analysis depends largely upon the investment in the contemplated product.

**Coordination of the Analysis Phase. . . .** Like preliminary screening, the analysis phase of new product investigation is coordinated in most firms either by a committee, by the new products department, or cooperatively by both. In companies favoring committees, the preliminary screening group may also coordinate the feasibility investigation. In other firms, these activities are kept separated. In large concerns with many projects under consideration, several teams or sponsor groups may be coordinating feasibility studies simultaneously. Team membership depends upon the research requirements. If the firm has a new products department, it is usually represented on each group, and part of the data gathering is done by that department. Naturally other areas and functional specialists must be called upon for help. In firms that do not rely upon committees and/or new products departments to coordinate idea analyses, this phase of product evolution will likely be directed by a designated member of general management, marketing management, sales, or R&D.[12]

When the feasibility investigation is complete, the data must be summarized with a recommendation—usually by the executive in charge of the research. Often segmental approvals by area heads are secured. Then, proposals are examined *in toto* by the executive committee of the firm and/or by the officials in charge of new products. They may approve the project, table it, or reject it; or they may authorize additional research before a final decision is made.

**Acquisition Screening. . . .** Organiza-

[12] See James H. Walter, "An Evaluation of the Process of New Product Idea Evaluation for Consumer Goods" (Bloomington, Indiana: School of Business, Indiana University, unpublished manuscript, 1960), pp. 67–107 for a detailed review of the preliminary screening and feasibility analysis phases of new product evolution.

tion for action is equally necessary if a company embarks upon an acquisition program. However, the screening arrangements for mergers are usually less complex than those required for internal evolution of products. The former is often done under the direction of the president, chairman, or a designated member of top management. Firms like the Rockwell Manufacturing Company use extensive evaluation checklists, and functional specialists within the firm are called upon as needed in the analysis process. Consultants are often used too, especially to conduct management audits. Generally, attention is given to the candidate's production facilities, inventories, finances, market position, and product lines.

## SUMMING UP

Most concerns are still experimenting with organizational procedures and techniques for new product evolution. There is no one best way that will fit every firm. The foregoing approaches must be adapted creatively to meet specific company needs and situations. Intelligent planning, an intense pioneering spirit, and continuity of effort are the key attributes in achieving success. New product planning, research, and development is still in its youth, but it is on the threshold of maturity.

## QUESTIONS

1. What are the chief sources of new product ideas?
2. How do companies organize for new product development?
3. Is it true that approximately four out of every five new products fail?
4. Explain the meaning of production and marketing fit.

## BIBLIOGRAPHY FOR CHAPTER V

ARTICLES:

Benson, Purnell H., and Pilgrim, Francis J., "Testing Less Desirable Product Possibilities," *Journal of Marketing*, Vol. 25, No. 5 (July 1961), pp. 65–68.
"How G.E. Stays on Top," *Sales Management Magazine*, Vol. 84, No. 5 (March 4, 1960), pp. 69–70.
"How New Products are Planned and Why?" *Printers' Ink, Vol.* 269, No. 3 (October 16, 1959), pp. 74–75.
Karns, E., and Mcgee, H. T., "Product Planning Aids Industry," *Iron Age*, Vol. 186, No. 21 (November 24, 1960), pp. 92–94.
McCarthy, E. J., "Organization for New Product Development," *Journal of Business*, Vol. 32, No. 1 (January 1959), pp. 128–32.

BOOKS:

Bursk, Edward C., *Text and Cases in Marketing: A Scientific Approach*. Englewood Cliffs, N.J.: Prentice-Hall, 1962. Section Six.
Buskirk, Richard H., *Principles of Marketing: The Management View*. New York: Holt, Rinehart and Winston, 1961. Part 3.
Faville, David E., *Selected Cases in Marketing Management*. Englewood Cliffs, N.J.: Prentice-Hall, 1961. Section Three.
Howard, John A., *Marketing Management: Analysis and Decision*. Homewood, Ill.: Irwin, 1957. Chapter X.
Lazo, Hector, and Corbin, Arnold, *Management in Marketing*. New York: McGraw-Hill, 1961. Chapter 5.
McCarthy, E. Jerome, *Basic Marketing: A Managerial Approach*. Homewood, Ill.: Irwin, 1960. Section C, Chapters 1, 2, and 3.
Phelps, D. Maynard, and Westing, J. Howard, *Marketing Management*. Homewood, Ill.: Irwin, 1960. Parts II and III.
Phillips, Charles F., and Duncan, Delbert J., *Marketing Principles and Methods*. Homewood, Ill.: Irwin, 1960. Chapter 23.
Tosdal, Harry R., *Introduction to Sales Management*. New York: McGraw-Hill, 1957. Chapter 2.
Westfall, Ralph, and Boyd Harper W., *Cases in Marketing Management*. Homewood, Ill.: Irwin, 1957. Section III.

# VI. Understanding Consumer Behavior

*M*ODERN psychology postulates that behavior is multi-motivated. In studying a single decision, we find interaction and influence of several motivational forces—some economic, others of a more psychological or sociological nature. In some instances, buying decisions are reached only after long and deliberate weighing of two or more conflicting urges—for example, the desire for economy against the craving for recognition.

Today the behavioral sciences are contributing significantly to our knowledge of consumer behavior. For instance, the concept of social class helps us to understand why certain groups buy what they do. While there is a definite relationship between income and social class position, the class concept gives a much fuller insight into spending habits than does level of income alone. A person's shopping habits are closely related to his social background, his attitudes, beliefs, customs and tastes.

Psychologists, sociologists and other behavioral scientists are used in motivation research. Motivation research is a phase of marketing research which attempts to relate behavior to underlying motives or drives both conscious and unconscious. This newer research is person-centered in that it tries to match the personality of the product with the self-images of consumers. Through motivation research, it is frequently possible to isolate those consumer personality variables which are relevant to the sale of the product or service under analysis. On such a factual basis, the product image can frequently be better adjusted to match the dictates of consumer preferences.

Marketing management has been relatively slow in using anthropological insights and approaches even though anthropology is also concerned with man and society. Among other things, anthropologists are well qualified to study and identify the differences which distinguish various nationality groups. They can, for instance, identify the subtle differences in customs and tastes between a Swede, a Dane, and a Norwegian, or between a Brazilian and an Argentinian. An anthropologist's analysis and interpretation of the customs of cultural groups can be of great value in developing foreign markets. The utilization of accepted domestic marketing practices in selling overseas may unwittingly violate a deeply ingrained cultural or religious taboo, or mos.

It is unfortunate that neither sociology, psychology, nor cultural anthropology can give us one theory which can explain all human behavior. Behavioral scientists have considerable disagreement among themselves, and we are still a long way from a general science of human behavior which could be applied automatically to marketing. However, behavioral scientists are contributing significantly to a more penetrating and rigorous analysis of consumers in their socioeconomic environment. As the body of knowledge about human behavior increases and is incorporated into marketing thought and practice, marketing management will continue to serve the needs of consumers more effectively.

# 33. The Rise of Consumership*

Nelson N. Foote, Sociologist, Consumer Behavior Research Program, Marketing and Public Relations Services, General Electric Company

*The affluent, sophisticated consumer of today wants specific qualities at the lowest possible price, and through word-of-mouth recommendation she or he knows what qualities can be gotten where. To the mobile consumer the stock of the stores of the entire area is a broad assortment from which to choose.*

The rise of consumership begins with the rise of income. The massive rise of incomes has generated recognition that we live in an affluent society; it began about 1946 in the United States, and is still continuing. The relative distribution of incomes has not changed during that period, and the distribution of personal assets has actually become more concentrated, but nevertheless millions of families have moved out of the economic situation wherein most of their expenditures are dictated by constraints. While discretionary income is quite a cloudy concept, it is the availability of additional funds, both now and in the future, that gives American consumers their unparalleled maneuverability in the market—their distinctive autonomy, not merely to choose among competing sellers, but to choose how much to buy, when to buy, and whether to buy at all. This power has always been possessed by the affluent, but now it is being exercised on a mass basis, and that is a postwar phenomenon, not even approached during the 1920's. Despite inflation, we are rich.

* Reprinted from *Marketing Precision and Executive Action*, Proceedings of the Forty-fifth National Conference of the American Marketing Association, June 20–22, 1962, p. 604. Edited by Charles H. Hindersman.

The first decade after World War II was a period of stocking up, of sheer quantitative acquisition. Like all parvenus, people went out and bought everything they had previously wanted, with little sense that a problem of choice existed. Home ownership shot up; households became saturated with major durables; wardrobes expanded until all previous closets were insufficient; menus diversified until all previous refrigerators were insufficient; children grew taller than their parents, and parents grew sidewise, until obesity became recognized as the leading national health problem. The year 1955 saw a binge of automobile buying that has not been equalled since.

As we now look back on it, 1956 was a major turning point in our economic history, although we did not realize it at the time. That was when industry indulged in the colossal burst of productive capacity, which has been haunting every manager since. And that was approximately the year, as we can see in retrospect, when consumers began taking a critical look at their previous conduct. The historian might generalize it as the year of transition from quantity to quality in the outlook and behavior of consumers. It was certainly the year when

235

discount houses really hit their stride in the marketing of consumer durables, the beachhead from which they have steadily moved into every other field of distribution, even challenging now the previous champions of merchandising efficiency, the food supermarkets.

In the durables market, the initial forms taken by the shift of emphasis from quantity to quality were the most obvious and direct (1) to get one's money's worth, and (2) to get products of greater dependability. These are interrelated, but represent two slightly different routes to a similar result. In the case of major appliances, for example, it has become increasingly common to shop in large outlets where money can be saved. [In marketing research, as one manifestation, it appears that price shopping is practiced most keenly by middle-income families, not by the highest or lowest] On the other hand, sheer price has not remained the sole criterion. Economy is not a pure function of price, and certainly not where original cost is accompanied by later operating costs, whether for fuel or for service. The service problem has of course been well publicized. The more equipment one owns, the more service he is bound to require. Even if he realizes that more complicated, automatic machinery inevitably creates more probability of breakdown, the annoyances become less tolerable. And so since 1956 we have seen consumers reaching deliberately either for better service on their equipment, or for equipment with higher dependability. Without going into details of changing brand shares, the evidence is by now conclusive that the consumer has been handsomely rewarding those firms which undertook to satisfy his demand for quality in these senses. [For those who built service into the product, rather than providing it later, the consumer has been happy to pay a price premium, and this develop-

ment has promptly shown up in the profits of those firms.]

For several years after 1956, it was none too clear what was happening. The success of the discount stores selling national brands was obvious. On the other hand, the success of national chains of department stores selling private brands was also obvious. Full-line national-brand manufacturers were perplexed by finding some of their products selling much better than others. Some of the latter have striven vigorously to make better product service available to consumers, despite the handicap inherent in being separated from their customers by a vast and diverse array of independent, multi-brand retailers. Others have striven to build more dependability into their products, uniformly across the whole line. And some have endeavored to accomplish both simultaneously. Yet the consumer, despite his increasing sophistication, has found it convenient to latch onto a few outstanding names and simply pass the word around that these were "the best." Almost without exception those so designated have been firms that specialized in that product, usually veteran conservatives, long known in the industry for soundness in manufacturing rather than for innovation or styling. To a lesser degree —that is, less clearly—consumers have seemed in recent years likewise to designate certain merchandising chains as simply "the best" for service, so that it has been hard to discern whether consumers have been rewarding the store itself or its private brand. In either case, the assurance of satisfaction has proven a powerful incentive to favorable discrimination.

It is worthwhile to dwell in some detail on what was happening in that period, now that it is somewhat clearer. First, it deserves emphasis that the specialists among the manufacturers who have experienced extraordinary success did not themselves change; they hewed to their previous policy of good workmanship.[It was the consuming public which changed; customers began about 1956 to put a much higher value on good workmanship.] Second, because everyone had been buying at a great rate, word-of-mouth recommendation has been an unusually feasible source of information for consumers seeking critical evaluations of quality, in a period during which purchasing through personally known and trusted local retailers was on the downgrade. And third, what is for some businessmen a reversal of common sense that they still find hard to accept, the maker who has been willing to specialize on a single quality product has not been forced to serve a minor segment of the market, but has emerged again and again with the biggest share of any competitor in that market. Probably this last point is the outstanding peculiarity of the past five years: Just as discretionary income has become a mass phenomenon, so has the quality-seeking customer. The same phenomenon is also affecting retailing, as will be discussed later.

Meanwhile the lesson of the success of the quality specialist has not been lost on his competitors. To achieve a high level of product dependability has become, in fact, no longer a promise of profitability, but simply a means of survival. It is the familiar spectacle of entire industries imitating the behavior of successful competitors which is bringing this half-decade of emphasis on dependability very rapidly to a close[When every brand of a given product can truly offer the same degree of dependability, then differences in dependability no longer offer the consumer a basis for brand choice. That is the situation we see developing around us now, even though the momentum they acquired by leading the quality parade will be fruitful for the specialists for several years to come.]

As stated at the outset, the rise of income is still continuing. Moreover, consumers are upgrading in many other ways; in average length of schooling, in reading and acquaintance with alternatives, in female employment, in leisure, and above all in practice and skill as consumers, that is, in consumership. And to put the matter in its most condensed statement, upgrading leads to differentiation. Or to put it another way, quality becomes plural.

In the case of durables, instead of defining quality as mere durability, we see consumers self-consciously seeking to discern other qualities to take into account in making their decisions among brands —and among products as well, since products more and more compete with other products. Hence we can foresee that the next champions of the marketplace are going to be those who prove ablest to implement the next definitions of quality to achieve salience in consumer attention. This problem of prediction is of course the topic which engages much advanced marketing research. In our shop, we jokingly call this problem "Which way is up?" And of course this has to be the point at which we shift back to the topic of retailing.

First let me express a violent personal prejudice. It appears to me that in the realm of distribution, to reverse the old adage, much knowledge is a dangerous thing. There is next to no science in retail merchandising as yet. Until there is, what passes as knowledge seems to consist of a vast mass of folklore, anecdote, precedent and rationalizations for present practice. The more such mental impedimenta a person in retailing has absorbed, the more he seems incapacitated for adapting to the changes in consumer behavior that structure his environment. Conversely, the less a person's mind is clouded by antiquated preconceptions, the more clearly he can perceive what is there before him. No kind of human behavior under the sun is as publicly observable as shopping. For the retailer, therefore, the required data are fully available. Hence what seems to be missing are mainly attention to the relevant facts, and possibly some concepts—not necessarily new—for organizing observation.

No doubt youth is a help in being free of preconceptions, as indicated by certain successful mass merchandisers who come to mind. But some older men have perceived clearly what was happening around them, and acted accordingly, and done equally well. In other words, the critical knowledge to consider is not the folklore of years of experience, nor the history of scholars, but understanding of the customer. Some of the quality specialists among manufacturers may have obtained their success virtually by accident, through merely adhering to their traditional strategy, but that cannot be said of the bold mass merchandisers who have so recently sprung onto the stage to challenge the giants. Their confidence does not come from firm adherence to tradition, but from clear and correct perception of consumer tendencies today.

Much is made in the trade press and in scholarly journals of the remarkable efficiency of these new forms of distribution. And certainly the speed with which they have learned to control inventory, eliminate overhead, and speed the flow of goods and money is impressive. They have also begun to adopt every technical device and administrative aid that has come along. But both operating knowledge and operating resources were at least equally available to previous retailers; the differing results lie in part to their differing readiness to utilize innovations and improvements in resources. But even the advantage of faster learning would have been insufficient if the mass merchandisers could not have achieved volume. As they themselves are the first

to explain, their efficiency depends on their volume. But despite some interaction —our old friend, the benevolent spiral— their volume was not generated by their efficiency. Their volume instead arises fundamentally from making the correct choices, from discerning more precisely and selecting more rigorously just what large numbers of consumers would recognize as the goods they were seeking. There is an underlying sympathy here between two parties each striving for correct identification of what one of them wants, that seems to get communicated.

The search for economy certainly was one of these, at the outset. The search for dependability was another; the discounters helped to make the quality specialist brands. The great chains that could offer economy through their private brands, and confidence in satisfaction through their service departments, aimed for both, as already sketched. But here the point is to emphasize that those who succeeded did identify what was wanted. It may not be the same ones who succeed tomorrow, but there is much reason to predict that the so-called revolution in retailing has only gotten started.

There are so many ramifications in trying to anticipate tomorrow's customer in tomorrow's store that perhaps the best way to focus on this matter of being right, through taking account of what is distinctive about the emerging situation, is through pursuing further the distinction between specialist and generalist, as applied to retail outlets.

Instead of starting with institutions as complex as Sears and Zenith, or Macy's and Korvette, let us take an ultrasimple example of achieving volume through selection. Chock Full o'Nuts, as few may realize, began operations during the depression. By offering a severely limited menu—changed daily—at a very low price, it got established quite early in New York, in the face of numerous low-price competitors. It greatly appealed to people who had to eat inexpensively but disliked the characteristics of most cheap eating places. The period of its most spectacular growth, however, has been during the period we have been discussing. Here was the perfect eating place for the sophisticated luncher who wanted only soup and a sandwich of the best quality, in clean and pleasant surroundings, among other customers like himself, who wanted to pay for the food only what it was worth. Many of the customers of Chock Full o'Nuts today are people who on other days pay three dollars for lunch in a restaurant where the menu covers four pages. William Black's discovery that he could obtain incredible volume through rigorous selection has been repeated in men's ties and girls' dresses; in greeting cards, drugs and appliances; even in medical services. In brief, it seems evident that quality specialists have succeeded in retailing as they have in manufacturing. But merely being a specialist is not enough. What is vital is to specialize in the right item for the right customer, who of course must be numerous.

Now right here is the place to restate for retailing the paradox of the past five years, that the quality position in the market can simultaneously mean the biggest market share in competition. The discount merchant builds his efficiency to a very large degree around handling only fast-moving items. He relies on location, price and showmanship to get volume for these items. Yet from the consumer point of view, assortment—breadth or depth of line offered—is a major attraction of an outlet. How is it then that customers seem to flock to stores with such limited offerings as are typical of either the discount department store or the discount specialty store?

[In brief, it certainly cannot be that the consumer, armed with more sophistication and equipped with more resources

than ever before, is deliberately choosing to restrict his own freedom of choice. People of low education and income tend to frequent the low-efficiency outlets, not our exponent of consumership. Instead, the answer has to be that the latter is finding what he is seeking in the high-efficiency outlets.]

The words segregation and discrimination have certain unpleasant connotations, but in retailing we are witnessing a growth of segregation concurrent with the growth of discrimination. The traditional retailer tried to satisfy every customer with his assortment; the selective retailer, by concentrating on only a segment of customers, can give them greater satisfaction with a narrower assortment. [Customers have never wanted assortment for its own sake, but as an inefficient way of finding (out) what they wanted (except perhaps for those who shop for recreation).] In the metropolitan communities in which most Americans now live, and with the mobility conferred by their high level of car ownership, the stock of the stores of the entire area becomes the assortment available to them. Hence each of these stores, even the most generalized, becomes in a sense a specialty shop. And it tends to specialize in those items which move fastest among the customers it attracts. Without the characteristic segregation of the suburbs, the narrow assortment of the suburban branch of a central department store would be a travesty.

Within the next several years, it seems safe to prophesy, discount department stores which compete in the same areas will become as differentiated from each other as they are now from traditional department stores, even though they may carry neither more nor less items in stock than at present. And from the consumer's point of view, this further differentiation will be magnificently welcome. He will eventually be able to buy almost anything under the sun, in a store which specializes in it, without paying any more than he pays now for what is considered a standard item, yet getting the quality he desires.

The arithmetic of market segmentation is bound to baffle any old-timer who does not recognize what has happened during very recent history. Yet there lie greater paradoxes ahead, even after the reality of achieving volume through selection is conceded. There is, for example, the phenomenon of matching.

In the past, a customer with a specific want tried to find it through a wide-ranging kind of search. Stores specialized, or departments specialized, in certain kinds of products, not so much in certain kinds of customers, save for tiny elite shops. Today the big and successful specialize in both products and customers. In the past, the manufacturer of a specific product likewise tried to find customers through a broadcast type of advertising and wide distribution through diverse outlets. Today such wide-ranging search for customers is too inefficient to support. Hence more than ever before the retailer has to become a more sophisticated type of marriage broker, who will bring together the parties who are seeking a match, with minimum exploration of unsatisfactory alternatives.

For the retailer to function effectively in promoting such matching, obviously both the consumer must know what he wants, and the manufacturer must decide what he wants to produce. The product that is suitable for every customer is gone. The manufacturer big enough to make every kind of product wanted by every customer is gone. The store big enough to stock every product made by every manufacturer is gone. Everybody is cherry-picking, not just the multibrand retailer. But for those who can find their matching partners, the cherry crops are bigger than ever before.

The prospects are pleasing, if each assumes he will find his match. But it cannot be too heavily stressed that choosing starts fundamentally with the consumer. The manufacturer and the retailer can collaborate with him in clarifying his choice and in implementing it. But beware of trying to circumvent or control that choice. The consumer today can reward his friends more handsomely than ever before, but in the same measure he punishes those who displease him.

## QUESTIONS

1. Does an expanding discretionary buying power complicate the marketing problems of the seller?

2. Is national advertising or user word-of-mouth advertising more powerful in influencing the sale of merchandise?

3. What are the values that middle-income consumers look for in shopping for merchandise?

4. What consumer attractions does a discount house offer?

5. What merchandising strategies should the manufacturer of consumer goods adopt to meet the rise of consumership?

# 34. Human Motivation—A Basic Factor in the Marketing Process*

W. Dwaine Richins, Associate Professor of Marketing, University of Oregon

*Buyers act like rational people. They decide after applying themselves thoughtfully to problems. Only a few decisions are made as a matter of habit and generally buyers have an interest in the social as well as the personal effects of their choices.*

Over the past thirty or forty years, educators and practitioners in the field of marketing have become progressively more interested in marketing research. We have applied research and statistical techniques to distribution with evident success. But it is becoming disturbingly evident to some of us that students of marketing are stepping with boldness of the novice into fully developed and systematized areas of study and research, where their inexperience is bringing deserved criticism and some discredit to the general field of marketing study. Specifically, this seems to be true as the efforts of marketing students to deal with economic, sociological, political, and psychological problems and questions.

There is no doubt that greater understanding, and aids for management decision in marketing, are realized through rigorous sales analysis and analysis of trading territories and through studies of channels of distribution, product sources, traffic movements, acceptance of product design, etc. But there is some serious question concerning the contribution students in marketing are making or should be expected to make in, for example,

income studies, studies of population problems, racial difference studies, studies of public opinion and its economic impact, and the study of basic effects of advertising and salesmanship in human motivation. Such research presumes a competency which is not typical of marketing people. Marketing students who venture into such studies sometimes fail to realize the depth of thought and research that has been achieved in these fields. It may be suggested that marketing people should be grateful borrowers from these areas rather than enter them as novices without the necessary training.

In two areas, particularly, it appears that marketing research and writing have been "invading" other disciplines—fields of social studies and of motivation. It is with the latter that this paper is particularly concerned.

An important objective of motivation study is the provision of information and ideas which may contribute to our factual knowledge and to the advancement of psychological, social, or economic theory. In business we are particularly concerned with the motivation of marketing decisions—with the mental processes and attitudes of buyers. This is a most difficult yet challenging field of investigation. A

* Reprinted with permission from *Oregon Business Review*, Vol. XVII, No. 12, December 1958.

common term used by marketing people for these processes is "buying habits"; but this term lacks a clear meaning and is often misleading.

"Buying habits" has a strong connotation of deterministic cause and effect associated with it. By "habit" we ordinarily have in mind attention and inclination toward some describable process or action which is acquired by repetition and which involves a decrease or loss in the power of resistance, even though this loss of resistance may be accompanied by an increase in proficiency or facility of performance. A connotation of doing something unconsciously or without premeditation also flavors the concept. As a consequence, a philosophical problem arises. From our cultural heritage we take as almost unquestioned the conclusion that everyone, except perhaps some victims of mental disorders, makes initiating decisions—that he consciously arrives at conclusions, that he thinks and acts creatively, and that he can be held responsible for the consequences of his decisions. Our judgements to commend or condemn rest upon the basic, often unexpressed, assumption that the individual wills his decisions and actions—therefore he must account. Yet it is common for people who are concerned with consumer behavior to accept habitual reaction as its most characteristic element.

It seems to me that the concept of buying habits cannot be defended as a satisfactory tool to explain anything more in the buying process than the term "habit" itself will allow—that is, instances of relatively minor significance, when buyers do, almost unconsciously or without premeditation, reach out and make a purchase. But the concept does not lend itself to explanation of the typical and certainly most important process of thinking, planning, reappraising, and deciding which characterizes almost all purchasing.

Related to the concept of "buying habits," with its cause-effect connotation, is the question so often asked by students of marketing and so often the title of speeches and articles—"Why do people buy (this or that)?" There is with this question, as with the term "buying habits," the fundamental assumption that, in some way, people are *caused* to buy. This assumption is particularly evident in the preparation of promotional and selling campaigns where immediate impact is the objective.

One must hasten to say, however, that psychological investigation does show that there are areas of human motivation in which actions and decisions are the result of stimuli and tensions which are not perceived by the individual; that there are, in other words, some near-causal factors associated with motivation. The effective use of propaganda techniques in promotion as well as politics, learning during sleep, response to subliminal stimuli, etc. provide evidence that action may follow stimuli without conscious decision intervening. However, to approach the selling function with the belief that this is the key to successful selling is, I believe, a basically eroneous, ineffective, and frequently damaging frame of reference. And satisfactory buyer-seller relations are not likely to result.

It is possible, with relative simplicity, for the marketing student to learn who purchased an item, or who influenced its purchase. It is, moreover, not difficult to find the amount and quantity of the purchase; but the basic problem of determining factors directly involved in consumer motivation remains a psychological problem—not a marketing problem. Is there an habitual reaction by individuals when they make their choices? If it is found to be so, then a cause-and-effect relationship may be assumed and the contributions of psychological research is largely one of discovering the nature of that relationship and interpreting it in such a manner that sellers can adapt the information in developing their appeals. If an habitual reaction is found not to be a proper description of the manner in which individuals purchase products and contract for services, then the term "buying habits" is a misnomer and a more appropriate term should be developed to describe how people buy. If we accept the term "buying habits," we must accept the concept that a cause-and-effect relationship exists to a significant degree between the efforts of sellers and the responses of buyers. Any study in this field would therefore be forced to investigate the assumption of cause and effect. But is there really a cause-and-effect relationship? Do we follow an habitual pattern in buying? These questions will, I think, be resolved more conclusively by the psychologist than by the marketing research man.

There are other more productive approaches to the understanding of the buyer-seller relationship than the somewhat conventional "buying habits" approach used in marketing. For example, suppose a person were to investigate buyers' overt and conscious experiences between the time when they first begin to feel some inclination toward a commodity or service and the time when they decide to buy or not to buy. One would expect to discover the problems which are characteristically faced by prospective buyers and the major and minor elements which are given consideration by buyers before they make their decisions to purchase. It may be found that there are elements of conscious thought process which are typical of buyers. It may also be found that some of these elements take precedence over others in frequency of occurrence, and a scale of importance might be developed to show which of these ingredients of decision are relatively most significant to buyers and therefore more to be emphasized by sellers in their appeals to consumers. The traditional

frame of reference expressed in the term "buying habits," and the basic assumption associated with it, may be shown to be improper or at least much less useful than it has been considered in the past. "*How* do people go about making their choices?" may be a much more effective research question for the marketing man than "Why do people buy?" What consumers consider important and how they go about satisfying their desires may then guide the salesmen's approach and the advertiser's appeal.

What do people consider when they make their choices? The factual data which would be useful in trying to answer such a question could be in the form of case histories for individuals of different age groups, different occupations, different income levels, different degrees of education, different racial backgrounds, and so forth, which would provide an opportunity to give numerical weights to the factors that people consider important to them in making purchases and in contracting for services. The quantitative results expressed in terms of frequency of occurrence would show the relative significance that people in general attach to the various factors and conditions involved in purchasing.

Such a study would probably disclose that, when a person first considers buying, a condition of imbalance occurs within him in respect to the products or services as they relate to incipient needs felt by himself or others for whom he buys. As the intensity of this imbalance increases within the individual, resistances are overcome in his mind to a degree that desire or want begins to be felt. At this point the individual might think in general terms of the generic nature of the product or may recall specific brands which have been impressed upon his mind through advertising. Perhaps he will then seek to learn where products of this nature may usually be obtained.

He will think of the places he customarily purchases items of this type. He may consult the classified section of the telephone book or he may ask other members of the family if they know where the product or service may be obtained. If he does not find satisfaction here, he may ask friends or neighbors for suggestions or he may telephone some store asking whether it carries the product or supplies the service. He may then search for specific items from which he may make choices to satisfy his feeling of want. When the consumer enters a store an opportunity is provided to develop in the buyer a sense of desiring a specific item in stock. This may be done by a salesman or, in case of a self-service store, by the manner in which the product is displayed or presented to the customer.

The customer enters the store when he hopes to find there some product of interest, but he has not been necessarily *caused* to do it, at least not in the generally accepted meaning of the term. This action is merely an element in a chain of events which he himself as a sovereign person considers necessary before choosing. At this point no desire for a specific product may have as yet developed.

Buyer interest is apparently a function of the anticipation of satisfaction felt by the customer at any moment in the buying process. The concept that an outside force impels a person to buy probably is not true, or at least not necessary. Motivation to make the purchase is an experience within the individual who makes the decision. It pervades the process of thought, however long or short, which precedes the act of purchase. The fact that it does occur should be simply accepted in marketing. How it occurs is a psychological problem which may some day be resolved by psychologists. Often the realization of cost, and a feeling of reluctance are great at the early stages of consideration. The want for an item during the early stages

may be light in intensity and at that stage comparison with another want may often take place. Reluctance to make an expenditure of any kind may also be strong. As desire matures, however, feelings of responsibility to family, social needs, or personal needs and interests gradually overcome the initial reluctance and a person develops a positive attitude toward the purchase and gradually directs himself toward its successful accomplishment. A clarification of this process of conscious thought would be a major contribution to selling.

To illustrate, let us imagine a family composed of a father, mother, and children who have interests in music and desire music lessons. The father is sympathetic but has many other demands for funds for other purposes. The father's reluctance is the greatest when he first hears of the request for lessons; but then he may consider the advantages and disadvantages to the family and the peace of mind which he himself would enjoy. Finally his sense of responsibility to his family may overbalance his reluctance to purchase and he may consent to investigate the possibilities. Thus a chain, ultimately leading to a purchase decision, has been started.

By investigation it may be possible to show the relative significance which people attribute to the various circumstances and conditions which become part of the processes of thought preceding a purchase. If the study indicates, for example, that people are concerned with the importance of the product to their professional status, and if this is found to be true in a large number of cases or just a few cases, then quantitative evidence (expressed in frequency of occurrence) as to the importance they attach to this factor would be secured. If individuals experience a feeling of loyalty to a firm or a city, if they feel any particular obligation to a specific store when they make their purchases, or consider other factors such as convenience or credit or assortment or salesmanship, the investigation may disclose these facts and form a basis for evaluating their importance in the purchase decision and consequently their significance to the seller in formulating appeals.

These quantitative tabulations might be expressed in percentages to indicate more clearly the relative importance of each of the numerous circumstances which bear upon the buying decision. For example, if we study the factors people consider important in the purchasing of a kitchen range, we may find that color is significant for say 11 out of 150. If this quantitative evidence were converted to a percentage figure, we would then have a useful expression of the importance of color. Other factors might be given the same treatment, such as style, convenience, design, power, accessories, and so forth, and a scale of quantitative results obtained. For example, 80 per cent of those interviewed may feel the style of a kitchen range to be of importance, convenience may be considered so by 15 per cent, accessories by 50 per cent. Sellers would be made aware of factors which are most significant to buyers and would be encouraged to phrase their appeals accordingly. We do not need to consider that any of the features of the range have been causal factors in purchasing. It is merely necessary to show to what extent they are given consideration by purchasers.

Other questions may disclose further factors involved when people plan to buy. When do they become conscious of first considering buying an item? Do they search for the item by themselves or do they often ask for the opinions of others? At what level in the thought process does the consumer ask himself such questions as: "Can I pay for it?" With these questions answered, we might then construct a scale of facts and conditions which are characteristically considered by buyers and thus establish the extent (in terms of frequency of occurrence) to which buyers concern themselves with these factors.

Anticipation of satisfaction from products and services may vary at different ages. For example, physical satisfaction may be extremely important in purchasing on the part of the very young, less important for middle-aged people, and its importance may further change as old age approaches. If we attempt to identify the different areas of anticipated satisfactions, we may find that the most important will include physical enjoyments and enjoyments derived from other experiences, such as the social, the intellectual, the aesthetic, and the acute experience of mastery.

Physical satisfaction is the pleasant experience enjoyed by the individual relative to the satisfaction of the needs of the body's functions and care. It may be found that the anticipation of physical satisfaction is less important than the anticipation associated with other satisfactions. It may be found that the importance people attach to the possession of physical things, that is, pride of possession (now this is mine!) is a stronger factor in the decision process than expected physical satisfactions. It is probable that anticipation of social satisfaction expected from products or services is an even more impressive factor. Our relationships to a group or groups are complex. A consumer may buy certain clothes, land, furniture, or services to fit the social group in which he finds himself, or in accordance with a desire to belong to some group, whether or not he is as yet accepted by the members of the group. Social satisfaction may be the strongest factor, for example, in a "well-set" table. It may not be the food or the linen and silver which are of greatest importance in the mind of the consumer; the thoughts and reactions of friends and associates who assemble around the table may be of much more significance to him.

The relationship of the individual to the social group in which he "belongs" may vary in accordance with his desire to dominate or lead or to just belong. More specifically, these relationships may be expressed in three major forms. First there is the desire of the individual to attain supremacy or guidance of the group, a dominant position which we call leadership. Sometimes the individual does not care to be a leader and yet wishes to maintain a defensive attitude toward other group members, an attitude of rivalry. Then there are those who are content to be members of the group and desire to be guided by some more dominant member or members. As these attitudes are disclosed in research, we can give them weight in accordance with the frequency with which they occur and thus indicate the quantitative importance which they seem to have in the buying process.

Intellectual satisfaction is one of the rich experiences of an individual. Individuals are inquisitive. They like to gossip. They want to hear news about products and services, to satisfy their desire for information. Intellectual satisfaction may be shown to rank relatively high as a concern of customers and to be highly useful for sellers in the creation of appeals.

Most consumers probably consider beauty to be important to them, as it is expressed in tone, color, design, and texture. Beauty is closely tied to emotional responses of individuals and may be considered one of the most significant types of satisfaction involved in purchasing, since taste is so pervasive in the choice of products and services. How often buyers consider this factor in the buying process needs to be understood and given its typical degree of importance.

The expectation of being able to master something or some situation may very well be one of the most impressive elements in the sequence of decisions leading up to the purchase decision. The sense of mastery over time and distance which is associated with the purchase of a new car, as well as the feeling of having arrived at a desired social level or of having acquired enough power under the hood so that one no longer feels inferior at a stop-light intersection—all these feelings in anticipation of purchase may be far and away the most frequently encountered elements in the car-buying process.

The importance to sellers of a scale of values which indicates the relative significance, in a quantitative sense, of the elements with which people are concerned in purchasing is apparent. For example, through sales promotion some sellers may be attempting to sell dining-room sets on the basis of anticipated satisfaction from the possession of the physical product itself, while research may indicate that a much more effective appeal would be that directed to the aesthetic or to the social satisfactions expected.

It might be shown that buyers' interests with respect to new or different products or discoveries is much greater than their interest in facts concerning specific features or economy or use. If this should be found to be true, then some of the appeals used in sales promotion which stress bodily comforts may be weak appeals compared with those which stress novel social or aesthetic considerations.

An attempt should be made to classify purchases according to the extent of thought and time devoted by buyers to the deciding process. The amount of money involved may not be a major criterion. The purchase of an automobile each year may not, for some consumers, be classed as a major purchase even though the item may involve a large expenditure. The ingredients in the thinking process of the individual are the important factors. The determining element in deciding what is a major purchase or what is a minor purchase is the number and the importance of the things considered by a person in making up his mind to buy. It is not the size or amount of the purchase that is important, but how long one attends to the matter before he buys and the elements he considers in reaching the buying decision. By use of individual case studies we may get closer to this process of consideration and learn how consumer thought processes evolve.

There is considerable evidence to support the theory that purchasing patterns and thought processes related to purchasing change and that a gradual evolution in the way we attend to things is taking place. Parts of the process seem to have changed little, but an historical comparison reveals significant differences. A study of the journals kept by George Washington, in which his purchases were entered with minute detail, indicates that most purchases of that day were of the nature of "bespoke merchandise" or goods made to the order of the individual who planned to use them. Several "fittings" were customary and delivery was slow. The artisan made each product and felt the pride of creation as part of his own satisfaction. Individuals did not expect immediate delivery and no doubt would have hesitated to accept an item too quickly after placing the order, thinking that the quality of workmanship might suffer or that the artisan had built or created the item for someone else. Purchasers attached importance to the fit and comfort of the product and the anticipated satisfaction of many years of service. Today, we usually assume the quality of an item to be standard or a satisfactory result of mass-production methods. We have little interest in the fact that the product was not produced for any particular individual. We are little interested today in the artisan who created the product and attach little importance to craftsmanship so long as the product fits our desires.

In Washington's time, use and style were most important considerations. Fashion was a minor consideration when compared with the use expected from the product. Today the wearing quality of an item may be relatively unimportant to a consumer when compared with the fashion of the item. Appropriateness, novelty, and design are much more important to many buyers today than are use considerations. Vehicles such as carriages were once built to last several generations. Wearing qualities were important to purchasers. A vehicle that was still in good condition after half a century was a prized possession. Today, depreciating values of automobiles indicate how greatly our concepts of what is important have changed. An automobile a few years old today is considered relatively undesirable. The ability of the automobile to provide transportation is not the fundamental basis for its valuation; it is rather the time factor, the age of the machine as this affects its social appropriateness. This is a reflection of what people anticipate in satisfaction in the purchase of the product involved. Historical comparison will reveal how the factors which people consider significant become less or more important as we go from season to season, from year to year, and from generation to generation.

The division of labor in marketing research involving buyer motivation needs to be more precisely clarified. We might well leave basic psychological research to the psychologists. While scientists in any area are hospitable to productive adaptation of the results of their effort, they revolt at the intrusion of the novice who touches the field lightly and then engages in profound dissertation. The researcher in marketing, particularly in motivation, is often guilty of this very thing and has contributed to bringing discredit upon marketing research in general.

It also might be well to give more weight to the assumption that buyers act like rational people; that they decide after applying themselves thoughtfully to problems; that they give varying degrees of importance to conditions relevant to their decisions; that they make a few but not many decisions as a matter of habit; and that generally they have an interest in the social as well as in the personal effects of their choices. If this assumption is true and if people with goods and services to offer can find out, to some degree of accuracy, those areas of concern with which buyers are involved as they move from the incipience of the buying process to its conclusion, selling appeals may be developed with more confidence and with more effect.

Primary motivation research should not be thought of as an area of marketing research. On the contrary, the businessman should keep abreast of basic psychological and sociological studies of motivation and seek to adapt these research findings as they seem to have useful application in economic endeavor. At the same time, greater effort should be devoted to describing and limiting an area which can be accepted more confidently as the proper area of consumer research.

And as a final observation—it is apparent that there is at present much concern (at least among reporters, editors, etc.) with aspects of the problem expressed in terms of "depth motivation," "subliminal advertising," "hidden persuaders," and so on. In reading such material, one becomes seriously concerned with the possibility that some at least of these writers and investigators are victims of the very concepts which they have created. Perhaps preoccupation with depth motivation and hidden persuasion is responsible for leading them toward the rather ridiculous assumption that economic men and women fall into two distinct classes—sellers, who must learn to manipulate the puppet strings, and buyers, who can be made to respond appropriately to such manipulation. It seems to me, however, that the basic strength of our economic system lies in the respect we have for the autonomy and individual responsibility of those with whom we deal and make transactions, and that to whatever degree we weaken that respect just to that degree are we weakening the structure of our whole socio-economic system.

## QUESTIONS

1. Is habitual reaction the most characteristic element in consumer behavior?
2. Does psychological investigation tend to show that there are unconscious motivations?
3. Can, perhaps, motivation research be effective in uncovering conscious but secret hopes, fears, dreams, and aspirations of consumers? Might not the uncovering of these private, but significant motivations be even more useful to the seller than digging for subconscious motivations.
4. According to the author, what are some of the thought considerations that a consumer probably goes through before making the final decision to purchase?
5. What social considerations influence the purchase of automobiles, clothes, and other merchandise that is consumed publicly?

# 35. "Familiar Affluence" Changing Buying Drives of Middle Majority*

Albert Shepard, President, Motivation Dynamics Inc.

*Emotionally, buying has become a more balanced and mature process; and on the rational level, buyers are increasingly more knowledgeable and more discriminative. Consumers buy for identity as well as for status. In buying for identity, the purchaser looks for products that express, confirm, and enrich his self-image.*

Why aren't the "Soaring Sixties" airbound? What happened to the buying boom fervently predicted by so many economists? What *are* the consumer market trends ahead?

Motivational studies yield a number of clues to these puzzling questions. They indicate a strong trend toward *selective buying* by members of the Middle Majority; a trend anchored in two basic factors. Emotionally, buying has become a more balanced and mature process; and on the rational level, buyers are increasingly more knowledgeable and more discriminative.

In many respects, this middle majority consumer of 1960 is not the same human being he was during the first 10 or 15 years following the war. No green "nouveau affluent" any longer, he is in the process of successfully adjusting his emotional life, and consequently his buying motivations, to his new circumstances.

Discontent with one's position, especially a grey and anonymous one, is a tremendous stimulus for action in an open democratic society. . . . However, achieving a new *status* is very far from achieving a new *identity*. Status is conferred by the outside world, identity is a self-oriented achievement. Status seeking is a restless demand for a favorable perception of one's position and role *by others*. Identity is a willing inner acceptance of his position and role *by the individual himself*. But acquiring such a comfortable sense of identity in changing circumstances is rarely an easy or simple process.

Case histories show, for instance, that a man who has seen himself as a "wage slave," and then becomes a property owner personally concerned with zoning laws, local elections, school problems, etc., etc., must radically adjust emotional patterns developed in childhood and early adulthood before he is able to see himself sharply and securely in his new role, or feel convinced that society too sees him in the same light.

*Attitudes toward products are an essential part of that process of readjustment.* The requirements and motivations of the identity buyer tend sharply to differ from those of the status buyer.

At whatever social level, the *nouveau affluent* of the '50s (like the adolescent similarly undergoing a crisis of identity), often tended to buy in order to convince himself and the world that he "belonged."

* Reprinted with permission from the January 2, 1961 issue of *Advertising Age*, p. 115. Copyright 1961 by Advertising Publications Inc.

249

He bought proofs and symbols. His constant fear that his slip might be showing opened the way to selling him through his eagerness to proclaim that he was in the know and did the right thing. *In contrast, the identity buyer is seeking and responding to products and experiences which express, confirm and enrich his accepted identity to his own eyes and the eyes of his family.*

What, then, happens in the market place when millions of people are given the impulse, the opportunity and the time to "reorganize" their identities satisfactorily? How do relationships to products and buying motivations change? What is in store for such products as the Buick, for instance, which was one of the first victims of the changing consumer motivations? A sales leader in 1955, Buick dropped to a secondary position beginning in 1958—a drop predicted by research a year previously. Findings showed that while Buick had not lost its status, it was increasingly seen as a "look alike" car with "cluttered" chrome, and "more for show than for go." In short, it was no longer felt to be in harmony with the growing identity consciousness of the customers. What can we learn from this case and similar examples?

## EIGHT STRATEGIC IMPLICATIONS

1. To a greater extent than before, the consumer searches for clues beneath the surface of advertising, of corporate images, of packages and labels, to see whether the manufacturer and the brand have kept pace with his own development. He knows that he has changed—that, in a sense, he has grown up; and he wants to be sure that there is awareness of and respect for that change, that the product offered to him *matches his new personality, self-image and buying criteria . . .*

2. The consumer wants the "genuine" article. His psychological need for flashy or gimmicky products has decreased. He wants products that *enrich* his personal and family life. He wants quality; not only reliability and good materials, but mainly *solid results* in meeting his needs. He wants to match his own *"worth"* with the "worth" of the products.

3. The consumer is more *economy conscious*, but he is willing to pay a higher price for such genuine quality—and *only for* that. We find for instance that today in the appliance field, emphasis is on lower priced lines largely because the higher priced lines have not convincingly demonstrated superior properties and results. Whenever such superiority is demonstrated, whether in the case of a Zenith tv set or a Sara Lee cake, consumers are still willing to lay out more cash. Demonstration and proof of *genuine* performance differentials, and the maintenance of a higher quality image will be an increasingly important competitive advantage in the '60s.

4. By the same token, we also find a growing rebellion against "frivolous" and artificial obsolescence. People will be less ready to buy products only because their color scheme or design has changed.

5. Middle majority men and women tend to be *strongly future-oriented* in matters of utilitarian products, building materials, appliances, cleaning fluids, heating systems, etc.; but they are *moderately future-oriented* in matters affecting taste and life style. They want not radical departures from the past but products which help them reach smoothly the *next step in self-fulfillment,* be it a rose bush, a new sauce for the old meat loaf, a cake mix with a more refined brand image.

6. People want products which *respect* their self-image, which are tidy and good looking, which don't stain, spill or smell, which enhance their newly found pleasure in structure and order.

7. Another level of this demand for respect concerns dissatisfactions with the present state of servicing and repairing the many mechanical appliances and contrivances in the home. Studies show that in this respect, consumers often experience a feeling of personal affront, as if the manufacturer had deliberately let them down or "taken them for a ride." Assurance of servicing will be an increasingly weighty buying motivation in the '60s.

8. Long range planning is on the increase. Respondents often talk of buying programs in terms of two or even three years. The great expansion of the range of products used in the American home leads to constant fights for *priorities* among the various product groups which best gratify the needs of a more deeply felt identity, such as those for greater stability, comfort, relaxation, self-esteem and self-improvement step by step.

That circumstance has important implications for advertising. Increasing attention will have to be paid to the specific role each medium tends to play in the course of the *entire purchase process* from the awakening of desire through planning, shopping, purchase rehearsal, brand decision and the final purchase act itself.

## QUESTIONS

1. The identity buyer seeks and responds to products and experiences which express, confirm, and enrich his accepted identity to his own eyes and the eyes of his family. Explain.
2. Distinguish between status and identity buying.
3. With which of the eight conclusions on consumer buying behavior do you agree?

---

# 36. Consumer Motivations in Black and White*

Henry Allen Bullock, Professor of Sociology and Chairman of Graduate Research at Texas Southern University

*The creation of an "integrated" marketing program that appeals equally to blacks and whites will be the only effective long-run method of reaching the mass market of 17,000,000 Negroes.*

Before advertisers can feel secure in the knowledge of how best to reach the Negro market, they must first truly understand the differences and similarities

* Reprinted from *Management Guide,* August 1961, p. 27. Published monthly by Developmental Research Institute, Inc.

between the motivations of Negroes and whites. They dare not assume that, as consumers, both races behave the same; for, as our studies show, they do not in many instances.

Because ad-men have not really understood the motivations of Negroes as consumers, they have tended to vacillate between dangerous extremes. At one end of the policy continuum are those who approach the market by direct appeal, selecting media and copy especially for Negroes. At the other end are those who use indirect appeal, beaming to the general market in the faith that Negroes too are thereby reached. However, though vast sums of money are used to implement both approaches, neither has made a significant impact on the mind and behavior of the Negro consumer.

**Those using the direct appeal tend to go too far.** They assume the Negro market to be more special than it is, and by this assumption miss the heaviest and most persistent purchasers. Two advertising patterns illustrate this fact:

There is the apparent belief that Negroes are highly superstitious—prone to use of self-medicaments as cure-alls, patent drugs for building sex potency, and hair oils or face creams to make them look like white people. Examples of these appeals are abundant. In 1959, the *Pittsburgh Courier*, a nationally circulating Negro weekly, carried the following advertisements:

"Lucky Hand Brand Oil—has been used by thousands of satisfied customers."

"Troubled? Love? Money? Problems? I'll help. Solution available if instructions followed."

"Presto Face Cream Bleaches, Beautifies. Makes skin like velvet."

Messages like these tend to fail in the long run because they appeal mainly to an unstable minority who are neither able to buy very much nor inclined to stick with any product very long. Also, they alienate the more stable majority whose ego cannot accept the self-image they impose. Consequently, this pattern has been useful only for those sellers whose

ethical values motivate them to seek a "quick killing," and then to withdraw or change the name of the product.

Another pattern using direct appeal operates through a series of radio outlets generally known as "Negro stations," mainly located in Southern cities, but some outlets in Northern cities. Beamed primarily at Negro audiences, the broadcasters utilize a program pattern consisting mainly of gospel music, rock and roll, and gulps of poorly read news. The shows are conducted by disc jockeys who take personality names like "Dr. Daddy-o," who was first presented through the sponsorship of the Jackson Brewing Company of New Orleans. The originator of this character attracted large audiences through his snappy jazz selections, his hep-cat lingo, and the novelty of a Negro's being on television. In fact he was so successful that a second Dr. Daddy-o sprang up in Houston. Since that time an entire army of eccentric radio personalities has paraded across the "colored air" —Mama Lou, Okey Dokey, Hot Ziggety, Deacon Sam, Miss Mandy, Hotsy Totsy, and a host of others.

**Since its appeal is highly specialized, this type of advertising misses the middle class Negro altogether.** Members of the more responsible upper class, along with a goodly portion of those comprising the bulging middle-class, are actually made hostile towards sponsors who use these disc personalities to push their products. They feel that this method shows disrespect for the Negro community and places an unwholesome stigma on it. Although this type of advertising must be successful for particular companies, the customers it attracts are of the "dollar down—dollar per week" variety.

**Just as there are advertisers who overplay their hand, there are also those who throw the cards away.** The latter group, using indirect methods, pour their spiels into the general channel of mass communication on the assumption that Negroes as well as whites are being reached and influenced by it. But copy used this way may fail to trigger the motivations of Negroes. It has prevented the identification with the sponsor or his product and has left them either indifferent or in doubt. Here are some examples:

One Negro woman of a dark complexion expressed this left-out feeling when she responded to a soap advertisement on TV by asking: "Now how can *any* soap make my skin white like that?"

One group of Negro men assembled in a barber shop also illustrated this left-out feeling. While viewing a television commercial that claimed some type of relief to be just a gulp away, one member of the group queried: "I wonder if they mean us?"

**Consumer motivations come in black and white. Although human needs are basically the same for all people everywhere, these drives tend to become plated with the compulsions, checks, and guidance systems of different cultures.** It is this cultural overlay that forms the foundation for all motivational differences between groups. This happens in the case of Negroes and whites because the two races live in worlds that are somewhat culturally separate; needs develop that are, in some instances, peculiar to each race.

*The facts and opinions which follow are drawn on the basis of interviews and questionnaires given to 1,643 Negroes and 537 whites in Atlanta, Birmingham, Memphis and New Orleans. It is the author's opinion that the conclusions presented in the study are generally applicable to Northern as well as Southern consumers.*

**Belongingness, one of the most common motivational forces with which advertisers must deal, hits black and white consumers at different spots but with equal force.**

Negroes want group identification; whites, feeling that they already have this, want group distinction.

More specifically, Negroes want to be identified with the general American society and all its peoples, while whites want to remain generally acceptable but particularly exclusive.

**The Negroes' need to belong grows directly out of the badge of inferiority which his communal isolation forces on him.** *Both* blacks and whites are conscious of this badge, and from this awareness stems a tremendous psychological force. *Both* races feel the pressure to define all things white as good and all things black as "bad," and from this contrast conception grows the first significant motivational aspects of racial segregation.

There have developed within the minds of colored people conflicting self-images. They are forced to hate and love themselves at the same time.

**Color consciousness dawns early in the minds of the Negro children and forms a reference scale by which they judge the "nice" and "not-nice."** Objectively evidencing this is the Doll Test which Kenneth and Mamie Clark conducted in order to observe racial identification as it relates to ego development and self-consciousness in Negro children. By allowing them to select a doll from among four models—each of which was exactly alike, except that two were brown with black hair and two were white with yellow hair —the experimenters were able to identify the children's color values. The results showed a definite tendency for the majority of the children to prefer the white dolls, considering them "most nice," desiring to play with them most, and judging them as not "looking bad."

Lurking in the background, however, is the other half of the Negro's split self-image. It is here that the Negro child learns to reshape this image in tones which he considers more acceptable. Even **as Negroes reject their color, they find it necessary to protect with equal vigor the dignity of their racial heritage.** When a group of 267 Houston Negro Junior High School boys were given lists of boxers and baseball players and were asked to rate who was best at each of these sports, the Negro athletes were far more highly rated than were whites, although objective judgment based on actual performance would have resulted in different rank order.

**Whites contribute to this love-and-hate conflict by the value they place on certain types of Negro achievement.** Although they attribute to Negroes a general status of "inferiority," their image of the race is not entirely consistent. In a field of physical prowess such as athletics, or in fields of special talents such as singing, and other forms of entertainment, they admit Negro "superiority" without apparent fear of shaking their position in the general society. For instance, several white Junior High school principals agreed with the Negro's ratings of athletics, and many whites chose Nat "King" Cole as one of the top pop singers.

**It is the Southern white consumers' strong and persistent feeling that they belong exclusively to themselves.** The sense of superiority which communal apartness fosters seems to make many of them more ethnocentric than Negroes and even less tolerant of people and ideas outside their local orbit. They want to remain to themselves, apart from non-white groups.

When white consumers were asked to complete this sentence, "*If I could change the world, I would . . .,*" the most repre-

sentative of their replies to it are as follows:

"Stop the neighbors' children from cutting across my lawn."
"Eliminate federal control over our lives."
"Destroy the United Nations."
"Do away with one worldism."
"Change the Supreme Court."

On the other hand, the most frequent replies of Negroes to the same sentence ran this way:

"Make all people the same."
"Establish brotherhood."
"Do away with war."
"Break down segregation."

**But whites also have the urge to belong-with those at the top of the heap.** They seek to identify with the "ideal American family," as one white consumer expressed it, but their definition of "ideal" is based on the status symbols of material achievement.

One man put it more explicitly: "The poor want to be well-to-do and the well-to-do want to be rich. If you have one automobile in your garage, the object is to get another."

One white housewife, a social leader in Houston's fashionable Memorial area, admitted to our interviewer: "My position just will not let me rest. I must always be on the prowl for something new."

In short, different consumers used different words, but the theme of compelling and distinctive belongingness was paramount.

**The drive to belong gives black and white consumers special kinds of market orientations.** One of the most important of these fostered among Negroes is the pronounced inclination of trade across racial-cultural boundaries, both as to the kinds of goods they buy and as to the places where they buy them. Of course some of this grows directly out of segregation, where rapid population growth places unrelenting, insurmountable pressure on area resources and facilities. Most, however, is attributable to the self-rejection side of the Negroes' split self-image.

Because of the combined weight of these two forces, Negroes trade in an atmosphere of scarcity and compulsiveness. New apartments made available to them fill quickly, no matter how high the rent. Houses vacated by whites are readily purchased by them, although the prices, in many cases, would appear to be out of their reach.

This is not only a response to the housing shortage. It also signifies the fact that they think it makes them less like themselves—more like white people and the general community norm.

**Furthermore, many upper- and middle-class Negroes have developed "country club ways" without a country club.** They're buying more playrooms, domestic bars for dispensing drinks, and lawns fenced and hedged to accommodate outdoor snacks and entertainment. Thousands of Southern urban Negro consumers go into the furniture, appliance, food, and liquor markets in search of products capable of feeding their country club aspirations. They like to appear "out of type" before their guests or when visitors come to town. Consequently they attempt to surround themselves with visible symbols of whiteness. And, where they find acceptance, they concentrate their patronage, to a greater extent than the white customers of the same stores do.

**Another need which we observe to be operative in the consumer behavior of Negroes and whites is that of security.** Some degree of insecurity seems to grow directly out of their respective social-cultural settings, and additional anxieties are apparently fostered by the goal block-

ages which they encounter in their pursuit of belongingness.

**The seed bed of the Negroe's fears appears to be the instability inherent in his family life, but the fertile soil in which these fears really grow must be identified as the even greater uncertainty which he experiences later.** The normal pattern of father and mother roles is characteristic of the families of both races, but the Negro family deviates more sharply from this norm. Its members are dependent solely on the mother to a greater extent.

The main reason for this is that a larger proportion of Negro families are headed by females. One fourth are so headed as compared to 14% of the whites. (These are averages based on 664,415 white and 237,355 Negro households of five leading Southern cities.) These figures represent a greater tendency toward family dissolution among Negroes—desertion, divorce, widowhood.

The personality-building power of this domestic pattern rests on its tendency to forge extremely close relationships between mother and child through its impact on child rearing practices. It is in this way that maternal dependency is taught and the matriarchy arises as the Negro child's greatest source of stability and anchorage.

Although this matriarchal feature gives Negro children some degree of security during their infancy, it exposes many of them to greater insecurity during their adolescence. They have to go to work at a relatively early age and, even when their mothers remarry, find little or no additional security. The small proportion of Negro elementary school children who enter Junior High is an indicator of the eroding effect of employment on children who are only entering the teens.

Influenced by such conditions, many of these children enter adult life with personalities already twisted by the insecurities from which they suffer. The interest pattern of Negro men appears more feminine, and that of Negro women more masculine, than in the case of whites. Negroes have higher tendencies than whites towards suspiciousness, oversensitivity, and some idea that people are against them or are trying to hurt them.

In a comparison of the frustration-aggression patterns of larger samples of Negroes and whites, researchers found racial and regional variation among subjects who responded to the Rosenzweig Picture-Frustration Study:

The Negro female, true to her traditional role in the monarchy, once again emerges as the dominant figure of the family—the one who meets frustration head-on. She directs her energy toward the sources of her frustration to a significantly greater degree than her white counterpart who is more inclined to turn her aggression on herself. Northern males, both black and white, join the Negro woman in this personality inclination, but the Southern Negro male is the most passive and self-blaming of them all.

Of course, in contrast to the strong *maternal* role among Negroes, there is a pattern of white *paternal* dominance. So it may be that, in the culture which Americans have built in the South, only the Negro woman and white man are free.

**Some degree of insecurity is fed into the experiences of Negroes and whites as a result of the differences in how fully each race shares in the economy. While whites worry about earning enough money to "get ahead" Negroes worry about getting enough money to keep what they have.** The southern city has developed a neat occupational rank order that reflects a top and bottom pattern so far as Negroes and whites are concerned. Though the expanding economies are drawing more Negroes into upper occupational classes which result in increases in the

income from gross wages, it does not alter thier relative social or economic position. Negro workers, therefore, derive their insecurity from this marginal position. They must cross racial boundaries, both spacial and social, in order to make their living. Their employers and supervisors are almost invariably white. Naturally, then, most Negroes define their position as uncertain and expendable.

**There are other worries that result more directly from short rations. Although Negroes have become somewhat adjusted to deprivation, poverty for a goodly portion of them is a constant threat.** Obviously their lower income places tremendous pressure on the family that tries to live according to the current American standard. Temporary unemployment is a serious and ever present threat. Illness is feared not so much as a harbinger of death as it is a cause of lost paychecks. The financial reserves of most Negroes are so small that unemployment compensation is, as some of them say, "a poor harbor."

Still, Negro families attempt to partake of all the gadgetry that characterizes American living standards. They tend to encumber through credit obligations a large portion of their future earnings. One Negro worker said: "We've bought so much stuff on time that to miss a payday makes us want to change our telephone number." These are not all of the Negro's economic fears, but they are the big ones —anxieties that grow chiefly out of the possibility that what one has will be taken away.

**The comparable worries of white consumers are basically characterized by the fear of not keeping up or moving ahead.** Contrary to outside appearances, desegregation in real estate inspires fears equal to those inspired by public school affairs. Such changes are putting pressure on white residential sections causing a noticeable degree of anxiety among those who cannot conveniently find escape from the Negroes who are rapidly becoming their neighbors. These people are not afraid solely of proximity of Negroes, per se, but of falling down the class ladder as a result of living among or near them.

The respective cultures of each race have planted fears and, to some degree, have erected defenses against them. The differences are in terms of degree rather than kind, although there are instances in which the security of one means insecurity for the other.

How, then, does this matter of security show itself in buying habits? When Negroes and whites go into the market place, there are essentially three patterns of insecurity that appears: fear of economic inbalance, uneasiness over store-customer relations, and fright imagery associated with particular kinds of products. These three anxiety patterns, though somewhat different in content, decisively join Negro and white consumers in the retail market.

**Negro consumers displayed almost common agreement about the use of credit as a method of bolstering their insecurities.** Almost three fourths favored credit buying, but felt obliged to display an elaborate system of rationalization to justify themselves. They generally concurred that credit is a wonderful means by which poor people can get some of the things they want, so long as they are able to stand each weekly or monthly note.

Over 70% of white consumers approved of credit buying as readily as did Negroes. However, the rationalizations behind their approval appear designed to protect their egos rather than their economic balance. According to them, buying on credit is all right provided people watch their interest rates carefully and not overburden themselves with payments. This kind of rationalization often shifts

to the type of object purchased, implying that size of monetary obligation should govern one's credit buying. Only a few justified credit buying on the basis of financial need.

**Most Negroes face downtown shopping with some feeling of security, especially when buying at stores in which they usually trade.** In speaking of her "at-homeness" in one of the stores, a Negro woman told us:

"When I first started trading there, I felt kind of strange. The place was so big and everybody seemed so busy, I thought they wouldn't notice me. But after a while I learned to like the place. I know where everything is and everybody seems glad to help me."

Another shopper said:

"When I would go there, I would get mad. I knew, with all the people they had to wait on, they would make the colored folks wait until last. But they don't do that anymore. Nowadays, they seem to take you as you come."

**According to whites, the atmosphere of bigness and formality characterizing most department stores presents no awe which they cannot overcome.** "I tell myself that the clerks are there to serve me," reported a housewife of the middle-upper class; "if it were not for us they would have no jobs."

Other defensive tactics were observed when consumers gave us an account of their feelings about contact with a sales-man.

**Negro and white groups agreed that readiness to talk with a salesman would depend on an emerging need.** They appear much more amenable to making contact with a salesman if, before the contact, their old car or refrigerator had given them trouble.

There were exceptions in both camps, however. A minority of the whites agreed that they would talk with a salesman provided they had already decided they were in the market for the item. A small but proportionally larger group of Negroes based their readiness to buy on the condition of the family budget.

Another set of racially common response patterns involved the kind of person the salesman would have to be in order to win attention.

For Negroes, the needs are confidence and trust. Therefore, they regard the salesman as a counselor whose personality inspires faith in his character or, at least, in his appeal.

Whites need affability and concession. They want to see the salesman as a person "on their side"—one who knows his product, but uses his knowledge in favor of the potential purchaser rather than the seller. Instead of playing up the product at all points, they want him to play it down at some.

**Consumers of both races want to feel secure as a result of the transaction.** Whites want security in their belief that they themselves made the decision to buy; that they have used good judgment and have driven a hard bargain. "I would expect to get complete satisfaction in service and guarantee—no regrets; no feeling that I have been taken" one white shopper said.

Negroes seek their security in the belief that they have not misplaced their confidence, and that the terms are low enough. "I would expect good service," said one. "I would expect the product to stand up, to give long service like the salesman promised, and I would expect the payments to be as agreed on."

What is more important about these replies is the emphasis which consumers place on the salesman as a person. Only three whites and two Negroes mentioned the company which the hypothetical salesman represented. This suggests that when a salesman makes contact with a

prospective buyer, *he* becomes the company. For that moment, at least, the destiny of the company is in his hands. Another important observation is that practically all of the consumers spoke deploringly of high-pressure sales tactics. Yet each one seems to expect the salesman to be a kind of lecturer or counselor. It seems that each buyer wants to have his mind made up for him, but he would like to feel that he did the job himself.

**Some degree of consumer insecurity is carried into the product area, but with more apparent racial difference.** Following are specific attitudinal patterns related to food and cigarettes.

**Food.** Many Negroes tend to view food basically as a means of sustenance, and eating mainly as a way of meeting biological needs. Beyond this point, eating is unnecessary and indulgent. The majority of these consumers also warned against the health hazard they believed to be involved. "He shouldn't overindulge because in his old age he may come up with a pressure condition" one Negro insisted.

Differing somewhat, a greater proportion of the white consumers conceive of eating as a self-indulgent and pleasurable experience. When asking about eating and drinking to satisfy appetites, many whites seemed startled and replied: "What other reason is there for eating and drinking?"

Statements like these suggest an indulgent attitudinal pattern which separates eating from its basic biological function and makes it a special ritual which serves a pleasant end. As more Negroes enter the upper classes, and as the entire population gets a greater share of our economic gains, we believe black and white motivations along these lines will grow more alike.

**Smoking.** Negroes and whites seem to share a common fear about cigarettes and what they term "excessive smoking." In general, Negro consumers pushed the pack-a-day habit into the region of abnormal consumption. But theirs was not so much a fear of lung cancer as an anxiety about physical or neurological incapacitation. Whites, however, expressed their fear of excessive smoking largely in terms of cancer.

So far as the brand concept is concerned, black and white consumers are not far apart. The majority of Negroes subordinated brand buying to the economy of the housekeeping. Most whites believed that knowing brands is a mark of consumer sophistication. Taken as a whole, both Negro and white consumers react to brand buying defensively. The former want to defend their budgets. The latter want to defend their egos.

Thus it can be readily seen how there is a clear division on certain market qualities and products between the two races. This makes it all the more important that marketers should be able to follow an integrated advertising policy and appeal to "consumer motivations in black and white" with a single, economical, effective approach.

## QUESTIONS

1. Belongingness hits Negro and white consumers at different spots but with equal force. Explain.
2. Although human needs are basically the same for all people everywhere, these drives tend to become plated with the compulsions, checks, and guidance systems of different cultures. Explain.
3. What three patterns of insecurity appear when Negroes and whites go into the market?
4. What are some of the differences and similarities between the motivations of Negroes and whites?

# 37. Motivation Research—Magic or Menace?*

James F. Engel, Professor of Marketing, The University of Michigan

*MR is not just a plaything of big business. It functions to "arm management's imagination" in marketing decision making by providing factual data to remove uncertainty concerning those forces giving consumer behavior its direction and intensity.*

In the past few years business journals have been full of articles on "motivation research" (MR).[1] The welter of conflicting claims and spectacular success stories crease, rather than dispel, confusion on unfortunately may have served to inthis important subject. Many discerning

* Reprinted from the *Michigan Business Review*, March 1961, p. 29.

[1] The reader who wishes to probe into the subject more deeply is referred to the following sources: Harry Henry, *Motivation Research.* (New York: Frederick Unger Publishing Company, 1958); Lawrence C. Lockley, *The Use of Motivation Research in Marketing,*

Studies in Business Policy, No. 97, National Industrial Conference Board, Inc.; "The $000 Billion Question: What Makes Her Buy?" *Printer's Ink,* October 18, 1957, pp. 35–37; Alfred Politz, "What Is Consumer Motivation Research?" *Proceedings of the Boston Conference on Distribution,* 1955, pp. 55–58; and John Paul, "A Psychologist Looks at Motivation Research," *Business Quarterly,* Winter, 1958, pp. 240–46.

businessmen have asked such questions as: "Just what is MR anyway?" "Can it be used only by manufacturers, or can retailers and marketers of services find a place for it?" "Is it just a fad that will pass in a few years?" "Does MR do away with traditional 'nose counting' research?"

This is the first of two articles designed to answer some of the many questions that have been raised. The reader should not look for easy "how to do it" suggestions. Instead, the subject will be approached from the point of view of the about the role of MR in management of his firm. This article will be devoted to a general review of the nature of the subject, and the concluding article will be addressed to more procedural issues, including methods used.[2]
average businessman who is concerned

## WHAT IS MR?

Each business firm, regardless of size and products sold, must make marketing decisions in an atmosphere of uncertainty. Perhaps the most important "unknown" the decision maker must face is the reaction of consumers to the product or service offered. Such questions as "What will happen if we change our advertising?" or "How will consumers like the new package?" are commonplace. It has become increasingly necessary in today's highly competitive business environment to undertake research activities to learn more about consumer behavior in order to provide a factual basis upon which to make decisions.

Analysis of consumer behavior begins with the fundamental assumption that all behavior is motivated. Through assessing the motives underlying manifested behavior, it is then possible to discover why behavior takes the forms it does. In more specific terms, MR may be defined as a

systematic attempt to ascertain those forces giving consumer behavior its direction and intensity. As such, therefore, MR is only one aspect of marketing research as a whole, discovering *why*—not what, how, where, or when.

## PUTTING THE CONSUMER "ON THE COUCH"

Research on consumer motivation has presented convincing evidence that the consumer follows logical patterns of behavior to attain more or less clearly defined objectives.[3] Moreover, it has become apparent that he buys not only on the basis of what a product or service will *do* for him performancewise, but also on what it *means* to him. Hence, emotional reactions to a product or service assume major importance. The problem for the motivation researcher is to discover with a useful degree of accuracy the *balance* of objective performance factors and subjective emotional factors underlying a consumer's purchase decision.

The information searched for may be located at one or more of three basic personality levels:

1. The conscious level. Often the consumer is clearly aware of why he behaves as he does and can freely stabilize these reasons if he so desires. Objective factors concerning product performance usually are conscious motives and are readily accessible through questioning.

2. The subconscious level. It frequently is necessary to go below the conscious level to find motives of which the consumer is not actively aware.

[3] The prevalence of logic and consistency in consumer behavior has been noted by many authors. See Wroe Alderson, *Marketing Behavior and Executive Action* (Homewood: Richard D. Irwin, 1957) Ch. VI; George Katona, *The Powerful Consumer* (New York: McGraw-Hill, 1960; John Paul, *op. cit.;* and James Morgan, "A Review of Recent Research on Consumer Behavior," *Consumer Behavior*, Lincoln H. Clark, ed. (New York: Harper & Brothers, 1958), pp. 93–124.

These reasons may be procured by aiding the individual in his thinking, or by inference from patterns of response to questioning.

3. The unconscious level. Freudian psychology has pointed out that basic behavioral patterns may be determined by desires located in the unconscious personality. It is impossible for the individual to restore these factors to conscious thought, so unconscious motives can be discovered only through extensive psychoanalysis.

In practice, level three is unattainable with the tools of MR as we shall see in more detail later. Therefore, two basic personality levels (conscious and subconscious) remain to be explored in the attempt to find "reason why" answers.

The problems of the motivation researcher are further complicated by the fact that he cannot always attain even conscious information with predictable accuracy. The individual may refuse to admit the true reasons for a particular purchase out of a fear that he may expose himself in an unfavorable manner. Instead he may offer only reasons which seem to be socially acceptable.

Research experience has shown that traditional direct questions permitting easy quantification and analysis are an ideal tool to uncover motives at the conscious level. Direct questions are thought to be inappropriate, however, for delving below the conscious. Hence, marketing researchers have turned in wholesale numbers to related social sciences for tools designed to reach deeper levels of the personality and to overcome reluctance to offer conscious information. Such exotic methods as the Rorschach Ink Blot Test and the cartoon test have come into relatively wide usage.[4]

Today the motivation researcher has at his disposal a large kit of tools to attain both conscious and subconscious motivational data. Hence it now is possible, as a result of cross fertilization with other social sciences, to apply methods designed to attain desired information.

## WHAT CAN MR DO FOR YOU?

It is often said that the concept of the "product image" is the most valuable product of MR. As Henry has observed:

What the consumer wants and buys is . . . the *total personality* of the product, which consists not only of its chemical composition and formulation, but also of the *ideas* which the public has about it. It [the product image] consists, in other words, of the picture which the consumer has in his mind of the quantities inherent in it, real or imaginary.[5]

In most fundamental terms, successful marketing efforts occur when the personality of the product is matched with the personality of the consumer. Through MR it is possible to isolate those consumer personality variables and desires which are relevant to the sales of the product or service under analysis. On such a factual basis, the product image can be "fine tuned" to match the dictates of demand.

## THE PRODUCT IMAGE

All types of marketing effort work together to form the product image: product design, branding and packaging, selling policies, price policies, channels of distribution, and services offered. For instance, visualize a piece of fine jewelry. The product itself may possess distinction; it is sold primarily through personal selling in exclusive jewelry stores; the

---

[4] Specific techniques and guides concerning their application will be discussed in more detail in the second article in this series.

[5] Henry, *op. cit.,* pp. 88–89.

price is relatively high; and the consumer is offered much in the way of point-of-sale service. The net result of this marketing program will be a "prestige" or "quality" image. If the manufacturer desires to sell primarily to members of upper social classes seeking a prestige appeal, then the product personality and consumer personality have achieved a close match. This would have been difficult, if not impossible, to achieve without a realization of what the consumer desires and *why*.

Assessment of the image of the product in the eyes of the consumer, then, is a major function of MR. Once the image has been determined, a foundation is formed for a more perfect matching between product attributes, marketing policies, and consumer desires in such terms as: "What advertising appeals will be most effective?" "Do we need personal selling to persuade the consumer to buy?" "Can we sell through discount houses?" "How can the product be changed to increase sales?"

The benefits of MR extend far past the manufacture and sale of consumer goods. For example, companies selling services also must adapt their "product" to consumer desires. In the sale of industrial products, on the other hand, objective performance factors tend to dominate over emotional motives; the product, nevertheless, must be fine tuned to demand. In the same sense, retailers face the identical problem with the product and service "mix" which is offered to clientele; the total output of a retail store, including products carried, prices, selling policies, and services must be matched to the dictates of demand.

## MISCONCEPTIONS HINDERING THE EFFECTIVE USE OF MR

If MR has so much to offer, then why isn't it more widely accepted in the busi-

ness community? This is a valid question, because for various reasons many managers and marketing researchers alike have failed to achieve a true understanding of what MR can do for them. Some of the common misconceptions and impediments to acceptance will be discussed in detail.

Perhaps the entry of the behavioral sciences into marketing research has been the primary source of confusion concerning MR. Established marketing research practitioners have tended to reject newer concepts, and, by the same token, behavioral scientists often neglected the rigorous statistical approach of traditional marketing research. Too many managers have taken sides in this controversy, thus hindering the acceptance of MR.

As we have seen, the traditional direct question of marketing research is ideally adapted to procuring conscious information, which newer psychological techniques are designed to probe below the surface of the personality. Hence, the traditional methods and psychological methods should be viewed as *complements*.

The split within the research profession has not been mended by the tendency to associate the term MR only with psychological techniques. This association represents an error in logic. It must not be overlooked that MR comprehends *all possible approaches to the determination of why consumer behavior takes its unique forms*. We cannot define an area of study by only one of the many types of techniques utilized.

## FEAR OF BEING SHOWN AS INADEQUATE

Some managers seem to have the erroneous impression that the use of research will, in some manner, place them in an unfavorable light in the eyes of superiors.[6] There is a feeling that "reason

[6] For an interesting discussion of this problem see J. W. Newman, "Working with Behavioral Scientists," *Harvard Business Review*, July, 1958, pp. 67–74.

why" data can be attained by an intelligent manager without resorting to research. Therefore, there frequently is a tendency to rely on "managerial determination"—the use of unaided management judgment and intuition to provide the answer as to why the consumer behaves as he does.

It is difficult, if not impossible, for the typical executive to place himself into the shoes of the consumer. He is too close to his product or service to assume this perspective without his judgment being severely biased. Also, important motivating factors may lie below the conscious level of the consumer's personality, and the consumer himself may not be able to supply the answer. The problems faced by an outsider "looking in" are obvious. The use of MR says nothing unfavorable about a manager's ability; rather it implies a keen awareness of marketing problems and a capacity for sound decision making. It is virtually imperative in many instances to resort to methods designed to "open the door" of the consumer's personality in order to produce a solid foundation on which to base strategic marketing decisions.

## FEAR OF FREUD

Any businessman not trained in clinical psychology naturally looks upon Freudian psychology as a mystifying unknown world. Motivation researchers have not helped the situation either by indiscriminately bantering about such Freudian terms as "oral gratification," "libido," and "Oedipus complex" without translation into everyday English. It is quite natural to fear the unknown, so it might be expected that MR would be rejected at least partly for this reason.

Freudian psychology provides a unique explanation of the inner workings of the unconscious mind. While it might be possible through extended psychoanalysis to

determine unconscious factors conditioning consumer behavior, such an approach is far beyond the scope of methods used in MR. Moreover, as Henry points out, we are not interested in the mainsprings of human behavior, but "with the escapements and regulators which can be adjusted in the interests of a manufacturer or advertiser."[7]

A key principle guiding the researcher is to find motives that are "manipulable."[8] We must be able to approach the consumer through persuasion with some hope of inducing him to act favorably toward our product or service. If motives are unconscious, it is extremely doubtful that they are manipulable in this sense. Imagine an advertising copywriter, if you will, attempting to design an ad which would capitalize on the fact unearthed by motivation researchers that consumers buy electric blankets because of a "yearning to return to the security of the prenatal environment of the womb."

MR relies on a great deal more than Freudian psychology. Marketers are interested in *all* reasons why a consumer behaves as he does. Such factors as performance of the product, color, durability, style, social pressures, and many more all are of importance. If deeper psychological reasons are discovered, they are only *one* type of useful information, not the only type.

## EXAGGERATED CLAIMS AND EXPECTATIONS

Some early practitioners of MR made unduly ambitious claims concerning its value to businessmen. In effect, it was alleged that psychological methods represent the "answer to the businessman's prayer." Such commercially motivated writing was bound to leave disillusionment in its wake after management soon

---

[7] Henry, *op. cit.*, pp. 30–31.
[8] *Ibid.*, p. 31.

discovered that MR is by no means a panacea.

All we can expect from MR is as accurate an estimation of consumer motives as present techniques will permit. As such, we will never have *the* definitive answer. Research cannot be a crutch, but only a starting point for creative and imaginative decision making by management.

## MANAGEMENT INERTIA

Finally, even though many up-to-date managements freely recognize the necessity of securing reliable estimates of consumer motivations, action based on this need frequently is overcome by inertia. There seems to be an inevitable tendency to stay with familiar paths and avoid uncharted areas.

The problem of inertia is particularly evident in larger corporations. By necessity, the large organization is committed to practices and procedures to permit efficient operation of the entire entity. Such procedures, of course, resist change. Hence, smaller firms may have a distinct advantage in that flexibility in operating policies more readily facilitates the constructive use of MR findings in decision making.

Also the well established older firm may tend to let matters coast as long as profit seems to be adequate and share of market stable. In this sense, the younger company fighting for differential advantage may be much more receptive to new management information-gathering devices for use as an aid in effective competitive strategy.

## CONCLUSION

MR is not just a plaything of big business. It functions to "arm management's imagination" in marketing decision making by providing factual data to remove uncertainty concerning those forces giving consumer behavior its direction and intensity. As such, it makes use of all methods designed to analyze why consumers behave as they do. The problems MR encompasses are common to all business firms, so MR is a tool which *any* company may find useful.

## QUESTIONS

1. Describe three basic personality levels.
2. Explain how the product image can be adjusted by the seller.
3. Should the seller manipulate motives or adjust the product to the motives?
4. Motivation research is just a starting point for creative and imaginative thinking. Explain.

# 38. Interdisciplinary Horizons in Marketing*

William Lazer and Eugene J. Kelley, Professors of Marketing, Michigan State University and New York University

*Marketing has reached a stage in its development as a discipline where critical evaluation of research findings and theories from other fields can add new dimensions to the field of marketing. More materials of other disciplines are likely to be incorporated in marketing in the future.*

The interdisciplinary approach to marketing includes utilization of contributions of the social and behavioral sciences, the physical sciences, and various areas of business administration and economics. The strength of the total approach lies in the addition of new dimensions and more meaningful perspectives to various marketing concepts, development of improved techniques for solving marketing problems, integration of findings and theories with marketing practice, and the development of a more widely applicable and generally useful body of marketing knowledge.

The potential promise of an interdisciplinary approach to the development of marketing theory was discussed by Wroe Alderson and Reavis Cox a decade ago. They wrote that "here and there in the literature of several intellectual disciplines are appearing the elements from which an adequate theory of marketing will be constructed."[1]

There has not yet been, however, any substantial acceptance of the development of a truly interdisciplinary approach to marketing knowledge. The use of other disciplines in marketing to date may be characterized as multi-disciplinary.

Individual marketers have brought specific problems to psychologists, sociologists, anthropologists, social psychologists, and other behavioral scientists. In many instances these specialists were able to find solutions. The problems were studied, however, from the limited perspectives of particular subject-matter areas. As a result, the needed cross-fertilization of ideas and the integration necessary to obtain more widely applicable generalizations and marketing concepts has not occurred on any large scale.

The point of departure and the focus of study differ with each of the disciplines underlying marketing. But there are frequently great similarities in the methodology and content of marketing and that of other disciplines. Marketing progress can be furthered by studying the similarities among disciplines rather than emphasizing the differences.

## BEHAVIORAL SCIENCE CONTRIBUTIONS TO MARKETING

Table 1 relates specific behavioral science concepts to particular problems being faced by marketing management. It

* Reprinted from the *Journal of Marketing*, national quarterly publication of the American Marketing Association, Vol. 25, No. 2, October 1960, pp. 24–30.

[1] Wroe Alderson and Reavis Cox, "Toward a Theory of Marketing," *Journal of Marketing*, Vol. 13 (October 1948), pp. 137–152, 142.

265

## TABLE 1
### Behavioral Science Contributions to Selected Marketing Management Problems

| | Psychology | Sociology | Social Psychology | Anthropology | Political Science |
|---|---|---|---|---|---|
| **Marketing Administration** | | | | | |
| Creativity, Problem Solving & Decision Making | Considerable | Some | Some | Some | Little |
| Leadership and Administration | Considerable | Considerable | Considerable | Little | Some |
| Organization | Some | Considerable | Considerable | Some | Some |
| Systems—Survival and Growth | Little | Considerable | Some | Considerable | Some |
| **Goods and Services Mix** | | | | | |
| Adjustment and Change | Considerable | Some | Considerable | Some | Little |
| Consumers and Consumption | Considerable | Considerable | Some | Little | Little |
| Innovation | Some | Some | Some | Considerable | Some |
| Products, Packages, Brands & Images | Considerable | Some | Some | Little | Little |
| Role, Status, and Symbols | Some | Considerable | Considerable | Some | Some |
| **Communications Mix** | | | | | |
| Attitudes and Opinions | Considerable | Considerable | Considerable | Some | Some |
| Communications and Information | Some | Some | Considerable | Some | Some |
| Individuals and Group Relations | Considerable | Considerable | Considerable | Some | Some |
| Motivations and Behavior | Considerable | Some | Considerable | Some | Some |
| Persuasion and Influence | Some | Some | Considerable | Little | Some |
| **Distribution Complex: Channels & Physical** | | | | | |
| Centralization, Decentralization & Integration | Little | Considerable | Little | Some | Some |
| Institutional Structure | Little | Considerable | Some | Considerable | Considerable |
| Wealth and Income | Little | Little | Little | Some | Some |
| Wants, Needs, and Goals | Considerable | Some | Considerable | Some | Little |

KEY:
▓▓▓▓ (solid)
||||||||||| Considerable significance
▒▒▒ Some significance
☐ Little significance

illustrates the value of the interdisciplinary approach in extending the frontiers of marketing knowledge and in helping to solve marketing problems. For example, such concepts as communication and information, motivation and behavior, creativity, problem solving, and decision making have significant implications for effective marketing management. They are being investigated from different vantage points by such disciplines as psychology, sociology, social psychology, anthropology, and political science.

Topics of interest to marketing managers are grouped according to four major marketing problem areas in Table 1. These areas are marketing administration and the three major components of an integrated marketing program. A unified goal-directed marketing program and its resulting marketing mix is comprised of three submixes. These are the *goods-and-service mix*, which includes product and pricing elements; the *communications mix*, which includes the functional areas of advertising, sales promotion, and personal selling; and the *distribution mix*, which is comprised of channels of distribution and physical distribution activities. The table illustrates the significance of the findings of several behavioral sciences to marketing management in solving specific problems within each of these areas.

These rankings are an attempt to relate in broad terms the degree of significance of the concepts. They were determined after an investigation of the literature of psychology, sociology, social psychology, anthropology, and several business administration areas. Specialists in these disciplines were consulted to substantiate the rankings. The rankings are necessarily subjective. Further research may result in modifications.

Many of the concepts cannot be conveniently classified as belonging to only one discipline. As intensive investigations are conducted into specific topics from an interdisciplinary perspective and as the multidimensional nature of concepts becomes more apparent, such tables will become more complex.

Psychologists, sociologists, anthropologists, and other social and behavioral scientists are not necessarily any more unified in the concepts they hold of their disciplines than are marketers. Complete agreement does not exist among these scientists as to the most promising lines of development for particular aspects of their subject-matter areas. The important marketing-subject area of motivation is an example. Motivation has been studied at considerable length by psychologists and other behavioral scientists. Rather than any one unified approach emerging, at least three major directions are being

followed by psychologists studying motivation.[2]

First, there is the approach of laboratory psychologists who have tended to focus upon the physiological aspects of psychology. Then, there are clinical psychologists who have concentrated on the role of certain psychological factors in motivation. This group tends to minimize the biological drives as influencing human motivation and behavior. The third approach is represented by Gestalt psychologists, particularly Kurt Lewin and his followers. Of the three, this latter approach may have the greatest significance for marketing people in studying human motives and other related questions.

This Gestalt approach is essentially socio-psychological in nature. It stresses the thesis that people do react to environmental factors. From the Gestalt viewpoint, motivations and behavior are analyzed as a function of the particular person, his inherent drives, and of the immediate environment of which he is a part.

These three different psychological approaches are cited to indicate that in the disciplines underlying marketing a variety of theories and avenues to the understanding of human behavior may exist. The basic problems in utilizing behavioral science concepts in marketing management are to evaluate and reconcile the various theoretical explanations and research findings relating to a subject. The attempt to integrate numerous, and often conflicting, explanations of behavioral scientists into a practicable solution can become a highly perplexing experience.

Also, for many of the problems facing marketing management, the behavioral sciences do not as yet offer useful concepts or methods. Indeed, "the behavioral

[2] Herta Herzog, "Behavioral Science Concepts for Analyzing the Consumer," paper given at the Conference of Marketing Teachers from Pacific Coast States held at the University of California, Berkeley, September 9, 1958.

sciences as they now stand do not provide a large reservoir of immediately useful analytical concepts and models."[3] This is not a reason for ignoring the promise of these disciplines. It is a challenge to begin realizing the potential.

### INTERDISCIPLINARY CONTRIBUTIONS TO MEASUREMENT IN MARKETING

Marketing practitioners and teachers are aware of the numerous measurement methods that have been developed by various subject-matter areas. The inter-disciplinary approach has been used by many measurement tools such as scaling and ranking techniques, personnel tests, various projective techniques, interviewing and questionnaire methods, statistical sampling and measurements, and mathematical models and programming.

Figure 1 specifies some of the more promising contributions to measurement in marketing by five disciplines: sociology, psychology, social psychology, statistics, and operations research. It lists specific measurement techniques from each discipline which have been, or may be, profitably applied to marketing research. These techniques may be useful in solving problems in such marketing areas as: advertising, product and price analysis, sales forecasting, locational problems, competitive strategy, and estimating market potentials. They contribute to more precise cardinal and ordinal measurements in marketing and facilitate the planning and controlling of marketing operations.

In many instances tools borrowed from behavioral sciences are adapted and modified by marketing researchers. Through refinements in application, the basic measurement techniques themselves are improved and marketing research thereby contributes to other disciplines.

This classification of measurement techniques merely suggests topics of interest. It is not comprehensive, and the categories are not necessarily comparable. There are a number of other important contributing subject-matter areas. Many of these techniques could be classified under several of the disciplines cited. In the figure this has been done only in a limited number of cases to avoid much duplication, but still to indicate the interdisciplinary overlapping of many of the methods of measuring specific aspects of human behavior.

## THE INTERDISCIPLINARY CONCEPT AND SYSTEMS ANALYSIS

The integration of the functional areas of business administration is an area where the interdisciplinary approach may be helpful. The problem is one of viewing a business enterprise as an operating system, as a whole. The impact of marketing, finance, production, or human-relations decisions on other aspects of company operations and on the business as a whole must be considered in a total cross-functional view of business enterprise.

Marketing administrators may be on the verge of a new level of sophistication in understanding marketing's role in the total system of business action. Managers are becoming increasingly interested in the interaction between the components of business enterprise. Forrester has pointed out that business achievement depends on the successful interaction among five sub-systems, the flows of information, materials, money, manpower, and capital equipment within the firm.[4]

These five sub-systems interlock to amplify one another within the total busi-

[3] G. L. Bach, "Some Observations on the Business School of Tomorrow," *Management Science*, Vol. 4 (July, 1958), pp. 351–364 at pp. 354–355.

[4] J. W. Forrester, "Industrial Dynamics, A Major Breakthrough for Decision Makers," *Harvard Business Review*, Vol. 36 (July–August, 1958), pp. 37–66 at p. 37.

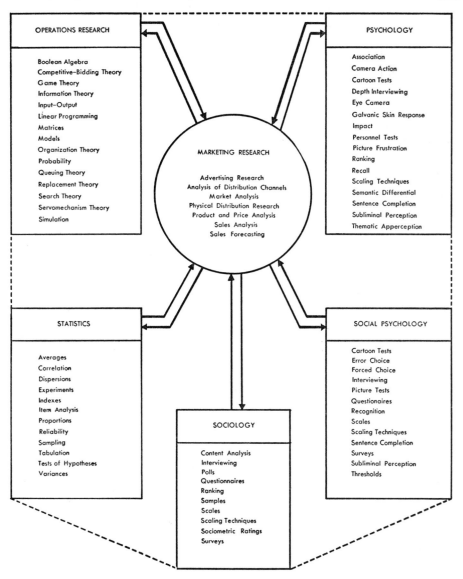

FIGURE 1. Measurement in marketing.

ness complex. Conventional functional thinking may not be adequate for an understanding of the effects of these interactions. It does not allow for anticipated impacts on decisions, policies, organizational forms, and investment choices within the firm.

Figure 2 indicates the relationship of interdisciplinary activity to a marketing management system. The disciplines listed in the area bordering the external noncontrollable forces can be useful in providing information and insights about marketing.

Consumers are the focal point of the entire system of business action. They are

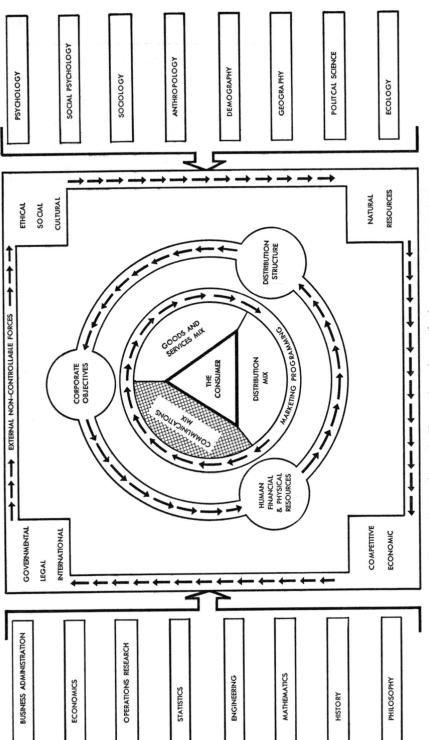

FIGURE 2. A schematic illustration of a marketing management system.

separated from firms attempting to serve them in space, time, ownership, valuation, and knowledge. These separations tend to increase in complex socio-economic systems. Sellers attempt to overcome the barriers of space and time by communicating to the consumer the want-satisfying characteristics of the product offered through the marketing program.

The marketing program is but one significant element in the total business system. Marketing decisions should be made in terms of their impact on the company as a whole and their contributions to over-all objectives. The human, financial, and physical resources of the firm should be factors in marketing decision making since the marketing program affects these factors. This corporate complex also includes the interrelationships and co-ordination of the activities of the manufacturing firm with distributors and dealers as part of their joint effort to serve the consumer.

The interdisciplinary approach can be useful in understanding and even predicting the influence of these external forces on marketing decisions. Figure 2 emphasizes that marketing and corporate decisions are influenced, perhaps determined, by various forces which are largely beyond the control of the management of an individual enterprise. These include competitive, social, political, legal, ethical, and international forces. Change is represented in the figure by arrows. As business systems become more complex, the rate of change increases with corresponding increases in the complexity of business analysis and decision.

The systems approach to business action is particularly important to marketing executives and educators. They have a unique opportunity to integrate business-management functions into a meaningful whole and to take leadership in advancing systems thinking in business administration.

This opportunity stems from two related developments. First, businesses in the future will become more marketing oriented. Second, the total marketing concept will be adopted in which marketing is viewed as an integral sub-system within the total system of business action.

The greatest long-run contribution of the interdisciplinary approach to the study of marketing and business systems may be that of influencing the ways of thinking about marketing and business problems. Marketing students and practitioners using the interdisciplinary approach should gain added insights into the nature and scope of marketing management activities. This is because a person's concept of marketing, or any other subject, depends largely upon the knowledge of the area gained through his own or vicarious experiences.

Marketing problems may be viewed as problems arising from the gratification of human wants and needs. As such, particular marketing activities become a part of the more general problem of raising the standard of living through satisfying the needs of human beings. The discipline of marketing in this perspective is seen as a contributing component of a broader science which encompasses man and his culture.

Acceptance of the interdisciplinary approach does not mean that marketing men must become psychologists or sociologists, nor does it mean that men trained in the behavioral sciences should move over completely to marketing. The relationship between marketing and other disciplines is a reciprocal one. Marketing is concerned with the study of human action in the market place, the study of the process of exchange and economic transaction and of the interacting efforts and responses of buyers and sellers in the market. This sphere of human action is essential to our economic system and the study of it is growing in importance.

The field of marketing provides a testing ground on which to verify, modify, and extend the hypotheses and relationships which have been described by various behavioral sciences.

The interdisciplinary approach can contribute greatly to a more penetrating and rigorous analysis of consumers in their socio-economic environment. As the body of knowledge about human behavior increases and is incorporated into marketing thought and practice, marketing management should be enabled to serve the needs of consumers more effectively.

The application of the interdisciplinary approach to marketing, however, is not a simple matter. Social scientists themselves experience great difficulty in communicating about and bridging disciplines. We are still a long way from a general science of human behavior which could be applied in marketing.

In the last analysis, it is likely to be the marketing men rather than pure behavioral scientists who will contribute most to the solution of difficult marketing problems and the development of mar-

keting thought. In the future, as in the past, the major advances in marketing knowledge probably will come from people who have a marketing background and who possess an intense professional interest in advancing science in marketing.

## QUESTIONS

1. What is meant by an interdisciplinary approach to marketing?
2. Distinguish between the behavioral approach and the interdisciplinary approach.
3. Distinguish between the approaches of the laboratory psychologists, the clinical psychologists, and the Gestalt psychologists. To make better use of the behavioral sciences, do we need to reconcile these differences in point of view?
4. We are still a long way from a general science of human behavior which could be applied to marketing. Explain.
5. How is operations research defined by the authors?

# 39. Anthropology's Contributions to Marketing*

Charles Winick, Graduate School of Business, Columbia University

*Of the social sciences which deal with man and society, only economics, psychology, and sociology have been widely used in marketing. Economics is at the core of much of the content of marketing; psychology has yielded a variety of interviewing and projective testing procedures; sociology has contributed concepts like social class.*

*Marketers have been relatively slow in using anthropological insights and approaches, even though anthropology is also concerned with man and society. This article considers why anthropology has been used relatively seldom, and how it has been and might be employed.*

The relative slowness of anthropologists and marketers in finding common ground is surprising.[1] Anthropologists have served as colonial administrators, in foreign-aid programs, and in other situations requiring a special sensitivity to foreign cultures. They have also developed sales-training procedures which involve the analysis of the rate of speech of salesmen with potential customers, through devices which measure the rate of interaction between people talking.[2] Another specialized industrial situation in which anthropologists have worked involves the application of their knowledge of the field of anthropometry or measurement of the body, in the design of products like chairs and knobs.[3]

Other anthropologists have worked on applied fields such as: reactions to disaster, the operation of internment and relocation centers, mental health, medical care, labor-management relations,[4] the culture of a factory,[5] community organization, social work,[6] military government, the cultural change associated with economic development,[7] contact between cultures, the nature of small-town life, behavior in extreme situations, the study of culture at a distance,[8] the reconstruction of the themes of a culture, relations among minority groups, the social structure of a hospital,[9] American national character,[10] and television.[11]

Although anthropologists have published their findings on America in very

* Reprinted from the *Journal of Marketing*, national quarterly publication of the American Marketing Association, Vol. 25, No. 5, July 19, 1961, pp. 53–60.

[1] John Gillin, "The Application of Anthropological Knowledge to Modern Mass Society," *Human Organization*, Vol. 15 (Winter 1957), pp. 24–30.
[2] Eliot D. Chapple, "The Interaction Chronograph," *Personnel*, Vol. 25 (January 1949), pp. 295–307.
[3] Earnest A. Hooton, *A Survey In Seating* (Cambridge: Harvard Department of Anthropology, 1945).

[4] Charles R. Walker, *The Man on the Assembly Line* (Cambridge: Harvard University Press, 1952).
[5] Eliot Jaques, *The Changing Culture of A Factory* (New York: Dryden Press, 1953).
[6] Franklin K. Patterson, Irving Lukoff, and Charles Winick, "Is Society the Patient," *Journal of Educational Sociology*, Vol. 30 (October 1956), pp. 106–112.
[7] Almost every issue of *Economic Development and Cultural Change* carries relevant articles.
[8] Margaret Mead and Rhoda Metraux, *The Study of Culture At A Distance* (Chicago: University of Chicago Press, 1952).
[9] Charles Winick, "The Hospital As A Social System," *New York State Nurse*, Vol. 26 (January 1954), pp. 9–13.
[10] David M. Potter, *People of Plenty* (Chicago: University of Chicago Press, 1954).
[11] Charles Winick, *Taste and the Censor In Television* (New York: Fund For the Republic, 1959).

273

accessible formats,[12] there has been little discussion of how their findings could be applied to marketing problems.[13] One advertising publication has published an article on the possibility of using anthropology in advertising.[14] The journal of applied anthropology, formerly called *Applied Anthropology* and now called *Human Organization*, almost never carries any material on marketing; and the national journal, *American Anthropologist*, also ignores the subject.

## ANTHROPOLOGY, SOCIOLOGY, AND PSYCHOLOGY

Anthropology is usually defined as the study of man. Such a definition is so all-inclusive that the field is generally divided into four sub-fields: archeology, cultured anthropology, linguistics, and physical anthropology. Archeology is concerned with the historical reconstruction of cultures which no longer exist. Cultural anthropology examines all the behaviors of man which have been learned, including social, linguistic, technical, and familiar behaviors; often it is defined as the study of man and his works. Linguistics is the comparative study of the structure, interrelationships, and development of languages. Physical anthropology is concerned with human biology and the development of the human organism, with special interest in race differences.

When anthropology is employed in marketing, it is usually cultural anthropology which is relevant. Cultural anthropology began with the study of primitive cultures, and its comparative analyses documented the different ways in which cultures have solved their problems of living.

Cultural anthropology has much in common with psychology and sociology. All three are concerned with the examination of man in his cultural setting. They differ in the emphases which they place on different elements of the relationship between a person and his environment. It can be said that all human behavior essentially is a function of the interrelations of personality, the social system, and culture.

Oversimplifying, psychology is concerned with personality, sociology addresses itself to the social system, and anthropology explores the culture. The interdisciplinary field of social psychology may draw on all three of these fields, and there are integrated social psychology texts which do so.[15]

A sharper focus on the differences among these three social sciences may be obtained by speculating on how each of the three might look at a family.

The psychologist would be interested in the personal adjustment and emotional health of each member of the family. He would want to examine their attitudes, mutual perceptions, and motivational systems. Their happiness or lack of it would interest him.

The sociologist would be concerned primarily with the dimensions of role and status within the family and with the number of different kinds of families. He would examine how the social structure created various kinds of internal arrangements which made it possible for the family to exist. He would be interested in the norms of behavior and the stresses and strains shown by the deviations from the

---

[12] Margaret Lantis, editor, "The U.S.A. As Anthropologists See It," *American Anthropologist*, Vol. 57 (December 1955), pp. 1,113–1,380.

[13] Richard C. Sheldon, "How The Anthropoligist Can Help The Marketing Practitioner" in W. David Robbins, editor, *Successful Marketing at Home And Abroad* (Chicago: American Marketing Association, 1958), pp. 209–304.

[14] Alan S. Marcus, "How Agencies Can Use Anthropology in Advertising," *Advertising Agency*, Vol. 49 (September 14, 1956) pp. 87–91.

[15] Steuart Henderson Britt, *Social Psychology of Modern Life*. (New York: Rinehart & Company, 1949 revised edition). S. Stanfeld Sargent and Robert C. Williamson, *Social Psychology* (New York: The Ronald Press Company, 1958).

norm and resulting from role conflict. He would study class membership as well as the rates of various kinds of behavior, such as the birth rate.

The cultural anthropologist would examine the technological level which the culture had reached and the interrelations of technology with culture. He would scrutinize the procedures for inheritance of property and how kinship was reckoned and described, and how the spouses got to know each other. He would study the family's food and housing. He would be interested in the language level and dialects and in who talked to whom. He would be concerned with how the age of different members of the family affected their behavior, and with trends in illnesses. He would study how the culture "rubbed off" on the family unit. The anthropologist thus does not have information which it would be impossible for the sociologist or psychologist to obtain, but he has a special sensitivity to certain facets of social life.

The sociologist and psychologist bring a powerful and varied arsenal of concepts and approaches to the study of social life. In what ways is the anthropologist able to contribute insights and experience toward the science of "marketology," and to what extent may they not be immediately accessible, for example, to the sociologist?[16] The anthropologist is especially trained to have empathy with groups other than his own and to "tune in" on their patterns of culture. Inasmuch as his training has exposed him to a wide variety of cultures, he can take a global view of a situation and see it in the context of a larger background. His training makes him sensitive to cross-cultural differences which may be of crucial importance in many different situations, because his en-

tire training is geared toward awareness of such differences.

Anthropology has less of the factionalism which characterizes psychology and sociology. This is not to suggest that all is serene in anthropology or that it has never been troubled by theoretical or methodological issues. However, even though anthropologists may disagree on something like the exact value of the contribution of a particular anthropologist, they would generally agree on what the cultural anthropologist looks for, and there are standardized check lists on how to view a culture.[17] In contrast, a psychologist's allegiance to the Gestalt, behaviorist, psychoanalytic, learning-theory, or perception schools is likely to influence what he does with a given problem. A sociologist's commitment to the structure-function, historical, ecological, "middle range," environmental-determinism, or demographic schools would largely determine the emphases of his approach to a problem. Since such divergent schools are less likely to exist in cultural anthropology, it is probable that anthropological guidance on a given marketing problem would be relatively consistent.

## WHAT THE ANTHROPOLOGIST KNOWS

The anthropologist is specifically trained to study national character, or the differences which distinguish our national group from another. He should be able to provide measures for distinguishing the subtle differences among a Swede, a Dane, and a Norwegian; or between a Frenchman and an Englishman; or a Brazilian and an Argentinian; or between a typical resident of Montreal and one of Toronto. The anthropologist is also a specialist in the study of subcultures. He would be able, in a

[16] Robert Bartels, "Sociologist and Marketologists," *Journal of Marketing*, Vol. 24 (October 1959), pp. 37–40; Christen T. Jonassen, "Contributions of Sociology to Marketing," *Journal of Marketing*, Vol. 24 (October 1959), pp. 29–35.

[17] Royal Anthropological Institute, *Notes and Queries on Anthropology* (London: The Institute, 1956).

city like New York, to differentiate the patterns of living of such disparate but rapidly homogenizing groups as Puerto Ricans, Negroes, Italo-Americans, Jews, Polish-Americans, and Irish-Americans.

Because almost any large community consists of a variety of subcultures, this awareness of subcultural trends can be especially useful. A more subtle area of special interest to anthropologists is the silent language of gesture, posture, food and drink preferences, and other non-verbal cues to behavior.[18]

Related to this is the anthropologist's professional interest in languages and symbols. He might, for example, be especially concerned about why a particular shape has special significance as a symbol in a society, or how the structure of a language or a regional speech pattern was related to how people think.[19]

Another area of concern to the anthropologist, because of its symbolic meanings, has to do with "rites de passage" or the central points in a person's life at which he may ritually be helped to go from one status to another, for example, birth, puberty, or marriage.[20]

Taboos represent a continuing area of interest to the anthropologist.[21] Every culture has taboos or prohibitions about various things, such as the use of a given color, or of a given phrase or symbol. The anthropologist is aware of the larger values of a culture, which represent the substratum of custom which is taken for granted and the violation of which represents a taboo.

The anthropologist's method is primarily the exposure of his highly developed sensitivity to the area in which he is working, via observation and extended

interviews with informants. Projective tests have also been widely used in anthropological studies. The anthropologist can bring a wealth of insight to marketing situations.

## USE OF ANTHROPOLOGY IN MARKETING

There are at least three kinds of situations in which the knowledge of the anthropologist has been employed in marketing: specific knowledge; awareness of themes of a culture; sensitivity to taboos.

### SPECIFIC KNOWLEDGE

Here are a few cases in which the specific knowledge of an anthropologist was applied to marketing situations.

A manufacturer of central heating equipment was planning to introduce central heating to an area which previously had used other heating. Since people generally grow up to accept a certain approach to heating which they take for granted, introduction of the new central heating posed marketing problems in coping with deeply imbedded consumer resistance to what would be a major innovation. An anthropologist was able to draw on his knowledge of the folklore and symbolism of heat and fire in order to suggest methods of presenting the new system, so as to make it as consonant as possible with the connotations of heat, even though the nature of the heating method had changed radically. There was considerable consumer resistance to the central heating, but it decreased substantially after the first year.

In addition to a marketing problem, the introduction of central heating also posed problems of public policy which the manufacturer had to overcome before he could obtain approval for the introduction of the heating equipment. The area was one

[18] Edward T. Hall, *The Silent Language* (New York: Doubleday & Co., 1959).
[19] Benjamin Lee Whorf, *Collected Papers on Metalinguistics* (Washington: Department of State Foreign Service Institute, 1952).
[20] Jan Wit, *Rites De Passage* (Amsterdam: De Windroos, 1959).
[21] Franz Steiner, *Taboo* (London: Cohen and West, Ltd., 1957).

which suffered from a declining birth rate, and officials were concerned about the extent to which central heating might cause the birth rate to decline further, because of their belief that heated bedrooms would cause a decline in sexual activity and ultimately in births. The anthropologist was able to point to some cultures in which the birth rate had declined and some in which it had not done so after the introduction of central heating. The anthropologist's data made it possible for the manufacturer of the central-heating equipment to discuss its probable effects realistically with the appropriate officials.

Another field in which the anthropologist has specific knowledge that other social scientists are not likely to have is that of clothing and fashion. The only empirical study of the fashion cycle in woman's clothing which has successfully been used for predictive purposes by clothing manufacturers was conducted by anthropologists.[22] In marketing situations, the anthropologist has often been able to combine his special knowledge of the needs of the body for clothing of various kinds at different ages, his sensitivity to what technology makes possible and his awareness of fashion.

For example, an anthropologist was consulted by a leading manufacturer of overalls for young children, a product which had remained unchanged for decades. He examined the product in the light of the special needs of children who wear overalls, the growing use of washing machines to launder the overalls, their relative frequency of laundering, and contemporary technology. He suggested that the overall straps have a series of sets of metal grippers instead of buttons, thus making it possible to use different sets of grippers as the child grew instead of

tying or knotting the straps. Noting that the straps often fall off the shoulders when children played, he suggested that the shirts which children wore under the overalls have either a loop for the straps to pass through or a synthetic fastener which faced matching material on the strap, so that the shoulder of the shirt could be pressed against the strap and remain attached to it until shoulder strap and shirt were pulled apart.

He also recommended that the seams of the overalls, previously single stitched, be double stitched like those of men's shirts, which have to withstand frequent launderings. The double-stitched overalls would be less likely to come apart as a result of frequent launderings in a washing machine. These recommendations were adopted, and within a few years substantially changed and expanded the nature of the overall market for young children. The children's parents were more pleased with the overalls because they lasted longer and looked better on the children, and they were far more functional than before.

The special knowledge of the anthropologist has been called into play where there are special subcultural groups to which the marketer wishes to address himself. One beer manufacturer wished to extend his market share among Negroes in a large eastern city in the United States. He was advised about reaching this group by an anthropologist who was familiar with the special subculture of Negroes, and who pointed to the profound effects of Negroes' caste membership on their purchasing behavior. The ambiguity of their role has led many Negroes to be especially aware of articles that have status connotations and of whether a brand symbolizes racial progress. Examination of the manufacturer's marketing program by the anthropologist led to several recommendations for change. The manufacturer began to help

[22] Jane Richardson and Alfred L. Kroeber, *Three Centuries of Women's Dress Fashions* (Berkeley: University of California Press, 1940).

in the support of several major social events related to the arts in Negro communities, and to stress that the beer was a national brand with quality-control procedures. He changed the content of his advertising in the direction of enhancing its status and quality connotations. These changes were all directed toward improving the status connotations of the beer to Negroes.

Guidance on related problems with respect to the Puerto Rican and Jewish markets has also been used constructively. Since 35 to 40 per cent of the population of the United States consists of minority subcultures, the anthropologist's contributions may be considerable.

Another situation had to do with the selection of specific symbols for various purposes. A major manufacturer of women's products was uncertain about whether to continue using the Fleur de Lis emblem on his package. Anthropological analysis of the symbol suggested that its association with French kings and other cultural connotations of maleness made it more masculine than feminine. The anthropologist's recommendations were confirmed by subsequent field testing.

In a related case, a manufacturer of women's cosmetics conducted an anthropological study of the comparative symbolism in our culture of women's eyes and mouth, which suggested that the eye tends to be experienced as a relatively protecting organ while the mouth tends to be experienced as more nurturing. This knowledge of the differences between the special meanings of eye and mouth could constructively be used in marketing the products, and especially in advertising. The advertising explicitly and implicitly mentioned the role of the eye in protection of the woman. It stressed the role of the mouth as the organ which both symbolically and literally gives love. This replaced the manufacturer's previous advertising, in which both eye and mouth were treated in the same way, as organs which could be made beautiful.

## AWARENESS OF THEMES

The anthropologist has functioned in situations in which he can use his special understanding of themes of a culture, oftentimes taken for granted.

A major chain of candy shops was suffering a decline in sales. A marketing-research study had established that the brand was usually bought as a gift, either for others or as a gift for the purchaser. The chain was unable to develop any ways of using this finding that were not hackneyed. Anthropological guidance on the symbolism of gift-giving enabled the chain to develop merchandising, packaging, and advertising formats for the gift theme. Anthropological study of the connotations of the major holidays suggested themes for window displays, and advertising of the candy in conjunction with the holidays. The chain's marketing strategy was revised on the basis of the anthropological interpretation and clarification of the marketing-research study. Anthropologists are the only social scientists who have systematically studied gift-giving and gift-receiving.[23]

Another example of anthropological interpretation of a marketing-research study was provided by a shirt manufacturer. The study had established that women buy more than half of men's shirts in a particular price range. The anthropologist was able to interpret this finding in the light of several anthropological studies of the relations between husbands and wives in America. The manufacturer had been thinking of placing advertising for his men's shirts in selected women's magazines. The anthropologist was able

[23] Marcel Mauss, *The Gift* (London: Cohen & West, Ltd., 1954).

to point to a number of studies of husband-wife relations which suggested growing resentment by men over the extent to which women had been borrowing and buying men's clothing, and which suggested that the proposed advertising campaign might not be propitious.

Another anthropologist's special sensitivity to the "rites de passage" helped a shoe manufacturer whose sales were declining because of aggressive foreign and domestic competition. The anthropologist was able to point to the extent to which shoes represent major symbols of our going from one stage of life to another, and to assist the manufacturer in developing methods for using the relationship between shoes and "rites de passage."[24]

A landmark along the road of an infant becoming a child usually is found between the ages of 4 and 6 when he can tie his own shoe laces. The manufacturer developed some pamphlets and other instructional material for parents on how to help children to learn to tie their shoe laces. Distribution by local retailers contributed toward making parents favorably aware of the brand's line for children in this age group.

The teenager signalizes her entrance into a new social world by her first high heels. Window displays and advertising which explicitly stressed the new social activities of the teenager wearing her high heels, and naming specific shoe models after teenage social events ("The Prom") contributed toward associating the manufacturer's name with the excitement of the new world symbolized by the high heels.

Older people see the wearing of special "old people's shoes" as the ultimate reminder that they are becoming old. The manufacturer was able to redesign his line

for older people so that it retained its special health features but still looked as stylish as any adult shoe, and had no visible stigma of "old people's shoes."

### SENSITIVITY TO TABOOS

Marketers may unwittingly violate a taboo, whether cultural, religious, or political, especially in selling overseas. Blue, for example, is the color for mourning in Iran and is not likely to be favorably received on a commercial product. Green is the nationalist color of Egypt and Syria and is frowned on for use in packages. Showing pairs of anything on the Gold Coast of Africa is disapproved. White is the color of mourning in Japan and, therefore, not likely to be popular on a product. Brown and gray are disapproved colors in Nicaragua. Purple is generally disapproved in most Latin American markets because of its association with death. Feet are regarded as despicable in Thailand, where any object and package showing feet is likely to be unfavorably received.

The anthropologist can cast light on taboos and on their opposite: favored colors and symbols. The reason for the people in a country or an area liking or not liking a particular color or symbol may be a function of political, nationalist, religious, cultural, or other reasons.

## SOME APPLICATIONS IN CANADA

Canada represents a special opportunity for the application of anthropology in marketing situations. Twenty-nine per cent of the country's entire population is in French-speaking Quebec, and over half of this number know no English. Canada thus offers a changing kind of bilingual and culture contact situation

[24] Charles Winick, "Status, Shoes, and the Life Cycle," *Boot and Shoe Recorder*, Vol. 156 (October 15, 1959), pp. 100-202.

with major cross-cultural differences for anthropological analysis.

Both the farm community and the industrial community of Quebec have been studied by anthropologists.[25] The re-evaluation of the nature of Quebec family and community life sparked by Dean Phillipe Garigue of the University of Montreal and a team at Laval University has led to renewed interest in Quebec on the part of anthropologists. Their studies have produced considerable information on styles of life in Quebec which should be translatable into marketing data on pricing policies, colors, package size, flavor and taste of various food items, texture of fabrics, automobile symbolism, product scents, and related subjects.

### SPECIFIC KNOWLEDGE

Perhaps the most frequent occasion for the anthropologist to demonstrate specific knowledge in Canada has to do with language. One laundry-soap company had point-of-sale material on its soap describing it as extra strong and the best one to use on especially dirty parts of wash ("les parts de sale"). After sales of the soap had declined, an anthropologist who was called in by the company pointed out that the phrase is comparable to the American slang phrase "private parts." This kind of mistake might have been avoided if anthropological guidance had been available before sales declined.

Some products do not sell well in Quebec because the English name may be almost unpronounceable to a French speaker, or the name of the product may be meaningless even when translated idiomatically. Even the English spoken in Montreal differs somewhat from the English spoken in Toronto, creating potential hazards for the marketers who may not

[25] Horace Miner, *St. Denis* (Chicago, University of Chicago Press, 1939); Everett C. Hughes, *French Canada In Transition* (Chicago: University of Chicago Press, 1943).

know, for example that a "tap" in a "flat" in Toronto is likely to be a "faucet" in a Montreal "apartment."

### AWARENESS OF THEMES

A study done by an anthropologist for a food manufacturer demonstrated the relationship between the purchases of certain food items and the gradual decline of the wood-burning stove which used to be a staple of Quebec farm kitchens. The wood stove would almost always have a stew pot ("pot au feu") simmering all day. Various ingredients were put into the pot to provide flavor. With the introduction of gas and electric kitchen ranges, it not only became relatively expensive to keep the stew pot going but the simmering could not be sustained because the pot would tend to boil rather than simmer.

This change was accompanied by some radical adjustments in food consumption which were of great relevance to food marketing. The manufacturer was able to begin distribution of canned soups and stews which soon found a very large market and rapidly replaced the "pot au feu."

### TABOOS

Alertness to taboos was illustrated by an anthropologist's suggestion to a manufacturer of canned fish for changing a series of advertisements which were appearing in Quebec magazines and newspapers, The same advertisement was run repeatedly. The advertisements showed a woman in shorts playing golf with her husband. The caption read that the woman would be able to be on the golf links all day and still prepare a delicious dinner that evening if she used the product. Every element in the advertisement represented a violation of some underlying theme of French Canadian life; the wife would not be likely to be playing golf with her husband, she would not wear shorts, and she would not be serving the particular kind of fish as a main course. In this case, the anthropologist was consulted *after* the series had been running for awhile.

## THE MARKETER AS AN ANTHROPOLOGIST

A good case could be made for the thesis that marketing researchers do more anthropological research on modern cultures than do anthropologists. Marketing researchers are studying national character, subcultures, themes, and ways of life. The kind of information which marketing-research studies seek on how people live and what products they use represent first-rate material for the cultural anthropologist.

The questionnaire, panel, audit, sales analysis, and other methods of modern marketing differ in degree but not in kind from the trained observations of the anthropologist, but there is no reason why the two methods cannot complement each other. Greater communication between these two fields can and should lead to mutual enrichment of both.

## QUESTIONS

1. Distinguish between anthropology, sociology, and psychology.
2. Describe some specific contributions of anthropology to marketing situations.
3. Have anthropologists made any specific contributions to the understanding of the fashion cycle in woman's clothing?
4. Explain how an anthropologist's familiarity with the taboos and mores of various foreign cultures help the manufacturer who sells abroad.

# 40. What Responding Behavioral Scientists Feel Their Disciplines Could Contribute to Certain Specialized Areas of Advertising*

Louis C. Wagner, Professor of Marketing, University of Washington

*This paper presents some of the contributions that anthropology, psychology, and sociology can make to various specialized areas of advertising according to a survey of opinion of social scientists in these three fields.*

Social scientists whose fields of specialization are Anthropology, Psychology,

* Reprinted from *The Social Responsibilities of Marketing,* Proceedings of the Winter Conference of the American Marketing Association, December 27–29, 1961, p. 259. Edited by William M. Stevens.

and Sociology were asked to indicate how their disciplines could contribute to the following four aspects of advertising: (1) Advertising management, (2) Advertising creativity, (3) Advertising media, and (4) Advertising research. Due to the fact that more psychologists and sociologists have been used by business firms as consultants, social scientists in these two fields felt that their disciplines had more applications to advertising than did specialists in anthropology. For additional information on the applications of these fields to marketing and advertising problems, the reader is referred to the references listed below.[1]

## CONTRIBUTIONS OF ANTHROPOLOGY

Only half of the responding anthropologists indicated that their discipline had any applications of value to the field of advertising. Those mentioning contributions felt that concepts developed in the division of cultural anthropology would be most valuable. In addition, it was pointed out that the field of linguistic anthropology could also be of value to advertising. Suggested applications of this discipline to the four areas of advertising are as follows:

[1] *General*
William Lazer and Eugene J. Kelley, "Interdisciplinary Horizons in Marketing," *Journal of Marketing,* Vol. 25 (October 1960), pp. 24–31.

*Anthropology*
Charles Winick, "Anthropology's Contributions to Marketing," *Journal of Marketing,* Vol. 25 (July 1961), pp. 53–61.
Richard C. Sheldon, "How the Anthropologist Can Help the Marketing Practitioner," in W. David Robbins, editor, *Successful Marketing at Home and Abroad* (Chicago: American Marketing Association, 1958), pp. 209–304.

*Psychology*
Hattwick, Melvin S., *How To Use Psychology for Better Advertising.* Englewood Cliffs, N. J., Prentice-Hall, Inc., 1950.
Pierre Martineau, *Motivation in Advertising.* New York: McGraw-Hill Book Co., 1957.
Walter A. Woods, "Psychological Dimensions of Consumer Decision," *Journal of Marketing,* Vol. 25 (January 1960), pp. 15–19.

*Sociology*
Philip M. Hauser, "Aspects of Sociology for Business," *University of Washington Business Review,* Vol. 20 (February 1961), pp. 3–17.
Christen J. Jonassen, "Contributions of Sociology to Marketing," *Journal of Marketing.* Vol. 24 (October 1959), pp. 20–35.

### MANAGEMENT

It was suggested that anthropology through a knowledge of cultures and cultural differences could assist management in making decisions as to when and where to employ advertising. This discipline could also be of value in appraising the ability of advertising to influence purchasing habits as well as to change purchasing habits of consumers.

This branch of the social sciences could also be of value in focusing attention on the decision making process in advertising as influenced by the knowledge of formal and informal organizations.

### CREATIVITY

It was pointed out that anthropology can assist the advertiser by providing an insight into the symbolic aspects of culture as well as mechanisms by which culture can be changed. In particular, a knowledge of cultures and the subcultural complexity of audiences may aid the copywriter. The selection of advertising themes can be helped by the anthropologist's understanding of themes in a culture. The studies made by this branch of the social sciences into the relationship of various members of a family to each other, such as the relationship of husband to wife, can be employed to secure a better understanding of buying influences and how these influences can be more effectively exploited.

In view of the importance of various sub-cultural groups in our economy, advertisers wishing to expand the market for their product among members of a racial group, can benefit from what the anthropologist knows about the special subculture of this race. In addition, American advertisers can be prevented from unwittingly violating a cultural, religious, or political taboo when selling overseas. The anthropologist may help the advertiser in selecting an effective layout or design by pointing out why a particular shape has special symbolic significance.

## MEDIA

Those responding to our questionnaire felt that this discipline could be of only general value in the media area. However, it was felt that use of advertising media could be assisted by providing information regarding the role of communication in culture and especially linguistics in relation to cultural value and perceptions. Anthropology could also help advertisers in media selection and appraisal by providing insights into the most effective modes of diffusion of new ideas in various cultural groups.

## RESEARCH

Relatively few anthropologists felt that their discipline would be of any help in the research area. Those who responded favorably felt that the main contribution of anthropology would be in the area of research methodology. In addition, a few respondents felt that their field would provide some help in identifying additional problems to be investigated.

# CONTRIBUTIONS OF PSYCHOLOGY

Nearly all psychologists responding to the questionnaire felt that their branch of the social sciences had contributions to make to advertising. Among the applications of this branch of the social sciences to advertising were the following:

## MANAGEMENT

The major contribution of psychology to advertising management was felt to be in the area of handling people employed in advertising. It was felt that this branch of the social sciences by developing knowledge about organization and decision theory, group psychology, and supervisor-subordinate behavior would help management in accomplishing its organizational objectives. In addition, their field has many contributions to make in the entire personnel management field. By application to problems of job analysis, testing and selection procedures, performance evaluation and motivation of personnel, psychology can assist any employer of advertising personnel increase the effectiveness of its manpower.

## CREATIVITY

In this area most respondents felt that this branch of the social sciences could make important contributions to the solution of creative problems. The body of knowledge developed by psychologists has application to the selection of effective themes and approaches.

The whole area of motivation research has drawn very heavily from the field of psychology. It was pointed out that the findings and methods of experimental psychology have been valuable to those interested in determining motivation. Social scientists in this field have developed techniques such as attitude scales, word association, and thematic apperception which can be used to probe into conscious and subconscious motivational factors.

In addition to knowledge which is helpful in understanding motivation, the psychologist can make important contributions to other creative problems in advertising. What psychologists know or do not know about perception, learning, attention, memory, and individual differences can be of value. For example, psychological theories can assist the copywriter in determining what appeals to emphasize, the number of appeals to include in the advertisement, the frequency with which appeals should be changed, the value of repetition, and adapting appeals to particular segments of the market. Psychological knowledge can help the artist and layout man concerned with the possible effectiveness of various methods of attracting attention, securing interest, and obtaining conviction.

## MEDIA

Most respondents felt that psychology had little or nothing to offer in appraising and selecting media. However, it was pointed out that this discipline might contribute an experimental approach of value in determining the relative efficacy of communication media.

## RESEARCH

Psychologists pointed out that many of the techniques developed in the fields of social, clinical and experimental psychology can be directly applied to advertising research problems. Their discipline has made important contributions to survey methodology particularly in the areas of interviewing, building of questionnaires, and sampling techniques. Psychological theories of human behavior also have widespread applications in the area of motivation research. Finally in studying the relative effectiveness of media or appeals, the psychologist's knowledge of experimental design is helpful to the researcher.

## SOCIOLOGY

Nearly all sociologists felt that their field had numerous contributions to make to advertising and tended to list more detailed applications than social scientists in the other two fields. Respondents to our questionnaire mentioned the follow-

ing ways in which their discipline could be of help.

## MANAGEMENT

It was pointed out that the sociologist can contribute to the effectiveness of advertising management problems by providing tools for the analysis of the decision making process by persons and groups. Knowledge of leadership principles, status and role theory, and functions of social conflict were stressed.

In addition, management decisions can be assisted by the sociologist's knowledge of groups and institutions. In particular, principles developed regarding small groups and bureaucracy as well as the nature and functions of institutions were mentioned. For example, small group research concerned with knowledge of leadership, motivation and incentive, group problem solving, and committee and group meetings may be particularly helpful. The theories and principles developed by the sociologist in this field can assist the advertising department in the decision making process as well as an agency in working effectively with a client.

The sociologist's work in the field of demography is of value in determining where to direct promotional efforts. Knowledge about the size, composition, distribution and dynamics of population is particularly useful. Of special interest to the advertiser is the increasing attention which the demographer is directing towards the making of current population estimates and population projections.

## CREATIVITY

Respondents to the questionnaire stressed the contributions which the sociologist has made in the area of motivation research. In particular, their studies of social class were stressed. These studies focus attention on the implications of class and status and describe the differential motivational patterns of various classes in our society. Contributions made by the sociologist in this area are helpful in selecting advertising appeals suited to influence particular groups.

The sociologist's knowledge of the leadership structure can also be of help in determining which individuals to influence in order to secure quick acceptance of new products or ideas. In addition, his studies of message diffusion can be of value in selecting effective media to use in a campaign.

Also, it was mentioned that social scientists in this field have undertaken experimental studies of the differential effects of various kinds of appeals.

### MEDIA

Sociologists replying felt that their discipline could make important contributions to media selection and evaluation through their study of the whole area of mass media and communications. In particular, they could provide a better understanding of the nature and role of the various media in influencing the thought and behavior of individuals and groups. Their knowledge would help understand the values, attitudes, and perceptions of the audience reached by media.

In addition, they pointed out that personal influence studies have related the effects of different vehicles to the composition of the medium's audiences.

### RESEARCH

Respondents pointed out that sociologists have made important contributions to knowledge in the area of survey research methodology. Their research has been particularly helpful in the areas of questionnaire construction; types of questions to ask; improvement of interviewing procedures; techniques of assaying the reliability and validity of response; and selection of better samples. They have also focused their attention on social structure variables which should be considered in the analysis of survey results.

Sociologistst also have been responsible for developments in other research techniques which can be of benefit to those engaged in advertising research. Social scientists in this discipline have made advances in: design of experiments, including experimental procedures and factorial designs; improved observational techniques; and in the use of mathematical models. The research in this field has made strides in more refined attitude measurement by means of latent analysis and scaling.

Finally, it was stressed that a study of sociology would insure that the necessary emphasis is given to an evaluation of the importance of the extent to which a person's reactions to advertising are influenced by his association with others.

## QUESTIONS

1. How might anthropological insights assist management in making decisions in the area of advertising?
2. What is thought to be the major contribution of psychology to advertising management?
3. What do sociologists think they can contribute to advertising ?

# 41. The Significance of Social Stratification in Selling*

Richard P. Coleman, Social Research, Inc.

*While the concept of social class has proven to be a very helpful tool to the marketing analyst, the time has come to advance to a more sophisticated application of social class to marketing problems. For example, it is important to recognize that differences as well as similarities exist within each class. This fact explains why some products such as color television, sales of which are not correlated with income generally, enjoy markets in each social class among relatively prosperous or "overprivileged" families.*

Dating back to the late 1940's, advertisers and marketers have alternately flirted with and cooled on the notion that W. Lloyd Warner's social class concept[1] is an important analytic tool for their profession. The Warnerian idea that six social classes constitute the basic division of American Society has offered many attractions to marketing analysts when they have grown dissatisfied with simple income categories or census-type occupational categories and felt a need for more meaningful classifications, for categorizations of the citizenry which could prove more relevant to advertising and marketing problems. However, in the course of their attempts to apply the class concept, marketers have not always found it immediately and obviously relevant. Sometimes it has seemed to shed light on advertising and merchandising problems and at other times it hasn't—with the result that many analysts have gone away disenchanted, deciding that social classes are not much more useful than income

categories and procedurally far more difficult to employ.

It is the thesis of this writer that the role of social class has too often been misunderstood or oversimplified, and that if the concept is applied in a more sophisticated and realistic fashion, it will shed light on a great many problems to which, at first glance, it has not seemed particularly relevant. What we propose to do here, then, is discuss and illustrate a few of these more subtle, more refined and (it must be acknowledged) more complicated ways of applying social class analyses to marketing and advertising problems. In other words, the purpose of this paper is to clarify *when* and in *what ways* social class concepts are significant in selling, and to suggest when they might not be as significant as other concepts, or at least need to be used in concert with other analytic categories.

## THE WARNERIAN SOCIAL CLASSES

The six social classes which are referred to in this paper are those which W. Lloyd Warner and his associates have

* Reprinted from *Marketing: A Maturing Discipline,* Proceedings of the Winter Conference of the American Marketing Association, December 28–30, 1960. Edited by Martin L. Bell.
[1] See W. Lloyd Warner, Marchia Meeker, Kenneth Eells, *Social Class in America* (Chicago: Science Research Associates, 1949).

observed in their analyses of such diverse communities as Newburyport, Massachusetts,[2] Natchez, Mississippi,[3] Morris, Illinois,[4] Kansas City, Missouri[5] and Chicago. These social classes are groups of people who are more or less equal to one another in prestige and community status; they are people who readily and regularly interact among themselves in both formal and informal ways; they form a "class" also to the extent that they share the same goals and ways of looking at life. It is this latter fact about social classes which makes them significant to marketers and advertisers.

Briefly characterized, the six classes are as follows, starting from the highest one and going down:[6]

1. The Upper-Upper or "Social Register" Class is composed of locally prominent families, usually with at least second or third generation wealth. Almost inevitably, this is the smallest of the six classes—with probably no more than one-half of one per cent of the population able to claim membership in this class. The basic values of these people might be summarized in these phrases: living graciously, upholding the family reputation, reflecting the excellence of one's breeding, and displaying a sense of community responsibility.

2. The Lower-Upper or "Nouveau Riche" Class is made up of the more recently arrived and never-quite-accepted wealthy families. Included in this class

are members of each city's "executive elite," as well as founders of large businesses and the newly well-to-do doctors and lawyers. At best only one and one-half per cent of Americans rank at this level—so that all told, no more than 2 per cent of the population can be counted as belonging to one layer or the other of our Upper Class. The goals of people at this particular level are a blend of the Upper-Upper pursuit of gracious living and the Upper-Middle Class's drive for success.

3. In the Upper-Middle Class are moderately successful professional men and women, owners of medium-sized businesses and "organization men" at the managerial level; also included are those younger people in their twenties or very early thirties who are expected to arrive at this occupational status level—and possibly higher—by their middle or late thirties (that is, they are today's "junior executives" and "apprentice professionals" who grew up in such families and/or went to the "better" colleges). Ten per cent of Americans are part of this social class and the great majority of them are college educated.

The motivating concerns of people in this class are success at career (which is the husband's contribution to the family's status) and tastefully reflecting this success in social participation and home decor (which is the wife's primary responsibility). Cultivating charm and polish, plus a broad range of interests—either civic or cultural, or both—are also goals of the people in this class, just as in the Lower-Upper. For most marketing and advertising purposes, this class and the two above it can be linked together into a single category of "upper status people." The major differences between them—particularly between the Upper-Middle and the Lower-Upper—are in degree of "success" and the extent to which this has been translated into gracious living.

[2] See W. Lloyd Warner and Paul Lunt, *The Social Life of a Modern Community,* (New Haven: Yale University Press, 1941).

[3] See Allison Davis, Burleigh B. Gardner and Mary R. Gardner, *Deep South* (Chicago: University of Chicago Press, 1941).

[4] See W. Lloyd Warner and Associates, *Democracy in Jonesville,* (New York: Harper & Brothers, 1949).

[5] The writer's observation on the Kansas City social class system will be included in a forthcoming volume on middle age in Kansas City, currently being prepared for publication by the Committee on Human Development of the University of Chicago.

[6] Some of the phrases and ideas in this characterization have been borrowed from Joseph A. Kahl's excellent synthesizing textbook, *The American Class Structure* (New York: Rinehart & Company, Inc., 1957).

4. At the top of the "Average Man World" is the Lower-Middle Class. Approximately 30 per cent or 35 per cent of our citizenry can be considered members of this social class. For the most part they are drawn from the ranks of non-managerial office workers, small business owners, and those highly-paid blue-collar families who are concerned with being accepted and respected in white-collar dominated clubs, churches, and neighborhoods. The key word in understanding the motivations and goals of this class is Respectability, and a second important word is Striving. The men of this class are continually striving, within their limitations, to "do a good job" at their work, and both men and women are determined to be judged "respectable" in their personal behavior by their fellow citizens. Being "respectable" means that they live in well-maintained homes, neatly furnished, in neighborhoods which are more-or-less on the "right side of town." It also means that they will clothe themselves in coats, suits, and dresses from "nice stores" and save for a college education for their children.

5. At the lower half of the "Average Man World" is the Upper-Lower Class, sometimes referred to as "The Ordinary Working Class." Nearly 40 per cent of all Americans are in this class, making it the biggest. The proto-typical member of this class is a semi-skilled worker on one of the nation's assembly lines. Many of these "Ordinary Working Class" people make very good money, but do not bother with using it to become "respectable" in a middle-class way. Whether they just "get by" at work, or moonlight to make extra, Upper-Lowers are oriented more toward enjoying life and living well from day to day than saving for the future or caring what the middle class world thinks of them. They try to "keep in step with the times" (indeed, one might say the "times" are more important than the "Joneses"

to this class), because they want to be at least Modern, if not Middle Class. That is, they try to take advantage of progress to live more comfortably and they work hard enough to keep themselves safely away from a slum level of existence.

6. The Lower-Lower Class of unskilled workers, unassimilated ethnics, and the sporadically employed comprises about 15 per cent of the population, but this class has less than 7 or 8 per cent of the purchasing power, and will not concern us further here. Apathy, fatalism, and a point of view which justifies "getting your kicks whenever you can" characterize the approach toward life, and toward spending money, found among the people of this class.

Now, we do not mean to imply by these characterizations that the members of each class are always homogeneous in behavior. To suggest such would be to exaggerate greatly the meaning of social classes. To properly understand them, it must be recognized that there is a considerable variation in the way individual members of a class realize these class goals and express these values.

For example, within the Upper Middle and Lower Upper Class, there is one group—called Upper Bohemians[7] by Russell Lynes—for whom cultural pursuits are more important than belonging to a "good" country club. As a result, the tastes in furniture, housing accommodations, and recreations exhibited by the men and women of this "issues-and-culture set"—leaning toward the avant garde and eclectic, as they do—are apt to be very different from those practiced by the more conventional, bourgeois members of these status levels. Nevertheless, to both the Upper Bohemians and the Upper Conventionals, displaying "good taste" is quite important, with the differences be-

[7] See Russell Lynes, *A Surfeit of Honey*, (New York: Harper & Brothers, 1957).

tween them not so much a question of good-versus-bad taste as one of whose form of good taste is preferred (though, to be sure, the Upper Bohemians are usually quite certain theirs is better).

Other sub-categories can be found in these higher classes and parallel kinds of sub-categories can be found in the Lower Middle and Upper Lower classes. Within the Upper Lower Class, for instance, there is a large number of people who are quite concerned with their respectability and spend much of their spare time in church trying to do something about it. Their respectability concerns are not quite like those of the Lower Middle Class, however, for they seem to care more about The Almighty's view of them than of their fellow man's. Thus, the Upper-Lower Class might, for certain analytic purposes, be sub-divided into Church-Going and Tavern-Hopping segments, although this would by no means exhaust all possibilities of sub-categorization here.

All of this is by way of indicating that the millions of individuals who compose each social class are not necessarily similar or identical in their consumption patterns, even though they are of equal status socially and share a set of goals and points of view which are class-wide. Thus far, the literature on social class in both marketing journals and sociological publications has emphasized the similarities of people within classes and rarely pointed out these variations. This has been necessary, of course, in order to properly introduce the concept and educate social scientists and marketers to its utility, but it has led on occasion to naive misuse of the concept and ultimate disillusion. In my view, it has come time for us to advance into a more sophisticated application of social class to marketing problems, which involves awareness of the differences as well as similarities within each class.

## SOCIAL CLASS VERSUS INCOME

Let us proceed now to stating the basic significance of this class concept for people in the selling field. In the first place, it explains why income categories or divisions of Americans are quite often irrelevant in analyzing product markets, consumers' shopping habits and store preferences, and media consumption. For example, if you take three families, all earning around $8,000 a year, but each from a different social class, a radical difference in their ways of spending money will be observed.

An Upper-Middle Class family in this income bracket, which in this case might be a young lawyer and his wife or perhaps a college professor, is apt to be found spending a relatively large share of its resources on housing (in a "prestige" neighborhood), on rather expensive pieces of furniture, on clothing from quality stores, and on cultural amusements or club memberships. Meanwhile, the Lower-Middle Class family—headed, we will say, by an insurance salesman or a fairly successful grocery store owner, perhaps even a Diesel engineer—probably has a better house, but in not so fancy a neighborhood; it is apt to have as full a wardrobe though not so expensive, and probably more furniture though none by name designers. These people almost certainly have a much bigger savings account in the bank.

Finally, the Working Class family—with a cross-country truck driver or a highly-paid welder as its chief wage-earner—is apt to have less house and less neighborhood than the Lower-Middle or Upper-Middle family; but it will have a bigger, later model car, plus more expensive appliances in its kitchen and a bigger TV set in its living room. This family will spend less on clothing and furniture, but more on food if the number of children is greater, as is likely.

One further difference: the man of the house probably spends much more on sports, attending baseball games (for example), going hunting and bowling, and perhaps owning a boat of some description.

The wives in these three families will be quite noticeably different in the kind of department stores they patronize, in the magazines they read, and in the advertising to which they pay attention. The clothing and furniture they select for themselves and their families will differ accordingly, and also because they are seeking quite different goals. This has become very clear in studies Social Research, Inc., has done for the *Chicago Tribune* on the clothing tastes of Chicagoland women, for the Kroehler Company on the place of furniture in American homes, and for MacFadden Publications on the purchasing patterns and motivations of their romance magazines' Working Class readers.[8] (These have been contrasted in turn with the motivations of Middle Class women who read service magazines.)

The Upper-Middle Class wife—even of the struggling young lawyer—usually buys all her public-appearance clothes at specialty shops or in the specialty departments of her community's best department stores; she feels constrained to choose her wardrobe according to rather carefully prescribed standards of appropriateness. In furnishing her home, she thoughtfully considers whether a given piece or a combination of pieces will serve as adequate testament to her aesthetic sensitivities, plus doing credit in turn to her husband's taste in wife-choosing. She pays careful attention to the dictates of the best shelter magazines, the "smart" interior decorators in town,

the homes of other women in her class, and maybe that of the boss's wife.

The Lower-Middle Class woman is more single-mindedly concerned with furnishing her home so that it will be "pretty" in a way that suits her and hopefully might win praise from her friends and neighbors. She tries to get ideas from the medium-level shelter and service magazines and is perpetually depressed because her home isn't furnished as much like a dream house as she would like it to be. In this she is quite different from the Upper-Lower wife who is apt to care more about having a full array of expensive, gleaming white appliances in her kitchen than a doll's house of a living room. Where the Lower-Middle housewife usually has a definite style in mind which she's striving to follow, the Upper-Lower woman simply follows the lead of newspaper furniture advertising (and what she sees when window shopping) toward furniture which is "modern-looking," by which she means the "latest thing" that has hit the mass market.

A great many more examples of differences in consumption patterns by class levels could be given, but the principal ones have been well reported already—facetiously by Vance Packard and seriously by Pierre Martineau;[9] for further amplification on this point the latter source is recommended. The significance to merchandisers and advertisers of these findings about motivational differences between classes is fairly obvious, the major idea being that for many products, advertising appeals and merchandising techniques must be differentially geared to the points of view reflected in these three main social classes. Advertising of brands or goods aimed at a specific class must

---

[8] This study has been published under the name *Workingman's Wife* (Oceana Press: New York City, 1959) by Lee Rainwater, Richard P. Coleman, and Gerald Handel.

[9] See Pierre Martineau, *Motivation in Advertising* (New York: McGraw-Hill Book Company, 1957) and "Social Classes and Spending Behavior," *The Journal of Marketing,* Vol. 23, No. 2, October 1958, pp. 121–130.

take into account the motivations of that class, and not try to sell everything as if it were an Upper Class or Upper-Middle status symbol.

Up to now, we've been talking about product areas—clothing, furniture, and residential neighborhoods—where the relationship between social class and quality of goods purchased is highest. In these things the so-called "Quality Market" and the Upper Middle (and higher) markets coincide. That is, the purchasers of highest quality clothing and highest quality furniture are more nearly from the Upper-Middle and Upper social classes than from the highest income categories, and so on it goes down the hierarchy. The correlation between price of goods purchased and social class is relatively quite high in these product areas while the correlation between price paid and annual income is lower than one might expect.

There is another group of products which are not linked in such a direct way with social class, but neither are they linked with income categories in any obvious relationship. The current car market provides an instructive example of this situation, for the nature of the market cannot be grasped by using one or the other concept exclusively. What is happening in today's car market can only be understood when income categories are placed into a social class framework.

## THE "OVERPRIVILEGED" AS "QUALITY MARKET"

Within each social class group there are families and individuals whose incomes are above average for their class. The Upper-Lower family with an income above $7,000 a year—sometimes a product of both husband and wife working, and sometimes not—is an example of this. So, too, is the Lower-Middle Class busi-

ness owner or salesman who makes more than $10,000 a year, but has no interest in either the concerts or country clubs of Upper-Middledom and hence is still Lower Middle Class. The Upper Middle Class couple with more than $25,000 a year at its disposal but no desire to play the "society game" of subscription balls or private schools is also in this category. These are what might be called the "overprivileged" segment of each class. They are not overprivileged" in the absolute sense, of course; they are "overprivileged," however, relative to what is required or needed by families in their class. After they have met the basic expectations and standards of their group in the housing, food, furnishing, and clothing areas, they have quite a bit of money left over which is their equivalent of "discretionary income."

In much the same way, each class has its "underprivileged" members; in the Upper-Middle Class these are the younger couples who haven't made the managerial ranks yet, the college professors, the genteel professionals, and a few downwardly mobile people from high-status backgrounds who are trying to hang on to what fragments of status they have left—for the most part these people are below the $12,000-a-year mark and they can barely meet some of the basic requirements of Upper-Middle life, much less experience any of its little luxuries; in the Lower-Middle Class these are the poorly paid bank tellers, the rows of bookkeepers in railroad offices, the school teachers with considerably more status aspiration than income; and in the Upper-Lower Class it is almost any family earning less than $4,500 or $5,000 a year, at today's rates of pay in metropolitan areas.

In the middle of each class's income range are its "average" members, families who are neither underprivileged nor overprivileged by the standards of their class.

You might think of this as the Upper-Middle Class family between $12,000 and $20,000 a year, the Lower-Middle family in the $7,000-$9,000 range, and the Upper-Lower family near $6,000 per annum. However, this word of caution is necessary: a lot of people in the middle income range of their class see themselves as underprivileged because they are aspiring to become one of the "overprivileged" in their class or to move on up the ladder to a higher class.

The relevance of all this to the car market is that when you look at this particular market today, you find it is the "average" members of each class, whether Upper-Middle, Lower-Middle, or Upper-Lower, who constitute the heart of the Low-Priced Three's audience; these are the people who are buying Fords and Chevrolets this year and last, and probably next. No longer is the Ford and Chevrolet market just a lower-middle income market, or (in class terms) a Lower-Middle or a Lower Class market. Rather, it is recruited from the middle income group *within each* social class. Indeed, the $15,000-a-year Upper-Middle "organization man" is apt to choose a Ford or Chevy from the Impala-Galaxie level or else a top-price station wagon once he ventures into this market, whereas the average-income Lower-Middle man will settle for a middle-series Bel Air or Fairlane 500, and the "average-income" Upper Lower guy either splurges for an Impala or "sensibly" contents himself with the spartan Biscayne.

While this has been happening to the Low-Priced Three makes the heart of the medium-price car market has relocated in the "overprivileged" segments of each class. Today, rich blue-collar workers are joining prosperous Lower-Middle Class salesmen and well-to-do Upper Middle Class business owners in buying Pontiacs, Buicks, Oldsmobiles, Chryslers, and even Cadillacs. In fact,

what there is left of big-car lust in our society is found at peak strength among the "overprivileged" Upper-Lowers or else among men who have achieved higher status, but grew up as kids in the Upper-Lower class and have not forgotten their wide-eyed envy of the big car owner.

Finally, as you may have guessed by now, the compact car market's heart is to be found in the "underprivileged" segments of each class (here we are speaking of the market for a compact as a first car). The overwhelming majority of Rambler purchasers, Falcon buyers, and foreign economy car owners come from this socio-economic territory. Thus, it is not the really poor who are buying these cheapest, most economical cars—rather it is those who think of themselves as poor relative to their status aspirations and to their needs for a certain level of clothing, furniture, and housing which they could not afford if they bought a more expensive car.

The market for compacts as second cars is somewhat more complicated in its socio-economic geography, being located in the middle range of the Upper-Middle Class, and the "overprivileged" segment of the Lower-Middle. The "overprivileged" Upper-Middle may have one as a third car, but he prefers either a T-Bird, a foreign sports car, a Pontiac convertible, or a beat-up station wagon as his second car, while the "overprivileged" Upper-Lower is apt to go for a used standard if he wants a second car.

If marketers and advertisers had assumed that the market for compacts was going to be the lowest-income or lowest-status members of our society, they would have seriously miscalculated in their merchandising and advertising approach. Rambler, for one, did not make this mistake. American Motors advertised its cars as "bringing sense into the auto market" and thus enabled people who bought one to pride themselves on the high-minded rationality they had displayed. Rambler owners, as they drive down the street, are not ashamed that they couldn't afford better—instead, as the company has told them to be, they are proud that they did not yield, like their neighbors, to base emotional desires for a car bloated in size beyond necessity and loaded in gadgetry beyond reason. Compact car owners have their own form of snobbery—what might be called "sensibility snobbery"—with which to content themselves and justify their purchase.

This analysis of the car market is one example of what I mean by the sophisticated application of social class concepts to marketing and advertising problems. There are many products and many brands which, like cars, are more nearly symbols of high status class within class than symbols of higher status per se. A color television set is such a product, or at least it was two years ago when Social Research, Inc., studied its market. At the time color television manufacturers were puzzled because sales were thinly spread throughout the income scale, without any noticeable increase in concentration until an extremely high level was reached. Furthermore, they were unable to see any particular relationship between social class and color set ownership, since about as many Upper-Lower Class people owned them as did Upper-Middles. However, when the two factors of income and class were put together, in the manner described above, it became clear that the color television market was concentrated among high-income or "overprivileged" members of each social class. Other products which bear this complicated relationship to class and income are the more costly brands and larger sizes of home appliances. Fairly expensive recreational equipment like outboard motor boats also tend to be in this category.

In summary, today's market for quality goods and quality brands is not necessarily drawn from what has historically been described as the "Quality Market" of Upper-Middle and Upper Class people, nor even necessarily from the highest income categories. Rather, in many instances, it is drawn from those people within each social level who have the most discretionary income available for enjoying life's little extras above and beyond the requirements of their class. Every merchandiser and advertiser ought to take a good hard look at what he is selling and ask himself if it bears this particular relationship to the class and income picture. If his product does, and if his brand is one of the more expensive, then he should merchandise it not as if it were just for social climbers or for the upper classes, but rather as part of the Better Life, U.S.A. If, on the other hand, his brand is one of the least expensive, then he is not just selling to the poor, but rather to those in all classes who feel it is only sensible on their part to settle for a brand such as his and save the difference for other things which are more important in their statement of social class aspiration and identity.

## SOCIAL CLASS ISN'T ALWAYS IMPORTANT

Now, to make the picture complete, it must be pointed out that Social Research, Inc., has found some products in which the income factor is all-important and the social class variable is relevant only to the extent that it is correlated with income. Perhaps the most perfect example of this is the market for air conditioners in Southwestern cities. There, everybody —except the sickly and the extremely old-fashioned—agree that air conditioning one's home is imperative if summer is to be survived with any degree of comfort. Consequently the expensiveness of a family's air conditioning equipment—whether centrally installed, or window units to the number of four, three, two, or one—is directly correlated with family income. It is not merely a function of discretionary income—as in our example about purchase of medium-priced cars; it is instead almost completely a function of total annual income. If more Upper-Middles than Upper-Lowers are fully air-conditioned it is only because more of them can afford to be; it is not because Upper-Middles as a group are placing higher priority on the air-conditioned existence.

Undoubtedly air conditioners are not alone in being classless—so that one more thing the marketer who uses social class in a truly sophisticated way needs to understand is that there can be occasions when it is an irrelevant variable. Realizing this, he will not become disenchanted with social class when he finds a marketing problem where it does not shed light or where it does not seem pertinent. Of course, he will want to make sure that in advertising such a product there is indeed no need to take class into account. After all, some apparently classless products are properly sold to the market in a segmental approach, appealing first on one ground to one class, then on other grounds to another.

There are other products—and probably air conditioning is one of them and children's play clothes may be another—where this is not necessary. For such products some factor, such as physical comfort (in the one case) or simple durability (in the other), is so basic in the consumer's consideration that all other motivations pale into insignificance beside it. There are even products, like beer, where the democratic approach—that is, a tone of "let's-all-be-good-fellows-together" is exactly right and segmental appeals or snob stories are all wrong.

Another aspect to the sophisticated em-ployment of social class refers back to the point made earlier that social class groups are not always homogeneous. It must be recognized that at times a product's market is formed by "highbrows" from the Upper-Upper Class on down to the Lower-Middle, or by "suburbanites" and suburban-minded people of all classes—in which case the social class variable may confuse a market analysis more than clarify it.

Particularly must merchandisers and market analysts beware of equating "Class" with "Brow"; for they are not synonymous. For example, the Upper-Middle Class and those above it are mainly middlebrow in taste (veering toward an all-American lower-middlebrow level of preferences in television shows and advertising messages) even though the majority of highbrows are found at this level. At times advertisers have made the mistake of assuming that the Upper-Middle Class should be appealed to in a highly sophisticated fashion—and though this is just fine if the product itself is likely to appeal primarily to the Manhattanized type of Upper-Middle, it is not correct if it is expected to sell to the kind of doctor in Dubuque who enjoys a visit to New York every now and then but would never want to live there.

In short, not only must the sophisticated marketer abandon social class in favor of income categories on occasion in his analysis and interpretation of a market, he must recognize that at times both income and class are superseded in importance by divisions of the public into brow levels, by divisions into "high mobiles" and "low mobiles," innovators and non-innovators, inner-directed and other-directed, urbanites, suburbanites, exurbanites, ruralites, and Floridians, or what have you. Usually, of course, fullest understanding of a market will require that social class be linked in with whichever sub-categorization proves pertinent from among those in the catalogue just recited, much as income and class were linked together for fullest comprehension of the car market.

As a final point, let it be noted that the way of life and the goals of people in each social class are in perpetual flux. Neither the "who" of each class nor "what motivates them" are constants to be assumed without continual re-evaluation. Right now, particularly, it is very clear that our society is changing. Every year the collar-color line is breaking down further. More blue-collar workers are becoming Middle Class as well as middle income and Modern, and a white-collar position is less and less a guarantee of Lower-Middle status. As a consequence of this, the Lower-Middle Class is perhaps somewhat more "materialistic" in outlook and slightly less "respectability" conscious than it was 25 years ago, or even 8. Meanwhile, for men and women to achieve Upper-Middle status without college backgrounds is becoming more and more difficult, so that this class is turning much more worldly-wise and well-read, much less conventionally bourgeois than it was in the zenith of Babbitt's day.

In short, the form of our society and its division into social classes is not fixed as of Yankee City in 1931, Jonesville in 1944, Kansas City in 1952, or St. Louis in 1960. We won't be able to say exactly

the same things about either the classes themselves or their relationships to specific markets by next year at this time. This fact about the American class structure, that it is not static, that it is in the process of change, is in itself important to merchandisers, to advertisers, to anyone in selling. Among other things, it means that undoubtedly they have played a part in past changes and can play a leading role in directing future changes. But of more direct concern here, to the marketing analyst it means that if he allows his stratification concept to become dated, his use of it will cease as of that moment to be sophisticated.

## QUESTIONS

1. Identify and describe the six social classes discovered by Lloyd Warner in his studies of various communities.
2. Within any one of these social classes, is the behavior always homogeneous?
3. What is meant by the "Overprivileged" as a "Quality Market"?
4. Is social class status always an important determinant of consumer behavior?
5. Are consumer income levels always relevant in measuring shopping habits, store preferences, and media readership?

## BIBLIOGRAPHY FOR CHAPTER VI

ARTICLES:

Bartels, Robert, "Sociologists and Marketologists," *Journal of Marketing*, Vol. 24, No. 2 (October 1959), pp. 37–40.

Jonassen, Christen T., "Contributions of Sociology to Marketing," *Journal of Marketing*, Vol. 24, No. 2 (October 1959), pp. 29–36.

Levitt, Theodore, "M-R Snake Dance," *Harvard Business Review*, Vol. 38, No. 6 (November–December 1960), pp. 76–84.

Lockley, Lawrence C., "Use of Motivation Research in Marketing," *Advertising Age*, Vol. 31, No. 37 (September 12, 1960), p. 98.

Martineau, Pierre, "Social Classes and Spending Behavior," *Journal of Marketing*, Vol. 23, No. 2 (October 1958), pp. 121–30.

Miller, Delbert C., "How Behavioral Scientists Can Help Business," *Business Horizons*, Vol. 3, No. 2 (Summer 1960), pp. 32–37.

"The Five Ages of Buying," *Sales Management Magazine*, Vol. 87, No. 12 (November 17, 1961), p. 26.

"The Senior Market," *Sales Management Magazine*, Vol. 87, No. 9 (October 20, 1961), pp. 35–38.

Woods, Walter A., "Psychological Dimensions of Consumer Decision," *Journal of Marketing*, Vol. 24, No. 3 (January 1960), pp. 15–20.

BOOKS:

Alderson, Wroe, *Marketing Behavior and Executive Action.* Homewood, Ill.: Irwin, 1957. Part II.

Boyd, Harper W., and Clewett, Richard M., *Contemporary American Marketing.* Homewood, Ill.: Irwin, 1962. Part II. Chapters 8–13.

Britt, Steuart, *The Spenders.* New York: McGraw-Hill, 1960.

Bursk, Edward C., *Text and Cases in Marketing: A Scientific Approach.* Englewood Cliffs, N.J.: Prentice-Hall, 1962. Section Two.

Centers, Richard, *The Psychology of Social Classes.* New York: Russell & Russell, 1961.

Clark, Lincoln H., *Consumer Behavior: Research on Consumer Reactions.* New York: Harper, 1958.

Dichter, Ernest, *The Strategy of Desire.* New York: Doubleday, 1960.

Henry, Harry, *Motivation Research.* New York: Frederick Ungar, 1958.

Hollingshead, August B., and Redlick, Frederick C., *Social Class and Mental Illness: A Community Study.* New York: Wiley, 1958. Chapter 4.

Katona, George, *The Powerful Consumer.* New York: McGraw-Hill, 1960.

Katz, Elihu, and Lazarsfeld, Paul F., *Personal Influence: The Part Played by People in the Flow of Mass Communications.* Glencoe, Ill.: Free Press, 1957.

Martineau, Pierre, *Motivation in Advertising: Motives That Make People Buy.* New York: McGraw-Hill, 1957.

Newman, Joseph W., *Motivation Research and Marketing Management.* Boston: Harvard University Graduate School of Business Administration, 1957.

Shaw, Steven J., and Thompson, Joseph W., *Salesmanship: Modern Viewpoints on Personal Communication.* New York: Holt, Rinehart and Winston, 1960. Part 1. Section C.

Smith, George H., *Motivation Research in Advertising and Marketing.* New York: McGraw-Hill, 1954.

Warner, W. Lloyd, *et al., Social Class in America.* New York: Harper, 1949.

# VII. Evolution in Physical Distribution

*I*T IS ESTIMATED that the volume of vending machine sales was close to $4 billion. From an early beginning of dispensing gum and candy, automatic vending has grown to the point where it can displace an entire retail service operation. Today in operation, mostly in suburban areas, are an estimated 3,000 semi-automatic drive-in markets with more to come. Apartment house vending, an accomplished fact now with milk, will perhaps be extended tomorrow to other food lines. Vending machine sales are growing rapidly and now exceed two billion dollars annually.

The discount house is another innovation that is drastically changing the retail industry today. Among others, specialty stores and department stores have been unable to ignore the explosive force of low-price, low-margin retailing generated by the discount stores. They are fighting back by eliminating some of the less desired services, by cutting prices in existing stores, by expanding cut-price basement operations, by adopting super-market techniques of self-service and checkouts, and finally by entering the discount field directly.

Wholesaling is in a state of flux. Both independent wholesalers and manufacturers branch warehouses are installing automatic materials-handling equipment in their warehouses to speed service and lower cost of operations. Many concerns are re-vamping their distribution systems through major programs of either contraction or expansion in number of warehouses depending upon the nature of goods handled.

One of the most significant post World War II developments has been the rapid growth and development of the rack jobber —a new type of independent middleman who services the larger food retailers by performing the complete in-store merchandising requirements of nonfood items. A rack jobber's service includes warehousing, in-store restocking, display and merchandising, prepricing and other valuable point of sale services.

As marketing managers strive to lower marketing costs, phys-ical distribution comes in for increased attention. It is now well

299

established that the cost of manufacturing a product is less than the cost of moving raw materials to plant and finished products to customers. Recent studies show that manufacturing costs account for only 41 per cent of final consumer prices, while nonmanufacturing costs account for 59 per cent. Of these non-manufacturing costs, physical distribution is likely the largest cost of doing business in most firms. Physical distribution management, chiefly the management of transportation and storage, must be accepted by businessmen as an important area. It must be treated as an integrated total system rather than several separate and distinct activities if it is to be effectively managed.

In a number of large operations, the planning of physical distribution is being centralized under one head. Experts in the field of distribution feel that the man for the job is the marketing manager. However, since in some instances the executive with the marketing manager's title is really the sales manager, given the title to pay lip service to the marketing concept, it is sometimes more expedient to set up a new marketing head with the title of physical distribution manager.

Splitting up responsibility for physical distribution and parceling it out among other functions creates "gray areas." Unless an integrated and coordinated plan of distribution management exists within a company, distribution functions tend to receive only second-class attention—often only the afterthoughts of people whose primary interests are elsewhere. Developing distribution into a major function is not empire building but sound organization planning.

# 42. Vending Machine Drive-In Forecasts New Food Retailing Technique*

*Kansas City, Missouri, drive-in is successfully pioneering an experiment which shows that Mrs. Consumer likes this revolutionary method of buying her fill-in groceries. The drive-in is a small convenience outlet using coin-operated vending machines to dispense two types of food merchandise—groceries and prepared foods.*

For about ten years now, retail food operators have been reading about the successes of drive-in grocery markets. Their growth, to say the least, is being watched closely by the entire food industry. It was only about eight years ago that a few hundred were in operation. Today, there are in operation an estimated 3,000 convenience stores. The last time Progressive Grocer counted (August 1959), there were 2,400 drive-ins in operation throughout the nation.

But now, over the horizon, looms a totally different and new concept of the drive-in. The inventors say that this revolutionary type of market could be the answer that many food store operators are seeking. Labor costs are reported lower than the conventional drive-in and net profits are reported high. This, of course, is what every operator wants.

## THE VENDING MACHINE COMBINATION DRIVE-IN

What is this new food retailing innovation? Here is about as good a definition as any: The vending machine drive-

* Reprinted from *Progressive Grocer*, The Magazine of Super Marketing, June 1961, p. 58.

in is a small convenience outlet using coin-operated vending machines, combining *two* types of food merchandise—*groceries* and *prepared foods*. The latter, of course, can be taken home, but are usually consumed on the premises.

## GENERAL DESCRIPTION

The only existing combination *grocery-prepared foods* drive-in is being operated at present as a pilot installation by the Vendo Company, Kansas City, Missouri. Vendo reportedly is the world's largest manufacturer of automatic merchandising equipment.

The name given to the new venture is "Stop 'N Treat." The unit is a specially designed structure of approximately 1,400 square feet and houses 14 coin-operated vendors.

## GROCERY SECTION

In this area, a wide range of grocery items are handled. These include bread, milk, bacon, eggs, coffee, frozen fruits and juices, and many other staple items —about 30 products in all.

This side...Take-Home Groceries

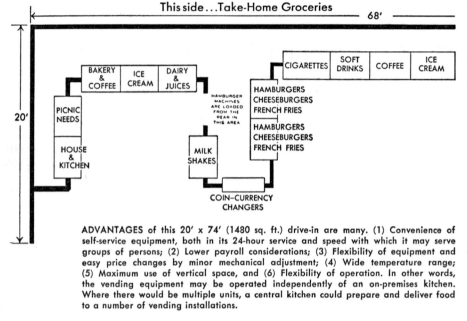

ADVANTAGES of this 20' x 74' (1480 sq. ft.) drive-in are many. (1) Convenience of self-service equipment, both in its 24-hour service and speed with which it may serve groups of persons; (2) Lower payroll considerations; (3) Flexibility of equipment and easy price changes by minor mechanical adjustment; (4) Wide temperature range; (5) Maximum use of vertical space, and (6) Flexibility of operation. In other words, the vending equipment may be operated independently of an on-premises kitchen. Where there would be multiple units, a central kitchen could prepare and deliver food to a number of vending installations.

From 100 to 300 individual units may be loaded at one time in a single cabinet, and products are served at room temperature, chilled or frozen, depending on the requirement. One machine, for example, sells both frozen and chilled products simultaneously from the same cabinet. Individual grocery items are loaded into separate compartments, in drums similar to lazy susans. In effect, these drums are stacked on top of one another, but act independently.

The customer sees a sampling of the various products within. When he has made his choice, he drops in his coins, opens the glass vending door and takes out the item he has selected. When the door is closed, the drum revolves and an identical product moves into place behind the vending window.

According to the Vendo Co., the obvious cost saving, using automatic merchandising of this type, lies in the labor factor. The only manual help required are people to load the machines.

Presently there are no items in the grocery selection in the drive-in that sell for more than 75¢. Even this, however, represents a major breakthrough in the sale of products from vending machines.

This year, the Vendo Company will have ready for the market a paper currency changer that should represent an important step towards the sale of more costly products through vending machines. Without such a device, people are not inclined to purchase higher ticket items, because they normally do not carry large amounts of change in their pockets or purses.

## WHERE DO CUSTOMERS COME FROM?

The Vendo Company feels that an automatic grocery, such as the Stop 'N Treat, is ideal for the customer in a hurry. A man returning home from work can quickly purchase a loaf of bread or a half-gallon of milk.

Persons returning home late at night

This side...Consume-On-Premises Prepared Foods

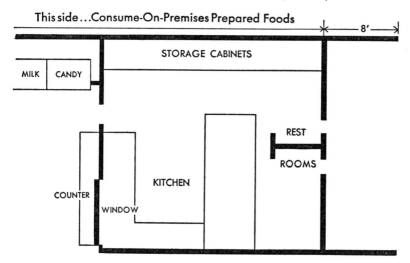

from the theater or a party may drop in at any hour and purchase the necessities for a complete breakfast—bacon, eggs, bread, butter, coffee and frozen, concentrated fruit juice.

The Stop 'N Treat driven-in features the best selling products of large super markets, and snack items, such as cookies, milk, potato chips and peanut butter are popular sellers.

Since the products in coin-operated vendors must sell themselves, just as is required in a modern self-service market, only name brands are being sold in the drive-in. Vendo officials reason, well known brands give the customer the confidence to buy from a vending machine.

## WHY STOP 'N TREAT IS POPULAR

Another advantage is 24-hour service. The drive-in sells around the clock, 7 days a week.

The Stop 'N Treat vending machines also utilize "grouping," much as a progressive super market does. Products that go well together, such as milk and cookies, bread, peanut butter and jelly,

are within close proximity to one another, stimulating the customer to purchase more items than he originally intended.

## PREPARED FOOD AND BEVERAGE SECTION

A kitchen where the majority of the prepared food items are produced is part of the facility, and functions as a service counter for change making and restocking between 11 A.M. and 12 P.M. Automatic service is available 24 hours a day, and is the only service during the hours between midnight and 11 A.M. Attendants who work the 12-hour shift in the kitchen stock the vendors for the early morning hours when the machines are unattended.

In the prepared food section, individual change making vendors serve fresh coffee, milk, ice cream, hamburgers, cheeseburgers, candy and cigarettes.

## PRICING

In general, the 24-hour service feature and convenience permits the drive-in slightly higher prices. Pricing are in increments of 5 cents only (no pennies) although it is possible to set the equipment to sell at prices of 17 cents, 29 cents, and so forth, with slight modification. All items, as formerly stated, in the grocery section are under 75 cents.

Items in the prepared food section approximate regular drive-in restaurant prices, and in most cases are lower. Example: hamburgers are 15 cents, French fries, 15 cents and milk shakes, 20 cents.

## AIMS AND OBJECTIVES OF VENDO OUTLINED

Arthur D. Stevens, vice-president in charge of commercial development at Vendo, made the following comment about this unique merchandising program:

"We are doing applied research on profitable and practical ways of applying automatic equipment to the sale of grocery products, and to the operation of the average restaurant, in addition to testing the appeal of coin-operated equipment in drive-in establishments. In no sense are we attempting to expand into a chain of automatic grocery stores.

"Automatic equipment will definitely be used in the super market of the future. It is only a question of when and in what form. This also applies to restaurants, where already there is a very real need for automated service.

"The Stop 'N Treat is located in a shopping area where there is a high traffic count. It is near a junior high school, and has other advantages of location. We are trying to create a situation with enough built-in attractions to draw a good patronage and provide a profitable operation as a guide to future similar developments."

## MORE FEATURES ABOUT STOP 'N TREAT

The unit is heated by reflected infrared rays from quartz lamps. The radiant heating system warms objects rather than air, eliminating the necessity of outer walls, and is the first unit of its kind to be used in the Greater Kansas City area. Fourteen fixtures mounted in the ceiling require a total of 25,200 electrical watts to heat kitchen, rest rooms and open vending area. Each area is thermostatically controlled so that unoccupied sections need not be heated.

The area is brightly lighted with fluorescent indirect lighting, and the quartz tube heating system also contributes an inviting golden glow for added night-time brilliance.

Vending equipment in the prepared food area is yellow and that in the grocery section is off-white.

Parking for 40 cars is available, and a 400 square foot patio accommodates those who wish to dine on the premises. Rest rooms are part of the main building.

The building, which has an angled folded plate metal roof, supported by exposed steel Y-beams, painted turquoise, was designed by Vendo in cooperation with Butler Manufacturing Co. and Dwight Horner, architect.

## QUESTIONS

1. What is the nature of the vending machine drive-in?
2. What types of customers patronize the vending machine drive-in?
3. Will automatic equipment be used in the super market of the future?
4. Will the vending machine drive-in reduce or increase costs?

# 43. The Big Revolution in Retailing*

*Everywhere that people shop, big things are happening. The "mass retailers," offering discounts on nearly everything, are spreading fast. New "membership" stores are taking business away from the discounters. Conventional department stores, battling both kinds of competition, are staying open nights, and trimming prices. Housewives are shopping more at "home" through catalgoues, and door-to-door salesmen. Merchants, meanwhile, are expanding at a hectic pace, despite warnings of a coming rise in store failures.*

All across America a retail revolution is under way that is affecting everyone who shops.

Major developments in the fast-changing retail scene:

"Discount" houses, springing up everywhere, are taking on more and more items—from mink and diamonds to automobiles. Supermarkets are pushing food into one corner, offering "everything under the sun under one roof."

"Closed-door" stores, giving discounts to select groups of customers, are expanding at a rapid rate. Door-to-door selling is showing new life. So is the mail-order business. Vending machines are grabbing more of the consumer's dollar with automatic restaurants and automated grocery stores.

Giant retail chains are expanding into new lines. The little retailer, more and more, is being forced to the wall. Dozens of new stores are opening up every week—despite warnings that the retail industry already is suffering from over-capacity.

To give you the latest on the marketing revolution:

The struggling discount houses of a decade ago now are flourishing "discount

* Reprinted from *U.S. News & World Report,* May 21, 1962, an independent weekly news magazine published at Washington. Copyright 1962, United States News Publishing Corporation.

department stores" featuring charge accounts, fancy fixtures and music.

**Jammed Shelves . . .** Supermarkets, more and more, are taking on the cluttered appearance reminiscent of the old general store. Shelves are crowded with items such as TV sets, movie cameras, clothing, hardware and shrubs.

Regular department stores, no longer able to ignore the "discounters," are fighting back. Some are opening their own discount chains. Others are using discount-house methods—for example, installing self-service departments and check-out counters, making customers pay for home delivery, staying open five nights a week.

As the battle heats up, many merchants are pushing for more-rigid enforcement of "blue laws" which call for Sunday closing. Discount houses often do as much as half of their weekly business on Sunday.

New steam is building up, too, behind the drive for "fair trade" laws. In Congress, bills have been introduced which would give manufacturers, in effect, the right to set retail prices on their brand-name products. More than 60 trade associations have endorsed the bill.

Behind all this upheaval in retailing is the scramble by stores of all kinds for the lush consumer market.

305

This year Americans will spend an estimated 234 billion dollars in retail stores. That's 15 billion more than last year's record and the biggest single market in the world.

To tap this fast-growing market, retailers have been expanding at a hectic pace. In the past year, hundreds of new stores were opened across the U.S. Dozens more are being opened every week. The number of discount stores alone, is expected to increase by 450 this year to a total of almost 3,000.

**Trouble Ahead?** . . . Retail-trade experts think that the fast pace of store expansion may mean trouble ahead for the industry. Some flatly predict a rising number of store failures.

Warns Malcolm P. McNair, retail-trade authority at Harvard graduate school of business administration: "There is now a general problem of overcapacity. The country is seriously overstored. One consequence is going to be lower retailing profits. Another consequence will probably be a marked increase in the number of retail failures. A shakeout appears to be inevitable."

**In Success, Danger** . . . From an investment banker who keeps a close eye on the operations of discount stores: "The very success of the discounters constitutes their greatest danger. Millions of square feet of space are being built. There's a wild scramble for new locations at increasing costs for land and building."

Says a retail executive in Chicago: "The little retailer—from the corner grocer to the small variety store—will be in hot water. The big chains, in nearly every line, will force him to the wall in the years ahead."

Already, trouble spots are showing up here and there. For example, in one New England city, discount stores mushroomed in number from one to 10 in two years. Competition got so stiff that two of the stores have had to sell out. In California, a number of closed-door discount houses are having to open their doors to anyone with a desire to buy.

In many cities around the country, merchants report that they are facing cutthroat competition. Price wars are flaring in gasoline, furniture, food, drugs, other lines.

**Battle of Stamps** . . . Even trading stamps are caught up in a war.

Shoppers now can get stamps with their purchases in a rainbow assortment. Some stores even use mechanical stamp dispensers.

Newest stamp color is plaid—introduced by the Great Atlantic & Pacific Tea Company. The giant food chain, long a holdout against stamps, finally adopted them late last autumn.

To meet the new competition, supermarkets and other stores around the country are luring customers with offers of extra stamps with every purchase.

As the stamp craze accelerates, sales of trading stamps are soaring. "Premium Practice," a trade magazine, reports that trading-stamp sales hit a record 618 million dollars last year—up more than 22 per cent over 1960.

**Competition: Fierce** . . . Intense competition is forcing all retailers to pay close attention to changing consumer tastes and shopping habits. One result is that many companies are expanding into new lines.

For example, A & P has just opened a general-merchandise store near Pittsburgh. Sears, Roebuck & Company recently opened a drugstore in Fort Worth, Tex.—the first of a chain. The Walgreen Company, nationwide retail-drug firm, has acquired two discount department-store chains.

F. W. Woolworth plans to open discount stores at the rate of one a month for the next 18 months. Grand Union, the food chain, now operates 21 Grand-Way discount centers.

Retailers have found that shoppers like a wide variety of products under one roof. Result: a fast growth in giant "one stop" shopping facilities.

For instance, Grand Central Super Center, near Minneapolis, is the size of 2½ football fields. It carries 125,000 items in its supermarket, bakery and 72 nonfood departments.

A Long Island discount department store is a block long and has 137 departments—from a supermarket to a pet shop. Grand-Way discount stores, when they first opened in 1956, carried 15,000 general-merchandise items, now carries 100,000 different items and a full food line.

May Department Stores Company, of Los Angeles, has broken ground in the San Fernando Valley for a store which will include a discount house, a fashion center and a supermarket.

**Cashing in on a Trend** . . . Americans now are spending a growing portion of their incomes for services—everything from dry cleaning and beauty care to trips abroad. Stores are trying to cash in on this trend.

Sears, for example, now offers local and international travel tours. A number of department stores have opened up rental services for the do-it-yourself group. Items available include such things as wallpapering kits, plumbing tools, garden equipment, banquet supplies and baby furniture.

Many department stores around the nation are opening up coin-operated dry-cleaning establishments. Some have installed beauty parlors.

A recent survey by the National Retail Merchants Association shows that a growing number of department stores are taking on operation of gasoline service stations, shoe-repair shops, fuel-oil deliveries and appliance repair.

**Upgrading an Image** . . . Discount houses are undergoing radical changes to meet demands of consumers.

A decade ago the discount house often was a dingy hole in the wall with pipe-rack fixtures and a limited assortment of merchandise. All sales were strictly cash.

Now it's hard to tell most discounters from their conventional rivals. Stores are bright and equipped with modern fixtures. Customers can charge their purchases—and have them delivered. More expensive lines of merchandise are being carried, in a greater variety of models.

As one discount-store official puts it: "We're trying desperately to upgrade our image."

Many stores are dropping the word "discount" from their title and are using instead such terms as "mass retailer" and "promotional department store."

**Mink and Washers** . . . E. J. Korvette, Inc., which runs a string of "promotional department stores" in the East, is about to open up a new outlet on New York's Fifth Avenue. The store will have crystal chandeliers and will offer mink furs as well as washing machines, diamonds as well as records.[1]

A New Jersey discount house has installed a $250,000 glass-and-steel mural in front of the store.

Says a Washington, D.C., department-store executive: "If a discounter lasts three years he begins to turn into a regular department store. Customers want the services and the frills."

From a retail consultant in New York: "Discount houses are forgetting how they started and why they succeeded. They have added services that approach in scope that of the stores they ridiculed— the conventional stores. One day they will wake up to find that they themselves are conventional and that a new crop of dedicated discounters has arisen."

As discounters provide more services, step up advertising, carry a broader line of goods, costs are beginning to creep up. This is seen as a threat to the discounters' biggest lure: low price tags.

**Bargains in Gems** . . . Bargain hunters have found that discount houses are of-

[1] This store has subsequently been opened.

fering big savings. Take jewelry—a fast-growing line among discount stores.

Medco, Inc., of Kansas City, Mo., offers to sell a $5,000 diamond or a $1,000 watch at any of its 27 outlets around the country at 25 per cent to 40 per cent less than conventional jewelry stores would charge. "No regular jeweler in the country can touch any of our prices," says a Medco official.

U-Save Department Store, a discounter in Portland, Ore., offers a $35,000 pair of jeweled pins for $23,750. A $30,000 bracelet is being offered for $22,500.

A number of conventional department stores now are trying to meet the prices of discount stores on specific lines.

For example, consider this comment from a Seattle store executive: "Department stores here are trying to compete pricewise. One store sends a man to the discount houses and gets their prices on items like TVs and appliances. The store then drops its prices on those items below the discount houses."

Department-store officials in the East mention toys as another example.

Says one executive: "Last Christmas a number of department stores slashed prices on toys. We lost money on them, but we got people in the store and they bought other things. It hurt the discounters' traffic."

**Stores with "Closed Doors"** . . . Closed-door—or "membership"—discount stores, now operating in 34 States, are continuing to prosper in most areas.

Sales last year reached 500 million dollars. Estimate for 1962: sales of 800 million. At least two dozen new closed-door stores are to be opened this year.

These stores sell only to members— Government employes, military personnel, union members, other select groups. Total membership is put at 3.5 million.

Members pay a small initiation fee, usually $2 or $3, and annual dues of $1. The stores do practically no advertis-

ing, offer no fancy displays or frills and hold down on sales personnel. Controlled membership keeps credit losses very low. Savings are reflected in lower prices.

In most cases, each department in a closed-door store is operated by a concessionaire, under a license agreement with management. The store merely collects a percentage of each department's gross sales.

**On Foot—and Wheels** . . . Door-to-door selling is also caught up in the retail revolution.

More and more companies are knocking on doors to sell everything from trees and tableware to dresses and dietary food. Sales last year: more than 2 billion dollars.

McCrory Corporation, which operates nearly 1,600 retail outlets, has put a direct sales force on wheels. The vehicle: a "Shopmobile"—a store on wheels, now making the rounds in Florida. Officials say it may be the forerunner of a fleet of such vehicles.

Shopmobile is the modern-day version of the old peddler's wagon. The idea is to reach the housewife who is "locked in" because the husband has taken the family car to work.

**Boom in Catalogues** . . . Less spectacular, but of growing importance, is this retail outlet: home shopping by catalogue. Once confined to people in rural areas, catalogue buying now has spread to cities and suburbs everywhere. Mail-order sales run into the billions.

Housewives, with catalogues, can avoid traffic snarls, parking problems and long queues for service or checking out, mail-order houses point out. An order can be written or simply phoned to the mail-order desk of the store.

The field is growing. J. C. Penney is preparing to move into the mail-order business. Some discount houses offer merchandise through catalogues. Some manufacturers are considering use of catalogues to sell their products.

**Push-Button Buying . . .** Another fast-growing field in retailing: vending machines.

Machines have been putting out items such as cigarettes, soft drinks and candy for years. Now elaborate machines are dispensing hot meals and groceries.

For example, Brass Rail Corporation has installed a completely automatic restaurant for General Electric employes in New York City. The menu includes 60 hot dishes. Food is prepared at a central production center, frozen and shipped to the restaurant.

When the dishes are placed in the machines they can be reconstituted to a fresh-cooked state at the drop of a coin.

About 700 GE employes are fed at the restaurant, which needs only two workers to handle the operation. Officials estimate that an ordinary restaurant, handling a similar number of diners, might require as many as 25 workers.

Automatic restaurants are already in operation in Chicago and Indianapolis. Others are planned in more cities.

**Automated Grocery Stores . . .** Coin-operated machines are also being used to automate grocery stores. In operation now: a unit which sells bakery goods, cereal, soaps, baby foods, canned fruits and juices.

Stores plan to set up automatic units outside the premises to serve customers after regular hours. Apartment buildings are also seen as a choice location.

Eventually, retail vendors are aiming for an entire store, taking care of shoppers' needs from food to clothing without the use of a single clerk.

Already, vending machines are a huge business. Sales last year reached 2.7 billion dollars, according to trade sources.

Machines are figuring in retailing in another way: in accounting, in keeping track of inventories, in watching sales— item by item. Computers are being used by more and more stores.

**Cash Registers Out?** . . . A major difficulty is getting a machine that can take information from a written sales slip. New kinds of machines are now tackling the problem.

For example, consider the "Uni-Tote." This system, now in operation, automates, through a complex of machines, much of the retailing process.

The ordinary cash register is replaced by a machine system which does all the calculations for the sales person, produces a printed sales slip and electronically checks the buyer's credit record. The system is so developed that if a customer is delinquent in his store payments, a light flashes.

The system transmits all the data to punch-card processing units. Billing and inventory control are automatic.

Everywhere you look, thus, a marketing revolution is under way. And the pace of change is quickening.

The outlook, as the experts see it, is for increased mass retailing, for more self-service, for larger shopping centers.

**Break for Consumers . . .** No letup is seen in the intense competition among retailers. Businesses will have to stay on their toes to survive and to prosper.

For consumers, developments in retailing are bringing real protection from rising prices, and improved chances of better quality.

## QUESTIONS

1. What are some of the most recent major developments in the fast-changing retail scene?
2. What is new in door-to-door selling?
3. What is meant by push button-buying?
4. Will future automation eliminate the cash register?
5. Why are many housewives shopping at home?

# 44. The Role of the Rack Jobber*

James J. Sheeran, Group Executive—Merchandising, Tatham-Laird
Advertising

*More and more non-food items are found in food outlets today.
This means that the servicing and merchandising of non-foods is
increasing in importance. This article discusses the most powerful
influence in the distribution of non-foods: the rack jobber. It examines his success, and points out some significant trends and opportunities in the rapidly changing area of non-foods marketing.*

A rack jobber is an independent business organization that services food retailers by performing the complete in-
store merchandising requirements of
non-food items. A rack jobber's service
includes warehousing, distribution, prepricing, displaying, and inventorying.

## FUNCTIONS OF RACK JOBBERS

In some respects the rack jobber, either
an individual or a company, is like a
"concession." He does not own the physical property on which he sells his merchandise, but he does control the merchandising procedures followed there. He
"borrows" space in food stores, and
draws profit from selling his service (including product) to food accounts at
slightly more than these accounts could
otherwise buy the *product only* from a
manufacturer.

The rack jobber provides in-store restocking, display, and merchandising at
the point of sale on a regular basis. He
sells on a guaranteed basis (not consignment). This means that slow-moving or
unsalable merchandise is picked up for
credit periodically, thereby assuring a

full profit to the retailer and preventing
losses through markdowns for clearance
and the accumulation of broken, outdated
merchandise.

The rack jobber performs at least thirteen marketing services:[1]

1. Assumes full responsibility for purchasing, warehousing, and delivery.
2. Assures a constant supply of the
   newest type of competitively pre-
   priced merchandise.
3. Co-operates with manufacturers in
   developing packaging and point-of-
   sale materials which will effectively
   sell non-foods through supermarkets.
4. Sells and delivers in less than case-
   lot quantities in relation to how
   each item sells.
5. Provides regular weekly (or semi-
   weekly) in-store restocking and
   display services.
6. Furnishes display services on special non-food promotions at the
   point of sale.
7. Develops tie-in promotions with
   food products that increase the
   sales of both food and non-food
   items.

* Reprinted from the *Journal of Marketing*, national
quarterly publication of the American Marketing Association, Vol. 25, No. 5, July 1961, pp. 15–21.

[1] "Advantages of Service Distributor to the Supermarket Operator," *Information Bulletin* of the American Rack Merchandisers Institute, 1960, p. 1.

8. Eliminates investments in warehouse and store back-up stocks.
9. Gives the supermarket operator a substantially greater profit (31 per cent) than the average profit on foods (19.5 per cent).
10. Picks up slow-moving and unsalable merchandise for credit or replacement.
11. Introduces new market-tested items in a merchandise rotation program.
12. Takes the risk out of handling seasonal merchandise.
13. Works to develop new and profitable non-food lines or departments for the supermarket.

There are over 800 rack jobbers in the United States. Most of them work on a local basis (one city), but several of the larger ones cover as many as five states.

From a central warehouse they serve a web of accounts, sometimes numbering as high as 1,500 stores. They compete for customers in the same area.

Not all rack jobbers carry a complete non-food line. Some specialize in health and beauty aids, carrying only one or two secondary lines such as electrical goods and hardware, whereas others may deal exclusively in housewares and soft goods. The economics and competitive activity of a territory dictate what lines a rack jobber will handle.

The average rack jobber may have a sales force consisting of a sales manager and an assistant, several sales supervisors, and a number of sales servicemen or routemen.

The sales manager normally has the responsibility of opening new accounts. He is on the alert for new business, whether new independent stores or new branches of a chain. If he deals with chain stores, he must get approval from the chain headquarters to deal with their branch stores. He is primarily concerned with selling the *concept* of rack merchandising to food outlets.

The particular products involved may be handled by the individual sales serviceman who is assigned to the account. Frequently the sales manager does not know exactly what items a store carries; but the sales supervisor who oversees the sales servicemen makes sure that the account is properly stocked and serviced. In addition, the supervisor indoctrinates, trains, and works with the servicemen to make sure of their continued efficiency.

The sales serviceman is the "backbone" of the rack-jobbing organization. He makes contacts with food operators on a weekly or semi-weekly basis and fully services the account. He operates out of a "vanette" or "walk-in" truck and is responsible for the complete servicing of the accounts he handles. The average number of calls for a serviceman may be eight to ten per day. His average daily sales volume varies between $600 to $800; and he has forty to seventy accounts that he covers exclusively.

The rack jobber services as high as 90 per cent of all supermarkets carrying *certain* non-food items. In *all* non-food categories, he represents the source of supply for about two-thirds of all supermarkets. For health and beauty aids (by far the biggest non-food item in a food store) about 52 per cent of food stores are serviced by rack jobbers, while the remaining stores buy direct from manufacturers or other wholesalers. Where space is at a premium, the rack jobber has been successful in securing about 15 per cent of food store floor space for the display and sale of his non-food merchandise.

## VIGOROUS NON-FOODS GROWTH

Since World War II, there has been a steady increase in the sales of non-food items. Today these products represent 5.2 per cent of total store sales, and there is every evidence that they will continue to grow. In 1950, sales of all non-foods were $0.2 billion. In 1958, food stores sold $1.8 billion, an increase of *800 per cent*. During the same period, the sales of regular food items increased only 81 per cent, from $27 billion to $49 billion. Thus, the rate of gain in supermarkets of non-foods over foods is almost ten times greater.

Exactly what are non-foods? Originally they took the form of toiletries and cosmetics (today called health and beauty aids) and housewares; but increasing demand and high-powered salesmanship added a number of other product categories to this list. Stationery, magazines, and toys soon followed, with phonograph records and soft goods later entering the picture. Presently these items form the basis for the non-food department.

There are a number of other items in food stores of a non-food nature, such as soaps, detergents, paper products, waxes and polishes, that are *not* distributed by rack jobbers. For the most part these are bought directly from the manufacturers or food wholesalers, and have always been considered food-store items. They had distribution in grocery outlets long before the advent of the rack jobber, and are not included in the figures relating to non-foods in this study.

Most important of the rack-serviced non-food items are health and beauty aids. This category contributes 2.3 per cent of total store sales, ranking above cookies and crackers, and soaps and detergents. Because of its high profit margin (average 32.5 per cent) and its relatively high turnover rate, its dollar profit per floor foot is $6.62 weekly as compared to an all-grocery item average of $2.88.

Housewares with 0.9 per cent of store sales and magazines with 0.6 per cent are the next most important categories. But soft goods with 0.5 per cent of store sales are pointed out as the real "comers" in

non-foods. They have the least distribution of any of the seven basic items, but are growing at a much faster rate. The other products—toys (0.4 per cent store sales), records (0.3 per cent), and stationery (0.2 per cent) round out the non-food category.

## PROFITABILITY OF NON-FOODS

These seven non-food items represent more total store sales than cigarettes and tobacco, all frozen foods, and all canned vegetables.

The performance of each of these items on a comparative basis—as to (1) percentage of total store sales, (2) margin of profit on sales, and (3) linear floor feet given to the item is shown in Table 1.

Although the figures in Table 1 reflect a substantial amount of strength for non-foods, their greatest strength lies in their *profitability*. Note that non-foods account for *5.2 per cent* of total store sales; but because of their wide margins and turnover, they earn *8.3 per cent* of all store *gross profits*.

If translated into sales and profit by space occupied, non-foods would compare with foods as follows:

Sales and Gross Profits
(by space occupied)[2]

|  | Groceries | Non-foods |
|---|---|---|
| Weekly sales per floor foot | $15.88 | $11.38 |
| Weekly gross profit per floor foot | $ 2.88 | $ 3.52 |

Space is an all important food store consideration, as is profit. The typical supermarket has 544 linear floor feet of gondolas and fixtures for display of merchandise; and 83 feet of this is given to non-foods. The weekly gross profit of

[2] Same reference as footnote 1.

## TABLE 1
### Performance of Non-Food Items in Food Stores*

| All Non-Foods |
| --- |

A. 5.2% of total stores sales—$943 weekly non-food sales
B. 31.0% margin on sales—$292 gross profit on sales
C. 83 linear floor feet—$1,046 items in all departments

*1. Health and beauty aids*

A. 2.3% of total store sales
$408 weekly dept. sales
B. 32.5% margin on sales
$133 gross profit on sales
C. 20.1 linear floor feet
381 items per dept.

*4. Soft goods*

A. 0.53% of total store sales
$99 weekly dept. sales
B. 31.9% margin on sales
$32 gross profit on sales
C. 9.8 linear floor feet
76 items per dept.

*2. Housewares*

A. 0.92% of total store sales
$158 weekly dept. sales
B. 33.0% margin on sales
$52 gross profit on sales
C. 10.5 linear floor feet
167 items per dept.

*5. Records*

A. 0.30% of total sales
$64 weekly dept. sales
B. 28.4% margin on sales
$18 weekly margin
C. 5.3 linear floor feet
94 items (titles) per dept.

*3. Magazines*

A. 0.58% total store sales
$110 weekly dept. sales
B. 26.0% margin on sales
$28.60 gross profit on sales
C. 12.3 linear floor feet
188 items per dept.

*6. Toys*

A. 0.35% of total sales
$63 weekly dept. sales
B. 33.2% margin on sales
$21 weekly margin
C. 96 linear floor feet
93 items per dept.

*7. Stationery*

A. 0.23% of total sales
$41 weekly dept. sales
B. 41.0% margin on sales
$16.80 weekly margin
C. 6.3 linear floor feet
47 items per dept.

* "Non-foods Are Big Business," *Progressive Grocer*, Special Report, 1959, pp. 3-7.

non-foods tops that of food items by about 22 per cent.

Even more impressive than the figures on gross profit is the *net profit* for non-foods. Against the average 31 per cent margin of profit that a typical food operator realizes on non-foods, very little is charged off to selling expense. The rack jobber takes care of ordering, shelf stock-ing, and displaying, and guarantees the sale. He thus eliminates store expenses for mark-downs and "throw outs." In effect, most of the food operator's costs of handling are borne by the rack jobber, and a store's cost of selling is lowered due to self-service.

As a result, the normal operating expense for non-foods is only about 11 per

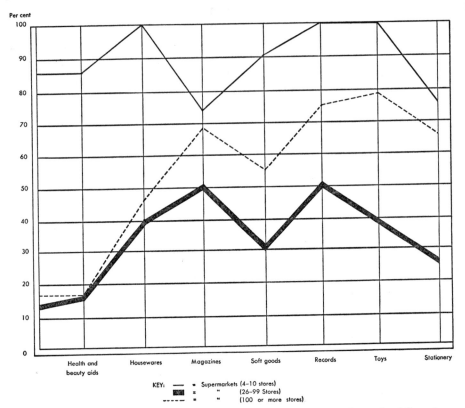

FIGURE 1. Outside servicing by rack jobbers and wholesalers of non-food lines.[3]

cent (including advertising, depreciation, insurance, interest, utilities, rent, trading stamps, labor and supervision, and taxes) leaving a *net profit* on sales of *20* per cent. Net profit for total food store operations average around *3* per cent.

## USE OF RACK JOBBERS BY SIZE OF CHAIN

All sizes of supermarkets use the services of rack jobbers. There is some support for the theory that relatively small supermarket chains (four to ten stores) use the rack jobber more consistently than larger chains.

[a] "The True Look of the Super Market Industry 1959," *Supermarket Merchandising,* Vol. 25 (May, 1960). p. 87.

Figure 1 shows that smaller chains rely in almost 85 per cent of cases on the outside servicing of the rack jobber. As a chain gets big and more "accomplished," it often tries to fulfill its own non-food requirements by buying direct from the manufacturer. As the chain gets bigger (over 100 stores), it tends to increase the use of outside servicing, and at this point in a chain's development, some 50 per cent of non-food items are supplied by an outside source—either a rack jobber or a wholesaler.

It would seem that small supermarket chains use outside servicing because of their inexperience, whereas middle-sized chains (26-99 stores) attempt to act independently and to consolidate non-food merchandising into their own operation.

The large chains, tend more toward the use of outside servicing.

## NEW RACK-JOBBING FEATURES

Two developments are evident in rack-jobbing today.

One is the establishment of *permanent personnel* (on the rack jobber's payroll) in the non-foods section of *very big* food stores. These people are assigned to their section to act as stocking and display men, and also as retail clerks. They are on hand to maintain their section in the store and to help the consumer buy the right products. This is much like the demonstrator concept of selling in department stores.

Another development is that of the *specialist soft-goods salesman* within the framework of non-foods. Some rack jobbers are training men to merchandise soft goods exclusively. The number of manufacturers willing to be represented in the food stores is increasing and so are the lines, especially since manufacturers have been willing to sell their major brands (as well as their "off" brands) to food outlets.

Both of these developments have raised the quality of soft goods in food stores. Included in this long merchandise category are hosiery, socks, bras, sportswear, baby pants, crib sheets, briefs, hats, towels, pajamas, sweat shirts, T shirts, slippers, slacks, sweaters, skirts, and rainwear. With the number of items growing longer and with a variety of styles and seasonal factors to be considered, *soft goods specialists* are needed.

The biggest factor in getting more business for a rack jobber is his service—how frequently he calls, how extensive his line, how well he merchandises. Free goods, premiums, and other standard inducements are used to a slight extent.

## PRICING

Pricing is fairly inflexible, but does vary within each non-food product group. On an average, the rack jobber sells at 31 per cent off retail to his accounts. He buys at close to 50 per cent off retail from his suppliers (manufacturers).

Discounts and pricing are as follows:

| Item | Approximate percentage discount from retail price to rack jobber (from manufacturer) | Average percentage discount from retail price to food store (from rack jobber) |
| --- | --- | --- |
| Stationery | 55 | 41 |
| Toys | 50 | 33 |
| Housewares | 50 | 33 |
| Health & Beauty Aids | 45 | 33 |
| Soft Goods | 45 | 32 |
| Records | 50 | 28 |
| Magazines | 40 | 26 |

Note that the figures in the first column are *approximate;* quantity purchases and periodic manufacturer-oriented promotions may cause these figures to vary from 3 to 5 per cent. Also note that the figures in the second column reflect an *average* discount.

The rack jobber gets roughly between 10 and 25 per cent of the retail selling price of an item as his profit. Considering his overhead (cost of warehousing, pricing, displaying, manpower, etc.), this is not a very high percentage of profit per item; but a rapid turnover and higher priced merchandise yield the rack jobber an adequate profit ratio.

In practically every case the food store could buy non-food merchandise *cheaper* on a *direct basis* from the manufacturer. For example, most manufacturers offer their direct accounts a 40 per cent off-retail discount for health and beauty aids. Obviously, buying from a rack jobber where a 33 per cent is offered yields less profit to a food store; but the fact that store personnel have to warehouse, handle, price and display the merchandise causes the 7 per cent difference to diminish considerably. In the final analysis, the 7 per cent added gross profit may translate into no additional profit over the 33 per cent that the rack jobber originally offered. This same profit problem exists for all categories of non-foods.

Most food accounts serviced by rack jobbers are billed within ten days after receipt of merchandise. They are billed at one price, which reflects the cost of the product and the cost of the rack jobber's service.

In the case of a shampoo that retails at $1.00, the food store that buys through the rack jobber will pay about 67 cents (if bought direct, the price would be 60 cents), while the manufacturer sells the item to the rack jobber for about 55 cents. The price of 67 cents to the food store includes the cost of warehousing, handling, displaying, etc., that the rack jobber incurs—there is no extra cost to a food store for these services.

## THE FUTURE OF THE
## RACK JOBBER

Rack-jobbing will grow; but the rack jobber will play a changing role in the future. The small indepndents that cannot get into the housewares and softgoods business without a tremendous output of money and effort will be prime targets for the services of a rack jobber. Strong competition, however, from food chain buyers, voluntary co-ops, and food wholesalers will seek to diminish his service. As food outlets grow larger and more diversified, they will tend to handle non-food merchandising themselves and switch their buying to a direct basis.

The rack jobber reasons that the food store cannot operate at peak efficiency by handling its own non-foods, especially since the cost of warehousing and handling is very high and since only 5 per cent of total store volume is at stake. Because of the tremendous number of items included in non-foods, he also maintains that the burden of display and product upkeep is too great for a food operator.

But the chains argue otherwise. They claim to have had "concession" operations before, which were integrated successfully and from which they realized a profit. In addition, they feel that they want to have control over every department in their store to make their profit worthwhile.

As this battle of "who is going to distribute what" goes on, a continual shift of buying policies is evident. In the last few years, such big chains as National, Kroger, Loblaw, and Safeway have tried *direct buying* of non-foods and then switched back to *rack jobbing*. Others have dropped rack servicing in favor of direct buying. Some food operations rely on rack jobbers for servicing only part of their non-food section and buy direct for the other part. But the rack-jobbing industry has steadily grown stronger.

Total sales of non-foods now exceed $2 billion annually. Compare that figure with those of other outlets that are in the business of *distributing non-foods* exclusively:

Annual volume of hardware stores is $2.7 billion
Annual volume of furniture stores is $4.9 billion
Annual volume of drug stores is $5.5 billion

No doubt years to come will see the non-foods segment of the food industry surpass in sales one of these *complete retail industries*. Consumers are spending more and more of their money in food stores; and this means even more business growth for rack jobbers.

### QUESTIONS

1. Is a rack jobber a retailer or wholesaler? What services does he offer?

2. What are two most recent developments in rack jobbing today?
3. What kind of future does the rack jobber face?
4. How is pricing handled by the rack jobber?
5. Is the sale of non-food items really profitable in food stores?

# 45. Tactics Vary as Firms Try to Cut Warehouse Costs, Speed Service*

Roger B. Rowand, Staff Reporter of *The Wall Street Journal*

*Some firms are successfully lowering their warehousing costs by cutting down on the number of storage points; Others are trimming costs by adding extra warehouses closer to customers. Still others are cutting distribution costs by merely altering methods and machinery in existing warehouses.*

By closing six warehouses scattered around the country and concentrating its inventory of 10 million books in a $2 million facility in Riverside, N.J., Macmillan Co., the publishing house, figures it is saving $200,000 a year.

Firestone Tire & Rubber Co., spreading its inventories closer to customers, has opened nine big new warehouses in the last six years and figures it has saved $750,000.

Although they have taken directly opposite courses, Macmillan and Firestone have identical goals: Reduction of the cost of getting their goods from the factory to consumer. And their efforts are being matched these days by a growing number of manufacturers who in recent years have watched soaring distribution costs tighten the squeeze on profits.

Distribution costs arise from a broad range of services which usually have no direct bearing on a company's product itself. These services include transportation, warehousing, selling, financing of credit sales or any other non-productive factor. The cost of this phase of business varies with industries, ranging from 10 cents of each dollar spent on rugged iron castings to 80 cents of each dollar spent on cosmetics. In the appliance industry, distribution takes 35 cents of each retail sales dollar, of which 15 cents is spent

* Reprinted from *The Wall Street Journal*, May 26, 1961, pp. 1 and 22. Copyright 1961 by Dow Jones & Company, Inc.

on selling and advertising and 20 cents on warehousing and transportation.

## FROM 22% TO 47%

"Surveys made by our staff for seven companies in the food, apparel, hardware and other consumer fields show the portion of the sales dollar representing their distribution costs has increased from 22% to 47% in the past five years," says A. T. Waidelich, vice president for engineering and research of Austin Co., Cleveland-based engineering, designing and construction firm.

Warehousing expenses loom large amid other costs of distribution and have become a major target of stepped-up corporate economizing efforts. Declares L. West Shea, managing director of the Material Handling Institute in Pittsburgh: "During production, most of the things done to an item increase its value, but as soon as it reaches the warehouse it can be moved one foot or a mile and its value doesn't change. Warehousing is purely an expense item and manufacturers are trying desperately to reduce expenses. As costs close in they are looking more and more at costs of warehousing and ways to cut them down."

For some concerns currently revamping their distribution systems, savings are coming in relatively small amounts through minor changes in warehousing procedures within existing facilities. For others, however, there have been major programs of decentralizing or centralizing operations.

Before Macmillan Co. set up its Riverside facility, its inventory was held in 40 binderies and in scattered warehouses. The company's inventory contains about 6,500 titles, with 350 to 400 new ones being added each year. Books were continually being shipped from one Macmillan office to another—at the com-

pany's expense. Almost no mechanical handling equipment was used in the small warehouses, says J. B. Bennet, Macmillan's secretary and general manger.

## CONSOLIDATED INVENTORY

Now, the publisher's system includes a consolidated inventory that is tightly controlled by Macmillan's New York City office and increased mechanization, featuring conveyors, two-way radios on fork lift trucks and a new machine that wraps single-volume offers at a rate of 600 an hour.

Customers are getting faster service, too, Macmillan says. Although the small warehouses frequently were close to customers, they often were out of items that were ordered and had to obtain them from other warehouses. Mr. Bennet says the new Riverside facility, with its mechanized equipment, is processing about 80% of the company's orders in less than 48 hours, compared with only 20% for all the small warehouses.

If centralization is working for Macmillan, why isn't it the answer for Firestone? A major factor is the widely different nature of their businesses. While many of Macmillan's orders are for a few books, which can be shipped easily and cheaply through the mails, Firestone's orders in many cases are for such bulky items as tires, major appliances and lawn furniture. With shipping costs such an important consideration, it would be impractical for Firestone to try to serve its nationwide network of dealers from a central warehouse.

Firestone currently is working the bugs out of an electronically controlled paperwork system at its Cleveland district warehouse. This warehouse supplies some 12,000 items to Firestone home and auto supply stores in a 300-mile radius covering five states. The company expects to cut the time required to process an order to even less than the 24 hours now needed. By using tabulating cards and a computer, the company will eliminate multiple handling and reproduction of customer orders, invoices and packing slips. The system, if successful, will be used in the company's 10 other home and auto supply warehouses, Firestone says.

## AID TO SALES

One Firestone warehouse man notes that sharp inventory controls can also help boost sales. He tells this story about the importance of speedy order filling. "A customer drove into one of our dealerships to buy a dome light for his car. The dealer said the customer needed a set of tires, too, and almost sold him a set. But as it turned out, the dealer hadn't yet received his new order of dome lights, so the customer left and the dealer missed not only that 10-cent lamp sale but the sale of the four tires as well."

Raytheon Co. of Lexington, Mass., like Macmillan, sells a lot of small products, including vacuum tubes, transistors and other electronic items. And, like Macmillan, Raytheon is centralizing its warehousing operations. It has closed all but its Westwood, Mass., warehouse and started using a new distribution system that includes air delivery and use of computers. Raytheon figures the system will save the company more than $380,000 a year. Major savings include $160,000 a year on warehouse rental and $177,000 a year on warehousing operating costs, says John T. Thompson, manager of the Distributor Products division.

Raytheon's new system works like this: Tabulator cards are inserted in each package of five electronic tubes leaving Raytheon's warehouse. As the merchandise is sold, the distributor collects the cards and files his replacement order without

doing paperwork. He simply sends in the cards which are identified by an account number, the type of merchandise and the price of the units he orders.

## "A SAVING OF 13 DAYS"

Western Union Telegraph Co. equipment accepts the punched cards and transmits information on them to the warehouse, where it is duplicated on other punched cards. A typical order of 5,000 tubes of varying types can be received in about 17 minutes, Raytheon says. It can be assembled in about 90 minutes and delivered to Boston's Logan Airport in an additional 45 minutes. "Orders from 3,000 miles away can be delivered within 24 hours, a saving of 13 days in some cases," says Mr. Thompson.

In some cases, companies are speeding service to customers and cutting distribution costs merely by altering methods and machinery in existing warehouses.

World Publishing Co., Cleveland, made a small change in its warehouse procedures that boosted employes' order output and saves the company a total of some $20,000 a year. Orders for the company's Bibles, dictionaries, and other books were formerly filled from warehouse shelves by men called "pickers" who pushed crates along a conveyor, selecting books as they walked. The crates were carried to packers who put the books into cartons for shipping. Now, order fillers pack books directly into shipping cartons as they are picked off shelves and former packers now simply seal the cartons. The savings arose from the reduced time needed in filling each order and in the cost of the crates, which lasted through only nine or 10 weeks of service and cost $2 each.

"As the selling price and manufacturing cost of books get closer to each other, we are forced to trim costs and the warehouse is the spot where it can  be done," says Leonard A. Charpie, World Publishing's vice president and treasurer.

## "CLOTHES ARE LIKE BANANAS"

Clothing is considered one of the most difficult items to warehouse efficiently. "Speed in filling orders and in keeping close control on inventory are essential in the garment industry," says B. L. Kamberg, marketing vice president of Bobbie Brooks, Inc., of Cleveland. "Clothes are like bananas—they don't sell well if they lie around very long."

Bobbie Brooks' Cleveland warehouse contains about one million garments of varying sizes, colors and styles. They are funneled through the warehouse from 48 scattered factories to 7,000 retail outlets around the country.

Until a year ago, clothing in the warehouse was transported on hand carts; the system was slow and cumbersome. Last summer, Bobbie Brooks revised its warehousing system.

The warehouse is criss-crossed by a network of almost two miles of· tubing that is open on its top and contains a notched V-belt conveyor. The belt carries clothes on hangers from trucks at indoor receiving docks to 22 storage areas within the warehouse. Boxed clothing, such as sweaters, moves on flat conveyor belts. Order fillers pick items from storage shelves and racks and start them zipping on their way via the notched V-belts to packers on an outbound network of overhead tubing or belt conveyor at a rate of about 50,000 garments a day.

By adopting this system and by using a computer for processing orders, the company says it has cut handling time in half and is shipping orders to retailers within 24 hours of receipt, compared with 72 hours previously.

## QUESTIONS

1. What merchandise characteristics determine whether a firm should centralize or decentralize its warehousing?

2. What are some of the special problems of warehousing in the garment industry?

3. What new warehousing innovations have been adopted by Raytheon Company of Lexington, Massachusetts?

4. What other methods of lowering warehousing costs are being tried?

# 46. Physical Distribution the Neglected Marketing Function*

Bud Reese, Associate Editor, *Industrial Marketing*

*In physical distribution there is great potential for improving customer service and reducing costs by the centralization of physical distribution planning under a physical distribution manager.*

He read the company's ads and talked to its salesman. He liked what he read and heard; and placed a trial order, to be delivered in six weeks.

That was seven weeks ago—and still no sign of the shipment. He has decided to wait another three days before canceling; *and he has decided to stick with his regular supplier.*

A lot of promotion and sales effort has gone down the drain, whether the shipment arrives in the three days or not. The cause of the waste is faulty physical distribution—not having the product at the right place at the right time.

## NOT UNUSUAL . . .

This situation is hypothetical, but similar situations are by no means unusual in industry today, say the nation's physical distribution specialists. These experts on the movemnt of finished goods to customers and distributors all seem to agree that:

*Sales are being lost and advertising claims are falling on deaf ears because of faulty physical distribution; and marketing men are primarily to blame for permitting this situation to exist.*

They say that marketing men have sadly neglected this important facet of their job—despite the fact that in the area of physical distribution there exists industry's finest opportunity to improve customer service *and reduce costs.*

They say that the movement of goods is over-managed, under-managed and mismanaged—at one and the same time. The purpose of this article is to examine the reasoning behind this rather unanimous belief, and to answer these basic questions:

1. Should marketing men concern themselves with the physical distribution of their company's products?

2. If physical distribution is a function of marketing, are industrial marketing men neglecting it?

3. What needs to be done to improve physical distribution? And what part do marketers have to play in this movement?

## WHY CONCERN YOURSELF?

"For the average firm, physical distribution consumes between 25% and 33% of each sales dollar [that is, the cost of warehousing, transportation, etc., make up from 25% to 33% of the total cost of products delivered at the customer's location]. A firm's longevity may well depend upon reducing this third highest cost of doing business [after labor and materials]."

That statement was made by Dr. Donald J. Bowersox, assistant director of business development for REA Express, New York, at a June meeting of the American Marketing Association.

And at an American Management Association conference, Paul A. Wassmansdorf, marketing administration consultant for General Electric Co., New York, said, "There is a growing belief that the costs of physical distribution which are not readily apparent are perhaps as great as the obvious ones. These are the costs that result from not having the right goods at the right place at the right time.

"The first, and possibly the largest of these costs is the cost of lost sales. Unfortunately, a great deal of work remains to be done in computing the cost of sales as a result of an unbalanced flow of goods. The preliminary work that has been done, however, indicates that the cost of lost sales is substantially larger than anyone has suspected . . . many sales are lost without the seller's knowing it."

A check with physical distribution executives and consultants brought out two more immediate reasons for marketing men to take a new, long look at the way their companies move their goods to customers and distributors. The two are closely related.

1. *The cost-service struggle.* Marketing and sales management are caught in the middle, between the field sales force asking for faster delivery and top management demanding cost reductions.

Field sales wants inventories maintained in each customer's backyard; but, maintaining many localized field inventories is an expensive habit.

2. *Less stocking by distributors.* And yet, the majority of the experts contacted by IM admit that industrial companies are being forced into adding more warehouses because an increasing number of industrial distributors are shirking their stocking function.

The manager of a newly established branch warehouse in Chicago said, "My company hated to create my job, but they had no choice. Distributors are becoming brokers, refusing to carry adequate stock. Our competitors face the same problem, and are establishing more branch warehouses; we have to go along."

## THE "BOTTOMLESS CUP"

Speaking at an American Management Association meeting, Jerome P. Shuchter, market research director of Federal Pacific Electric Co., Newark, N.J., told why his company's marketing and sales management decided to devote more attention to the problem of physical distribution:

"We backed into our general warehousing policy some ten years ago. With sales expanding rapidly and freight costs mounting, we had to reach an understanding about the function of warehouses. Two different concepts were under consideration:

1. "The 'emergency stock' theory. Were warehouses to be used only to provide local emergency stocks to our distributors? Under this theory, bulk shipments would normally be made directly from our central warehouse in Newark.

2. "The 'bottomles cup' theory. Were warehouses to be a full-dress distribution channel, with large stocks avilable locally? Under this theory, our distributors could stock lightly and be asured of an unlimited secondary source of supply.

"On the table were surveys backing the emergency-stock viewpoint. They showed the tremendous inventory saving that could be achieved through this approach.

They showed conclusively that direct LCL [less than car load] shipments to customers were more economical than through use of the warehouse as a dog-leg station.

"We reached an easy decision that day —and had to toss it out the next month! The pace of industrial and corporate growth almost passed us by. There was no way in the world we could hold to the emergency-stock concept if even one of our major competitors took the road to all-out customer service through large local backup stocks. And many of our competitors did take that road. The bottomless-cup theory carried the day."

Judging from what has been said and written on the subject, Federal Pacific Electric is just one of many industrial companies to be forced into bottomless-cup physical distribution. The function of having the product at the right place at the right time, of meeting customer service demands, has become an important determinant of sales effectiveness. But . . .

## "MOST NEGLECTED"

In his AMA speech Dr. Bowersox said, "Among the many problems consuming the time and talents of marketing executives, those most neglected relate to physical distribution."

At the same meeting, Philip F. Cannon, vice-president of Barrington Associates, New York, stated, "I don't want to be so trite as to say—as other speakers over the years have said—that there is no more promising field for improvement than physical distribution; but that is really the way I feel. Allow me, if you will, to say at least this much: I think that in physical distribution there is a great potential for improving customer service and reducing costs. And, this potential stands relatively unexploited. This is virgin territory."

Why do these men feel that physical distribution is being "neglected" by marketing men?

Mr. Cannon explained it this way. "The fact that physical distribution, as something other than a cost factor, has received very little attention suggests that perhaps there is something peculiar or particularly difficult about this function.

"The fact is, however, that the technical, procedural and operational aspects of physical distribution do not pose any more difficult problems than are found in manufacturing or selling. The real reason for the neglect of physical distribution, I believe, is that it is usually not organized very well. Too many physical distribution functions are left to fall between the chairs, creating many 'grey areas' where objectives, policies and organizational lines are at best fragmentary, if they exist at all. Most commonly, the functions of distribution are split haphazardly between manufacturing and sales . . .

"Not infrequently, in discussing job responsibilities with senior marketing executives, we have had them wryly add, 'Oh yes, another part of my job includes liaison with the plant shipping department.' "

## WHO DOES WHAT?

In his book, "Modern Marketing Management," Ferdinand F. Mauser, marketing professor at Wayne State University, wrote, "All too often . . . inter and intraplant flow of goods are under traffic, and the control of regional warehouses and inventories are under the jurisdiction of the sales department."

The manager of a warehouse on the outskirts of Chicago said that in his company, traffic, finished goods inventory control and order processing are directed by the controller; planning of warehouse space is done by the planning manager;

order status inquiry is headed by the sales manager; and the factory manager controls finished goods materials handling and warehouse management.

Mr. Shuchter of Federal Pacific Electric said that before his company woke up to the importance of physical distribution, "We had no . . . really consistent concept of the distribution function. True, we did have a traffic manager; someone did schedule shipments; someone did back the process with production schedules; someone did modernize and lay out new warehouses; and someone from the marketing department did bird-dog the activity, policing warehouse expenses and counting inventories. But, all these activities were carried on in different departments, with insufficient common direction and policy."

The physical distributions specialists say that because of this hodge-podge of authority, customers receive incorrect answers to their order status inquiries; orders are not processed with dispatch; and, in general, customer service suffers severely.

## WHAT'S THE ANSWER?

What is the answer to the Hydra-headed distribution problem. Centralization of physical distribution planning, obviously—but under whom? And just what would this person administer?

Here, again, the experts seem to agree. They say that the man for the job is the marketing manager. But, they are quick to qualify their suggestion. They realize that the man with the marketing manager title in many companies is really the sales manager, given the title to pay lip service to the "marketing concept."

In such cases, the experts suggest that a new marketing title be established, as is being done by an increasing number of companies; the title being that of physical distribution manager.

## THE ONLY WAY

Why couldn't the job simply be given to the sales manager, or the production manager, or the controller?

Mr. Shuchter answered this question bluntly: "There has never been a sales manager who thought he had too much inventory—or a finance manager who thought he had too little. There has never been a production manager who thought production runs were long enough—or a sales manager who didn't prefer smaller, more frequent runs."

Mr. Cannon was more specific as to what happens to physical distribution when it is under sales or manufacturing:

First, here are some things that he said can happen when distribution is sales-directed:

1. "Sales is naturally inclined to provide customer service at any cost, i.e., it might well over-invest in branch warehouse inventories [Mr. Bowersox said that for a typical warehouse it takes about 75% more inventory to satisfy 95% of customer sales from stock than it does to satisfy 80%], incur excessive LCL or LTL shipping costs, and so forth.

2. "The traffic department is called upon to serve other divisions or functions of the business, such as manufacturing and purchasing; its position under sales may limit its ability to render corporate service.

3. "Branch warehouses tend to be located automatically with branch sales offices, even though the organization and location of selling functions in a territory bear no relationship to the economics of warehouse location.

[John T. Thompson, general manager of distributor products, Raytheon Co., Westwood, Mass., has stated that field warehouses frequently create availability problems rather than solve them, and sometimes they inject a communications delay point.]

4. "Sales executives get saddled with an operating function for which they may have little training, and less understanding—physical distribution economics." (Mr. Mauser wrote that, "Out of habit, sales departments often promise deliveries on the 1st and 15th. The distribution executive who creates an awareness of the importance of staggering promised delivery dates induces a smoother and less costly outgoing flow merchandise. The sales department should be checked to determine what the lag time is between the customer's placing the order and its actually arriving in the shipping department. Such a check may reveal delays which often mean the difference between high and low transportation costs and between prompt deliveries and less satisfactory ones. It is often surprising to discover the extent of internal delay to which an order is subjected.")

Now, here's what Mr. Cannon said might happen when distribution is directed by manufacturing:

1. "Operations are restricted under the dominance of the manufacturing point of view, which generally tends to be introverted and which cannot evaluate objectively the needs of marketing for physical distribution support.

2. "Distribution is treated as a subordinate and secondary function that does not merit first-rate, top-drawer attention from manufacturing executives."

## QUALIFICATIONS

What would be the qualifications of this physical distribution manager? Would he be a traffic manager with planning authority?

Most physical distribution specialists say "no" to the idea of a glorified traffic manager. They say that the traffic manager's preoccupation with detail and with

activity that is massively routine usually disqualifies him for the job of physical distribution manager. The right man for the job would be:

Appreciative of the fundamental nature and importance of physical distribution in corporate planning.

Familiar with distribution costing. "On a national average," says Dr. Bowersox, "transportation services account for less than 25% of the total cost incurred in marketing logistics [physical distribution]. A total cost perspective provides the analytical framework necessary for a penetrating evaluation of alternative distribution systems. It is interesting to note that astute distribution planning will often lead to higher transportation cost . . . total cost is the fundamental concept."

Appreciative of the need for exacting research to support distribution planning. In place of crude approximations, fictitious averages and intuitive guesses, distribution planning must be the result of effectively utilizing electronic data processing and quantitative techniques.

Dr. Bowersox explained that many advancements in this area of quantitative techniques have mushroomed under the catch-all label of operations research, including a technique commonly called linear programming. He said, "While much criticism can be voiced on the relative sterility of OR in providing significant pay-offs to date, if quantitative techniques do hold the promise of significant pay-offs, it is reasonably certain they will be realized first among logistics problems.

"The foundations for this prediction are simple: many elements of total cost distribution are quantifiable and can be approximated by near linear relationships. . . . It is safe to generalize that better than 90% of historical distribution planning lacked the benefits of system logic, mathematical structure and, in many cases, even advanced statistical analysis.

The history of distribution planning represents an era of stagnant check-lists and static formulas."

## CENTRALIZE WHAT?

So much for the man; now for his job. Here's what the majority of the experts contacted by IM say should be administered by the physical distribution manager:

1. *Transportation and traffic* — the movement of inbound materials to the factory, and the movement of finished goods from the factory to final customers, branch warehouses and regional distribution centers, another factory, freight forwarding or classifying points.

2. *Finished goods inventory control* — The method of a company's data processing system may dictate the assignment of the responsibility for actual maintenance of the inventory records elsewhere; but where circumstances warrant, it may be logical for distribution to maintain these records, particularly where branch warehouse inventories are concerned.

Sales and finance would, of course, have the major voices in determining levels of inventory; but, finished goods are the immediate physical responsibility of distribution, which serves as the connecting link between sales and manufacturing.

3. *Location of branch warehouses* — First, sales would define service, in terms of number of days between the date of an order from the customer and the date of its delivery to the customer. Then it would be the distribution manager's responsibility to maintain at least this level of service. As was pointed out earlier, the organization and location of selling functions in a territory bear no relationship to the economics of warehouse location.

4. *Operation of branch warehouses* — Sales management skills and energies are best devoted to selling, not in handling the routines of warehouse operation.

5. *Order processing and administration* —This would include: (1) acknowledgment, done under policies issued by sales; (2) credit review, done under policies, procedures and current credit ratings issued by the treasurer's office; (3) pricing, done under strict formulae and price lists issued by sales; (4) order editing, done as specified by the controller and by sales; (5) invoice preparation and mailing, as prescribed by the controller; (6) reorder from production—inventory replenishment according to formulae emanating from manufacturing, as well as from distribution.

Many physical distribution specialists claim that order processing time can be cut from a third to a half through organization of the various facets under one man.

6. *Customer service* — Distribution should also be concerned with answering inquiries on order status from salesmen and customers. Distribution would not, of course, be responsible for technical service.

7. *Materials handling*—Manufacturing has historically been responsible for this function, say the experts. They point out, however, that in-process materials handling methods are not readily applicable to finished goods handling.

8. *Package design*—Merchandising and sales aspects of package design are not the concern of physical distribution. However, package design as it affects the handling and transporting of merchandise are his concern.

## IMPROVEMENT

Are the physical distribution specialists correct in suggesting that planning of the movement of finished goods to customers and distributors be centralized? Compare the improvements in customer service and the reduction of marketing costs possible through proper physical distribution management with the distribution system of the early growth days of Federal Pacific Electric, as described by Mr. Shuchter:

"Sam O'Toole was the 1949 version of Ramac. He guided the destiny of our stock from its source for many years. With orders and memos tucked in every pocket, he charged through each day as though it were the decisive moment in human history.

"Emergency! The ABC Distributing Co. placed an order for 12 400-amp, three-pole, solid neutral switch devices three months ago. The order, it seems, has been misplaced and now the salesman, Sam's buddy, is on the phone crying his heart out: He faces cancellation of the $600 order and other reprisals too terrible to mention. The card inventory shows zero.

"Enter Sam O'Toole. From the dark recesses of the stockroom he drags out three of the precious devices. His friend, Jake the foreman, will convert two from similar units. Up in the factory Sam has spotted five almost-complete assemblies coming down the line. He drags the plant manager (no lesser mortal will do) to the spot and stands panting as the foreman is ordered to stop all work until the devices are complete.

"That's ten down and two to go. In a flash Sam has wired the people at the St. Louis warehouse that the switch they will receive today is to be air-freighted back to Newark. And finally Sam calls a Paterson distributor who is sure to help him out by returning a switch he has in stock. His task complete, Sam calls the salesman to promise shipment of eight switches today and four tomorrow, and knows in his heart that this was a job well done. (Sam, by the way, was also the best pitcher our softball team ever had.)"

## 1965

As for the future, in an American Management Association report on physical distribution, A. W. Greene, editor of *Distribution Age,* Philadelphia, wrote:

"In 1965 there will be many physical distribution managers. They will come from traffic and transportation, from warehousing, from industrial engineering, from production, marketing and sales. Each will have greater scope and greater breadth of vision than the present pioneers of distribution management.

"I see such a man at his desk. It's a clean desk, except for rows of push-buttons, intercoms and other executive gadgets. Behind him, and on all sides, there are live charts and graphs, pulsating with electronic recordings of up-to-the-moment inventories at all distribution points. There are direct wire communication lines to all points.

"As the distribution manager of 1965 sits in his white tower of control, his telephone rings. An angry voice is heard: 'Nine weeks ago I sent you an order for three sizes of your model X-5 components. You promised seven-week delivery. As of now, I haven't received a single unit. If I don't get this shipment by the end of the week, cancel the order!'

"Well, . . . maybe in 1966 . . ."

## QUESTIONS

1. What percentage of sales is consumed by physical distribution typically?
2. Who should manage physical distribution?
3. What functions should be administered by the physical distribution manager?
4. What changes in physical distribution may take place by 1965?

# $47.$ The Logistics of Distribution*

John F. Magee, Head, Operations Research Group, Arthur D. Little, Inc.

*The choice of distribution system each company makes will have a significant impact on product design, plant investment, and organization. Industrial logistics and trends in logistics technology will receive increasing attention from business.*

American business is awakening to a new, exciting opportunity to improve service and reduce costs—better management of the flow of goods from plant to user. Capitalizing on this opportunity means:

Thinking of the physical distribution process as a *system* in which, just as in a good hi-fi system, all the components and functions must be properly balanced.

Taking a fresh look at the responsibilities, capabilities, and organizational positions of executives in traffic, warehouse management, inventory control, and other functions which make up the over-all system.

Re-examining the company's physical plant and distribution procedures in the light of technical advances in such areas as transportation, data processing, and materials handling.

In this article I shall first examine the pressing need for improved management of comparnies' distribution systems. Then I shall outline some of the most promising ways by which progress in "industrial logistics" can be achieved, with special attention to the implications of technological advances for policy, the problems of getting started wtih a new look at a company's system, and the steps that

should be taken in making a good distribution study.

## STUBBORN PRESSURES

The need for progress in distribution is a product of not one but several trends—trends in costs, in product-line policy, and in the market place. More often than not, the challenge posed is to the system as a whole, not just to the particular part or function where trouble is most obvious.

### RISING COSTS

For years, businessmen and economists have looked with mixed feelings on the increase in distribution costs in our economy. Over the past half century, tremendous strides have been made in reducing the costs of production, but these feats have not been duplicated in other areas. If the over-all efficiency of companies is to continue to improve, management must turn its attention increasingly to holding distribution costs in line. Physical distribution costs in particular, estimated by some to represent the third largest component in the total cost of business operation, are a logical center for management attention.

The problems of cutting these costs pose certain new and interesting questions

* Reprinted from *Harvard Business Review*, July–August 1960, p. 89.

for business. Whereas in many production operations it has been possible in the past to substitute a machine for human labor and to cut the cost of one operation without seriously disturbing the rest of the production system, this is hardly the case in efforts to cut physical distribution costs. Indiscriminate cost reduction in any one of the individual cost elements, such as inventory maintenance, warehousing, transportation, or clerical activities, can have a disastrous effect on the efficiency of the system as a whole. To illustrate this point:

Suppose we cut inventories. Certainly a reduction in inventories will save capital investment and the costs of supplying capital, and it may save some expenses in storage, taxes, and insurance. On the other hand, an indiscriminate reduction in inventory levels may seriously impair the reliability of delivery service to customers and the availability of products in the field. An inventory reduction which saves money but destroys competitive position is hardly a contribution to a more effective distribution system.

We can cut transportation costs, perhaps, by changing to methods showing lower cost per ton-mile, or by shipping in larger quantities and taking advantage of volume carload or truckload rates. But if lower transportation costs are achieved at the expense of slower or less frequent movement of goods, we face the risk of: (a) cutting the flexibility and responsiveness of the distribution system to changes in customer requirements; (b) requiring greater field inventories to maintain service; (c) creating greater investment requirements and obsolescence risks.

Similarly, blanket refusal to allow cost increases in any one part can wipe out opportunities to make the system as a whole more efficient. For instance:

New methods of high-speed data communications and processing may in fact increase the clerical costs of operating the distribution system. On the other hand, they may cut down delays in feeding information back to govern production opertaions and to control lags in getting material moving into the distribution system in response to customer demand. Thus, they may actually cut *total* distribution system costs because of their impact on improved production and inventory control.

It takes a careful analysis of the total physical distribution system to know whether net costs will be increased or decreased by efforts to cut the cost of any one component.

PROLIFERATING PRODUCT LINES

Physical distribution systems in recent years have been put under tremendous pressure induced by changes in product-line characteristics. Until recently, for example, products like typewriters, light bulbs, appliances, and plumbing fixtures were largely utilitarian, with differences in product characteristics rather closely related to function. A typewriter manufacturer did not have to worry about matching typewriter color to office décor or type style to company "image." Light bulbs used to be white and sometimes clear, and they varied by wattage. Now, however, typewriters come in pastels and two-tones. Light bulbs are sold not only to provide light but atmosphere, with a corresponding increase in the number of products that have to be shipped, stocked, and controlled. Appliances and plumbing fixtures are available to customers not only in the classical antiseptic white, but in a wide range of color and style combinations. In short, style and individuality have become strong competitive weapons.

In an almost unending list of products in the consumer field, variations in color, packaging, and other features have imposed heavy burdens on the distribution system. In the marketing of industrial goods, variations in grade, color, and size have had a similar impact. In paper manufacture, for example, the wide variety of package sizes required for consumer products has led carton manufacturers to demand correspondingly wide ranges of kraft board roll widths from paper manufacturers, and these demands have created difficult problems of scheduling, inventory control, and distribution.

The growth and change in product-line characteritsics in both consumer and industrial products have meant that manufacturing plants have had more items to make, and the distribution system has had more items to handle and stock. More items mean lower volume per item and

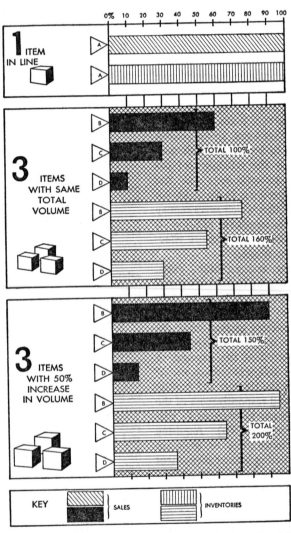

Exhibit I. What happens to inventories when the product line is broadened?

correspondingly higher unit handling inventory and storage costs. Take, for example, just the impact on inventory requirements of substituting three items for one:

Suppose we have substituted items B, C, and D for an old item A. If sales among these items are broken down 60% to B, 30% to C, and 10% to D, with no over-all increase in sales compared to the volume on the old item A, then Exhibit I shows what is likely to happen to field inventory requirements—an increase of more than 60%. (This figure is based on characteristic relationships between inventory and sales in companies with which I am familiar. In general, the larger the sales, the lower inventory can be relative to sales. Thus, product D with 10% of sales needs a much higher proportion of inventory than product B, with 60% of the sales.)

At a carrying cost of 20% a year, this increase represents a handsome expense for maintaining competitive position.

Let us be optimistic, however, and assume that items B, C, and D do more than yield the same total volume; let us assume that total volume increases by 50%. Even so, the inventory requirements would double, and inventory cost per unit sold would increase over 30%—a substantial source of pressure on the distribution system.

These figures illustrate the impact of small-volume items on the cost of operating the distribution system. Yet diversity of product sales is characteristic in American businesses, whether selling in consumer or industrial markets. Exhibit II shows the typical relationship between the number of items sold and the proportion of sales they account for. The figures are based on the records of a large number of firms in the consumer and industrial products fields. The exhibit reveals that while 10%–20% of total items sold characteristically yield 80% of the sales, half of the items in the line account for less than 4% of the sales. It is the bottom half of the product line that imposes a great deal of the difficulty, expense, and investment on the distribution system.

ALTERNATIVE COURSES

Increased cost, selling, and product-line pressures suggest that management should take a hard look at alternative distribution patterns, as a means of cutting logistics costs without a major sacrifice in service. Here are a few of the possibilities:

The company can carry central stocks of low-selling items only. To get the right balance of transportation costs, handling costs, and service, it may be necessary to stock these items at one central point and ship them against individual customer orders as the latter arise, perhaps by expedited service or air freight.

For many items in the line, a good compromise may be to carry some low- or middle-volume items in only a few large regional warehouses, as a compromise between the excessive storage costs incurred from broad-scale stocking and the transportation and service penalties incurred by attempting to meet demand from manufacturing points alone.

Warehouse points can be consolidated. With improvements in transportation and in mechanical material- and data-handling methods, large opportunities exist in many businesses for cutting down on the number of field warehouse points. With increased volume through the individual warehouses, carrying a broader product line at the local points begins to make greater economic sense.

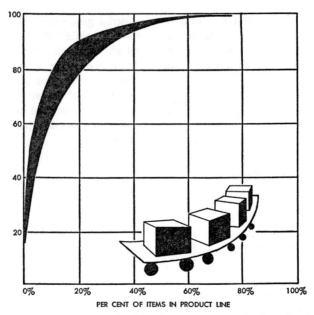

PER CENT OF ITEMS IN PRODUCT LINE

Exhibit II. What fraction of total sales is accounted for by what fraction
of total items in the product line?

### SALES-GENERATING CAPACITY

The first and most basic job of the distribution system is to get customers, to turn interest and orders into sales. As business has grown more competitive and the public has become harder to please, management has focused increasing attention on the *quality* of its logistical operations. What can be done to make products more readily available for purchase in local markets? What improvements can be made in backing up product merchandising and advertising programs with adequate deliveries and service? Obviously, questions like these are affected by cost considerations, but as marketing objectives they deserve individual attention.

In analyzing the capacity of a distribution system to produce sales, executives will do well to examine three key characteristics:

1. *Location.* It has been estimated, for example, that from 5 distribution points a company can reach 33% of the U.S. consumer market within a day; while from 25 warehouse locations, 80% can be reached in one day.

2. *Inventories.* Judging from my own and associates' experience, approximately 80% more inventory is needed in a typical business to fill 95% of the customers' orders out of stock than to fill only 80%.

3. *Responsiveness.* The ability of a system to transmit needs back to the supplying plant and get material needed into the field determines how quickly the busines can shift with changes in customer preferences to meet demand with minimum investment and cost.

### REVOLUTION IN TECHNOLOGY

The pressures on distribution methods have led to exciting new technological advances for getting goods to the user at lower cost to the company—with less labor and materials expended and less capital tied up in inventories and facilities. When these advances are introduced in proper balance, the distribution process can better meet the needs of the consumer. Major technological changes are now taking place in transportation, information handling, and material handling. Let us examine each of them in turn.

### COSTS VS. TRANSPORT TIME

Transportation thinking has been dominated too long by preoccupation with the direct traffic bill. Too much attention has been paid to transport cost per ton-mile and not enough to the contribution transportation makes to the effectiveness of the distribution system as a whole.

Railroad rate structures are to an outsider an eye-opening illustration of what can happen when a transportation system is put under the cost-per-ton-mile pressure for too long. Rail rate structures, despite frequent attempts to introduce some rationale, have degenerated into an unbelievable hodgepodge of unrealistic and uneconomic rate compromises as the roads have succumbed to the pressure of giving each shipper the lowest cost per ton-mile, often at the expense of service. While improvements in equipment, such as the introduction of the diesel locomotive, have led to greater efficiency on the track, in some cases at least the longer trains and increased classification problems that have resulted have meant little or no net increase in over-all distribution efficiency. The gap between traffic and marketing thinking is painfully evident in many companies' distribution methods; little has been done to relate transportation methods and service to the objectives of the distribution system in support of marketing efforts.

Transportation costs are important indeed, but they are only part of the story. For example, think of the value of materials in transit:

Data collected on sample shipments in various parts of the country indicate that material may spend one to two weeks in transit and that the capital value of assets tied up in the transportation system may, depending on the pressure for capital, add as much as 1% to the economic cost of the goods.

Service, or reliability of the transport system, is also important. Goods must get to the user promptly and reliably, to permit him to operate systematically with low inventories.

The direct and indirect costs of damage in transport are another large item in the traffic bill that at times gets overlooked in the pressure for low cost per ton-mile.

Clearly, transport time is one of the key determinants of the efficiency of the distribution system. Its impact is not vivid or dramatic, and executives do not always appreciate what a difference it makes, but in a great many companies it is a significant factor in financing. To take a simple illustration:

Suppose that in a company doing an annual business of $100 million, time in transit is reduced from 14 days to 2. Time between reorders is 14 days, communication and processing time is 4 days, and field stocks average $12.5 million. In such a situation the reduction in transit time might well lead to a reduction in distribution inventory investment of $6 million, made up of: (1) a reduction of $3.3 million in transit, i.e., 12 days' sales; (2) a reduction of $2.7 million in inventories required to protect customer service resulting from a faster, more flexible distribution system response.

### SPEEDING UP SERVICE

Changes in transportation leading to improved opportunities in distribution have been truly revolutionary since World War II. Major superhighway

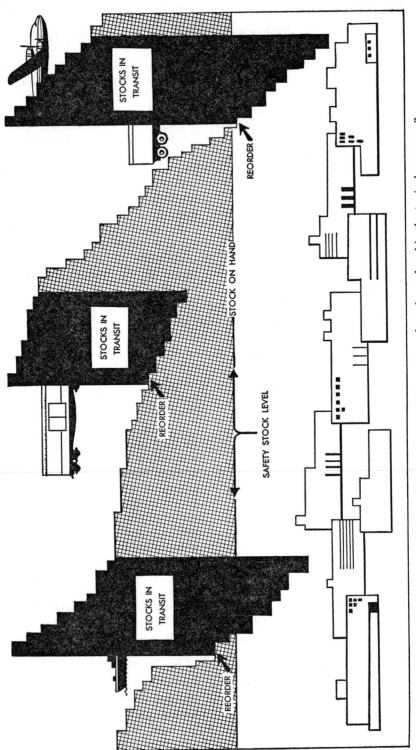

EXHIBIT III. What is the characteristic inventory pattern of stocks on hand in the typical company?

systems have been built, truck speeds have increased substantially and so have trailer capacities. The growth in the use of trucking for industrial distribution is now well known. The stimulus from subsidies is only part of the story; trucks have been able to compete at characteristically higher ton-mile costs because they have offered speed, reliability, and flexibility to shippers.

Without doubt, railroads are responding to this challenge. A recent survey showed that almost all Class I railroads are offering some form of piggyback or expedited motor-carrier service. At least some railroads are showing new merchandising awareness in concentrating on customer service. Whether the industry will be able, in the face of inherent limitations, to reverse the decline in its share of manufacturers' freight business is still an open question.

Air freight represents a challenge to both rail and over-the-road haulers. Today most industry executives still tend to view air freight as a luxury, as a service available for "orchids and emergencies." However, the trend in air freight rates has been sharply downward in recent years. With new planes coming into service, even further reductions can be projected—down to 8 cents to 12 cents a ton-mile from present-day rates of approximately 22 cents. Much depends on the success of efforts to develop aircraft equipped for freight handling and for flexible operation under a wide range of conditions (for example, modest runway lengths), and to build up the ground service needed to match air-handling speeds so as to avoid the danger faced by the railroads—the collapse of service as a result of concentration on mass, low-cost, terminal-to-terminal movement.

### IMPACT OF NEW METHODS

What is the significance of the ferment in transportation methods? For one thing,

improvement in local truck service opens up opportunities to serve wide-flung markets through fewer and larger distribution points. With larger distribution centers, the chance that mechanized material handling and storage systems will pay off is enhanced, and inventory requirements are reduced through consolidation.

To suggest the size of the opportunity, one analysis with which I am familiar showed that cutting the number of field distribution points for a national product line from 50 to 25 would increase total transport costs 7% but cut inventories 20% and cut *total* physical distribution costs 8% (the latter representing roughly a 1% cut in the total cost of delivered product). This was accomplished at the cost of serving a few small markets— about 5% of the total—with second-day instead of first-day delivery.

Rapid truck or air service increases the feasibility of relying on shipments from a few central points to back up service. Here are two ways in which this can be employed:

(1) The many low-volume items in the typical product line, the items on which local storage and handling costs outweigh the penalty costs of expedited shipment, can be held centrally and moved to the market where they are needed. For example, the bottom 50% of the product line, which as EXHIBIT II shows often accounts for only 4% of sales, may require 25% or more of the warehousing costs and inventory capital charges. Turnover of the stocks of these items is often only one eighth that of the high-volume half of the line. In a *relatively* high number of cases, special shipments could be made at a cost well below that of storing the items at local distribution centers.

(2) If there are substantial reserve stocks designed to protect customer service located in the field, it is possible to pare them down in the knowledge

that additional supplies can be moved in promptly to meet sudden customer demands.

In a typical distribution system a large share of the inventory—as much as 90%—is carried to protect delivery service to customers in the face of fluctuating demand and system delays. This safety stock is most likely to be used at the end of the reorder cycle, when stocks hit their low point before new receipts. EXHIBIT III illustrates a common situation, with safety stocks being partly depleted at intervals just before a new shipment arrives. During the period of the first reorder cycles, however, stocks will not be touched at all; this is the case before the second reorder in the illustration (middle of the chart) comes in. Note that inventory in transit represents a fairly significant proportion of the whole.

How much of safety stocks is actually used depends on the reorder system and level of service maintained. Typically, the last 10% may be needed only once or twice a year—a turnover rate roughly one sixth the average; and the last 30% may be needed only two to four times a year. Warehouses and inventory carrying charges on this portion of inventory, then, may easily run to 10%–20% of the sales they make possible.

There is an opportunity in many companies for management to cut material held in the field and back up customer service through regularized high-speed delivery service. This possibility will deserve increasing attention from management as the costs of high-speed transport, communication, and data processing drop.

### INFORMATION PROCESSING

Revolutionary data-processing methods were noisily battering at established business methods some six or seven years ago, but the impact was more in noise generated than in accomplishment. Now that a lot of the superficial excitement has died away, however, a broad and solid structure of accomplishment in modern data-processing techniques is quietly being built.

For one thing, computers seem to have become much more broadly accepted than anticipated. When the earliest internally programed machines were announced, computer manufacturers' optimistic estimates were in the dozens. Today the number of machines installed or in the process of installation is in the thousands. In support of computing or processing facilities, great improvements are taking place in communications systems, especially systems designed to feed into or out of computers. In distribution management, fast, reliable communication is equally as important as fast, reliable processing.

The use being made of modern information-processing equipment in distribution is just as significant as its broad market acceptance. For instance, machines are being used to maintain local inventory balances, forecast near-term demand, employ forecasts and inventory balances as inputs in calculating item orders, prepare tentative purchase orders, allocate item balances among stock points, and draw up production schedules and work force requirements. These are not mere compiling and accounting functions, nor is it fair to call them "decision making." In these functions, the machine sytems are interpreting rules or procedures to work out the decisions implicit in them in light of the facts of the situation. In other words, the equipment is doing what we would like intelligent clerks to do: diligently following policy and weighing costs to arrive at day-to-day actions.

The forecasting function in particular

deserves special attention. I refer not to the longer term economic forecasts, annual business forecasts, or even shorter term (e.g., quarterly) business predictions, but to short-term forecasts of sales, item by item, over the replenishment lead time. These forecasts are made implicitly or explicitly in every inventory control system. In most companies they are left up to the individual stock clerk or inventory controller to make as best he can, usually with little or no training or guides. Management will spend hundreds of hours of industrial engineering time simplifying or improving a job method here and there to take a few pennies out of labor cost. Yet the stock clerk making inventory control forecasts may, through his control over product distribution and assets tied up in inventories, be costing his company many pennies indeed.

Many people still argue that one cannot forecast routinely because intuition and background knowledge count too heavily. They fail to recognize that objective procedures for short-term prediction of item sales have the same merits as, say, routing and tooling lists in a shop. Experience leaves little doubt that great gains can be made by substituting powerful systematic methods for casual or unrecognized ones.[1]

CHANGES IN MATERIAL HANDLING

Mechanization is slowly spreading from the making of things to their handling in distribution. For instance:

One company in the clothing industry has installed a new data-processing system first to handle sales orders and then inventory control and production-scheduling systems. At the same time, it has been developing a bin-and-conveyer system which will permit economical mechanization of order-filling

[1] See Robert G. Brown, "Less Risk in Inventory Estimates," HBR July–August 1959, p. 104.

activities. The goal toward which both of these efforts are directed is a unified system in which the customer order not only serves as an input in automatic order handling but will also, after suitable internal mechanical processing, activate the warehouse system to select and consolidate the customer's order. This customer order data will also be processed internally for inventory management and production planning purposes.

How will such changes in warehousing and materials handling influence the planning of distribution systems? The effects will take at least three forms:

1. *Integration of systems for (a) material storage and transport and (b) information handling*—This development should create opportunities for significant "automation" of the distribution function and for reduction of manual drudgery. Ultimate full-scale mechanization of materials handling will not only require redesign of warehouse and transport facilities, but will have an impact on design of products and packages as well.

2. *Pressure to reduce the number of distribution points or warehouses*—Mechanized warehouses cost money. One way to improve the efficiency of capital utilization is of course to increase throughput.

3. *Pressure to concentrate ownership of warehousing facilities*—Mechanization takes capital. This factor will be another force behind the tendency for manufacture, distribution, and maintenance service to become integrated under one ownership roof.

## GETTING STARTED

Some managers view the opportunities presented by changes in distribution technology with about the same air with which a bear views a porcupine: the possibilities look interesting, but where can you start to get your teeth in? Improvements in distribution efficiency cost money. Higher speed, more flexible transport generally costs more per ton-mile. Mechanized warehousing systems or material-handling systems are not cheap. The cost of working out, installing, and testing new information-processing systems may make direct clerical cost savings look like a rather thin return on investment. In fact, direct payoffs from distribution changes (e.g., modified transport methods leading to a direct cut in transport costs) may often be small or nonexistent. The payoffs, often handsome ones, are more likely to be indirect, coming about from "tradeoffs" such as paying a higher transport bill to save material investment, putting in warehouse investment to cut over-all shipping costs, and so on.

Because tradeoffs so often are involved, it is not always easy for management to get an aggressive, functionally operated group of people to think *through* the problems. It is not easy for men in production, sales, warehousing, traffic, merchandising, and accounting to grasp other functions' needs or express their own needs in terms which make the advantages of tradeoff and balance clear. Many times the distribution *system* has been run too long as a collection of more or less independent *functions*. Any changes, any tradeoffs to get the system into better, more economical balance, any modifications to take advantage in the whole system of new technical developments— these are bound to be disruptive and to some extent resisted.

The difficulties in facing up to a searching look at the distribution system are not confined to the individual functions concerned. Some of the toughest

questions arise at the general management level. For example:

What degree of sales service is the system to provide? How far will the firm go to meet customers' service desires? What standards are to be used to judge investment in facilities and inventory so that it can be weighed against any cost savings that are made possible?

What policy will the company take toward ownership and operation of the distribution, transport, warehousing, and information-processing facilities? Will the company operate its own facilities, lease them, contract for services, or rely on independent businesses to perform some or all of the necessary distribution system functions?

What is the company's policy toward employment stabilization? To what extent is the company prepared to pay higher distribution costs to absorb demand variations and to level employment?

APPROACH TO THE ISSUES

Grappling with all of these problems is like untangling a tangled skein of yarn. Each decision has an impact on other choices and for this reason is hard to pin down. The distribution problem is a system problem, and it must be looked at as such. If it is examined in total and if the experience and methods available for studying it are used, the issues just mentioned can be resolved in an orderly, mutually compatible way.

In my experience, three key conditions have, when present, made for a sound distribution system study and an effective implementation program:

(1) Recognition by company management that improving distribution means examining the full physical distribution system.

(2) Use of quantitative systems analysis or operations research methods to show clearly the nature of tradeoffs and the relation between system operation and company policies.

(3) Cooperative work by men knowledgeable in sales and marketing, transportation, materials handling, materials control, and information handling.

In the following sections we shall see the need for these conditions asserting itself again and again as we go through the steps of making a good distribution study.

## MAKING THE STUDY

How should a distribution system study be made? What principal steps should be taken? As far as I know, there is no formula for the approach. The relative emphasis put on different phases of the study can vary. as can also the degree of detail; the order of analysis can be changed; and so on. But there are important steps to take at some point in any study, and I shall discuss them in logical order.

1. *Data on the company's markets should be organized in a helpful way.*

The distribution system study starts with a study of customers. This does not need to be a field interview program; to a large extent what is required is the organization of market facts which are available. Occasionally, a moderate amount of skilled field interview work may be desirable to obtain customers' estimates of service requirements and their comparison of the company with its competition.

A great deal of useful information can be obtained by analysis of sales data.

Here are some of the key questions of interest:

Are we servicing several fundamentally different markets through different distribution channels? Are these markets located differently? Do they buy in different patterns, in different quantities, and with different service and stock availability requirements?

How are our sales distributed among customers? We have found that the top 10% of a company's customers characteristically account for from 60% to 80% or even more of its business.

Do the same customers tend to buy our high-volume items as well as slow-moving items? The answer to this question has an important bearing on how the slow-moving items, for which distribution and sales service costs are often relatively high, should be handled. Few companies seem to have really examined this problem, though strong opinions on it exist in most.

2. *Statistical analyses of product characteristics should be made, with special attention to the nature of sales fluctuations.*

Sometimes the facts about products can be established fairly readily. An example is the susceptibility of items in the line to spoilage or damage. The degree to which sales volume is concentrated among a few fast-moving items (as illustrated in Exhibit II can often be ascertained rather quickly, too. But data of this kind do not tell us nearly enough. Statistical analysis is needed to establish certain key sales characteristics of the product line, all related to the *variability* of item sales. The significance of variability must be emphasized. Business managers are used to thinking in terms of averages or average rates, but the answers to many important questions affecting

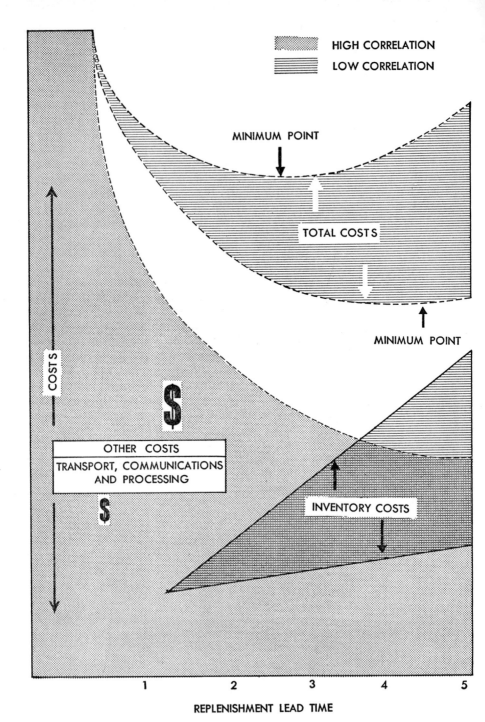

distribution system design depend on the characteristics of short-term sales variations about the average.

Most items exhibit unexpected day-to-day variations in sales about the average or expected level. In some cases the fluctuations are extremely wide and short-term in character; in other cases they are quite steady and predictable. The statistical characteristics of these variations determine in a very significant way how a distribution system will work and how it should be designed to operate economically.

3. *In analyzing sales variations, special attention should be paid to size, time, area, and volatility.*

Executives interested in the practical implications of short-term sales variations might focus on the following questions:

How big are the ups and downs? The magnitude of sales variations *over the replenishment lead time* will determine how large the inventory of an item must be to maintain a desired level of delivery service. The amount of an item on hand at a field point or on order must always equal the maximum reasonable demand over the lead time. Thus, the bigger the sales fluctuations, the more inventory of an item must be carried in the distribution system— at local warehouses, at the factory— to provide a given level of delivery service.

Are the variations correlated from one time period to the next? If one day's sales are above or below average, are the chances considerably better than 50-50 that the next day's sales will be above or below average, too? If sales are highly correlated from one week to the next, or from one month to the next, this means that the range of accumulated variation over the replenishment lead time increases nearly

in proportion to the lead time itself. Doubling the warehouse lead time would nearly double the range of sales variations and the inventory requirements, while cutting the lead time in half would cut inventory requirements nearly in proportion. If sales are not correlated from one period to the next, chance variations tend to offset to some degree; doubling the lead time would increase inventory requirements only 40%–50%, while cutting it in half would cut inventories 30% or so.

High correlation in sales puts a premium on cutting lead times to make the distribution system react faster, perhaps through more expensive but higher speed transport, communications, and sales-information processing. By contrast, lower correlation means it may be more economical to let lead times lengthen and save expense in information handling and transport at the cost of somewhat higher inventories. EXHIBIT IV illustrates all this graphically for a hypothetical firm:

The dotted line represents transport, handling, and data-processing costs, tending to fall as a longer lead time permits less frequent reordering and slower, less expensive methods of shipment. The solid lines represent unit inventory costs, increasing nearly in proportion to lead time in the case of high sales correlation (dashed line) and at a slower rate in the case of low correlation (black dashed line). The higher the correlation, the further the point of minimum total cost is shifted toward the left—that is toward a shorter lead time—even in the face of higher transport, handling, and processing costs.

Are sales variations correlated between areas or markets? Is an unexpected increase in an item's sales in, say, the Pittsburgh area likely to co-incide with an increase in Cleveland, or are variations unrelated from one market to another? Some causes of expected sales variations may affect a wide geographic region (e.g., weather, rumors); others may be related entirely to local conditions (e.g., individual customers' plans).

The degree of cross-correlation in chance sales variations occurring in different markets has a significant influence on warehouse location decisions. For example, if the cross-correlation is low, so that chance variations in sales in one market tend to offset those in another, there is a potentially substantial economy in consolidating warehouses, in having fewer distribution points to serve the same total market. But if the cross-correlation is high, little would be saved to offset possibly greater transportation costs.

How do sales variations compare among items? Are sales of high-volume items relatively more stable than sales of low-volume items? Generally (but not always), one finds evidence that the higher the sales volume of an item, the more stable will be sales, relatively speaking. Differences in the sales volatility of products influence distribution system choices. The more changeable the sales of an item, other things being equal, the better the chances that centralized stocking in regional distribution centers or plants will be advantageous.

4. *Inventory functions should be examined and related to other company needs.*

Characteristically inventories are made up of: (a) stock in transit; (b) supplies arising from periodic shipments; (c) reserves carried to protect service in the face of unusual demand (safety stock). In some businesses, inventories are also carried to accommodate seasonal sales patterns and to permit a smoothed load to be put on manufacturing. These inventory functions and methods for analyzing have already been discussed in HBR[2] and there is no need to outline them again here. Suffice it to say that one important job in a distribution study is to identify the functions actually served by inventories and to characterize the factors—e.g., transport times, reordering principles used, and service requirements —that are responsible for existing inventory levels and costs.

5. *The costs of warehouse storage and handling, traffic or freight, and clerical procedures should be determined.*

Many of these costs are difficult to obtain from normal company accounting records or engineering studies; direct unit costs often just are not maintained in these records. However, statistical analyses of operating cost records can often serve quite adequately.

Warehouse costs are as good an illustration as any of the approach I have in mind. Included here are:

a. *The costs of holding inventory—* These are generally related to the average or maximum inventory level in a distribution center and include space rent (including maintenance and janitor services, heat, and so on) and inventory costs (taxes, obsolescence and spoilage, and especially the cost of capital tied up in inventory). In our experience, careful study of the storage bill typically yields costs of 20%–35% per year on the capital value of the inventory, depending on the financial resources and policies of the company.

² See John F. Magee, "Guides to Inventory Policy: Part I. Functions and Lot Size," January–February 1956, p. 49; "Part II. Problems of Uncertainty," March–April 1956, p. 103; "Part III. Anticipating Future Needs," May–June 1956, p. 57; and Robert G. Brown, op. cit. See also John F. Magee, *Production Planning and Inventory* (New York, McGraw-Hill Book Company, Inc., 1958) and Robert G. Brown, *Statistical Forecasting for Inventory Control* (New York, McGraw-Hill Book Company, Inc., 1959).

b. *The costs of handling*—These include the costs of physically moving material into and out of storage or through terminal marshaling areas.

What is wanted here are cost factors which can be used to calculate the warehousing and handling costs under different system plans. These factors usually take the form of:

A fixed charge per warehouse per year × number of warehouses (the fixed charge is generally $5,000–$10,000 per warehouse per year, depending on the character of space).

Warehousing cost per year per unit in inventory × average inventory in the system.

Handling cost per year per unit through the warehouse.

These cost factors can be built up from an engineering study or derived from statistical analysis of existing cost data. They will, of course, differ for different types of facilities and operating methods. For example, a mechanized warehouse operation will of course have a quite different order of costs from a nonmechanized operation.

Clerical cost factors for alternate operating systems can be derived in similar fashion. Transport costs must also be collected, usually in the form of specimen rates collated with shipment volumes for alternate transport methods. Such possibilities as in-transit privileges, "marriage" of shipments, and forwarding schemes should be reviewed.

6. *Management should analyze alternative distribution plans on paper.*

The effect of alternative numbers of warehouses, changed locations, different transport methods, and different response times should be tested, using the methods of inventory analysis and programming techniques. Existing manufacturing capacities and locations may be used as a starting point. Alternatively—or as a second step in the analysis—the effect of changes in manufacturing facilities, in capacities, or in the product assigned to individual plants can be tested.

The first broad system studies are used to see where the biggest payoffs or traps may be. On paper, it is possible to make some arbitrary changes in lead times, warehouse locations, plant capacities, flexibility, and so on to see what the gross impact on distribution costs will be and thus whether detailed implementation studies are justified. It is important that the system study be based on current demand conditions, such as gross volume, product mix, and regional balance, as well as demand conditions projected roughly five to ten years ahead.

The facilities analysis is a step-by-step process. As the studies proceed, they will indicate potentially useful modifications in the distribution system. For example, a high concentration of sales among a few customers may indicate the need for special distribution plans, or the degree of concentration among products and the statistical characteristics of demand will suggest the need for regional stocking, changed warehouse numbers or locations, or similar alternatives. Again, an inventory study may indicate payoff possibilities in reducing lead times, in modifying service standards, or in introducing new, more flexible transport and handling methods.

Generally, as a result of broad analyses of facilities and operations, special studies will be indicated. Such studies as these may be in order:

Detailed analysis of the information-processing methods and costs to (a) take advantage of advancing technology to improve forecasting and control and (b) cut replenishment lead times.

Investigation of the costs of employment variations and manufacturing changes. Additional inventory—

or changes in production technology— may be justified to minimize these costs. If so, however, the additions or changes should be clearly recognized; "manufacturing cost" is too often a lame excuse for careless, inefficient management of materials in distribution.

Study of product redesign or regrouping, especially where the product line may have evolved without much thought having been given to logistics concepts.

Analysis of special ordering procedures, stock locations, and transport methods for handling low-volume items.

## ORGANIZATION PLANS

Distribution system management poses some puzzling organization problems to the typical, functionally organized firm. Distribution is not a sales function; it is not traffic management; it is not a manufacturing responsibility. It is an aspect of *all* of these functions. At the same time, the effectiveness of its managers will determine the conditions under which men in the individual functions must work.

Most companies prefer not to put all aspects of distribution management— sales order processing and analysis, field stock control, warehouses, traffic, production control—under one organizational unit, but to divide responsibility among several interested units. Such a division leads, however, to difficulty principally because of failure to (a) recognize the need for specific coordinated distribution systems planning, (b) specify planning and control responsibilities, and (c) set up performance measures consistent with over-all system efficiency and with assigned responsibilities.

In revising an organization to meet current needs and in keeping it up to date, executives should try to have five questions uppermost in their minds:

1. What are the necessary planning steps, policy decisions, and operating decisions to be made?
2. Who is the right person to make each of the decisions?
3. What information does he need, and how can he get it most expeditiously?
4. Does each person know how to recognize an emergency calling for nonroutine action? Does he know how to resolve it?
5. What performance measures reflect what is expected of each person in terms of the operation of the whole system?

## CONCLUSION

To sum up, a number of pressures have piled up on today's distribution systems. As manufacturing efficiency has increased and product cost has come down, costs have grown. Physical distribution costs are a significant share of these.

Business in many fields is becoming increasingly competitive, with competition taking new forms, including availability of goods and reliability of delivery. Product changes are forcing new pressures on the distribution system— more items to carry, faster obsolescence, lower unit sales and inventory turnover. In particular, changes in merchandising practices, such as the introduction of style as a merchandising weapon, have significantly complicated the distribution problem. Pressures for improvement in logistics also include internal forces—for example, the need to stabilize production and insulate production levels from short-term fluctuations in sales.

In the face of these trends, a number

of revolutionary changes have taken place. Substantial improvements have come about in essentially all forms of transportation methods. Tremendous strides forward have been made in information-handling methods, including schemes for assimilating and processing data dealing with product demand and with the need for replenishment. Materials-handling methods, ranging from mechanized stock keeping to extensions of the pallet concept to eliminate item-by-item handling, have been gaining acceptance. Finally, and perhaps as important as improvement in physical facilities and concepts, there has been progress in ways of looking at the logistics problem and at methods for analyzing distribution systems.

### LONG-RUN IMPLICATIONS

So far, we have seen farsighted companies taking advantage of the changes I have described by redesigning their distribution systems to cut costs and increase the support given to sales programs. The next step is now beginning to be felt—the insinuation of distribution concepts into certain aspects of long-term planning ad capital budgeting, especially the analysis of facility requirements, the location of distribution points, and the determination of financial requirements to support distribution.

Of course, we must avoid the trap of thinking that all management problems will be resolved in terms of efficient distribution. Nevertheless, the long-range impact of distribution-system thinking on production, on product design, and on manufacturing location may be substantial. Perhaps one of the most significant changes will be in concepts of organization, in the assignment of functions and responsibilities. Efficient physical distribution poses a challenge to business in integrating what is essentially a system

approach with the functional approaches that hitherto have tended to govern business organization planning.

In the long run, at least two possible directions are open for making a wide variety of products available in local markets. On the one hand, manufacturers can move toward centralized manufacture, with the specialty or small-volume items being made in enough volume to permit reasonable manufacturing economy and then being moved rapidly, perhaps by air freight, to the local markets as needed. On the other hand, management can try to achieve diversity through superficial differences built into a few basic product lines. Low-cost mass transport methods, perhaps rail freight, can be used to move parts and components from centralized manufacturing points with heavy equipment into widespread local assembly or modification plants. At the local points, the final touches can be put on the product to meet customer demand.

One thing seems sure: the choice of distribution system each company makes will have a significant impact on product design, plant investment, and organization. Industrial logistics and trends in logistics technology will receive increasing attention from business, along with markets, capital resources, and product development, in the formulation of corporate plans for the decade ahead.

## QUESTIONS

1. The need for progress in distribution is a product of several trends. Explain.
2. What recent changes in transportation have led to improved opportunities in distribution?
3. How should a distribution system study be made?
4. What organizational problems does distribution system management pose?

## BIBLIOGRAPHY FOR CHAPTER VII

ARTICLES:

Edelman, Franz, "Accounting and Operations Research – Example of a Problem in Marketing Channels," *N.A.A. Bulletin,* Vol. XLI, No. 6 (February 1960), pp. 27–36.

Evans, J. K., "When and How Should You Sell Through Distributors," *Industrial Marketing,* Vol. 44, No. 3 (March 1959), pp. 41–44.

"Integrating Your Transportation for Profits," *Duns Review & Modern Industry,* Vol. 73, No. 6 (June 1959), pp. 60–66.

Sherman, B., "Vending Industry's Fabulous Economic Future," *Commercial & Financial Chronicle,* Vol. 192, No. 5984 (September 8, 1960), p. 12.

Silberman, Charles E., "The Discounters Choose Their Weapons," *Fortune,* Vol. LXI, No. 5 (May 1962), pp. 118–20 and 18–188.

Weiss, E. B., "Vending Machine Era Now Begins," *Advertising Age,* Vol. 31, No. 24 (June 13, 1960), p. 96.


BOOKS:

Beckman, Theodore N., and Davidson, William R., *Marketing.* New York: Ronald, 1962. Parts III and IV.

Bursk, Edward C., *Text and Cases in Marketing: A Scientific Approach.* Englewood Cliffs, N.J.: Prentice-Hall, 1962. Section Four.

Buskirk, Richard H., *Principles of Marketing.* New York: Holt, Rinehart and Winston, 1961. Chapters 13, 14, and 15.

Converse, Paul D., Huegy, Harvey W., and Mitchell, Robert V., *Elements of Marketing.* Englewood Cliffs, N.J.: Prentice-Hall, 1958. Chapters 10, 11, 14–16.

Davis, Kenneth R., *Marketing Management.* New York: Ronald, 1961. Chapter 4.

Faville, David E., *Selected Cases in Marketing Management.* Englewood Cliffs, N.J.: Prentice-Hall, 1961. Section IV.

Lazo, Hector, and Corbin, Arnold, *Management in Marketing.* New York: McGraw-Hill, 1961.

Levitt, Theodore, *Innovation in Marketing: New Perspectives for Profit and Growth.* New York: McGraw-Hill, 1962.

Mauser, Ferdinand F., *Modern Marketing Management: An Integrated Approach.* New York: McGraw-Hill, 1961. Part VI.

McCarthy, E. Jerome, *Basic Marketing: A Managerial Approach.* Homewood, Ill.: Irwin, 1960. Section D.

Phillips, Charles F., and Duncan, Delbert J., *Marketing: Principles and Methods.* Homewood, Ill.: Irwin, 1962. Parts III and IV.

Smykay, Edward W., Bowersox, Donald J., and Mossman, F., *Physical Distribution in Management.* New York: Macmillan, 1961.

Tousley, Rayburn, Clark, Eugene, and Clark, Fred, *Principles of Marketing.* New York: Macmillan, 1962. Parts III and IV.

Westfall, Ralph, and Boyd, Harper W., *Cases in Marketing Management.* Homewood, Ill.: Irwin, 1961. Chapters 31–39.

# VIII. Sales Promotion

*IT IS LOGICAL* to think of sales promotion as including those marketing activities that contribute directly or indirectly to the promotion of profitable sales. Thought of this way, sales promotion becomes an inclusive term which embraces publicity, advertising, personal selling, and point of sale promotion.

While it has not been emphasized in marketing literature, publicity can be an important factor in building a favorable image for the firm and its merchandise. In the modern marketing department the publicity function is placed in the public relations section. Publicity considerations frequently come first in the planning and timing of a promotional campaign since a substantial amount of company news concerns its new products. To have news value, the press story must precede the advertising or appear simultaneously with it. Besides product publicity, there are numerous other company activities that are newsworthy, and it is the task of the public relations staff to be alert to the possibilities and keep the communications media informed through timely press releases.

With about 385,000 active brand names competing for shelf space in retail stores today, the individual manufacturer, even if in business for a long time, finds it difficult to establish and maintain the reputation of his products. The traditional way the large firm has sought to gain consumer recognition, acceptance, and perhaps even preference has been through national and retail advertising. But with so many hundreds of nationally advertised brands fighting for the consumer's attention, a manufacturer can spend huge sums on national advertising and not be sure of what effect, if any, it has on his sales. In self-defense he may continue these huge outlays, but relies heavily on point of sale promotion and retail advertising to sell his merchandise to consumers.

While the consumer is frequently confused by the claims of superiority of so many different competing, nationally advertised brands, he is coming more and more to rely on the retail advertising of reputable local merchants. Today a large number of consumers look to the advertising of their favorite stores for guidance in the selection of outstanding values. Salesmen fight for point of sale space at the retail level. The prestige of the firm, its reputation for quality with customers, and its price either help or hinder the salesman's efforts, as the store buyer looks at such tell-tale factors as turnover and profitability to guide his purchasing for his customers.

The firm that offers truly superior quality and service at attractive prices can also depend on gaining consumer acceptance and preference through the medium of word-of-mouth advertising. Today's mobile and gregarious consumers are quick to share their experiences, and in the final analysis it is this consumer power to recommend or veto that makes or breaks a promotion.

Aside from retail advertising, the value of much of national advertising is open to question. A substantial portion of such expenditures are purely a defensive reaction to competition. However, with the enormous capacity of the new computers to make an almost infinite number of calculations, a reliable measurement of the effectiveness of much of national advertising looms on the horizon as a distinct possibility.

For many products of equal quality, point of sale promotion is necessary. If effectively executed, point of sale merchandising coordinates advertising with personal selling. Among other things, it stimulates wholesale and retail sales personnel, and makes the promotional campaign more meaningful to shoppers through informative window and interior displays.

Gradually, the salesman's role has evolved away from the traditional function of high pressure. Today's professionally trained salesman has to play many different roles as he is confronted with a variety of complex situations. Among other things, he has to be a communicator of information, a problem solver, a planner, a public relations expert, and a trainer. In many lines of work, a salesman has to be a technical expert, a business consultant, and even a market analyst in the case of a media representative.

Personal selling is still the single most powerful, vendor-generated promotional force. It is expensive but an indispensable tool of sales promotion. Personal selling is a unique, hard-to-replace force in modern marketing because it makes possible two-way communication of ideas between a seller and buyer. It is the only form of sales promotion that can encourage and make immediate, on-the-spot use of responses from buyers.

# *48.* Promotion*

Albert W. Frey, President American Marketing Association and Professor of Marketing, Graduate School of Business, University of Pittsburgh

*Marketing management needs to find ways and means of making better decisions in the promotion area. The promotional mix generally includes publicity, advertising, personal selling and point of sale promotion.*

The purpose behind any study of the problems of promotion is to make improvements in the concepts and techniques of marketing available to the marketing manager so that he in turn may make better decisions. While a great deal of empirical data is available in the field of promotion, there is still much to be done, much to know. Our present knowledge is relatively meager.

Marketing management, for example, needs to find ways and means of making better decisions in the promotion area. Because not enough is known about how promotion decisions should be made, the degree of guess-work employed in this area today is far too great. Marketing men also know too little about how consumers arrive at *their* decisions, and how they will respond to any influence the marketing man may attempt to exert upon them. Basically, then, there is a strong need for better *executive* decisions made in the light of more extensive and more accurate knowledge of the factors that influence *consumers'* decisions.

* Reprinted from the First International Seminar on Marketing Management. Published as a Special Supplement to *Business Horizons*, School of Business, Indiana University, February 1961.
This article is prepared by Jean C. Halterman.

## DEFINITIONS

There may be considerable difference of opinion concerning what is to be included in each of the promotion activities: personal selling, advertising, sales promotion, and publicity. For purposes of this discussion, the following definitions are used:

*Personal selling* refers to the efforts of salesmen when they call on customers and prospective customers in order to induce purchases.

*Advertising* is the preparation of visual and oral messages and their dissemination through paid media for the purpose of making people aware of and favorably inclined toward a product, brand, service, institution, idea, or point of view.

*Sales promotion* is concerned with the creation, application, and dissemination of materials and techniques that supplement advertising and personal selling. Sales promotion makes use of direct mail, catalogues, house organs, trade shows, sales contests, premiums, samples, window displays, and other dealer aids. Its purpose is to increase the desire of salesmen, distributors, and dealers to sell a certain brand and to make consumers more eager

351

to buy that brand. Personal selling and advertising can go only so far in these decisions; sales promotion provides an extra stimulus.

*Publicity* is like advertising in some respects but differs in that it is used at the discretion of the media to which it is sent, media are not typically paid for using it, there are no established media rates for publicity, and the company or institution by which or for which it is released is often not identified with the message.

In short, personal selling tends to move the product through the distribution channels toward the consumer; advertising tends to move the consumer toward the product; and sales promotion and publicity facilitate both these activities.

The importance of definitions is not confined to placing workable delimitations on discussions of advertising, selling, and sales promotion. In budgeting, particularly, the business executive must be concerned with definitions, with what should be included as advertising, what as sales promotion, what as publicity, and what as public relations. For purposes of comparison, control, and executive management, then, definitions of the various promotion activities must be clearly stated.

## FUNCTIONAL INTEGRATION

Decisions in marketing deal with the ends and means, with strategy and tactics, and with the achievement of the right quantity and quality of each type of marketing effort. Strategy in the promotion area must be in tune with strategies in other areas—such as production and pricing—and the total strategy must consist of a profitable optimum combination of *all* marketing activities.

The offering to consumers is a com-bination of the product, package, brand, service, and price. This offering is implemented through the tools of promotion—personal selling, advertising, sales promotion, and publicity—and through decisions related to the marketing organization and policies such as decisions concerning distribution channels. Most of the factors in these areas can be controlled, at least in part, by the business firm. Yet the manager must be concerned also with additional factors of the environment, including the market and competition, over which he has no control at least in the short run.

While decisions have to be made concerning organization and policies—whether, for example, to sell to discount houses, or whether to use advertising as a component of the marketing mix—these occur less frequently than decisions in the promotion area. Decisions in this area must be made with regard to three broad categories of specific objectives: company, marketing, and advertising (or other elements of promotion). Within this framework, the basic, though not mutually exclusive, questions concerning the effective use of the promotion tools at reasonable cost are: (1) whether to use the tool (personal selling, advertising, sales promotion, publicity) at all, (2) how much to use it, (3) how to use it, (4) how to control its use, and (5) how to measure its effectiveness.

## QUESTIONS

1. Distinguish between publicity and advertising.
2. Distinguish between personal selling and sales promotion.
3. Distinguish between personal selling and advertising.
4. What are some of the factors that determine the amount of each of these activities in the promotional mix?

# 49. A Basic Guide for Developing Publicity*

Bernard E. Ury, Director Public Relations, Harshe-Rotman Inc.

*Methodical, painstaking planning, plus creative execution and careful follow-through are as essential in good publicity as they are in any other phase of corporate activity. Under the marketing concept publicity becomes a valuable marketing tool in major, medium-sized and smaller firms.*

What makes a good industrial publicity program tick? Where do the ideas come from? Just what should be publicized? How do you deal with so-called "trade secrets" that could be turned into good publicity?

If you have anything to do with industrial publicity, these are questions you must answer. Publicity has become a standard marketing tool of practically every major industrial company, and is rapidly being adopted by the medium-sized and smaller firms.

The big question today is not, "Shall we have publicity?" Rather, it is, "How do we get the most out of it?"

Our own experience in developing programs for small, medium and large corporations indicates that waiting for the big brainstorm to strike is the least effective way to develop publicity. Inspiration has its part, but perspiration is 90% of the program.

Methodical, painstaking planning, plus creative execution and careful follow-through are as essential in good publicity as they are in any other phase of corporate activity. If you want to make the most of your publicity activities, then the following suggestions may help.

* Reprinted from *Industrial Marketing*. Copyright 1959 by Advertising Publications Inc., 200 E. Illinois St., Chicago 11, Ill.

## ESTABLISH OBJECTIVES

If your management walked in and asked, "Just what are the objectives of our publicity activity?", could you answer the question? Or would you utter pious sentiments about "building the corporate image?"

If specific 1-2-3 objectives aren't forthcoming, sharpen your pencil, get out your note pad, and start thinking. A good starting point is the classic McGraw-Hill advertisement that appeared in 1958 and is still being quoted. You may remember it. It pictured a hard-boiled individual glaring straight at you and saying:

*"I don't know who you are.*
*I don't know your company.*
*I don't know your company's product.*
*I don't know what your company stands for.*
*I don't know your company's customers.*
*I don't know your company's record.*
*I don't know your company's reputation.*
*Now—what was it you wanted to sell me?"*

The well-rounded publicity program answers all of these questions, not just one or two at the expense of the others.

**353**

By and large, product publicity forms the bulk of most industrial publicity programs. By product publicity, we mean publicity focused on the product itself and its uses. This is good, but if the program is limited to this category, the company will miss out on other opportunities to build profits.

A company today sells more than a product or service. As a matter of fact, product differentiation is becoming less and less of a fact. The McGraw-Hill ad points out the other key factors that help determine the sale—the salesman himself, his company, its principles, its customers, its record and its reputation. These are every bit as important as the product, and they should not be neglected in the publicity program.

FIVE STEPS TO FOLLOW

If you want to make your publicity efforts truly productive for the entire company, not just the product alone, do the following:

1. Obtain a statement of management policy from your president. Certainly your objectives must be in line with the company's.

2. Study the annual reports issued by your company, plus any other materials which may contain expressions of policy. These will often add meaning and substance to the statement provided by your president.

3. Research all available marketing data from your sales and marketing departments. This is an especially important source of valuable product publicity. You must know what your best-selling products are, where the markets are, and where future potential lies.

4. Check your directors of manufacturing, engineering, personnel, and other key departments to learn what their objectives are. Very often you will find

common areas of interest. At the same time, you will establish the necessary basis for working with these people. Their help can be valuable to you.

5. Have your written objectives checked by all interested parties. This is one good way to get them on your team and to convince them that their help is essential.

## FIND KEY PUBLICITY AREAS

Like an iceberg, nine-tenths of a company's publicity potential is below the surface. You have to dig to find it. This is not easy. As a matter of fact, unless you have a reporter's "nose for news," you may not know a good publicity idea when you see it.

In this respect, it often helps—if you're a company public relations man—to call in a professional outsider to do this digging for you. Competent professionals, because publicity is their full-time job, can pay for themselves in the time they save you in locating fruitful publicity assets.

To do this job, our firm recently developed a six-part, 60-point checklist covering every conceivable corporate activity that might be a treasure trove of publicity. The essentials of the checklist can be boiled down as follows:

1. MANAGEMENT ACTIVITIES

Publicity about your management is an excellent way to give personality to your company and make it less of a machine. Industrial customers, like other humans, react most favorably to personal things. Identify your company with its management and you achieve corporate personality.

How do you do this? You can make sure that personnel changes and promotions are announced in the press. You can issue releases on important speeches and statements made by management, and you can suggest occasions when such statements might be issued. You can draft forecasts and industry opinions attributable to your executives.

Going further, you can build stories around management people as interesting personalities in their own right. Your president may be a flower grower, an amateur rancher, or have a prize stamp collection. Others on the management team may have accomplishments that make good local news copy. If your biographical file on your management is up to snuff, you can pick out personality topics that will win friends for your company.

In the same category are stories about your company's history and its future. Don't overlook any chance to publicize the fact that your company is growing, even though the growth may be only a 5,000-square-foot addition to the machine shop.

If yours is a publicly-held company, be sure the annual report as well as dividend actions, mergers and acquisitions are well publicized. Stockholders are among your most important publics. Favorable publicity about your company's progress is a powerful way of holding their good esteem.

## 2. PRODUCT PROMOTIONS

The lazy way is to issue a short blanket release when a new product is announced and then forget about it. The better way is to examine every facet of product use that can be turned into a story.

For example, your new product may have a host of different uses for different industrial areas. Your news story for each area should be different and pinpoint the specific use for that trade area. This same new product may involve design features that would be interesting to readers of design and engineering publications. Similarly, new materials may be used in the product which would make a good story for publications in the materials field.

Once a product is announced and in use, don't neglect it. There are many ways you can continue to reap valuable publicity for old products. Among the most powerful of these is the case history, the story that tells how your company's product or service is working for customers.

You can hunt for case histories through your sales representatives. Prepare a short bulletin for them requesting leads on product applications. Follow up by contacting the customer and obtaining the facts. Case histories are effective testimonials. In reprint form, they can be used by your sales force as customer literature and for direct mail. The same case histories can often be the basis of a good advertising campaign.

There are other ways you can publicize existing products. For instance, a new use may be uncovered. Recently an angle-finding device was introduced for machinists. Then a salesman happened to show it to an auto muffler installer. The device simplified the job of aligning the muffler. A story on this new use brought responses from muffler shops across the country.

Even if you don't have a specific use to report, you can point out untapped uses through publicity. Your engineers can help you with this. If the product is relatively new, the engineers can also help with an article telling how it should be used. Such stories are especially valuable if technique is important, as it is, for instance, in the plastics molding field.

Check with your sales department to see if any product-use trends are shaping up. Write to your company's suppliers, offering to supply them stories for their house organs and advertisements telling how *their* products are used in *your* products. Ask your service department to help you develop an article on how your products can be maintained.

Finally, don't overlook this very important area of product publicity: Giving your distributors and dealers local support. You can do this by providing them with fill-in type releases that they can offer to their local newspapers, quoting themselves as the source. For example:

Your company introduces a new drill press. First, you obtain appropriate national trade publicity. Now the presses begin moving to the field. To accompany them, you prepare releases for your distributors to use in announcing availability of the drill press locally. Your distributors will thank you for the support, and your sales curve will reflect your efforts.

### 3. SALES ACTIVITIES

Here is a sticky area which some managements will not open for discussion because they believe "it's no one's business what our sales activities are like." But it *is* someone's business—your salesmen's. Forceful publicity can be highly important in keeping morale high, and in building acceptance of salesmen by customers and prospects.

It is important to make sure that all sales appointments and promotions are announced both nationally to trade publications and locally to newspapers in areas where these events take place. It is important to publicize awards won by your sales people. If they attend a national sales conference, it is important to announce the fact in a home-town release.

Why is it important? Because your sales representative must sell himself as well as his company and product. The better known he is, the easier it is for him to sell.

National sales conferences offer publicity opportunities. One astute public re-

lations director took advantage of the fact that the 1958 recession was turning into a 1959 boom. When his company held a national sales meeting, he sent releases to the home-town papers of every man attending. These releases quoted the local man as reporting that the boom times were with us again, and reported on general company trends to back up the statement. Result: Effective local publicity that established each representative as a sales person who was also an authority on economic matters.

Has your company recently completed an effective sales campaign? Never mind if management won't release figures. The techniques you used are just as important to many trade publications, and can help establish your company as an aggressive promotion-minded firm.

Do you publicize your exhibits in trade shows and conventions? Do you seek to attract the local newspapers to visit your booth, and offer to set up an interesting shot for the paper? These are all legitimate publicity opportunities.

If your company has a sales training program, you can often build stories around it for trade magazines and even local newspapers. Such publicity is a pat on the back for those who attend the program. It also helps recruit sales candidates.

Speaking of sales activities, don't forget to make reprints of important publicity and send them out to your sales people. Keep them informed of what your publicity is doing for the company and for them. Reprints of product publicity are especially valuable as material to leave with prospects and as enclosures for direct mail.

### 4. MANUFACTURING AND ENGINEERING

Publicity of manufacturing and engineering know-how builds customer confidence and strengthens the quality story your company wants to tell. At the same time, this type of publicity builds the morale of supervisors and employes, and helps recruit technical personnel.

Here is a brief list of factory topics that you should check on for possible publicity value:

New tools, procedures, and processes.

Unusual manufacturing and testing steps.

Superlative operations (biggest, fastest, smallest, etc.)

Employes with unusual manufacturing jobs.

Speeches or papers to be given by technical personnel.

Honors awarded to technical personnel.

Technical personnel appointments and promotions.

Some of the best manufacturing and engineering publicity is obtained by making it a policy to invite trade editors to visit your plant. This is best done on an individual basis so that the editor, if he finds something worth writing about, can have it on an exclusive basis.

A common stumbling block in manufacturing and engineering publicity is the "trade secret"—the process, tool, or technique that management doesn't want competitors to know about. Sometimes these secrets are, indeed, secrets. But many times they are not. Competitors already know about them, and restrictions on publicizing them merely deprive the company of promotional ammunition.

This point was illustrated recently when a United States company opened a plant in Canada. The Canadian managers prohibited any publicity on the plant's facilities, even though these facilities were the same as those in the United States plant which had received wide publicity. When this inconsistency was pointed out, the Canadian managers agreed to a publicity program and were well pleased with the results.

It is up to you to spot inconsistencies in any secrecy policies your management may have. Where more good than harm can come from publicity, you should stress this point to management.

### 5. PERSONNEL ACTIVITIES

Although the primary value of publicizing personnel activities is internal, some aspects lend themselves to marketing concepts. For example, achievements in safety, waste prevention and cost-cutting can be publicized to establish the fact that your company is efficient. Retirements and service awards convey the idea that long-term craftsmen work at your company. Publicity of good labor relations can forestall doubts that your company can deliver as promised.

### 6. PUBLIC RELATIONS ACTIVITIES

More and more, business men are proclaiming that business must broaden its public responsibilities if it is to win public approval and combat socialistic trends. While business must make a profit to exist, progressive executives are emphasizing extra-curricular activities which help protect the right to make that profit.

That is why companies are entering into community activities, holding open houses, establishing grants and scholarships, and doing many other things in similar areas. Publicity attention given to these activities is essential if your company is to be credited for them.

## FOLLOW-THROUGH AND REPORTING

"What have you done for me lately?" is one way management expresses its desire to know what your industrial publicity program is accomplishing. Never take for granted that every story you prepare and place will be seen by top management, or that these executives know completely what you're doing. You must follow through and report to them.

By follow-through, we mean that every activity you undertake should be accounted for. You may not score perfectly on every story idea, but you should account for them all. Where you didn't score, try to find out the reason, so you can increase your publicity efficiency the next time.

Where you did score, make sure you have proof, such as a clipping or tear sheet, and interpret this proof in terms of its meaning to the company's objectives. This is an essential part of reporting.

Reporting to management is important for two reasons:

First, management has a right to know what you're doing. Informed executives will be more cooperative and act more intelligently in your behalf.

Second, regular reporting is the best way of keeping your program in line with company objectives. You must get "feedback" from management to gauge your success.

Just as there are two reasons for reporting, so are there two types that you should consider. One is the spot report on a major fast-breaking achievement, such as a full-length feature article in a major trade magazine. The other is a report-in-depth about your activities over a given period, such as a month, a quarter, or a year.

Spot reporting is valuable to fill in the gaps between formal reports made periodically. Reprints or Thermofax copies of major stories as they appear, circulated among top management and sent out to field sales force, are good to help dramatize what you're doing.

Formal periodic reports give you the opportunity to review your own work and prepare a document that will keep management sold on industrial publicity. This report is best prepared in written form, delivered orally, and then discussed with management.

These recommendations are a far cry from the sporadic hit-or-miss industrial publicity efforts that were characteristic some years ago and that still exist in isolated areas. They add up to a program every bit as methodical and productive as any other corporate activity. They make it possible for marketing to be fully integrated, and to be that much more profitable for the company.

## QUESTIONS

1. What different types of company activities can be publicized?
2. What type of the company forms the bulk of industrial publicity?
3. What is the principle criterion used by media to determine whether to publish a story sent in by the publicity department?
4. What five steps are recommended to make the publicity effort truly productive?

# 50. Publicity Alone Launches a New Product for GE*

Hudson S. Day, Manager Instrument Equipment Sales, Instrument Department, General Electric Co.

*The development of a significantly improved product is of major interest to potential customers and the news of its availability can be effectively and economically communicated via publicity releases to trade publications.*

A marketing man doesn't often get the chance to see exactly to what extent publicity can help promote a new product. The reason is obvious: publicity is normally a sidecar to space advertising and other promotional efforts, and its results are obscured in the total returns.

Thanks to a rather unusually handled new product campaign, however, we at General Electric's Instrument Dept. were able to get a good look at publicity's impact "in the raw." The results were striking. We drew two conclusions: (1) this arm of the marketing function can be a surprisingly efficient one, and (2) it's easier to net good press coverage than many think, provided the job is done right.

## AN "INDUSTRY FIRST"

The product was our now-well-known industrial mass flowmeter. Developed by GE in cooperation with Black, Sivalls & Bryson, a major manufacturer of equipment for the oil and gas industry, the flowmeter came through to marketing early in 1959 with an okay to shoot the works. However, production was not scheduled to begin until early 1960.

The true mass flowmeter is simply a device that measures the flow of liquid and gases directly in pounds. Other flowmeters used by industry measure volume. As any engineer knows, to convert volume readings to pounds means either time-consuming calculations or, in the case where these corrections are not made, frequent inaccurate readings. Our instrument eliminates these drawbacks.

We knew we had something of paramount interest to the natural gas, petrochemical, petroleum, chemical, steel, and many other industries. The problem now was to prepare the market.

## A MAJOR PROBLEM

There was one major problem complicating promotion; namely, we were essentially breaking news of a product that wouldn't be ready for production for almost a year.

This would rob impact from an all-out advertising splash. It just didn't seem practical to spend thousands of dollars on advertising which would have a bid-for-action of, "Please give us a call next year." We wanted to get the development story disseminated more economically another way.

And economically it had to be. As a

* Reprinted from *Industrial Marketing.* Copyright 1960 by Advertising Publications Inc., 200 E. Illinois St., Chicago 11, Ill.

GE department we sell a tremendous variety of instruments to many markets, and our promotional dollars, while liberal, have to be weighed carefully for their ability to produce sales. Because there weren't going to be any flowmeter sales in '59, we set economy as a major factor in our plan.

### UNORTHODOX

After a series of meetings with the department's ad manager, P. M. Johnson, we came up with a practical, if somewhat unorthodox, plan. In effect, we decided to spend nary a dollar on space advertising that year.

H. D. Hexamer, handling our press relations out of the GE Apparatus Sales Div. news bureau in Schenectady, N. Y., was to carry the brunt. It was his job to get us maximum coverage in the trade press.

For back-up, an eight-page bulletin was produced and ready by June. Stress was placed on internal promotion, and the department sales staff set about, via letter and personal meetings, to brief our field sales force—GE's Apparatus Sales Div.

Trade show activity was also a factor. Black, Sivalls & Bryson (which is also marketing the flowmeter under agreement with General Electric) introduced the product to the petroleum industry at the Tulsa oil show, and we sent personnel to help man the booth. In addition, both our firms featured the flowmeter in separate booths at the ISA instrument-automation show in Chicago.

Inherent in 1959 plans was the intention to hold off space schedules until the second quarter of 1960, when the flowmeter would be "on the shelf" and we would be ready and budgeted to launch a full-scale space campaign.

Publicity, trade shows, internal promotion and bulletin back-up—that was the entire scope of the program. Here's what resulted:

### RESULTS

Between June, 1959, and the end of the year, stories about the flowmeter ran in 70 trade publications. This was no arbitrary list; each magazine was directed to at least one major potential market. And the average story size was no mere new product blurb, but rather ten full column inches.

Publicity netted us over 1,500 direct customer inquiries; trade shows another 300. We are presently carrying on customer negotiations at maximum capacity, and there's no doubt at all as to where the vast majority of our leads came from.

So, we got good publicity. But more important, we saw dramatized some very germane points:

1. It pays to bring the press relations expert into your promotion planning meetings at an early date.

2. Bona fide news may get good press coverage on its own merits, but the *best* coverage takes experience, and careful planning.

3. (This may come as a surprise to some.) Just because you have something important to show the press, *you do not necessarily need a press conference.*

### NO PRESS PARTY

Original promotional plans, when GE news bureau publicist Hugh Hexamer came into the picture, called for a rather elaborate press conference schedule. We were toying with the idea of gathering trade press editors in New York just prior to the Tulsa oil show, giving them a thorough indoctrination on the flowmeter, then flying those who were interested to the show itself, where BS&B had the product on display.

Mr. Hexamer voiced a contrary view; namely, that the story of our product, its design, development and significance, could be completely told on paper. Why, then, go to the time and expense of a press conference? Editors, he volunteered, can find press parties time-consuming and expensive.

On these grounds we turned off the press conference idea and ended up with one simple, inexpensive publicity endeavor—a news release, fact sheet, and four photographs distributed to every trade publication serving potential flowmeter market areas.

It was from this alone that, during the last six months of 1959, our message reached a theoretical audience of nearly 8 million via the business press.

The fact that the release was successful stemmed from far more than just the revolutionary nature of the product. Behind it were:

A careful description of the flowmeter's development and design.

A discussion of its true significance, including a look at its wide application possibilities.

Good quality photographs showing the instrument and analyzing its internal make-up.

A careful compilation of all these into a package that would stimulate the interest of editors of every publication deemed useful.

Painstaking care in distribution, which involved an intimate knowledge of markets and a familiarity with both horizontal and vertical books reaching specifying influences within these areas.

An added twist was provided by Black, Sivalls & Bryson. Because of BS&B's renown throughout the oil and natural gas industries, it was mutually decided that it should take up the publicity reins among the trade publications serving these markets. The package BS&B distributed under its own letterhead ended up being the same as ours, but supplemented by several of its own photos showing the flowmeter in actual field application.

ADS FOR '60

Last year's story of flowmeter promotion is a story of publicity *without* space advertising, not *instead* of it. Regardless of other promotional plans, it is always our philosophy at General Electric to integrate publicity into a new product campagn regardless of the latter's direction.

This year, as part of our continuing campaign, we are running two-page announcement ads primarily in publications aimed at the petrochemical and steel industries. An extensive direct mail campaign will pinpoint management and key operating personnel within important market areas to further spotlight the flowmeter and its benefits. Trade show participation and internal sales-force promotion will continue at an accelerated pace.

But publicity is far from being spent; our first successful application has already been documented by a second news release that went out early this year. Signed articles and further application stories will follow.

"FLAGRANTLY OVERLOOKED"

Had we elected to advertise the flowmeter last year, publicity would have been used regardless. No doubt our returns, with the necessary integration, would not have been mtaerially different. Playback during 1959, to us, was simply a dramatic demonstration that publicity —without a doubt the most flagrantly overlooked tool in a sales manager's chest —is a vital arm of the marketing function.

It isn't necessarily within a sales manager's bailiwick to know how to produce good publicity. But he *should* know that with a thorough advance knowledge of the product and its markets, a publicist versed in his field can put a substantial boost into a new product campaign. Whatever the budget—$4,000 or $400,000 —bring the publicist into the fray. The production costs are dramatically low, and the words he can put in print will do much to build a favorable sales climate of awareness, interest and demand.

## QUESTIONS

1. In general, should the publicity on a new product precede, appear at the same time, or follow the advertising?
2. Why did management decide to initiate the promotion of the mass flowmeter through publicity alone?
3. What lessons were learned by the publicity department?

# 51. Sandage Defines the Role of Advertising, Predicts Its Greater Use to Attain Social Goals in Future*

C. H. Sandage, Head of the Department of Advertising, University of Illinois

*Advertising is both an instrument and an institution—so criticize it as an instrument, not as an institution, just as you would criticize schools or churches, but not education and religion. Basically the functions of advertising are to disseminate information, persuade, and educate.*

Several times in our recent history, advertising has been under attack by various groups and individuals. We are currently witnessing a renewal of such attack.

It is not my purpose now either to indicate the nature of criticism or to attempt to provide direct answers to the critics. Instead, an attempt will be made to look at advertising in somewhat of an abstract manner and consider some of

* Reprinted with permission from the May 15, 1961 issue of *Advertising Age.* Copyright 1961 by Advertising Publications Inc.

the functions that society has assigned to it.

Let us first make a clear distinction between advertising as an institution and advertising as an instrument. It may help in our understanding if we leave advertising for a moment and consider some well recognized institutions and the instruments that have been developed to perform the functions expected of those institutions.

The institution of religion is old and honored. It is supposed to perform many functions for society, the primary one being to serve the spiritual needs of man. To accomplish the functions that society expects religion to perform, certain instruments have been developed and individuals recruited to man and operate the instruments. In the case of the institution of religion, the instrument has generally been the church and the practitioner— the priest, minister, or rabbi.

We might also refer to the institution of education. Important functions here are to transmit to the present generation the knowledge of the past, to promote a continual search for truth, and to cultivate the mind of the individual. The instrument is the school and the practitioner the teacher.

## COMPARE EDUCATION, ADVERTISING

Few would criticize either religion or education at the abstract level. Many, however, will criticize, and with justification, individual churches or schools and individual ministers or teachers. But even the criticisms of instruments and practitioners are never carried to the point of advocating their elimination, but rather to suggest that practitioners use the instruments in a wholesome or proper manner.

The institution of advertising has been assigned certain functions by society. The most important of these are to communicate on a mass basis to (1) inform, (2) persuade and (3) educate consumers in respect to products, services and ideas. The instruments used are the advertisement and the mass media. The practitioners are the advertisers and their agents. In any critical evaluation of advertising it would seem highly important to distinguish between the institution and the instrument and practitioner.

One might properly ask how institutions get started. They are basically created to serve the spiritual needs of man.

ations of society. Some are formal with the sanction of law, while others are informal with only the general sanction of society. In all cases, however, they are accepted as a fundamental part of a culture. They generally come into being from a social or economic need and are assigned, either by accident or design, basic functions which it is believed are necessary to the proper growth and development of society.

Let us, then, examine the three functions of information dissemination, persuasion, and education as they are related to the institution of advertising and the needs of society.

### 1. DISSEMINATE INFORMATION

If we go back in history before our great industrial development, low cost transportation, and division of labor, when individual communities were largely economically self-sufficient, we would find some of the instruments of advertising being used, but certainly no development on an institutional level. There was no need for the dissemination of information about products or services on a mass basis. Consumers' needs were minimal, and the sources of supply were generally near at hand. Personal observation and word-of-mouth communication seemed adequate as aids in the purchase of most products.

The need for the dissemination of information about products and services on an organized and mass basis developed with the growth of industrial concentration and the diffusion or scattering of buyers. This information function was assumed by or assigned to advertising.

Thus, today, we accept this as one of the basic responsibilities of advertising in our economic and social order. People need or want to know what products and services are available to them. With the great multitude of items that are produced for human consumption it is no easy task to merely keep oneself informed of the existence of such items. In essence, then, society has said that producers of goods also have the responsibility to inform consumers of their existence.

The information function of advertising of course goes beyond this. It requires the dissemination of information as to where products and services can be found, their quality characteristics presented in terms of consumer needs and wants, and the cost to the consumer.

This information function could be supplied by a government agency, but in a free or quasi-free market economy, society has chosen to have this function performed by entrepreneurs operating on a free and competitive basis. Naturally the attribute of honesty is expected from those who practice in the field of advertising although it is recognized that some dishonest people will find their way into the field. This fact, however, does not diminish the importance of the function any more than the presence of some dishonest teachers might diminish the importance of education.

## 2. PERSUADE

Another function or role of advertising in modern society is that of persuasion. There is no clear line of demarcation between information and persuasion. Often information is itself highly persuasive, but there are important differences between the two. To persuade is to urge, advise, induce, or give reasons for taking specific action.

Psychologists tell us and a little introspection will confirm that people tend to be lethargic, indolent, and passive after their body needs are met. Persuasion is necessary to get people to extend and enrich the range of their wants and, therefore, their lives. For most people, rewards must be offered to get them to stretch

their physical efforts or their minds beyond a certain minimum. Students must be persuaded to study, laymen to go to church, citizens to vote, and consumers to reach for the abundant life.

Since advertising has been concerned primarily, although not exclusively, with persuasion at the level of consumption of goods and services, it is to this point that major attention will be given here. It is this function that led the historian, Professor David Potter of Yale, to characterize advertising as the institution of abundance. He considers abundance in strict material terms. He indicates that abundance could not have been achieved without the persuasive power of advertising.

Modern society emphasizes the right of every person to be employed. To achieve this, high level consumption is essential. Arno Johnson has been pointing out for some time that, if we are to keep our economy operating on a level to provide employment to all who wish to work, consumers will have to learn to live better in the future than they are living now. This will require persuasion.

This is the function of advertising. It is to persuade husbands to provide their families with automatic washing machines, an occasional dinner out, a flower for Valentine's day, a trip to some of our national parks, a second car for greater family independence of movement, and new carpeting for the home. It is the function of advertising to persuade consumers in general to pay taxes, make contributions, or vote bonds for schools, churches, parks, highways, community symphony orchestras, community beautification, and aid to unfortunate neighbors at home or abroad.

Some say that such persuasion causes people to live beyond their means. Another point of view is that such persuasion causes many people to stretch their means to match their ambitions. This is

often done through investment in education to raise one's earning capacity, multiple wage earners in individual families,
or moonlighting on the part of the principal breadwinner.

It is not necessarily germane here to
examine whether persuasion directed to
enhance material abundance is good or
bad. It is perhaps sufficient to observe
that our modern culture encourages this
and that the institution of advertising is
performing a function dictated by the culture itself.

### 3. EDUCATE

The functions of information and persuasion are generally accepted as ones
to be performed by advertising. It would
seem appropriate to add to these the
function of consumer education. This
latter function is also closely related to
information and persuasion. It might
properly be called judicious or enlightened persuasion. It is concerned not so
much with passing along information or
urging people to act without thought, but
more with the development of judgment
on the part of consumers.

The function of consumer education
impinges somewhat on the general institution of education, but since the general
institution has not assumed a significant
role in this area, it is important that the
responsibility for this be assumed by
some agent of society. It is an appropriate function for the institution of advertising to perform.

In this respect, it should be recognized
that we operate in an economy of abundance where the ultimate power of the
consumer is supreme. The consumer, generally, is in a position to buy or not to
buy in the case of a large percentage of
the goods and services available or that
can be made available. The ultimate freedom to chose is his.

Our social ideal is an economic democracy built on the solid foundation of

consumer choice. Freedom to choose
what will be bought is as vital to this
economic democracy as freedom of citizens to elect is vital to political democracy. But just as the success of a political
democracy depends upon an enlightened
and educated citizenry, so does the success of a consumer oriented economic
democracy depend upon educated consumers.

It is in the performance of this function of consumer education that the role
of advertising can flower in the future.
Of course there will be those who will
object strenuously to having advertising
perform this function. Criticism will
come on the grounds that effective education cannot result when individual
"educators" are biased and are interested
in presenting only the good side of their
wares.

But let those critics be reminded that
this is the very essence of education in
civic affairs. The latter is built on the
principle of the competition of ideas
where proponents and opponents are
permitted to present their arguments to
the electorate. Freedom of speech and
freedom of access to citizens are pre-
served so that all who wish to hear may
have that opportunity. Faith is placed on
the ultimate wisdom of citizens to make
a choice that will provide maximum satisfactions to the majority.

There is one fundamental difference
between freedom of choice in civic affairs and freedom of choice in respect to
products and services. In the political area
choices are made by and for a total
grouping of people whereas, in the area
of consumption, choices are made by and
for the individual.

This concept of consumer education
places high emphasis on human dignity.
It assumes that the individual has the
right to decide for himself what products
or services will bring him the greatest
satisfaction. It assumes that, if the indi-

vidual has not developed to a point where he can exercise effective judgment in making choices, he can be educated to that point. It recognizes that there will be errors in judgment in the learning process but holds that this is much less serious than to have consumption decisions dictated to the individual. In short, freedom of the individual to choose is rooted deeply in the basic philosophy of the inherent dignity of man.

## LIFE INSURANCE OR A TRIP TO EUROPE?

Perhaps this concept of the educational function of advertising can be clarified with an illustration and a comparison. There are many advertisers of many kinds of products and services competing for the patronage of consumers. Each advertiser presents his case with conviction and hopes it will be accepted. Descriptive materials and persuasive literature are made available to consumers for review and analysis. One group of advertisers provide material that extolls the merits of investing in stocks, bonds, savings and loan associations, or insurance companies. These messages emphasize the values of postponing consumption in order to have greater consumption rewards in the future.

Opposed to the idea of current saving are advertisements that present the merits of spending now for such things as a trip to Europe, a new home, a second automobile, a pleasure boat, or a new lawn mower. What a conflict this must set up in the minds of consumers. What comfort it would be to some to have a single authority figure make the decisions. But how much education in consumerism would result under the rule of authortiy?

Compare this with the process of education in our schools where we insist on presenting students with conflicting ideologies, hypotheses, theories, and descriptive matter with the knowledge that this will help to develop discrimination, enhance judgment, and sharpen the intellect. Universities purposely include on their staffs professors with differing beliefs so that students can become acquainted with the existence of such differences and thus strengthen their own independence of thought.

We might relate this also to our political democracy where we refuse to shelter the citizen from undemocratic ideologies. Instead, we insist on a free market place for the distribution of divergent opinions. We hope and believe that the citizen will be wise enough, or will develop the wisdom, to judge what is most appropriate and satisfying to him and vote accordingly.

In an economic democracy we need the same faith and foresight. We need to recognize that milk producers and coffee roasters should be free to present their respective arguments directly to consumers rather than to a commissar as a means of determining which beverage or how much of each shall be distributed.

Advertising should not be expected to carry the full load of educating the consumer in buying judiciously so that maximum satisfaction will be achieved. But it must, and will, assume greater responsibilities along this line in the future than it has in the past.

In performing this function, advertising will continue to be guided by the principles already emphasized, namely, the freedom of consumers to choose and the capacity of consumers to learn to make judicious choices from the great number of alternatives available to them. Advertising will continue to resist efforts to subject consumers to a paternalism, however benevolent, that dictates what will be made available or denied to them. Advertising will not be taken in by the pleas of those who consider the consumer as ignorant, gullible, and not capable of making his own decisions, and thus should have a guardian appointed to shape his economic life. Intsead, advertising will strive to raise the level of understanding and sharpen the faculties of discrimination and judgment wherever these are found to be inadequate.

Admittedly, much of the education of consumers as undertaken by advertising at the present stage of its operation will be concerned with material things. At the generic level, it will be to present the merits of high level consumption, increased wants, and aspirations for a better material life. Both individual and social goods and services will be involved.

At the specific level, such education will involve the presentation of the merits of competing products where what is claimed for one product is in conflict with claims made for another. By this process, however, the consumer has evidence that will assist him in making a decision.

Perhaps society has assigned to advertising the job of presenting the case for an abundant material life. There is no other institution that accepts this function to a significant degree. Religion is charged with the responsibility of presenting the case for the spiritual and moral man, medicine for the healthy body, and education for a highly cultivated intellect. The individual can best make judgments in respect to the whole self only after he has heard and evaluated the case of each proponent.

Let it be emphasized that reference to an abundant material life is not to be confused with materialism. One can strive for or attain an abundance of material things without making them objects of worship or being devoted to them for their own sake.

Throughout history, man has been striving to free himself from the shackles of economic want. Economists, philosophers, and governments have concerned themselves with the development of means whereby this could be achieved. In the face of a dearth of material goods in the past, philosophers, churchmen, soothsayers, and others often built a glorious picture of the value of abstinence and the satisfaction gained from economic denial.

However, in many cases the individual was admonished to not give up hope, but rather to expect a rich reward in the hereafter. Abstinence and denial were presented as a kind of investment which would pay off handsomely in the future. Interestingly enough the rewards were often presented in material terms, such as mansions in heaven and streets paved with gold. Why should we not rejoice when we can now have our mansions, highways paved with smooth cement, and beautiful parks carpeted with deep green velvet?

## ABUNDANCE ISN'T MATERIALISM

It is not the abundance of material things, but our attitude toward them that might be bad. If we use things unwisely or view them in a manner that will reduce the satisfaction we gain from them, it indicates a kind of consumption illiteracy. That there is some unwise use and immaturity of attitude toward material good is obvious. Such consumption illiteracy breeds a feudal approach to product distribution. The best protection against feudalism in this area is the development of high literacy in consumption. This is a challenge that society gives to advertising.

Major attention has purposely been given to advertising in relation to goods and services. This is because, historically, advertising has been concerned much more with material things than with nonmaterial matters. There is, however, no reason to limit advertising in this manner. In fact, there has been a very sharp growth during the past decade in having the institution of advertising assume important responsibilities in informing, persuading, and educating people on a systematic and mass basis in respect to many non-material issues.

To document this we have only to look to the great work of the Advertising Council. Here the same instruments and the same people who perform the functions of information, persuasion and education in terms of goods are performing the same functions in presenting the case for highway safety, the Red Cross, love of thy neighbor, tolerance, better schools, blood donation and many other social goals.

Perhaps it is in this role that we will see the greatest development of advertising in the future. Radio Free Europe is essentially an advertising undertaking. It is probable that advertising will be called upon more and more to join with other institutions to develop and promote through mass information and education a positive program for freedom.

It is possible that advertising can plan an important role also in laying foundations for eventual peace in the world. This issue is one we tend to leave to politicians and statesmen, but perhaps it should become the increasing concern of all. Is it not possible that the forces that brought economic abundance to America could be implemented to bring eventual abundance to the world? Would this not remove the greatest single cause of war? To paraphrase Lincoln's statement that "no nation can long exist half slave and half free," might it not be equally true that no world can long exist half rich and half poor?

Of course advertising cannot, in itself, create riches where poverty now exists, but it can stimulate desire and encourage people to develop themselves to a point

where they can achieve their goals. If advertising is truly the institution of abundance as Professor Potter has indicated (and there is no reason to believe otherwise), then it will play a vital role in developing abundance in other areas of the world.

## NEEDED: HIGH QUALITY PERSONNEL

If advertising is to meet the challenge and perform the functions assigned to it by society, it must have practitioners of a high order. They must be dedicated people, imbued with a professional spirit. Charlatans must be discouraged from entering, but if some get in, methods must be devised to expel them.

The future need for dedicated, professional people in advertising is great. Efforts must be made to increase the number of such people in both absolute and relative terms. Leading universities in this country are helping to meet future needs by offering professional programs in advertising education. Progress in meeting the goals set for advertising by society will be hastened if we can attract increasing numbers of students with keen minds and dedicated spirits to enroll in these education programs and thus prepare themselves for careers in advertising.

We have had and still have some outstanding statesmen in the field of advertising practice. They have had and are having a wholesome influence on the character and development of the profession. One needs only to examine the contributions of a man like James Webb Young to appreciate true statesmanship in advertising.

On the other hand, there are too many examples of men who engaged in advertising practice only long enough to accumulate sufficient wealth to permit them to transfer their talents to what they call public service. Some of these people, after leaving advertising, have spoken or written disparagingly of the field they left. It would appear that these people led the life of the hypocrite while practicing advertising. They failed utterly to sense that advertising has basic functions to perform that are vital to the economic health of a nation and the proper servicing of consumers in a free society.

Those who believe that advertising has no relationship to or interest in public service do not comprehend the true functions of advertising. Surely it is as much in the public interest to minister to consumer needs and wants through self-appointed entrepreneur servants as it is for elected or government appointed servants to minister to the civic needs and wants of citizens. Failure to recognize this fact will reduce the effectiveness—and the happiness—of the practitioner.

Not all of the blame for having men and women with a non-professional attitude in advertising practice should be laid at the door of the individual. Too many persons have drifted into advertising practice or come in by accident. Too many employers have gone out on the street to entice bright young men and women to join the staff or have raided the staffs of other employers with the inducement of higher pay. Some employers have even rejected college graduates who majored in advertising, preferring those who concentrated in history, political science, or French. It is this philosophy of employment that breeds defection among the truly gifted and makes for unhappiness among the mediocre who are caught in a field they had never aspired to enter.

This is in no way a criticism of education with a major in areas other than advertising, but rather an attempt to place emphasis on the element of personal and professional interest. Without interest and belief in what one is doing

or wishes to do, both personal development and contributions to society will be stunted. The men and women who wish to enter advertising should do so not for purposes of mere monetary gain, but because they believe it is an honorable calling and one which will permit them to benefit society.

Leaders in advertising should spearhead, now, a drive to recruit people with this viewpoint, encourage them in an education for professional advertising service, and provide internship facilities for them when they graduate from college. With such a program for the development of future personnel, we should be able to look forward to continued advancements in performing the functions assigned to the institution of advertising by society.

## MAINTAIN ACCESS TO MEDIA

The instrument which practitioners use to perform the functions of advertising is the advertisement—the commercial—the informative, persuasive, educational message. But the message is of no value until it is delivered to consumers. It is therefore essential that advertisers be afforded freedom of access to the mass media. They must also have the freedom to present their messages without censorship (except as imposed by the law or moral code). These things are especially important where the advertising of ideas is involved, but also important in the case of products and services.

The right of people to know what products are available is as significant as their right to know who divorced whom. The right of access to media is as vital as the right to mount the soap box and speak, or the right to assemble to hear the speaker. If those who control the media provide access to one person and deny access to his competitor or protagonist, they are, in fact, serving as licensers or gatekeepers. They thus exercise the power to determine what shall be made available and what shall be denied to people.

In these modern times, with the great diffusion of people, freedom of speech is a hollow freedom if he who wishes to speak is denied access to modern facilities that permit the distribution of speech on a mass basis. It is not suggested that access be provided without cost, but rather as paid space or time to all who wish to avail themselves of such facilities.

We are dealing here with an issue that some would say impinges upon the freedom of the press. This is an issue with many ramifications and it shall not be developed at length, but it cannot be ignored. Let us emphasize, however, that the advertisement is the only modern instrument that permits persons to speak effectively to masses of people at a minimum cost.

Freedom of the press does not give the owner of medium freedom to discriminate among advertisers of competing products or ideas nor to censure what is presented in the advertisement. The "press" is not a term that applies to the total property the publisher or editor uses, but rather only to that part that deals with the news and editorial content. When the owner makes his property available to others for advertising purposes, a part of the service provided is the transfer to those who use the property of the rights and privileges that pertain to the press.

It is recognized that this line of reasoning does not now have the force of law. Where this has become an issue in the courts, it has generally been held that owners of media can deny access and can, within the limits of the Sherman or Clayton acts, discriminate among advertisers. In general, media owners have provided freedom of access on a voluntary basis. Should this situation change appreciably in the future, it will be incumbent upon society to force freedom of access if the functions for advertising are to be performed effectively.

Society expects much of advertising. The functions assigned this institution are significant ones and vital to the economic and social growth of free people. Its future role will be determined largely by the quality of practitioners who enter the profession and by the availability of the mass media on an unrestricted basis.

## QUESTIONS

1. Discuss the three basic functions of advertising.
2. Is advertising both an instrument and an institution?
3. What are some common abuses of advertising as an instrument?
4. To forestall government control of advertising, what voluntary measures are being used by the business community to weed out spurious advertising?

# 52. Can We Compare Media Effectiveness?*

*This article describes a small but significant first step in the comparison of media effectiveness. While the experiment was not completely free from limitations, it did provide researchers with a reasonably efficient tool for measuring media effectiveness.*

Is it possible to come up with a dollars and cents evaluation of the relative effectiveness of various media? This has long been a big question in the minds of media researchers and advertisers. How does a 4-color full-page ad in a magazine compare with a one-minute network TV announcement, for instance? Or how does each compare with a full-page newspaper ad? So far, no one has been able to find an answer to such a question. That is, until Dr. Jaye Niefeld, director of research at Keyes, Madden & Jones, Advertising, presented his study of the Florist's Telegraph Delivery campaign.

The study, which may well be the first valid evaluation of its kind, was presented at a recent meeting of American Management Association's Media Research Discussion Group. It measured the relative effectiveness of TV, radio, newspaper and outdoor advertising, and covered these media from January through June, 1960. The study uses the criterion of sales volume versus advertising dollar invested, to determine which medium— and later which combination of media— would be most effective.

A group of three test markets was set up for each medium (magazines were excluded because of the difficulty in reducing their scope to three test market cities). Another group of three comparable markets was set up in which the over-all national media mix was run in

order to determine whether or not the test markets in general might be expected to reflect the national sales trend.

The test markets used were the following cities: Television—Spokane, Wheeling-Steubenville and Madison; Radio— Bakersfield, Grand Rapids and Charlotte; Newspaper—Fresno, Wichita and Charleston (W. Va.); Outdoor—Tacoma, Des Moines and Columbus (Ga.).

Using an index of 100 each for the national average increase in number of orders and value of orders, the index for increases in number of orders in the three control markets was 99; for increases in value of orders it was 95. These figures indicate that the test markets would have been very close to the national average had they not been used for test purposes.

Here's the way the media stacked up against each other: Outdoor scored 179 in number of orders and 131 in value. Radio had 102 for number and 101 for value—very close to the national average. Television scored a 42 for number of orders and, the lowest of the group, 46 for the value of orders. Newspapers scored the low for number at 37 and slightly higher than TV with 63 for value of orders.

While the findings show outdoor advertising with a substantially higher score than other media, Dr. Niefeld cautioned advertisers that the results were valid for this industry only—and perhaps only for this campaign. It was due solely to the

* Reprinted by permission from *Sales Management Magazine*, November 4, 1960.

**371**

## CHARACTERISTICS OF TEST MARKETS

| Item | TV | Radio | Newspaper | Outdoor | Average |
|------|------|------|------|------|------|
| Population .................. | 860,300 | 907,300 | 1,014,100 | 832,400 | 903,522 |
| Number of households ........ | 257,700 | 264,600 | 304,800 | 238,400 | 266,375 |
| Effective buying income per household ............. | $6,155 | $6,196 | $5,733 | $6,327 | $6,103 |
| Number of F.T.D. members .... | 51 | 50 | 57 | 42 | 50 |
| Value of annual F.T.D. sales per household ............. | $1.16 | $1.20 | $1.12 | $1.15 | $1.16 |
| Advertising budget for the test period ............ | $4,790 | $4,620 | $4,710 | $4,517 | $4,659 |

unique position F.T.D. holds in its industry that the usual conclusion-inhibiting variables could be eliminated. F.T.D. has only one small competitor that does virtually no advertising. Consequently there were few competitive factors present to complicate the study.

In order to provide for proper payment of its 11,000 member florists, F.T.D. directs all orders through a central clearing house, thus, making it possible for researchers to collect unusually accurate sales data.

However, there are other factors that must qualify the study findings—the suitability of a given advertising message to the various media involved, for example. The literalness and completeness of the TV dramatization may have spelled out the appeal in too much detail. AMA discussion critics were quick to point out that television could have been used much more effectively had its message been limited to simple identification spots. With products such as flowers, color also becomes a strong factor. Neither television nor newspapers had the color advantage that outdoor ads had.

Keyes, Madden & Jones also questioned the degree to which a single medium can be used as a valid measure of its own effectiveness, and wondered how much certain combinations of media might show the individual one to better advantage.

Yet in spite of all these limitations, the real significance of the F.T.D. study should not be overlooked. It provides researchers with the first reasonably efficient tool for measuring media effectiveness.

### QUESTIONS

1. Did the experiment prove conclusively that outdoor advertising is the most effective producer of sales?
2. Are any of the criticisms of this experiment valid?
3. Can you suggest other experiments that might be tried to measure the relative effectiveness of various media?

# 53. Advertising: Electronic "Buyers" of Media*

Peter Bart, Staff Reporter of *The New York Times*

*Electronic computers are invading the advertising—agency business. They will be used in devising media plans for agency clients. The computers will help decide how to make the most efficient use of radio, television, newspapers and other media in carrying out clients' advertising programs.*

On the seventh floor of Batten, Barton, Durstine & Osborn's executive headquarters is a large but completely empty room. It is an eerie room. A specially constructed air-conditioning system purrs quietly, but there is no other noise. A raised metal platform covers most of its floor space, but there is nothing on it.

The room, however, is a very important one to B.B.D.O. management. It shortly will house a $1,250,000 electronic computer that will open up new vistas for the agency's media department.

Electronic computers, of course, have long been used in various industries, but in the advertising-agency business they are both new and controversial. B.B.D.O. and the several other agencies that are installing electronic "brains" will use them in devising media plans for agency clients. The computers will help decide how to make the most efficient use of radio, television, newspapers and other media in carrying out clients' advertising programs.

The introduction of the electronic computers symbolizes the important change that has taken place over the last decade in the role of the agency media man.

* Reprinted by special permission from *The New York Times*, July 15, 1962. Copyright by *The New York Times*.

## OLD-TIMER WAS ORDER-PLACER

The old-time media man was basically an order-placer. If a client desired to start a saturation radio-spot campaign, a time-buyer would negotiate with the necessary radio stations or networks. A space-buyer would perform a similar function with magazines and newspapers.

Today's media man, however, is more strategist than order-placer. As the cost of advertising has continued to soar, advertisers have increasingly turned to agency media departments for guidance on how to gain maximum mileage from their advertising expenditures. Media departments, therefore, have expanded in size, and media directors have risen in the agency hierarchy.

This evolutionary change has culminated in the installation of the big "brains." Media planners, theoretically, will be able to feed into the computers data describing the types of customers that their clients would like to reach. The computers will then produce a list of media that can accomplish this with greatest efficiency. If a company thinks it can sell its product to teen-age girls and young mothers, the computer should

**373**

be able to indicate precisely how these markets could be reached at lowest cost.

This prospect may be a delightful one for the agency media planners. But for many other people, it is somewhat frightening.

The old-line media salesmen are worried, for example, that their services may no longer be relevant to agency operations. Their job is to visit media men and "sell" them on the qualitative and quantitative advantages of their particular station or periodical. They fear that the agency media men may now say, "Don't tell it to us, tell it to the computer."

Many of the more thoughtful executives of advertising media also are concerned. There already is too much of a tendency to judge media solely "by the numbers," they say. Now that computers have been brought into the picture, the numbers fetish may get completely out of hand.

## MAGAZINE EDITOR
## GIVES VIEW

Curtiss Anderson, editor of *The Ladies Home Journal*, argues, for example, that media planners even now rely too much on quantitative factors. "A magazine can't be judged purely in terms of statistics," he asserts. "You have to read a magazine, and consider whether it is a serious publication which people will believe and rely upon. These criteria can't be measured, but they are terribly important."

Another magazine editor puts it even more strongly. "The media boys decide whether we survive or die," he says. "Yet, how often do you see anyone at an agency media department reading magazines—they're just looking at sheets of data."

The agency media men themselves say all this is alarmism. The advent of the computer, they say, will not take the human element out of media planning. If anything, it will give agency officials more time to evaluate qualitative factors.

## COMPUTER IS BACKED

Herbert Maneloveg, vice president and director of media at B.B.D.O., puts it this way: "The principal value of a computer is that it forces the explicit statement of a problem and requires organized thinking toward its solution. You can't just take a computer's answer and call it quits. The computer merely serves as a general guide."

One possible result of the introduction of computers, says Mr. Maneloveg, is that magazines with specialized circulations may get a larger share of advertising.

Media men have leaned toward television in recent years, because it offers mass numbers, often at a lower cost-per-thousand viewers of the ad than other media. But now, with the help of the electronic "brains," media men will be able to place more emphasis on readership selectivity—they may be able to pinpoint their markets with greater efficiency, he says.

Whatever the pros and cons of the computers, agency media departments continue to realign their staffs to meet their broadened responsibilities. Many agencies have media planning groups that formulate broad media strategy and guide the work of the buyers. Benton & Bowles has gone so far as to abolish the traditional demarcation between time and space buyers.

"All too often," says Bern Kanner, vice president for media, "the print buyer would end up fighting the time buyer for his portion of the total budget. The rivalry did no one any good."

As a result, Benton & Bowles' buyers

handle both print and broadcast media. Their work is guided by a media-analysis section, whose job is to analyze media studies and systematize the mass of data that flows into the agency.

Though the media planning and analysis specialists at many agencies are charged with the main responsibilities for stretching advertiser dollars, the buyers also often make significant contributions towards this end. Many agency buyers have good sources of information at the various media—sources that help them to make the "smart buy."

An example of how this process works occurred recently at a major agency. One of the agency's clients was eager to buy spots on a prime-time network show, but there was nothing available. Then an agency buyer heard from a network contact that a major advertiser had encoun-

tered budget problems and wanted to cut back his commitments. The buyer promptly negotiated for the spots—much to the irritation of the agency for another sponsor on the show, who also would have wanted the additional time segments for another of its clients.

Thus, contacts in the right places can often help both an agency and a client. And no agency, at last report, has any plans to use a computer to negotiate with television networks.

## QUESTIONS

1. Will electronic computers eliminate media salesmen?
2. The electronic computer will enable media men to place more emphasis on readership selectivity. Explain.

# 54. Sales Training*

Steven J. Shaw, Professor of Marketing, University of South Carolina

*Personal selling is a unique, hard-to-replace force in modern marketing because it makes possible two-way communication of ideas between a seller and buyer. It is the only form of sales promotion that can encourage and make immediate, on-the-spot use of responses from buyers.*

Personal selling is a unique, hard-to-replace force in modern marketing because it makes possible two-way communication of ideas between a seller and buyer. To borrow a term from cybernetics, a salesman gets feedback from the

prospect in response to what he says and does.

Because personal selling is the only form of sales promotion that can encourage and make immediate, on-the-spot use of responses from buyers, the salesman will always play an indispensable role in marketing.

* Reprinted from the August, 1961 issue of *Advertiser's Digest*. Copyright, 1961, by Publishers Digest.

The pool of information already organized under the typical college and university selling course can equip the student with knowledge pertinent to all areas of management from personal relations to marketing policy. The universal applicability of the salesmanship course stems from its interdisciplinary nature. Educational psychology, social psychology, sociology, and cultural anthropology all contribute to its subject matter.

If this is true, then why is the selling course under fire from certain business leaders and college administrators? The criticism stems from the belief held by many that salesmanship is a narrow skills-type course useful only for training students toward a career in selling. And it is true that over the years the basic principles of salesmanship have been neglected in favor of techniques practiced in selling, and the course has evolved or degenerated into an extremely vocational subject.

Under the pressure of a short training period, sales training directors in industry have tended to skip principles in favor of techniques. Even college instructors, while working in a more leisurely classroom atmosphere, have had to conform to the vocational trend. Moreover, teachers of salesmanship and other business subjects have always been under the pressure of inquisitive students who want to know how and not why.

Then, too, text writers, aiming at mass adoption, have tended to emphasize current sales techniques and practices without adequate identification of the psychological concepts from which many of these practical techniques have evolved.

If the salesmanship course is to contribute fully to the professional development of students, then the behavioral principles underlying the sales techniques and practices must be carefully spelled out. Study of these underlying principles would give the student greater insights into the selling process and more self-

confidence in using his knowledge, whether he later became a salesman of merchandise or of ideas to businessmen.

For instance, an undertsanding of the psychological concepts of projection and identification can help the student of salesmanship to handle objections and use testimonials more effectively. How these concepts might be applied to specific selling situations is illustrated in the following examples:

## PROJECTION

Underlying certain types of buyer objections is the psychological mechanism of projection. Here the prospect blames someone else for his disinterest in buying. In this way, he can state an opinion without leaving himself open to attack.

For instance, a purchasing agent may look at a product and say, "Our engineers won't like that. They won't be interested." The salesman might ordinarily react to this with annoyance. He might consider this an attempt to block his path to the engineering department.

But the salesman familiar with the defensive mechanism of projection would recognize the decoy, and his strategy might be to question the prospect further to determine why he himself is not interested.

## IDENTIFICATION

The effectiveness of testimonials in selling depends upon the psychological mechanism of identification. A prospect gains confidence in a product when it can be identified with a person or company about whom he has a favorable image.

But testimonials are frequently misused. For one thing the salesman must be careful not to assume that the customer will view the person offered as a testimonial in the same light as he does. If the salesman is trying to sell Mr. A and intends to influence him by pointing out that Mr. B has already bought the product, he had better find out first how A feels about B.

Thus, it can be seen how an understanding of the concept of identification can help in the effective use of testimonials. In the same manner it can be shown why a study of such psychological concepts as rationalization, compensation, aggression, submission, and other similar ideas would give greater insights into the selling process.

A behavior-oriented course in salesmanship not only should incorporate some of the older psychological concepts underlying all selling techniques, but should also add newly developed ideas. For instance, psychologists have demonstrated that telling does not always result in communication. Several companies are now teaching sales trainees to use planned sales questions in place of "canned" sales talk.

Drawing-out techniques—asking questions that require an explanatory answer, asking the other person to explain further, repeating the last few words, and remaining, silent—tend to overcome the prospect's resistance. The prospect sells himself while talking about his needs.

In developing the new behavior-oriented salesmanship course, the content can be enriched further by adding pertinent concepts from sociology and cultural anthropology. For example, in the past it was usual to think of social class and income groups as practically synonymous.

However, from the studies of sociologists and cultural anthropologists has come the realization that a person's social-class setting—his attitudes, beliefs, customs, and tastes—has a greater influence on his spending habits than does his income.

The following examples illustrate phases of selling where knowledge of social-class theory can be helpful to the salesman:

## QUALIFICATION OF PROSPECTS

Familiarity with the particular attitudes, beliefs, customs and tastes of each of the classes can help the salesman select the group and sub-groups with which he can best establish rapport. In general, an individual will be a better prospect if his personal characteristics and background are similar to those of the salesman.

## PERCEPTIVITY TO CLASS NEEDS

Aside from basic physical and economic needs, a prospect has requirements which spring from his social-class background. The desire to live up to the cultural patterns of one's social-class position appears to be a compelling reality to most customers.

## USE OF CENTERS OF INFLUENCE

Upper-class members exercise great influence and power. C. Wright Mills points out in his book, *The Power Elite* (Oxford University Press), an example of how a member of the upper class pushed through the idea that his city should be the national headquarters for an International Trade Council. Once the financing and other important questions had been settled, within hours, it was decided to bring in others by declaring the project a community affair!

The salesman who cultivates the friendship of upper-class members in his community probably can increase his sales productivity. Upper-class endorsement of the salesman and his products can mean an endless chain of sales through the operation of the sociological processes of emulation and conformity.

Finally, the new salesmanship course could also adapt some of the behavioral concepts developed by psychologists and sociologists who have contributed new ways of thinking about the behavior of man as a consumer. Of significance to salesmanship theory are such concepts as self-image and product symbols.

Of particular importance is the idea that an individual's behavior, while it may appear irrational to others, is purposeful and in harmony with his image of himself. This self-image is reflected in everything he does, including his choice of merchandise and services.

Closely related to the self-image concept is the idea that a product may have a variety of different meanings, depending upon what it communicates to different people when they look at it or use it. Of course, selling tactics and strategy must be kept in tune with the prospect's image of himself and the product.

These are but a few examples of the psychological and sociological concepts that can be integrated into the salesmanship course. Placement of more emphasis on these behavioral principles can transform salesmanship from a narrow vocational course to a broader communications subject that would stress principles of business persuasion common to both selling and nonselling situations.

## QUESTIONS

1. In what way or ways is personal selling a unique force in modern marketing?
2. What psychological principles are being applied to selling techniques?
3. In what specific ways can knowledge of sociology help the salesman understand his prospects?
4. In what ways might training in cultural anthropology help a salesman?
5. Why are we so slow in applying behavioral principles to the buyer-salesman relationship?

# 55. A Philosophy of Selling*

W. R. Bennett, Professor of Marketing, University of Alabama

*Salesmen play many roles in their problem solving activities. The salesmen find themselves in different roles at different times or in several conflicting roles at the same time. What are some of these roles?*

What is a salesman? A salesman is a problem solver. He exists because people and companies have problems that can be solved with the salesman's product or

* This paper is part of a speech given at a meeting of the National Society of Sales Training Executives in French Lick, Indiana, June 13, 1962.

service. Thus, sales training is training in problem solving. Problem-solving skills must be developed because the salesman's success is determined by his ability to use what he knows to solve his and other people's problems. The purpose of sales training is to give the salesman a set of decision rules so that he will solve the problem the way management would if management were there.

Selling is characterized by *diversity* while much sales training seems to focus attention on the *similarity* of salesmen's problems. I suggest that the salesman finds himself in many roles in his problem-solving activities and that cases should be built around these roles to teach him how to use what he knows in solving problems. The way in which the salesman sees his role influences his behavior in handling the problem. For example, if the salesman sees himself in the role of a small business consultant, he will conduct himself quite differently than if he is in the role of simply communicating company promotional ideas. What are the roles of the salesman? We must recognize that most salesmen find themselves in different roles at different times.

## COMMUNICATOR

Every salesman plays the role of communicator. He must communicate the merits of the product or service and company policy to the customer or prospective customer, while at the same time communicating the events in the market to management. The salesman is the company's link with the market, and, as far as the customer is concerned, he is the company. He represents the power and prestige of his company, and whatever he does reflects this power and prestige or lack of it.

## PROBLEM SOLVER

Problem solving is the fundamental reason for the salesman's existence. Prospective customers have problems whether they recognize them or not. The salesman's function is to fit the features of his product to the needs of the customer. Often knowledge in depth of the product

and the prospective user's problem is necessary to do the job. Selling is the first level of marketing management. The salesman has the problems of marketing management in a simpler form. He must manage his territory, must coordinate company policy and approaches to the market as they relate to the particular account, and he must adapt what he knows to the buyer's situation.

## PLANNER

The feedback we get from our graduates in selling indicates that a principal function of many salesmen is planning. Planning may be short term, like planning tomorrow's interview, or long term, like planning the strategy to be used in developing an account for a year or more.

## PERSUADER

The salesman's principal role may be that of persuading prospective buyers to act now on the basis of their feelings concerning the salesman's product. For example, in life insurance selling the salesman can usually convince the prospect that insurance is a fine institution. The prospect will usually agree that he needs additional life insurance but *not now*. The salesman must have motivating stories and other devices to show the prospect the importance of quick action. He must know how to use these devices in a skillful manner. In other words, he must be what we sometimes call an expert closer.

## PUBLIC RELATIONS

The salesman's principal job may be to keep the customer happy in his dealings with the company. This may involve seeing certain key people or it may involve handling ticklish personal situations. For example, relatively few of the book publishers' salesmen who call on college professors make any attempt at a sales presentation. Instead their function is to keep the customer sold on their house. The book publisher's salesman also finds himself in the role of *market analyst*. His job is to find what books are being used, the views of the professors concerning these books, and the professor's views concerning educational philosophy, trends in the field, etc. These men also serve as editorial consultants to writers and prospective writers, yet they are called "book salesmen."

## DIAGNOSTICIAN

The salesman may find that this principal task is to identify and solve business problems of his accounts. For example, the oil company salesman frequently finds himself in the position of having to examine a small retail business, the service station, to find why it isn't doing more business. If an accounting, personnel, or some other type of problem exists, the dealer may be unable to buy gasoline and accessory products. The salesman's task is to find the problem and correct it.

## SMALL BUSINESS CONSULTANT

In many situations the salesman has the responsibility of making sure the dealer is a successful business man. His work is finding problems and suggesting solutions. He may be concerned with accounting, housekeeping, location, hours, personnel, and other problems. We have developed a case at Alabama built around this relationship.

## TRAINER

Many salesmen who call on dealers tell me that their principal problem is the training of dealer sales people to sell their product properly. Thus the salesman finds that his success depends on his ability to multiply himself through others.

## EDUCATOR

The salesman may find that his success is determined by how much he can teach groups of people. For example, the investment salesman frequently conducts classes to inform neophyte investors on procedures for getting into the market. The pharmaceutical salesman has the problem of informing doctors, nurses, and hospital personnel concerning the merits and uses of new products.

## DISPLAY MAN

In some types of selling the salesman must show the customer how to promote and sell his products. In the grocery business salesmen often find that their success is largely determined by their ability to think of promotional ideas and to set up effective merchandise displays.

## TECHNICAL EXPERT

Salesmen sometimes find they must be technical experts in the products or services they sell. The business machine salesman must be an expert in the use of his equipment and often must plan new systems built around his product. This task calls for a high degree of knowledge and the ability to apply that knowledge to specific problem situations.

## MARKET ANALYST

The salesman's success may be based on his ability to find and analyze the needs of the market. The life insurance salesman must be able to analyze the market that he can best serve in order to be successful. The media salesman must often make extensive studies of the market for a particular product before he can sell his services. For example, the radio time salesman may have to make extensive studies to show that the particular market segment at which the business is aiming actually listens to the station under consideration.

## NEGOTIATOR

In the selling of some industrial products, the salesman is given a considerable amount of discretion in negotiating the final price. The salesman's skill as negotiator determines his success.

These roles call for quite different skills and knowledge. They may also call for quite different backgrounds. Selling is characterized by diversity while much sales training seems to focus attention on similarity of salesman's problems.

## QUESTIONS

1. What seems to be the principal defect of traditional sales training according to the author?
2. Is the salesman a one-way or two-way communicator?
3. Which of the enumerated roles of the modern salesman seem to you to be the most important?
4. Can you suggest several ways in which salesmen serve as business consultants to small retailers?

# 56. Sales Promotion Sells More than Advertising*

**Robert M. Graham, Field Sales Manager, Indian Head Mills**

*For many types of products point of sale promotion is the prime impact force on the consumer. If properly executed sales promotion coordinates advertising with personal selling. Among other things, it stimulates wholesale and retail sales personnel and makes the campaign theme meaningful to shoppers through informative window and interior displays.*

We don't believe that advertising sells!

We believe that if we took full page ads, properly created, in full color, in every magazine published in America, ran them simultaneously with the best TV

* Reprinted from *Advertising Requirements*, now *Advertising & Sales Promotion*, June, 1960, p. 33. Copyright 1960 by Advertising Publications Inc., Chicago, Ill.

show on the air and wrapped it up with car cards, outdoor spectaculars, cooperative newspaper ads in every newspaper and a direct mail piece in every mail box —we'd only show a slight increase in retail sales of Indian Head brand all purpose cotton cloth.

Now, if anyone would like to finance

such an experiment, we'll be glad to furnish our product as the item for testing —but I definitely feel that I'd prove our contention that advertising will not sell our product.

But if I *do* find a volunteer who *will* finance this biggest of all saturation programs, I'm going to do my best to sell him on allowing me to coordinate an intelligent sales promotion program with his advertising extravaganza and then we will sell our product—in box car numbers.

Because I believe that sales promotion *sells!* And all of that advertising would give me a foundation for a wonderful, glorious sales promotion program.

Sales promotion is the single most important function in the marketing of Indian Head brand fabrics. Advertising, market research, product development, packaging—they all rank behind sales promotion in the selling program of our fabrics.

And this situation stems from the fact that our top management—Jim Robison, the president, Charlie Wood, the vice president, marketing, Earl Rushon, vice president and general manager of the finished goods division and Pete Scotese, vice president and general sales and advertising manager—have strong, positive opinions, based on experience and results, which make a program of sales promotion the primary activity around which the remainder of each quarterly marketing program is planned. Sales promotion is the star of the show—all other marketing functions are supporting players.

Many of you will recall the terrific impact of the Textron brand name at the close of World War II. Major department stores in every part of America ran promotions which were based on the theme, "It's Textron time at So and So's." The Textron brand name was advertised—yes —but so were thousands of others.

But what brought about this terrific impact of the Textron name? It was sales promotion. And it was the aggressive, logical, what-will-it-do-for-me presentation to retailers of Textron's sales promotion program which blasted department store top mangement out of their easy-selling, World War II lethargy and resulted in more powerful promotions than many stores had ever conducted either before or since.

Let me give you a very quick run-down on one promotion held in 1948. The Textron people contacted top management at J. L. Brandeis in Omaha early in the year with the proposal that this major department store run a storewide "It's Textron Time at Brandeis" promotion in early October, aimed at pulling up the store's sales graph sag which invariably follows the Back-to-School volume of late August and September. With the complete blessing of the store's entire executive management, a total of 10 salesmen, sales promotion girls, district managers and New York executives of Textron's various divisions met in Omaha one hot Saturday in July. By Sunday night the largest sample room at the Fontanelle Hotel was set up with displays of every product produced by the entire Textron Corp.

On Monday, beginning with the top people from the store, the story was presented individually to every Brandeis executive and buyer concerned. By Tuesday noon, every item had been ordered for the appropriate department and at the wind-up luncheon, the top Brandeis and Textron executives outlined the detailed promotional plans which included a special section in the *Omaha World Herald,* special departmental displays on every Textron product in each department concerned plus *every* show window around the entire store.

It goes without saying that such carefully integrated sales promotion resulted in record volume days for the store and in record sales with the store on every item promoted.

By 1952, Textron's management had begun a 180° move from their original idea of operating as an integrated, vertical textile operation to their present character as a widely diversified, multiple divisioned corporation. In February of 1953, Jim Robison formed his own independent corporation, Indian Head Mills Inc. and bought the mills, trade names, patents and copyrights of the Nashua Division of Textron. Manufacturing only Indian Head brand all purpose cotton cloth, and with an annual volume of only $11.5 million, this new, independent corporation could no longer indulge in the million dollar annual advertising extravaganzas it had enjoyed in its years as a Textron division.

The officers of the new corporation, except for the treasurer, were all sales trained. Every man had personally participated in the fabulous Textron promotions—management was *sold* on sales promotion—and knew that where advertising had to be purchased, publicity and sales promotion could be earned.

With this complete belief in sales promotion, an organization was established with the emphasis on complete coordination among field sales, merchandising, packaging, and the limited advertising program which volume would allow.

Let's start with the product—what kind of promotion can best produce the desired results from a selling program based on an unusual combination of positives and negatives inherent in the corporation, and the product and distribution of Indian Head fabrics?

To answer that we need to know those strengths and weaknesses. And here are some of the important ones as they appeared to be on that day when Indian Head became an independent company:

On the positive side we had:

1. The oldest registered trademark in textiles—the name Indian Head.

2. A saturated distribution with the fabric in at least 95% of all desired retail outlets.

3. A strong distributor organization to completely service the small retailers and give fill-in service to the major stores.

4. A product with strong consumer acceptance and some consumer demand.

5. An established, experienced field sales force, most of whom had demonstrated excellent selling and promotional ability.

6. A top management composed of sales and sales promotion minded men— with every key executive having his life's savings (and all he could borrow) invested in the company.

On the negative side we had:

1. Only one fabric to sell, where our men had become accustomed to carrying a broad line of piece goods, linens, beddings, shower curtains, draperies, etc.

2. Limited capital with no reserve to pay for even a single major mistake.

3. Strong new competition appearing on the horizon in the form of new synthetic-fiber cloths, blends, new crease resistant finishes and a fashion trend toward prints against solid colors.

4. A shift of piece goods purchasing by the consumer from branded lines in department stores to private brand fabrics in chains or price promotion goods from small specialty retailers.

5. The post-war change in department store management from merchants who know goods to controllers who only know figures, resulting in many piece goods departments being moved from traffic loca-

tions on the good floors to an isolated area on the higher floors.

6. Aggressive competition among apparel manufacturers creating a market in which a consumer could buy satisfactory garments as cheaply as she could make them at home.

Management carefully evaluated these pros and cons and decided we would need to take two steps as rapidly as possible:

1. Educate consumers on new end-uses for the product.

2. Broaden the range from one solid color fabric in one width to several widths in various weights with the possible addition of prints to meet the fashion trend.

Our first promotion, still on the one basic width of solid color cloth, was to advertise—in a single half-page ad in the *Ladies' Home Journal*—an easy to make Christmas table cloth.

Of course, this ad contained every element of being promotable:

1. It was a new end use, something *new* to talk about in calling on the buyer.

2. The item advertised could be easily displayed at the point of purchase of the fabric to be used.

3. The majority of consumers did not have a special tablecloth especially designed for holiday use, creating plus business for both the store and the manufacturer.

4. The entire promotion met a critical need in the piece goods department where volume during the Christmas season is usually at its lowest ebb.

Our first diversification promotion was completely successful. We sold out at every stock level—retail, wholesale, mill stocks—on the colors adaptable to Christmas tablecloths.

Immediately following this promotion, we launched our broadened range of fab-

rics—a wider width of the same fabric, a line of prints on the basic cloth, and finally a heavier *and* wider fabric of the same basic character.

Our diversification of end-use ideas in advertising and in-store promotions extended to bedspreads, vanity skirts, dust ruffles, pillow tops and most successful of all—we promoted our fabrics for cafe curtains, shorty draperies and various other window treatments.

Today more than half of the yardage of our fabrics moving to the consumer through retail stores is purchased for the making at home of decorative items rather than garments. And this has been done with limited advertising budgets, primarily founded on the premise that the advertisement must *first* be promotable and *then* be appealing to the consumer.

Expansion since our formation has resulted in our field sales force again carrying a broad line of products for sale to department stores, dry goods wholesalers and the specialty manufacturing and distributing organizations who use our items.

This diversification of product line presents many problems. All of us know that we like most to sell what we know most about. To combine the talents of a superior sales promotion man with the ability to write a balanced volume of business on a variety of products with various types of customers requires a peculiar breed of salesman.

It's not awfully difficult to find a man who can take a sales-promotion-designed ad on piece goods to a store and get the buyer to agree that he will back the promotion with goods, display the supporting model items and run a local ad. On the other hand, to have the same salesman prove equally effective in selling a utility company on buying our electric blankets to give free with every clothes dryer purchased in their service area—and on the next call successfully establish our Pequot

No-Iron sheets and pillow cases in a trading stamp catalog—this takes versatility and an unusual amount of flexibility.

It's when the peak season on electric bedcoverings coincides with the only time to sell linen calendar towels, sheets and pillow cases for January white sales and the sew-it-at-home Christmas tablecloth promotion that, both in the field and at the home office, we sometimes find ourselves going in opposite directions at the same time.

This is when we face our greatest challenge in keeping our sales promotional programs simple, workable and interesting.

So let me tell you briefly what we do to *try* to avoid the conflicts of product pressures and what we *still* would like to accomplish in improving our promotional planning.

Right now I have six salesmen sitting at department store buyers' desks (or awaiting their turn to see the buyer) in Boston, Buffalo, Philadelphia, Baltimore, Pittsburgh and Miami. Six other men are presumably checking wholesalers' stocks in Louisville, Minneapolis, Chicago, Kansas City, New Orleans and Fort Worth. Our San Francisco man is driving up the Freeway toward the city and our Los Angeles representative is driving out toward San Bernardino.

In every salesman's brief case (or more hopefully on the buyer's desk) is a promotional package on Pequot Easy-Care No-Iron sheets and pillow cases showing the cooperative newspaper ads run by the major retail stores in the New York metropolitan area, a summary of the cooperative advertising program, illustrations of the ad mats available and suggestions for easy to make interior or window displays.

On Stevens linen towels, the season is opening on 1961 calendar towels and each man has a sample line of actual calendars, a colored catalog to leave with the buyer for reorders, a glossy photo of the display fixtures available to retailers at no additional cost with a modest order, sample ad mats and a summary of the Stevens cooperative advertising program.

In addition to his sample line of electric bedcoverings, the salesman carries a cooperative advertising program outline and a supply of colored brochures showing the major items and illustrated suggestions on how to install a Nashua automatic electric sleep shop in the buyer's department. Along with ad mats he has radio and TV copy.

Our current package on Indian Head brand all purpose cotton includes a reprint of our current national ad, appearing in five publications, copies of direct mail pieces—one sent to retailers we sell direct and the other to retailers who buy from our wholesalers, copies of our latest consumer leaflets available to retailers for distribution to consumers, a booklet containing suggested departmental and window displays and finally actual cafe curtain panels as illustrated in our national ad, available to our customers at a token charge.

These promotional packages are supplied quarterly on each product line, usually one each month (but occasionally two). By placing these in the salesmen's hands in a carefully controlled relationship to his territory coverage plan and the seasonal aspect of the product, we hope to eliminate any feeling that he is being tugged and hauled in different directions simultaneously, yet get his emphasis on the right products at the right season.

Our seasonal priority at this time is on our line of fabrics—Indian Head brand all purpose cotton in white, colors and prints.

Let's take the current Indian Head piece goods package and have a quick look at the way it was put together. The ad was created by our advertising agency, Nathan Fein Inc., with the counsel of Pete Scotese, my boss, and Ed Concheiro, the assistant advertising manager. During preparation and again prior to its final approval, it passed through the hands of our merchandising department, our promotional gals, our field sales office and our outside public relations counselors, Ruder and Finn. In each instance it was analyzed on the basis of its potential support of that operation's effectiveness and plans were drawn to get the most possible mileage in each area from the finished ad.

Merchandising recommended the product patterns and colors and geared production to support the estimated increase in sales.

Our promotional gals selected the styles of window curtains to be illustrated and selected the Vogue pattern from which the model's dress was made. They also worked with an allied supplier, Coats and Clark Thread Co., on preparing the consumer booklet giving instructions on "how to" make the curtains.

The field sales office checked out the attitude of key accounts toward buying and displaying actual model curtains and worked with the advertising department in the preparation of the direct mail pieces and the suggested interior or window displays. A direct letter from the field sales manager to all of our franchised wholesalers pointed up the power of this promotion, outlined all of the supporting activity: the national advertising, the direct mailing to the wholesalers' customers and the availability of consumer leaflets and actual model curtains. Enclosed was also an adequate supply of bulletins for the wholesaler's salesmen outlining the program.

Our public relations counsel developed the newsworthy fashion aspects of the advertisement and prepared mailings to radio, TV and publications' fashion editors, including an offer to support their presentations with free consumer booklets.

We'd like to build our promotions on better advertising, so we constantly feed ideas from our customers, our salesmen and our management group through advertising department to the agency. How can we get more and better ideas from more people so that the agency can produce better ads?

True Utopia would be just around the corner if we could get the thousand largest department stores in America to install departmental and window displays bringing our ad to life in three dimensions and featuring the actual product ready for sale. How can we improve our point-of-purchase sales aids, our model items, our display ideas?

We know that there's an alarming dilution in the presentation of a promotion between the sales meeting presentation or the bulletin covering the package and the actual "pitch" made by our salesmen. And we know the tangy elixir is reduced to almost clear water by the time it passes through all of the communications filters between our office and the smaller retailer, as he gets the story from the average wholesaler salesman. How can we dehydrate our communications so that *our* salesmen and the *wholesaler* salesmen are sure to have the concentrated essence to which they need add only their fluid vocal presentation, coming up with the original full-strength message?

We face these problems, knowing that we will never reach perfection—but we're certainly going to keep striving toward that goal.

The only successful advertisements are those which answer two questions—"What is it? What will it do for *me*?"

We try to weave this basic fundamental into every sales promotion so that it becomes the dominant pattern in the sales promotion velvet we present. And be- cause we want this "What will it do for me?" to stand out so clearly, we have a formula—the double-U formula:

$$\frac{2\ U}{I} = A \text{ successful sales promotion}$$

And it works because if we'll put in twice the quantity of what it will do for you, the buyer, to one part of what I want, the program is accepted with enthusiasm by the salesman, it retains its full strength as it passes through the filters of communication and repeated presentations and fulfills the promise of success it seemed to have on the day it was finalized in the home office.

## QUESTIONS

1. Is it true that point of sales promotion can sell more than advertising?

2. In the marketing of what types of products is point of sales promotion the most important?

3. In the marketing of what types of products is advertising the single most important promotional force? Can you think of any products in the promotion of which advertising is the single most important agent?

4. In what large area of marketing is personal selling far more important than either advertising or point of sale promotion?

# BIBLIOGRAPHY FOR CHAPTER VIII

ARTICLES:

Christian, R. C., "Marketing Men to Succeed Admen in Future," *Advertising Age,* Vol. 31, No. 43 (October 24, 1960), p. 112.

Evans, K. J., "How to Use Sales Promotion to Cut Selling Costs," *Industrial Marketing,* Vol. 44, No. 6 (June 1959), pp. 134–139.

Henry, Porter J., "Can Machines Teach Salesmen to Sell?" *Sales Management,* Vol. 89, No. 2 (July 20, 1962), pp. 38–39.

Kelley, Eugene J., and Lazer, William, "Basic Duties of the Modern Sales Department," *Industrial Marketing,* Vol. 45, No. 4 (April 1960), pp. 68–83.

McGary, Edward, "Propaganda Function in Marketing," *Journal of Marketing,* Vol. 23, No. 2 (October 1958), pp. 131–139.

Weinberg, A. M., "Publicity; Extra Pay-Off For Your Exhibit," *Sales Management,* Vol. 85, No. 2, Part 2 (July 15, 1960), pp. 114–21.

Weiss, E. B., "The Vanishing Salesman," *Sales Management,* Vol. 88, No. 10 (May 18, 1962), pp. 48–55.

White, Irving S., "The Functions of Advertising in Our Culture," *Journal of Marketing,* Vol. 24, No. 1 (July 1959), pp. 8–14.


BOOKS:

Buskirk, Richard H., *Principles of Marketing: The Management View.* New York: Holt, Rinehart and Winston, 1961. Chapter 20.

Canfield, Bertrand R., *Public Relations, Principles, Cases and Problems.* Homewood, Ill.: Irwin, 1959. Chapter 17.

———, *Salesmanship: Practices and Problems.* New York: McGraw-Hill, 1958. Chapters 1–4.

Dunn, S. Watson, *Advertising: Its Role in Modern Marketing.* New York: Holt, Rinehart and Winston, 1961. Chapters 1–3, 33, and 35.

Edwards, Charles M., and Brown, Russell A., *Retail Advertising and Sales Promotion.* Englewood Cliffs, N.J.: Prentice-Hall, 1959. Chapters 18–21.

Greif, Edwin C., *Modern Salesmanship: Principles and Problems.* Englewood Cliffs, N.J.: Prentice-Hall, 1958. Chapters 1–2.

Gross, Alfred, *Sales Promotion.* New York: Ronald, 1961.

Haas, Kenneth B., *Professional Salesmanship: Persuasion and Motivation in Marketing.* New York: Holt, Rinehart and Winston, 1962. Chapters 19 and 20.

Pederson, Carlton A., and Wright, Milburn D., *Salesmanship: Principles and Methods.* Homewood, Ill.: Irwin, 1961. Chapters 1–3.

Sandage, C. H., and Fryburger, Vernon (eds.), *The Role of Advertising: A Book of Readings.* Homewood, Ill.: Irwin, 1960.

Shaw, Steven J., and Thompson, Joseph W., *Salesmanship: Modern Viewpoints on Personal Communication.* New York: Holt, Rinehart and Winston, 1960. Parts 2 and 3.

Wright, John S., and Warner, Daniel S., *Advertising.* New York: McGraw-Hill, 1962.

Zacher, Robert V., *Advertising Techniques and Management.* Homewood, Ill.: Irwin, 1961. Chapters 1–4.

# IX. Pricing

*I*T IS DIFFICULT to establish universal rules as to pricing policies in business and industry as these policies must be tailored to meet the competitive situation of individual firms. Nor will a single method of setting price serve all of a larger firm's needs, for this firm ordinarily runs into a whole host of special situations calling for unique strategies. Many firms could benefit from following the multi-stage approach to pricing, for it insures that adequate consideration is given to the basic long-run factors that determine a firm's market success. Although this method does not yield a single price, it does provide an orderly sequence in which to narrow the range of alternative prices that deserve detailed consideration.

The pricing function cannot be tied down to a special department—either line or staff. It is an all-pervasive type of function which is influenced by forces within the company as well as by forces of the external market. To support top management in determining its basic pricing policy, it is the practice of larger companies to bring into conference top men from the major departments—from marketing, from manufacturing, from finance, and from research and engineering. In medium-sized and smaller organizations, this same totality of viewpoint should be represented.

In top management conferences on pricing policy, the marketing department may ask for more attractive styles and stress the importance of lower price ranges; the finance department may emphasize the need for larger profit margins; the engineering department might point out the technical difficulties of attaining the desired quality level; the manufacturing department would certainly be interested in cost of production at different volume levels—and so on all through the company, each separate group emphasizing its particular problems and interests.

The consideration of these many viewpoints is essential to a sound decision. Major pricing decisions must reflect all facets of the company's internal operations and problems and then be assessed against the external market factors which exert their own pressures on the total situation. The all important external factors of consumer preferences and competition can be carefully appraised through the firm's marketing research department. With regard to the management of the pricing function, marketing research and sales are invaluable in terms of feedback. Both departments can provide continuously a vast amount of information which top management needs to appraise the effect of external consumer reaction and other market force on the company's pricing structures. This feedback is an essential element in balancing external forces with internal forces in order to arrive at a sound pricing policy.

Although cost should play a vital part in pricing, analyses of demand, of competitive environment, and of political effects are also major considerations. For reasons that are easily understood, the use of cost-plus formula pricing is widespread. Despite its popularity, cost-plus pricing has serious limitations since it disregards demand, it does not reflect competition adequately, and it places too much emphasis on historical costs.

More research should be done on how customers will react to various prices. Huge sums of money have been spent in researching customer motivations in regard to advertising and promotion but amazingly little has been done in regard to the psychology of alternative pricing policies and strategies.

# 57. Pricing—An Area of Increasing Importance*

Charles M. Hewitt, Professor of Business Law, Indiana University

*The government, competition, middlemen, and customers play an important part in price decisions. More research should be done on how customers will react to various prices. Huge sums of money have been spent in researching customer motivations in regard to advertising and promotion but amazingly little has been done in regard to the psychology of alternative pricing policies and strategies.*

Some years ago, Joel Dean commented that, although pricing is of central importance to economic theory, most American business executives felt that it was their least important worry. There are many reasons why pricing decisions have demanded a larger share of executive attention in recent years.

Overcapacity, increased competition from foreign-made goods, higher labor costs, automation, and certain recent demographic trends have contributed to both overproduction and a tendency towards sharply increased price competition in many industries. Evidence of the impact of these competitive pressures on the marketing levels of various industries shows in trends toward scrambled merchandising and the use of nontraditional distribution channels, the decline of fair trade, and diverse attempts by manufacturers to obtain controlled distribution. On the other hand, nonprice competition, with a growing stress on product and promotion policies, seems to be the basic competitive strategy in European mar-

kets. For the present, at least, European markets appear to be growing fast enough to absorb the increasing supply of goods. There are signs, however, that competitive pricing may be on the increase in many European countries.

Paradoxically, this purported lack of executive interest in pricing can be rationalized either as evidence of rigorous competition or as evidence of some form of monopolistic power or collusion among competitors. Under highly competitive conditions, the entrepreneur has little choice as to the price he may charge if he is to sell his goods. His crucial decisions are cost decisions rather than price decisions. Likewise, under conditions of monopoly or collusion the cooperating firms will usually pay little attention to prices once they are set. The tendency is for such prices to remain stable until fresh circumstances warrant a reappraisal. In an industry dominated by a few large firms selling fairly similar products, prices tend to be uniform and stable even though there is no collusion among competitors. Each firm soon realizes that price cuts will be promptly met by competitors, and that all stand to lose unless

* Reprinted from the First International Seminar on Marketing Management, p. 108. Published as a Special Supplement to *Business Horizons*, School of Business, Indiana University, February, 1961.

393

the demand and/or cost situation in the industry is unusual.

Most firms have some—but not un-limited—discretion as to the prices that they can charge. However, primarily be-cause a few firms apparently do have a considerable range of discretion over their prices, controversy has arisen over whether businessmen should consider so-cial objectives as well as profit objectives in setting their management policies.

Writers who argue that businessmen must assume more social responsibility reason that the firms with the discretion-ary power over prices must exercise re-straint if an inequitable allocation of na-tional resources is to be avoided. Some critics of this social responsibility thesis assert the over-all effectiveness of com-petition and deny the existence of sub-stantial discretionary economic power. Other critics make the alternative argu-ment that some monopolistic price stabil-ization power is essential to encourage investment and innovations. The innova-tion process, rather than price competi-tion, is viewed as the real mainspring of lower prices and better goods to con-sumers.

Still other critics of the social responsi-bility thesis argue that the free enterprise system cannot function efficiently unless there are effective competitive market checks on the extent of private economic power that might be wielded by entre-preneurs. These critics reason that sub-stantial discretionary economic power must be curtailed either through vigor-ous antitrust action designed to invigorate competitive forces or through various forms of government surveillance or regulation. These critics tend to mistrust various social concepts that portray busi-ness managers as "trustees" of the public interest. They particularly dislike the "baronial" or *noblesse oblige* aspects of these concepts.

## CONCEPTUAL APPROACHES

### COST-ORIENTED APPROACH

It has been suggested that there are three basic approaches to pricing.[1] A dis-cussion of these approaches serves to demonstrate some of the complexities in-volved. Various studies indicate that cost-oriented pricing practices find widespread use in both the manufacturing and the marketing sectors of industry. Typically, a forecast of sales is made, followed by an estimate of total unit cost at some standard or expected operating rate. To this basic cost figure is added a percent-age markup as profit. It will be noted at the outset that this method involves circularity of reasoning. In estimating the standard operating rate, an estimate of price must be used; the operating rate selected sets the costs, which, in turn, establish the price.

### ECONOMISTS' APPROACH

Cost-plus pricing practices are criti-cized by economists on many grounds. Under conditions of competition, eco-nomic theory predicts that unit prices will tend, in the long run, to be equal to total average unit costs (including a normal profit). But no necessary relationship exists between price and costs in either the short run or market (inventory) period.

A good part of the criticism of cost-plus pricing is directed against account-ing practices. Economists argue that the accounting costs utilized in cost-plus pric-ing are theoretically and factually un-sound. Accounting costs do not allow for many implicit or opportunity costs and do not properly handle such items as depreciation reserves, dividends on pre-

[1] This discussion is an elaboration of some ideas pre-sented by Professor Alfred R. Oxenfeldt of Columbia.

ferred stock, and capital gains and losses. More important, the economists argue that accounting costs involve the use of historical averages, while current pricing decisions should be based on present alternative-use values and marginal analysis. For pricing, the manager should compute the added cost for the last unit (or batch of units) to be produced, and the price should be set where the added cost will be equal to the added revenue generated. In some situations, this marginal cost may exceed the average cost as computed by the accountant—in others, it may be less.

In addition, the economists charge that accounting costs frequently include irrelevant "sunk" costs and that pure cost-plus pricing does not give due regard to conditions of demand. As was stated previously, if profits are to be maximized, the price must be set at the point where the marginal costs of producing and selling just equal marginal revenue generated. While theoretically sound, the marginal approach to pricing offers many practical difficulties. This is particularly true for the typical multiproduct firms. It is extremely difficult to estimate the marginal costs for specific products under such circumstances. Various studies indicate that businessmen do not think in marginal terms when setting prices.

Perhaps the major contributions of the economist to pricing practice have been in the area of demand analysis. Various concepts of elasticity and cross-elasticity of demand have been of significant value to marketing research and to practical decision-making. Even a highly simplified linear demand-schedule concept helps to clarify thinking as to the relevant factors that may determine the slope (elasticity) and position (magnitude) of the demand for a firm's products.

More sophisticated demand concepts involving game theory, and additional elements of realism are in the process of development. The ultimate success of approaches of this type will hinge on the degree to which the key considerations affecting pricing decisions can be quantified.

## MARKETING MANAGERS' APPROACH

The marketing manager should recognize that the theoretical arguments of the economists—granted their premises—are sound. At the same time, the marketing manager should recognize that in many, if not most, real-life situations the premises are unrealistic and that, of all marketing decisions, pricing decisions are the ones most often involved with problems that concern delicate and unpredictable human relations. It should be recognized that, as a topic for study, pricing should be handled by the behavioral sciences.

Consider for a moment the parties having a more or less direct interest in the pricing policies of a firm. First, within the firm, the price set usually represents a compromise. The finance department recommends one price, the marketing department another. The actual price is nearly always a result of an interplay of power politics within the firm.

Second, customers play an important part in a price decision. How will they react to various prices? Huge sums of money have been spent in researching customer motivations and attitudes in regard to advertising, packaging, and promotion; but amazingly little has been done in regard to the psychology of alternative pricing policies and strategies.

Third, middlemen are parties directly affected by pricing decisions. The price morale among dealers and distributors. Computing the long-run costs under such that might maximize profits for the firm might cause huge losses in money and circumstances frequently involves "guess-timating" in a type of political theory of games situation.

Fourth, the reaction of competitors is often the crucial consideration imposing practical limitations on pricing alternatives. Winning your competitor's customers with salesmanship or superior products is one thing; attempting to win his customers with price cuts is quite another.

Fifth, potential competitors as well as present competitors must be considered in setting prices. One writer[2] has suggested the following considerations for the purpose of setting price with potential competition:

1. How easy and cheap it is to get into the business, that is, the height and importance of barriers to entry

2. How much potential competitors know about the profitability of the present producers of the product

3. Whether product acceptance has developed to the point where the "specialty" is maturing into a "commodity"

4. Whether the other aspects of merchandising competition make the producer an easy mark for an invasion

5. Whether the buyers are numerous, highly concentrated, and technically well informed

6. The demands of the firm's suppliers (including suppliers of labor) are frequently influenced by the prices set by the firm.

In addition, the government must be considered as a party particularly interested in pricing. It is doubtful that some of our larger firms would be hailed before the antitrust authorities if they were to adhere strictly to the marginal cost optimum price policies advocated by economists.

The foregoing gives some indication of why a relatively simple concept like the marginal pricing concept suggested by economists can be no more than a starting point for setting prices. How then can the marketing manager set prices? The answer seems to be that he may have to use all of the concepts discussed plus those that he can develop which may have a special significance for his particular situation.

Professor Oxenfeldt has suggested a multistage approach to pricing designed to narrow the range of alternative prices at each successive stage.[3] The stages are as follows: selecting marketing targets; choosing a brand "image"; composing a marketing mix; selecting a pricing policy; determining a pricing strategy; and arriving at a specific price.

It is observed that these steps call for considerably more information than that normally utilized by economists. Markets, for example, are not viewed as homogeneous masses of people but as specific individuals or peer groups, which should be identified and served in particular ways.[4] While a brand "image" is in part a reflection of price, no simple price-quantity sold relationship is assumed.

In summary, the marketing manager understands that the selection of a pricing policy involves a consideration of the interest of all of the parties previously identified and may involve setting price by a process of eliminating alternatives. He properly views pricing as only one element of his marketing mix and utilizes market research not only to set prices, but also as a means of keeping past policies under periodic review.

[2] Joel Dean, "Pricing Policies," in Fiske and Beckett, eds., *Industrial Accountants' Handbook* (New York: Prentice-Hall, Inc., 1954), p. 608.

[3] Alfred R. Oxenfeldt, "Multi-Stage Approach to Pricing" *Harvard Business Review* (July–Aug., 1960), p. 125.

[4] John A. Howard, *Marketing Management* (Homewood: Richard D. Irwin, Inc., 1957), p. 92.

The atomic age portends tremendous gains in productivity and an increasing variety of competing goods and services. There are also signs that international and domestic barriers to free competition may be breaking down. Education, advertising, and increasing amounts of discretionary spending power will mean better-informed and more selective consumers. It seems reasonable to assume that there will be a gradual reduction in the amplitude and duration of the cyclical swings that have periodically afflicted industrial nations. A public policy based on free competition has the best chance for survival in an environment of steady economic growth.

All of these factors indicate that pricing may become an increasingly important element in the marketing mix. In the world of tomorrow, increased competition may decrease the range of discretion in pricing, but the opportunities for error will still remain.

## QUESTIONS

1. More research should be done on how customers will react to various prices. Explain.
2. Distinguish between the cost-oriented approach and the economist's approach to pricing.
3. What should be the marketing manager's approach to pricing?
4. What factors have contributed to the tendency towards sharply increased price competition?

# 58. The Role of Price in the American Business System*

Joel Dean, Joel Dean Associates

*The tools for making correct pricing decisions are improving. Among these are a scientific approach to the measurement of demand elasticity, economic and statistical cost research and engineering predictions, electronic data-processing and computer techniques, and new tools and broader experience for market testing of new products and promotional pricing.*

The basic job of price in the American competitive business system is to do for a free economy what a master economic planning and control commissar does in

a collectivist economy. Price rations and allocates inputs (materials, men, and money) to their highest and noblest economic use in producing the goods and services wanted in a free, competitive economy. Price also rations and allocates the output of our economy, using the

* Reprinted from *Pricing: The Critical Decision,* AMA Management Report Number 66. Copyright 1961 by the American Management Association Inc.

mechanism of the competitive marketplace instead of wasteful waiting lines or ration coupons. In fact, the efficiency of our market price system in supplying incentives, guidance, and control is more and more recognized, admired, and imitated by our Communist competitors.

The effectiveness of price in performing these vital functions depends in large part upon the responsiveness of price to dynamic changes in conditions and outlook as regards demand and supply. It is the responsiveness of price which brings about corrective action. The role of price, then, is to adapt our business system to changes in what society wants from it and in what our scientific revolution and growing capacities make us capable of turning out. The function of price is to direct, motivate, and control this adaptation to change.

Pricing decisions, therefore, need to be adapted to changing conditions, of which the following are important:

1. Technological progress is being speeded up by the revolution in industrial science.
2. The number of new products is growing by leaps and bounds because of research spending on a vast scale.
3. The demand for services, both pure and product-attached, is becoming wider and more insistent because of higher living standards.
4. The ranks of our foreign competitors are being swelled by the entry of new and stronger members.
5. Legal restrictions are being tightened by the present administration in Washington.

## FASTER TECHNOLOGICAL PROGRESS

The accelerated rate of technological progress has four important impacts upon pricing decisions:

1. The basic discoveries get more quickly translated into commercial realities and have their effect on the pricing of existing products sooner. Greater fluidity and faster communication of research discoveries among industries and among countries facilitate speedy commercialization. The rapid pace of the research race and the specter of obsolescence motivate prompter introduction of innovations. This acceleration is made practical by advances in innovation economics.
2. The duration of the shelter which the product innovation enjoys in its pioneering stages is shortened. The market power of the new product is more quickly reduced by competitive imitation and improvements. The price elasticity of demand for the novel product changes more rapidly. Insensitive to price in the pioneering stages, it can quickly become highly price-sensitive. The period during which the innovator has wide discretion in setting prices is, therefore, briefer.
3. Commercialization of research—that is, the entry of competitors into a field—is speeded up, thereby forcing the pace of pricing adjustments of the defenders. New entrants in some industries no longer need to spend years building a reputation in order to compete with established firms. Successful drug firms have been created almost overnight through technological innovation, and we have seen the birth of whole industries, such as missiles and electronics, in a single decade.
4. The circle of rivalry of a product is expanding fast. In our technologically advanced, affluent society, there are now many alternative directions of spending of discretionary income. Thunderbirds compete with pleasure boats; trips to Europe with

mountain cabins. Greater "shiftability" of demand and response to relative prices (as well as relative promotional pull) generally result from this intensified competition for the consumer's dollar. Broad and rapid changes in the composition of demand are likely as a consequence.

## POPULATION EXPLOSION OF NEW PRODUCTS

Our scientific revolution drives product innovation forward at such a rapid pace that we are experiencing a "population explosion" in new products. The fast proliferation of new car lines by major automobile producers is but one example of the trend toward bigger product families. Bigger families make policies of product-line pricing more delicate, intricate, and important.

Greater population density of substitute and alternative products is another trend which has important pricing consequences. Twenty years ago, for example, there was a sharp three-way choice in foods: fresh, frozen, and canned. Markets were sharply defined and price differentials generally wide. Today the range of choice has been widened and the market segments blurred by the introduction of frozen-uncooked, frozen-completely cooked, frozen-partially cooked, as well as by the multiplication of grades and brands of fresh and canned foods. As a consequence, relatively small price differentials can cause relatively large shifts in consumer patronage.

Another impact of the product population explosion is the rising importance of "target pricing"—that is, tailoring product and anticipated production costs to yield a specified margin or rate of return. Cited by some as a sign of market power and price stickiness, it is actually

more often a sign of intense direct and substitute competition. The manufacturer must prove to himself that he can build a product profitably to sell at a given price, because he knows he can't charge any more and still get volume sales. An illustration of this is the experience with compact cars. Target pricing and profit planning do not, however, guarantee success, but they do provide "birth control" pricing which guides new product planning to the *economic* satisfaction of consumer desires.

## INCREASED DEMAND FOR SERVICES

The postwar increase in the demand for services has taken two directions, which are difficult to distinguish at the borderline but distinctive in impact on practical pricing problems. These are (1) the increased demand for pure services and (2) the stepped-up demand for services that are built into products.

**Pure Services . . .** As far as pricing decisions are concerned, some implications of the increased demand for pure services are as follows:

1. There are likely to be increases in price, because most pure services consist mainly of labor, and productivity gains will consequently be relatively low.
2. These price increases for services (many of which are considered necessities, such as medical services) will contribute to the uproar about inflation and have far-reaching consequences—for example, increased antitrust activity.
3. Our technological ingenuity has not been able to keep pace with the growth in the demand for pure services. However, where manufacturers are able to find cheaper substitutes for these services, pricing discretion

will be, at least temporarily, increased. We need only consider the revolution in educational techniques to see this.

4. Insight gained from pricing and price behavior in pure services will have a carryover to product-attached services. Some lessons to be learned are that underlying shifts in composition of demand are occurring; prices are dependent on the rate at which supply can be expanded; the price of a product should be based on the price of substitutes; and an estimate of the future availability of substitutes needs to be built into price policy.

**Product-Attached Services . . .** Decreases as well as increases in the demand for services built into products are occurring. Services such as credit and delivery in supermarket and in discount-house merchandise are being dropped at the same time that other services are being built into precooked or frozen foods.

In general, the postwar shift in demand toward a richer mix of services has been a gradual one whose impact has been hidden in some industries by the worldwide restocking of durable goods. Hence, the shift, which is not likely to be reversed, may have gone further than is widely recognized.

Shifts in the comparative advantage gained by providing product-attached services at different points along the processing and distribution road confront sellers with altered risks and opportunities in pricing. The direction is usually toward *more* attached service. Technical advances and economies of scale in production reduce the cost of building in more services. Moreover, because the consumer has more money (and therefore places a higher price on leisure) and because there are more working wives,

the value of these timesaving services has been increased.

In pricing the bundle of product-attached services, the high opportunity value of the service component can be fully reflected during the period of innovational shelter from competition. As the market power from a pioneered product is eroded by competition, the comparative cost advantage of mass production tends to play a more dominant role in pricing. For the smaller companies in an industry, correct pricing of product-attached services can be a way of existing alongside of much larger competitors who have economies of scale in making the product but have no comparative disadvantage in supplying the associated services.

In pricing, we should recognize that product-attached services constitute a joint product. We should build in services that are economical from both the customers' viewpoint and our own—that is, services that we have a comparative advantage in supplying. We must also price so as to recognize the inelasticity of demand for a built-in service, where it exists. Finally, we should differentiate prices, because elasticities of demand for components of this joint product-service package may vary by customer groups.

A new dimension of pricing is introduced by the manufacturer's discretion in manipulating the size of the service component of his product. First of all, competition in providing services can be discriminatory with greater impunity and greater adaptability to the need of the individual buyer than can explicit pricing. Second, cyclical adjustments of the service component can be more delicate and less disturbing to competitors. Finally, services built into a product are sometimes capable of producing shelter from competition through patents or through peculiar skills which present an unusual pricing opportunity.

## THE WORLDWIDE ARENA OF COMPETITION

The power of imports to police domestic prices and impart price elasticity to domestic demand will probably steadily increase. The main causes for the inroads that foreign competitors have made are as follows:

1. The liberalization of foreign trade and the reduction of trade barriers.
2. The narrowing of our margin of superiority in productivity, coupled with the wide disparity in hourly wage rates.
3. The stimulus to investment in new plants and equipment in war-torn economies in West Germany, England, France, and Italy, caused by highly favorable tax treatment of depreciation in those countries.
4. The appearance of new nations which are industrializing urgently. The long-run outlook for American producers is made more gloomy because ordinarily a higher proportion of the gains from higher productivity go to labor in the United States than in rival industrialized nations. This handicap is accentuated by our high tax rates and comparatively unfavorable tax treatment of depreciation.

A number of mistaken pricing attitudes also militate against a satisfactory solution. One is the notion that American technology produces such a wide margin of superiority that we are sheltered from foreign competition and that, therefore, our pricing problem is merely a parochial one. Another is the conviction that the quality superiority of American producers and their ability to adapt products to fit our peculiar needs will always shelter them from foreign competition. Third, there is the idea that passing on higher wage rate is only a problem of

public relations—that our prices can go up indefinitely. Fourth, we have the notion that price cuts won't increase total sales of the domestic industry—that is, that American industry faces no price competition and little price elasticity of demand.

Erroneous economic notions like these will be eventually changed by the realities of the marketplace, but the learning process is likely to be a costly one. New competitors may gain a foothold while management, decoyed by questions of "price discipline," loses time that it should be using to ferret out and deal with the real problems—or at least those that management can do something about—the problems of cutting costs and developing new products.

As far as pricing policy is concerned, the basic long-run problem is a national one. It cannot be solved by the pricing policies of any individual manufacturer. Meeting foreign competitors' prices down to the level of our incremental cost is the indicated short-term response. But it is not a long-term solution: our incremental cost may be higher than the foreign competitor's full cost. Therefore, even the best pricing response will only buy time; and time is not worth much unless either the national response or the cost-and-product response of the individual manufacturer produces an ultimate solution.

For the individual manufacturer, non-price actions in the form of research, promotion, wage negotiations, and renewed efforts to increase productivity by mechanization and greater efficiency are more important than pricing adjustments.

## THE CHANGING LEGAL ENVIRONMENT

The legal setting of price decisions is also changing. These changes are particularly perplexing because the laws of economics lead to pricing decisions or policies which are frequently at odds with the Sherman, Clayton, and Robinson-Patman Acts.

Legal changes are susceptible to quicker reversal than are other changes in the environment of the price maker. Pendulum-like, they swing through cycles: from extended policing by government of pricing practices to periods of complacency, when there is renewed confidence in the policing power of intensified competition to force upon business men a willingness to keep their own house in order.

The increased concern of the Government is less likely to be expressed by new legislation than by vigorous enforcement of existing legislation. With the intensification of the cold war and a growing recognition of the need to put our resources to their most efficient use, it is possible that Congress may be induced to modify the present pricing legislation which inhibits this optimum use. The Robinson-Patman Act, for example, may deny the consumer, and the economy as a whole, the full benefits of well-established economies of scale. Incidentally, one of the critical differences between our economy and the Soviet economy is belief in economies of scale. In Soviet Russia, there is full faith, and no inhibitions, about complete utilization of savings of size. In our country, in contrast, economies of scale are always suspect and have to fight their way against vigorous government opposition.

Paradoxically enough, at the same time that there is increasing competition in industries traditionally oligopolistic, we find greater Government concern with pricing activities in these industries. Evidence of this is to be found in the drug and electric-industry hearings; the audit of consent decrees, initiated very early in the new administration; and the call

to government purchasing agents, military and non-military, to report all instances of price identity to the antitrust agencies.

This paradox is explained by the tendency to confuse the behavior of individual prices with the price level. Holding down the price level is more appropriately the domain of monetary and fiscal policy. Trying to control it through the antitrust division is a mistake. However, it is a mistake of public policy that private business must live with and take into account in its pricing decisions. It must realize that antitrust audits are necessary. A company would do well to conduct seminars in the economies of strictly legal pricing, such as some perceptive manufacturers have inaugurated since the "electrical cases."

## A LOOK AT THE FUTURE

The economic function of price remains the same: to allocate input and ration output. But the institutional environment for particular pricing decisions is constantly changing. Price will probably perform its economic functions even more effectively in the future because (1) the step-up in antitrust activities will deter collusion and prevent thwarting of the economic function of price; (2) the adequacy of capacity means relatively large shifts in sales may result from small changes in price; and (3) the distorting effect of sharp movements in the overall price level on the function of relative prices will be reduced.

The need for economically correct pricing decisions will become more pressing. We must face up to the fact of more intense competition where it exists and not be blinded by the "administered price" myth or the "orderly market" myth. Price behavior is determined by the structure of industries and markets, by supply and demand conditions, and not by wishful thinking. The penalty for incorrect pricing decisions is becoming more prompt and devastating because the catch-up of capacity with demand in many industries will compel more competitive pricing. Moreover, accelerated technological progress will create additional substitute competition and hasten obsolescence. Finally, the rising competence and capacity of foreign manufacturers will police the pricing of more American firms.

Oligopoly is simultaneously becoming more common as the structure of competition and less powerful as a pricing force. The combined effect of (1) scale economies, (2) geographical separation of competitors, (3) quality-strata separation, and (4) specialized products will make oligopoly more and more common in America. It will become the typical economic structure of competition in industries where price making is managerially important.

The tools for making correct pricing decisions are improving. Among these are (1) a scientific approach to the measurement of demand elasticity, by controlled experiments and other objective research; (2) economic and statistical cost research and engineering predictions, which can provide relevant cost forecasts for pricing; (3) electronic data-processing and computer techniques, which speed up and reduce the cost of the analysis of both demand and cost data; and (4) new tools and broader experience which are available for market testing of new products and promotional pricing.

## QUESTIONS

1. What effect does the elasticity of demand have on prices in a monopolistic industry?
2. The worldwide arena of pricing helps to impart price elasticity to domestic demand. Explain.
3. Describe some specific effects of our legal environment on pricing.
4. What factors will make oligopoly more and more common in America?

# $59.$ Multi-Stage Approach to Pricing*

Alfred R. Oxenfeldt, Professor of Marketing, Graduate School of Business, Columbia University

*The author presents a long-run, policy-oriented approach to pricing which should reduce the range of prices considered in specific situations. This new approach calls for the price decision to be made in six successive steps, each one narrowing the alternatives to be considered at the next step.*

Of all the areas of executive decision, pricing is perhaps the most fuzzy. Whenever a price problem is discussed by a committee, divergent figures are likely to be recommended without a semblance of consensus. Although unanimity in marketing decisions is a custom more remarkable in its occurrence than in its absence, agreement in pricing decisions is even more rare.

This article accordingly presents a long-run, policy-oriented approach to pricing which should reduce the range of prices considered in specific situations and consequently improve the decisions which result. This approach, which to the best of my knowledge is new, calls for the price decision to be made in six successive steps, each one narrowing the alternatives to be considered at the next step.

Is this method just another mechanical pricing formula? Hardly, for it is my conviction that the quest for mechanical pricing methods is unduly optimistic, if not downright naïve. Nevertheless, many businessmen consistently employ almost mechanical formulas for pricing. They do this even though they scoff at the claim that there are reliable fixed formulas for handling personnel problems or making

advertising or capital outlay decisions. Certainly, experience has not produced recipes that guarantee correct decisions in any sphere of business. The best of them only apply under normal conditions, and it is most rare indeed that conditions resembling normalcy prevail.

On the other hand, many discussions of pricing present a long list of factors to be "taken into account," carefully weighed and balanced, and then subjected to a process called "judgment." While a specific price is thus arrived at, this does not alter the fact that intelligent and experienced business executives using the method will arrive at widely different price decisions—all based on the same information.

Yet, even if mechanical pricing formulas are the hope of the optimistic, it would be excessively pessimistic to resign ourselves to a *formless* consideration of all the relevant factors and to a random exercise of judgment. Many things are known about the subject that would be extremely helpful to those responsible for making such decisions.

## SEQUENTIAL STAGES

In order to organize the various pieces of information and considerations that

* Reprinted from the *Harvard Business Review,* July–August 1960.

bear on price decisions, a multi-stage approach to pricing can be a very helpful tool. This method sorts the major elements in a pricing decision into six successive stages:

1. Selecting market targets.
2. Choosing a brand "image."
3. Composing a marketing mix.
4. Selecting a pricing policy.
5. Determining a pricing strategy.
6. Arriving at a specific price.

The sequence of the stages is an essential part of the method, for each step is calculated to simplify the succeeding stage and to reduce the likelihood of error. One might say that this method divides the price decision into manageable parts, each one logically antecedent to the next. In this way, the decision at each stage facilitates all subsequent decisions. This approach might also be regarded as a process of selective search, where the number of alternatives deserving close consideration is reduced drastically by making the decision in successive stages. Of course, one could arrive at the same result by simultaneously considering all the factors mentioned—but it might require a computer to do so.

While it appears that this approach is applicable over a broad range of industry and trade, the great diversity of business situations precludes the possibility of its being a universally applicable method. No rigid approach, and certainly not the one presented here, offers a guarantee of reaching the best—or even a satisfactory —price decision. It must be adapted to prevailing circumstances; consequently, information, experience, and the application of rigorous logic are required for its optimum utilization.

## I. MARKET TARGETS

A going concern is "committed," confined, and tied down by several important circumstances which can be altered only over a considerable period of time. It must live with many conditions, even while it may attempt to alter them. Also, an operating business possesses specified resources on which it will strive to capitalize in achieving its objectives. For example, a firm will have:

A fixed production location, given physical facilities, and a particular production and sales labor force.

A set of distribution arrangements through which the firm generally sells, including particular distributors with whom it has established relationships.

Contracts with suppliers, customers, laborers, and lenders of funds.

A portfolio of customers who have a definite opinion of the firm's reliability, and the quality of its offerings and service.

These commitments and resources of a firm contain pricing implications. Mainly, they determine the type of product that it can make, the type of service it can render, and its probable costs of operation. What is more, these circumstances form the basis for the most fundamental pricing decision that management should make—namely, the types of customers, or market segments, it will attempt to cultivate.

By virtue of its fixed commitments, then, a firm is limited to the several market segments it can reasonably hope to capture. It has customer connections on which it can capitalize, and it has a variety of strengths and weaknesses that limit its choice among potential submarkets for intensive cultivation.

Two examples drawn from the TV set industry will help to clarify this crucial first stage. Certainly, no two firms could possibly exemplify all situations, nor is it possible for an outsider to explain satisfactorily why specific decisions were made in specific cases. However, these illustrations are intended to indicate what factors management must consider if it is to apply the multi-stage approach. They do *not* describe how management reasoned or what would have been the best decision under the circumstances.

## ZENITH RADIO

First, consider the pricing problem of the Zenith Radio Corporation at the time it started to produce TV sets in 1948:

This company, which is one of the two largest TV set producers now, dropped out of the automobile radio business in order to manufacture television sets. (At that time, it was the largest single producer of automobile radios, but this business was not very profitable.) Zenith possessed these resources and was subject to these commitments and limitations that could have influenced its selection of market targets in the TV business—

It had production facilities in Chicago that had been designed for and used in radio production for many years; its labor force and supervisory personnel were familiar with the electronics business. The firm had substantial manufacturing skills in electronics because of its work for the military, during and after World War II. Zenith could assess its manufacturing capabilities as very substantial, but not outstanding.

Financially, Zenith was also in a very strong and liquid position and could readily have undertaken heavy expenditures at this time.

But Zenith's outstanding resource was a distributor and dealer organization that was as good as that possessed by any other firm in the nation. Its dealers commanded strong loyalty among their clientele not only in small communities but also in large cities— a most vital fact in view of the technical character of TV and the great power that retailers wield over consumer choices of such products. Here Zenith was helped by the fact that it had acquired an excellent reputation for quality products in radios; for many years, it was the Cadillac of the radio industry. Zenith management, like all other radio manufacturers who entered the television business, decided to sell its sets through the distributor organization it had already created; its distributors, in turn, would sell them mainly to dealers already buying Zenith radios.

There were also several other peripheral advantages. Zenith was closely identified, in the minds of many consumers, with hearing aids which were widely advertised as much on grounds of moderate price as in terms of high quality. Further, Zenith started to telecast, experimentally, in the Chicago market even before World War II and had some local identification as a telecaster, as well as a manufacturer. Its products were strongly favored in the Chicago market.

In summary, Zenith Radio could count on its strong distributor and retail organizations as its outstanding resource, while recognizing that it did not possess any particular advantage in costs of manufacture or quality of product and, in fact, that its behavior in the television business was necessarily circumscribed by its radio and hearing aid business. Zenith's management would have required very strong reasons to choose as its market targets customers who were very different from those who bought its radios and hearing aids.

Under these circumstances, Zenith management might have decided to attempt to reach customers at almost all levels of income. Partly, it could do this by including "low-end" and promotional models in its line; partly because television sets were sold on installment credit involving modest monthly charges; and partly because, at least in the early years, television purchases were spread rather evenly over all income groups.

On the other hand, Zenith management, as its first step, might well expect to cultivate particularly those consumers who were conservative and quality-conscious, who felt a strong loyalty to particular appliance retailers, and who were located mainly in small cities and towns. On this basis, the Zenith customer targets would not include "snobs" who, at that time, favored the Dumont brand and, to a lesser degree, the RCA set. Also they would not include bargain hunters. Rather Zenith's customers would be the kind of people who feel that "you get what you pay for." (Zenith would presumably capitalize on its strong position in the Chicago area by special measures aimed at that market.)

COLUMBIA BROADCASTING

Now contrast Zenith's position with that of Columbia Broadcasting System, Inc. when it started to produce and sell TV sets under its own brand name in 1953:

CBS resources and commitments were altogether different from those possessed by Zenith, with the result that the two companies could have been expected to cultivate different market targets. Specifically, in the case of Columbia Broadcasting—

CBS executives were primarily familiar with the management of entertainment talent and the creation and servicing of a network of stations. Although its phonograph record and Hi-Fi phonograph business did involve a type of production and distribution experience, CBS was completely new to major appliance manufacturing and possessed no suitable distribution facilities whatsoever for appliances.

In addition, CBS acquired production facilities when it entered the TV business that were of relatively poor quality. The size, location, equipment, plant layout, and employee facilities of the Air King firm, which CBS acquired, were widely recognized as mediocre or below. Many people familiar with that company and with the TV industry strongly doubted that Air King's management was capable of establishing a prestige national brand and producing the high quality product needed to support a quality reputation.

On the other hand, CBS had some genuine pluses in its favor. Its radio and television networks were the largest, and enjoyed great prestige at the time CBS entered the TV set business. Also, by virtue of its telecasting facilities, it could advertise its sets during unsponsored programs at virtually no out-of-pocket cost. It could, moreover, get the advertising support—mainly through testimonials from outstanding personalities like Arthur Godfrey, Edward R. Murrow, Jack Benny, and others—for little or no cost. *

To what kinds of customers could a firm with these resources and limitations appeal?

One way that CBS might have adjusted to its particular combination of resources and weaknesses would have been to select as its chief consumer market target the metropolitan customer who is anxious to be associated with prestigeful figures, vulnerable to advertising over radio and TV, prepared to pay a premium price, and relatively unfamiliar with or insensitive to technical performance features.

But this market target would hardly have been very large in the first instance; moreover, CBS management must have recognized that many other firms were cultivating this type of customer.

It would appear, then, that CBS was compelled to select its market targets mainly in terms of distributors and retailers, rather than ultimate consumers. Whereas Zenith already possessed a strong distributor and dealer organization, CBS had to construct one. Only after it secured representation on the market could it hope to sell to consumers.

CBS management must have realized that whatever it did in an effort to win distributors and dealers would also influence the kind of customers it could hope to attract. For example, if it had to extend big markups to distributors and retailers to get them to handle its sets (combined with the fact that its production facilities were mediocre), CBS would be compelled to charge a relatively high retail price for its sets. In turn, it would have to rely on intensive advertising to persuade consumers to pay these higher prices and find methods of making its sets appear luxurious and worth the high price.

In addition to having to accept the fact of a relatively high-price product, CBS would feel pressure to concentrate on customers in the large metropolitan centers, because of the need to build large sales volume rapidly in order to get its production costs in line with those of its competitors. Even as early as 1953, the large metropolitan markets were pervaded by severe price competition among set manufacturers and relatively little emphasis on quality and brand loyalty on the part of retailers. Independent distributors were leaving the business because of great manufacturer pressure to gain heavy sales volume. Hence CBS could not have much hope of obtaining strong independent distributors for its line in most metropolitan markets, but would have to look ahead to a considerable period during which it "supported" both distributors and key retailers to obtain an organization that would distribute its sets.

## OTHER CASES

Zenith and CBS have been cited as companies that would have been justified in placing relatively little weight on price in their selection of target submarkets. These companies mainly had to avoid alienating customers by charging prices that were far out of line with other companies' prices. Not all TV set manufacturers could have taken this approach, however. Thus:

Companies like Admiral, Emerson, and producers of private brands were under pressure to cultivate customers who place heavy emphasis on price. Why? Because in some cases they lacked the personnel and financial resources to sustain a claim of quality and style superiority; or, because their experience in the major appliance business before adding a line of TV receivers could have indicated that they had won acceptance mainly among customers who want moderate quality at prices below the average; or, finally, because their chief asset was a very efficient manufacturing organization that could imitate the products of their more progressive rivals at low cost.

Other industries offer clear examples of firms that selected as market targets persons who were not particularly interested in high intrinsic quality or style. Specifically:

A fairly obvious example is the Scripto pencil, which offers satisfactory performance at minimum cost. Apparently the customers Scripto selected for intensive cultivation were those who would want a pencil to write with and not for display, a pencil they could afford to lose or misplace.

Some producers of private brands of aspirin likewise have selected as market targets those persons who know of the fundamental similarity of aspirin quality and who actively desire to minimize their outlays for this product.

These examples illustrate a point that may not have been particularly clear in the discussion of the Zenith and CBS examples: *one important criterion in the selection of market targets is customer awareness of and sensitivity to price.*

## II. BRAND "IMAGE"

Once management has defined the submarkets it wishes to cultivate most actively, it must select the methods it will use to achieve its goal.

Success in the market place for more and more products seems to depend on creating a favorable•general image (often vague and formless) of the product or company among prospective customers. The selection and development of this image become of prime importance and have a direct bearing on price, as will be explained subsequently. A favorable image is especially important when one sells consumers' goods, but only rarely is it completely unimportant even in the sales of producers' goods. Buyers' very perceptions are affected by their prior attitudes, the actions and opinions of others, first impressions and early associations. It is a rare firm that can ignore the total impression its potential customers have of it and of what it is selling.

The firm's selection of its company and brand image should be dictated by the types of customers it is trying to attract. Submarkets may be likened to targets at which the seller is firing, and "images" are powerful weapons that can be used to hit the targets.

Almost every going concern has invested—often very heavily—in the creation of a favorable image. Most businesses know what image they wish to achieve and are concerned lest they or their products fail to have a favorable "meaning" to potential customers. At the very minimum, almost every management knows there are certain images that customers might have of it and its product that would prove disastrous.

The type of image a firm can create of itself and its wares depends to a considerable degree, again, on its fixed commitments and resources. With its physical and personnel resources, there is a limit to what it can do to alter the prevailing opinions—for they reflect all that the company was and did in the past. In that sense, the basic commitments limit the type of image a firm can establish, how much time it will require to establish it, and the cost. Even as brand image is frequently an effective weapon in cultivating particular submarkets, price helps to create the brand image. It is for this reason that the selection of a brand image which is consistent with the firm's market targets implies particular forms of price behavior.

Let us carry our original examples a little further. Given the market targets that they might have selected, as explained earlier, what brand image could Zenith and CBS try to create?

### ALTERNATIVE QUALITIES

As in the selecting of market targets, every firm has only a few *reasonable* alternatives from which to choose its desired image. For example:

Zenith already possessed a brand image that contributed strongly to its success in the radio and hearing aid business. Even if another image might have been advantageous for its television business, Zenith's management could hardly afford to injure the bird already in hand. Consequently, Zenith would be obliged to perpetuate for its TV line the brand image it had already established in its other activities. As it happened, that image was altogether suitable for its TV set business.

To implement this line of thinking, Zenith would be obliged to establish the image of a "premium" product and of a company that was old-time, conservative, and mainly concerned with quality and craftsmanship. Above all, it would seek to avoid high-pressure selling, emphasis on price, and shoddiness of product. In styling, it could pursue a safe policy of including a wide variety of styles, while being especially careful not to alienate its conservative small-town customers with models too far in the vanguard of modern design.

CBS faced a very different choice with regard to brand image. It, too, could not afford to jeopardize its eminent position in the radio and TV network field, for those activities were very profitable and would always remain its major sources of income. Except for this limitation, CBS had a relatively free choice of brand images.

CBS could well undertake to be the style leader in the industry. This image would be consistent with relatively inefficient manufacturing facilities, concentration on selling in the metropolitan market, and the necessity of charging a high retail price. It would appear that few brand images other than for advanced styling and for gimmicks would have been consistent with the resources and limitations on CBS at this time.

In contrast to Zenith and CBS, other TV set producers sought a brand image that did have an important price ingredient. Again, most producers of private brands, Admiral, Emerson, and others, often featured price in their advertising and apparently sought to sensitize prospective customers to price. They could purposely become identified as firms that were not afraid to discuss price and that seemed confident they offered better values than their competitors.

Many firms outside the TV set industry attempt to establish a brand image that has a heavy price ingredient. Among producers, one finds Caron boasting that its Joy perfume is the most expensive, and Chock-Full-of-Nuts implying much the same thing about its coffee. Without being explicit, some retailers seem to claim that no stores charge more than they—and, strangely, this image is a source of strength. The retail world is full of stores that claim that they are never knowingly undersold; on the other hand, it is difficult to name manufacturers who claim that their product is the cheapest on the market—probably because of the implication that theirs is also the brand of lowest quality. (Automobile manufacturers occasionally claim to be the "cheapest of the low-price three," but none has occupied that position long.)

## III. MARKETING MIX

The third stage in multi-stage pricing calls for the selection of a combination of sales promotion devices that will create and re-enforce the desired company and product brand image and achieve maximum sales for the planned level of dollar outlays. In this stage, a role must be assigned to price. The role in which price is cast should be selected only after assessment is made as to the relative effectiveness and appropriateness of each sales promotion device that might be employed. The short-term gains of certain sales promotion devices may entail injury to the image objectives of the firm. Conflicts of such a nature must be resolved at this stage.

Then, too, a firm might achieve precisely the *desired* image and still find customers very hard to get. It is not enough to establish the desired image; it must be an *effective* image. Furthermore, even though a firm may establish highly favorable impressions of itself and its wares, the company and its products must live up to the image they foster. Not only must its product be "within reach" in price, but it must be accessible by being offered through convenient channels of distribution, and must be sold in outlets where customers like to buy.

The third stage builds directly upon the second. The need to conform to the prior decision about company and brand image greatly limits the number of price alternatives that a price setter can reasonably consider.

The marketing mix decision at this stage need not be translated into specific dollars and cents amounts to be devoted to each sales promotion device; however, it does at least call for crude answers to the following questions:

How heavily to advertise?
How much for salesmen?
How much for product improvement?
How much of an assortment to carry?
How large an inventory to hold?
How best to provide speedy delivery?
How much emphasis on price appeal?

The composition of a marketing mix (arrived at by answering the type of questions just listed) is admittedly very difficult and highly subjective. But the job is facilitated greatly when answers are subjected to the test of conforming to the desired company and brand image and to the firm's fixed commitments.

Few firms can afford to switch "images," usually because they have invested heavily in them in prior years and should, therefore, not abandon them lightly.

Moreover, past images persist and blur any future attempts at image building. Although it cannot easily scrap its brand image, a firm can vary its marketing mix within moderate limits and remain consistent with the image it seeks to create. Thus, the selection of an image sets limits and gives direction to the decision about the elements to be included in the marketing mix. In that way, it facilitates the decision and also increases the likelihood that it will be correct. However, it does not isolate a single marketing mix as the only correct one.

MARKETING THE IMAGE

How might have Zenith, CBS, and other TV set manufacturers composed a marketing mix, if they had reasoned about market targets and brand image along the lines of the foregoing discussion? Let us see:

In Zenith's case, price clearly would have had to be subordinated as a sales appeal. The company could have placed major emphasis on quality of product, subdued advertising, and reliable service, while placing its product with retailers who would enhance the reputation of the brand. By these measures, Zenith could have re-enforced the image of a high quality and reliable producer.

In the case of CBS, the role of price in the marketing mix would not have been subject to much control. As explained, it might have been forced to charge a high price; if so, most of its other actions would have been dictated by that fact. It could have relied very heavily on radio and TV advertising to generate consumer preference, and justified its high price by adding externals to the set—particularly attractive styling, an expensive furniture appearance, or special features of some sort. It could not have reasonably hoped to get very much support from retailers who commanded strong loyalty among their patrons.

Other TV set producers adopted quite different market mixes from those that Zenith and CBS would have selected if they had reasoned along these lines. Some, however, apparently had noœconscious marketing mix philosophy and, therefore, seemed to improvise and stumble from one crisis to another. Nevertheless, in their bids for patronage, some TV set producers apparently place relatively heavy reliance on advertising (including mainly RCA, General Electric, Westinghouse, and Sylvania). Others made strong quality claims (like Dumont and Andrea). Still others placed chief emphasis on styling (Magnavox).

## IV. DETERMINING POLICY

The fourth stage in multi-stage pricing calls for the selection of a pricing policy. But before a pricing policy can be determined, answers to the following questions must be obtained:

How should our price compare with "average" prices in the industry? Specifically, should we be 2% above or 4% below the average? And, when we speak of the average, which firms' prices are we going to include in the computation?

How fast will we meet price reductions or increases by rivals?

How frequently will it be advisable to vary price? To what extent is stability of price advantageous?

Should the firm make use of "fair trade" price maintenance?

How frequently should the firm run price promotions?

These are simply illustrative of the aspects of a pricing policy which management can and should spell out—in proper sequence. By virtue of having made the evaluations and decisions called for in the first three stages, management will find itself limited in the number of choices on these points.

In addition, each company must take account of the valuations placed on its product-service "package" as well as the valuations of rival products by the market segments it is most anxious to cultivate. On the basis of such considerations, plus its target market segments and marketing mix, it will decide whether it can afford to charge much more or less than its rivals.

### "BRACKETING" THE PRICE

Before proceeding further, let us summarize. Surely, a price setter would be some distance from a specific price decision even after completing the fourth step. We must ask ourselves whether he would not also have covered considerable distance toward a price decision. By taking account of the firm's basic commitments and resources, the images it desires to establish, its decision about marketing mix, and the selection of a detailed pricing policy, has not the price setter reached the point where he is very strongly circumscribed in the price decision he will ultimately make? To illustrate Step Four, let us carry our two main examples—Zenith and CBS—about as far as they can be taken and see what pricing policy these companies might have adopted:

If the Zenith management had selected the market targets set forth here and made the same decisions regarding brand image and marketing mix, it would have had little trouble in selecting a pricing policy. It would have felt obliged to charge a price somewhat above the average in the market and to minimize emphasis on price in its advertising. Moreover, it could have varied price relatively infrequently to the consumer—except possibly in some of the large metropolitan markets where neither consumers nor retailers are loyal to anything or anyone, except their own pecuniary interests.

In Zenith's pricing policy, the preservation of distributor and retailer loyalty would have figured very prominently in its thinking. It would be compelled to sacrifice long-term price advantages in order to protect its distributors and retailers from financial loss due to price change.

CBS, on the other hand, need not have concerned itself much with dealer and retailer loyalty. It had none and must have realized that it would not have been able to create a loyal distribution structure unless it were willing to make very large financial outlays. If it had reconciled itself to a not-too-loyal distributor and dealer organization, CBS could have conducted sales promotions and varied price frequently and by large amounts. It could have emphasized price in these promotions, but presumably only when combined with strong emphasis on alleged high quality and superior styling. CBS need not have felt obliged to match the prices charged by its competitors, but it could not have afforded to have its retailers' margins be out of line on the low side.

Since it commanded no loyalty from its retailers, CBS was, in fact, compelled to buy their sales support. This it could do, primarily by offering a higher than average margin. (CBS could also have attempted to solve its distribution problem by granting exclusive privileges to a small number of retail outlets. In the case of the TV industry, such a policy has been used successfully by Magnavox. However, this company had already sewed up the strong quality retailers who were capable of producing large volume. As a

result, CBS was shut out of this pattern of distribution.)

Although Zenith and CBS apparently would have been obliged to charge more than the average by the foregoing line of thinking, other TV producers were wise to take a very different tack, mainly because of their different resources and commitments. For example, Admiral and Emerson have tended to charge somewhat less than average, while General Electric has not adopted a very consistent price position.

## V. PRICING STRATEGY

It is difficult to draw a sharp line between policy and strategy, but it is possible and useful to make some sort of distinction between them. Policy is formulated to deal with anticipated and foreseeable situations of a recurrent type. However, markets frequently are beset and dominated by *special* situations that basic policy was not designed to meet. For example:

A Congressional committee might threaten to investigate the company's or the industry's pricing arrangements.

A sizable firm may have fallen into a desperate financial situation so that it was forced to raise cash through a liquidation of its inventories.

A large new firm may have entered the market.

Business may have fallen off precipitately for the entire industry or economy.

The company may have introduced a model that is either a "dud" or a "sure winner."

Special situations like these ordinarily require an adjustment in price—and the formulation of a strategy to guide management in setting price *during the time that the special situation* endures.

There generally are several strategies which would be compatible with the firm's basic commitments and resources, its market targets, its image objectives, its convictions about the relative emphasis to attach to various elements in the marketing mix, and its specific pricing policies. Others would be incompatible with earlier decisions and therefore might endanger precious values. A threat to one's very survival might justify a scrapping of these, but impetuousness, shortsightedness, or avarice would not. Explicit recognition of these earlier stages of the pricing decision should prevent hasty short-run actions that are painful, but quite common.

No effort will be made to discuss the Zenith and CBS examples in connection with the formulation of a pricing strategy. They have already been stretched far enough to illustrate the application of the multi-stage approach to pricing—especially in the most difficult stages. The reader might, however, speculate about how, within the framework of the approach outlined here, both Zenith and CBS management could have responded to a great pricing crisis in the TV set industry. This occurred in the fall of 1953 when Westinghouse suddenly reduced its TV sets by approximately 20% during the very heart of the selling season. We may speculate that adherence to decisions regarding market targets, brand image, marketing mix, and price policy would have prevented both Zenith and CBS from reducing their prices to the levels set by Westinghouse Electric Corporation.

charge. Nevertheless, he usually will have some range of price possibilities that are consistent with the decisions made in the preceding five stages of the price decision. How may he best select among the alternatives?

To the extent that he is able, he should be guided by the arithmetic of pricing—that is, by a comparison of the costs and revenues of the alternative prices within the zone delimited by the prior stages of his pricing decision. Once he has taken into account his market targets, brand image, marketing mix, pricing policy, and strategy, he can afford to ignore everything but the calculations of costs and revenues. *The first five stages of decision are designed to take account of the business considerations which may be ignored if one selects price solely on the basis of prevailing cost and revenue conditions.*

It often is impossible to obtain reliable information about sales at different prices; this difficulty is present whatever method of pricing one employs. But the multi-stage policy approach facilitates research and experimentation into demand conditions by limiting the number of alternatives to be considered.

The price that would be established under this multi-stage policy approach would rarely be the same as that set by balancing marginal cost and marginal revenue. The former probably would exclude, as incompatible with the firm's basic commitments and resources, desired brand image, and so on, the prices that would be most profitable in the very short term.

## VI. SPECIFIC PRICE

Here is the final step—the selection of a specific price. At this point, the price setter will usually find himself sharply circumscribed in the specific sums he can

## THE ADVANTAGES

*First, this approach breaks up the pricing decision into six relatively manageable pieces.* In that way, it introduces order into the weighing of the many considerations bearing on price. This approach, therefore, should increase the likelihood that all major factors will be taken into account and that their large number will not overwhelm the price setter.

*Second, this method of pricing reduces the risk that the price setter will destroy the firm's valuable investments in corporate and brand images.* Also, it requires the price setter to determine and take into account the limitation on the firm's freedom of decision. In that way, it would discourage the pricing executive from undertaking what he is powerless to accomplish. Similarly, the multi-stage policy approach should militate against a short-run policy of opportunism that would sacrifice long-term values.

*Third, the multi-stage policy approach to pricing should be valuable to those executives who are compelled to delegate pricing responsibilities.* In the first place, high-level executives are virtually required by the method to make the decisions for several stages, which thus limits their dependence on their subordinates. In the second place, as explained, it simplifies the making of a price decision so that greater success can be expected. Then, too, its use should make it easier for subordinates to raise questions and obtain advice from their superiors, should they be unable to reach a decision.

*Fourth, this approach to pricing puts considerable emphasis on the intangibles that are involved in pricing—particularly on the total impression that customers have of the vendor and of the things he sells.* Price is far more than a rationing device that determines which potential customers will be able to afford to make a purchase. Generally it is one of the most important actions in creating an impression of the firm among potential customers. Especially as tangible differences among rival products shrink, these intangibles will grow in significance for marketing success.

## THE LIMITATIONS

*This approach does not indicate all the considerations that should be taken into account at each stage in the pricing decision.* In other words, the price setter is compelled to isolate the significant factors operating at each stage and weigh them for himself.

*Second, this approach does not indicate what price to charge in any specific situation.* The most that can be claimed for it is that it narrows down the zone of possible prices to the point where it may not matter a great deal which particular price is selected. As stated at the outset, one must beware of any pricing method that does lead to a single price, for such a method could not possibly take into account all of the special circumstances which are relevant to a price decision and which vary so greatly from market to market and from time to time.

*Third, this method does not guide price setters in recognizing the factors that dominate the market at any time and in knowing when to switch basic strategies.* Also, there may well be more than one dominant condition which must be considered in selecting a basic strategy.

On balance, then, the multi-stage approach to pricing at best only takes an executive fairly close to his ultimate destination. Although the multi-stage policy approach does not do the whole job of pricing, the part of the job that is left is relatively easy to finish in many cases. Where this is not so, one can only assume that the task would be almost hopeless without the assistance of a method that reduces the pricing decision to a series of relatively manageable steps in a prescribed sequence.

## CONCLUSION

The multi-stage policy approach outlined here differs from usual approaches to pricing in two major respects. First, it demands a long-range view of price by emphasizing the enduring effects of most price actions on company and brand image. One might say this approach constructs a policy framework for the price decision. And, second, it allows the price decision to be made in stages, rather than requiring a simultaneous solution of the entire price problem. *

## QUESTIONS

1. In what two major ways does multi-stage approach to pricing differ from usual approaches to pricing?
2. What are some of the differences in the pricing problems at Zenith Radio and Columbia Broadcasting?
3. Describe each of the six stages in multi-stage pricing.

# 60. Concerning the Fine Art of Making a Profit*

D. F. Houlihan, Partner, Price Waterhouse & Co.

*In this period of the profit squeeze businessmen must learn to make careful analyses of profits by products to chart shrewd course through the siren songs of certain business myths and fallacies about pricing.*

All of you undoubtedly remember the story set forth in Homer's *Odyssey*, in which Ulysses plugged the ears of his crew and strapped himself to the mast of his ship so that he could listen to the sirens without heeding their call. By so doing he was able to steer his ship safely between Scylla and Charybdis.

Businessmen are in somewhat the same position as Ulysses, except that not all of us have plugged ears nor are we tied to the mast. Ulysses was able to take advantage of the experience of others and, recognizing that danger, took adequate preventive measures to keep himself from making an unwise move. Today the dan-

* Reprinted from the *Price Waterhouse Review*, Autumn 1961, p. 1.

gers are not always as clearly recognizable as those which confronted Ulysses.

## THE SIREN SONG OF VOLUME

Take the siren call of "volume." This is an insidious call which holds the lure of profitability through spreading overhead over a greater number of units thereby reducing unit costs. Now there is no question but that increased volume produces increased profits—provided that the cost of getting this volume does not exceed the profit it brings. It is often possible to reduce both the selling price and the unit cost so that both the customer and the supplier profit. This is good sound orthodox economics—the basis of industrial health and progress. The siren begins to call, however, when we start to say, (1) why not build volume by setting prices so that different classes of customers or products bear disproportionate shares of the cost or (2) why not set some prices so that we cover our direct cost but not our full costs and instead of making a true profit make a "contribution to overhead." Then a steady, strong, restraining hand is needed. The argument is strong and skill and restraint are needed to avoid wrecking the ship.

Under this concept, we determine those costs which are direct—that is, "out-of-pocket" costs which vary proportionately with volume. We treat this cost determination as being a basic figure, and any recovery in sales prices in excess of this direct cost as representing a marginal contribution. This contribution is supposed to pay all of our plant fixed costs, such as supervision, depreciation, insurance, taxes, and also costs of marketing, distribution, etc., and to provide us with a profit over and above all costs.

Now this siren, volume, sends out her beautiful song. We hear from this, that if we can attain sales over and above those we would normally expect and can make them at prices which exceed the direct costs and contribute something to our marginal income, we are providing a benefit for the company by increasing its profits. We are gaining volume. There is no indication, however, as to who is supposed to pay for the overhead, marketing, distributing and the profit that should exist at a normally anticipated volume.

Once we start cutting sales prices we are in for real difficulty as you gentlemen know only too well. The problem is that Gresham's law applies to prices. "Bad prices drive out good." Unless you can so restrict the impact of your "bad" or marginal prices that they will not affect the bulk of your business, a new and

lower price level almost certainly will result—for all sales. In some industries bad prices can be established overnight; in some others it can take several years—but established they will be.

I do not mean to imply that the additional information furnished management for pricing decisions by the separation of variable and fixed costs should be withheld simply because it might be misused. If properly used and, possibly, restricted to special situations it can serve a useful purpose. My point is that such data be used with great discretion. When a sales pricing policy based on marginal costing is combined with a sales commission plan where salesmen are paid on volume, the need for discretion is doubly strong.

A case in point as to how to use marginal pricing right. One company, during a temporary recession, employed the principle of direct costing, or covering its out-of-pocket expenses, to obtain a new relatively large account. In going after this business it took into account three points: (1) due to the nature of the business, which involved a high degree of service, it would be difficult for another company to take the account away from them once the customer had been satisfied, (2) the current recession would be temporary, and (3) the improvement in general business conditions would support an increase in price over the long term which the customer would be willing to pay.

Fortunately for this company, all the factors upon which the original low price bid was made worked out, and this customer is now paying what might be considered reasonable trade prices.

There are other similar cases where a company wishes to break into a new territory or introduce a new product or perhaps make a bid on a large contract. In such cases it is helpful to management to know the direct cost of the products to be sold. By adding to the direct cost the expenses of marketing, distributing and administration, management will know the "out-of-pocket" break-even point of such products. Although it might be good business to make certain sales on this basis, the company should ascertain that the remaining sales will be made on a basis that will cover the full overhead and their share of marketing, distributing and administrative expenses and profit. Management must ever be alert to the danger of fixing for most of their products selling prices on the basis of direct costs.

Let me give you an example of the difficulties that can arise from this concept. This example comes from an industry where the relationships of costs and profits are easily seen. We were requested to assist this company to determine why it was not profitable, and to determine what could be done to help it make money. We found that the company did not know its costs and as a result was preparing bids on an unsound basis. By revising their methods of costing and record-keeping, we were able to provide management with information as to the fixed and variable costs which could be used as a reliable basis upon which to make estimates for pricing bids.

In working with the officials of this company, we assisted them in analyzing the information they were able to obtain in regard to their competitors' bids on a number of contracts. When we used the knowledge of the industry of this company's officials and the cost information developed from the company's records, it became apparent that their competitors were bidding for contracts on a basis which would barely recover the direct labor and materials and other direct costs of performing the contract. This industry was in the doldrums and companies were fighting for business merely to keep their organizations together.

What was the result? Our client, in order to keep his organization together, was forced to submit bids on the basis of his direct costs. This made the competition even more cutthroat than it had been before. A number of the weaker companies in the industry have been forced out of business. Neither we nor our client know the final answer in this case, because it will be a number of years before our client finds it necessary to replace major pieces of his heavy equipment. His cash reserves are rapidly disappearing. Major maintenance work on his equipment is being deferred and he is becoming less efficient—with resulting higher costs. What will happen when he can no longer operate with his present equipment is not at all clear, although at this moment it would seem that this could be another company that will go out of business. Here is one of those shipwrecks caused by heeding the siren song of volume.

## THE SIREN SONG OF FULL COVERAGE

Another siren is the one that chants "the full line and national distribution" as a sure source of profit. One of the children of this siren is the "loss leader" or its more respectable cousin, the "low profit" item as a business-getter. This is a dangerous policy from the viewpoint of profitability. The "loss leader" can well become the major product because it becomes so easy to sell and so good to buy; the rest of the line might be disregarded. Once this has occurred it becomes extremely difficult to correct for buyers can be just as smart as sellers. It must, however, be corrected if an industry is to be profitable.

In an industry with a great variety of products, it becomes difficult to know just what is the loss leader or low profit item without adequate information. It becomes difficult also to assess what would represent a reasonable line of products for any company which can be sold on a profitable basis. Many companies today are reappraising their marketing policies and pricing policies to eliminate the loss leader and to make each product stand on its own feet. It is only in this way that any company is able to formulate desirable pricing policies and desirable product line policies.

Many distributor organizations today are engaged in analyzing profitability of operations by product line and are completely revising their concepts of customer service from the viewpoint of carrying a full line. Products that do not pay their own way on a "net" profit basis are being discontinued if they cannot be made to pay. This is being done with the advice and assistance of the manufacturer of the product, as the manufacturer realizes that the distributor must have a profitable operation if he is to stay in business. No manufacturer can operate successfully with a weak distribution organization and losses on a continued basis will lead to nothing else. Adequate analysis on a *net profit* basis of products is essential if sales emphasis is to be placed on the proper product.

## THE SIREN SONG OF TAKING ALL ORDERS

A third siren is the one that sings of the necessity of taking all orders—large or small. She sings also of calling on all customers every week or oftener—"to make sure we get all the business." Have you ever stopped to figure out the cost of getting and filling an order? In my long experience in business, as well as the experience of my associates in our consulting activities, we have reached a general conclusion which we call the "80-20 rule." 80% of the volume of sales will be made up of 20% of the items; 80% of the sales will come from 20% of the customers; 80% of the inventory will be in 20% of the items. This generality applies in many

activities of industry, and it is uncanny to see how this same pattern recurs from company to company. This sounds interesting but how can we take advantage of it?

If 80% of our customers provide only 20% of our sales, what are we doing to minimize the cost of carrying on business with these small customers? Do our salesmen call on these small customers with the same frequency as on large customers? Do we give these customers the same prices, do we provide them with the same service as the large customers? Let me cite an example I encountered recently. In establishing pricing schedules, this company set a price of $2 a thousand for a certain item for sales in quantities up to 20,000. Our study of the costs of this company disclosed that there was a fixed cost of $8 an order just to receive the order, write the acknowledgment, schedule the production, make the billing and collect the account. In addition, the company had the cost of calling on the customer and paying a commission. No sale of $40 could be profitable. Yet a substantial *number* of the company's orders for this product were for quantities of 5,000 to 15,000, although these orders constituted a minor part of the volume. Here was an activity which was costing more to carry out than could possibly be received in gross profit on these orders. Disclosure of these costs and discussion of the problems with sales management led to a revision in sales emphasis and in pricing policy.

Another example of the costs involved "in making sure we get all the business" is that of a division in a very large company. This division had developed a new product which would require marketing through slightly different channels than the rest of its products, and there was a need for an increased sales force to provide this marketing effort. Officials of this division, which incidentally was highly successful profitwise, decided to take a look at the possibility of staffing this new sales activity from its existing personnel since the development and training of a completely new sales force would be extremely costly. Therefore, a detailed survey was made of the existing policies on customer calls and of the possibility of estimating what would happen if the frequency of calls was reduced.

Analyses of all of the data regarding customer calls and customer purchases, by use of sophisticated mathematical techniques, revealed that customers reacted to sales calls in a manner similar to that of a learning curve—that is, buying was rather slow at first in relation to the number of calls, but after the customer had become "indoctrinated," the sales did not vary proportionately with calls. By carefully plotting the customers' buying habits in relation to the number of calls, it was found that the number of calls could be reduced by 50%, with a loss in sales of perhaps 3% to 4%. To state it another way: half of the company's sales force was being used to secure 3% to 4% of the total volume. This, you will admit, is not a very productive use of sales time.

This company took the plunge. It transferred half of its sales force to the new product and introduced it very successfully. Its sales of the old products dropped by about 2%, but by slightly changing the emphasis of the salesmen in their calls this ground has been regained. Here was a substantial saving which resulted in increased profits for even this highly successful division.

## GOOD MARKETING MANAGEMENT

This is an area where marketing management can contribute substantially to the profitability of company operations. But to make such determinations, sales management must be in a position to make informed decisions—they must have information such as the following:

1. How many calls do salesmen make in each territory, to each customer? How much does each call cost, including salaries, expenses, car allowances, and the like?
2. How much business are we getting from specific customers or classes of customers as a result of these calls, and what size are the orders?
3. What does it cost to reach various classes of customers through promotional and advertising activities?
4. How much does it cost to receive and edit an order, schedule it, ship it, bill it and collect the receivable?
5. What is the minimum size order in various product classes which can be profitable, considering the foregoing fixed costs of doing business?
6. In view of the costs disclosed by these studies, how adequate is our pricing policy for various order sizes?
7. Do we have a realistic discount policy in view of the fact that orders, and not total business during the year, are often the deciding factor in determining profitability of business?

## REDESIGNING ACCOUNTING PROGRAMS TO MEET MARKETING NEEDS

If my experience has been any indicator of the conditions in your industry, I would suspect that your marketing personnel get very little information from your accounting personnel in forms which are really usable for control of marketing costs. It has been my experience that accountants have been attempting to deal with marketing and distribution costs only in broad generalities and have provided little in the way of useful data to marketing management. Marketing managements have to think in terms of individual calls, individual customers, individual orders. Accounting reports have just not been designed to provide this type of data. I think accountants are beginning to realize this, and I believe that many will be very happy to work with the marketing people to improve the information. It is in this area of marketing and distribution that cost control and cost reduction must be obtained in the future since manufacturing costs in most companies are well controlled and can produce relatively little in the way of future cost reductions, except for relocation of plants in certain instances.

rocks of nonprofitability? In navigation we do this by carefully charting our course through the use of precise instruments which tell us exactly where we are, and through the use of charts developed by experience which show the rocks and the shoals ahead. In business we must do this through quite similar procedures—through analyses of profits by products, through analyses of costs of doing business. To be useful, such data must be developed in substantial detail so that we have some basis for estimating the results of alternative courses of action. Thus, I think we can increase profitability in our companies by proper use of carefully developed cost data—particularly in the areas of marketing and distribution.

## CHARTING OUR COURSE THROUGH THE SIREN SONGS

It is unfortunate that we cannot plug our ears or tie ourselves to a mast to prevent reacting to these siren songs. But we must make decisions and we must take into consideration the actions of our competitors. How then can we prevent our companies from being piled up on the

## QUESTIONS

1. How can marketing management contribute substantially to the profitability of company operations?
2. What are some of the pitfalls of volume sales?
3. How might the accounting department contribute more effectively to profitability analysis and pricing?

## BIBLIOGRAPHY FOR CHAPTER IX

ARTICLES:

"Are Your Volume Discounts Legal?" *Sales Management,* Vol. 84, No. 11 (June 3, 1960), pp. 33–37.

Griffin, Clare E., "When is Price Reduction Profitable?" *Harvard Business Review,* Vol. 38, No. 5 (September–October, 1960), pp. 125–32.

Newman, L. E., "Diseases that Make Whole Industries Sick," *Harvard Business Review,* Vol. 39, No. 2 (March 1961), pp. 87–92.

"Ohio Judge Declines to Ban Price Cutting on Cosmetics Items," *Advertising Age,* Vol. 33, No. 1 (January 1, 1962), p. 12.

Tarpey, L. X., "What About the Good Faith Defense?" *Journal of Marketing,* Vol. 25, No. 1 (July 1960), pp. 62–65.

"What's the Profit in that High-Volume Contract?" *Sales Management,* Vol. 84, No. 6 (March 18, 1960), pp. 89–90.

Wright, W., "Direct Costs Are Better for Pricing," *N.A.A. Bulletin,* Vol. 41, No. 8 (April 1960), pp. 17–26.


BOOKS:

Backman, Jules, *Price Policies and Price Practices.* New York: Ronald, 1953.

Beckman, Theodore N., and Davidson, William R., *Marketing.* New York: Ronald, 1962. Chapters 29–31.

Buskirk, Richard H., *Principles of Marketing: The Management View.* New York: Holt, Rinehart and Winston, 1961. Part 5.

Christenson, Charles J., and Vancil, Richard F., *Managerial Economics: Text and Cases.* Homewood, Ill.: Irwin, 1962. Chapter 2.

Converse, Paul D., Huegy, Harvey W., and Mitchell, Robert V., *Elements of Marketing.* Englewood Cliffs, N.J.: Prentice-Hall, 1958. Chapters 5 and 6.

Dean, Joe, *Managerial Economics.* Englewood Cliffs, N.J.: Prentice-Hall, 1951. Chapters 7–9.

Howard, John A., *Marketing Management.* Homewood, Ill.: Irwin, 1957. Chapter 12.

Lazo, Hector, and Corbin, Arnold, *Management in Marketing.* New York: McGraw-Hill, 1961. Chapter 12.

Oxenfeldt, Alfred R., *Pricing for Marketing Executives.* San Francisco: Wadsworth Publishing Company, 1961.

Phelps, D. M., and Westing, J. H., *Marketing Management.* Homewood, Ill.: Irwin, 1960. Chapters XI–XIV.

Shubin, John A., *Managerial and Industrial Economics*. New York: Ronald, 1961. Chapter 5.

*The Marketing Job*. New York: American Management Association, Inc., 1961. Pp. 238–269.

Tousley, Rayburn, Clark, Eugene, and Clark, Fred, *Principles of Marketing*. New York: Macmillan, 1962. Chapters 26–28.

# X. Ethical and Moral Responsibilities of Marketing

$\mathcal{T}$*HE MANAGEMENT* responsibility, viewed objectively in its job of problem solving, should include a consideration of ethical and moral decisions. Society is a complex maze of institutional influences. Executives responsible for the business institution must wrestle with the moral and ethical problems involved as the business firm does not and cannot operate within a profitable vacuum, impervious to outside influences. An alternative might be to ignore the consideration of ethics or morality; but, what of the consequences? Religious, social, political, and economic values become mixed with the values of the business community, while the business community values are a result of evolutionary forces of attitudes, beliefs, and mores of the total environment.

Business firms are not correctly viewed as social, missionary agencies, but rather as profit making institutions, taking economic risks and performing economic services. To assume this does not relieve the businessman from the burden of weighing the ethical and moral issues as his business decisions are made. Hazy thought and quick judgment may create a feeling toward the problem of ethics and morality that it is one of only current emphasis. Upon serious study, however, we become acquainted with a constant stream of human conduct over centuries of business and social history. The complexities of the industrial environment, the influence of government, recognition of the worth of reputation as a business asset, have enjoined to forceably enter ethical and moral "decision making" into the ever growing assortment of positive business decisions.

Society makes demands upon the business enterprise, and, thereby, upon those who are responsible for the policies of the enterprise. It makes no difference as to the ease or practicality of measurement of these demands whether or not they exist. Management's alternatives encompass at least two possible actions. Ethical and moral issues can be ignored on the basis they cannot be measured, or because it may be felt they can be relegated to minor significance; or they can be positively accepted as a variable requiring managerial decision, and of significance in business operation.

The evolution of business activities within our social environment is a matter of historical record. People, as business policy makers, employees, or as customers, are like merchandise. They have varied with the passage of time. One of the lessons of the historical evolution of business within the social community is that moral and ethical problems have not been placed into a formula-like mold for a simple managerial solution. It does reveal an elusive but an ever persistent variable of ethical and moral action interrelated with problems of pricing, personal selling, advertising, personnel, product design and packaging; indeed the entire scope of business activity.

Classical economists have emerged from moral philosophers; management creeds have resulted from an awareness of ethical attitudes. At the moment, formal textbooks may not devote important segments of their material to ethical and moral decisions. This is not a denial of the problems involved. It is a tribute to the complexities involved.

# 61. Management Ideology: Myth and Reality*

Thomas A. Petit, Director of the Breech School of Business Administration, Drury College, Springfield, Missouri

*When there is strain on the management role, ideology serves as a "reduction gear" enabling executives to integrate into business life changes in social goals to which they become sensitive by participation in other spheres of life.*

A controversial issue in contemporary managerial literature is whether management's prime responsibility is to maximize profits or to take a leading role in achieving broad social goals. This is a false issue because it perpetuates the unrealistic dichotomy between the economy and society established by the classical economists in the late eighteenth and nineteenth centuries.

Myths about management ideology will continue to be confused with reality until management is viewed within the framework of society, of which the economy is but a sub-system. It is the thesis of this article that although the need of executives for an ideology is imperative, in the nature of things there cannot be a unique and permanent management ideology.

## CLASSICAL MANAGEMENT IDEOLOGY

In classical economic theory the entrepreneur is motivated by the lure of profits to expand the output of the goods for which consumers clamor and to cut back

* Reprinted from *California Management Review,* Winter 1961, p. 95. Copyright 1961 by The Regents of the University of California.

the production of less desirable goods. His ideology is delightfully unambiguous: do everything possible to maximize profit short of failing to live up to contractual obligations and committing fraud. The only values to consider are those which can be expressed in money terms and which affect in some way the profit position of the enterprise.

Because of the overlap between entrepreneurship and management, the classical entrepreneurial ideology has become associated with management. According to orthodox economic theory, management's first and only responsibility is to the owners of the enterprise. It is the executive's function to do everything in his power to maximize the firm's profits and to protect the interests of shareholders.

The validity of the classical management ideology can be no greater than that of the model of pure competition of classical economics from which it is derived. Yet it was not till long after most economists frankly admitted the failings of the model of pure competition on theoretical and empirical grounds that it was recognized by some members of management that there might be more to their job than making money.

427

The classical economists committed what Alfred North Whitehead called the fallacy of misplaced concreteness (i.e., mistaking an abstraction for the reality which it represents) when they proceeded from a few general laws of human nature directly to a delineation of economic behavior in specific societies. They did not recognize the importance of social organization and institutions and cultural value-orientation in linking individual psychology and concrete behavior.

Life was conceived as essentially an economizing process because all activity was thought to be undertaken in order to increase pleasure or lessen pain and man's human resources are limited. One consequence of such a conception of life is that economic organization is of vastly greater importance than social organization.

Even today many economists are not willing to consider economics as an aspect of the general science of human behavior. According to some theorists economics has no reference whatsoever to factual data. The central question for them is, how would a thoroughly rational person behave in a competitive world of scarce resources? In this view economics is merely a deductive study of comparative values.

The factor which ultimately did more than anything else to undermine the model of pure competition in the United States was the concentration of economic power which occurred from 1880 to 1905. During this period the structure of the American economy was transformed by the formation of trusts, mergers, holding companies, patent-licensing agreements, interlocking directorates, and joint sales agencies. As a result of this mass consolidation movement the large, multiplant, vertically integrated corporation that we call big business emerged as our preeminent economic institution.

## COMPETITION FOR GIANTS ONLY

According to the model of pure competition each seller's actions are forced in the way that a chess player must move his king when it is put in check. It is the pressure of the monolithic and impersonal market that insures an economic result in the best interests of society. The structural requirement for this result is the decentralization of economic power. Each of the buyers and sellers who come into contact in the exchange process is so small relative to the total market, that he has no choice but to accept the going market price.

Because of the concentration of economic power in the hands of big business, competition today is between giants rather than pygmies in many markets, and the giants have a good deal of discretion over their pricing policy. Prices are determined administratively rather than taken as given by the market.

A major conclusion of a recent study of big business is that many large corporations price their products as though they were public utilities. The fewness of sellers also makes possible a variety of collusive and independent activities to avoid price competition (e.g., overt agreements to fix prices or output; price leadership; uniform cost accounting systems and pricing formulae; basing point pricing). Furthermore, nonprice competition in advertising, packaging, and product innovation attenuate the assumption of price competition.

## CONSUMER NO LONGER SOVEREIGN

Nonprice competition also seriously weakens the restraint placed on firm behavior by consumer sovereignty in the classical model. According to the doctrine of consumer sovereignty the end of economic activity is consumption, so the consumers ultimately determine what is produced in the economy. They allocate their income among the goods competing for their custom in such a way as to maximize their consumption satisfaction, and this insures the optimal allocation of resources in the economy.

The validity of this doctrine must come into question in an economy in which producers strongly influence consumption behavior through advertising, product innovation, and sales promotion. In addition, according to Galbraith the cultural climate is such that consumption is the means and production the end rather than the reverse.

The weakening of the constraints on firm behavior of competition and consumer sovereignty struck a body blow at liberal economic theory from which it has not recovered. Oligopoly theory has been developed to make more realistic the model of how the economy works, but it has become bogged down in indeterminacy and offers no basis for unique predictions.

For a long time the significance of the crumbling of the foundations of the theory of pure competition for classical management ideology was not clearly perceived. So long as there was confidence that firm behavior ultimately is determined by the motive of profit maximization, the classical management ideology could be sustained. Economists might worry about how to make competition more effective so the economy would work according to their model, but businessmen could go their own way sure that they weren't "in business for their health." However, the concentration of economic power which led to the decline in competition and consumer sovereignty also emancipated management from the domination of the shareholders and relieved it of the necessity of maximizing profits.

## STOCKHOLDERS NOT MANAGERS

Few of the individuals who hold stock in big business participate in any way in the management of the firm. Most shareholders feel that their stake in the enterprise is not large enough to warrant taking an active interest in management. Furthermore, they recognize that the task of managing big business is so complex, technical, and time-consuming that it is impossible for an outsider to do it justice. As long as dividends are regular and considered to give an adequate return on investment, stockholders are content with the incumbent management. It is only rarely that they rebel and attempt to oust an existing management.

The separation of ownership and control of big business has shorn the owners of any entrepreneurial function and they have become *rentiers*. The top management officials of most large corporations tend to be self-perpetuating oligarchies. They are members of the board of directors and in general, they dominate the board. There is no legal reason why big business management cannot be entirely self-selective if it chooses.

The autonomy of management means that it is not compelled to have the uni-dimensional profit motive the entrepreneur was suposed to have had in the nineteenth century. Executive incomes are semi-fixed and are not related in any set way to the profit experience of the firm. The independence of management from the shareholders makes it possible to emphasize other objectives such as the prestige of management; the position of the firm in the industry; the long run survival value of the firm; and the welfare of employees and customers. Beardsley Ruml thinks that profit is a kind of score in a competitive game which gives the winning management recognition. It may reasonably be concluded that while profits must be earned to maintain management in power, there is no necessity that they be maximized. If management is under no compulsion to maximize profits the classical management ideology is not valid and there is no unequivocal rule of action to guide the behavior of executives in operating the firm.

## SOCIALLY RESPONSIBLE MANAGEMENT

The implications for the classical management ideology of the weakening of the social controls over management have not been lost on many top executives. Some of them have searched for a new credo and have invented the ideology of "socially responsible management," which is assuming the proportions of a new orthodoxy.

They contend that the corporation is such a powerful institution in American life that it is socially disastrous to conceive of it as merely a profit-making organization. Whether management likes it or not its function must change, they argue. It must accept its full responsibility for the way in which the activities of big business affect society. If it does not, the corporation "may be in danger of eclipse because of its failure to safeguard the environmental conditions that nurture its survival and growth.

It is frequently suggested that the proper function of management is to administer the enterprise for the welfare of several groups in addition to the shareholders (e.g., employees, customers, suppliers, the community, government), impersonally arbitrating among their various interests. This approach appeals to many management men because of its moral tone, and it is being articulated explicitly in the company creeds and management philosophies which big business has publicly announced in recent years.

Among the overt manifestations of the new orthodoxy are participation by executives in political affairs, corporate giving, support of educational institutions, various employee welfare measures, community relations, and intensified public relations campaigns. These activities are considered essential to safeguard the position of the corporation, and sometimes they are justified on this basis alone. According to Richard Eells, "A prudent regard for all the interests that merge in making the business a going concern now and in the future is, in fact, the only way to protect and to augment shareholder equity."

But it would be a mistake to think that social responsibility of management is merely a public relations gesture that has as its objective the protection of the firm's profit position. As Theodore Levitt points out, "Self-conscious dedication to social responsibility may have started as a purely defensive maneuver against strident attacks on big corporations and on the moral efficacy of the profit system. But defense alone no longer explains the motive." There is a sincere desire on the part of responsible executives to gain the respect of the general public by utilizing their considerable power for the common good. The focus is on the corporation as a social institution and the pursuit of profit is secondary in importance to the public interest.

## THE "NEW FEUDALISM"

The new orthodoxy has its opponents as well as proponents; there has been a strong revival of the classical management ideology as a reaction to the doctrine of management responsibility to society. Theodore Levitt, who has written one of the most incisive rebuttals of the new orthodoxy, says "the business of business is profits . . . In the end business has only two responsibilities—to obey the every-day face-to-face civility (honesty, good faith, and so on) and to seek material gain." He foresees the new orthodoxy leading to "a new feudalism," with the corporation investing itself "with all-embracing duties, obligations, and finally powers—ministering to the whole man and molding him and society in the image of the corporation's narrow ambitions and its essentially unsocial needs."

Others fear that so much capital, talent, and energy will be devoted to essentially social welfare measures that the corporation will not be able to get on with its job. This is objected to on moral grounds because the interests of the shareholders will be sacrificed for those of other groups. Those who view management within the traditional motivational framework of profit maximization argue that the exercise of managerial powers to benefit anyone but the shareholders is illegitimate and not in the best interests of society in the long run.

Kelso and Adler say, "For the management of a corporate enterprise to dispose of what rightfully belongs to its stockholders without their free, present and affirmatively expressed consent is despotism, and it remains despotism no matter how benevolent or wise management is in acting for what it thinks to be in the 'best interests' of its stockholders."

## NEW MANAGERIAL ELITE

But the most fundamental objection to the new orthodoxy is that it srikes at one of the foundations of capitalism, the separation of political and economic power through the institutional device of private property. According to one line of thought we are in danger of coming under the domination of a management elite as powerful and as unresponsive to the popular will as the bureaucratic industrial leaderships which operated the prewar Nazi and Fascist economies and the one which controls the contemporary Soviet economy.

This is the eventual outcome predicted by James Burnham in his pioneer work *The Managerial Revolution,* and according to sociologist C. Wright Mills we have already reached this stage in the United States. Mills denies that the American people govern themselves economically or politically. He thinks that power of a generalized nature is concentrated in the hands of a political, economic, and military elite. Autonomous big business management is in the driver's seat in the economy and it has a smooth working relationship with the warlords and the politically powerful.

## WHICH IS RIGHT?

Which is right, classical management ideology or the new orthodoxy? The former is solidly based on a refined theoretical system, which is itself erected on misleading if not invalid assumptions. The latter has more claim to realism, but it is not based on any theoretical foundation. Of the two, the new orthodoxy is less guilty of the fallacy of misplaced concreteness, but it too is described and discussed within the frame of reference of traditional liberal economic theory which treats the economy as a discrete entity not subject to the laws of society.

Man does live in society and he must come to grips in some way with social laws which are human in origin and application. Economic activities are influenced, just as every other aspect of man's social behavior, by the society and culture in which he lives. To get at the reality of management ideology the frame of reference must be a specific society with a unique social organization and system of values.

## THE STRAIN THEORY
## OF IDEOLOGY

The business executive is not a robot who functions only within and for the corporation. His role as businessman is just one of the parts which he plays in the social drama. He also participates in society as husband, father, neighbor, voter, taxpayer, and citizen. Associated with each role is a mode of behavior which is culturally determined and socially recognized.

The executive must conform to the behavioral norms which apply to his various roles in some minimal degree if he is to enjoy the benefits bestowed on the individual by his society. This is not a simple matter because many of the demands made upon him in the various roles he occupies are inconsistent with one another.

This strains the management role and gives rise to stress in the individual.

For instance, a rising junior executive may find it expedient to remain silent on a political issue if his views differ with those of his superior because an overt difference of opinion may hurt his chances for promotion. The individual must protect himself against the tension produced by conflicts between his different roles if he is to survive and function effectively in the various areas of life in which he participates.

## SEPARATION OF BUSINESS
## AND ETHICS

One solution is to avoid conflict by keeping the roles and their associated behavioral norms and values in airtight compartments so that the contact which is a necessary precondition for conflict never occurs. This approach to the problem is difficult to maintain, and it is much less common today than in previous eras. In *The Folklore of Capitalism* Thurman Arnold reproduces a newspaper report as it appeared in *The Washington Post* on July 12, 1937 of the testimony of John E. Edgerton, former president of the National Association of Manufacturers, before the Senate committee holding hearings on the Black-Connery wages and hours bill in 1937:

Baldish and grim-faced, his sandy eyebrows knitted in a scowl, Edgerton had told the committee that he had "allowed" a number of grandmothers to work for $6 a week during the depression "as a human thing."

Apparently shocked by his testimony, both Republicans and Democrats joined in close examination of the aggressive witness. . . .

Edgerton burst out: "Why, I've never thought of paying men on a basis of what they need. I don't inquire into what they want. I pay men for efficiency.

"Personally I attend to all those other things, social welfare stuff, in my church work." (Here the crowd in the hearing room roared with laughter.)

Edgerton, glaring at the spectators, sneered:

"Of course, some people don't know about that sort of thing, church work and so . . . *But that's the feeling side of life, church contributions and church work. That's not business.*"

Few businessmen today hold such a fragmented view of the world, and not many who do would care to admit it. But they have the same psychological need as Mr. Edgerton to avoid conflict between values. As businessmen they are sometimes compelled to take actions which are contrary to the demands of their other social roles in the family and community.

Management ideology fulfills the vital function of resolving and alleviating the anxieties and doubts caused by the conflict between business and nonbusiness norms and values. Thus management ideology has a psychological rather than an economic origin. It is an essential part of the executive's psychological equipment to meet the demands of his occupation. This suggests that in order to understand the phenomenon of management ideology it is necessary to first know why there is strain in the management role.

## STRAIN IN MANAGEMENT ROLE

There must be a high degree of social control over management; it is one of the most important roles in the social system because of the emphasis placed on economic well-being in our value system. We are a materialistic people in the sense that we place a much higher value on human comfort and pleasure in the present life than contemplation of a life hereafter.

Sustained economic progress is one of our most cherished goals. Consequently, we are rationalistic in organizing economic resources, and we have confidence in man's ability to eventually subjugate nature. Managament is bound to play a key role in achieving the goal states of such a value system.

It is because of the importance of the management role that executives feel so much strain in their business life that they need an ideology. They share this need with congressmen, bishops, generals, and other individuals to whom society has allocated a large measure of power as one of the facilities to be exercised in

the performance of their roles. If incumbents of management roles had the same degree of control over social and nonsocial objects as newsvendors there would be as little need for a management ideology as there is for newsvendors' ideology.

A second cause of strain is the nebulous nature of management role expectations. The function of management essentially is to organize, coordinate, and direct disparate talents and activities to accomplish collective goals. This tells us little about what to expect from an executive in any particular management situation. There is a wide variety of possible approaches to the same management objective, and for this reason management will always be more of an art than a science. If the role expectations of management were as explicit and circumscribed as those of the occupational role of the mailman, there would be little room for discretion and the second source of strain would not exist.

## WHY MANAGERS ARE CONSERVATIVE

But what is the cause of conflict which gives rise to the strain? To answer this question the relationship between society and its economic sub-system, within which management functions, must be examined. The economy is the sub-system of the society which is chiefly concerned with means. It is in the political sphere that the question of ends is resolved.

Because of its key role in the economy, management is in the forefront of the process of adapting economic means to ends. In the broadest sense the role expectations of management consist of a generalized readiness to carry out society's will in the economic sphere. The strain arises because of the impossibility of achieving a smooth articulation between the ends of societal goal states and the means of management role expectations.

Societal goal states are uncertain in the short run because they are formed in the crucible of interaction between values and events. Values are relatively stable in the long run, but events are in constant turmoil. Some events continually further the emergence of goals associated with particular values and others hinder them, and it is not till long after the battle is over that the turning point can be assessed. Society is always moving in some direction, but at any one time it is difficult to interpret the social drift.

This is the reason for the conservatism of businessmen. Like judges, executives tend to be reluctant to exercise their power to take the lead in directing the course of social change. It seems paradoxical that management is one of the most conservative groups in society because it is in the vanguard of technological progress. On this point James Worthy says, "the philosophy of liberalism is by and large more natural and comfortable for the modern businessman and better fitted to the needs of his role than the philosophy of conservatism."

This view has much to recommend it, but it overlooks the importance for social stability of a lag between changes in societal goal states and their implementation in the economy. If management were to become the architect of social progress the economy would engulf the society.

It is part of the burden of management that it must forever follow the uneven and winding trail of social consensus. Because social change is a more or less permanent condition and management is by temperament and social necessity conservative, there will always be strain in the management role. When it becomes clear what the social consensus is, executives adapt their behavior to the new status quo and adopt an appropriate ideology so that the level of strain in the management role can be reduced.

## "THE FELT NECESSITY OF THE TIMES"

Strain in the management role serves the invaluable social purpose of forcing executives to reorient their role expectations in line with the current social drift so that the economy is integrated with the rest of society. Management ideology is merely the reduction gear which enables executives to integrate into their business life the changes in social goals to which they are made sensitive by their participation in other spheres of life.

In his search for the wellsprings of the common law, Oliver Wendell Holmes was impressed with the turning, twisting convolutions the law had taken historically. He concluded that there were no ultimate truths which had been successively refined to form the corpus of law, but rather the law was a reflection of the tortuous path which the social organism had traversed. The only interpretation consistent with the facts was that the law was molded in conformity with "the felt necessity of the times."

Justice Holmes' reasoning has just as much relevance for management ideology as the common law. The classical management ideology had a powerful sway over men's minds in the late eighteenth and nineteenth centuries because it was consistent with a profoundly important shift in direction of the social organism.

For the complimentary societal goals of social equality and the dignity of the individual to be achieved a much more rapid development of economic resources than had ever occurred in the past was necessary. The profit motive was essential to secure the degree of motivation required for the successful exploitation of the new technology of the Industrial Revolution.

The mistake made by the classical economists was to think that the profit motive is instinctual, whereas the truth is that the profit motive and all that it stands for can be an important motivation only so long as it conduces to movement in the direction of societal goal states. The current confusion over profit maximization versus social responsibility of management is simply a reflection of the difficulty of interpreting the contemporary social mandate.

**QUESTIONS**

1. Why is it necessary to view management within the framework of society?
2. What does the idea of socially responsible management have as its goal?
3. In what way does the consumer's position in the economy involve managerial responsibility? Discuss.
4. Does the structure of business complicate the problem of responsibility to society? Explain.
5. Where are the strains in management's role in our value systems? Discuss.

# 62. Ethical Theory, Societal Expectations, and Marketing Practices*

Clarence C. Walton, Associate Dean, Graduate School of Business, Columbia University

*Corporate leaders would agree that the economic objective of competitive policy in a market economy is to promote good performance in which progress through technological change is encouraged, and the economic activity contributes to, or at least does not interfere with the achievement of equally important social and political goals.*

A market—manned by millions of wholesalers, retailers, advertisers, warehousers and the like, and servicing hundreds of millions of consumers both here and broad—is bound to generate an occasional uneasiness over its performance. Seizing upon its deficiencies, the critics have mounted a rather sustained attack.

* Reprinted from *The Social Responsibilities of Marketing*, Proceedings of the Winter Conference of American Marketing Association, December 27–29, 1961. Edited by William D. Stevens.

If, at times, the criticisms have been lacking in logic they have never been found wanting in temerity of conclusions. "Waste-makers," "Hidden persuaders," "hucksters," are not terms calculated to raise the merchant to any high level of public esteem. Are these descriptions adequate? Is the marketing man's consciousness conscienceless? Are high and low positions in marketing peopled by greedy and grubby denizens? Or have we evolved market institutions that perform economic functions with a high degree of efficiency? And are these functions carried out in what can be fairly described as "ethical" ways? Perhaps on close examination there may be seen in the market a magnificently intricate and symmetrical mechanism which keeps customers supplied with need, businessmen excited by profits, and the total society satisfied with its merits.

It may be fairly conceded that the attractions and motivations of the marketplace are not found in high moral ideals; indeed marketing institutions and practices may be developed in a morally neutral climate to satisfy material wants. Yet, these institutions and practices must not collide with other values in the social system. And when they promote concern over higher values, then marketing practices can be said to contribute to a more just and humane society.

A self-adjusting market, isolated from the rest of the community and operating under its own exclusive autonomy, may have been the ideal of the nineteenth century. It is not the reality of the twentieth century. There is a range for greater judgment and greater choice which are primary ingredients of an ethical act. The assignment is to discover where moral guidelines are to be sought: in the Church? In business itself? In philosophical inquiry?

## I. INTRODUCTION

Philosophers' condemnations of man's cupidities and theologians' fulmination against human frailties are as old as Plato's *Republic* and as new as Rabbi Finkelstein's now-famous *Fortune* blast against the current business ethos.[1] To concede that material affluence is not

¹ Louis Finkelstein, "The Businessman's Moral Failure," *Fortune,* September, 1958, pp. 116 ff.

moral influence, that power is not probity, or economic security the equivalent of safety is to germinate a paradox. The paradox begins to press home when we are told that television has turned the high art of polity into the low cult of personality, and that the marketplace has despoiled judgment, debased tastes, invaded individual sovereignties, and eroded moral fibre.[2] If, indeed, these are the ample symptoms of the working out of a Gresham's law of ethics, then Marx's prophesies of the eventual doom of free-market economies appear readied for fulfillment.[3]

Yet for all its alleged weaknesses, no less an authority than Reinhold Niebuhr holds firmly that the economic realm, above all else, has become the "strategic testing ground of the adequacy and relevance of a religio-moral worldview."[4] The significance of the observation is the more striking when it is realized that traditional religious attitudes reveal an anti-economic bias. "The careful, calculating, economizing way of life is neither prophetic nor poetic. It counts the costs; it asks for reward; it has no fine frenzies; it is humdrum, commonplace, even a little sordid"[5]—yet the economic way of life becomes the stage where the drama of Everyman is to be worked out. If Niebuhr's observation is correct then the relationship of the business order to so-

² Vance Packard's name and particularly *The Hidden Persuaders* (London: Longman, Green, & Co. 1957) come immediately to mind. More devastating criticisms have come from Eric Fromm, *The Sane Society* (New York: Rinehart & Co., 1955), and Will Herberg, *Judaism and Modern Man* (New York: Farrar, Strauss, & Young, 1951), esp. pp. 16–23. The phenomenon is not unique to the United States. Viewing the French scene, Reverend Joseph Thomas bemoaned: *"Materialisation des hommes, materialisation du corps social, tel est le jugement qu'on doit porter sur notre societe quand on l'etudie objectivement." "Le mieux-etre materiel est-il le tout de la vie d' un peuple?" Chefs d'Enterprise* V (Octobre, 1961), p. 15.

³ *Manifesto,* (New York-New York Labor News Co.,) 1933) p. 15.

⁴ *An Interpretation of Christian Ethics,* (New York: Meridian Books, 1956), p. 165.

⁵ Kenneth Boulding, "Religious Foundations of Economic Progress," *Harvard Business Review,* Vol. XXX, (May-June, 1952), pp. 33–41.

ciety's total value structure—always relevant—becomes crucially important.

The modest objective of this inquiry is to explore such relationships from a general and theoretical framework.[6] Although involved with three basic notions which have been identified as *ethical criteria*, *societal expectations*, and *marketing practices*, respectively, it is patent that each concept has its own solar system. The following questions are most germane:— what *ought* and *ought not* to be done by the market; what should we *like* the market to do beyond the ethical imperatives; and what *is* the market actually doing. The range moves from the obligatory to preference systems to actual practices. The trilogy, while suggestive of focus, fails to penetrate the heart of the matter which is the interplay of values in a pluralistic society. Involved is the total *social system* by which is meant the observable structure and organization through which basic human needs are satisfied. These needs relate to man's religious, political, cultural, sexual and economic life, and the activities carried out according to socially acceptable norms in order to achieve certain objectives. Since norms embody values, it is evident that the social system is "held together by its internal agreement about the sacredness of certain fundamental moral standards."[7]

As thus construed, the system is geared to accomplish the social good—defined by Newman as less the purusit of a theoretical absolute and more a choice among warring alternatives. To understand and to achieve the good impose the necessity for effective dialogue between men of different intellectual persuasions but of equal good wills. It assumes that peace and liberty, equity and security constitute the good society.[8] What are our sacred and fundamental values? How are they determined and expressed? What priorities prevail when value systems clash? How are refinements made without injury to the polity?

Three broad categories can be usefully employed to treat of such questions and they may be classified as (1) theological norms, (2) philosophical ethics, and (3) the business *ethos*. The first class involves the Church where matters of faith and sectarian allegiance influence and guide human behavior; the second category looks to values that can be rationally discovered by all men; and the third embraces a host of commitments and expectations which characterize an advanced industrialized society. While the classifications are less than fully satisfactory, they have merit in permitting the development of important distinctions between the supernatural and the secular orders; otherwise, there is the real danger of developing something akin to social monophysitism[9].

## II. THE BASIC TERMS: LEVELS FOR VALUES

A. *Theological Norms*—may be roughly described as standards for conduct which flow from those basic views of Deity and of man and which are often

---

[6] Reliance on the generalist view carries an important caveat for it means that in this short treatise certain details will be insufficiently treated—a weakness common to the macro approach. When the occasion warrants, therefore, the author assumes a risk in expressing opinions on trends for which supporting empirical data may be presently inadequate. In such cases note will be made that it is an informed opinion and not an established judgment.

[7] "In an inchoate, dimly perceived, and seldom explicit manner, the central authority of an orderly society, whether it be secular or ecclesiastical, is acknowledged to be the avenue of communication with the realm of sacred value." Edward Shils and Michael Young, "The Meaning of the Coronation," from the collection edited by Seymour M. Lipset and Neil Smelser, *Sociology: The Progress of a Decade*, (Englewood Cliffs: Prentice-Hall, Inc., 1961), p. 232.

[8] Terence Kenny, *The Political Thought of John Henry Newman*, (London: Rutledge, 1957), pp. 77–88.

[9] An ancient Christological heresy which held that the divine and human natures of Christ fused to form a distinct third nature even as gold and silver combine to form electrum.

derived from Revelation; from the point of view of the communicant, such standards remain above the realm of debate. They are fixed values and hold the highest priority because they reflect God's will. Exchange of views is difficult, even when undertaken, because each religion clothes its most subtle values within an elaborate ritual[10] which has profound significance to the adherent and is often meaningless to the outsider. Perhaps Plato was right when he declared flatly in the VIIth Epistle that the really profound insights are not communicable; hence poetry, allegory and myth are always necessary. The religions of the Bible are convinced that their roles in the American Commonwealth are "vastly more than a subordinate sociological datum performing an increasingly peripheral function in society. The religions want to be a source of culture, determining its nature from a point of reference beyond it."[11] Whether the Churches are achieving such an objective is difficult to say in view of the conflicting nature of the data and the contradictory opinions held by theologians themselves. For example, Gerhard Lenski's studies of Detroit offer substantial evidence that religion colors the daily behavior of men at both the personal and social levels. Installment buying, savings, attitudes toward work, and political preferences are influenced by the socio-religious group to which one belongs.[12] Yet others, like Rabbi Finkelstein and John Courtney Murray, are far from persuaded that religion has any appreciable influence on

American social behavior or institutions.[13] Two factors suggest support for the former view. In the first place there is evidence that business practices are being conditioned by religion and the efforts of Quaker businessmen associated with Walter Lamb is a case in point.[14] Secondly, there are clear signs that the Churches are taking a more positive and direct position on contemporary mercantile issues.[15] There are even small signs of reciprocal interests by the business community. Perhaps it is unlikely that anything will develop to approximate the sixteenth century experience of Tomas de Mercado, a theologian at Salamanca, who was earnestly requested by the Seville merchants (then engaged in making the town the trading center for all the Spanish-American possessions) to provide them with a primer in business morality,[16] but it is worth noting that the committee on business ethics set up under the aegis of the Commerce Department does include clergymen. Looking ahead a decade, businessmen might reflect nostalgically on the easy homiletics of the

[13] Finkelstein, loc. cit., and John Courtney Murray, *We Hold These Truths*, (New York: Sheed and Ward, 1960).

[14] T. H. Blum, "Social Audit of the Enterprise," *Harvard Business Review*, Vol. XXXVI (March–April, 1958), p. 77 and esp the now-celebrated article by O. A. Ohmann, "Skyhooks: With Special Implications for Monday Through Friday," *Loc. cit.*, Vol. XXXIII (May–June, 1955), pp. 1–9. The most recent attempt to develop empirical data has been reported in part by Rev. R. C. Baumhart, "How Ethical Are Businessmen?," *Harvard Business Review*, Vol. XXXIX (July–August, 1961), esp. p. 168.

[15] See, for example, the report on the 1959–60 steel strike from the Special Committee of the National Council of Churches of Christ in the U.S.A., *In Search of Maturity in Industrial Relations*, (New York: 475 Riverside Drive, 1961), and the sharp critique by James Kuhn, "Piety and Maturity in Labor Management Relations," *Christianity and Crisis*, Vol. XXI (March 6, 1961). This difference of opinion within the "Protestant family" has not parallelled the acerbity of the quarrel over *Mater et Magistra* between liberal Catholics (represented by the Jesuit editors of America) and the conservative Catholics of William Buckley's persuasion as reflected in *The National Review*.

[16] The primer was written in 1569 and entitled *Suma de Tratos y Contratos*. See Bernard Dempsey, *Interest and Usury* (Chicago: Loyola University Press: 1960), for a critical commentary, p. 126.

[10] See Lyman Bryson *et al.*, eds., *Symbols and Values: An Initial Study*, (New York: Harper and Brothers, 1954), esp. Chs. 4, 5, 7, 10 and 12.

[11] William Lee Miller, "Religion and the American Way of Life," *Religion and the Free Society* (New York: The Fund for the Republic, 1958), p. 4.

[12] *The Religious Factor* (New York: Doubleday Co., 1961). Support of this view is given in the two new volumes edited by James Ward Smith and A. Leland Jamison, *Religion in American Life* (Princeton: Princeton University Press, 1961).

*Organization Man*—and with a wish to return to the conformities which characterized the fifties.

What conclusions may be drawn so far as religious influences on the market? Clearly, Churches are reaching into the marketplace to make known religious views as they relate to a variety of business problems, including wages and working conditions, Sunday shopping and sympathy strikes, competition and advertising.[17] If this development expands, the market faces discipline from external forces for the first time in the century— a development not to be taken lightly by either minister or marketer.[18]

B. *Philosophical Ethics*—is here employed to denote the nature of right and wrong, good and evil as clarified by analysis and discussion. It can employ with equal effect either the deductive or inductive methods but its essential characteristic—as distinguished from religious ethics—is its complete reliance on human reason working with human materials: man's nature and man's institutions. However one views the intricate technical debates between absolutists and relativists,[19] between natural-law theorists and pragmatists, or between those who

lament or ignore the decline of a public philosophy,[20] one is driven inexorably to fall back to an image or "model of man" as the ultimate arbiter of such differences.[21]

Now the model of man depends largely on three assessments as these touch on (1) his capability for rational judgment, (2) his capacity for exercising free options among defined alternatives, and (3) his basic motivations. Ever since Freud the whole thrust of psychology has been into examinations of man's irrational impulses. Herbert Simon assures us that "however adaptive the behavior of organisms in learning and choice situations, the adaptiveness falls far short of the ideal of maximizing postulated in economic theory. Evidently, organisms adapt well enough to 'satisfice'; they do not, in general, 'optimize'."[22] The evidence is however, far from conclusive[23] to suggest abandonment of a theory which, flowing from scholastic thought through classical economic theory, underpins representative government, personal responsibility, consumer sovereignty, and the Western legal system.[24] There is postulated there-

---

[17] Encyclicals like *Rerum Novarum* and *Mater et Magistra*, and the studies sponsored by the Federal Council of Churches are clearly concerned with matters that cannot be viewed as strictly related to dogma. See G. C. Tracy, S. J., ed., *Five Great Encyclicals* (New York: The Paulist Press, 1939) for the earlier papal encyclicals. The America Press of New York published in 1961 the English text of *Mater et Magistra*. The Protestant study was summarized by Marquis Childs and Douglass Cater, *Ethics in a Business Society* (New York: The New American Library, 1954).

[18] This is said because there are substantial differences in ethical approaches to social problems. The differences are brilliantly developed in succinct form by Norman St. John-Stevas, *Life, Death and the Law* (Bloomington: Indiana University Press, 1961), Ch. 1. A longer treatment but of equal competence is by Edward Duff, *The Social Thought of the World Council of Churches* (London: Longman, Green, 1953), esp. pp. 93–106.

[19] That all is not relative in human affairs is argued persuasively by R. L. Humphreys, "Human Nature in American Thought," *Political Science Quarterly*, Vol. XIX (June, 1954), pp. 266–271. We agree with this position.

[20] See Walter Lippmann, *Essays in the Public Philosophy* (New York: The New American Library, 1955), and David Truman, "The American System in Crisis," *Political Science Quarterly*, Vol. LXXIV (Dec., 1959), pp. 481–493 for contrary views. The nub of the matter in Lippmann's view is that institutions in Western society are unworkable without relevance to a natural law. "Alexander had discovered empirically what Zeno was to formulate theoretically—that a large plural society cannot be governed without recognizing that, transcending its plural interests, there is a rational order with a superior common law," p. 83.

[21] See Richard Bendix, "The Image of Man in the Social Sciences: The Basic Assumptions of Present-Day Research," *Commentary*, Vol. II (1951), pp. 187–192.

[22] Herbert Simon, *Models of Man: Social and Rational* (New York: John Wiley & Sons, Inc., 1957), p. 261.

[23] See Arnold M. Rose, "A Study of Irrational Judgments," *The Journal of Political Economy*, Vol. LXV (October, 1957), pp. 394–402. "True intransitivity (irrationality) in making choice or judgments appears to be a very rare phenomenon, if it exists at all," p. 401. See also Warren J. Bilkey, "The Vector Hypothesis of Consumer Behavior," *The Journal of Marketing*, Vol. XVI (October, 1951), pp. 137–151.

[24] See Anthony Downs, *An Economic Theory of Democracy* (New York: Harper & Brothers, 1957).

fore, as the first attribute of an ethical act, the capacity for rational decision by seller and buyer on the market; business practices which help or hinder rational choice are tinged with philosophical implications of an ethical nature.

When attention turns to the second problem, the area of individual freedom, the assessment is more difficult. Thirty years ago, John Dewey felt that "personal motives hardly court as productive causes in comparison with impersonal forces"[25] and that the range for individual initiative and action was indeed narrowing to the point of insignificance. Even with this stricture, Dewey allows more latitude than the classical market concept with its assumption of automatic governance by the impersonal forces of supply and demand.[26] There is postulated as the second characteristic of an ethical act freedom to choose. The practical issue is the measure of freedom accorded to producer and to consumer on today's markets.

The third and final problem to be touched upon relates to the purposes of human actions. Is human destiny fulfilled by service to others or to the self? The medievalists put the emphasis on the supernatural order. Man's gaze was firmly fixed on heaven even as his tired eyes and tortured back bent to search the earth's fruit. The Renaissance ruptured this ideal and, later, John Locke and Adam Smith erected a new intellectual structure designed to emancipate man from religious or governmental bondage.[27] If Locke was the forerunner of laissez-faire and Adam Smith its most eloquent spokesman, both were urging a hedonism at variance with the earlier views. Self-interest rather than service was the keyword but the real achievement was the equation of self-interest with public good. Economic justice was to be served in the new dominion not by ethical precept but by impersonal laws of supply and demand.

Yet it must be observed that in the whole school of English classical economics self-interest becomes a dominant factor *only* in economic transactions. What is often forgotten in our concern with the classic *Wealth of Nations* is that Smith earlier rejected the notion that self-interest was the primary determinant of historical progress[28]—a conviction shared by Ricardo and John Stuart Mill.[29] What the classicists asserted, therefore, was that a whole range of interests and motives—such as charity or social service—transcended the marketplace but that economic justice was so uniquely promoted by market mechanisms that no outside intervention by either Church or State was necessary.

In the nineteenth century people as intellectually apart as Marx and Leo XIII challenged the beneficences of the market. Marx denounced self-interest as the "most violent, mean, and malignant passion of the human breast."[30] And Leo XIII, in the 1891 encyclical on labor, felt equally that self-interest had run rampant. Shared in common was a rejection of Smith's invisible hand as the deft manipulator of a just society. Thus was joined the historic debate between

[25] John Dewey, *Individualism: Old and New* (New York: Minton, Balch & Co., 1930), pp. 35–36.

[26] See Edward Mason, "The Apologetics of Managerialism, *Journal of Business*, Vol. XXX (Jan., 1958), pp. 1–11, and Karl Polanyi, *The Great Transformation*, (Boston: Beacon Press, 1957).

[27] See C. A. Czajkawski, *The Theory of Private Property in John Locke's Political Philosophy* (South Bend: Notre Dame Press 1941), & Eli Ginzberg, "The Pleasures and Pains of Economic Man," Bryson, *op. cit.*, pp. 427–432.

[28] Adam Smith, *The Theory of Moral Sentiments*, Part VII, pp. 542–611.

[29] A. A. Young, "The Trend of Economics," *Quarterly Journal of Economics*, Vol. XXXIX (Spring, 1953), esp. pp. 175–181.

[30] *Capital*, Vol. I, Introduction, p. 15. For good interpretation see M. M. Bober, *Karl Marx's Interpretation of History*, (Cambridge: Harvard University Press, 1948), Ch. 4. See also the encyclical *On the Condition of Labor* in G. C. Treacy, *op. cit.*, pp. 1–39.

those who placed a primacy on self-interest and those who placed emphasis on service, between those who counted the gains and others who measured the cost, between men who relied on self-adjusting market and others who would put constraints upon it. While the classical position of strict laissez-faire has been substantially modified there remains the conviction that a more-or-less freely operating market is preferable if the other extreme involves centralized control over prices, wages, and production. This leads directly to the question: can such a market promote justice? Before responding to the question there is required some rough working definition of justice itself.

Now justice, even in the most mechanistic terms, involves two elements: *equality* and *proportionality*. Equality (exchange of equivalents) has traditionally been the kind of justice to which the market could and should make a major contribution; proportionality or equity (allocating fair shares) has been variously assigned to private philanthropy and to the government. It is the contention here that the market should continue to focus on the former and that equity is not a primary purpose in the exchange function.

The argument, summarily stated, rests on the premise that the market is not exclusively an impersonal and automatic mechanism; that it not only permits but relies on human judgment and choice; and that the market judgment and choice should be properly directed to exchange justice (sic, a transactionalistic ethic) and not to problems of social justice.

C. *Business Ethos*—It is clear, then, that the transactionalistic ethic limits moral responsibility in the market to "the most fundamental relationship in the business world"—that which prevails solely between buyer and seller.[31] Even within this narrow spectrum, exchange justice was frequently denied its vital principle by total reliance on ruthless competition and rugged individualism. The real danger now is that in attributing a new dynamic quality of personal freedom and responsibility to the exchange function we expect too much. The full range of justices demanded by a complex, twentieth-century, industrialized economy cannot be met by the market; therefore, what might be called market ethics and what is often termed business ethics are not identical and never will be. The business ethic is primarily a problem for management as it seeks to discharge obligations to a variety of claimants such as stockholders, workers, consumers, suppliers, local communities, and to the public at large.[32]

And ethos will embrace value systems and expectations that have been reasonably well-defined and soundly approved. An affluent society may suggest as reasonable expectations fulfillment of ambition to own one's own home, to have quality and variety in clothing, to be able to join a social club or two. A technological society may face problems of chronic unemployment or depressed areas where the ethos will impose upon management responsibilities for retraining workers, or for assuring job security even at the cost of increased profits. In a word, the ethos shifts markedly with time and circumstances and is concerned, more and more, with equity.

[31] Frank Sharp & P. G. Fox, *Business Ethics: Studies in Fair Competition* (New York: Appleton Century Company, 1937), p. 13. Peter Drucker goes beyond this but carefully limits managerial authority to business performance. *The Practice of Management* (New York: Harper & Brothers, 1954).

[32] Manley Howe Jones, *Executive Decision Making* (Homewood: Richard D. Irwin Co., 1957), is philosophically oriented in its treatment of social objectives for business. He is concerned with the company's ideological, political and legal environment and not simply with more narrowly conceived economic ends. See pp. 280–298.

The point can be illustrated in terms of business power. How internal disciplines are to be developed and managed provided a spacious arena for debate. Some see in the self-perpetuating oligarchies the emergence of the corporate conscience which presumably would make the new lords temporal the guardians of the larger society.[33] Some see the emergence of ethical behavior less in terms of ennobled business motives and more in structural changes within the business order itself.[34] Some would go even further to institutionalize both corporate conscience and corporate structure into a formally organized government pattern.[35]

Since it is patent that a whole host of values is being transformed it may be appropriate to suggest wider use of a concept called the *marginalist ethic*.[36] According to this notion, traditional criteria are challenged vigorously when a society enters a period of dynamic change. Thus, in the nineteenth century, employers who provided for workers beyond market wages soon found themselves at a competitive disadvantage with producers who did not. Soon they refused to accept such responsibilities. Such a development represented a decline in business morality from the older acceptance of trusteeship. But the change can be constructive. Accommodating values to affluence may improve traditional ethical standards by according to workers greater participation in decisions affecting the work life, or by providing

relief from long hours of fatiguing toil. What is involved in marginalistic ethics, of course, is no ethical standard but a device for appraising change in the value systems of society. It seeks to relate the continuum to change: to insist on certain minimum absolute values while allowing wide scope for pragmatic assessment.

## III. SOCIETAL EXPECTATIONS

At a level lower than ethical imperatives and lower than the ethos is a substratum of somewhat inchoate ambitions which can be called *societal expectations*. More specifically, these expectations are generated by knowledge that the traditional theory of scarcity has been modified by affluence, that buy-now-pay-later can be economically prudent (something absolutely alien to the Puritan mentality), that thrift is not always a virtue, that leisure may indeed be more humanly constructive than work, and that property no longer allows untrammeled personal control over its use. Like Gompers' old formula for labor unions, the American consumer wants more.

These expectations have begun to thrust upon the country some disturbing contradictions. We demand efficiency and competition but are uncertain that the traditional alliance between the two is a sound one; indeed, a determination of what constitutes monopoly and what constitutes competition is based less on economic and more on legal criteria.[37] The fact that a high value has been attached to competition does not mean that the concept of itself is an ethical one. While

[33] A. A. Berle, *The Twentieth Century Capitalist Revolution* (New York: Harcourt Brace, 1954).

[34] Courtney Brown, *The Businessman of the Future.* Address to Life Insurance Office Management Assoc. (Chicago, Nov. 10, 1961).

[35] Earl Latham, "The Anthropomorphic Corporation:," *Amer. Econ. Review,* Vol. XLVII (May, 1957), *Proceedings,* pp. 303–31.

[36] Goetz Briefs claims to have first developed the idea in *Untergang des Abendlandes, Christentum and Socialismus* (Freiburg: Herder Publishing Company, 1920); fuller and more systematic treatment is found in Werner Schoellgen, *Grenz-moral* (Dusseldorf: Bastion Publishing Co., 1946).

[37] Irston Barnes, "Competitive Mores and Legal Tests in Merger Cases: The du Pont-General Motors Decision," *The Georgetown Law Journal,* Vol. XLVI (Summer, 1958), pp. 564–632. As Barnes points out, the Supreme Court itself tried the case as a violation of the Sherman Act for eight years before turning—almost as an afterthought—to section 7 of the Clayton Act.

we have not gone nearly so far as Learned Hand who argues that "as a principle of universal application competition defeats itself" since it always leaves the "group worse off than it would be without it," there is a clear ambivalence in our current thinking.[38] Perhaps in basic conviction we are moving toward the Italians who, according to Professor Vito, never rated competition "highly in the general opinion and conviction."[39]

Or let us turn to the contrary pulls imposed on business by a commitment to full employment, and the expectation that the private business sector would assume primary responsibility for its implementation. To achieve full employment involves a per capita increase in Gross National Product which, in turn, can be achieved through increased government expenditures, increased net export, and increased domestic consumption. In a society already at high levels of consumption this means aggressive salesmanship to sell more and more goods if the private sector is to contribute to steady employment. And yet this takes the market perilously close to accepting the wisdom of ultra-special pressure campaignings in advertising and in public relations. It is related to the oft-stated criticism that the market is immoral because it urges man to increase his desires rather than concentrate on his needs.

There is also the expectation of improved products due to technological innovation. Some may see in this expectation a rationale for what Schumpeter called "creative destruction" and still others may feel that the response is planned obsolescence where the product's life is

deliberately shortened and the consumer asked—and unethically in this view—to pay hidden costs. The advance of science has proceeded so intensively of late that property and work—the two pillars of economy—have "at length fallen" with consequence for the traditional morality. The problem, we are told, may be to "find people qualified to consume the increasing abundance of goods produced by a declining number of workers" and the "traditional morality," like the "conventional wisdom" appears inadequate for the assignment.[40] And finally, there is a growing expectation that business has financial responsibilities to schools, to hospitals and to community projects in a manner reminiscent of those once assumed by the medieval *casa*. Here, literally, the consumer is being taxed for philanthropies he may actually disapprove of.

The foregoing catalog is more suggestive than exhaustive. Yet, it illustrates some of the basic contradictions being foistered upon the business community and helps to explain why any application of simplistic ethical formula to the market is misleading and why the new business ethos is still so amorphous.

## IV. MARKETING PRACTICES

Thus far, two major conclusions may be drawn. The first holds that while the Churches are urging their views upon business with greater vigor than ever before, there is not great likelihood of early agreement among theologians on any practical moral code for business. Even if agreement were reached there is little evidence to suggest a willingness on the part of the business to abide by such norms. The second conclusion relates to

[38] Learned Hand, *The Spirit of Liberty* (New York: Vintage Books, 1959), p. 29. Even Alfred Marshall admitted that perfect functioning of competitive markets would not yield automatically ethically acceptable results. *Principles of Economics.* (London: Macmillan, 1948), p. 29 of eighth edition.

[39] E. H. Chamberlin, ed., *Monopoly, Competition and Their Regulation: Papers and Proceedings of a Conference held by the International Economic Association* (London: Macmillan Company, 1954), p. 57.

[40] Gerard Piel, *Consumers of Abundance* (New York: Center for the Study of Democratic Institutions, 1961), pp. 3, 5 and 7.

the business sector itself. In the face of contradictory demands by society there is grave doubt that the business community will effectively develop a satisfactory ethos on the basis of industry codes, adjustments in federal statutes, advertising or selling practices. To say this is not to deny the possibility of a more rational or ethical ordering of marketing institutions. The question here is simply where initiative for guideposts can be secured.

Yet recent anti-trust cases, congressional hearings on the drug industry, and efforts by a distinguished committee of experts to draft a code of business ethics remind us constantly that the market is being assessed by criteria that transcend the sheer profit-and-loss calculus. So the problem essentially is to give greater logic and clarity to these criteria and it is submitted that philosophical ethics has much to offer. Indeed, as an initial basis for inquiry and assessment, one might ask if the market today is encouraging more rational decision-making and more rational consumer behavior? Is it encouraging greater freedom of choice for seller and buyer—even recognizing that gains for one of these parties may mean losses for the other? Is it promoting the growth of hedonistic culture or is the push for greater consumption justified by need to maintain, for example, high levels of employment and growth? If a judgment must be rendered it is the contention that, on the whole, the ethical dimension is being expanded by current market practices. The conclusion beggars support.

If a simple model of the economy embraces the production and sale of goods and services, and their purchase and consumption,[41] it is evident that marketing is concerned with the selling

[41] William A. Kovisto, *Principles and Problems of Modern Economics,* (New York: John Wiley & Son, Inc. 1957), p. 53.

and buying aspects only.[42] Yet the dynamic aspect, missing from such a definition, can be supplied by considering marketing practices as the production of customers (especially regular ones) just as manufacturing is the production of goods. Thus a product improvement designed to attract new customers is a marketing practice. So is a new store, or air conditioning, or a new product or service. Greater convenience in purchasing, and better terms of payment, communication which enhances the customer's knowledge of the product and perception of its value, also fall within this definition.

It should be noted carefully that such marketing practices seek customers who, by definition, are freely choosing agents not coerced into buying. Indeed the distinction between customer and consumer is an important one for the latter suggests recognition of the ethical element of freedom of choice.

But what of those marketing practices which are allegedly designed to blunt judgment and literally "force" a choice? Here advertising becomes the *bete noir.* The advertising fraternity defends itself on grounds that it promotes economic growth and sales while the critics argue that current advertising promotes too much sale of the wrong goods at the wrong prices. Yet both plaintiff and defense rest their cases on what may be a false assumption, namely, the power of advertising itself. This sense of power is overdrawn. A more realistic view suggests that advertising is akin to casting

[42] Theodore Beckman, Harold Maynard, William Davidson, *Principles of Marketing* (New York: The Ronald Press, 1957), p. 4, Sixth Edition. Marketing "covers all business activities necessary to effect transfers in ownership of goods and to provide for their physical distribution. It embraces the entire group of services and functions performed in the distribution of merchandise from producer to consumer, excluding only operations relating to changes in the form of goods normally regarded as processing or manufacturing operations."

in a stream when the fish are biting. It does not lure fish into hitherto uninhabited waters. Industrial, retail-store and mail-order house advertising are geared to market receptivity. Only in cosmetics, remedy goods, and so-called luxury items is advertising effective in creating demand but expenditures in this area are only a small amount of the total expenditures for advertising purposes. Viewed in this context there is not really much room for the "hidden persuaders." And since there are luxury items are they not in the area where less careful calculus of the costs is ethically permissible? And is not the responsibility here more the purchaser's than the vendor's?[43] If one adds the realities of modern life (small suburban homes located some considerable distances from the place of work) it would appear that the American male has neither room nor time for extensive luxury purchases. And even the American woman, after completing expenditures on necessary food and clothing items for herself and children, is not likely to be an overly gullible creature.

If attention is shifted from customer to marketer we note a major development in forecasting that holds promise for greater ethical performance within the market. Forecasting techniques have improved substantially over the past decades and this means ultimately more effective predicting and satisfying of real demand, better control over inventories, and less pressure to create artificial demand or to tamper erratically with prices. From this point one could go on to assert that reasonable expectations make for a a more ethical and orderly society and the farther removed marketing practices are from the "oriental bazaar" mentality

the more efficaciously does the market perform.[44]

If there is emerging a healthy "plus" factor for believing that both sellers and customers are operating in an institutional framework where rational decision making is more, rather than less, likely, what of the second ethical criterion—the element of free choice? At the consumer level it would be hard to argue that such choice does not, in fact, exist in an affluent society. Of all the cruel prisons to freedom none is worse than the dungeon of poverty. In terms of range of goods, in terms of possibilities for knowing the range, the American customer is really a monarch by contrast to other times and other societies.

The most persistent charge of violation in this regard is in terms of "planned obsolescence." But there is a waste factor built into every dynamic process and some of it is deliberately contrived to achieve other goals. "Built-for-life" is not always a blessing as some of the antiquated dwellings along Riverside Drive amply demonstrate. If product change and product design are part of the culture then some measure of obsolescence is tolerable and necessary. This strikes cruelly at the folklore of thrift and frugality but it is one of the prices society is asked to pay to achieve other things. Given a choice between full employment with a planned rapid turnover of products versus the older ethos of thrift and frugality at the cost of unemployment, there is little doubt what option the American people will select.

Now this does not mean a defense of marketing practices which deceive the customer but such offenses can be corrected by guarantees adjusted to the life

---

[43] One of the most thoughtful studies on this aspect has recently been completed by Thomas Garrett, *Some Ethical Problems of Modern Advertising* (Rome: The Gregorian University, 1961) especially Ch. 8.

[44] Paul Lazarsfeld points out that the "empirical study of individual choices or decisions . . . has remained largely undeveloped." *Social Science Research on Business: Product And Potential* (New York: Columbia University Press, 1959), p. 103.

of the product. If a customer knows that one television set will last five years and a second will last fifteen for double the price, there is no assurance whatever that it is to his best interest to buy the latter —given the state of modern technology and the fashions of modern life.

Finally, what of motivations? Are they basically moving away from narrow self-interest toward a loftier plane? The present state of the question is so murky that the best that can be expected are a few reasoned opinions. Plausible arguments have been developed for holding that "Adam Smith's recognition of self-interest as a perennial and durable spring of human conduct is as true today as it was in his time;"[45] that the marketplace responds to the ring of coin and not to moralistic preachment. Yet here again institutional changes of first magnitude are in the making. For example, marketing research is showing first signs of losing its special functional identity as it seeks to relate demand to production. If this develops then the marketing specialist becomes less concerned with his specialty and more concerned with the total process. As a generalist he will tend to relate parts to the whole—to be concerned with the totality. And one of the primary attributes of ethical behavior is precisely this kind of view and this kind of concern. Clearly, there is no necessary connection between an "overview" and more ethical behaviour but in the context of business today there is sufficient grounds for holding that such a relationship will in fact prevail.

Nor is this the full story. Ours is an "organization life" and in the economic order group life is being influenced more significantly by that large association known as the corporation. By definition, the corporation is a voluntary association and so long as it remains true to its origins it can survive only as it holds the allegiances of a wide variety of clients. Unlike the seller in Adam Smith's view, the corporation looks to a life eternal and its objective tempers and restrains temptations to shortcut either morals or mores. It relies spatially on mass markets and the very impersonality of this market demands stability in pricing, quality of goods and servicing. Hit-and-run tactics are effective with the pirate's ship but impossible for the citadel, and the corporation is the citadel in the modern economy.

## V. CONCLUSIONS

Lamentations over the decline of a "traditional morality" which emphasized thrift and labor not infrequently ignore another aspect of the older ethic; namely the conviction that economic practices operated exclusively under their own laws and, hence were immune to, and unaffected by, other ethical considerations. Glorified was the individual with his immediate self-interest. But the glories have been tarnished and many of the old realities dissipated. Corporations, with long-term interest in society at large, have replaced the small seller and the corporation must be, like Caesar's wife, above suspicion. Corporate leaders would agree that "the economic objective of competitive policy in a market economy is to promote good performance—good in the sense that resources are used efficiently (if not ideally), that progress through technological change is encouraged, and the economic activity contributes to, or at least does not interfere with the achievement of equally important social and political goals. . ."[46]

[45] E. G. Nourse, *Price Making in a Democracy* (Washington: The Brookings Institute, 1944), p. 449.

[46] Almarin Phillips, "Policy Implications of the Theory of Interfirm Organization," *American Economic Review: Proceedings*, Vol. LI (May, 1961).

Motivations may still be largely self-centered and hence "conscience alone, whether of public trustees or of Christian businessmen, is not enough."[47] But the institutional mechanisms are changing to provide wider latitude for personal responsibility. It is a hard skeptic indeed who, given prevailing market conditions, would not view the widening scope for personal responsibility with greater enthusiasm than the old iron law of supply and demand. Then, too, history has a long and grim verdict to pass on the ethical planes which prevailed in poverty-ridden societies. Affluence brings its problems but also its opportunities. Finally, improvements in pricing, forecasting and distribution suggest strongly a more effective and more efficient satisfying of consumer demands. The ideal moral economy

of the Ralph Barton Perry's vision[48] may not be realized but surely Professor Henry Oliver is correct when he perceives some major "trends toward a new moral philosophy for Business."[49]

## QUESTIONS

1. What is the conflict of goals corporate leaders face in our market economy? Discuss.
2. What are the characteristics of the market that are sensitive to moral or ethical issues? Explain.
3. Explain the "levels for values".
4. Distinguish between philosophical ethics and business ethics. Discuss.
5. Is there evidence of the charge of a decline in "traditional morality"? Explain.

[47] William C. Frederick, "The Growing Concern Over Business Responsibility," *California Management Review*, Vol. II (Summer, 1960), p. 61. See also Reinhold Niebuhr, *Interpretation of Christian Ethics*, p. 165.

[48] *The Moral Economy* (New York: Charles Scribner's Sons, 1909). See also Robert Bartels, *Business Ethics: Compliance or Conviction* (Los Angeles: University of Southern California, 1961).
[49] *Business Horizons*, Vol. I (Spring, 1958), pp. 33–43.

---

# 63. How Much Control Can Business Endure?*

Earl W. Kintner, law partner Arent, Fox, Kintner, Plotkin & Kahn

*Are Americans unwilling to grapple with the naked concept of power? Is our present distribution of economic power sound? The recent chairman of the Federal Trade Commission examines this distribution, and shows why the antitrust laws are a principal guarantee of its enduring quality.*

Explosive things are capable of producing great good and great evil. Thus,

\* Reprinted from the *Journal of Marketing,* national quarterly publication of the American Marketing Association, Vol. 25, No. 2, July 1961, pp. 1–6.

TNT can be used to erect a dam or destroy a city. So it is with concepts; and of all concepts, none is more explosive than that of power.

In fact, all man-made holocausts that

humanity has endured have been caused by disputes over the allocation of power. Whenever two human beings associate, one question inevitably arises: Who shall exercise the power of decision? The omnipresence of this struggle is felt in the family, the work group, the tribe, the municipality, the nation, and the world.

The question is basic. Think for a moment of how many forms the elemental query takes: democracy or totalitarianism, centralism or localism, the individual or the state, parent or child, teacher or pupil, union or management. All human relationships and all the adjustments that they imply involve, at bottom, the problem of the proper allocation of power.

No man can stand above the agonizing struggle to answer the basic question that every society—using that word in its most fundamental sense—must resolve. Probably the vast majority of human relationships have been organized on a totalitarian basis. In this connection, note that we call our government and way of life the "American Experiment." Our permissive, plural, decentralized way of life was a very new thing only a minute ago in the history of mankind.

## IS POWER AN ALIEN CONCEPT?

Examinations of the naked concept of power have been infrequent in the American experience. Somehow we have always preferred to use other terms. However, it may be refreshing to dissect the anatomy of power without benefit of euphemism.

The American system in all its aspects—political, economic, and social—places individualism at the highest point on its scale of values. We have never wavered from the theory that the power of decision should be dispersed as widely

as possible . . . that each citizen is capable of, and entitled to, determine his own fate. Our faith in individualism has cost us dearly at times, but we have reaped inestimable benefits from it.

Of course, there are limitations on the individual exercise of power. Rampant individualism means anarchy, not freedom.

Dr. Johnson once said, "Power is always gradually stealing away from the many to the few, because the few are more vigilant and consistent." This pithy description illuminates a great deal of human history. The transition from unrestrained individualism to unrestrained tyranny is very swift. One need only say "Athens" or "Rome" to prove the point. The American people, dedicated as they have been to the principle of individualism, have nevertheless found it necessary to evolve a series of restraints on individualism through trial and error. The first element in the equation that is the American government describes these restraints.

Any government necessarily must impose some restraints. Lord Melbourne opined that "the whole duty of government is to prevent crime and to preserve contracts." This is a very skeletal idea of the role of government, but it does encompass restraint, however minimal that restraint may be. At first we were content with an absolute minimum of restraint. But as the industrial revolution gained impetus and as our society became more complex, the need for more sophisticated restraints became painfully evident. In the dawn of our industrial development, some few used their individual freedom without regard to the many.

Tolstoy described 19th Century Czarist Russia in terms that describe any nation in the midst of industrial revolution: "If the arrangement of society is bad and a small number of people have power over the majority and oppress it, every victory over nature will inevitably serve only to increase that power and that oppression. That is what is actually happening."

Restraints upon rampant individualism were necessary in America, and restraints were imposed. But the *nature* of the restraint devised has a peculiarly American cast.

## THE EVILS OF CENTRALIZED POWER

Americans posit the centralization of power as an absolute evil, regardless of whether that power be political or economic. Just as we reject the unchecked exercise of the power of decision by the state, so also do we reject the concentration of power in a few private hands. The centralization of a nation's economy may well lead to the centralization of its polity. A brief reference to the status of guilds in early mercantile economies is enough to establish the point.

By guarantees against the undue concentration of political power, by the system of checks and balances embodied in the Constitution, by the adoption of the Bill of Rights, and by the subsequent extension of suffrage, Americans by the late 19th Century had demonstrated an effective solution to the problem of determining the proper allocation of political power. When our political system was organized, devices to insure the dispersal of power were woven into the basic framework of government.

Viewed in one light, the separation of powers is nothing more than a means of insuring that autocracy will not gain a foothold through the exercise of total governmental power by a single entity. Viewed in the same light, federalism is no more than a device to insure the decentralization of power. The dispersal of power is not a total answer to autocracy;

but insofar as formal organization of government can prevent autocracy, the American adaptation of these two basic devices provides a firm barrier to centralization.

But as the frontier closed, and as the potentialities of the corporate form of business organization in reaping the fruits of the industrial revolution were realized, it became obvious that a pattern of private autocracies was enveloping the American economy.

Americans are activists. They are not disposed to apathy in the face of a threat to their vision of the good society. It became clear that some means had to be devised to shake off the spread of private economic autocracy.

Consider the intellectual picture at the moment of decision. By that time a large number of Continental theorists had grappled with the problem. Saint Simon and the other academic socialists had long since published their answer to concentration of economic power in private hands. Karl Marx had completed his labors at the British Museum. The authors of the Paris Commune had furnished a brief augury of things to come. This chorus of Continental voices sang one song: The answer to the undue concentration of economic power in a few private hands was the concentration of economic power in the state.

But in America a people wedded to the dispersion of power would not easily accept statism as a reply to monopolization. The instrument devised to snip the tentacles of monopoly was the antitrust laws. Instead of transferring economic power from one monolith to another, a method was invented to promote dispersal of power among private entrepreneurs. The major premise of antitrust is an unshakable belief in the efficacy of a competitive, free enterprise economy. The ideal to be realized is unlimited opportunity for entry into the market place, unlimited opportunity for self-development, and the resolution of economic issues by the unchecked exercise of free market forces.

In draining power from monopolists, only a minimum of power was transferred to the state. The sole reason for that transfer was to provide a governmental device for the dispersion of monopolistic power and the prohibition of harmful economic aggrandizement.

## A LESSON FROM ANTITRUST LAW

One example taken from the body of antitrust decisions illustrates the depth of the American commitment to the decentralized private exercise of economic power. In 1951, the U. S. Supreme Court decided the case of *Kiefer-Stewart Company* v. *Joseph E. Seagram & Sons,* 340 U. S. 211. An Indiana wholesale liquor dealer sued the Seagram and Calvert Corporations for treble damages under Section 1 of the Sherman Antitrust Act. The complaint charged that the respondent had conspired to sell liquor only to those Indiana dealers who would resell at prices fixed by Seagram and Calvert, and that this agreement deprived the petitioner of a continuing supply of liquor.

So far this seems like a standard antitrust action; price fixing has long been held to be illegal *per se.* However, when this case went to trial, the evidence showed that the distiller had fixed *maximum* prices above which the wholesalers could not resell. The U. S. Court of Appeals for the Seventh Circuit held that there was no violation of the Sherman Act, because an agreement to fix maximum resale prices was not anti-competitive in effect. Rather, such prices promoted competition and aided the consumer.

To the surprise of many, the Supreme Court reversed. It held that agreements fixing maximum resale prices "crippled the freedom of traders" in the same manner as agreements to fix minimum resale prices. It is the restraint upon the ability of traders to sell in accordance with their own judgment that the Sherman Act reaches.

Thus, we see that price fixing, even when done with a laudable motive, that of securing lower prices to the consumer, is illegal *per se.* At first the result seems anomalous; but if we refer again to the notion of a pluralistic decentralized society, all becomes clear. It is the exercise of power by a dominant concern to the detriment of the establishment of market conditions by the aggregate of individual decisions that is condemned. Far from being anomalous, this decision shows that the American people, speaking through its judiciary, are willing to commit themselves to freedom even where centralism would seem to provide highly desirable short-term goals.

To be sure, antitrust was not the only American answer to economic concentration. The fruits of Populism were many. Another American device forged in that time of crisis was the economic regulatory agency. Although the regulatory agency inevitably presupposes a transfer of some economic power to the state, the employment of this device represents a minimal transfer. The industries chosen by supervision were, without exception, industries peculiarly affected with a public interest and industries not adapted to the checks and balances imposed by unlimited competition. They were industries in which concentration of power was inevitable; and it was inevitable that a democratic nation would require a diaspora of private power.

But there was never a complete transfer of power. The regulatory agencies have never warred against private enterprise. They have merely insured that private enterprise affected with a public interest performed its responsibilities in a reasonable manner, and every agency was swathed in an elaborate net of guarantees against the unbridled exercise of power.

The American answer to the problem of monopoly has been a good one. There has been no attempt to convert unlimited private power into unlimited governmental control. Instead, the single thrust of our political effort has been to guarantee individual freedom by limited governmental regulation. There has been no departure in theory from the ideal of a plural, decentralized, permissive society dedicated to individualism.

## THE CONTRADICTORY PRESSURES

Unfortunately there have been departures, and pressures for still more departures, from these ideals in practice.

Acceptance of the idea that free enterprise bestows unparalleled benefits upon our nation does not negate the conclusion that the consequences of economic freedom have been and can be painful to many individuals and groups within the nation.

These painful consequences have led many to attempt a reshaping of the meaning of free enterprise in the mold of self-interest. To these people economic freedom may mean freedom to receive governmental subsidies to maintain uneconomic or dying industries. Or it may mean freedom to seek legislation to restrain competition and promote the stability and security of an industry or segments of an industry.

Contradictory pressures to present at least a façade of devotion to national economic ideals and at the same time to protect economic positions that could not withstand unrestrained competitive pressures have produced some public statements that are glaringly contradictory.

One of the most distressing habits of speech common to some businessmen is the tendency to say something like this: "Yes, of course I believe in free competition . . . but what *my* business (or *my* market, or *my* industry) really needs is less competition and more stability." These businessmen place their reliance upon legislation, not competition, to secure the prosperity of their enterprises.

No intensive search is necessary to uncover examples of this distressing tendency. Bills that would extend resale price maintenance, provide territorial security to dealers in various commodities, erect barriers to market entry, and establish or expand exemptions from the antitrust laws are introduced in great numbers in every session of the Congress. Proposals of this character are naked departures from the concept of economic freedom embodied in the nation's antitrust and trade regulation laws. For implicit in these laws is a recognition that the freedom to start a business, to win markets through fair competition, and to make business decisions independently cannot be enjoyed, absent the risk of displacement by stronger fair competitive efforts.

Even as we extol the benefits of economic freedom, we must recognize that no free society can guarantee every individual complete insulation from painful consequences.

## THE NEW CHALLENGE

The preservation of the ideal of a free-enterprise economy from the threat engendered by the rise of the trust was a signal accomplishment. The governmental devices designed to preserve economic individualism have, on the whole, been very successful.

However, new challenges threaten this ideal and new responses are continually needed. The pace of change defies description. The velocity and intensity of economic evolution approaches a state of constant revolution. New ways of accomplishing economic tasks proliferate. In space technology, for instance, we are seeing the onset of what may be a significant trend in economic organization. The rise of the government-sponsored, non-profit corporation and the university-sponsored, non-profit corporation and the development of ever more sophisticated relationships between prime contractors and sub-contractors may have unforeseen consequences in the allocation of industrial power.

There is nothing sinister in these new developments. They are simply one indication of the constant need to assess the impact of organizational innovation on our traditional ideals.

Another massive challenge facing the American pattern of economic organization is the Gargantuan need of awakening populations faced with the task of expanding a narrow industrial base to meet the ever-rising expectations of ever-increasing populations. Another factor now shaping the future is the prolonged and unremitting struggle now taking place between statism and individualism.

Many thoughtful citizens are actively debating the question of whether an economy dedicated to individualism and the profit motive can adequately satisfy great public needs for education, research, resources development, foreign aid, and defense.

A clear look at the shape and pace of change does not reveal either that our ideal must be abandoned or that the instruments that we have devised to effectuate that ideal have become obsolete.

The best way to answer challenge is to set imaginative and daring men free, not to impose more shackles on human activity. Mankind is best served in a society where the power of decision is dispersed—where an educated and responsible citizenry is capable of wise and effective solutions to national problems by the aggregate of wise and effective individual decisions.

Economic individualism, then, must be defended. The antitrust and trade-regulation laws will continue to be the most effective weapons in the conduct of that defense. So long as we insure that entry to the market place and opportunity to compete in the market place are not foreclosed by coercion or unlawful combination or stifling monopoly, then the creative and talented individual —our ultimate, last, and only hope—will have the opportunity to exercise his talents.

So long as the free play of competition guarantees that the obsolescence means failure, we need not fear change. Compliance with the antitrust laws by responsible businessmen and vigorous enforcement of the antitrust laws by responsible government agencies, therefore, become primary duties of those immediately charged with the defense of the national belief in free enterprise.

## THE QUESTION OF GOALS

"It is all very well to talk of preserving the reward of the daring free enterpriser," you may say, "but the nation may yet flounder if the wants satisfied by an abundantly productive free-enterprise economy are idle wants. A nation can flounder very quickly if the imaginative enterprisers devote themselves to producing kewpie dolls and electric highball stirrers when space vehicles and cyclotrons are what the nation needs."

It may be granted that dedication to free enterprise is bootless if free enterprise is doomed to end on a dungheap full of tail fins and discarded comic books. However, the necessity for some sort of hierarchy of national goals does not dictate an abandonment of freedom in favor of centralism. Rather, that need calls for an increased emphasis on enlightened individualism. Sacrifice is not incompatible with individualism, nor is excellence. *The good society cannot be achieved by the imposition of goals on a subdued populace.* The good society is composed of good individuals. As citizens, we can ultimately insure excellence only if we as citizens demand excellence.

The business community has very special responsibilities in the pursuit of excellence. The business community is skilled in the gathering of intelligence and the formulation of programs on the basis of that intelligence. It is supremely skilled in the art of persuasion.

Accordingly, if the business community wishes to insure the preservation of all the concepts embodied in the phrase "free enterprise," it must engage in a concerted effort to raise the national standards, to explain the perils that face this nation, to identify the tasks that must be accomplished, and to reinforce the will to accomplish them.

The business community has a special responsibility for education in a free society. It has the responsibility for improving the qualitative as well as the quantitative aspects of American education. Truth makes men free. The spread of truth insures that freedom will endure. Only by awakening a universal thirst for truth and by providing a means to slake that thirst can we even approximate the good society.

Democracy is a most hopeful way of life; but, unlike statists, the advocates of democracy can promise no Utopia. The dreams of free men are bounded by the limitations of the human condition. But the condition of intelligent, free men and women is not an ignoble one. A promise

that problems will be faced and solutions will be sought, that tragedy will be endured and that perseverance will not fail, is far more noble than any promise that cares will cease.

## RESPONSIBILITIES OF BUSINESS

Our deepest responsibility is to insure that the promise of the open society and the promise of free enterprise are realized. Business must meet the bewildering variety of demands now being made on our economy without surrendering freedom.

Inevitably this means that business must pledge renewed devotion to the principles embodied in our antitrust laws. Free enterprise cannot survive contamination either by monopoly or by statism. The best way to avoid both of these perils is to attain maximum compliance with the antitrust laws.

No one need be afraid that advocacy of vigorous enforcement of the antitrust laws is tinged with wide-eyed radicalism. Indeed, these laws are conservative in the truest sense of that much-abused term. They represent an undertaking by government designed to prevent still wider undertakings by government; for, if competition is abused and monopolistic practices become widespread, unfettered control over the economy will inevitably pass to the state.

The struggle for the preservation of free enterprise imposes great burdens upon the government also. Governmental agencies charged with enforcement of the antitrust laws and the proscription of unfair trade practices must exploit every resource available to them to insure that competition is free and fair. The malefactor must be restrained with swiftness and certainty, in order to deter others who may be tempted. And every businessman willing to accept the responsibilities that freedom brings must be educated in the letter and the spirit of the ground rules of competition, so that no one may transgress through ignorance.

But governmental proscription or regulation of economic activity must be limited, in the main, to the promulgation and enforcement of the "ground rules" under which fair and vigorous competition may take place, and to the penalization of those who wax strong through unfair methods. The government in its regulatory role fails if the monopolist or the predator imperils the freedom of the market place; it also fails if an iota of the freedom of individuals is sacrificed unnecessarily in the effort to contain the monopolist or fence in the predator.

Woodrow Wilson wrote, "Human nature is much the same in government as in the dry-goods trade. Power and strict accountability for its use are the essential constituents of good government." The prescription can be completed by stating its obverse: Human nature is much the same in business as in government. Exercise of power by the individual and strict accountability for its use are the essential constituents of free enterprise.

## QUESTIONS

1. What scale of value is basic in the American social, political, and economic system? How does this scale of value become involved in making business decisions? Explain.
2. Discuss the problem of contradictory pressures in the competitive system.
3. How does regulation and power become an important problem in our economic society?

# 64. Salesmanship and Professional Standards*

David J. Schwartz, Professor of Marketing, Georgia State University

*The unprofessional status of much personal selling is a serious obstacle to recruitment of qualified young people for this activity. Further, because many of the most capable young people do not enter selling, the over-all marketing effort of our economy appears weakened.*

## CRITERIA OF A "PROFESSION"

There can be no absolute or unqualified answer to the question, "Is personal

* Reprinted by permission from *Atlanta Economic Review*, September 1961, p. 15. Published by the Bureau of Business and Economic Research, School of Business Administration, Georgia State College.

selling a professional activity?" Rather, this question can be answered only in terms of the degree to which personal selling, as practiced today, meets the generally accepted criteria established to designate a "profession." Five such criteria of professional practice were used for purposes of this study.

### 1. INTELLECTUAL PREPARATION

*Formal preparatory education* is generally considered a primary criterion of a professional activity. Generally this criterion is met only with accepted prescribed knowledge obtained in colleges and universities. Ministers, teachers, medical doctors, and architects obviously qualify in this regard. Salesmen generally do not. While an increasing number of companies require sales applicants to have earned a college degree, more often than not no specific degree is made mandatory. Many companies appear to place just as much value on a liberal arts degree as on a degree in business administration.

### 2. CONTINUOUS LEARNING AND DEVELOPMENT

A mark of a profession is *emphasis on further learning and development* above and beyond formal educational preparation. This learning and development takes on many forms, such as postgraduate study, seminars and conferences, reading of literature in the field, and creative research. This criterion is quite subjective. Many salesmen meet this test. However, many others appear to make no effort to become better informed and more proficient.

### 3. SERVICE ATTITUDE

From long-standing tradition, professional activities have specified the *"service first"* attitude. Two marketing authorities sum up this criterion as it pertains to salesmen:

The opportunity to benefit mankind generally, or specifically one's clients or one's patients, is in many cases a more dominant motive than is financial return. Many salesmen are so motivated; many are not. The test comes to the salesman just as it does to the physician, the accountant or the attorney when he knows that by giving incomplete, vague, or perhaps inaccurate advice, his fee or commission might be larger than if he told the whole truth. Some salesmen meet the test; others fail.

### 4. ADHERENCE TO ACCEPTED ETHICAL STANDARDS OR CODES

A fourth characteristic of a professional activity is adherence to a set of accepted guideposts which define *ethical practices*. These codes generally spell out matters pertaining to compensation for services rendered, such as split fees, competition with other members of the profession, soliciting work, use of advertising, and related items. No industry-wide codes of ethics are found in selling today.

### 5. PUBLIC RECOGNITION AND RESPECT

A final criterion of a professional activity is the *attitude of the public* toward that activity. In order to be "professional," a group engaged in an activity must be recognized as a profession by people outside their activity. Salesmen as an occupational group do not meet this test.

## EVIDENCE OF LESS-THAN-PROFESSIONAL SELLING

There is evidence that much personal selling is conducted on a less-than-professional basis. The following examples illustrate unprofessional conduct in selling:[1]

1. The salesman who suggests to a purchasing agent that he can make some

---

[1] These are some of the practices revealed by statements made by salesmen attending sales seminars conducted by the author.

extra money if he places his purchases in the right places. Sharing the commission with the person who is doing the buying.

2. The salesman who attempts to pry information from purchasing agents regarding bids submitted by competing companies.

3. Misrepresentation of actual price of product. Quoting one price at order time and billing another price at invoice time.

4. Discussing business affairs of other companies with customer.

5. Trickery used to obtain interview with prospect, such as, "I'm just making a survey and I'd like to have your opinion."

6. Taking orders and promising delivery on dates known to be impossible.

7. Failure to take the responsibility for errors made in shipment.

8. Telling customer that competitor is dishonest or no good.

9. Purposely overselling an account, that is, selling more than the customer logically needs.

10. Adding items to a given order without a customer's knowledge or consent.

11. Calling on customers when lacking the technical information needed to provide service.

12. Begging for business. Making appeals based on personal handicap or under charitable organization sponsorship.

13. Quoting prices on last year's model when customer thinks the price refers to this year's model.

14. Neglecting to find out what customers really need and continuing to sell on the basis of assumptions of what they need.

15. Calling secretaries or other office employees to find out competitive quotes that have been submitted.

## LACK OF DIGNITY IN SELLING

The personal behavior of many salesmen attests to nonprofessionalism—for example:[2]

1. The use of slang, profanity, or off-color stories in the sales interview.

2. Wearing gaudy, loud, or distasteful clothing.

3. Chewing gum, smoking cigarettes, eating candy or peanuts in the presence of customers.

4. Eating onions, garlic, or drinking alcoholic beverages before calling on customers.

5. Failure to dress properly or, specifically, being sloppily dressed.

6. Boisterousness—loud jokes.

7. Exhibitionism. Dressing in such a way as to be an "attention-getter."

8. Romeoism—the salesman who must stop by desk of each girl in the office to "charm" her.

9. Know-it-all—the salesman who is never wrong and appears to be an expert on everything.

10. Lack of sincerity—not really believing in what one sells.

## ILLEGAL MARKETING ACTIVITIES

Most investigations of the Federal Trade Commission are concerned with various marketing practices. These violations, while not always involving salesmen directly, do nevertheless reflect on the behavior of salesmen. Insofar as business practices are concerned, it seems that much more "cheating" is associated with marketing than with any other business function.

False advertising, misrepresentation, misbranding, and false labeling are examples of the many violations of the Federal Trade Commission legislation.

[2] *Ibid.*

Unquestionably, such violations of legislation pertaining to fair competition does much to lower public acceptance of personal selling.

### SALESMEN OFTEN NOT SOLD ON SELLING

Part of the reason behind low public acceptance of selling can be traced directly to salesmen themselves.

In a summer-1960 survey of 6,000 members of the National Association of Women's and Children's Apparel Salesmen—men who averaged twenty-three years in outside commission selling and who had an average compensation of $9,600 before income tax deductions—half of the 2,000 respondents were not particularly enthusiastic about selling as a career.

In a survey, recently published, salesmen were asked to rank fifteen different

### TABLE 1

How Salesmen Compare Themselves with Members of Other Occupations in Terms of Ethical Conduct

---

Cumulative Rankings
(Most Ethical to Least Ethical)

---

1. Engineers
2. Teachers
3. University Professors
4. Doctors
5. Salesmen to Business and Industry
6. Corporation Top Management
7. Lawyers
8. Editors and Publishers
9. Salesmen Selling for Resale
10. Production Workers
11. Government Officials
12. Retailers
13. Advertising Men
14. Door-to-Door Salesmen
15. Automobile Salesmen

Source: Based on confidential responses to the American Salemen's national salesmen's panel as reported in *The American Salesman,* January 1961, pp. 48–53. Reproduced here with permission of *The American Salesman.*

occupations in terms of ethical conduct. Four categories of salesmen were included in the list—those selling to business and industry, those selling for resale, door-to-door salesmen, and automobile salesmen.

The results show that salesmen rate other salesmen low on the scale. Further, it is interesting to note that two other categories of marketing personnel—retailers and advertising personnel—also were rated very low. (See Table 1.)

## EFFECTS OF UNPROFESSIONAL STATUS

Damage resulting from unprofessional status is twofold. First, unprofessional status appears to discourage talented people from entering selling. Second, because the best human resources are not attracted to the selling occupation, total output of the economy is lowered.

### UNPROFESSIONAL STATUS HARMS RECRUITMENT

The fact that selling is widely regarded as an unprofessional activity has two negative influences on recruitment of individuals. First, young people put selling way down on their list of occupational choices. Much potential sales talent therefore never enters the field of selling. Second, many people who harbor prejudices toward selling enter the field much later in life than is desirable. Often a person with, say, an accounting background or an engineering education initially wants no part of selling but later finds that this occupational choice is a much more direct avenue toward job success.

The impact of a professional regard for a job classification cannot be taken lightly in terms of recruitment. T young individual contemplating a career in medicine knows before he begins that society—his friends, his relatives, teachers, neighbors, and others—will have a high opinion of his job choice. This is not true of selling. Individuals contemplating a career in this activity are aware that many in their social group will not be impressed by their career choice. In fact, there will be some in the social group who will feel that the individual is a failure.

### UNPROFESSIONAL STATUS PRODUCES ECONOMIC LOSS

Most executives, economists, and educators agree that one of the principal tasks of our economy is to discover ways to put more goods and services in the hands of the ultimate consumer. To the extent that the marketing arm of industry is weakened because of insufficiently capable and qualified sales personnel, all industry suffers.

It has been estimated that the field of selling needs one million new and qualified individuals to help perform the demand-creation function. In this connection, the following observations are pertinent:

But even more important than mere numbers is the need for nearly a million *top caliber* salesmen who can persuade consumer to buy if the nation is to enjoy a $150-billion increase in its national product.

That's the stark fact that leads sales and marketing executives queried by *Printers' Ink* to agree unanimously ⸱here is indeed a *crisis in talent* facing ⸱⸱⸱or instance, Tom McCall, a ⸱loyment agency head who ⸱⸱⸱ recruiting, says ⸱⸱⸱ industrial selling ⸱ $8,000 and

$12,000, he now finds only six to eight qualified applicants out of every 400 who apply. Another example: the personnel head of a large company says they regularly fill only 90 per cent of their sales-job openings. Reason: there just aren't enough qualified men.

That's the heart of the problem. No one doubts that sales could get its million more men. But it doesn't want "people who can't do anything else" and turn to sales. It wants capable, persuasive men who want to sell and will be effective salesmen.[3]

## OBSTACLES TO PROFESSIONALIZING SELLING

### LACK OF ACCEPTABLE DEFINITION OF "SELLING"

One factor which complicates efforts made to professionalize selling is the lack of an acceptable definition of selling. All people who sell bear the title of "salesmen." One might liken it to saying that anyone who works in the field of medicine is a doctor, or that anyone that helps build a house is an engineer. No provision in the customary definitions of selling is made for different grades or levels of selling. There appears to be as much difference between a salesman selling door-to-door and a salesman selling advertising for a large agency as there is between a hospital orderly and a surgeon. Since retail sales people and door-to-door sales people are much more frequently exposed to the public, the typical young person tends to think of a salesman as someone in a store or someone pushing the doorbell.

*New Terminology.* There is much reason to believe that many people fear the word "salesman" and what it stands for.

[3] *Printers' Ink,* March 27, 1959.

As a result, many companies hope to disarm prospective buyers by calling their salesmen something other than "salesmen," such as educational consultants, field editors, financial consultants, representatives, account executives, and media representatives. The public forms its impressions of salesmen by their deeds and actions—their behavior—rather than the terminology printed on their business card.

### VAGUE REQUIREMENTS FOR PROFESSIONAL EDUCATION

Earlier in this paper it was stated that a principal requirement of a profession is intellectual preparation. There is virtually no agreement as to what constitutes the proper intellectual preparation for a career in selling. In fact, there is no agreement as to the proper curriculum for a career in the *general* field of business.

### LACK OF ENCOURAGEMENT BY SALESMEN'S UNIONS

Unions generally rely on the contracts made with employers to spell out what constitutes minimum standards of performance. No provision is made which calls for members to do their best to treat customers fairly, to advance themselves professionally, and to strengthen the reputation of selling. Unions might well attempt to raise the performance standards of their members and to upgrade the members' thinking with regard to their responsibilities to customers and to employers.

## FAVORABLE TRENDS IN PROFESSIONALIZING SELLING

Some positive actions have been taken which are intended to elevate selling to a higher status.

### PI SIGMA EPSILON

There is only one professional college fraternity devoted to professionalizing selling—Pi Sigma Epsilon, founded at Georgia State College in 1951.

The rapid growth in chapters and membership of this professional fraternity can be interpreted as evidence of a definite need for such an organization in American colleges and universities.

The objective of Pi Sigma Epsilon can be summed up in three words "Develop Professional Salesmen." One of the operational goals of Pi Sigma Epsilon is to bring the advantages of selling to the attention of young college men. On most college campuses there is virtually no effort made to explain the pros and cons of a selling career to college students.

### CODE OF ETHICS

A second example of efforts underway to make selling a truly professional activity is found in codes of ethics adopted by various salesmen's groups.

The nation's largest organized body of organized outside salesmen, the National Association of Women's and Children's Apparel Salesmen, has developed a code of ethics for its 12,000 members. This group, composed of independent contractor salesmen, functions as a trade association. It lists as one of its principal objectives obtaining "adherence to the NAWCAS Code of Ethics."

The progressive leadership of this association is aware that unethical practices of one member cast a negative reflection on other members. Therefore, practices is regarded as a responsibility.

The code of ethics adopted forced by this association below.

### THE NAWCAS CODE OF ETHICS

This long needed code for our industry can only become 100% effective when all manufacturers recognize the need for NAWCAS, and when, they, too, subscribe to the same high standards which NAWCAS has set for all its members to follow:

1. Honest performance of salesman's duties and the obligation of the salesman to perform a full and complete day's work.
2. Intelligent, truthful and conscientious representation of his product.
3. Diligent effort at all times to bolster the reputation of his firm, refraining from derogatory remarks.
4. Create goodwill in order to promulgate a better relationship between salesman, manufacturer and buyer.
5. Notification to employer of termination of employment in sufficient time for replacement.
6. Fair notice to the manufacturer on termination of contract during the season.
7. Return all samples within a reasonable time.
8. Refrain from promises to buyers that the firm will not be able to fulfill.

additional lines only with the nwledge of his employer.

fulfill any agreements himself and his em-

IGNATIONS

anding example selling to pro-
L. U. profes-

of the National
Apparel Sales-

sional designation program developed by the life insurance industry.

The need and background for this program is explained as follows:

If practiced as it should be, life underwriting meets all the requirements of the professional concept. As a calling, it is so fundamentally useful to society and so inherently noble in its purpose as to inspire the practitioner to make it his full-time life's work. It also involves a deep science and in its practice an expert knowledge of that science. Life underwriters can be of inestimable service to clients by way of counsel and guardianship.

The day is passing when the underwriter is content to know only the technique of salesmanship and to rely on motivation of his prospects by subtle appeals to their emotions. Instead, he is stressing the intelligent analysis of human problems and the extending of professional advice of a high order.

The efficient underwriter needs a broad business education—including economics, business finance, personal finance, social problems, taxation, business and insurance law, law of wills, trusts and estates—in addition to life and health insurance fundamentals—if his services are to be of maximum value to his clients. The Chartered Life Underwriter program covers these subjects.

The C. L. U. designation is therefore a professional one. It does more than denote that the holder of it has met certain academic standards by passing a series of examinations. Primarily, it serves to indicate that the underwriter has spent time and effort in preparing himself to render a high type of service to the public and will continue to merit the confidence of the public by keeping abreast of the times.[5]

The C. L. U. designation program involves a specific curriculum or program of studies.

**The C.P.C.U. Designation. . . .** The success of the C. L. U. program provides encouragement for a professional designation for salesmen engaged in property and casualty insurance underwriting.

The designation Chartered Property Casualty Underwriter (C.P.C.U.) can be awarded only to those career persons who furnish satisfactory evidence of meeting the professional concept. For this purpose the American Institute has established and will enforce high qualifying standards of moral character, education and experience. The C.P.C.U. recognition, therefore, signifies that the holder has met not only the educational qualifications, but also fulfilled an experience requirement.[6]

### OTHER FAVORABLE TRENDS

Several other indications that selling is becoming more professional can be mentioned. Chief of these are: (1) The trend toward knowledge as a requirement for selling. More and more companies now provide some form of formalized training than at any time in the past. (2) The upgrading of requirements for entering selling. Many companies today will not employ anyone in a sales capacity who is not a college graduate. (3) The licensing requirements now in effect in many states for persons selling real estate, insurance, and securities.

[5] American College of Life Underwriters Catalogue, 1960–61, p. 10.
[6] American Institute for Property and Liability Underwriters Announcement, 1960–61, p. 9.

## SUMMARY

There is much evidence that, generally, present-day selling does not meet professional standards. This evidence is based on numerous examples of unprofessional conduct, behavior patterns of many salesmen, much illegal marketing activity, and lack of respect for selling by salesmen themselves.

The unprofessional status of much personal selling is a serious obstacle to recruitment of qualified young people for this activity. Further, because many of the most capable young people do not enter selling, the over-all marketing effort of our economy appears weakened.

Raising selling to professional status is hampered because of the sweeping definition given selling and because the educational requirements for a selling career have not been established.

Despite the general lack of professionalism in present-day selling, several favorable trends are in evidence. These include development of fraternal organizations to encourage professional selling, establishment of codes of ethics by trade groups, and development of professional designation programs in the insurance industry.

## QUESTIONS

1. Why is the problem of ethics morality related to "Profes business activities? Explain.

2. Is there any evidence of s less than professional selli ties? How does this affe decisions? Explain.

3. In what way has there tempt to professionaliz cuss.

# 65. Sales Ethics: Truth and Taste Needed?*

*Sales ethics has come up out of the swamp, but it still has a long swim ahead. Areas of most concern to responsible businessmen are price-cutting, conflict of interest and antitrust. All are critical, but concentration on any one of them, at the expense of a general sales-ethics policy, is fundamentally wrong.*

A purchasing agent in Omaha leaned over his desk last week and opened a sports magazine to a page he had marked. "Here she is," he said to the salesman across the desk from him, pointing to an expensive imported shotgun. "I know you're not a sportsman yourself, but I just thought I'd show it to you in case you were wondering what to get me for Christmas."

On a train headed for Atlanta, another salesman was toting up his expense ment for a three-day trip. He paused end of the column as he did a tal calculation, then entered 20 he day's total in the "enter-

fore, in the bar of a ee salesmen came to nt not to cut each greement they all bably be forced to month.

cases the sales- ting their com- hat would have rofits. But per- nt, they were ation and the d advertising

programs which their companies had built up to help them sell.

## I. THE PROBLEM

Advertising ethics has come under heavy fire in recent years. Sales ethics, because it directly affects only the few individuals involved and isn't apparent to the mass audiences reached by advertising, has managed to keep out of the limelight for the most part. But recent government actions now are bringing sales ethics out of the shadows—notably the Congressional investigation into, and the Federal Trade Commission action against, three major manufacturers of electrical equipment for price collusion in bids for government contracts.

These actions are forming a pattern, and the pattern is repeating itself on a less spectacular scale and in many other places besides Washington, D.C. New York City had its own price-fixing scandal the winter of 1960–61, for example—involving companies selling salt to the city sanitation department for cleaning streets. A few months later a Federal grand jury indicted a major automaker and three dealers' associations of conspiring to prevent the sale of their cars below list price. Hardly a week goes by without several such actions being taken against some area of the sales function.

Clearly a great deal of ethical malpractice exists in the sales-management area, and the public—as represented by the government and law-enforcement agencies—is getting fed up with it. So are many corporate officers, who realize that most ethical malpractices undermine their marketing programs and usually take sizable bits out of tight-squeezed profits.

This doesn't mean that sales ethics is getting worse. Most executives agree that it has improved, because of tighter government regulation, and the increasing awareness of the importance of public relations and reputation in business. "There are still abuses, but we've come a long way from the darkest days around 1955," an auto executive said.

But even though sales ethics isn't getting worse by and large, it isn't getting better fast enough to please a great many top corporate officials. There is a growing awareness that a tremendous problem still exists, and that something must be done about it.

## II. AREAS OF ABUSE

Moreover, there are strong indications that this awareness is growing particularly fast. Some examples:

An interest survey that Research Institute of America, New York, conducted among sales managers showed a high level of interest in sales ethics. Another RIA study, this one conducted on all levels, from managers down to rank-and-file salesmen, posed hypothetical problems in ethics, brought forth much more thoughtful replies than expected. "Before this year, we'd never elicited any inkling of interest in sales ethics problems," said Jack Tarrant, director of RIA's development division.

A three-day American Management

Association personnel conference this fall devoted a full panel discussion to the subject of business ethics. The panel was headed by Theodore V. Purcell, S.J., associate professor of psychology and industrial relations at Loyola University, Chicago. An increasing number of such seminars on ethics have been cropping up in business conventions lately.

Last summer the Harvard Business Review surveyed 1,700 of its readers—mostly top management men—on the subject of ethics, found about half of them believe that "the American business executive tends to ignore the great ethical laws as they apply immediately to his work. He is preoccupied chiefly with gain." Four out of five executives affirmed the presence in their industry of unethical practices, many of them directly related to sales, such as bribes, excessive gifts, call girls, price discrimination, price fixing.

National Industrial Conference Board polled top executives of 130 manufacturing firms on the subject of business ethics, found that most of them believe conflict-of-interest is the major problem area. This is a question that frequently affects upper sales-management levels, when, *e.g.*, a sales executive holds a large stock interest in a supply or customer firm. NICB found an increasing concern with this problem among the executives polled. One out of three companies represented in the survey now has a written policy statement on the subject of conflict-of-interest. Last year, when the study was made, the ratio was one to ten. One metals company has set up a special "conflict-of-interest committee," made up of three board members, to review and recommend on conflict-of-interest cases.

A *Printers' Ink* survey of sales executives found a wide belief that many unethical sales practices are on the increase. Specifically:

misrepresentations of merchandise—judged on the rise by 45 per cent of respondents

demands for kickbacks—named by 38 per cent

price gouging—32 per cent

abuse of co-op advertising—25 per cent

income-tax maneuvering—19 per cent

excessive demands for entertainment—16 per cent

padded expense accounts—six per cent.

Some of the comments these executives appended showed concern verging on disgust with present sales ethics, and a conviction that the situation is getting steadily worse. "It seems many more people accept less than the highest ethics in business," said Robert Graham, sales education director at Diebold Inc. Some her comments:

he percentage of market is impor-
a company; when this percentage
company will occasionally 'cut
—Glen Palmer, national sales
Lustra Corp. "Today most
rimarily interested in the
r profit. Services, pres-
l seem to be passé"—
s manager, New York
any.

Printers' Ink survey
ent of a group of
lemned the wide-
s reciprocity (de-
r also buy from
and 80 per cent
bsmanship.

Geasing number
Moles immorality
Michess figures as
board of American
to seek the
ee Bristol,
Iyers Co.;

T. "Jeff" Wood, vice-president of Procter & Gamble.

## III. VULNERABLE SALES

Business immorality is by no means limited to the sales function, all of these men have pointed out. But sales is particularly vulnerable for several reasons. Sales impinges on the highly sensitive antitrust areas of price-fixing, for example. It's an axiom (to be taken with a grain of salt) that whenever two salesmen get together, they are bound to discuss prices.

The very fuzziness of federal legislation invites violation in some cases—or at least careless behavior by sales personnel. One company president told the National Industrial Conference Board, "There are many areas of business which are covered by ambiguous and even conflicting laws. As a result, a manager cannot get a precise answer to the question, 'What is legal?' To obey one law is to break another. Under these circumstances a manager can only do the best he can, and hope for the best."

Another company president—in the chemical industry—said, "Even a mature executive with high business ethics can run afoul of the law unknowingly if he does not have adequate legal counsel and judgment enough to know when to use it. The law, particularly with regard to antitrust provisions, is far from clear, and the wise executive will call in an experienced 'pilot' to steer the ship through such unfamiliar waters."

The salesman and sales executive are constantly plunged into such "gray" regions, where it's next to impossible to decide what is right. Research Institute of America's Jack Tarrant described one such situation that arises occasionally in almost every company. A price change is coming up and the information leaks to salesmen before the official announcement. A customer of long standing and close friendship, tipped off by rumors, asks a salesman, frankly, if there's a price change coming. "In this situation, the salesman looks like a heel no matter what he says," Tarrant said. "If he spills the news he's betraying his own company. But if he doesn't, he'll look like a traitor to his customer a few weeks later when the price does change."

There are particular ethical pitfalls in sales, also because salesmen handle sizable amounts of travel- and entertainment-expense money—and are constantly engaged in confidential dealings involving much larger merchandise orders. Add to this the pressure of stiff competition in most industries, and almost any sales job becomes a potential ethical trap.

In some industries ethical malpractices are practically endemic—especially in the retail field. There are supermarket operators who cheerfully admit that their profit all comes from rakeoffs on cooperative advertising—their actual food operations barely break even. Profit-taking on co-op may not be illegal, due to the spread between local ad rates (which the supermarket operator pays) and national rates (at which he bills the manufacturer); but the ethical status of this practice is open to question—and possible eventual legislation.

It's also well-known that kickbacks to buyers are widespread in supermarkets and other types of retail stores. A Cleveland chain-store merchandising manager was amazed recently when he walked into one of his company stores and stood face to face with an end-aisle display he'd never authorized. A grocery *clerk* (not even a manager) innocently revealed that a salesman had offered him a new wristwatch to put the display up. *He didn't even realize he was taking a bribe.*

The relationship between manufacturers and dealers or distributors are strewn with enticements. The manufacturer's control over dealer conduct is extremely tenuous, especially in the automobile field. Under present legislation it's difficult for a manufacturer to cut off a dealer because he chisels on service or treats customers unethically in other respects.

Another ethical pitfall exists for many old companies, because legislation and sales ethics may have changed considerably since the companies' early policies were formulated. An executive in the National Industrial Conference Board study pointed out, "Many procedure which were perfectly legal and ethic 15 or 20 years ago would not be le today."

## IV. BLAME AT THE TOP?

The answer to many of these p lies in a firm policy statement management. The NICB study s written policy statements are more common, not only in conflict-of-interest but also cover such potential antitru price fixing.

The top-level policy sta able, first, because it se an example for ethic more important, it ta off the hook. About th to a buyer's request valuable "Christmas but we have a fi against that. You fast it would run we bought ever present like that,

The dilemma the case of an ing an immin

top management's fault. The only valid solution to this dilemma is for top management not to leak the information in the first place.

In view of the repeated temptations that salesmen are bound to face in these areas, any company that does not formulate firm top-management policies is cutting the ground out from under its ...les force. There's danger in limiting ...e statements to the touchy areas of ...ct-of-interest and price-fixing, too.

...eral executives note that the only ... that most companies have taken ...ield of business ethics have dealt ...lly with either possible conflicts-...t or adherence to antitrust laws ...in reaction to the over-publi-...akes of a few," the National ...onference Board study points ... executives often share the ...chemical company president ...that 'an elaborate defense ...up against a specific prob-...ouble is most apt to occur ...er in the future.'"

...nts in any case are only crucia...ntrol is an even more trated ...as is graphically illus-eral Ele... the remarks of Gen-in the ...nan Ralph Cordiner, brought a...he antitrust actions tric and A... Westinghouse Elec-Without ...rs last year.

ment's respo...odge top management case, Cordine...n the price-fixing impossible for ...ut, "It would be edge of the pr... to have knowl-different produc...he hundreds of marketplace by th...ffered at the 3-million catalog ...ny. There are the available varia... representing product lines. Each ... our many ... has hundreds or ...department offered at different pr...ds of items not expect to monitor a...d I would ...individual

prices or the day-to-day transaction involved . . .

"Equally, I am unaware of the suggested retail price in Chicago for a 15-cubic-foot General Electric refrigerator. . . . The suggested retail price is the responsibility of the General Electric distributor serving the dealers in Chicago.

"The officers of the company, of course, have the general function of seeing that customers continue to receive good value and service. . . . But the basic responsibility to see that such values and service do in fact exist for a particular customer must remain with those to whom the responsibility has been delegated. . . . I cannot recall a single instance, since I ceased to have operating responsibility . . . many years ago, when on my own initiative I originated or quoted a price to a customer."

And, Cordiner pointed out, the price-fixing that prompted last year's charges took place in the face of a firm, written company policy of many years' standing, expressly prohibiting any understandings on prices with competitors, or any other actions that violate antitrust legislation. This is one of only six mandatory policies in effect at GE.

## V. THREE-WAY APPROACH

An effective attack on the problem of sales ethics requires a three-pronged approach, combining clear-cut policy statements by top management, indoctrination of salesmen and meticulous controls. All three of the electrical-apparatus manufacturers involved in the recent price-fixing case have taken strong steps in all three areas.

Westinghouse Electric revised and reissued its Management Guide on Legal and Ethical Conduct—a one-page statement spelling out the company's policy "to comply with all laws governing its operations and to conduct its affairs in keeping with the highest moral, legal and ethical standards." The guide specifies the penalties for infraction—"which may include reprimand, probation, suspension, reduction in salary, demotion or dismissal—depending on the seriousness of the offense. Clear-cut price-fixing or bid-rigging acts, or illegal activities with competitors to divide or allocate markets or customers, will result in dismissal."

A six-page memo explains just how this policy is to be enforced, and where responsibility for it lies.

Even before these steps were taken, Westinghouse had mapped out a program of rigid controls. Division and department managers are obliged to investigate all prices being quoted, bid or charged, to determine that they were not arrived at collusively—and file certificates with the general counsel's office that they had done this.

A second set of certificates must be signed and filed by salesmen each time they attend a meeting (including civic organizations such as chambers of commerce), stating that no discussion of price-fixing took place. A third set of certificates is filed by certain individuals with pricing responsibilities, after each *phone conversation* with personnel of competitors.

Westinghouse is also stressing ethics in its sales training. The field-training program includes three conferences devoted to business ethics and laws. The Westinghouse sales-personnel development workshop also carries lectures and discussions in an "intensive two-day program aimed at stimulating personal development and high moral standards."

General Electric took similar steps, instituted tighter legal reviews of oper-

ations, new auditing techniques, designed to turn up clues to malpractices, intensified teaching and instruction by the legal-services department. Executives all down the line were urged to develop more effective controls.

The drug industry—another area that has come under governmental fire for actual and alleged malpractices in sales—is less eager to talk about the subject of sales ethics. Most companies reportedly give their salesmen careful instruction, taking special pains to see that the salesmen don't misrepresent the capabilities of drugs, and many of these companies have high ethical reputations. But sales abuses are still widespread in many areas, drug officials allow.

And most executives agree that sales abuses are still common in most other industries. The significant development in recent months is the widespread awakening of management desire to control these abuses. Sales ethics—along with business ethics—is moving out of the area of sermonizing and into the area of scientific control and management—along with all other aspects of successful marketing.

## QUESTIONS

1. Discuss some of the ethical problems corporate officials feel are of immediate concern.
2. Discuss the findings of the *Printers' Ink* survey on unethical sales practices. The executives' comments voiced what concern? Explain.
3. Explain how business activities are vulnerable to reactions to business morality.
4. Do you feel the problem of sales ethics can be solved? Discuss.

# 66. Is There a Public Side to Private Price-Making?*

Irwin M. Stelzer, Vice President of Boni, Watkins & Jason

*Some increased government intervention in pricing appears inevitable. The absence of competition need not be proved in order to justify regulation. Substantial inequities in bargaining positions, socially unacceptable price behavior rooted in inelasticities of supply or demand may also evoke regulation.*

Economists long ago abandoned the notion that prices and output are determined in large measure by the unimpeded operation of impersonal market forces. The spotlight now being thrown on the problem of administered prices represents only the most recent and perhaps best publicized effort to demonstrate what few responsible executives would, in private, deny—that the prices charged for the bulk of our national output are, within varying limits, determined by corporate officials. The presidents of major corporations do not buy the daily newspaper to discover the prices their firms' output will bring that day.

Awareness of the range of discretion open to business administrators has been sharpened by the recently published Brookings Institution study, *Pricing in Big Business*, by Kaplan, Dirlam and Lanzillotti. The frequency with which executives cite as a pricing objective the achievement of some "target" rate of return on investment raises the question of whether or not some form of public-utility-type, cost-plus-fair-return pricing has now come to dominate non-regulated industries.

An apparent impossibility of maintaining anything like an unconcentrated, purely market-directed economy inevitably leads to a consideration of how current antitrust efforts can be integrated with some other form of control over various industries.

And by control we do not necessarily mean utility-type regulation. This author has, in past years, had sufficient experience with utility-type regulation to be aware of its potential (although not unavoidable) dangers: regulatory delay, complex and expensive quasi-judicial hearings, eventual identification of the regulators with the regulated, etc. Nevertheless, it must be realized that the choice in many instances is no longer between government regulation, on the one hand, and a "free" market, on the other. Rather, the choice is between government regulation *in some form,* or private administration by managers remotely responsible, at best, to scattered and impotent stockholders.

What must be clear is the regulation need not be, as tradition would have it, a response to *monopoly*. In the words of one prominent economist, Dr. Alfred E. Kahn of Cornell University, ". . . the presence or absence of competition is not in itself and in all situations a complete and sufficient test of whether or not government intervention is required . . .

* Reprinted from *Challenge,* The Magazine of Economic Affairs; published by the Institute of Economic Affairs, New York University. January 1960.

Markets in the real world—even markets that may fairly be termed competitive—are typically highly imperfect. The processes by which supply adjusts to demand and demand to supply are often so slow, so inexact, so painful that they impose intolerable hardships—in some instances on buyers, in other instances on sellers. In such instances, economists have long recognized, government intervention may be perfectly appropriate to supplement and even on occasion to supplant the unregulated pricing mechanism, even in the absence of obvious monopoly power."

To fully understand the meaning of this position, it is necessary to examine various instances of public participation in the pricing process. The free enterprise-oriented reader should attempt to overcome his immediate—and, from many points of view, desirable—negative reaction to any government intervention, no matter how mild. If the community decides that its welfare requires some form of "regulation," obstinate resistance to it may eventually result in even more stringent measures, such as *direct* government operation.

The term "regulation" is generally taken to mean direct control by government over pricing, so as to keep profits at "fair" levels. So defined, regulation was first applied to such local monopolies as water works, electric and gas distribution companies, street railways and telephone companies. The complete absence of competition, actual or potential, in the supply of an essential service led to what has come to be known as public utility regulation. Government commissions assumed the role of the absent competitors by keeping profits at "normal," "fair" and "reasonable" levels. The disintegration of Adam Smith's "invisible hand" was compensated for by the extension of the long arm of government into the pricing process.

Gradually, however, both the reasons for and the nature of such regulation changed. A general awareness of the need for regulation to correct malfunctionings of the price system led to its extension into nonmonopolized fields. Since such regulation was designed to serve a different need, it inevitably took a different form.

## DRASTIC EXAMPLE

In some instances (natural rubber, coal and agriculture) government intervention in the pricing process was designed to set minimum prices. Such action was deemed necessary because socially intolerable price fluctuations resulted from major lags in the adjustment of output to price changes. The natural rubber industry provides a most dramatic example of conditions which, to a lesser degree, prevail in much of agriculture. It takes about six years for the rubber-bearing Hevea tree to reach maturity. For a period of at least that many years, therefore, price increases cannot result in substantially expanded production. Under such circumstances, it is not surprising that a 343 per cent increase in rubber prices between 1921 and 1925 called forth only a 75 per cent increase in Far Eastern exports of rubber. By the time the plantings of the early 1920s reached maturity, demand had slackened. Trees could not, however, be unplanted; native labor could not readily move into other occupations. Consequently, a 95 per cent price decline over the next few years had no immediate impact on production. This "miserable market performance" (to quote Kahn) was due to imperfections and inelasticities, not to monopoly. While the nature of appropriate government intervention in such a case may be argued, the need for some policy program other than complete *laissez faire* would seem clear to most economists.

Regulation of rates charged by such different groups as employment agencies, landlords and producers of natural gas is also justified by such socially intolerable price inelasticities. The strategic position of employment agencies in the 1930s, combined with the basic bargaining weakness of their job-hunting "clients," created a potential for abuse. At least one Supreme Court Justice, in a leading case involving the regulation of employment agencies, indicated his awareness "that employment agencies . . . deal with a necessitous class, the members of which are often dependent on them for opportunity to earn a livelihood, are not free to move from place to place, and are often under exceptional economic compulsion to accept such terms as the agencies offer."

## EXTREME INELASTICITY

A similar situation exists in the case of natural gas. Quite apart from the question of concentration, government regulation would be justified here by the unequal bargaining positions of producers and pipelines, and extreme inelasticity of supply and demand. The return permitted to pipeline buyers by the Federal Power Commission is computed as a per cent of their net investment (rate base); as investment in facilities is depreciated, this rate base inevitably declines. Only by building new facilities—which means getting more gas—can pipelines shore up their rate bases. They are, therefore, under considerable pressure to buy. Most producers of natural gas, on the other hand, derive the bulk of their revenues from oil operations. They can and do sit on gas reserves. Humble Oil Co. can forego some current gas revenue, if by doing so it can increase pressure on buyers to raise offering prices. Little wonder that the new contract price of natural

gas has trebled in the postwar period, while the consumer price index rose by only 26 per cent. It is unlikely that price increases of this magnitude were regarded to call forth discovery of supplies which would not otherwise have been uncovered, while demand inelasticities—the householder is in no position to scrap his gas-burning heating equipment—insure producers of the ability to charge the rates they want. Regulation in such a situation should become, if not agreeable to producers, at least understandable.

The implications of the above remarks for many American industries must be faced. The absence of competition need not be proved in order to justify regulation. Substantial inequalities in bargaining positions, socially unacceptable price behavior rooted in inelasticities of supply or demand may also evoke regulation. This regulation may, for the time being, take the form of Kefauverish supervision of prices. Company executives already operate with the clear understanding that steel price increases will have to be explained to a Senate committee, crude oil price cuts to a state legislature and gasoline price wars to a House committee. They may lament such "interference" in a theoretically non-regulated industry, but live with it they must. The knowledge that this quasi-regulation is the inevitable consequence of inelasticities will, perhaps, enable them to resign themselves—a course to be preferred to resigning their positions—to this fate.

It should be emphasized that this alternative is not a terribly far cry from the present mixed regulatory pattern. For the present, those industries being regulated on a utility-type basis will remain in that status. In fact, a realization that historical trends have tended to reduce demand inelasticities in, let us say, rail transportation, may lead to a relaxation of regulation. A broad category of industries manufacturing nonessentials—textiles, automobiles, etc.—will probably continue subject only to such pressures as result from antitrust enforcement and occasional Congressional interest in specific problems. A final group, in which there are inelasticities and inequalities of bargaining power between buyers and sellers, will face the continued scrutiny of Congressional committees and a drumfire of criticism calling for more direct regulation. Recent inquiries into drug pricing contain such potential: purchasers of drugs are unable to bargain effectively with large drug manufacturers over prices. The reasonableness of the industry's price structure, therefore, becomes an appropriate source of inquiry. The industry can do little save cooperate.

Some increased government intervention in pricing appears inevitable. Still further intervention, however, is often unwittingly invited. Thus, in requesting protective import restrictions the domestic oil producing industry brought upon itself government supervision of residual fuel oil prices. Should prices rise, quotas will presumably be increased. In the words of one high industry official, this is "very ominous" and "has all sorts of implications." By reducing the elasticity of supply, the oil industry, in effect, invited an increase in government participation in pricing.

## QUESTIONS

1. Why have economists abandoned the idea that prices and output are determined in large measure by unimpeded operation of impersonal market forces? Discuss.
2. Explain alternatives involved in achieving balance desired in government and business.
3. Explain the characteristics of some of our regulatory problems.

# BIBLIOGRAPHY FOR CHAPTER X

ARTICLES:

Andlinger, Gerhard R., "The Crucible of our American Business Creeds," *Business Horizons,* Vol. 2, No. 3 (Fall 1959), pp. 34–44.

Austin, Robert W., "Code of Conduct for Executives," *Harvard Business Review,* Vol. 39, No. 2 (Sept.–Oct. 1961), pp. 53–61.

Buggie, Frederick D., "Lawful Discrimination in Marketing," *Journal of Marketing,* Vol. 26, No. 2 (April 1962), pp. 1–8.

"Busines Ethics: Too Much Gray Area," *Fortune,* Vol. LXII, No. 3 (September 1960), pp. 127–8.

Cahill, Raymond F., "Criteria for Busines Morals," *Atlanta Economic Review,* Vol. XII, No. 6 (June 1962), pp. 8–10.

Demos, Raphael, "The American Image of Success," *Harvard Business Review,* Vol. 39, No. 2 (March–April 1961), pp. 45–50.

Freedman, Robert, "The Challenge of Business Ethics," *Atlanta Economic Review,* Vol. XX, No. 5 (May 1962), pp. 7–12.

"Have Corporations a Higher Duty than Profits?" *Fortune,* Vol. LXII, No. 3 (August 1960), pp. 108, 146–53.

Kennedy, William F., "The Ethics of Conspiracy," *Atlanta Economic Review,* Vol. XII, No. 8 (August 1962), pp. 14–17.

Levitt, Theodore, "The Dangers of Social Responsibilities," *Harvard Business Review,* Vol. 36, No. 5 (Sept.–Oct. 1958), pp. 41–50.

Orton, Vrest, "Decay of Ethics," *Journal of Retailing,* Vol. 33, No. 2 (Summer 1957), pp. 61–62.

Sullivan, A. M., "Business Ethics: Policy or Principles," *Dun's Review and Modern Industry,* Vol. 76, No. 4 (October 1960), pp. 58–72.

BOOKS:

Beckman, Theodore N., and Davidson, William R., *Marketing.* New York: Ronald, 1962.

Bowen, Howard R., *Social Responsibilities of the Businessman.* New York: Harper, 1953.

Converse, Paul D., Huegy, Harvey W., and Mitchell, Robert V., *Elements of Marketing.* Englewood Cliffs, N.J.: Prentice-Hall, 1958.

Dimock, Marshall E., *A Philosophy of Administration.* New York: Harper, 1953.

Fenn, Dan H., *Management's Mission in a New Society.* New York: McGraw-Hill, 1959.

Houser, Theodore V., *Big Business and Human Values.* New York: McGraw-Hill, 1957.

Selehman, B. M., *A Moral Philosophy for Management.* New York: McGraw-Hill, 1955.

Sharp, Frank C., and Fox, Phillip G., *Business Ethics.* New York: Appleton-Century, 1937.